THE NEPTUNE BOOK OF
TENNIS AND RACKETS

THE NEPTUNE BOOK OF
TENNIS AND RACKETS

James Bruce

Sponsored by
Neptune Investment Management

Copyright © 2015 by James Bruce

First published in Great Britain in 2015 by
James Bruce
Chalcot House
Westbury, Wiltshire BA13 4DF

The right of James Bruce to be identified as the Author of the Work has been asserted by him in accordance with the Copyright, Designs and Patents Act 1988.

2 4 6 8 10 9 7 5 3 1

All rights reserved. No part of this publication may be reproduced, stored in a retrieval system, or transmitted, in any form or by any means without the prior written permission of the publisher, nor be otherwise circulated in any form of binding or cover other than that in which it is published and without a similar condition being imposed on the subsequent purchaser.

British Library Cataloguing in Publication Data.
A CIP catalogue record for this title is available from the British Library.

ISBN 978 0 9930969 0 7

Printed and bound in Great Britain by
CPI ANTONY ROWE LIMITED
Bumper's Farm, Chippenham, Wiltshire SN14 6LH

CONTENTS

Preface 7
Sponsor 8
Acknowledgements 9

Part I
TENNIS

How Tennis Began	13	Seventeenth-century Tennis	51
Why Tennis?	18	Eighteenth-century Tennis	61
Keeping the Score	20	Nineteenth-century Tennis	71
Basic principles of play	23	Twentieth-century Tennis	85
Development of the Racquet	25	Twenty-first century Tennis	112
Development of the Ball	28	Ladies' Tennis	118
The Medieval Game	31	Historic Tennis Photographs	125
Sixteenth-century Tennis	35		

Part II
RACKETS

How Rackets Began	131	Ladies' Rackets	183
Nineteenth-century Rackets	143	Rackets in the USA and Canada	185
Twentieth-century Rackets	154	Rackets in India	193
Twenty-first century Rackets	179	History of the Rackets Ball	195

Part III
TENNIS AND RACKETS CLUBS

Aiken Tennis Club	201	Le Jeu de Paume de Fontainebleau	238
Ballarat Tennis Club	204	Greentree	241
Le Jeu de Paume de Bordeaux	206	Haileybury College	243
Boston, The Tennis and Racquet Club	208	Hampton Court, The Royal Tennis Court	244
Bristol Real Tennis Club	211	Hardwick House	248
Cambridge University	213	Harrow School	251
Canford School	216	Hatfield House	254
Charterhouse School	219	Hobart Tennis Club	257
Cheltenham College	222	Holyport Real Tennis Club	259
The Racquet Club of Chicago	225	The Hyde Tennis Club	261
Clifton College	228	Jesmond Dene Real Tennis Club	263
Detroit Racquet Club	230	Lakewood, the Georgian Court	266
Eton College	232	The Leamington Tennis Court Club	269
Falkland Palace	236	Lord's, Marylebone Cricket Club	271

Malvern College	274	The Racquet Club of Philadelphia	314
The Manchester Tennis and Racquet Club	276	Prested Hall	318
		The Queen's Club	320
Marlborough College	279	Radley College	325
Royal Melbourne Tennis Club	281	Romsey	329
Middlesex University Real Tennis Club	283	Rugby School	330
		St Paul's School	332
The Montreal Racket Club	285	RMA Sandhurst	335
Moreton Morrell Tennis Court Club	287	Seacourt Tennis Club, Hayling Island	337
Newmarket Real Tennis Club	290	Southwest of France	341
Newport, The National Tennis Club	292	Tonbridge School	347
New York, The Racquet and Tennis Club	295	The Tuxedo Club	350
The Oratory	300	International Tennis Club of Washington	355
Oxford University	303		
Paris, Société Sportive du Jeu de Paume et de Racquets	306	Wellington College	357
		Winchester College	359
Petworth House	309		

Part IV
Further Information

Courts being Created or Revived	365	The Tennis & Rackets Association	403
Disused courts	372	Championship Records	411
Stické	394		
Building and Restoring Rackets and Real Tennis Courts	398		

Important Bibliography 433
Contributors 434
Photographic Acknowledgements 435
Index 437

PREFACE

BAGSHOT PARK

Morys, Lord Aberdare, was a great champion of Tennis. As a newcomer to the sport as well as the Tennis & Rackets Association back in the 1980s I remember him well. He always spoke with passion and knowledge, so it should be no surprise that his book, *The Willis Faber Book of Tennis & Rackets*, which was originally published in 1980 quickly became the best reference on the two sports. Morys updated the book in 2001, just a few years before he passed away.

Perhaps I should warn the unwary browser before you delve further that the 'Tennis' referred to here is the original, and to the purist, the only true game of Tennis from which most modern racquet games are descended. Tennis has been around in a documented form since the Middle Ages and probably existed in some form well before then. Lawn Tennis, on the other hand, has only been around since the middle of the nineteenth century and came about due to the invention of vulcanised rubber and a ball that could bounce on grass.

What comes across clearly from this latest edition is that both Tennis and Rackets are alive and thriving. There is a whole new chapter on ladies' Rackets which has developed rapidly over the last few years and now has its own British Open singles championship. Perhaps the most intriguing chapter is on the development of new courts and the restoration of others; apart from the record of renaissance it is wonderful finding out where some of these courts are.

James Bruce, Morys' son, has done an excellent job in updating and refreshing his father's work, thus ensuring that the newly titled *Neptune Book of Tennis & Rackets* will continue to be the foremost reference book for years to come.

HRH The Earl of Wessex, KG GCVO
Patron, Tennis & Rackets Association

SPONSOR

I am enormously grateful to Neptune Investment Management for sponsoring this update of my father's book which has been re-worked to incorporate the fascinating events of the 21st century to date.

JAMES BRUCE

FOREWORD

It gives me great pleasure to help James Bruce with the updating of this invaluable book his father first wrote in 1980.

Real Tennis and Rackets are two sports which have a long and valuable history, both here in the UK and in many countries overseas. To ensure that such memories and facts are remembered is of real historical importance to both games, and this book provides such a lasting memory.

The modern era has seen many changes to both sports and, through our lead sponsorship of Real Tennis and Rackets in the UK, we are pleased to see the games continue to thrive at all levels.

I sincerely hope you enjoy taking a journey through the annals of history of both these great sports.

ROBIN GEFFEN
CEO, Neptune Investment Management

NEPTUNE INVESTMENT MANAGEMENT

Neptune is an independent and privately owned UK-based fund management company that offers a range of equity funds to clients, from individuals to institutions.

At Neptune, we pride ourselves in nurturing and developing talent whether this is in our own employees or through our sporting, arts and educational partnerships.

We have been a key sponsor of Real Tennis in the UK since 2008 and Rackets since 2010. We are committed to improving the standard of both games from grass roots through to professional level, and championing their development and popularity.

To learn more about Neptune and our investment insights, visit **neptunefunds.com**

Sponsored by
Neptune Investment Management

ACKNOWLEDGEMENTS

First and foremost I would like to express my gratitude to Roddy Bloomfield, without whom this book would have never seen the light of day. Roddy edited the original 1980 edition written by my father, and did most of the spade-work for the 2001 update. Six years ago he encouraged me to start thinking about another update and to begin with the Championship Records. The latter update duly appeared in 2009, following which I began to address the whole book. My aspirations on this front received a big boost in 2011 when Robin Geffen agreed that Neptune Investment Management would act as sponsor, and from then it took three years to bring everything together. Throughout these six years Roddy has acted as my mentor, providing invaluable advice and introductions every step of the way.

It was Mervyn Dunnington-Jefferson who inspired me to write a whole new chapter on building and restoring courts, not only providing a huge amount of information but also introducing me to Jim and Duncan MacKellar of Armourcoat. I'm sad that he never saw the finished book but at least he managed to review that particular chapter. Simon Inglis's research on Joseph Bickley for his book *Played in London* was also immensely helpful.

Howard McMorris and Mike Garnett made my task of retrieving information from North American and Australian clubs respectively immeasurably easier by either writing pieces themselves or enlisting the support of others. Davis Anderson and James Zug both surpassed themselves by composing two North American chapters each. Mike's own books on Real Tennis were a huge source of information for the greatly expanded chapter on disused courts, as was Nick Harding's extraordinary ability to unearth disused Rackets courts. David Best was incredibly helpful in providing a much more comprehensive chapter on the Tennis & Rackets Association. Graham Tomkinson's own book on Stické was a major source of information for this expanded chapter. Paul Mirat provided all the information for the new South West of France chapter in his inimitable style.

I have tried to keep track of all those who helped on individual club chapters or provided photos and these generous souls are listed as Contributors or under Photographic Acknowledgements at the end of the book. Frederika Adam and Tim Edwards were a goldmine of new photos for the UK, as was Michael Do for the USA and Mike Garnett for Australia. Frederika Adam and Chris Davies were immensely helpful on the New Media piece. Chris was also a constant source of general support, particularly providing key contacts or introductions. Towards the end, he and Howard Angus did a huge amount of vital proof-reading. Howard reviewed the sections on 21st century Real Tennis and Rackets, and was also immensely helpful updating the pieces on Rackets balls and racquets.

The Oxbridge employment websites provided me with two talented creative writers – Charlotte Mungavin and Julia Huschke – and, along with my own undergraduate children Augusta and Robert, they were also immensely helpful in editing a lot of the information.

Lastly my appreciative thanks go to HRH The Earl of Wessex for writing the Preface.

James Bruce

Part I
TENNIS

A ball game illustrated in the tomb of Beni Hassan.

HOW TENNIS BEGAN

GAMES OF BALL were just as much a part of ancient civilisations as they are of today's world. The earliest known illustration of a ball game comes from the ancient Egyptian tomb of Beni Hassan, built before 2000 BC, which depicts two women astride the backs of two other women, evidently playing ball. In another tomb, the shrine of Hathor in the Temple of Deir-er-Bahari, built about 1500 BC, the Pharaoh, Thotmes III, is shown holding a stick in one hand and a ball in the other. In the background are two other figures, probably priests, also holding balls.

Robert W. Henderson, formerly librarian at the New York Racquet and Tennis Club, is the greatest expert on the history of Tennis. In his authoritative book on the origin of ball games, *Ball, Bat and Bishop*, published in 1947, he has shown that such early ball games developed from religious ceremonies, often connected with the fertility celebrations of springtime. He suggests that the ball may originally have represented the most significant part of man – his head. It seems natural that a ball should have come into use early in man's history as a result of the innate urge to throw, hit or catch small round objects such as stones or apples. It is known that balls featured in certain rain-making ceremonies performed by women, and this could explain the illustration in the tomb of Beni Hassan.

In Islam similar religious rites are known to have existed, often involving large groups of contestants wielding sticks and stones and resembling a primitive form of hockey. In Persia games were played on horseback and are reminiscent of a form of polo, with large numbers of horsemen on either side.

Herodotus asserted that the Lydians originated ball games, and Polydorus Vergilius wrote a book of inventions in 1499 in which he said:

> *Dice, Tables, Tennis and Cards were found of the Lydians, a people of Asia, and begun not for any lucre or pleasure, but for a Common-wealth. For when the Countrey had great scarcenesse and want of Corn, insomuch that it was not able to suffice the people, they mitigated and swaged their hunger and scarcity by taking their meat moderately one day, and by applying such sports and pastimes the next day, to drive away the tediousnesse of their famine and hunger.*

Ball games of a sort were part of the great civilisations of Greece and Rome. The Greeks were exponents of physical fitness and the ball played a part in their gymnastic exercises. Homer in the sixth book of the *Odyssey* relates how Nausicaa, daughter of Alcinous, the King of Phaeacia, goes to a river to do the family washing. While the clothes are drying she plays ball with her companions. One of the girls misses a catch and the ball falls into the river. The cries of the girls awaken Odysseus. Bajot in his *Eloge de la Paume* published in 1854 quotes Anne Lefèvre, later Dacier, who wrote on this episode:

> *Eustace (a twelfth-century bishop of Salonica) believes that it is the game of* hephetinda *or* phennis, *in which you try to take each other by surprise; you make as if to throw the ball to one of the players, but you throw it to another who doesn't expect it. Sophocles wrote a drama on this Homeric subject which he called* pluntrias *and in which he showed Nausicaa playing this game. It was a great success. I wish it had survived so that we might see what art could make of such a subject. However, this game which Homer here describes, was common even among women.*

For their gymnastic ball games the Greeks used the word Sphairistike, borrowed by Major Walter Wingfield in 1873 for his game of lawn tennis. According to Hieronymus Mercurialis, author of *De Arte Gymnastica* published in 1572, the Greeks had at least four different ball games, which he labelled 'the little ball, the great ball, the hollow ball and the inflated ball'. The first three were of various sizes and were thrown from player to player as part of gymnastic exercises. The great ball was something like a medicine ball filled with sand.

The game with an inflated ball was called *episcyrum* and resembled a primitive form of rugby football. Two sides took part and evidently attempted to drive the ball through their opponents' defence to score a goal.

Mercurialis also identifies four Roman ball games according to the type of ball used – the *follis*, the *trigonalis*, the *paganica* and the *harpastum*. The *follis* was a large leather ball filled with air. It was propelled by the forearm, which was protected by an arm-guard (*bracciale*). An illustration shows it to be the game of Pallone, though it is very doubtful that this was really played by the Romans.

The term *trigonalis* suggests a threesome and the game seems to have involved three players probably positioned in the shape of a triangle. The ball was passed between them and the object was to prevent it from touching the ground. Evidently this led to considerable exertion as it was usually followed by a warm bath. The *paganica* was a country game played with a ball of skin stuffed with feathers. *Harpastum* seems to have resembled the Greek *episcyrum* using a leather ball.

These old Roman ball games are mentioned in contemporary writings but not in detail. Several references occur in Martial's *Epigrams*, in one to Atticus praising the merits of a good run rather than boxing, wrestling or ball games, he mentions all four of the games identified by Mercurialis.

'Neither *pila* [presumably *trigonalis*] nor *follis* nor *paganica* prepare you for a warm bath – nor striking at a dummy with a blunt sword. Don't twist your arms on the wrestling mat nor dash to seize the dusty *harpasta*.' (BOOK VII. 32). Later he lists all four balls:

'Pila Paganica. *This ball which swells with tightly pressed feathers is less flaccid than the* follis *and less compact than the* pila' [presumably again trigonalis] (BOOK XIV. 45)

'Pila Trigonalis. *If you know how to defeat me with your cunning left-handers, I am yours. You don't? You fool, give me back the ball*' (BOOK XIV. 46)

'Follis. *Go away young man; quiet old age suits me; it is fitting for boys to play with the* follis, *and for old men*' (BOOK XIV. 47)

'Harpasta. *These the pansy-boy, who enlarges his neck with wasted effort, swiftly seizes on the dusty ground of Antaeus*' (BOOK XIV. 48)

The game of Follis *as illustrated by Mercurialis.*

As in fives, it was clearly an advantage to play equally well with both hands. Martial writes of Menogenes: 'he will take the warm *trigonem* with either right or left hand.'

Certainly there were competitive ball games, played with hand and foot. Manilius writes in the first century AD:

Let Feasts unbend the Clowns, let Labour yield
To Sport and Mirth, and Pastime Crown the Field;
None give so sure, and none avoid the Fall
So well; or catch and turn the flying Ball.
To vigorous Stroak their active Arms command,
Or with their Foot supply the place of Hand,
Or when in Sport they shall the Ball divide
From Hand to Hand, and toss on every side;
Now throw the flying Globes, and now retain,
Or play them back upon themselves again.
Now back, now forward, round, and every way
O're all their Limbs the active Balls shall play,
As taught to know their meaning, and obey.

But they were normally associated with the Baths, where Petronius introduces Trimalchio to his readers:

Then all of a sudden we noticed a bald old fellow in a reddish shirt who was playing ball with some long-haired slave-boys. It wasn't the lads who made us stop and stare, though they were well worth a good look; it was the old boy their master. He had house-slippers on his feet and was doing things with a green ball. If a ball touched the ground, he wouldn't pick it up. A slave stood by with a bagful and handed out a new one to the players. And we observed another novelty. Two eunuchs were posted on opposite sides of the group. One held a silver jerry; the other counted the balls – not when they were in play, caught and hurled from hand to hand, but when they were missed.

We gaped a bit at these pomposities, but then Menelaus (Agamemnon's assistant) bustled up. 'That's the chap at whose table you're going to eat,' he said. 'In fact, you're at this moment watching the prelims of the dinner.'

No sooner had he got this information out than Trimalchio cracked his fingers. The eunuch with the jerry rushed up at the signal and held it out. Trimalchio went on playing as he relieved his bladder, then he called for a basin of water, dipped in his fingertips, and wiped them on the head of one of the young players.

Gianni Clerici in his magnificent book *500 Anni di Tennis* even suggests that the Romans played with a racquet, and cites a passage from Ovid's *Ars Amatoria*. However, Ovid is surely referring to board games, resembling dice, draughts and backgammon, rather than to any ball game.

Galen, one of the pioneers of medicine writing in the second century AD, highly recommended exercise with the small ball. He considered it superior to other gymnastic exercises and listed several of its advantages such as relative safety, modest cost, little apparatus and no waiting. He pointed out that it was useful in exercising every part of the body, including the eyes, and was adaptable for all ages, and the weak as well as the strong. He recommended it to doctors for convalescent exercise.

Clearly at this point the ball was still mainly associated with gymnastic exercise and games had not yet been formalised. Galen was a good example of his own precepts, living to be 100 years old.

The first reference to a formal ball game occurs in a letter from Sidonius Apollinaris, a fifth-century Bishop of Clermont in Gaul, then overrun by the Visigoths. Addressing Eriphius, he writes:

Tired at last of this long rest, we felt a desire to do something. Presently dividing ourselves into two companies, according to age, the first loudly called for a game of tennis, the others for a table and dice. I was the first to make a move for the tennis; for, as you know, I love it as much as my books. On the other hand, my brother Domicius, a man of great elegance and love of sport, got hold of some dice, rattled them, and rapped his dice-box as though he was sounding a trumpet to summon the players to him. As for us, we had a long game with the scholars, in order to refresh our limbs, numbed by a too long rest, by this healthy exercise. The noble Philimathius himself, as the Mantuan poet says, Ausus et ipse manu juvenum tentare laborem, *constantly mingled with the tennis-players. He excelled at it when he was younger; but when he had been frequently hustled from the middle, where they stood upright, by the shock of some player running against him; when, at other times, going within the base, he could neither bar the way nor get out of the way of the ball, as it flew before him, or came upon him, and found a difficulty in recovering himself from his falls, being frequently overturned, he was the first to leave the game, panting and greatly heated. The exercise had caused his liver to swell, and he suffered a sharp pain. I stopped shortly afterwards, by way of charitably stopping at the same time as he, and thus relieving our brother from the annoyance of his fatigue.*

With the spread of Christianity through Europe, many pagan buildings and pagan rituals were adapted to new use. Temples became churches, spring rites became Easter festivals and with them many ball games were translated. First in Spain, later in France, Easter festivals are known to have been associated with ball games of a primitive sort.

Early in the twelfth century at Auxerre in S.W. France, it was the custom on Easter Day for a ball to be handed to the Dean by a student priest. A procession entered the church and the ball was thrown from one person to another as they advanced up the aisle. Similar ball ceremonies existed at Auxerre in 1396 when the chapter issued an ordinance on the presentation of balls by new canons on the first Monday after Easter; and in 1412 another ordinance was issued limiting the size of the ball. It was not until 1538 that the old custom was finally abolished by order of an ecclesiastical court.

At Vienne, the Archbishop himself threw a ball into the midst of the congregation and some form of game was played.

In the thirteenth century at Nevers, the canons used to play at Easter and the bishop himself gave instructions for refreshment to be served to all members of the choir who took part.

These rituals had their critics. Jean Beleth, a theologian from Paris, disapproved of bishops and even archbishops taking part in these ball games at Christmas and Easter in the cloisters or episcopal palaces; he condemned them as pagan practices. This is the first mention of ball games being played in a cloister. William Durandus, Bishop of Meaux in 1326, quoted Beleth in support of his case against ball games; it is clear that they took place mainly in Meaux, Auxerre and Troyes.

To regulate the practice, several ecclesiastical councils issued edicts. Pierre de Colmien, Archbishop of Rouen in 1245, forbade priests to play. St. Charles Borromeo, Archbishop of Milan, allowed only young priests in training to play. Jean de Longueville forbade his priests to play often in public, especially with laymen. Others acted as did the Council of Sens in 1485 and 'forbade all priests and all in holy orders to play tennis without shame in a shirt and in indecent undress'. An early illustration in the Bodleian Library shows just such an episode.

Until the last years of the twentieth century, the prevailing view was that the likely origin of Tennis lay in cloisters. The available evidence – the shape of the court and early references to, and illustrations of, the game being played in ecclesiastical circles – seemed to indicate that this was the case.

However, more light has been shed on the matter by Dr Heiner Gillmeister, a Chaucerian scholar and linguist, in his book *Tennis: A Cultural History*, first published in Germany in 1990, and also by Roger Morgan in *Tennis: The Development of the European Ball Game*, published in 1995. Gillmeister, who has meticulously studied evidence provided in contemporary literature and illustration, theorises that the origins of the game lie in medieval tournaments, especially the Pas d'Armes, in which knights on one side try to storm entry to a castle defended by the other side. He suggests that this knightly exercise was adapted by humbler folk into a game played in the open outside the walled city, which seems somewhat far-fetched.

Morgan takes a different view. He has unearthed a great many street games originating in Europe that included aspects of modern Tennis in their rules, such as scoring in 15s and the use of chases. This is in sympathy with Antonio Scaino da Salò, an Italian scholar who published the first-ever treatise on Tennis,

Tennis in a cloister.

Trattato del Giuoco della Palla, in 1555. Scaino writes of various different types of game, modified to suit the location of the court and the equipment of the player.

Morgan points to the unsuitability of the size and shape of a cloister and to instances of Tennis being played in church buildings despite the existence of a cloister. Evidence that the game spread from street to closed court and not the reverse may be seen in the need for adapting the old open-air rules. Chases, which in the original game were marked at the point where the ball was 'stopped', were not possible in the closed court. The rule was altered to marking a chase at the second bounce. The winning areas of the street game became the winning openings (dedans, grille, trou, lune) of the closed court. Such a transition seems far more credible than the reverse from closed court to the street, or indeed from Pas d'Armes.

Morgan suggests that the penthouse (which gives the court its cloister-like look) was of no significance in the early days and was in fact no more than the canopy providing shelter for shoppers in medieval streets. The association of the game with the church may have derived from the fact that ecclesiastical buildings provided walls and buttresses where the game could be played without interruption from pedestrians.

We are still left, however, with what Morgan describes as a 'tantalising gap from Greco/Roman times to the Middle Ages'. How did the Royal Tennis court of Henry II at the Louvre, described by Scaino in 1555, emerge from the multifarious forms of court elsewhere? Who decided on the positioning of the galleries and the penthouse? How did the tambour come to be inserted and why was the grille provided? It is tempting to think that there was a prototype somewhere and that these features formed part of an existing building, a castle perhaps, or an ecclesiastical building. Perhaps we shall never know.

Professor Nicholas Orme of Exeter University accepts the probable street origin of Tennis and that there were a great variety of rules depending on local geography. What is certain is that the game finally became well established when taken up by the aristocracy in the fifteenth and sixteenth centuries and more sophisticated courts began to be built for their use. I am indebted to Roger Morgan for allowing me to make use of his recent research into the drawings of Androuet du Cerceau, an eminent French architect of the sixteenth century. He was put on to this source of information by Cees de Bondt of the Dutch Real Tennis Association. Between 1545 and 1586, du Cerceau designed many châteaux, some of which included one or more Tennis courts. He was employed as a designer and architect by the royal family and received a pension from them for the last ten years of his life. His designs of Tennis courts differ from the known model at the Louvre. The penthouse is supported at intervals by pillars all around the court and there are no dedans, grille or tambour. Morgan refers to these courts as 'pillared galleries'. They occur in many of du Cerceau's designs and some possibly pre-date the Louvre court of 1555. Some were sited in moats and use the outer walls of the châteaux as the main walls of the courts. Existing turrets and buttresses were incorporated and this may be the origin of some of the unusual features of the Tennis court. Features differed from court to court. Just as the game in the street took various shapes according to the location, this seems to have been the case too with the development of closed courts.

Research work carried out in Italy by Cees de Bondt, covering the period 1450 to 1789, shows the existence of a considerable number of 'Pallacorda' courts built by the great aristocratic families of Italy, including Medici, Gonzaga, Este and the ecclesiastical princes in Rome. These varied in size and layout, becoming more standardised in the late sixteenth century.

The popularity of Tennis at this time in France is attested to by several contemporary witnesses. Jerome Lippomano, Venetian Ambassador to Henri III for three years from 1577, wrote that there were more than 1800 Tennis courts in Paris and at least a thousand écus (an ecu was three francs) were spent on the game every day. 'The French enjoy the game and play with marvellous grace and dexterity,' he said, and they 'eat four or five times a day without any rule or fixed hour. Little bread or fruit, a lot of meat and pastry.'

Francesco Gregory d'Ierni, who accompanied the Papal Legate, Alexandre de Medicis, Cardinal of Florence, to Paris in 1596, writes of '250 tennis courts, very beautiful and very well equipped, which they say, before the recent wars, gave employment to some 7000 people.' This figure may be an underestimate according to Thomas Plater in his *Description of Paris* in 1599. 'Some allege,' he writes, 'that there are about 1100 tennis courts in Paris; admittedly there are only half that number, but it is still a respectable figure.'

Another witness is Sir Robert Dallington, secretary to the English Ambassador to France, who wrote in 1598:

As for his exercises, there is danger but of one in France, and that is tennis play: this is dangerous (if used with too much violence) for the body: and (if followed with too much diligence) for the purse.

As for the exercise of Tennis play...it is more here used than in all Christendome besides; whereof may witnesse the infinite number of Tennis Courts throughout the land, insomuch as yee cannot finde that little Burgade, or towne in France, that hath not one or more of them. Here are, as you see, three-score in Orléans, and I know not how many hundred there be in Paris: but of this I am sure, that if there were in other places the like proportion, ye should have two Tennis Courts for every one Church through France. Methinks it also strange, how apt they be here to play well, that he would thinke they were borne with Rackets in their hands, even the children themselves manage them so well, and some of their women also, as we observed at Blois.

There is one great abuse in this exercise, that the Magistrates do suffer every poore Citizen and Artificer to play thereat, who spendeth that on the Holyday at Tennis, which he got the whole weeke for the keeping of his poore family. A thing more hurtful than our Ale-houses in England, though the one and the other be bad enough.

And of this I dare assure you, that of this sort of poore people, there be more Tennis Players in France, than Aledrinkers, or Malt-wormes (as they call them) with us.

The testimony of such people has to be believed. In conclusion the name *jeu de paume* was applied to innumerable variants of the game in the streets and the chateaux; some were played in the open, some in covered areas. They had their own versions of the rules depending on their location and were played by old and young, rich and poor. As Dr Gillmeister has pointed out, historians have concentrated their attention on the doings of the king and court and have overlooked the popularity of the game among the ordinary people of France and other countries in Europe.

WHY TENNIS?

Tennis was known in its early days as *cache, jeu de bonde* and, eventually, *jeu de paume*. The first of these names is from the Northern French dialect of Picardy and was adopted into Scots at an early date, although it does not appear in a written source (in the form of *caich*) before the last decades of the fifteenth century. Picardian *cache* reappears in the fifteenth-century Dutch *kaetsspel*, the sixteenth-century *Katzball* and *Katzenspil* in German, and the Scots *caichepule*, found in 1526. James VI of Scotland (James I of England), advising his son Henry in 1598, recommended 'playing at the cache'. Why then did the English call it Tennis?

It is an intriguing question which has long puzzled historians. Many ingenious theories have been advanced, most of them unsatisfactory. One suggestion was that it was played five-a-side, making a total of ten players; another that it derived from *tenes bound*, an old Norman expression referring to the tendons or cords protecting the hand; another that it came from the Greek *phennis* or the Latin *teniludium* or *tenere* (to catch), or the German *Tenne* (a threshing floor), or even from the old Egyptian city of Tinnis, famous for its fabrics which may have been used to make Tennis balls. Another suggestion was that it derived from Tennois or Sennois in the Champagne district.

Most of these theories suffer from one great defect: they don't explain why a foreign word should have been used to describe a French game.

A plausible explanation seems to be that given by John Minshew in his *Guide into Tongues* published in 1617. He derives it from the French imperative of *tenir* (hold) – 'which word the Frenchmen, the only tennis players, use to speake when they strike the ball at tennis.' If French players used to call out *tenez* (i.e. hold or take heed) before each service, it could be that their English pupils came to call the game by this term.

That the English were not the only ones to choose this word for the name of the game is shown by a curious extract from the *Cronica di Firenze* by Donato Velluti, writing between 1367 and 1370, but referring back to an event in 1325.

Thomas of Lippaccio was an ecclesiastic endowed with a benefice on the other side of the mountains [i.e. beyond the Alps], beautiful in form, tall and courageous as a lion. He sold the benefice referred to and came over here [i.e. to Florence] for there had arrived 500 French courtiers that were the handsomest and finest set of people I ever saw, with plenty of money, all noblemen and great barons, among whom I saw one who was taller by a whole head and neck than any tall man, and his foot more than half an arm long. Almost all of them were killed at the defeat of Altopascio. He played all day with them at ball, and at this time was the beginning in these parts of playing at tenes.

This suggests that the Italians, too, used *tenes* to describe what the French called *jeu de paume*, although later they came to call it in their own language *giuoco della corda*.

But what evidence is there that the French players did call out *tenez* before serving? The difficulty lies in the fact that such customs are not normally recorded by writers about a game. Consider, for example, the game of Rackets in which the marker calls out 'play' after each good stroke. This is certainly not recorded by writers on Rackets and should the custom cease a researcher 500 years hence would have great difficulty establishing its use.

However, the remarkable fact is that some evidence does exist that a warning cry was given before serving, although in Latin, the *lingua franca* of the day, rather than in French. The first of such evidence comes from the *Colloquies* of Erasmus. These were written as Latin exercises for his students in Paris and became a standard school textbook. He first published them in 1518, but added to them in later editions, including a section on sport in 1522.

The part on Tennis is in the form of a dialogue between Nicholas and Jerome. They draw lots for side and Nicholas wins the service. Before he serves Jerome says to him, 'Well, good luck. Serve the ball on to the penthouse. If anyone serves without warning, that service is not good.'* (*Qui miserit nihil praefatus frustra miserit*). Then Nicholas serves, calling out: *Hem, accipe igitur*. Later he serves again using the words *Rursus accipe pilam*. So it looks as if the server was required to give warning before serving and it seems likely that Erasmus uses the word *accipe* as a translation of the French *tenez*.

Antonio Scaino is unfortunately not very helpful on this particular subject, but at one point he refers to the duty of the captain of each side to call and reply at the beginning of the rally.

The vital key occurs in a Latin/French phrasebook written in 1580 by a Frenchman, Maturin Cordier, under the title *Commentarius Puerorum*, which includes a section on Tennis, '*Ludus Pilae Palmariae*'. The game is three-a-side with a pint of wine at stake. The players toss for sides in the modern manner by spinning a racquet, the alternatives being *pluye* (rain, probably 'rough') and *beau temps* (fine, probably 'smooth'). The server calls out '*Tenez, j'y mets*' (look out, I'm serving), and this is translated: *Excipe: ecce mitto*. Here surely is the proof. *Excipe* or *accipe* is the translation of *tenez*, used by French players before serving.

Cordier goes on to confirm what Erasmus had written, that a word of warning was required before serving, although in this case he used the word *jouez* rather than *tenez*. One player says: '*Ton coup ne vault rien: car tu n'as pas dict, Jouez*' translated into Latin very similar to that of Erasmus – *frustra misisti: utpote nihil praefatus* (your service is not good because you didn't call 'play'). He defines *jouez* as a word uttered by the server and in his Latin translation uses *excipe*.

In the light of this sixteenth-century evidence, it seems almost certain that the server had under the rules to give a word of warning and that the word used in French was either *tenez* or *jouez*. *Tenez* would seem to be the earlier word and no doubt gave rise to its use to describe the game in England.

In the present Basque game of *rebot*, the server

---
*Translated by Craig R. Thompson, 1965.

has to warn his opponents either orally or by gesture that he is about to serve and his opponents have to acknowledge the warning. In the *Petit Manuel de la Longue Paume* by Edmond Collin, written in 1891, rule thirteen is: *On avertit chaque fois que l'on tire* (one gives warning each time one serves).

A much later writer, R. Frissart, in a curious pamphlet of 1641 entitled *Carmen de Ludo Pilae Reticulo*, dedicated to Cardinal Richelieu, illustrated the war between Louis XIII of France and Philip IV of Spain in terms of a Tennis match. They spin a racquet for sides; the French king chooses smooth (rectos) and wins; so he serves crying out, '*Excipe.*' He uses the same *excipe* on several other occasions when he serves and so does the Spanish king when it is his turn to serve.

Gillmeister refers to a children's game called *tenee-ui* played in the Rhineland Palatinate and evidently developed from contact with French neighbours. A similar game is known in English-speaking countries as cat, and both games are played with a short wooden stick, tapering at both ends, rather than with a ball. In *tenee-ui* the server cries out *tennee* and the receiver replies *ui* suggesting the French *oui*.

A similar exchange of cries was observed in the Faroe Islands by Jens Christian Svabo, watching children playing a similar sort of game in 1781/2. In that case they called out *exebiti* or *exaksebiti* and the reply was *roti*. The first two words are clearly *excipite* or *accipite* and the reply is derived from *parati* (ready).

Gillmeister also calls in evidence a poem on the battle of Agincourt, describing the siege of Harfleur in terms of a Tennis match. There are three extant versions of this Middle English poem, but the two labelled the B-version and the C-version by Dr Gillmeister are of special interest. In these a big gun, before serving its 'ball', is heard to exclaim:

B. *Tenys seyde the grete gonne,*
   How felawes go we to game.
C. *Than sayd the greate gunne,*
   Holde felowes we go to game.

This evidence from the Agincourt poem is reinforced by a Shrewsbury clergyman in the 1420s, one John Audelay, calling back to memory Henry's feat of arms in another poem:

With tenes hold he ferd ham halle
With tenez! hold! he frightened them all

This certainly seems to suggest that Minshew was right in his etymology of the word and that *Tenez* or 'hold' was the normal word of warning before service.

Keeping the Score

One practice in Tennis that dates back to its very earliest days is scoring in points worth 15 each until a total of 60 is reached to win one game. The first mention of this scoring in 15s occurs in the Middle English poem on the Battle of Agincourt, mentioned in the previous chapter. Henry V, having laid siege to Harfleur, places his guns in position.

> *My gonnes schall lye upon this grene.*
> *For they schall play with Harflete*
> *A game at the tenys as y wene.*

Other siege-engines are placed on a hill

> *To marke the chase whan they play well.*

Three great guns are brought forward – London, Messyngere and Kynge's Daughter. London fires first:

> *'XV be fore' than sayd London, in same,*
> *Hys ball foull fayre he gan throwe.*

Messyngere fires next:

> *'XXX his myne' sayd Messyngere,*
> *'I woll hit wyn if that I may.'*

Kynge's Daughter fires the third shot:

> *The Kynge's Doughter sayd 'Harke how they play,*
> *Helpe my madonys at this tyde.'*
> *XLV, 'that nys no naye'.*

The next evidence is contained in the Middle Dutch didactic treatise of 1431 *Dat Kaetspel Ghemoralizeert*, and the third in a poem written in 1439 by the French prince Charles d'Orléans while imprisoned in England:

> *J'ay tant joué avecques Aage*
> *A la paulme que maintenant*
> *J'ay quarante-cinq.*

(I have played Tennis so much with Time that I am now 45).

Confirmation in Latin comes from Erasmus's *Colloquies* of 1552 during the game between Nicholas's side and Jerome's. Nicholas's side wins a love-game and the points are clearly described in Latin – *Quindecim, Triginta, Quadraginta quinque*. Modern usage of the word forty is merely a shortened version of the original forty-five. Even when Maturin Cordier wrote in 1580, it was not unusual to abbreviate the rather clumsy forty-five. In Latin it was *quadraginta quinque* and this, he tells us, was shortened to 'quadra' by the young.

In 1431, Jan van der Berghe in Holland had posed the question why 15s, but he could find no satisfactory answer. The first attempt at explanation was made by Antonio Scaino in 1555. He argued that there are three degrees of victory in each game:

1. The simple, when both players score points in the course of a game.
2. The double, what we now call a love-game.
3. The treble or furious, when one player reaches 40-love and his opponent wins the next five points and the game.

Who wouldn't be furious!

Betting was frequent in those days and the treble victory brought a triple reward to the backer. This being the finest achievement of all, Scaino reasoned that the 5 points necessary should be multiplied by the three degrees of treble victory to arrive at the magic number 15.

Scaino's typically medieval exposition is not very satisfactory. A more likely account is given by a French scholar, Jean Gosselin, writing in 1579 his *Déclaration de Deux Doubtes qui se trouvent en comptant dans le Jeu de Paume*. He confesses that he has found no previous authority on the subject and that the origin is buried in antiquity. He goes on to propound two theories of his own. The first is based on the fact that the number 60 often represented a complete whole in medieval times. A physical sign or sextant, the sixth part of a circle, consisted of 60 degrees; each degree was made up of 60 minutes, each minute of 60 seconds. It was natural therefore to take the figure 60 to represent a game, and the four points which made up the game were each worth 15 in consequence.

On the whole, this theory of Gosselin's seems to be the most satisfactory of any. Undoubtedly, in the Middle Ages the number 60 had a significance which it is now more usual to find attached to the number 100. It would be quite logical therefore to divide the game into four equal stages of 15. Gosselin's other theory was based on geometrical figures and is extremely complicated. It revolves around various measurements, particularly a *clima*, which is 60 feet in length and in breadth. Once again he finds the magical number 60 and proceeds to divide it up into four equal parts of 15.

More modern writers have propounded other theories. One ingenious theorist of 1885 pointed out that in French courts there are 14 chases marked on the floor. Thus, if the marker calls any number from 1 to 14, it means a chase. He suggests that the number 15 was therefore chosen for the first point won, so that there could be no confusion with a chase. This theory fails because there were no chases marked on the floor at the time when scoring by 15s was first used.

In 1913 A.E. Crawley advanced a theory based on the division of the clock into 60 minutes, made up of four quarters each of 15 minutes. In 1920 he added another based on the sexagesimal system of coinage in use in France in the fourteenth century. Both these ideas lend weight to Gosselin's theory of the segment: they are added proof of the medieval significance of the number 60 to denote a whole. From that point its division into four equal parts is a natural step.

The origin of the word deuce is fortunately simple. It was often the habit in France to call *à un* instead of 40, meaning that the player was within one stroke of winning a game. When both players reached 40, the rules required the winning of two consecutive points (advantage, game) and the score was called *à deux*. The old score *à un* has fallen into disuse, and *à deux* has developed into deuce in English.

More difficulties arise in tracing the origin of the term love to mean nothing in Tennis scoring. An unlikely theory, albeit ingenious, ascribes its derivation to a corruption of the French word *l'oeuf*, the egg. It is argued that the figure nought was familiarly known in France as an egg, in the same way that in this country a nought in cricket is called a duck's egg. However, there is no evidence to support this theory. Malcolm D. Whitman is probably nearer the mark when he argues that the use of the word love to mean nothing is as old as the English language. He quotes a saying of the year 971, apparently from an entry in the *Oxford English Dictionary*: *ne for feu, ne for nanes mannes lufou* – the equivalent of the modern 'neither for love nor money'. Love is equivalent to nothing, also, in such phrases as 'a labour of love' and 'to play for love'. In Latin the world *gratis*, meaning literally for favours or for love, is used in English to mean for nothing.

The origin of the word service may lie in the ancient practice of having a servant to play the first stroke. Henry VIII employed a man in this capacity and in the ancient Italian game of *pallone* a *tripolino* delivered the service. Such servants at tennis were known as *nackets*, who were also expected to stop chases and act as marker. The word comes from *naquets* in French and according to Roger Morgan in *Tudor Tennis* they were also well known as artful layabouts.

Another ancient aspect of Tennis, and one that has continued to give it a very special charm right up to the present day, is the chase, derived from the French *chasser*, to hunt or chase. The chase developed from the earliest Tennis of all: *longue paume*, which was *jeu de paume* played in the open. A large open space was required and often five players on either side would face each other across the cord or net. The ball was originally struck with the hand on the volley or at the first bounce and the players would seek to hit it as far as they possibly could. If one side failed to get the ball up, it made a chase – not at its second bounce as today, but at the point where it ceased to roll. The players would seek to stop it rolling as quickly as possible to reduce the length of the chase that they in turn would have to play for.

In such conditions, chases were marked by placing some object on the ground. In Erasmus's *Colloquies* it is clear that Nicholas and Jerome were playing *longue paume*. Erasmus uses the word *terminus* for chase – the point at which the ball ceases to roll. Nicholas says, 'Mark the chase with a shell or stone, or with your cap if you prefer.' And later, having made the chases, he remarks, 'We have two quite long chases.'

Most people associate Basque games with the *chistera*, the basket used in various games of *pelota* or *jai-alai*. In fact, the *chistera* dates from 1857, but the games played with the bare hand, the gloved hand and the bat date back to the origins of Tennis.

Rebot, one of the most ancient of these Basque games, incorporates the chase. Unlike most Basque games, *Rebot* is played by two teams across a centre line – very similar to *longue paume* except that both ends of the court are bounded by a wall. One side has a smaller area to defend than the other and the way of forcing a change of side is by making a chase – as in Tennis.

The chase is made at the point where the ball ceases to roll or is stopped, and is made on the smaller side of the court only. It is marked by a branch or a small flag on that side. It is played for as in Tennis, when one side reaches 40 or there are two chases.

The two sides then change ends and the centre line is deemed to be at the point where the chase was made. This means that the opponents have an even smaller area between the new centre line and the back wall to make a better chase.

The first mention of a chase being scored at the second bounce is made by Juan Luis Vivès, a friend of Erasmus, who also wrote a Latin exercise book for students in dialogue form. He had studied in Paris, but came to England in 1522 where he lectured on philosophy at Corpus Christi College, Oxford. He received an allowance from Henry VIII and obviously knew Tennis well. He wrote his *Leges Ludi* in 1539, and one of his two characters explains that 'the ball, indeed, is either returned on the volley or at its first bounce. For on its second bounce it is dead and a mark is made where it struck the ground.'

An illustration of an early seventeenth-century court at Tübingen in Germany shows a marker holding a special object used to mark a chase before the development of chase lines.

Scaino explains that the making of a chase when the ball stops rolling is not appropriate for the game of *courte paume*, played in a court with a back wall. 'In the court game,' he writes, 'they insist on the chase being marked at the point where the ball hits the ground at its second bounce, this being the custom in almost the whole of Tuscany and, in my opinion, a very excellent custom, worthy to be accepted by valiant and esteemed players.'

The first known illustration showing chase lines marked on a court is an etching in *Grosser Herren Stands und Adelichen Haus-Vatters* by F.P. Florin, published in Nuremberg about 1719.

An early seventeenth-century court at Tübingen, showing the marker with his chase-marking equipment.

BASIC PRINCIPLES OF PLAY

To the uninitiated Tennis appears to be a very complicated game, but in reality – apart from the system of chases – it is not. Lawn tennis is derived from it and the two games have much in common. Both are played over a net and in either singles or doubles. Both require the ball to be returned either on the volley or after it has struck the ground once, although in Tennis it may rebound off the walls before striking the ground for a second time. Both are scored in games by points of 15, 30, 40, deuce and advantage; and in sets won by the first player to reach six games, although in Tennis the winning margin can be a single game, i.e. 6–5.

In Tennis, however, there are certain openings in the walls of the court that give the player who strikes a ball into them an outright point. These are the dedans, the grille and the winning gallery (see plan). The court has another feature, the tambour, off which the ball comes at an awkward angle, not easily anticipated.

Service at Tennis is always delivered from the dedans end; the ball has to bounce at least once on the penthouse, in between a line marked on it at the centre of the court and its join with the far end (hazard end) penthouse; another line on the back penthouse limits the distance it may roll round towards the grille. As in lawn tennis it is an advantage to serve and a player will seek to remain on the service side as long

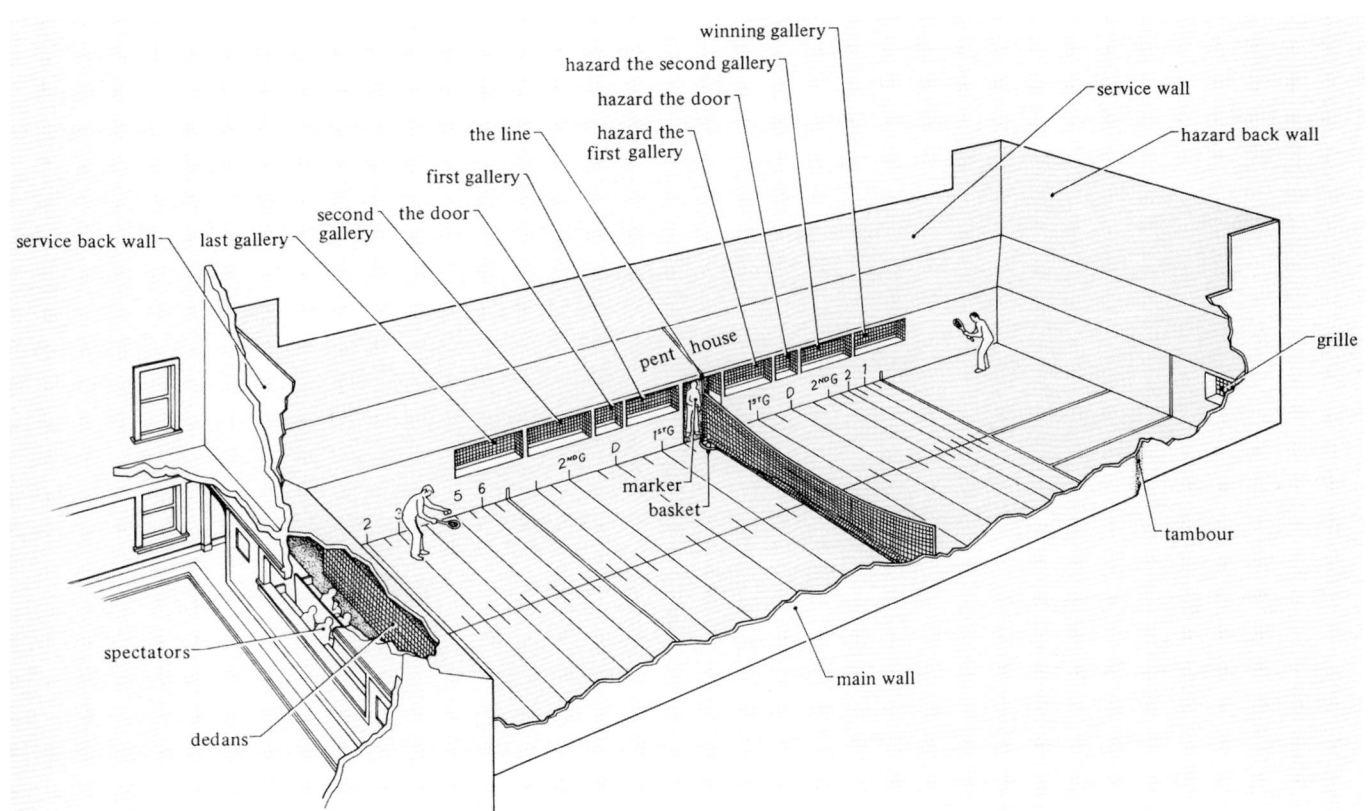

Plan of a Tennis court.

as possible. The only way the receiver can cross over and gain the service is by means of a chase.

A chase is made when a ball strikes the ground on its second bounce anywhere on the service side or on the receiver's (hazard) side between the net and the winning gallery. In most ball-games the ball would be 'dead'; at Tennis it makes a chase at the point on the floor where it bounces for the second time. Lines across the court enable the scorer ('marker') to record accurately the exact spot. A chase is also made if the ball enters any of the galleries – except, of course, the winning gallery. Each gallery has its own name (see plan).

The chase lines are numbered on the service side from the back wall at yard intervals from 1 to 6. Thereafter lines are drawn opposite the galleries and are described by the name of the appropriate gallery. On the hazard side there are only two yard chases after the second gallery; between them and the back wall no chase can be made. On both sides, the nearer the back wall the chase is made, the better it is for scoring purposes.

When a chase is made, neither side scores a point; the relevant chase (e.g. chase 2 – chase 5 – chase the last gallery) goes into cold storage for the time being. When there are two chase or when one player is within a point of winning a game, the players change ends and play off any outstanding chases. The player who made the chase now has to defend it; his opponent attacks it. To win the chase the attacker must make a better chase than the one being played. In other words he must ensure that every ball he plays will bounce on its second bounce between his opponent's back wall and the line of the chase being played. The defender will seek to return any such shot before its second bounce, but, if he judges that it will fall at a point worse than the chase being played, he will leave it and win the point.

The need to bring the ball sharply down off the back wall and thereby make a better chase is responsible for the typical cut shot of the Tennis player, not appropriate in the different conditions of lawn tennis.

One other difference in scoring between the two games can cause confusion. At lawn tennis the server's points are called first (e.g. 15–40); at Tennis, because service can change in the middle of a game, it is the winner of the last point whose score is called first.

DEVELOPMENT OF THE RACQUET

WITHOUT DOUBT TENNIS was first played with the bare hand – indeed it was known in its country of origin as *jeu de paume* (palm game). Anyone who has seen young Basques hitting a hard ball up against a *'fronton'* (the large front wall) will know the strength and skill that can be developed. However, it was not to be expected that everybody was tough enough for such painful sport, and gloves came into use. An excellent example is the Basque glove known as a *passaka*, used for an ancient game played in a *trinquet* – a form of court, developed from the hazard side of a Tennis court. Then followed wooden bats, *battoirs*, and eventually a *battoir* with a head strung with sheep gut – a primitive racquet.

Chaucer's use of that word in his *Troilus and Criseyde* – when Troilus says, 'But kanstow playen raket, to and for, Nettle in, dok out, now this, now that Pandare?' – has led to theories that the racquet was used earlier. Robert W. Henderson has asserted that Chaucer's 'raket' was in fact a game of dice, but Heiner Gillmeister, who has had several scholarly articles published on Chaucerian problem words, believes that Chaucer, to judge from the context, had in mind some form of Tennis, although whether 'raket' referred to the game itself or to some sort of implement we have at present no means of knowing.

The case of Margot has also been cited as evidence of an early use of the racquet. About 1427, 'came to Paris a woman called Margot, rather young, from twenty-eight to thirty years old, who was of the country of Hainault and played better at hand-ball than any man had seen; and she played very strongly both forehand and backhand, very cunningly and very cleverly as any man could, and there were but few men whom she did not beat except the very best players. And it was the court in Paris where the best play was in the rue Grenier Saint-Lazare, which was called the Petit-Temple.'

It has been argued that if she played a backhand she must have had a racquet, but this is not necessarily so. It is perfectly possible to play a backhand shot with the hand and may even be desirable in some circumstances – especially if one hand is stronger than the other.

Transition from hand to racquet comes later – at the beginning of the next century. Pasquier (*Recherches sur la France* 1596) cites the evidence of an old man of over seventy-six who told him that in his youth he had been one of the leading players of Tennis in his day, but that the game had been quite different because they played with the hand only – and while some played with the naked hand, others, to make it less painful, wore double gloves. Still others, more confident, gave themselves some advantage over their companions by wearing cords and tendons, in order to hit the ball better and with less trouble, and this came to be general practice. Finally came the racquet, at first a very primitive instrument but gradually developed into what we know today. Pasquier was born in 1528, which would suggest that the old man was talking about the latter part of the fifteenth century.

For a considerable time both hand and racquet were used. When Henry VII entertained Philip, Archduke of Austria and King of Castile, at Windsor in 1506, he laid on some Tennis.

> *After the horse was Bayted Bothe Kyngs went to the Tennys playe ... where played my Lord marques (of Dorset) the Lord Howard and two other knights togethare, and aftere the Kynge of Casteele had scene them play a whylle, he made partye with the Lord marques and then played the Kynge of Casteele with the Lord Marques of Dorset the Kynge Lookynge one them, but the King of Casteele played with the Rackete and gave the Lord Marques XV. and after that he had pled his pleasure and arrayed him selfe agene it was almost nighte, so both Kyngs Retorned agayne to their Lodginges.*

Clearly the racquet gave the King of Castile an advantage over the Marquess of Dorset, for which compensation was made by a handicap of 15. Even so, the racquet must have been a pretty primitive affair to have given a mere 15 to the opponent playing with his hand.

A few years later, in 1522, Erasmus in his *Colloquies* includes this dialogue:

> NICHOLAS: *We'll sweat less if we play with a racket.*
> JEROME: *No, let's leave the net to fishermen. Using your hand is finer.*

Jerome's answer is a pun in the original Latin – the word *reticulum* meaning both a racquet and a net.

The derivation of the word *racquet* has usually been attributed to the Arabic *rahat* meaning hands, but this is hardly tenable on linguistic grounds. Heiner Gillmeister, in an article published in *Journal für Geschichte* in March 1980, argues for a French origin of the word, which would be in keeping with the fact that most Tennis terms are French. As already mentioned, the earliest recorded name of the game was *cache*, the Picardian equivalent of the French *chasse*. The English words *catch* and *chase* mirror the different pronunciation in France of what was originally one word. In Picardy the verb *racacher* was used to denote the return of the ball, and a noun *racache* has survived in Picardian children's language meaning a sort of bat. It would seem probable, then, that some variant of these two words was the origin of 'racquet', rather than a remote Arabic word, the use of which was confined to medical writings throughout the Middle Ages.

Even in 1555, when Scaino wrote his magnificent treatise, there were still courts built for play with the hand, and he includes plans for an open and a covered court; but clearly his own preference, and no doubt that of most of his contemporaries, was for the game with the racquet.

In 1539, Vivès in his *Dialogues* describes a contemporary French racquet strung with fairly thick gut, somewhat like the sixth or bass string of a lute.

By the end of the sixteenth century, the racquet was the accepted thing and hands were only used to grip the racquet. In his Italian/English phrasebook of 1591, John Florio makes no mistake in having one of his characters call out: 'What ho, boy, bring hither some balls and some rackets.'

Tennis racquets did not become the powerful instruments they are today until much later – probably the eighteenth century. The racquet described and illustrated by François de Garsault in his *The Art of the Tennis-Racket-Marker and of Tennis* published in 1767 is the immediate ancestor of a modern racquet with a much longer handle than had previously been used. One noticeable difference is that in those days, the vertical strings were twice the thickness of the horizontal strings and that the latter were wound round each of the vertical strings instead of being threaded through them as they are now. This was the sort of racquet used by Barcellon and Masson, and by Barre and Biboche.

Somewhere about 1856 the system of stringing changed; gut of equal thickness was used and the horizontal strings were threaded through the vertical. The French were the best makers of Tennis racquets and they included Borrelly, Lavergne, Tison and Leclercq. John Dynan and his son in the seventeenth century are the first known English makers and in about 1780 even the French acknowledged that an English professional Pilet (or Pillet) made a racquet as good as theirs.

The great name in French racquet-manufacture in the nineteenth century was Brouaye, an apprentice of Leclercq. His racquets, with their striking green centre-piece, are easily recognisable. They were as popular in

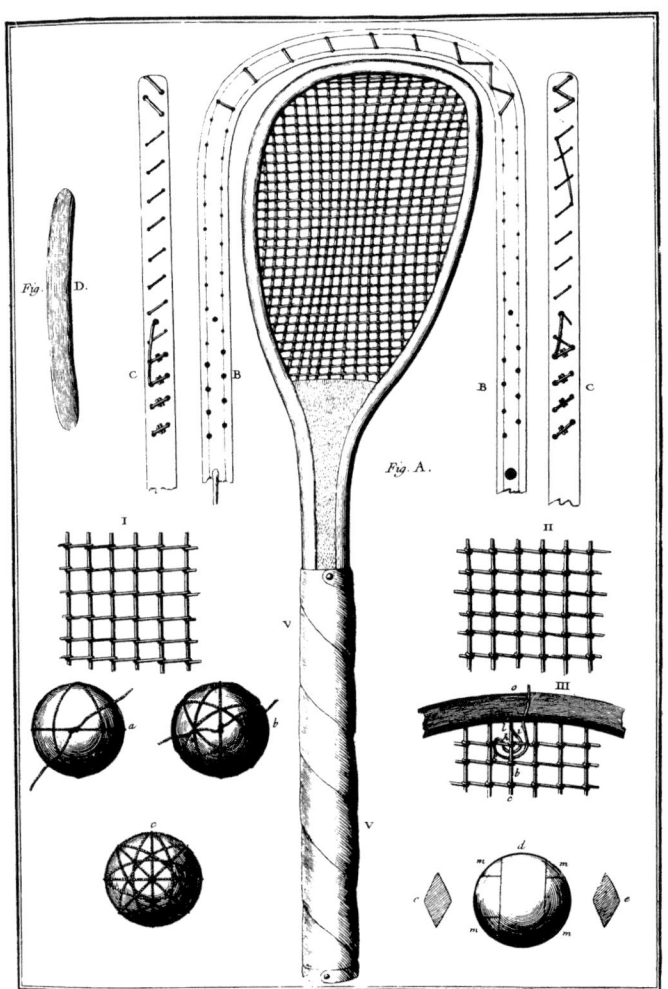

De Garsault's racquet of 1767.

England as in France, although there were a number of English manufacturers such as Watkins, Pittman, Wilson, W. Birt, Cox, John Case and his son Henry Case.

The earliest known makers of Rackets racquets were Pittman and Wilson.

In about the 1880s, two London firms began to make first-class Tennis racquets: Prosser of Holloway Road, and Nusser of Dean Street, Soho. About 1913 Bennett, an apprentice of Nusser, started a new firm in Cambridge. In 1915 Nusser was interned as an enemy alien and his business was taken over by one of his principal assistants, G. Wilson. Other English makers of this period were Alfred White of Hampton Court and Arthur Twinn of Cambridge. In France two new firms started business, Gell and Cabart. The firm of H.J. Gray & Son was founded in Cambridge in 1855 by the Rackets champion of 1863–66 to make Rackets racquets.

In the twentieth century, Tennis and Rackets frames have evolved from a single ash hoop into a frame consisting of ash, hickory and, latterly, vulcanised fibre and willow laminations. Adhesive tape was used to bind the throat and shoulders of Rackets racquets. The introduction of modern adhesives has meant that the use of a wood screw to strengthen the throat is no longer necessary.

There have been a number of frame developments in recent years. Tennis frames have either the traditional square or rounded handles. One model, designed by former world champion Wayne Davies, features one less ash lamination to lighten the head. Another incorporates additional vulcanised fibre laminations inside and outside the head, which provide a stiffer, more durable frame. Paint finishes have improved and most clubs now have models specially made up in their own club colours. An unsuccessful attempt to launch a graphite Tennis racquet resulted in a change in the laws to stipulate that the racquet must be made of wood or wood-related materials. Synthetic gut has replaced the natural variety and some professionals use alternative stringing patterns. Synthetic grips are now fitted to the handle.

Early nineteenth-century racquets from Petworth House.

In America, Bancroft of Rhode Island ceased production in the 1980s, having tried to manufacture Tennis frames in the Far East. Harrow Sports took over Bancroft and in 2005 started producing Real Tennis and Rackets racquets using the same factory in Pakistan. Grays of Cambridge remain the predominant manufacturers of Tennis and Rackets racquets. Grays were forced to close their factory in Benson Street in 1986 when graphite replaced wood in lawn-tennis and squash racquets, but production of Rackets and Tennis frames was transferred to their former sawmill in the nearby village of Coton, where production continues to this day. The firm continues to be wholly owned and controlled by the Gray family.

Development of the Ball

Balls for Tennis have been made in much the same way since the game began. It was necessary to have a fairly hard, round ball that would bounce true on a stone surface and balls were made of leather or cloth stuffed with wool or hair. It wasn't until the use of rubber was understood that balls suitable for bouncing on grass were developed and lawn tennis began.

As one might expect, the first mention of ball-making comes from France, where it is recorded that in 1292 there were thirteen professionals (*paumiers*) making balls in Paris alone. French balls were exported to other Tennis-playing countries. When in 1386 French knights informed John I, King of Castile, that John of Gaunt and the English were preparing a military expedition against him, he replied:

> *When you left me last year I charged you to bring me some balls from Paris on your return to this country so that we might play a game of Tennis. But it would have been better had I charged you to bring me a helmet and good armour.*

In England there was strong opposition to foreign balls. In 1463/4 a petition was submitted to Edward IV to ban the import of a wide range of articles including 'Tenys Balles'.

> *'Pyteuously shewen and compleynen unto youre wisdomes, the Kynges true people, Artificers, Handcrafty men and women' of London and elsewhere in England and Wales have 'been gretely empoveryshed and greviously hurt and hyndred of their wordely encreace and daily livyng' by goods imported 'by the handes of Straungers beyng the Kynges Ennemyes'.*

A century later a State paper of 1559 lists what were considered to be excessive imports, among them 'Balles, viz. Tennys balles, £1699'. And in 1591 Hugh Williams and Richard Kyd petitioned the Queen for a licence to make hand-balls and Tennis balls. They submitted that they could make better and cheaper balls than imported ones, which were sold at arbitrary and excessive prices, and that it would give employment to many poor working people. Evidently there was a duty on imported balls, for they offered to reimburse the Revenue by means of a tax.

But the main manufacturer of Tennis balls between about 1450 and 1550 was the Ironmongers' Company. Their records show receipts for balls supplied by them over nearly a hundred years, varying in price from one shilling to 1s 8d a gross.

Italy, too, was producing its own balls. In 1470 Galeazzo Maria Sforza ordered 100 balls from Florence, specifying that they should be a little larger than last time so that they would bounce more.

Evidently the standard of French balls had started to decline by 1480, when Louis XI, a keen Tennis player, issued a decree on 24 June that balls were to be stuffed with good hide and wool wadding and were not to contain sand, ground chalk, metal shavings, lime, bran, sawdust, ash, moss, powder or earth. The weight of these balls was about 1oz – very light compared with a modern ball of $2\frac{1}{2}$ to $2\frac{3}{4}$ozs, but of course they were for use by the hand or a fairly flimsy racquet. The improvement in the quality of balls was further ensured in 1537 when François I granted letters patent to the professionals, authorising them alone to sell balls in the vicinity of Tennis courts. Finally, in 1581, Henri IV granted a charter to the master professionals of Paris which included standards for the manufacture of balls.

Esteufs, for use by the hand, had to weigh just under 1oz and be covered with sheepskin and tightly stuffed with wool; *balles*, for use with the racquet, had to weigh about 1oz and be covered with new white cloth and stuffed with pieces of cloth tightly tied with good thread. In other words the ball, though lighter, was made in exactly the same way as it is today.

In 1539, Vivès in his *Dialogues* describes a contemporary French ball in contrast to that used in Spain. 'They hardly have any large balls as we do here [i.e. in Spain], but use smaller balls than yours, much harder and covered in white leather. The stuffing is not made of cloth as yours is but usually of dogs' hair and that is why they don't often play with the hand.'

The change from a leather cover to a cloth cover was noted by Sir Robert Dallington in 1598: 'You observe here [i.e. in France] that their Balles are of cloth, which fashion they have held this seven yeares: before which time they were of lether, like ours.'

In England balls were often stuffed with hair, normally dogs' hair, but if we are to believe Shakespeare, sometimes human hair:

> DON PEDRO: *Has any man seen him at the barber's?*
> CLAUDIO: *No; but the barber's man hath been seen with him; and the old ornament of his cheek hath already stuffed tennis balls.*
> (*Much Ado about Nothing*)

A very interesting early ball found in the rafters of Westminster Hall is now in the Museum of London; it is made of leather stuffed with hair.

A press for making Tennis balls.

De Garsault (1767) gives a detailed account of the making of a ball together with illustrations, but a complete do-it-yourself guide was published in 1977 (*How to Make the Real Tennis Ball from Core to Cover* by Richard Hamilton and Anthony Hobson).

In England between the wars, Tennis balls were made by Gradidge of Woolwich and A. Tompkins of Brighton. Balls from Prince's and Queen's were sent to A. Tompkins for re-covering, although at Queen's some were re-covered by E. Ratcliff and F. André. Alf White re-covered the balls at Hampton Court and for some of the private courts; at Manchester they were re-covered by J. Ronan and George Cooke under the direction of Charles Feldon.

In the Second World War both Gradidge and Tompkins ceased production of balls; for some time after the war there was a sufficient stock and little demand. The first stimulus to renewed production came from America. There a machine-made ball had been in use, extremely hard and very difficult to play with – especially for beginners. An approach was made to Dugald Macpherson for a supply of 3000 balls from Britain.

Macpherson sought the help of Henry Johns at Lord's, who had learnt the art of ball manufacture from Alf White. Johns made a dozen balls for approval and they were accepted. He tells the rest of the story himself:

> *As they were hand-made with strips of cloth torn from old coats and flannel trousers, I needed a great many pairs of trousers and lots of coats. Material was unobtainable as clothing was rationed and we were still using clothing coupons. All the old materials used had to be torn in $^3/_8$ in. strips which took hours and hours before the actual making of the ball was started. I then asked the Americans which 'fall' was it they wanted them by, as the contract would take me at least six years (dollars bought most things those days except time). They settled for as many as could be made at any time, in fact the 3000 balls took five years to complete.*
>
> *I was greatly assisted in this enormous exercise by George Beton and George Ferguson both at Lord's at this time. They made the kernel of the ball about an inch in diameter and I built them up to the required size and correct weight and tied them. My wife, Mona, and Mrs Beton had learnt to cover and re-cover them as required and this shortened the time-factor considerably.*

Jimmy Dunn of Philadelphia was originally the only source of balls in the United States. He taught himself how to do it at the suggestion of Sammy Van Alen, and trained members of his staff in the art. Other professionals in the USA are skilled at re-covering both Tennis and Rackets balls.

The difficulty of ball production stimulated experiment and help was forthcoming from Guy Bassett-Smith of Dunlop although there was never any question of commercial gain. In 1960 he persuaded Sir Reay Geddes, then managing director of the company, to agree to the idea that the technical department of Dunlop Sports Co. at Speke be given the task of developing a machine-made ball with characteristics similar to the hand-made ball.

The department began by taking apart a typical ball from Manchester and found the best part of a Crimean War tunic in it.

The cover presented no difficulty; the normal lawn-tennis ball Melton cloth was suitable. The problem lay in finding a ball of normal weight with the same bounce characteristics. After patient experimentation, a ball was evolved by using a squash ball core and moulding pressureless lawn-tennis ball-compound around it. On first trial these balls were considered too lively and this was rectified by the addition of sawdust to the compound. Dunlop moulded the balls in manually operated presses and supplied them in quantities of about 200 dozen. Thanks to David Sealey, the sales and marketing manager of Dunlop, these were offered to clubs at manufacturing cost.

However, balls could not be relied upon to perform in the same way in every court and were temperature dependent. Attempts to develop a manufactured ball continued, but without any further success. A return to traditional methods seemed the best solution and at present the balls are made by the club professionals. Nevertheless, efforts have been made to standardize the balls and in the UK most are now constructed with a cork centre covered by several metres of half-inch cotton webbing. Every court in Britain now uses fluorescent yellow cloth to cover the ball.

THE MEDIEVAL GAME

It wasn't long before the attractions of Tennis spread from the street to the castle and it became the game of kings. Philippe IV of France, known as the Fair (1285–1314), had a court at the Hôtel de Nesle, which he bought in 1308, but there is no evidence that he played. The first French king who certainly played was his successor Louis X, the Quarrelsome (1314–16), and he owed his death to it. He played Tennis with great vigour in the forest of Vincennes, drank a beaker of cold water and went to rest in a nearby grotto. There he caught a chill, which turned to fever and he died.

It is likely that Louis X had been playing a game of *longue paume*. Side by side with the street game *courte paume* there developed an open-air game which needed no court. *Longue paume* never achieved the same degree of popularity as its sister game, but nevertheless it has survived into the twentieth century. In 1929 there were ninety-eight societies of *longue paume* in France, where it was played mostly in Picardy, and in Paris in the Luxembourg Gardens where it is still played.

Jean II, the Good (1350–64), also certainly played. His treasurer recorded a payment of 144 écus in 1355 for 'two sheets of Brussels cloth, bought to make four pairs of robes, lined with miniver, which the King gave to certain people to whom he had lost at Tennis.'

His son, Charles V (1364–80) was a keen player despite his poor health. He seems to have had a primitive court in the Louvre itself; he also played in a court on the rue Froidmantel, adjoining the Palace to the west, and in another, which he had built, in the rue Beautreillis.

Longue paume *in France.*

Charles VI (1380–1422) played and we know that in 1394 he lost 300 francs which he had to borrow from Jacques de Montmor, the Governor of Dauphiné. His brother, the Duke of Orléans, also incurred considerable debts at Tennis and must have been a keen player. Tennis being thus popular at the French court it was natural that in 1414 the Dauphin should send Henry V of England a present of Tennis balls, with the advice that he would be better employed playing games than making war.

Shakespeare records the English king's reply as follows:

> *When we have match'd our rackets to these balls,*
> *We will, in France, by God's grace, play a set,*
> *Shall strike his father's crown into the hazard.*
> *Tell him he hath made a match with such a*
>   *wrangler,*
> *That all the courts of France will be disturb'd*
> *With chaces.*

Shakespeare based his *Henry V* on *The famous victories of Henry V* of 1598, in which the Dauphin's presents are described as a 'guilded tunne of Tennis balles and a carpet'.

The incident is also described by several other writers. Thomas Otterbourne, living at the time, was the first to mention it. A fifteenth-century manuscript describing the Battle of Agincourt, Caxton in his continuation of Higden's *Polycronicon* printed in 1482, Hall in his *Chronicle* of 1548, and Holinshed in 1577, all give accounts of the same incident, although varying in detail.

In the reign of Charles VII (1422–61), France produced the first known lady player, Margot, who has already been mentioned (see page 25).

Louis XI (1461–83) took a keen interest in the game, as is shown by his decree on the manufacture of balls (see page 28).

From existing evidence, Tennis was played in Scotland, from the reign of Alexander III (1249–86), before it was played in England. Alexander's mother was a Frenchwoman, Marie de Couci, and the ties between the two countries were always strong. For King James I of Scotland it was fatal. He was at the Blackfriars Monastery in Perth when, on the night of 20 February 1437, a band of at least eight assassins led by Sir Robert Graham broke into the royal apartments. They slew a page on the staircase and rapidly approached the room where the King was alone with the Queen and some of her attendants. On hearing the noise of their approach, the Queen and her ladies sought to bar the door, but the traitorous Sir Robert Stewart had removed the bolts. The story that Catherine Douglas thrust her arm through the bolt staples seems to be of later invention. Meantime, the King had tried the windows but found them strongly barred. Seizing an iron poker from the fireplace, he prized up a plank in the floor and lowered himself into the drain of the lavatory ('thordure of the privay'). The only exit from this stone channel was a small square hole at the bottom intended for cleaning, but alas 'he maid to let stop hit well iij dayes afore hard with stone, bicause that whane he played there at the pawme the ballis he plaid withe oft ranne yn at that fowle hole, for ther was ordeyned without a faire playing place for the kyng.'

However, he remained hidden until he thought that all was quiet and then called up to the ladies to lower sheets down to him to pull him out. Unfortunately, one of the ladies, Elizabeth Douglas, fell in and the disturbance led to the discovery of the King's hiding place. He put up a stout fight but unarmed he was no match for his murderers and was killed.

James IV of Scotland also played Tennis as we know from the Lord High Treasurer's accounts.

At the end of the century another Tennis casualty occurred. Charles VIII of France, although mis-shapen and stunted in body, was an affable man who loved his wife, Anne of Brittany, and his château at Amboise. Here he built a Tennis court which was the scene of his death. (The remains of the court are still visible.) An eye-witness described the event.

> *The King left Queen Anne of Brittany's room and took her with him to watch the tennis players at the moat of the château where he had never taken her before; and they entered together a gallery called Haquelabac, the entrance of which was in disrepair, and the king struck his forehead against the lintel of the door, although he was quite small, and then watched the players for a long time and talked to everybody. Suddenly he fell backwards and lost the power of speech; it must have been two o'clock in the afternoon and he remained there until eleven o'clock the same night.*

He was succeeded by his cousin, Louis XII (son of Charles, Duke of Orléans), a charming and well-liked young man who delighted in playing Tennis with his subjects, especially the citizens of his native Orléans.

But the popularity of Tennis had one drawback in the eyes of medieval kings and governors – it diverted the populace from more warlike sports, such as archery. So, while king and court continued to play with

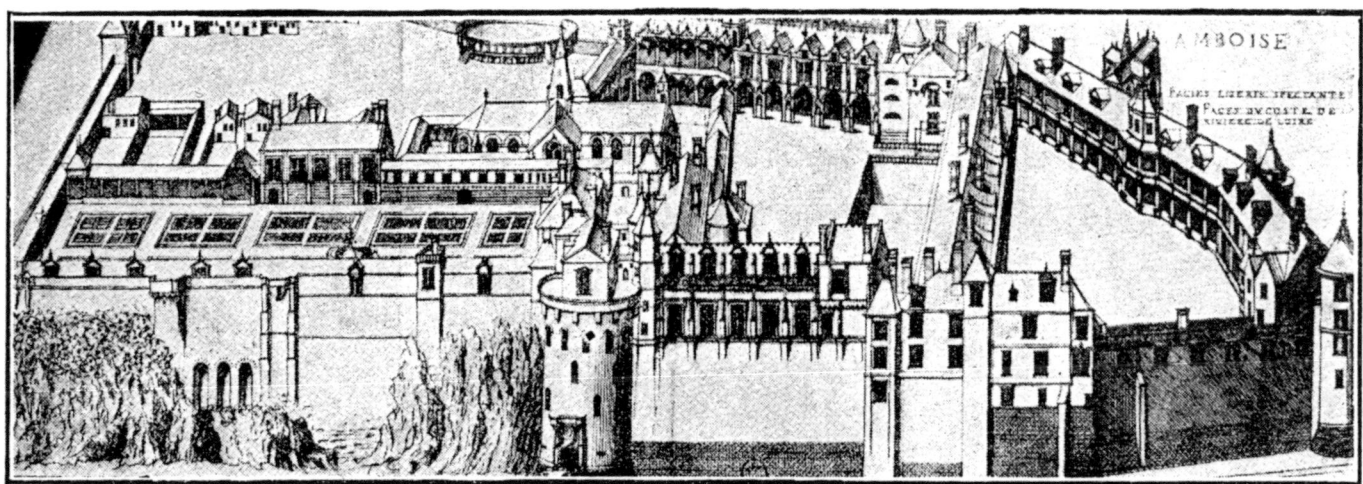
The Château d'Amboise.

increasing keenness, it was forbidden to the humbler subject, though seemingly with little effect. Philippe IV of France was the first to prohibit it in 1292 and Charles V re-enacted the ban in 1365, the very same year that Edward III of England decreed:

> June 12. To the sheriffs of London.
> *Order to cause proclamation to be made that every able bodied man of the said city on feast days when he has leisure shall in his sports use bows and arrows or pellets or bolts, and shall learn and practise the art of shooting, forbidding them under pain of imprisonment to meddle in hurling of stones, loggats and quoits, handball, football, club ball, cambuc, cock fighting or other vain games of no value; as the people of the realm, noble and simple, used heretofore to practise the said art in their sports, whence by God's help came forth honour to the kingdom and advantage to the king in his actions of war, and now the said art is almost wholly disused, and the people indulge in the games aforesaid and in other dishonest and unthrifty or idle games, whereby the realm is like to be without archers.*

This was followed by a further prohibition in 1388 by Richard II, specifically including Tennis under the name *les jeues as pelotes* (*pelote* being the French for hand-ball). Servants and labourers were to have bows and arrows and to use them on Sundays and holidays, but, he adds, 'it is not the King's Mind that any prejudice be done to the Franchises of Lords, touching the Forfeitures due to them.'

Prohibition followed prohibition in France and England as each king came to the throne, although the Mayor of Paris slightly modified the complete ban in 1397 by permitting Tennis to be played on Sundays only. Henry IV confirmed it in 1410, imposing a penalty of six days' imprisonment on convicted offenders, a fine of twenty shillings on Mayors and Sheriffs, and six shillings and threepence on Constables who failed to put the Act into execution. Later Acts of 1476 and 1477 increased the penalty to forty shillings and six days' imprisonment and finally to twenty pounds and three years' imprisonment – a very stiff penalty indeed.

The first record of a prosecution under these Acts occurs in Canterbury about 1396. William Terrey was summoned before the Burgmote for permitting divers men to play 'le Closhe and le Tenesse' in his house.

In Lydd, Tennis was obviously so popular that public announcements were frequently necessary to forbid it, as these accounts show:

> 1429. *Itm paid to a man crying the Watch to be kept by the sea-side and that no man should play at the tenys.*
> 1462. *Itm paid for two Cries one for tenys-players and the other for the Watch.*
> 1476. *Itm paid for a proclamation made for tenys-players, dyse-players and boyle-players 1d.*

Further prosecutions are recorded in Oxford in 1450 when 'Thomas Blake, currier, William Whyte, Barber and John Karyn, glover, "husbandmen", appeared before us Master J. Beek, DD and Master Gilbert Kymer, Chancellor of this kindly University of Oxford and Comissary General (of the Bishop of Lincoln) with their hands on the Holy Gospels abjured the game of tennis within the City of Oxford and its precincts.'

At Exeter they even played illegally in the cloisters of the cathedral, as appears from this reply of the Bishop, Dean and Chapter to the Mayor's Articles in 1447:

Art. 5. Atte which tymes and in especiall in tyme of dyvyne service, ungoodly ruled peple most custumabely yong peple of the saide Comminalte within the saide cloistre have exercised unlawfull games as the toppe, penny prykke and most atte tenys, by the which the walles of the saide Cloistre have defowled and the glas wyndowes all to brost, as it openly sheweth, contrarie to all good and goostly godenesse…

In 1451 the canons of the Collegiate Church of Ottery St Mary and their lay friends defied their bishop's ban on 'tenys' and 'by vain, foul and prophane words, by senseless and swelling oaths, by torrents of unlawful perjuries, they shamelessly occasioned such brawling, contention and yelling in the sacred churchyard that the devotions of Christian people coming there to pray for souls departed were vilely and damnably disturbed.' (Letter from Professor G.R. Dunstan to *The Times*, 3 May 1977).

Detail from an early print showing the two original courts at Fontainebleau – marked 8.

SIXTEENTH-CENTURY TENNIS

WITH THE ACCESSION OF the kings of the House of Angoulême in France and the House of Tudor in England there began the golden age of Tennis which was to last throughout the sixteenth and seventeenth centuries.

In France, François I, Henri II, Charles IX and Henri IV were all keen players. It was the fashionable game at Court, and despite continued prohibition for the ordinary citizen it was much played throughout the country.

Herald of this golden age was the young François I, strong, healthy and handsome, a dashing cavalier who loved chivalry and splendour and violent exercise, a patron of the arts as well as sport. Here was a monarch very different from the ugly and depraved kings of the previous century. He played Tennis from his youth, and in order to be able to play whenever he wanted he built courts at all his principal residences. At the Louvre he built a new covered court by the rue d'Autriche in 1530. At Fontainebleau he built an open court near the fountain of Diana and two more covered courts at the Château of Saint-Germain.

The setting of one of these, in the forest above the Château de la Muette, has been described as 'paved with large paving stones, with pillars at intervals, on which were engraved in relief salamanders, the arms of France, and the letter "F" surmounted by a crown, which went right round this beautiful terrace on which one strolled, and from which sometimes one saw the hunt pass…and in particular there was a very lovely covered tennis court, which was on this terrace and from which there was a very lovely view.'

The King was evidently a useful player and always attracted a good audience, including the ladies of the Court with Catherine de Médicis at their head. It is said that 'a certain Monk, while playing with the King against two lords, made a brilliant stroke which decided the set in the King's favour, who then exclaimed "Ah, that is the stroke of a Monk". "Sire", replied the monk, "whenever it may please you, it shall be the stroke of an Abbot". An Abbey happened to be vacant at the moment and this the Monk received' – as he undoubtedly deserved.

It has been stated that the King played a match against the Emperor Charles V at Orléans, but there is no evidence of this. It has also been said that he played with Benvenuto Cellini. The King gave Cellini a triangular château up against the city wall, called Le Petit Nesle, which was unfortunately already let to the Mayor of Paris, although the latter made little use of it. However, he objected to Cellini moving in and it required violence to install the new tenant. Once in residence, Cellini writes: 'I had a tennis court in my castle from which I drew considerable profit.' He also tells of another pitched battle fought with stones, pikes and arquebuses without ball to expel a distiller who with the King's permission moved into the Tennis court and its lodgings. Cellini won this second battle and the King merely laughed at the incident. He does not mention playing Tennis with the King, which he surely would not have omitted were it in fact true.

François was envious of Henry VIII's navy and, determined not to be outdone, founded Le Havre and ordered a man-of-war even larger than Henry's famous *Great Harry*, which was over 180ft long with a burden of over 1000 tons. *La Grande Françoise*, built at Le Havre in 1532, was a third longer with a 2000 ton burden. She was four-masted with a mainmast of 25ft girth (nearly 8ft diameter) and 210ft high. She included a forge for mechanical repairs, a windmill to grind flour, a baker's oven and a private chapel. Between the castles, a Tennis court filled the waist of the ship with a huge awning stretched above it. The vessel attracted hundreds of sightseers and she was finally launched in September 1533. She did not go very far. Halfway across the harbour she disappeared into the estuary and grounded. She was freed and taken back to her berth, but on 14 November in a terrific storm she capsized at her moorings and sank. Eventually she was broken up and the St François district was built from her timbers.

The floating Tennis court experiment was repeated, however:

> *On the 3rd December 1539 the King embarked on the River Loire bound for Orléans; and the City Councillors sent ahead of the King to Gien ten or twelve boats, all covered in satin, on which were galleries, rooms, chimney-pieces and other furniture after the fashion of ships and there was one specially for the King, on which there were four rooms, galleries and a Tennis court.*

Orléans was a thriving centre of Tennis which was particularly popular with the university students. There were forty courts in the city at the beginning of the sixteenth century, and some complaints that the sport was interfering with the young gentlemen's studies. Later, in 1556, the situation was sufficiently serious for a complaint to be made to the Duke of Orléans, who ordered eighteen courts to be closed. The students at Poitiers, too, were addicts of Tennis and had twenty-two courts on which to play.

Rabelais brought the young Pantagruel to Orléans, where he met the students and learned to play Tennis. He soon mastered it and when he graduated in law, one of his fellow students wrote of him:

> *Un esteuf en la braguette,*
> *En la main une raquette,*
> *Une loi en la cornette,*
> *Une basse dance au talon*
> *Vous voyez là passé Coquillon.*
>
> *A ball in your pocket*
> *A racket in your hand*
> *A law in your hat*
> *A low dance at your heel*
> *You see you have passed the examiner.*

The Dauphin François inherited a love of sports from his father, but unfortunately died at the age of eighteen in a somewhat similar way to Louis the Quarrelsome, having taken a cold drink while hot from playing Tennis – according to the doctors of the day. His brother Henri, who succeeded in 1547 as Henri II, had less charm than his father but had the same liking for vigorous exercise. He was certainly one of the foremost Tennis players of his day, if not indeed the best in the land. He built a second court at the Louvre, also on the rue d'Autriche side of the castle, at the other side of the main gates from his father's court. It was also a larger court than usual, as Henri was very fond of playing doubles – or even trebles, with three players on either side of the net.

A contemporary described the King playing Tennis: 'At the large tennis court in the Louvre, dressed in white, wearing a doublet and a straw hat, he hits the ball enthusiastically; there is no formality except that the net is lifted when he wishes to go under it.' The white clothes lend a very modern touch to this picture, although designers today would hardly include a doublet and a straw hat. He must have been a delightful partner, for he shared his winnings with those on his side and paid all their losses himself. Henri's sporting activities led to his death. He took part in a tournament to celebrate the wedding of his daughter Elizabeth to Philip II of Spain and was mortally wounded in the eye by the lance of Montgomery, son of the Captain of the Guards.

His son François II was only fifteen and a sickly boy, who lived to reign for only one year. He was succeeded by his ten-year-old brother Charles IX, but effective power fell into the hands of Henri II's widow, Catherine de Medicis, who was faced with a critical situation in the rivalries of the Catholic and Protestant factions. She was naturally a leader in women's fashions and one of her hair styles was known as the racquet style (*coiffure en raquette*), so called because the hair was criss-crossed in bands in the same way as the racquet-makers crossed their strings. She evidently brought up Charles to play Tennis, for a drawing shows him at the age of two with a racquet in hand.

Charles was weak, lazy and melancholic, but as the Venetian ambassador reported in 1561 'passionately fond of tennis and riding'. He fell under the influence of Admiral Coligny, much to the dislike of the Catholics, for Coligny was the political leader of the Huguenots. Catherine de Medicis was alarmed at the thought of this Protestant influence on the King and the result was an attempt to assassinate Coligny on 22 August 1572. Charles, as was his wont, was playing Tennis in the Louvre at the time, as described in the following account of the incident:

> *It was about 10.30 a.m. The Admiral left the Council... In front of the Louvre he met the King, who had just heard Mass celebrated at 10 o'clock in the Petit Bourbon chapel, and out of deference to the Sovereign he immediately retraced his steps and accompanied him to the tennis court, where the King and the Duke of Guise, having made a match with Téligny, the Admiral's son-in-law and another gentleman, played for a while. Leaving the tennis court the Admiral took the rue d'Autriche... Then,*

Charles IX as a child.

being wounded by a shot from Maurevert's arquebus, he ordered Messrs de Piles and de Mouneins...to go without delay and inform the King of the attempt on his life. His orders were carried out at once. At that moment Charles IX was informed of the attempted assassination. Coligny's messengers had found him still in the tennis court and all witnesses agree on the spontaneous fury and bitterness with which he greeted the news. 'Will I never have any peace?' he exclaimed. 'Always new troubles.' Then throwing his racket on the ground he returned to the Louvre.

The attempted murder of Coligny brought things to a head. Catherine de Medicis and the Catholics realised that they could not let matters rest without imperilling their position. Charles gave in to his mother's advice and on 24 August, St Bartholomew's Day, at 1.30 in the morning, the alarm bells at St Germain-l'Auxerrois gave the signal for a massacre of the Huguenots. Coligny was killed. All the Protestant leaders were slaughtered except for the royal princes, Henri of Navarre and the Prince de Condé, who were imprisoned in the Louvre. In Paris alone three or four thousand Huguenots were killed.

One lucky man to escape was a certain Nompar de Caumont la Force, afterwards Marshal de la Force.

He was thirteen. The bodies of the three Caumonts lay at the end of the rue des Petits-Champs, near the city wall, where they had fallen. At about four o'clock in the afternoon, the doors of some houses opened, people appeared and approached the bloody scene. A professional from the Tennis court in the rue Verderet saw on the leg of one of the murdered Huguenots a cotton stocking which might suit him. He turned over the corpse, which was facing the ground. The youth of the face stirred him. Softly he said, 'Alas! He is only a poor child. Isn't it a shame. What wrong could he have done?' The child's head (it was that of Jacques Nompar) rose slowly, the mouth murmured, 'I am not dead, please save my life.' The man put his head down again. 'Don't move, for they are still here,' he said, and went away. Then came back. 'Get up,' he said, 'for they've gone.' Jacques Nompar put over his shoulders the dirty cloak that the man threw him. He walked in front of his saviour, who made pretence of beating him.

Later this Tennis professional received a pension from Marshal de la Force for his services and the Marshal became a keen player.

This kindly professional was no doubt one of those whose statutes had only recently been granted by the King. Originally the Tennis professionals had been members of a fraternity of makers of racquets and brushes. There were at least two branches of this fraternity in Paris in 1457, one of them meeting in the Chapel of St Barbe, their patron saint. Their arms show two types of brush and one racquet.

Some time during the sixteenth century they broke away from the brush-makers and established their own corporation, calling themselves *maîtres-paumiers raquetiers* – master professionals and racquet-makers. They adopted new arms and François I gave them letters patent. Charles IX granted them statutes in 1571.

The preamble to these was: 'Charles, by the grace of God, King of France, Tennis being one of the most honourable, worthy and healthy exercises which princes, peers, gentlemen and other distinguished persons can undertake, and which is today as much or more played and practised than any other by all the good towns of our kingdom, we have agreed the said requests and

A member of the guild of racquet- and brush-makers.

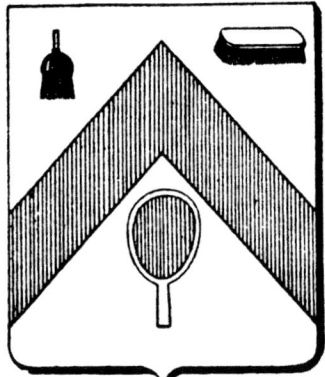 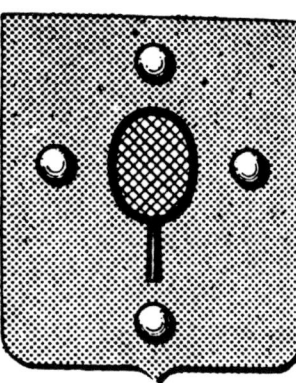

The arms of the racquet- and brush-makers and the later arms of the master-professionals and racquet-makers.

pleas of the Master Professionals…' The statutes go on to establish three grades of professional: the apprentice (minimum three years), the associate, and the master. The master could manage one court and employ one apprentice; he could also run a billiard saloon. A police licence stipulated the hours of opening and forbade play on feast days or during High Mass, the sermon and vespers, and banned the lending of money to players. The statutes also endowed the corporation with extensive rights over the manufacture of balls and racquets. These statutes were later confirmed by Henri IV and Louis XIII.

Besides the master professionals, associates and apprentices, there were many others employed at each court. There were markers, of whom two were required for each match, one to stand in each of the doorways leading into the court, marking the chases. The score was kept by the marker on the service side by recording the games won in chalk on the stone floor. It was also the duty of a marker to massage players and to look after them when the game was over; this usually meant rubbing them down with a towel.

A similar guild of professionals is known to have existed in Florence in 1550.

The delicate King Charles did not long survive and died in 1574 at the age of twenty-four. His successor was Henri III, amusing and full of charm but effeminate in manner. He liked wearing costly clothes, necklaces and scent, and was even known to dress up as a woman for some Court festivities. He played Tennis but, as his demeanour suggests, does not seem to have been outstanding.

Henri of Navarre succeeded him in name, but he was not recognised by the still powerful Catholic League which was dominant in Paris. He had to fight for his throne against the League and its allies, the King of Spain and the Duke of Savoy. He was a brave man and a gallant soldier, popular with his Protestant subjects and merciful to his Catholic enemies. After four years of civil war, he sacrificed his religious principles to political practicalities and on 25 July 1593, at Saint-Denis, attired in white, he was accepted into the Catholic church and entered Paris as the acknowledged King of France.

He played Tennis wherever he found an opportunity and his early wanderings enabled him to visit courts in many parts of the country. Brought up in Béarn, he played frequently at Pau in the court in the rue du Château. In the disorders of 1569 this court was demolished to provide material for the fortification of the château, but it was soon reconstructed. The builders were ordered to be as economical as possible by Jeanne d'Albret, Queen of Navarre, Henri's mother, 'in order that our very well-beloved son may take some pleasure there.' He also played at Lectoure, Montauban and Nérac, where the Court established itself. In Paris he played in the court of the Sphère and in the two courts at the Louvre, and according to one version played Tennis in the Louvre when he was confined there on the morning of St Bartholomew.

After he became King of France, Henri IV played frequently and there are many accounts of his Tennis activities.

On 18 March 1590, the town of Nantes paid homage to the King who refreshed himself and passed the time by playing Tennis against the bakers of the town. They won his money and did not wish to give him his revenge, because they said that they had agreed to play a maximum of three sets. The King, to get the better of them, had it announced the next day that a small loaf would cost a penny-ha'penny, at which the bakers, very embarrassed, came to ask His Majesty to have mercy on them and to take whatever revenge he wished, except on their bread.

Three days after his conversion to Catholicism,

the King played tennis at Saint-Denis and, noticing that the court was full of ladies who wanted to watch him but could not because of his bodyguard, asked the latter to withdraw so that the ladies could watch him at their ease . . . and the same day the Duke of Elbeuf came to find the King in the tennis court at Saint-Denis. On seeing him the King left the court and said, 'I must meet this fat boy'.

Arriving in Paris on 15 September, after the surrender of Amiens, the King played Tennis the whole afternoon of the next day in the court of the Sphère. On 24 September, he was still there, his shirt torn at the back, his grey shoes tied in a 'dog-leg' knot; and not being able to get to the ball because he was tired, he said that he felt like a stumbling donkey.

The King mixed love and politics with his sport.

At the Sphère court, the Marchioness [of Verneuil, by whom he had three illegitimate children] and the Mesdames de Sourdize and de Sagone went every day to see him play; he allowed himself to borrow money from Madame de Monceaux, whom he caressed much and kissed in front of everybody; this did not prevent him from watching the Spaniards and he was ready when the moment came to abandon Tennis and love to throw himself upon Amiens with that flexibility of movement which tennis taught him.

And in 1598 after receiving the Spanish envoys,

the King went to play tennis in his court at the Louvre. Marshal de Biron had the court and the King partnered him against Prince de Joinville. There were foreigners there who watched him play; he was also watched by the ladies, amongst whom the Duchess of Beaufort was outstanding; the King made her unmask herself so that the Spaniards could see her more easily.

He went on playing until almost fifty and wrote to the Queen in 1601, 'You are awaited here with the greatest enthusiasm. Enough of writing – I am off to play tennis. I kiss you a thousand times.'

There are many entries in the royal accounts of the payment of the King's debts at Tennis, and it has been assumed that he cannot therefore have been a very good player. It should be remembered, however, that only his losses were recorded and his gains were received personally by him after each match. He was particularly careful not to let his winnings find their way into the treasury. On one occasion he put them in his hat, exclaiming 'by the belly of St Gris, I'll keep these to be certain no one will rob me, for they will not pass through the hands of my treasurer.' Naturally Henri IV built some new courts for himself. One was at Fontainebleau, where there already existed an open-air court. Henri built a covered court beside it, somewhat larger as, like Henri II, he preferred to play doubles. Another he built at Compiègne.

The vigour with which the game was played in France led to the occasional casualty. Poet Jean Passerat lost an eye through playing Tennis and Montaigne in his *Essays* wrote of a Tennis tragedy.

Captain Saint-Martin, twenty-three years old who had already given pretty good proof of his valour, while playing tennis was struck by a ball a little above the right ear, with no sign of contusion or wound. He did not sit down or rest, but five or six hours later he died of an apoplexy that this blow gave him.

An interesting court still exists at the Château of Suze-la-Rousse in the Drôme department of southeast France. It was built in 1566 (the story says in three days and nights) about fifty yards from the main entrance to the Château, when Charles IX paid a visit to Count François de la Baume Suze with the Queen Mother, Catherine de Medicis, and the future King Henri IV. It is an open court with a narrower and longer tambour than usual.

During this same period Tennis began to flourish in England under the Tudors. Henry VII played frequently, as his expenditure testifies, despite the fact that he re-enacted the restrictive legislation of previous reigns. His accounts tell us also some of the places where he played – Woodstock, Wycombe, Westminster, Sheen and Windsor. Westminster is an interesting location for there is no evidence of a court there; he may have played in one of the inner courtyards or perhaps even in Westminster Hall. The latter seems doubtful as it was then in use as law courts.

Nothing is known of a court at Wycombe, but a court at Woodstock is mentioned again in 1634 on the side of the house facing the town. Sheen Palace had a dramatic history. Built by Edward III, who died there, it was demolished by Richard II in 1394 out of grief at the death of his wife, Anne of Bohemia. Henry V rebuilt it, but in 1498, the very same year that Henry VII played Tennis there and while he was still in residence, it was totally destroyed by fire. It was again re-built by the King, re-named Richmond Palace and was to be the place where he, and later Queen Elizabeth I, died.

The site of the court at Windsor is shown in a view of the castle produced by John Norden in 1607 (page 41). It was in the old moat by the Round Tower, at the spot where now stands the equestrian statue of Charles II. It was an open court approached by a covered way from the keep. At Windsor Henry VII entertained Philip, Archduke of Austria and King of Castile in 1506. Philip was on his way from the Netherlands to take possession of his throne in Castile and had been driven to shelter at Weymouth by rough weather at sea. Henry entertained him with hunting, horse-baiting and Tennis, as described on page 25.

Henry VII also built a court at Kenilworth Castle in 1492/3. Very recently excavations at Woking Palace have revealed what is thought to be another Tennis court built by Henry VII. If so, it is the oldest surviving court in the British Isles of which anything remains.

Henry VIII was a great lover of sport and was especially keen on Tennis which he played frequently as a young man – and frequently lost, as the royal accounts bear witness. A contemporary author writes that 'the Kynge thys tyme (1510) was moche entysed to playe at tennes and at dice, which appetite, certayn craftie persones about hym perceyuynge, brought in Frenchmen and Lombardes, to make wagers with hym, and so he lost moch money.' A typical entry in Henry's accounts for 1519 reads:

to young Care for my lord's losses at tennis 8s.

As time went on he seems to have grown more reckless and Tennis debts are recorded in 1530 of forty-five shillings and in 1532 of forty-six pounds thirteen shillings and fourpence. The latter sum, lost by the King to the Cardinal of Lorraine and Monsieur le Guise, was a considerable one in those days compared to our present debased coinage. It is interesting to find that the very same day the King lost one hundred and sixteen pounds thirteen shillings and fourpence at dice to the same Cardinal, Lord Norfolk, Lord Suffolk and his Master of the Household. Many other interesting payments connected with Tennis are recorded in these accounts. It is clear that a certain Anthony Ansley was the King's professional, who supplied balls and racquets, and accompanied the King to play in various courts – even to France on one occasion in 1532, to play at Calais. Other courts mentioned in the accounts were at Richmond, Greenwich, Windsor and the Moore. The court at Richmond was the same as that at Sheen previously mentioned. The court at Greenwich formed part of the old Palace built by Humphrey, Duke of Gloucester, known as the Manor of Pleazaunce. The Moore court lay in the Manor of Rickmansworth and belonged to the Crown.

A good picture of the King at play in such courts as these was given by the Venetian Ambassador, Sebastian Giustiniani, writing in 1519.

His Majesty is twenty-nine years old and extremely handsome; nature could not have done more for him; he is much handsomer than any other sovereign in Christendom; a great deal handsomer than the King of France; very fair, and his whole frame admirably proportioned. On hearing that Francis I wore a beard he allowed his to grow, and as it is reddish, he has now got a beard which looks like gold. He is extremely fond of tennis, at which game it is the prettiest thing in the world to see him play, his fair skin glowing through a shirt of the finest texture.

Rawdon Brown in his *Four Years at the Court of Henry VIII*, adds in a note:

The shirts worn by persons of condition at this period were bordered with lace and curiously adorned with needlework. One which had belonged to Arthur, Prince of Wales, made of long lawn, and beautifully embroidered with blue silk round the collar and wrists, was in the possession of the late John Gage, Esquire, Director of the Society of Antiquaries.

On his way to and from the court, Henry evidently wore a black and blue velvet jacket, for in an inventory of his wardrobe in 1517 occur two entries listing: 'iij

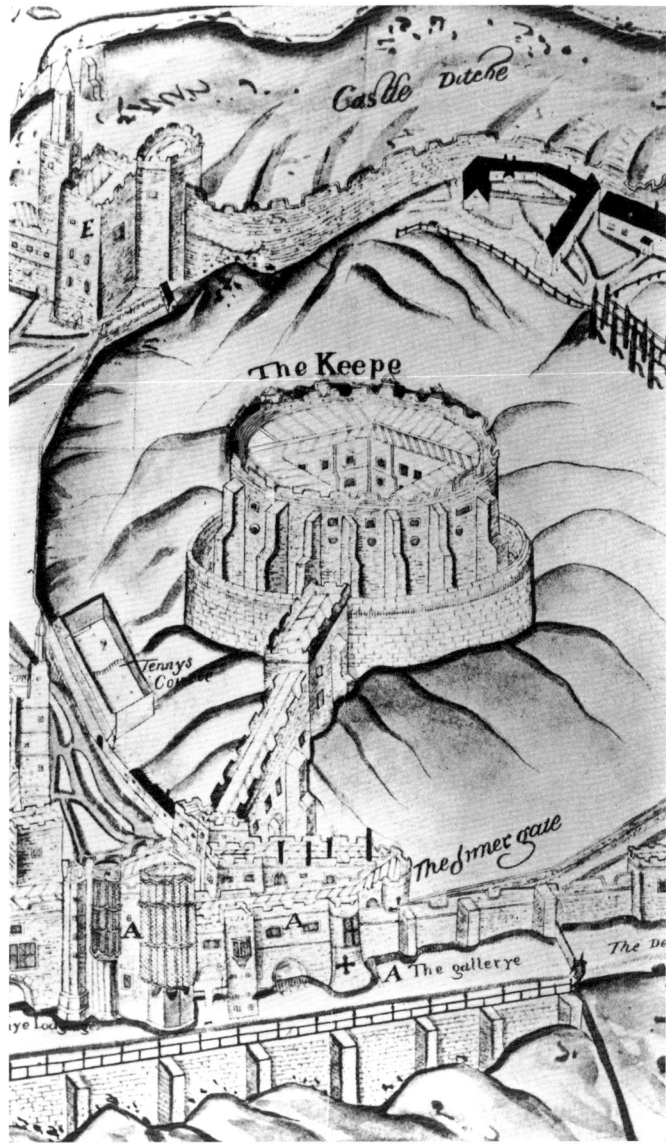

The court at Windsor Castle in 1607.

and in his suite in the Palace of Bridewell. Henry had built a long gallery, decked with tapestry, between the two, spanning the Fleet river and breaching the City wall. Here Hall records 'on Saturday the Kyng and the Emperor played at tennice at the Bayne against the princes of Orenge and the Marques of Brandenborow and on the Princes syde stopped the Erle of Deuonshyre and the lorde Edmond on the other syde, and they departed euen handes on both sydes after XI games fully played.'

How they managed to end up level after eleven games must remain another Tennis mystery! The Prince's partner was Albert, Marquis of Brandenburg, made a Cardinal in 1518. The two 'stoppers' were the Earl of Devonshire and probably Lord Edmund Howard, a member of the King's retinue at the Field of the Cloth of Gold. 'The Bayne' probably means the bath, and it seems likely that baths and Tennis court were combined in the same building – much in the same way as modern clubs combine games and swimming pools. It is not clear whether the court itself was at Blackfriars. Later evidence proves the existence of a court there in 1593 and certainly until 1918 a place named 'Tennis Court' existed off Church Entry, Carter Lane, Blackfriars. Expert research into the layout of the Dominican priory at Blackfriars, however, has not revealed the site of any Tennis court.

As might be expected of so keen a player as Henry VIII, he built several courts at his various palaces. One of them was at Hampton Court, where Tennis continues to be played to this day.

As a result of the research of Dr Howard Colvin, much more is now known about the early history of Tennis at Hampton Court Palace than hitherto. The first court, probably wooden, occupied the site of the present one and may have been built in Cardinal Wolsey's time. In 1532/3, Henry VIII built a new covered court at the northern end of the east front of the palace; its site is shown on the plan of the palace drawn up in George I's reign (marked AAAA, page 42). It measured 83ft x 27ft overall – much the same as the larger covered court at Whitehall. The two courts were connected by a gallery, the remains of which form the present garden wall. A description of this new court emerges from the accounts.

1. *Freemasons wourking upon all such dorys, wyndows and scouncyons for the new lodginges by the Tenys playe (April 1529).*
2. *8 standards and 2 staybarres for 2 wyndows servyng the new lodgings betwixt the galary and the Tenys playe. do.*

yerds qrto of blacke Velwete for a Tenes Cote for the Kings grace' and 'iij yerds qrto of blew Velwete for a Tenes Cote for the King'.

An item in the royal accounts gives an interesting sidelight on the King's Tennis shoes: 'It'm for sooling of syxe paire of shooys with feltys, to pleye in at tenneys, of oure greate warderobe.'

In May 1527 the King injured his left foot playing Tennis and was forced to wear an easy slipper of black velvet for a time.

Great festivities took place in London in 1522, when the King received the Emperor Charles V. The two monarchs left the Palace at Greenwich on Friday, 6 June and came to Blackfriars. The Emperor was lodged in the guest-house of this Dominican priory

3. *Laying of gutters over the tennys play.*
4. *A vayn servyng for the stone typis at the gabull ende of the new Tennys play.*
5. *Payntyng and gyldyng of the vane uppon the type of the Tennys play, the Kynges armys wrought with fyne golde in oyle…4s.*
6. *To John Wylkynson for 200 redd ocker for pensellyng of the new tennys play at 20d. the 100.*
7. *For 12 wyndows of new glass, sett in the tennys play, every wyndow of 3 lightes, so the middle lights contain 39 footes, and every syde lyght conteynyng 36? ft. In the lesser wyndowys 3 lyghts.*
8. *Carpenters workyng in makyng the hassardes in the close Tennys play agaynst the Kynges cummyng, every of them ratyd for every 9 howres 8d.*
9. *Master Wyre-drawers payd for the wyndows of the New Tennys Play some at 16d. the day, others at 8d.*
10. *Also payd to John Budd of Chiselhurst for 4000 and a hundrithe pavyng tiles for the Close tennys play at Hampton Court of hym bought and delyverd at Hampton Court, at 16s. the thousand, by convencion 65s. 7d. (Nov. 1532).*

It is clear from these accounts that the court was roofed and that the floor was constructed of paving stones. There were twelve windows, glazed and protected from stray balls by wire netting. There were lodgings at either end with windows allowing a view of the court.

York House was the property of the See of York and the London residence of the Archbishops of York when Thomas Wolsey succeeded to the Archbishopric in 1514 (becoming a Cardinal the following year). During his tenure he made many structural improvements to the building and entertained lavishly. Often he was host to the King there, and when in 1529 he fell from grace, Henry VIII was quick to seize the opportunity of acquiring the property, especially as his own Palace of Westminster, badly damaged by fire in 1512, was in a poor state of repair.

Once in possession, Henry wasted no time in embarking on an ambitious building programme and he renamed the palace Whitehall. As a keen sportsman and Tennis enthusiast, he made sure that Tennis courts were included in the building programme. There were

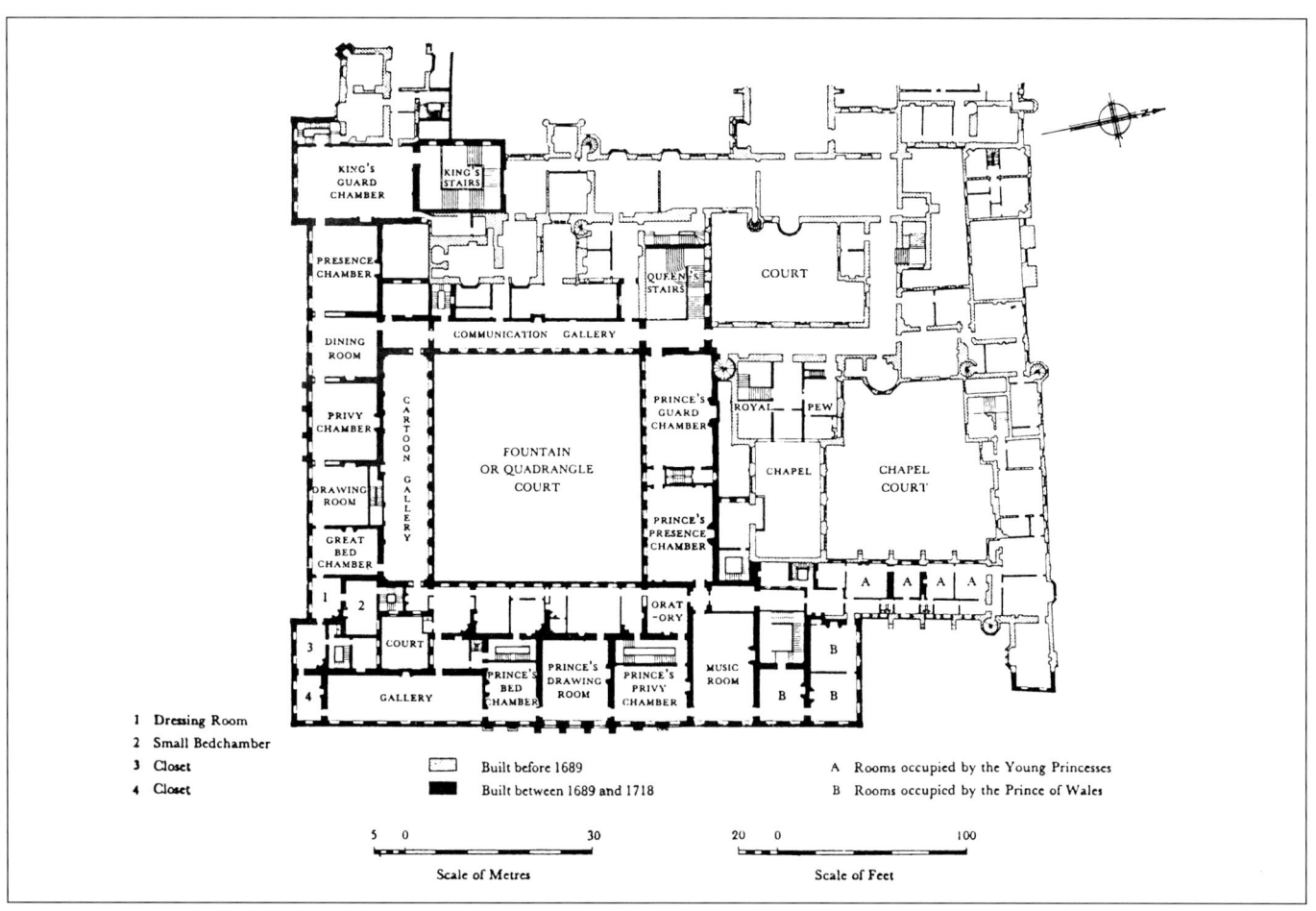

A plan of the royal apartments at Hampton Court in the reign of George 1, showing the site of Henry VIII's court, marked AAAA.

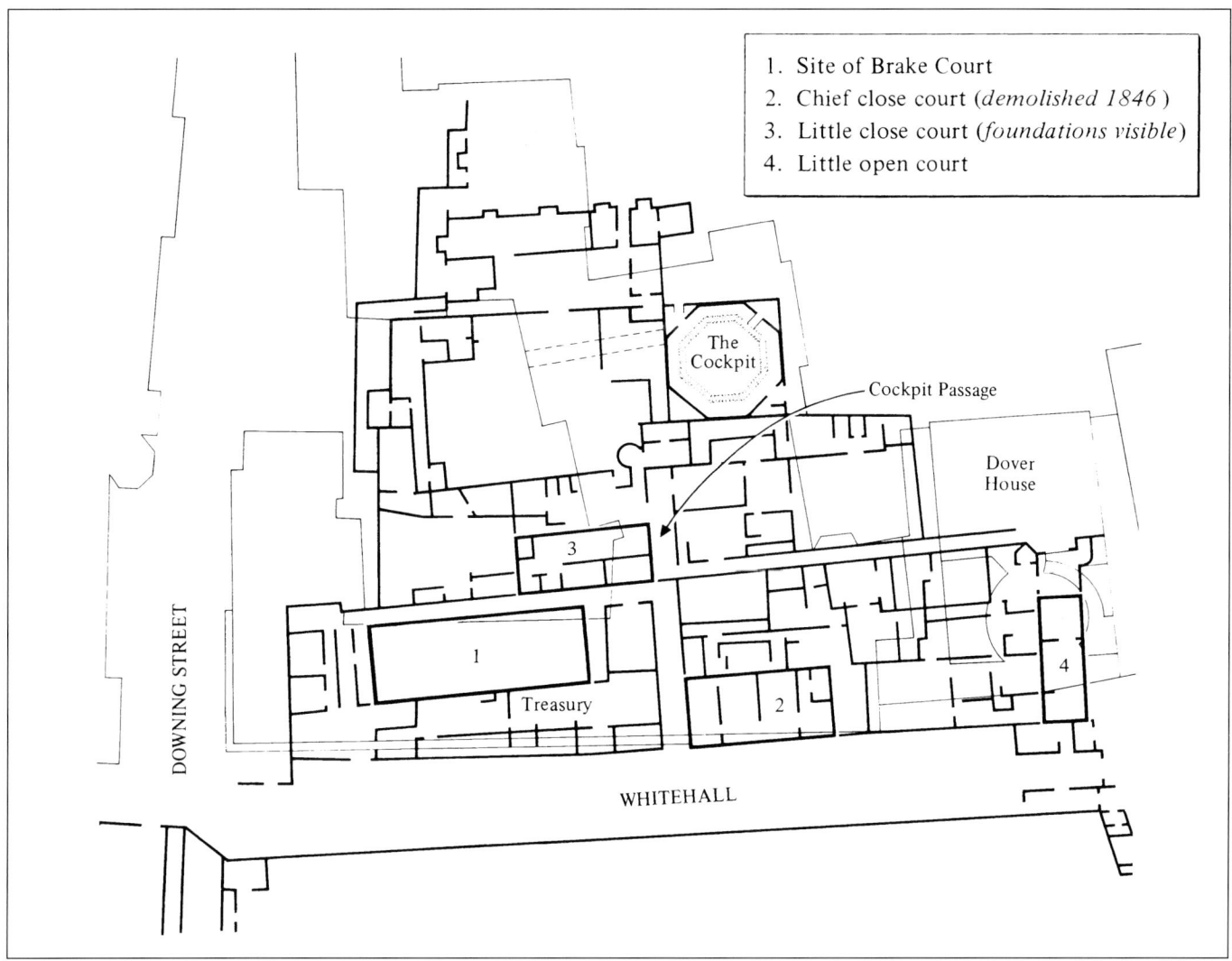

The approximate sites of Henry VIII's four Tennis courts, superimposed on John Fisher's plan of Whitehall in 1670.

four in all, two covered courts and two open. Their location is shown in the plan (above).

The most famous of these courts was the large open one south of the cockpit passage and known as the Brake – and it is another mystery of Tennis why it should have been so called. Rabelais, writing in 1532, brought Gargantua to Paris to play Tennis with his friends at the 'Braque', and in his *Dialogues*, written in 1539, Vivès mentions the most famous court in Paris called the 'Braccha'. This was the court known as the *Jeu du Grand Braque Latin*, place de l'Estrapade, which bore the sign of *un chien braque* – a pointer. The King may have adopted the same name for his own great court because it was so well-known in Paris.

Great it certainly was. The paved area covered 5213 sq. ft and it must have measured about 130 ft long x 40 ft wide. (Compare that with the present Lord's court, which measures 96 ft x 31 ft) It was even larger than the great court at the Louvre (illustrated by Scaino) which measured 114 ft x 37 ft 8 ins; but Henry VIII was always eager to surpass the French. No doubt in this huge court, as in the Louvre, it was usual to play three-a-side, if not four. It was also used to play *pallone* or balloon ball and was sometimes known as the balloon court.

The Brake remained a royal court in the early Stuart age. In 1604 it was repaired at a cost of £200, and later a dressing room was added for the use of Henry, Prince of Wales, when he played there. But it met its match in Oliver Cromwell, who turned it into a garden.

The main covered court lay just north of the Brake, fronting the street, and it was very much smaller than a modern court. The exact measurements are known to us from an interesting list of courts compiled in 1615 by the Clerk of Works at Petworth, who gives them as 78 ft x 22 ft. This may seem very small for an important court, but it has to be remembered that racquets were not the powerful instruments used today and that for the first half of the sixteenth century it was still quite usual to play with the hand, often protected by a thick glove.

This court, with its turrets and battlements, was a familiar landmark in Whitehall and although it, too, fell into disuse in Cromwell's time, its street façade survived until 1846 when it was demolished to make way for Sir Charles Barry's new Treasury offices.

There were two even smaller courts. One of them was open, and also appears on the Petworth list, with measurements of 72 ft x 18 ft. It adjoined the Tiltyard gallery and a building account of 1599/1600 suggests that it may have had wooden walls – 'lathing and laying of plaister with lyme and here (hair) on Tymber walles in the Tennys Court next the gallery to the tylte'. This court, too, disappeared under Cromwell.

The smaller covered court was sited west of the Brake at the end of Bowling Alley – its size is not known but from existing plans it would seem to have been about 60 ft x 18 ft. It was re-roofed in 1601, but in 1604/5 it was adapted for use by Princess Elizabeth as a kitchen and offices. Her lodgings were later used as a residence by Cromwell, until he moved to the main buildings of the palace in 1654. The foundations of this court can still be seen from Cockpit Passage, in the Cabinet Office.

The King built St James's Palace for himself and Anne Boleyn and naturally he included a Tennis court. It was situated in the angle between St James's Street and Pall Mall. In 1533 the keeper of St James's Park was put in charge of this 'Tenys playes'. Henry himself continued to play with great keenness, at least as late as 1538. In 1534 the Spanish ambassador wrote to the King's ex-partner, the Emperor Charles V, that 'there have been dances and games of tennis, and the King exercised himself in both.' A little later the same author wrote that 'on St Andrew's Eve, instead of going to vespers, he [Henry] played Tennis with the [French] Admiral, and next day with another…' In 1538 some young Englishmen being educated in France told how they had seen the King play Tennis when he was supposed to be ill in bed.

The names of two holders of the office of Master of the King's Tennis Plays in Henry VIII's reign are known from an appointment of 9 December 1543:

Thos. Johns, a page of the Chamber. To be master of all the King's tennis plays within the palace of Westminster and elsewhere in England vice Oliver Kelly dec.

It is interesting to note that in the late twentieth century another Johns, Henry, became one of the most highly regarded professionals in the game.

Repressive legislation continued. Acts of 1535/6 and 1541/2 imposed such fines as 'fyve markes for evry moneth' and forty shillings for every day that a Tennis court was kept open. Anyone playing was liable to a fine of twenty shillings except at Christmas. Noblemen, however, and those with an income of over £100, were allowed to possess a court on their property. Others required a licence. In 1542 such a licence was granted to William Griffiths to keep a Tennis court in the Parish of Allhallows-the-Less, for the use of strangers born out of the King's dominions. In 1543 another licence was granted to Richard Kynwolmershe and his wife Elizabeth, to keep a Tennis court in the City for the recreation of 'young lords, knights, gentlemen and merchants'.

Bad sportsmanship seems to have been severely punished in Tudor days, at least within the precincts of a royal palace, for in 1541, 'Sir Edmund Knevet of Norfolk, Knight, was arraigned before the officers of the Green Cloth for striking one master Cleer of Norfolk within the Tennis Court of the King's House. Being found guilty he had judgement to lose his right hand and to forfeit all his lands and goods.' He besought the King that he might lose his left hand instead so that he might live to do the King good service with his right. Henry pardoned him.*

Although with the death of Henry VIII Tennis lost a great patron, it continued nevertheless to be very popular. Among the effects left by the young Duke of Suffolk on his death in 1551 were nine racquets. Etienne Perlin in his description of England and Scotland in 1558 reported that 'you may commonly see artisans such as hatters and joiners playing at Tennis for a crown, which is not often seen elsewhere, particularly on a working day.' He didn't much like the English, writing: 'England is a good land with bad people, as the Spanish say,' and 'the people of this nation mortally hate the French… and we call them "or son" (whoreson).'

Queen Elizabeth I was a keen spectator of Tennis. John Nichols in *The Progresses of Queen Elizabeth* relates how ten Somersetshire men played Tennis in front of her window, 'to so great liking of her Highnes that she graciously deyned to behold their pastime more than an houre and a halfe.' If Nichols's timepiece was functioning correctly, we can conclude that the Queen

---

*Holinshed is the source of this story. According to Fuller's Worthies, it happened to Sir Edmund Wyndham not Sir Edmund Knevet.

would today be a regular visitor to the centre court at Wimbledon. On one occasion she was involved in an ugly scene, recounted in a letter from Thomas Randolphe to Sir Nicholas Throckmorton, dated 31 March 1565, at 'Edenbourge'.

> *Latlye the Dukes G. (of Norfolk) and my L. of L. (Leicester) were playinge at tennes the Q. beholdinge of them, and my L. Rob. being verie hotte and swetinge tooke the Q. napken owte of her hande and wyped his face, wch the Duke seinge saide that he was to sawcie and swhore y^t he wolde laye his racket vpon his face. Here vpon rose a great troble and the Q. offendid sore wth the Duke.*

In 1577 it was reported that 'the Queene said she would have a gallerie from her Bed Chamber [in Windsor Castle] to go along over the Porter's lodge throughe the Cunstable's lodginge, and a Tennis Courte at thend.' The plans of the surveyor, Henry Hawthorne, for this gallery and Tennis court still exist. They show the projected court, measuring 76 ft x 28 ft westward of the Inner Gatehouse outside the wall of the Middle Ward. A window of several lights was to be made in the gatehouse turret from which the Queen might look out on the Tennis court below. The gallery was built in 1583, but not the Tennis court. Instead a new brick-built court was erected on the site of the old wooden one.

A new Master of the Queen's Tennis Plays, William Hope, was appointed on 22 April 1584; he held the office until his death eight years later. He was succeeded on 21 December 1592 by Edward Stone, 'footman'. The fee was 8d a day from Michaelmas 1591.

An interesting application for an exclusive licence was made in 1592 by one Thomas Bedingfield, 'for moving her Majesty to grant a licence for keeping certain houses in London and Westminster for playing at dice, cards, table-play, bowling and tennis, and to grant the forfeiture of others that keep such houses or places and use such plays contrary to statute.' For he says, 'She has power to grant such licences; the number of houses is at present very great, and many are kept by persons to whose houses the honester sort will not resort, whereby the worst sort have greater liberty to do evil; it is therefore meet to reduce the number, appoint good order and forbid from such places those who are not fit to play.' He goes on to propose that no one shall be allowed to play 'in the forenoon of any Sabbath day or during evening and morning prayers on holydays; that no swearing or blasphemy be suffered in any such places'. Lastly, 'none but noblemen, gentlemen and merchants, or such as shall be entered in the Book of Subsidies at 10*l.* in land or goods, shall be suffered to play within any such houses.' Five years later, in 1597, another grant reveals the existence of a Tennis court at Ludlow Castle. It was a 'grant to John Hartgell, on surrender of Rob. Bery of the portership of Ludlow Castle, and of the tennis play there; fee 4*l.* a year, to be taken out of the issues, fines, etc. assessed before Her Majesty's Council of the Marches of Wales.'

A picture of a game of Tennis in Elizabethan days is given in *The Parlement of Prattlers* by John Eliot, published in 1593.

THE TENISE-PLAY

JOHN: *Shall we play a set of tenise you and I?*
NICHOLAS: *Let's go to the great Bracke at White-hall.*
JOHN: *Where is the maister that keepes the tenise?*
MAN: *Here I am, sir, what is your pleasure?*
JOHN: *Giue us some soft and gentle shooes here. Rackets and bals bring here, ho.*
NICHOLAS: *Well play.*
JOHN: *I haue fifteene.*
NICHOLAS: *A losse, marke that chase there.*
JOHN: *Fifteene all.*
NICHOLAS: *This racket is not worth a rush.*
JOHN: *Some more rackets, ho.*
NICHOLAS: *Now giue me a faire ball. I cannot take a ball aboue hand, nor at rebound.*
JOHN: *The chase is mine.*
NICHOLAS: *I am thirtie.*
JOHN: *Thirtie all.*
NICHOLAS: *Aske standersby, I touched it not.*
JOHN: *Fortie fiue.*
NICHOLAS: *At dews then.*
JOHN: *A ball, I haue the advantage. The set is mine. I will bande a ball more than six-score paces mounting, with this racket which you refuse. Looke here.*
NICHOLAS: *O diuell! what a firking stroke is that! You haue an arme of yron.*

A sidelight on sixteenth-century behaviour after a game of Tennis is provided in George Chapman's *An Humourous Day's Mirth*, where the following dialogue occurs:

Enter Catalan, sweating.

CAT: *Boy, I prithee call for a coarse napkin. Good morrow, gentlemen! I would you had been at the tennis court, you should have seen me beat Monsieur Besan, and I gave him fifteen and all his faults.*
LEMOT: *Thou did more for him than ever God will do for thee.*
CAT: *Jaques, I prithee fetch me a cup of canary, three parts water.*

Evidently a coarse napkin took the place of the modern towel and a cup of canary with three parts water was the equivalent of the modern shandy. Sporting manners, however, have much improved and nowadays one would expect a sweating Catalan to offer his vanquished opponent a drink.

In Scotland, Tennis continued to be popular and James V built a court in 1539 at his palace of Falkland, Fife – where he later died of a broken heart, leaving the Scottish throne to his daughter, Mary, Queen of Scots. This court is still in use and a description of it can be found in Part III. It is the only remaining example of a *jeu quarré*.

Tennis was not exclusively royal. It seems to have flourished at Oxford despite official disapproval, and the annals of Merton College (today the landlords of the sole remaining court in Oxford) record in April 1492: 'Holt plays tennis and that in public. Comes late to Church.' This refers to Richard (or Robert) Holt, a Fellow of Merton from 1487 to 1493. Later, in 1508, Michael Clowe, William Philips, Richard Andrewes and Henry Busby were each fined sixpence for keeping 'tenys playes'. Seven years later two of them were convicted again of the same offence and fined a further sixpence each. Since the full penalty under the Act of 1495 was 'imprisonment by the space of a day in the stokkis openly', it doesn't appear that the law was very strictly enforced in Oxford.

In the year 1530 there were two Tennis courts in Oxford at Smith's Gate. The evidence of their existence is interesting. Under the Act making certain games illegal, the City Constables were to collect all tables, cards, dice and balls and to burn them in the market-place on market-days. A similar mandate was given to the Vice-Chancellor in respect of the University. The Mayor alleged that the Vice-Chancellor had failed to carry out his duty and had returned the equipment to the scholars. The Vice-Chancellor retorted that the City authorities 'allways do mayntene opynly unlawfull gamys of the tenys, as yn two houses of the rent [i.e. house property of the city] lying next to Smyth Gate, oon of the est side and a nother yn the west side, takyn more rent of the tenants of the said houses for the maynteyning of the said plays yerely.'

These two courts belonged to the City as opposed to the University; they were open courts and were on the present site of Hertford College. The one on the west side of Cat Street soon disappeared, but the other, which at its south end abutted on New College Lane, can be traced down to about 1690, when it was converted into two houses.

The first known University court was built by Christ Church shortly before 1546, in Blue Boar Lane, St Aldate's, on the same estate that included the Unicorn Inn. In 1587 the property was leased to John Lante MA, who later built the Merton Street court.

In about 1572 a new court was built in Oriel Street which remained in use until 1860, when it was converted into billiard rooms. In 1878 the site was acquired by Oriel College and the old Tennis court converted into lecture rooms. After 1945 it became a bicycle store and table tennis area. Between 1990 and 1994 it was converted into 22 student rooms above 2 lecture rooms on the ground floor. A curious feature of this old court was that a niche was cut in the centre of the main wall by the net hook to accommodate the marker. Presumably that was thought to be an improvement on the use of one or both of the doors, but it must have been a position of great danger.

Another court in Oxford is recorded in a lease of 1577, described as 'a certain sphaeristerium called le tenys court' on the east side of Vinehall Lane (now Alfred Street), somewhere at the back of the London and County Bank.

In 1595 Merton College granted a lease on Postmaster's Hall to John Lante MA which included 'a tennise court of late built and erected thereon by the said John Lante'. This was on the site of the present court, which was built about 1798. Tennis was popular in Oxford and J. Earle, a Fellow of Merton, wrote in 1628, describing an Oxford undergraduate: 'The two markes of his Senioritie, is the bare veluet of his gowne and his proficiencie at Tennis, where when hee can once play a Set, he is a Fresh-man no more.'

Oxford was very poorly provided with courts compared with Cambridge, where there were at least ten courts in the sixteenth and early seventeenth centuries:

Corpus Christi College in Penny-Farthing Lane. At some date between 1487 and 1515 the walls of a building intended for a bake-house and granary were carried up to sufficient height to play *pila palmaria*. In 1569 this court was converted to student rooms and a new roofed court built, shown in Hammond's map of Cambridge in 1592. It was pulled down in 1756.

Christ's College. Built 1564/5. Repaired 1597/8. Pulled down 1711.

Emmanuel College. Built 1584 or earlier. Originally roofed, but roof removed 1632. A College Order of 29 October 1651, reads:

The key of it shall be in the keeping of the Deane, who is to take care that the door is kept lockt, and none suffered to play during the howers hereafter mentioned, viz. from one of the clock till three in the afternoon and from eight of the clock at night till three the next morning; unless any of the fellows desire to play there in any of these howers, who may take any fellow commoner with them; yet soe as they cleare the court, shutt the doore, and return the key to the Deane at their comeing away.

This court was pulled down at some date before 1746.

Peterhouse. First mentioned 1572. Still in use 1677.

St John's College. A wooden building in 1573/4 near the Master's garden. Pulled down 1598/9. Second court built on the other side of the river 1602/3.

Jesus College. First mentioned 1566/7. Rebuilt 1603/4.

King's College. A roofed court that certainly existed in 1569/70. Mention of 'chambers in the tenise courte', 1579.

Queen's College. Built before 1531. At east end of garden opposite the great gate. Accounts contain many entries recording repairs.

Trinity College. A court at the south-eastern corner of the college was repaired in 1585/6. Pulled down 1598. A new court was built in 1611 between the end of the north range of Nevile's court and the river, at a cost of £120. Two Tennis court keepers were appointed. Pulled down 1676 to make way for the Library.

Pembroke College. Abutting on Tennis Court Lane. Court built or re-paved in 1564. Rebuilt in 1734. Pulled down 1880.

Five of these courts – Corpus Christi, Christ's College, Emmanuel, Peterhouse and Pembroke – are all clearly marked and numbered on David Logan's plan of

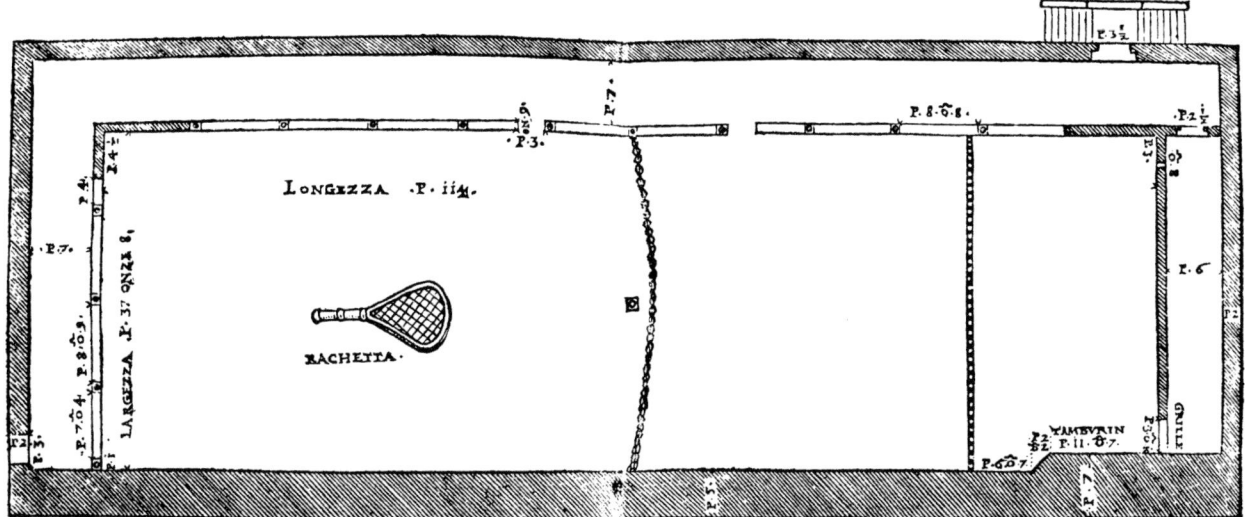

Scaino's plan of the court at the Louvre.

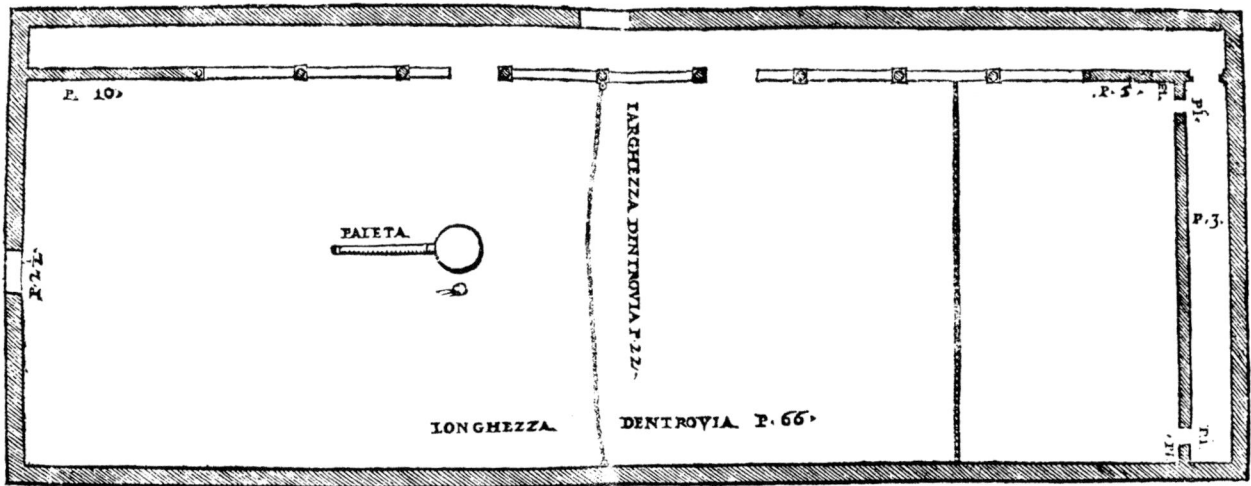

Scaino's plan of a jeu quarré.

Cambridge in 1688. A sixth – St John's – is clearly shown but not numbered. The courts at Christ's College, Emmanuel and St John's also appear in the views of these individual colleges.

Another new court was built by Sir Henry Sidney, President of the Council, at Ludlow Castle.

The popularity of Tennis in the sixteenth century was by no means confined to England, France and Scotland. It was extensively played elsewhere in Europe; and it was in fact an Italian, Antonio Scaino da Salò, who wrote the first-ever treatise on the game in 1555.

Antonio Scaino came from Salò on Lake Garda. He worked at the University of Padua, where he lectured on Aristotle and St Augustine, and became a friend of the Duke, Alfonso II, who was a keen Tennis player. It was a disputed point in a game of Tennis that inspired Scaino to write his *Trattato del Giuoco della Palla*.

So enthusiastic was Scaino that he tells us that all the best people played Tennis – Julius Caesar and Alexander the Great included. And he tells us of the great players of his day – Gian Fernando the Spaniard and Gian Antonio the Neapolitan, who played with the hand, and Laches and Verdelot, Frenchmen, who played with a racquet. Gian Fernando used to practise by using two cords stretched across the court less than a foot apart and playing the ball between them.

Scaino tells us of six different games:

1. *Pallone* is an open-air game usually played by four players on each side, using a large ball made of goatskin and filled with air. Each player wears an arm protector (*bracciale*) made of wood on his forearm, and with this he strikes the ball. Scaino includes a diagram showing the ball, the pump for inflating the ball and the *bracciale*. *Pallone* continued to be played in Italy up to the eighteenth century and an interesting picture in the MCC Museum at Lord's shows a game in progress.

2. A similar game uses a smaller air-filled ball struck with a kind of wooden bat (*scanno*), also illustrated by Scaino.

3 and 4. *Longue paume* is Tennis played out of doors, using either the bare hand or a racket. The balls for both *longue* and *courte paume* are the same, being stuffed with wool shearings, but the ball used for hand-play, larger and heavier than that for use with a racquet, is more loosely stuffed to avoid injury to the hand.

5 and 6. *Courte paume* (called by Scaino the cord game) is Tennis as we now know it, but played either with the hand or with a racquet.

Scaino includes two plans of Tennis courts. One is of the court at the Louvre in Paris, built by Henri II, and apart from its great size, this closely resembles a modern Tennis court. One slight difference is the entry to the court which is by a door on either side of the net (where the door gallery is today). In these doorways stood the two markers who kept the score and recorded the chases.

The cord (net) from which Tennis derived its Italian name, *giuoco della corda*, is clearly shown. It was a simple rope across the court with a fringe hanging from it to make it easier to determine whether the ball had gone over or under the cord. Scaino tells us it must be 3½ ft above the floor at the centre.

The other plan is of a smaller court, known in France as a *jeu quarré*. The court at the Louvre, with dedans, grille and tambour, was called a *jeu à dedans*. The *jeu quarré*, of which the only remaining example is at Falkland Palace, had certain distinguishing features. It had no dedans and no tambour. Instead of the dedans it normally had various other winning openings which differed from court to court.

In Scaino's court there is one such winning opening on the service side, a square hole (*trou*) in the centre of the court 2½ft x 1½ft and 4½ft above the floor. On the hazard side the court illustrated is unusual in having no grille, but two small openings 1 ft from each corner, 10 ins square and 5½ft above the floor.

In the normal *jeu quarré* there was another winning feature called *l'ais*. This was a board 6 ft high by 1 ft wide attached to the back wall on the service side in the corner by the gallery wall. The *trou* was usually found in the opposite corner of the service side, about 16 ins square.

In some courts there was a further winning opening high up on the back wall of the service side. This was a round hole 8 ins in diameter known as *la lune* – and a ball struck into it won a whole game outright. In the print of the court at Tübingen (on page 22) there appear to be two *lunes*, one at each end.

To complete his thorough survey Scaino includes two more diagrams of open and covered courts for Tennis played with the hand.

But of all the various ball games, Scaino considered the cord game to be the best:

Countless are those who place the cord game above all others, and among them I number myself. It is a game of great majesty and truly worthy of Gentlemen. Therefore we conclude by saying that, of all Ball-Games, the rarest and most honoured is the cord game.

It is suitable for children, youths, men, almost for old men, too. It is dear to the jovial, pleasing to the melancholy, the serious and the severe, and suited to almost all humours and temperaments.

What shall we say of the great gladness and contentment that the victor feels after a long and tiring battle? So great are they, indeed, that, unable to hide them, he jumps about, visibly and infinitely rejoicing in his victory. [Compare the scorer of a goal in modern football.]

It is quite clear from all the evidence that courts differed very greatly in those early days and the rules had to take account of all sorts of natural hazards – especially in the case of *longue paume*. For example, Scaino discusses the way to treat a ball that lands on a passing cart and is then returned from the cart by an opponent. He advises that such a stroke is good if the ball was still moving on the cart, but if not, then a chase is made at the point where the cart was when the ball came to a stop; or, if a ball enters the window of a house and is returned to the court from another window, that is not good. He also records that there are often doorsteps of stone or wood or other such protuberances in Tennis courts which can lead to difficult decisions when struck by the ball.

He asserts that the ball is good if it hits one of the nails or hooks to which the net is attached and then passes over the net; a net cord is good in France but not in Italy.

Scaino also gives some tips to young players, emphasising in particular the need to watch the ball carefully, to keep to the centre of the court and to make good use of the back wall. Muddles between doubles partners were just as familiar then as now, and Scaino mentions that it is often effective to play the ball between two or more opponents, for each may well leave it to the other and neither return it. He particularly praises the cut stroke at which the French excel, and stresses the importance of constant practice.

All this advice reads very familiarly to modern ears and there is little difference between Scaino and a modern professional when it comes to coaching. But in the matter of what to wear for a game of Tennis, times have changed. Stockings, says Scaino, must be supple to allow the legs to bend; they may reach to the knee or, in 'modern' fashion, right up to the waist. The shirt must fit closely, provided the arms are free; and the shoes shall be light, soled for example with buffalo skin. Keep fit, says Scaino, and avoid a fat belly.

Curiously, he devotes one chapter to football, played twenty, thirty or forty to a side at Padua. He doesn't consider it so artistic a game as Tennis, but nevertheless it gives great pleasure to the spectators, especially when the players dash about in great disarray and fall upside-down almost as in a real battle.

Tennis seems to have been played in all the main Italian cities, as one might expect, but few traces of it remain today. We know it was played in Mantua in 1560, for the problem of 'whether or not it is allowed to play ball on Sabbaths and Holidays' by Jews was referred to the famous Rabbi, Moses Ben Abraham, later known as Moses Provençal. Mantua at the time was a haven for the persecuted Jews, thanks to the liberal policy of the Duke of Mantua, and there were probably some 2000 resident at the time. The Rabbi's ruling gives some glimpses of the game as it was played there.

Special buildings had been erected for it and some of them had open windows; occasionally the ball would go out through them, and 'the Sabbath is thus desecrated by the transfer of an object from private grounds to the field, which has the status of a quasi-public thoroughfare.' On the other hand, it was an advantage that the floor was of stone, thus obviating the need for minor repairs on the Sabbath. The ball was played, either with a kind of scoop, similar to the Basque *chistera* as used in *pelota*, or with 'small bows laced with guts, and netted with strings'.

Moses Provençal was particularly outspoken against the current habit of gambling on Tennis matches and condemned the practice of avoiding the prohibition of cash stakes on the Sabbath by betting in foodstuffs, such as flour and potatoes, later readily convertible into cash. 'Also,' he continues, 'it is not uncommon for the game to be conducted while the sermon is being preached in the Synagogue: this is by no means permissible.' He concludes that Tennis might only be played on the Sabbath with the hand; to use a racquet was not allowed as 'the case was analagous to that of playing musical instruments on those days which were interdicted by the Rabbis, for fear that the player might attempt to mend the instrument that broke.'

Galeazzo Maria Sforza, a son of Duke Francesco Sforza, built three courts in or near Milan in the 1470s. Other courts were built around this time in Ferrara, Urbino, Florence, Mantua, Padua and Rome. In Rome in 1606 a young painter, Caravaggio, quarrelled with a friend over a game and killed him. A poem by Francesco Bracciolini, 'Lo Scherno degli Dei' in 1618 probably alludes to this tragedy and was the inspiration for the painting *Death of Hyacinth* (executed circa 1618–20), currently in the Musée Thomas Henry in Cherbourg. We know that Tennis was introduced into Venice in 1595 and at least four courts seem to have existed there. There was also a court in Turin in 1620.

In Spain, too, Tennis was well-known in royal circles, and like Louis X of France, two Spanish kings, Henry I in 1217 and Philip I in 1506, both of Castile, are said to have died as a result of drinking cold water after an energetic game.

The Hapsburg king, Philip III, was another royal patron of Tennis. 'He was at the age of twenty-four of small stature, but healthy and of a good complexion; very religious and an example of goodness and good manners. He ate well, but drank no wine; amused himself in hunting, which led him to be constantly in the country; he willingly undertook journeys; and passed the rest of his time in playing tennis and dancing.' The court in the Alcazar Palace in Madrid was repaired for him by the municipality and a corridor built from the Palace to the court for greater ease of access. Vivès, writing his Latin exercises in 1539, introduces a dialogue on the difference between the games in France and Spain. Scintilla has just returned from a visit to Paris:

> BORGIA: *Do they play there in the same way as here?*
> SCINTILLA: *Almost, except that the manager of the court provides shoes and caps for the players.*
> BORGIA: *What are they like?*
> SCINTILLA: *The shoes are made of felt.*
> BORGIA: *Wouldn't these shoes suit us here?*
> SCINTILLA: *Perhaps on a paved floor. In France and in Belgium they play on a flagstone floor, flat and level. The caps worn in summer are lighter, but in winter they are thick and fitted with straps under the chin, so that they do not come off.*
> BORGIA: *Here we only tie our caps under the chin when the wind is strong.*

Throughout central Europe the game flourished and at least one court existed in every main town and city. In the German states, forty-six towns possessed at least one court. The game was introduced to Vienna by the Emperor Ferdinand I, Charles V's younger brother, who had learnt it in his birthplace, Spain. In Sweden Eric IV built a court in Stockholm.

In Prague there were four courts, of which the most important was the royal court, known as Rudolf's *Ballhaus* in the castle gardens. This was built by an Italian architect for Ferdinand I about the year 1568 and was much patronised by the Emperor Rudolf II (1576–1612), who was a keen player. When his health deteriorated he remained a keen spectator and used to watch matches in progress, hidden from general view. The French Marshal Bassompierre described in his memoirs how he played a game in Prague in January 1604 against Wallenstein with Rudolf II watching:

> *Playing tennis against the great Wallenstein, who was acting as the Emperor's great chamberlain since the death of Peter de Mollart a week previously, the Emperor came to see us play through a blind (jalousie) in a window that overlooked the court, and stayed there a long time.*

In the early eighteenth century this royal court was used as a theatre, and in 1757 was heavily damaged during the siege of Prague. Later it became an arsenal and by 1945 was a total wreck. The magnificent exterior of the building has since been beautifully restored, but not, alas, the Tennis court itself.

There is a curious set of eleven sixteenth-century pictures, each of which includes a view of a contemporary Tennis court. The series tells the story of David and Bathsheba. David is depicted twice – once gazing longingly from a balcony upon a nude Bathsheba beside a pool and once handing sealed instructions to her husband Uriah at the castle gate. The background to each picture contains a number of sports, Tennis most prominently, but also archery and a form of bowls. So far as the Tennis courts are concerned, some show a game of doubles, some singles. Most include markers sitting on a bench inside the court; three of them show markers actually marking a chase. In one there appears to be a sort of tambour, in another a winning-gallery. The pictures are individually owned in England, the United States, Italy and Australia. Their origin is another mystery of Tennis.

In *Royal Tennis in Renaissance Italy* Cees de Bondt says the principal literary source of inspiration for the paintings were the writings of Antonio de Guevara's *Relox de Principes (Diall of Princes)* of 1529 and more in particular his *Del Menosprecio de la corte y alabanza de la aldea (A Dispraise of the Life of a Courtier)* published in 1539. Guevara served Holy Roman Emperor King Charles V of Spain as preacher and chronicler from 1526 onwards. At the end of the Preface Guevara refers to the main theme of the paintings, the adultery of David and Bathsheba as described in the Bible, and goes on to bitterly attack extravagance and excess at Court and suggest that Courtiers seek refuge in the purity and quiet of the countryside. However, when indulged in by a Ruler whose virtues far exceeded his vices, such excess was to be exonerated. His writings also contain many references to Tennis.

The layout of the paintings appears to be based on a description of the gardens of the Abbey of Thélème in Rabelais' *Gargantua* published in 1534, which feature many of the pastimes seen in the paintings including tennis, bowls, falconry, the maze and swimming-pool. In *Gargantua* the same theme of excess is satirised and ridiculed (*Fais ce que voudras*) with Thélème being depicted as one hundred times more sumptuous than any Renaissance chateau. So it may well be that Rabelais' description of Thélème was also the source of inspiration for Guevara's *Menosprecio*.

SEVENTEENTH-CENTURY TENNIS

The arrival of Bourbon kings on the French throne and Stuart kings in England did not signal an immediate decline in the popularity of Tennis, which continued to thrive for the first half of the seventeenth century.

Louis XIII was taught early to play Tennis. At eleven he was receiving lessons from a professional, Pierre Gentil, and at thirteen he played regularly three or four times a week, either in the court in the rue de Grenelle-Saint-Honoré, or at St Germain. Here is an extract from his doctor's diary:

> The 19th February, 1614. Goes by carriage to play tennis at Grenelle. The 28th, goes to the court at Grenelle; washed at M. Leclerc's; he eats there. 1st June, goes to the court at Grenelle, where he was struck in the teeth by a ball from the Chevalier de Soubré; he bleeds a little. 21st, plays tennis at St Germain-en-Laye.

Later in the year he went on a tour of western France and played Tennis whenever he had the chance. The same diary records games at Orléans, Châtellerault, Poitiers, Mirebeau, Angers, Nantes and Le Mans. He suffered another slight accident playing at Nantes, where he was struck by a ball in the right eye. He then fell ill and there are no further records of his play until 1617, when he returned to the Tennis courts.

Unfortunately, his doctor died that year and detailed records cease but he certainly retained his liking for the game and presumably continued to play. At any rate he played at La Rochelle in 1628, just after the capture of the town from the Huguenots, although he was seized by an attack of gout in the middle of the match.

One Tennis professional of the day was a certain La Lande; the King writes to Cardinal Richelieu that he had not been paid either his journey money or his fee.

The great popularity of Tennis necessitated the first common book of rules, and this was compiled by a master professional, Forbet. In 1592 he devised the earliest known rules, comprising twenty-four articles, which were published in 1599. They were re-edited and re-published in 1632 by Charles Hulpeau, under the title *Le Jeu Royal de la Paume*.

It is remarkable how closely these ancient rules resemble those in use today. Basically they differ on points of detail. The set consists of four or six games; in the case of a four-game set, if three games all is reached, a player has to attain a lead of two games to win it. The height of the net at the centre was to be such that a man standing at one end wall could just see the foot of the wall at the opposite end – with no mention of how tall the man should be! When there were two markers they stood in the two doors; when only one he stood in the door on the service side. If a marker's decision was disputed, a player could appeal to the spectators, whose majority decision was final.

Betting was normal on all matches and governed by rules. Very fairly, the winner was responsible for meeting such expenses as lost balls, bread, wine, firewood, shoes and markers' fees. The frontispiece of Hulpeau's book is an excellent reproduction of a seventeenth-century *jeu quarré*, although strangely enough it does not show the *ais*, mentioned in the text. In this particular court there seem to have been two *trous*, no *ais* and no *lune*.

An interesting description of a match in a *jeu quarré* is contained in Frissart's pamphlet of 1641, describing a game of Tennis between the French and Spanish kings, resulting in victory for the French. In this court there were a *trou*, an *ais* and a *lune*.

Naturally enough, Alexandre Dumas has his three musketeers play Tennis, but d'Artagnan calls the game off for fear of the power of Porthos's hitting.

A curious print by Jacques Callot records another casualty, but in this case resulting in a miraculous recovery. It shows a river scene near Mont St Michel, where the Prince's son has been killed by a blow from a Tennis ball. He is brought back to life by Jean Porcelet, Bishop of Toul.

A Tennis court in 1632, from Charles Hulpeau's book.

Louis XIII died in 1643 and was succeeded by his eldest son as Louis XIV, *Le Roi Soleil*. He was just four on his accession, but was soon on the Tennis court learning to play. Saint-Simon writes that, 'he excelled at dancing, pall-mall and tennis'.

In 1658, Louis paid a visit to Dijon, and 'passed part of his afternoons playing tennis in the Salamander court'. He also carried out some repairs to the court at the Louvre. But after Mazarin's death the burdens of state fell heavily upon him and he played less Tennis, preferring billiards, which he could play after the day's work was over.

However, he still enjoyed watching the best players, and was often to be seen at Fontainebleau on wet days until in 1702 a disastrous fire burnt out both courts there. He granted the best professionals the privilege of being allowed to advertise twice-weekly matches in Paris. Those favoured in this way were two Jourdains, Le Pape, Clergé and Sercot.

A steady decline in the number of courts in Paris is recorded by the Dutch ambassador who wrote in 1657 that there were 114, although he was surprised there were not more. This compares with the 250 reported in 1596 (see page 17).

But there is no doubt that, in general, Tennis remained very popular in France. A Sicilian visitor wrote in 1692 that 'the young people amuse themselves with every sort of physical exercise, and especially Tennis.'

Some players, then as now, did not enjoy losing. One is reported to have had a habit of throwing balls, ball-baskets, racquets, clothes, and finally even himself into the grille. Another, more sporting, used to give a crown to his servant to go outside and utter a few strong oaths on his behalf.

An interesting account of the correct dress for Tennis occurs in the statutes of the master professionals of Bordeaux in 1684. 'No master professional may keep a court unless he has linen for the use of players: that is to say four dozen fine cloths to make caps, two dozen shirts, six dozen half-cloths for wiping, twelve pairs of trousers, the same number of vests, socks, shoes of leather and shoes of wool and eight pairs of sheets.' No doubt the woollen slippers and sheets were for use after the game, when waiting one's turn to be rubbed down by a marker.

As in France, so in England Tennis continued to be popular during the first half of the seventeenth century. James I was well aware of the merits of the game and recommended his eldest son, Prince Henry, to play. In his *Basilicon Doron*, written in 1598, when the Prince was aged four, he writes:

And amongst all vnnecessarie thinges that are lawfull and expedient, I thinke exercises of the bodie moste commendable to be vsed by a young Prince, in suche honest games or pastimes, as may further ability and maintaine health. For albeit I graunt it to be most requisite for a King to exercise his engine, whiche surelie with idlenesse will rouste and become blunt; yet certainly bodily exercises and games are verie commendable; as well for bannishing of idlenesse (the mother of all vice) as for making his bodie able and durable for trauell, whiche is necessarie for a King, but from this compte I debarre all rumling uiolent exercises as the fitball meither for laming nor making able the useris thairof, as lykeuayes sicc tumbling trikkis as onlie seruis for comædians and gysairis to uinne thaire breade with, but the exercises that I uolde haue you to use (althoch but moderatlie not making a crafte of thaime) are rinning, leaping, urestling, fensing, dansing & playing at the cache.

The 'cache', usually spelt 'caitche', is the old Scots name for Tennis and the first public edition of 1603 reads 'playing at the caitche or tennise'.

No doubt for Henry's benefit, the King repaired the Brake Court at Whitehall. 'By Order, 2nd of September 1604. To Andrew Kerwyn, paymaster of His Highness's works, the sum of 200*l*., in prest, parcel of a more sum, limited by the said Privy Seal, towards the repair of the great Tennis-Courte, commonly called the Brake of Whitehall.' In 1612 he built a dressing room for the Prince, described as 'a small buildinge between twoe Brickwalls, adjoyneing to the Tennis-Courte or great Brake, beinge for the Prince to make himselfe ready in to play at Tennis there.'

Henry seems to have been hot-tempered on the Tennis court, and on two occasions was involved in a fierce quarrel. On the first he is said to have struck, or offered to strike, Robert Carr, Earl of Somerset, his father's favourite. On the second, Henry disputed a point of play with the young Earl of Essex. So violent was the argument that Henry called the Earl, 'son of a traitor', and Essex struck the Prince on the head with his racquet, drawing blood. The affair was reported to the King who pardoned Essex when he heard a full account of the incident. He told Henry that the boy who had struck him would never be slow to smite his enemies for him. Another of the Prince's opponents was Sir John Harington. In a letter of 1609, Henry wrote to Sir John, 'When I see you (and let it be shortlie) you will find me your better at Tennis and Pike. Good Fellow, I write your friend, Henry.'

It was a great loss to the country when, in his eighteenth year, he fell ill and died. Thomas Birch, who wrote his biography in 1760, criticises his self-neglect. He would go swimming in the Thames after supper with a full stomach and this, according to Birch, stopped his nose bleeding but caused the fatal fever. On 24 October he played a great match at Tennis (probably at the Brake) clad only in his shirt despite the cold weather, and on going to bed complained of lassitude and headache. On 6 November he died.

His greatest diversion was at Tennis [Birch writes] *in which, it is acknowledged, he neither observed moderation, nor what suited his dignity and person, continuing often three or four hours at it.*

King James's second son, the Duke of York, later Charles 1, was equally keen on Tennis. In the Exchequer records, under the date 6 December 1610, is entered, 'By order, to Jehu Webb, master of His Majesty's Tennis plays, the sum of 20*l*. for his attendance in teaching the Duke of York to play at Tennis, now one whole year ended at Michaelmas last, 1610, and for furnishing him with balls, racquets and other necessaries within the said year.' Another entry, on 8 November 1611, is authority to pay twenty pounds per annum and twenty pounds already due to John Webb, Master of the Tennis Plays, for instructing the Duke of York in that exercise, and providing racquets and balls for him. That the young Duke was no sluggard where Tennis was concerned is shown by a later entry which reads, 'Messenger to fetch Mr Clemman to come to his Highness next morning at St James by six in the Tennis Court, to play the match with Sir Thomas Howard.' He was also on occasion as impetuous as his elder brother and in 1618 quarrelled with the Duke of Buckingham in the court.

The Duke's Tennis teacher, John Webb, had been appointed 'master of the King's Tennis plays at Westminster, etc' on 7 February 1604. Three years later it is recorded that he was granted the moiety of £1600, old debts due to the Crown, to be recovered by him, and was confirmed in the office of 'Master of the King's tennis play throughout England'.

Two years later, in 1609, we find him suing Sir Thomas Knyvet, Knt, Lord Knyvet, John Freeburne and Roger Rolles in the Court of Common Pleas, alleging that they 'wrongfully, and without judgment, disseised him' of the office of Master of the Tennis-plays. He won his case, for the court held that the office of 'master of the King's Tennis-plays in Westminster, etc' included 'the tennis-plays for the King's household, and not only for the tennis-play when the King himself plays in his royal person; for the King is the head of his household, and therefore *a digniori parte*, the tennis-plays for his household may well be called the King's tennis-plays.' The record of the case mentions two courts at Whitehall, 'the close tennis court' and 'the Brake'.

John Webb's duties seem to have included the provision of balls, yet there existed another office – that of 'brinder or keeper of ballons and bracers for the tennis court', granted to Alex Narne, Gentleman waiter, for a fee of 2d a day with all profits, probably in 1604.

John Webb retired in January 1618 on a pension of £120 p.a. He was succeeded by Gideon Lozier and John Webb, who was probably his son. John Webb died in 1656.

The royal courts in London were the Brake at Whitehall and that at St James's, built by Henry VIII and repaired by James I. An interesting list of other courts existing in 1615 in the City is included in the Records of the Clerk of Works at Petworth, then the property of the Earl of Northumberland. The first two courts on the Petworth list are two other Whitehall courts; the larger covered court and the smaller open court. The other courts listed are 'Sommersett house, Essex house, Fetter lane, Fleetestreete, Blackfriers, Southampton, Charterhouse, Powles chaine, Abbchurch lane, St Laurence Pontne, Fanchurch streete, Cruchedfriers'.

The Charterhouse court was originally the court of Howard House, belonging to the Duke of Norfolk, on the site of the Carthusian monastery at Smithfield. In 1611 Charterhouse School was founded and soon afterwards the old Tennis court was converted to a boarding house for forty scholars, who at one time included John Wesley. It continued to be so used until 1872, when the school moved to its present site.

Many courts existed outside London. Henry VIII's court at Hampton Court flourished and James I included Tennis in the revels he organised there at Christmas 1604. The court at Windsor is shown in Norden's *Description of the Honor of Windesor*, in the year 1607. King James built a palace including a Tennis court at Newmarket, and in 1624 issued a warrant for the building of a court at Theobald's.

Courts also existed at this date in Ireland. In 1609 Lord Howth and Sir Roger Jones were involved in a brawl which led to bloodshed in a court in St Thomas's Street, Dublin.

By this time the old restrictive Acts were ignored, but it still required a licence to run a Tennis court. In 1620 James I granted to Clement Cotterell,

for the Term of his Life, sole Power and Authoritie to appoint, assigne, nominate and license such Persons as he shall think good, to have, maintain and keep, within the severall Places hereafter mentioned and not elsewhere, the severall nombers of Bowling Allies, Tennis Courts and suchlike Places of Honest Recreation, as are likewise in theis Presentes hereafter particularly mentioned, sett down and appoynted…videlicet…within the said Citties of London and Westminster, and in any place or places within two miles of the said cities, fowarteene Tennis Courtes.

This figure of fourteen courts is valuable confirmation of the accuracy of the Petworth list.

Charles continued to play Tennis enthusiastically on coming to the throne. On 6 November 1626 a warrant was issued to pay Thomas Hooker, keeper of the Tennis court at St James's, £798 3s 2d for balls and other accessories and for betting debts.

A later document of 1627 contains an instruction to Lord Treasurer Marlborough concerning 'his Majesty's pleasure that Hooker, the Tennis-court-keeper, be paid.'

The Treasury seems to have been very lax in settling the King's debts to Thomas Hooker, for after his death his wife, who succeeded him as keeper of the King's Tennis court at St James's, entered the following petition in 1637:

Before the death of her late husband, Thomas Hooker, there was due to him £3000 in 1630 whereof he abated £1000 for renewing the lease of the tennis court, and by his will left the other £2000 for the portions of his children. In May 1633 petitioner received £1000 and for the King's play since 1630 to 2nd May 1636 there is due £632. 7s. 0d. Prays a Privy Seal for £1632. 7s. 0d.

It seems likely that Charles I built the present court at Hampton Court Palace in about 1625, on the site of the old wooden court.

He also kept the Whitehall courts in good repair. A warrant of 21 October 1634 is addressed 'to the survayer, to cause the 3 Tennice courts at Whitehall to bee mended in places needfull'. In 1635/6 he re-paved the Brake court and money was paid 'to Nicholas Stone, Maurice and Richard Flewellein and other Masons…for taking up all the Purbecke paving in the Brake, and new squaring and layinge downe againe, V^{m}CCxiij foote of the said stone.'

About this time an investigation into the escape of a prisoner from the gatehouse mentions a certain Mr Gibbons, who keeps 'the Tennis-court in the Fields, unto whose house noblemen resort there and eat'. This reveals the existence of a new court in Lincoln's Inn Fields, built about 1633. It was situated in Bear Yard, Vere Street, Clare-market, and was usually known as Gibbons' Tennis court. Charles Gibbons lived close by the court until his death in 1668. This was one of two new courts near Lincoln's Inn Fields, built in this reign. The other was known as Lisle's Tennis court and was situated in Portugal Street on the site of the Royal College of Surgeons' Museum, blitzed in the Second World War.

In about 1634, the first of two courts was built in James Street (now Orange Street) off the Haymarket.

View of Hampton Court showing the present court as built by Charles I and the outer walls of Henry VIII's previous court.

It fell into disrepair and in 1680 Charles Hatton wrote to his brother:

> *Yesterday ye roof of ye Tennis cote in ye Haymarket fell down. Sir Charles Sidley being there had his skull broke, and it is thought it will be mortall.*

Even the outbreak of Civil War in England did not dampen the King's enthusiasm for Tennis, and he was playing the game with Prince Rupert in the Oriel Street court at Oxford on 28 December 1642 when a messenger arrived from Parliament with proposals for 'articles of accommodation'.

The match was 'at Mr Edwards his tennis court'. This was Richard Edwards, a surgeon, who was granted the lease of the property on 12 October 1636.

The King's absence from London was much lamented, and a pamphlet printed for NV and JB in 1642 is entitled: 'A Deep Sigh breathed through the lodgings at Whitehall, deploring the absence of the Court and the Miseries of the Pallace'.

It begins, 'A Pallace without a Presence! A White-Hall clad in sable vestments! A Court without a Court!', and later it reads:

> *There is no presse at the Wine-Sellor Dores and Windowes, no gaping noise amongst the angry Cookes in the Kitchings, no wayting for the opening of the Posterne-dore to take water at the Stayres, no racket nor balling in the Tenis Court...*

On one occasion the King found himself short of a Tennis suit and had to obtain Parliament's consent for the necessary material to be sent from London to Oxford. On 8 November 1643, it is recorded:

> *George Kirk, master of His Majesty's robes, applies for a pass for John Daintrey, one of the grooms in the office, to go to Oxford with his servant with 4 dozen of gloves, which are much wanted by His Majesty, and 4 yards of taby, 2 ells and $\frac{1}{4}$ of taffety to be a tennis-suit, and 2 pairs of garters and roses with silk buttons and other necessaries for making up of the said suit. Permission was granted by Parliament and it was ordered that John Daintrey shall have a pass to Oxon with a servant to carry down some things for the King's Majesty.*

At Oxford, Thomas Burnham keenly promoted Tennis. He had obtained a sub-lease of the Merton Street court in 1647 and issued a farthing token inscribed with a Tennis racquet and ball and the words, 'Thomas Burnham at ye tennis Court in Oxford'. In 1667 he leased the Oriel Street court and in 1670 the Unicorn in Blue Boar Lane, 'where he built a fair and stately Racket court...covered overhead which it was not before.' He died in 1676, but his wife continued the business.

Tennis continued to be played in the Blue Boar Lane court until about 1835.

Oliver Cromwell did not approve of Tennis, and courts were put to military use.

John Hooker laid claim to the Tennis court at St James's. Probably he was a son of Thomas Hooker, whom Charles I had rewarded so generously for his services as Tennis court keeper at St James's. John Hooker received a peremptory order in July 1649 to hand over the key of the court of Colonel Thomas Pride, 'to enable him to quarter his soldiers there'.

A survey of the St James's Tennis court, made by order of Parliament in 1650, sheds some light on its construction.

> *One house called the Tennis Court built with bricks and covered with tiles and paved with tiles. The tiles well fitted and joined containing by admeasurement 100 ft. of assise in length and 35 ft. in breadth, also one leanto or walk lying on the east side of the said Tennis Court consisting of the length aforesaid, also one garden belonging to the same enclosed round with a strong brick wall of 20 ft. high, now in the occupation of John Hooker gentleman and is worth per annum £47.*
>
> *We find that the late King by his letters patent bearing date the 12th day of August in the 7th year of his reign did grant to Thomas Hooker gentleman in consideration of his good service all that aforesaid Tennis Court and other the aforesaid premises for and during the full end and term of 80 years to commence at the end expiration or future or other determination of a former lease which did determine on the 25th day of March 1643 yielding and paying yearly during the aforesaid term of 80 years the sum of 12s. 4d....so that the aforesaid Thomas Hooker is the immediate tenant and hath yet to come 77 years and a half on the 29th day of September next ensuing...*
>
> *The lessee covenants to repair uphold maintain and keep this Tennis Court and houses in good repair at his own cost and charges...*
>
> *Examined for William Webb, Surveyor-General 1650*
> *Ric Heinwood*
> *Rowland Brasbridge*
> *John Brudenell*

Charles Gibbons' endeavours to build another court in 1654 found no favour in Puritan eyes.

> *October 17th. Petition of John Tilson, gentleman, and others, to the Protector and Council, to prohibit Charles Gibbons, a tennis-court-keeper near Lincoln's Inn Fields, from erecting another tennis court, to the disturbance of his neighbours and ill example of others in this time of reformation, he having one already which entertains company at unseasonable hours.*

After the Restoration this court became a well-known theatre, but later it was used for sundry other purposes until finally burnt down in 1809.

Even under the Commonwealth, the office of Master of the Tennis Plays evidently continued, for on 8 March 1656 when John Webb died, Ralph Bird was appointed. He held office for a few years only, being replaced at the Restoration.

In exile, the Court continued to play Tennis in France. Charles I had brought up his sons, Charles and James, to play – a print of James at the age of eight in 1641 shows him racquet in hand in an open court, probably the Brake in Whitehall, and accounts at Petworth record his playing there in 1647/48. When John Evelyn visited France in 1649 he wrote:

> *...on 13 September the King invited the Pr. of Condy* [Prince de Condé] *to supper at St Clo's* [St Cloud]. *There I kissed the Duke of Yorks hand in the Tennis Court, where I saw a famous match 'twixt Monsieur Saumeurs* [perhaps Paul de Saumur] *and Col Cooke, and so returned to Paris.*

A letter from Sir Edward Hyde to Sir Edward Nicholas, dated 1657, reports that

> *The King spends his time not unpleasantly, nor uselessly, having entered into another kind of conversation with Don Juan, than is natural to an* incognito *condition. Yesterday they played at long poume, a Spanish play with balls filled with wire, and tomorrow they have a match at tennis.*

Another story tells that Charles was playing a game of Tennis when news was brought to him of Oliver Cromwell's death in 1658.

The year 1660 marked not only the restoration of the monarchy, but the restoration of Tennis as the royal game. Charles II was the most enthusiastic monarch since Henry VIII to play it.

It was seldom that he passed a day without visiting the Tennis court as early as there was light enough to see clearly. In the summer he was there at five in the morning; on 5 October 1660, at eight, he told Clarendon at Council, 'I am now going to take my usual physicks at tennis.' It was in the Tennis courts that grave interviews were granted; when the Lords of the Hamilton party came in 1678 to press their cause against Lauderdale, they kissed hands in the lobby of the court; and it was in 1679 that he had his first serious illness from the chill which he caught, after a hard game, by sauntering along the waterside in St James's Park. He also played frequently at Hampton

Court and Stephen Charlton wrote to Sir R. Leveson in January 1661 that 'the King is in very good health and goes to Hampton Court often and back again the same day, but very private; most of his exercise is in the Tennis-court in the morning when he doth not ride abroad.' And in another letter he writes: 'His Majesty's only recreation as yet is at tennis [at Whitehall] by 5 o'clock in the morning for an hour or two.'

Charles was far from content with the courts that he found in England and immediately upon his restoration set to work to rebuild and restore them. He began in 1662 to build a new court at Whitehall, partly on the site of the Brake and partly on Lord Sandwich's garden, to replace the three courts of his father's reign. He issued a warrant in May of that year to 'pay Unto Thomas Cooke, his Ma^{ts} Servant, the Summe of 1500*l*. out of the Receipt of his Ma^{ts} Customes, to be by him employed in the building and erecting of a Tennis Court in the place of the Brake at his Ma^{ts} Pallace of Whitehall'. He sent Robert Long down to Hampton Court to take measurements and evidently entrusted to him much of the new construction. Long was paid for 'superviseinge & orderinge the workmen at the New Tennis Court nere the Cockpitt'. In fact, the court was commonly known as 'Long's'.

Samuel Pepys several times mentions the construction of this new court. On 26 July 1662, he notes: 'Here I find that my Lord (Sandwich) hath lost the garden to his lodgings, and that it is turning into a tennis-court.' Accounts of the Lord Chamberlain give details of some of the materials provided for the new court. A warrant of December 1662 was, 'to provide and deliver to Capt. Cook, Master of His Maties court at Whitehall…two chavres of two foot and an halfe wide in the seat one footstoole two velvett cushions, one velvett Carpett with gold fringe…Curtayne cloathes for the Tennis Court sixty yards of each side in length and six yards of each side deep in breadth, a corde, and Tarpaulin to goe round the court on the outside and black Bayes for the ends of the Court.' At the same time a bed and bedding were provided at the court for Robert Long, the marker, so that he might always be at hand.

There was a slight set-back some months later, and on 24 June 1663, Pepys writes, 'This day I observed the house, which I took to be the new Tennis-court, newly built next my Lord's lodgings, to be fallen down by the badness of the foundation or slight working, which my cozen Roger and his discontented party cry out upon, as an example how the King's worke is done.'

By the end of the year, however, the court was completed and Pepys watched the King play there on 28 December 1663. 'Walking through Whitehall I heard the King was gone to play at Tennis, so I down to the new Tennis-court, and saw him and Sir Arthur Slingsby play against my Lord of Suffolke and my Lord Chesterfield. The King beat three, and lost two sets, they all, and he particularly, playing well, I thought.' On 4 January 1664, he again visited the court and commented, 'but to see how the King's play was extolled, without any cause at all, was a loathsome sight, though sometimes, indeed, he did play very well, and deserved to be commended; but such open flattery is beastly.' He made another interesting visit to the court on 2 September 1667, and records it as follows:

I went to see a great match at tennis, between Prince Rupert and one Captain Cooke, against Bab May and the elder Chichly; where the King was, and Court; and it seems they are the best players at tennis in the nation. But this puts me in mind of what I observed in the morning, that the King, playing at tennis, had a steelyard carried to him, and I was told it was to weigh him after he had done playing; and at noon Mr Ashburnham told me that it is only the King's curiosity, which he usually hath of weighing himself before and after his play, to see how much he loses in weight by playing; and this day he lost four and a half pounds.

The site of this new Whitehall court is clearly shown on a Survey of the Royal Palace of Whitehall made in 1670 by John Fisher. It was surrounded by the apartments of Captain Cooke, Master of the Tennis Court. Charles himself kept a bed at the court. In 1673 he made over a 'Red Damask Tennis Court Bedd, with all things thereunto belonging' to the Duke of Monmouth. A few years later in 1677 an order was issued to the Master of the Robes to provide

a new bedd for his Ma^{ts} service in ye Tennis Court at Whitehall, (vizt.) a crymson damaske bedd with silke fringe of severall coloures, the bedd to be somewhat larger than ye other, the bedstead, quilts, bedding and blankets to be fitted up as for his Ma^{ts} other bedds, with one elbow chaire and 2 stooles with covers of crymson serge…2 window curtaines and a Portugall matt under the bedd.

The new court appears to have been about the same width as a modern court, but somewhat longer. The overall dimensions given in a plan of 1793 are: width 39ft 1in (compare Hampton Court 39ft 7ins) and length 118ft 1½ ins (compare Hampton Court 110ft 11ins).

The other royal courts were certainly not neglected. The court at Hampton Court was repaired and in 1672 a warrant was sent 'to certify unto you his Maties pleasure that you provide and deliver...unto Thomas Cook Esqr Master of his Maties Tennis Courts such a proporcon of netts curtaynes and lynes for his Maties tennis Court at Hampton Court as Mr Cook shall inform yr L^dpp shall be necessary and convenient for his Maties service.'

In 1669 it was decided to convert the old Tudor court into lodgings for the Duchess of York (wife of the future James II). This conversion was completed in 1674 at a cost of £3000.

Another new court was built at Windsor. The old Tudor court still existed as late as 1672 when it was shown in a drawing by Wenceslas Hollar of the Upper Ward of Windsor Castle. Being an open court it was not in a very good state of repair. In 1676 it was decided to build a new covered court. The Treasury receipt of that year reads, 'Received of Mr Topham by order of King Charles the Second for a peice of ground sould to his Matie called Old Hawes to erect a Tennis Court – sixty pounds.' It was built south of the Lower Ward within the grounds of the Duke of St Albans' Lodge and is shown in Kip's views of 1709, which reveal a magnificent covered court measuring about the same as the new Whitehall court. Warrants of 1678 and 1679 show that it was furnished similarly to the courts at Hampton Court and Whitehall, with curtains, nets, lines, black hair-cloth and 'andyrons tongs'.

This court was still standing in 1742, but in 1782 the Queen's Lodge and later the Queen's Mews were built on the site.

King Charles also played in his court at Newmarket. Cosmo III, Grand Duke of Tuscany, described him playing there in 1669. 'After dinner the King, with the Duke [of York] and Prince Robert [Rupert], went on horseback to a place at a little distance from Newmarket and amused themselves with the game of tennis.' The King and the Duke of York also paid many visits to the James Street court.

Interesting figures for the number of courts in London in 1669 are provided by an Italian resident, who wrote,

before the Fire there were six different tennis courts, all built in the French fashion. Now there are only four, two having been burnt. The finest is that belonging to the King, just opposite the Palace, with which there is communication by a gallery over an arch. The King has a bedroom there to change his clothes in, the window of which, guarded by an iron grating, looks upon the game. They generally play there three times a week, in the morning, in vests suited to the purpose.

Accounts show that the King continued to play later in his reign. Payments of the Wardrobe for 1679 show the following items bought for him:

Making a Paire of Tennis drawers   xxx^d
1 Ell of Taffata for Tennis drawers   xxi^s vi^d
1 Ell of Taffata for Tennis drawers   xxi^s vi^d
To John Pate for Shoos, Goloshoes, tennis shoes,
  Slippers & Bootes   lxxxxiij l. x^s

In 1682 the Tennis court bills submitted to the Master of the Great Wardrobe amounted to £111 12s 10d.

On Charles II's restoration there was considerable competition for court appointments. One of the first claimants for the post of Master of the Tennis Plays was Simon Smith, who had married John Webb's widow and claimed large sums of money owed to Webb on his death by the late King. His claim failed, however, and he had to be content with the post of Master of the Otter Hounds. Thomas Cooke was appointed Master of the King's Tennis Plays with Horatio Moore as his successor on his death.

Robert Long, who described himself as 'Clerk of the Chapel to the late King and keeper of balloons and paumes and of tennis shoes and ankle socks to his Majesty when Prince', petitioned in 1660 for the post of Groom of the Great Chamber. He was not successful but was compensated later the same year when appointed 'Marker in his Maties Tennis Courts, on the death of Mr Timothy Plesaunt'. A few months later, 'John Dynan ye younger, after the Decease of John Dynan, his ffather' was appointed 'Rackett Maker'.

Another claimant was John Hooker, who had laid claim to the court at St James's during the Commonwealth. He received £100 in 1662 in satisfaction of Tennis debts owed to him by Charles I.

Thomas Cooke remained Master of the King's Tennis Plays from the Restoration until 1689. However, in 1675 he transferred his rights in the Brake at Whitehall only, to Charles Cornwallis for the sum of £1500. The Crown granted Cornwallis a twenty-one-year lease on the Brake at a nominal rent with the stipulation that on the death of Cooke or on the expiry of the lease the property should pass to Horatio Moore.

When James II came to the throne in 1685, he confirmed Captain Cooke's position as the royal professional and by warrant of 17 June arranged for him to have the 'Bed, Bedding, etc. belonging to ye Bed which his late Matie used to lye in at ye Tennis Court at Whitehall'.

However, the King had many other preoccupations and little time for leisure pursuits.

On the accession of William and Mary, Horatio Moore lost no time in asserting his claim to be Master of the King's Tennis Plays elect. In April 1689 he issued a caveat that 'no grant pass relating to the place of Master of the Tennis Courts, till notice be first given to Horatio Moore, Esq., at Mr. Wait's house, a salesman, at the Golden Hart in the Strand, near the Savoy.'

The next month he made a petition for the grant of the office, alleging that he was entitled to it in reversion and claiming that it was vacant – presumably because Cooke was by this time an invalid. His claim was referred to the Attorney-General.

Another claimant was Henry Baker, a solicitor to the Treasury, who alleged that Cooke 'is above eighty and is bedrid' and sought to have Moore passed over in his favour.

The final decision was made by a grant dated 15 November 1689. The office of 'master of our Tennis Courts and Tennis Plays at Whitehall Hampton Court and elsewhere built and to be built for our Royall Disport and Recreation within this Our Kingdome of England' was granted to Henry Villiers. Excepted from the grant was

> *all that Tennis Court with the appurtenances and other buildings there situate on a parcell of ground called the Brake adjoyning to the Cockpitt within Our Palace of Westminster built by Thomas Cooke Esquier and by his late Majesty King Charles the Second in the Twenty Seventh yeare of his Reigne granted to Charles Cornwallis Esquier for Twenty One yeares.*

The grant was made to Henry Villiers 'for and during the naturall life of Thomas Cooke Gent'. He was to receive eightpence a day and £120 a year from the Exchequer.

Meanwhile Robert Long, the King's marker, secured the appointment of his son, also called Robert Long, to

The smaller seventeenth-century court in Stockholm.

succeed him in office. On 28 November 1669 'Robert Long ye younger, marker at Tennis and keeper of ye Long Paulims in order without ffee' was appointed 'to commence in ordinary with ffee upon the first avoydance or decease of his ffather'. His father died seven years later.

Under the Stuarts none of those repressive acts so common in Tudor times was passed. Tennis was in no way discouraged, and the only action taken was to regulate the amount of gambling on this and other sports by an 'Acte against deceitfull disorderly and excessive Gaming' in the year 1675. Import duties continued on foreign equipment; racquets were liable to duty at eightpence each and balls at £2 per thousand.

The granting of licences for public courts was part of the office of Groomporter. In 1678 John and Samuel Garrard were appointed to succeed Thomas and William Neale in that office with the oversight of 'all common billiard tables, bowling grounds, dicing houses, gaming houses and common tennis courts and the power of licensing the same'.

Tennis was popular throughout the seventeenth century in Europe. Two courts were built at Strasbourg in 1602; there were two at Leipzig, one in Berlin, several at Cologne, and the pattern repeated itself elsewhere on the continent. At Regensburg, a court was specially built for the meeting of the Diet of the Holy Roman Empire in 1652, and when the Diet met in Prague in 1663 the *Ballhaus* there was put at the disposal of visiting delegates.

In Switzerland there were courts in Basle, Berne, Geneva and Neuchâtel. In Sweden a magnificent royal court was built in Stockholm in 1627; it was 104ft long by 44ft wide and 28ft 4ins high. The original master professional was Mikael, but he was replaced in 1635 by a German called George Sippel.

Gustavus Adolphus II was a keen player and during the siege of Ingolstadt in 1631 expressed a desire for a game with his officers in the fortress court, but he did not succeed in capturing it.

The royal court being unable to meet the demand, another smaller court was built in the vicinity by Sippel between 1648 and 1653 on ground provided by the Empress Christina. This second court was eventually converted into a chapel in 1725.

In Vienna there were four courts. One of these, attached to the Imperial Palace, was burned in 1525 but reconstructed on a new site and eventually in 1741 converted into a theatre. Another remained in use until 1855 when it became first a museum and then the Chancellery (known as the *Ballplatz*).

In the seventeenth century, Tennis also spread to the New World. It is historically consistent that the first evidence should be in the form of a prohibition.

Peter Stuyvesant, Governor of New York, on 30 September 1659, proclaimed 15 October 'a day of Universal Fasting and Prayer. In order that it may be the better put into practice, we interdict and forbid during divine service on the day aforesaid, all exercise and games of tennis, ball-playing, hunting, fishing, ploughing and sowing…'

EIGHTEENTH-CENTURY TENNIS

The decline in the popularity of Tennis which had begun by the end of the seventeenth century continued throughout the eighteenth century. Many old courts disappeared altogether and others were put to other uses, particularly as theatres.

Louis XV had been taught to play Tennis as a boy, but he was too lazy to play much. However, he built a new covered court at Fontainebleau to replace the two burnt down in 1702. This court was remarkable in having a niche in the main wall just under the net hook where the stakes were to be placed. Louis also reconstructed the Château at Compiègne, which involved the demolition and rebuilding of the Tennis court.

The Prince de Condé built a new court at Chantilly, but the game was generally in decline, except among students and soldiers. A decree of 30 May 1708 forbade Tennis court owners to allow students into the court during their working hours or to accept books or working equipment in settlement of debts. On 3 January 1731 they were forbidden to allow soldiers into the courts.

One keen player of this period was Philippe Egalité, father of Louis Philippe. He was playing in the Caille court at Orléans in 1787 when he received a letter from Louis XVI pointing out that he was to be exiled to Villiers-Cotteret instead of Orléans. He immediately dropped his racquet and departed, comforted no doubt by the fact that there was also a Tennis court there where he could continue to play the game. To him is attributed the 'coup d'Orléans', a ball hit into the dedans after hitting the service wall.

Two books have provided us with a good knowledge of the game in France at this period, and of some of the great players. The authors were François de Garsault and de Manevieux.

François Alexandre Pierre de Garsault (1673–1778) was a member of the French Royal Academy of Sciences which published a comprehensive encyclopaedia of arts and crafts. His most interesting book *The Art of the Tennis-Racket-Marker and of Tennis* was part of that encyclopaedia and was first separately published in 1767. It is a goldmine of information on every aspect of Tennis in the eighteenth century.

Scaino was the first to give us details of the *jeu quarré* as distinct from the *jeu à dedans*. De Garsault gives us a complete description and plan. The winning openings are the grille (3ft 4ins high x 2ft 9ins wide) on the hazard side; the *trou* (16ins square) on the service side, at floor level in the corner with the main wall; and the *ais*, a board (1ft wide and 6ft high) attached to the back wall in the corner with the gallery wall. There is no tambour.

The plan of the court still shows two doors, but only one marker is employed and he stands in the doorway on the service side, carrying a racquet to protect himself. He also uses this racquet to raise the centre of the net when players change ends to allow them to pass beneath. He keeps a record of sets and games won by each side with a piece of chalk on the flagstone at his feet. In a *jeu quarré*, there being no dedans, the balls were kept in the last gallery.

It is interesting that de Garsault was the first to mention the winning gallery. He describes it as the last gallery on the hazard side, but he makes it clear that a ball entering it wins a point outright. The chases are marked by lines and half-lines painted along the joints of the blocks of Caen stone, each 1ft square, with which the floor is laid. There are fourteen chases on the service side but evidently none on the hazard side.

Clothing is supplied by the Master of the Court – caps, shorts, trousers, pullovers, stockings and shoes at an all-in charge of fifteen *sous* or at four *sous* each article except the cap which costs two *sous*.

The wearing of a cap might seem curious to us today, but perhaps with shaven heads on which to fit a full-bottomed wig, it was a necessity for keeping out the cold, especially in open courts. Certainly Vivès, writing in 1539, was familiar with the cap.

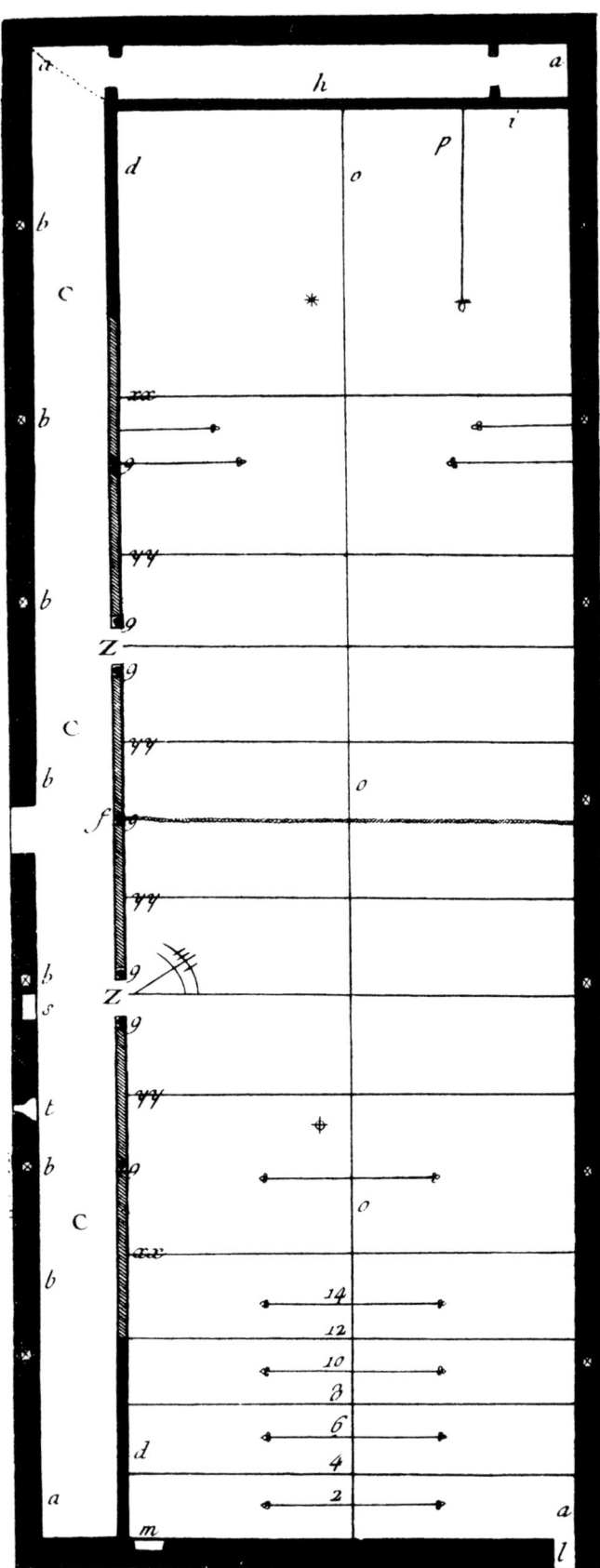

Plan of a jeu quarré *from de Garsault's book.*

Dressing-gowns were also supplied if required. The shoes were low-heeled or heel-less, made of undressed buffalo or calf hide, and tied with string. A buffet was provided including bread, wine and beer and in the corridor under the penthouse roof was a conduit for urine.

After the game, players were rubbed down in front of a good fire, but no beds were provided, since to sleep after a hard game and a good rub-down had resulted in fatal accidents.

De Garsault's book contains detailed instructions on the manufacture of both racquet and ball, together with diagrams. He also gives us a recipe for blacking the inside of the court.

Take half a hogshead of ox blood, fourteen bushels of lamp-black, the gall of ten oxen to dissolve the lamp-black, and a bucket of urine to give sheen to the composition, mix it all cold.

Imagine the smell of a newly painted court – and he recommends doing it twice a year!

Between 1751 and 1780 Messrs Diderot and d'Alembert were publishing the twenty-three volumes of *The Encyclopaedia or Reasoned Dictionary of Sciences, Arts and Crafts by a Society of Men of Letters*. Twelve volumes of plates accompanied the Encyclopaedia and in Volume IV, published in 1765, appear nine plates, very similar to those in de Garsault's book. Plans of a *jeu quarré* and a *jeu à dedans* are included and additional plans show a bird's eye view and a cross-section of these courts.

There is a slightly different illustration of a *jeu quarré* with a doubles match in progress, but all the features of the court are the same. However, there is no illustration of a *jeu à dedans*, but an additional plate shows a billiard room and the construction of a billiard table. There are also copious illustrations of implements used in the manufacture of racquets and balls closely resembling those in de Garsault's book.

De Manevieux's book, published in 1783, is less technical but full of interest. He describes the two sorts of court – *à dedans* and *quarré* – but differs in ruling that to win a point outright on the *ais* of a *jeu quarré* the ball must strike it full toss. He goes on to describe the ball and the racquet, the rules and the method of scoring. In one *quarré* court in Paris, he tells us, as well as the *trou* and the *ais* there is another opening on the service side known as the *lune*. It is round, 8ins in diameter and 5ft off the floor. A player putting a ball into the *lune* wins a whole game outright.

However, he points out, most amateurs prefer the *jeu à dedans* and many master professionals had altered

Players of the eighteenth century properly dressed, including cap.

their *jeux quarrés* into *jeux à dedans* so that not many *jeux quarrés* existed in France.

He warns against the use of damp clothing.

Every player who intends to play several matches knows the need for a change of clothes, especially in the summer; but he must be sure that the shirts or vests that the master professional hires out to him are properly dry, since in a busy court, where the pro. is providing several shirts every day, the servant often only gives them a very hasty wash; each evening she takes all the shirts and clothes used during the day, shakes them in cold water while still impregnated with the player's sweat and hangs them out at once on a line. The mistress of the house thinks that it is useless to iron these clothes as they will be used the next day, so she folds them up half dry; a player impatient to play, only complains about the coldness of this shirt for as long as it takes him to put it on and is soon in the court. As soon as he starts to play the warmth of his body causes the damp in the shirt to evaporate and he finds himself surrounded by steam as if he were in a steam-bath.

De Manevieux also tells us of the leading players of his time. Of the professionals of the 1740s and 1750s, he singles out Clergé, Farolais, La Fosse, Guillaume Barcellon and Barnéon. Barcellon was the King's professional (*paumier du roi*) in 1753 when his portrait was painted by E. Loys. His eldest son, Pierre, published a book entitled *Règles et Principes de la Paume* in 1800. Of his contemporaries, de Manevieux praises the pre-eminence of Raymond Masson, whom he considered better than all the previous five, and next to him, Charrier, the young Barcellon and Bergeron. This young Barcellon was probably Guillaume's nephew, Jean-Pierre, who married Pierrette Masson, Raymond

Raymond Masson.

Masson's sister. Of English professionals, he mentions two – Pilet and John Mucklow, Keeper of the Haymarket (James Street) court. In all he calculates there were about 160 professionals in circulation in France and abroad.

Masson is the first of the really great champions of Tennis whose achievements are on record. He was born in 1740 and by the age of twenty-five he was the outstanding player of his time. He could give 15 to his nearest rival, the elder Charrier. He won one remarkable match, watched by Louis XV and his court at Fontainebleau, against Clergé and Charrier, giving them half 15.

Against amateurs he had to submit to even greater handicaps such as on one occasion being seated in a barrel from which he had to emerge to play each stroke. All this was despite the fact recorded by de Manevieux that he wore spectacles.

Another rare distinction enjoyed by Masson was his wife's prowess at Tennis. De Manevieux remarks that at the age of twenty-eight, Mme. Masson too was a skilful player.

As the century advanced, the number of Tennis courts in France declined. By 1767 there were only twelve master professionals in Paris, and in 1771 a decree forbade the recruitment of apprentices because of the small number of courts. When de Manevieux wrote his book in 1783, there were fifty-four courts in France, thirteen of them in Paris and three in Lyons. Not, perhaps, very many compared with the great days of the two previous centuries, but still a considerable number.

The French Revolution had a devastating effect on Tennis and the aristocracy, although curiously one of the first events took place in a Tennis court.

Although Louis XIII had a Tennis court at the royal palace of Versailles, it is very odd that during the reign of Louis XIV this was demolished and never replaced; courts existed at all the King's other palaces – the Louvre, Vincennes, Fontainebleau, Compiègne, Saint-Germain. All that was available to the Court in 1684 was a game of *longue paume* in the avenues of the Trianon. For the story of the court at Versailles, I am indebted to M. Charles Vatel's book of 1883.

In charge of the royal Tennis courts (*maître paumier du roi*) at this time was Jean Bazin, proprietor of the court at Saint-Germain-en-Laye. He had a son, François, and a daughter, Jeanne, married to another Tennis professional, Nicholas Cretté. The three men determined to remedy the Versailles omission and to build a court on a site owned by them in the rue l'Hôtel-de-Lorge.

They planned the building with great care and the specification dated 1686 was minutely detailed. The floor was to be of Caen stone, white, without vein or marl, laid firm and level. The ceiling was to be painted blue, decorated with *fleurs-de-lis* in gold. Above the entrance was to be carved the royal emblem, a rising sun. Clearly it was expected that Louis XIV would play there.

It was also specified that the work should be completed in four months – and it was. But unfortunately, *le Roi Soleil* was unable to open it – he was ill throughout the year, underwent a major operation in November and was in bed until January the following year. So it was left to the Dauphin to confer royal approval on the court, which he did by playing there three days after it opened in December 1686.

However, it was not long after the King's recovery that he played Tennis on the new court, with all the pomp and ceremony that was then observed. It was the duty of one official (*le porte-manteau*) to hand the balls to His Majesty with one hand while with the other he held his sword. After he had played, the King was rubbed down in front of his officers and courtiers. He had to meet all the expenses, whether he won or lost, including a suitable meal for all his courtiers, laid on by the master professional.

Little is recorded of the court during the reigns of Louis XV and XVI. Neither King played there as far as is known, but certainly others did and it was well used. So it was readily available for the great event of 20 June 1789 which made history.

The King had summoned the full States-General, which comprised the Nobility, the Clergy and the Third Estate, to meet at Versailles in May 1789. But deadlock ensued on the seemingly important question of whether the three Estates should meet together or separately. Exasperated at the delay, the Third Estate met in the main hall on 17 June and voted to establish itself as the National Assembly, and this was followed on 19 June by a vote in the House of Clergy to meet with them. The King and his advisers were seriously alarmed at this prospect. They immediately announced a royal session of the States-General and troops occupied the main hall, where the Assembly had held its meetings, to prepare for it.

Bailly, President of the National Assembly, satisfied himself that the hall was occupied and a discussion ensued among the members on an alternative meeting-place. It is said that the suggestion of the Tennis court was made by Dr Joseph-Ignace Guillotin (a man of initiative, says M. Charles Vatel). Here the National Assembly met at 10.30 a.m. on 20 June 1789 and took the historic oath:

> We swear never to dissolve and to meet whenever circumstances demand until the Constitution of the realm is firmly established on solid foundations.

This oath was unanimously approved and members were required to sign it individually. One demurred, but repercussions were averted by the President, who pointed out that one man's refusal to sign was witness to the liberty of their cause.

On the first anniversary of this historic oath, a bronze plaque was affixed to the wall of the court and ever since it has been regarded as a very special monument to the history of the French Revolution. In 1791 Jacques-Louis David was commissioned to paint a picture of the Tennis Court oath, 30ft x 20ft, for the sum of 36,000 *livres*.

In England, a parallel decline in the popularity of Tennis set in with the arrival of the Hanoverian monarchs. But in the first few years of the century further improvements were carried out to the court at Hampton Court Palace, which itself had been extensively rebuilt by Sir Christopher Wren. In 1700 Horatio Moore had submitted an estimate of £365, to include the laying of a stone floor 'without which no Ball can give a true bound'. But King William III preferred a brick floor, presumably for economy. In the event, however, the floor was laid with 1070 ft of Ketton stone.

Despite this, the King was not interested, and ordered the court to be fitted up as a 'Drawing Room' with an additional 'Side Kitchen' and a 'Necessary House for Persons of Quality'. He used to hold evening assemblies in the court.

The last flicker of royal interest was shown by Frederick, Prince of Wales, eldest son of George II, who played Tennis. Horace Walpole alleged that his death in 1751 was caused by a blow from a Tennis ball three years earlier.

The office of Master of Royal Tennis Courts continued. On 19 February 1708, Thomas Chaplin was appointed on the death of Horatio Moore. His appointment is described as:

> *A grant unto Thomas Chaplin of the office of Master or Keeper of the Tennis-court near the Cock-pit in Whitehall, and all other Tennis-courts which Horatio Moore, Esq., deceased lately enjoyed, with the buildings and appurtenances thereunto belonging, during her Majesty's pleasure (except the ground, building, and lodgings adjoining to the same Tennis-court near the Cock-pit, which are now enjoyed by the Duke of Montagu and Earl of Rochester, or either of them), with the fees of eightpence per diem, and 120l per annum, payable quarterly, out of the exchequer.*

He was confirmed in office by King George I on his accession to the throne in 1714. He died in February 1728 and was succeeded by Charles Fitz-Roy.

The name of the marker in the James Street court at this time is also known, for a notice in the *Daily Courant* of 7 February 1732 reads: 'On Saturday last died Monsieur Latell, Marker of the King's Tennis Court in the Haymarket.'

In 1762, Richard Beresford succeeded Charles Fitz-Roy. He was replaced, from May 1764 to October 1765, by William Chetwynd Jr, but returned as Sir Richard Beresford and held the office until his death in 1791. In that year, Charles Meynell took over. Finally, in 1815, the Rt Hon. William Beresford was appointed. In his case, for the first time, there is no mention of the court at Whitehall, which had been demolished in 1809.

Some time before 1720 a new court was built in James Street, Haymarket, immediately adjoining the previous court and to the west of it. By this time, the old east court had been adapted for use as a theatre, but the new court came to be the centre of Tennis in England. A plan of the site indicates that the court measured overall 110 ft x 43 ft, identical to a modern court.

In 1757 it was taken over by Thomas Higginson, who seems to have specialised in the provision of facilities for Tennis and Rackets in the capital. An advertisement in the *Daily Advertiser* of 28 October 1742 reads:

> *To all Gentlemen that like the Exercise of Tennis, Fives or Billiards. There is a complete Tennis-Court, with a Tambour, and everything that makes it as good a Tennis-Court as any in England, at 1s. a set single, or 6d. a set double; with Fives-playing in the Tennis-Court, and Billiards at the same place. It's near the Bull and Gate Inn, Holborn, and near Lincoln's Inn Fields, by the Duke of Newcastle's, next door to Adlam's Coffee-House, opposite little Turnstile. It's kept by*
>
> THOMAS HIGGINSON
>
> *who keeps a Fives-Court at the bottom of St Martin's Street, on the left hand in Leicester-Fields. It's for Fives-playing only either with Racquets, Boards, or at Hand-Fives, at 2d., 3d., or 4d. a Game.*
>
> NOTE, *Any Gentleman may bespeak either Court for their own playing, and Care will be taken to keep it for them. Tennis-playing at 8d. a set with Tossing-Balls and Racquets, on agreeing before they begin to play, or else not less than 1s. a Set. Boards, Racquets, and all sorts of Ball, sold at the Tennis-Courts, Holborn.*

A subsequent advertisement states that the Holborn court adjoined the 'Six Cans' tavern.

Thomas Higginson opened a new court in Great Windmill Street in 1743 and advertised its facilities on 12 December:

> TO ALL GENTLEMEN LOVERS OF EXERCISE
>
> *The New Tennis-Court in Great Windmill Street, facing St James's, Hay-Market, is completely finish'd and open'd, with complete Dressing-Rooms, and everything fit for the Reception of Gentlemen, at 2s. for a six-game Set, with Advantage Game, or at 1s. or 8d. for four-game Sets. This Court is built after the Manner of that in James Street.*

> NOTE, *Another Tennis-Court in Holborn, or near to that Corner of Lincoln's Inn Fields turning up on the left Hand for the Duke of Newcastle's, with Tennis at 1s. or 8d. for four-game Sets, which is much cheaper than any other Courts in London, for they are 3s. 6d. a Set...*

By 1744 the court in St Martin's Street had been adapted for Tennis as well as for fives and Rackets, as an advertisement of 23 February makes clear. It was a *jeu quarré*, anglicised in the advertisement as a 'Carry-Tennis-Court':

> *There are now three new and complete Tennis-Courts built by Thomas Higginson.*
>
> *These are the one in Windmill Street, price 2s. 6d. for a six-game set, or at 8d. or 12d. a four-game set 'when the Court's at Leisure'. The one at Holborn, where tennis is 8d. or 1s. in four-game sets.*
>
> *And the other Tennis-Court is in St Martin's Street, next Door to the Stable-Yard, near Hedge Lane, Leicester Fields; it's built like the Tennis-Courts at Oxford or Cambridge; it's made out of the Fives-Court into a Carry-Tennis-Court; Tennis at 8d. or 12d. for a four-game Set.*

> NOTE, *Any Gentlemen may bespeak either Court for their own Play for any Day or Hour; or Fives-Playing; in either Court, with Tennis and other Balls, till they are wanted for Tennis, at 2d., 3d., or 4d. a Game.*

Thomas Higginson ran these three courts and the James Street court until his death in 1783, when John Mucklow took over at James Street.

Another fine court was built at Bath, the fashionable watering place, and thanks to the research of Mr R.R. Henshaw more is known about this court. He quotes the *New Bath Guide* for 1779:

> *Adjoining to the Riding School is erected an elegant and commodious Tennis Court by Richard Scrace, which was opened for play in 1777. The plan was presented to Mr Scrace by the Earl of Pembroke, and the dimensions of the Court were the same as that of the Duke of Orléans and Masson's in Paris – here are dressing rooms, dresses and everything necessary to render it as agreeable as possible. The terms of the play are the same as in London.*

The court was built of Bath stone and the original flagged floor can still be seen. Adjacent are the changing rooms. The tambour still stands, and the markings of chases 1, 2 and 3 are visible. There also remains an *oeuil de boeuf* in each gable end. It stands in Morford Street and is now an industrial museum. There is evidence of two additional courts in Bath.

Other new courts, outside London, were opened in Liverpool in 1750 and at Goodwood by the Duke of Richmond in 1760.

Another Tennis enthusiast was Francis, fifth Duke of Bedford. He built a court and riding school at Woburn Abbey in 1792 to a design by Henry Holland, which included a covered walk from the house and central dressing rooms serving both activities. A 'master of the court' and a 'tennis boy' were added to the household staff, the master being paid a salary of £84 per annum. Nets were supplied by Samuel Thatcher.

Unfortunately, this old court was gutted by fire in the early twentieth century, and in 1950 the discovery of dry rot necessitated the demolition of the whole building.

A primitive form of Tennis was also played in Wales. In keeping with history in other countries, the first known mention of the game is its prohibition in Cowbridge in 1610:

And also that there be noe tenyse playinge within the highe streate uppon payne of iij s iiij d. to be levied uppon every of them that playethe.

An early Welsh Tennis player was the martyr, Philip Evans, a Jesuit priest born in Monmouthshire in 1645. During the scare caused by the Titus Oates 'plot' he was arrested and imprisoned in Cardiff Castle. He was condemned to death, but the execution was deferred for eleven weeks during which time he was well treated and even allowed to play Tennis. He was on court when informed that he was to be hanged the next day, but he insisted on completing his game before returning to his cell.

About 1777 a court was built in Cardiff adjacent to the licensed premises attached to Nell's Brewery, once the Kemeys-Tynte Arms, later the Tennis Court Inn and then the Buccaneer. Before this court was built, a ball game was played against the north wall of St John's church tower and led to the usual prohibition as appears in the churchwardens' accounts of 1777:

To the Cryer for Proclaiming against Playing Ball against the Church 6d.

This court still existed in 1851, but can only have been of a very rudimentary sort, certainly an open court. There was another court in Chepstow.

Ball games of a sort were played in other parts of Wales. Three 'courts' existed at Llantrisant, and there was keen rivalry between Llantrisant and Cowbridge; a match between the two teams would draw a crowd of several hundred people.

John Richards, in *The Cowbridge Story*, gives an account of this game, which resembled fives or a primitive form of *jeu de paume*:

One of the most exciting games played at Cowbridge until the year 1880 was ball tennis. A very large high walled tennis court existed in East Village on the site now occupied by the Pavilion Cinema. The court was originally attached to the Tennis Court Inn which afterwards became the Wheelwright's Arms occupied by Mr Richard Aubrey, wheelwright. This game of tennis was played with the bare hand using a hard ball slightly larger than a golf ball and made of layers of rubber covered with white soft leather. The balls could not be purchased ready-made but were manufactured in the Borough by the local expert. The hop or tamp was extraordinary, and at the start of the season the players' hands would become red and swollen, later gradually hardening and becoming capable of the task. Competitions with players from other courts were a regular and popular feature arousing great enthusiasm in the Borough. Some of the last experts playing on the Cowbridge court were the brothers Traherne of Llantrisant, and the two Cowbridge stars Edmund John and John George, coal merchant. The pneumatic rubber ball was introduced about 1870 and replaced the hard leather ball.

At Nelson, games were played against the wall of the public house, now called the Nelson Inn, and much betting took place on the outcome. Sometime during the nineteenth century the present handball court at Nelson was built by some of the coal owners, and matches took place against teams from the Rhondda Valley. The large wall is reminiscent of a Basque *fronton*. The popularity of these games, even on Sunday, was noted by John Taylor, the poet, in his *Journey through Wales*, published in 1859:

There is no such zeale in many places and parishes in Wales; for they have neither service, prayer, sermon, minister, or preacher, nor any church door opened at all, so that people do exercise and edifie in the church yard, at the lawful and laudable games of trap, catt, stool-ball, racket, etc., on Sundayes.

TEN [381] TEN

which means they can play as long as they please, without ever having occasion to stoop for a ball.

As to the odds at tennis, they are by no means fixed, but are generally laid as follow:

Upon the first stroke being won between even players, that is, fifteen love, the odds are of the single

game	7 to	4
Thirty love	4	1
Forty love	8	1
Thirty fifteen	2	1
Forty fifteen	5	1
Forty thirty	3	1
The odds of a four game set when the first game is won, are	7	4
When two games love	4	1
Three games love	8 to	1
When two games to one	2	1
Three games to one	5	1
The odds of a six game set when the first game is won, are	3	2
When two games love	2	1
Three games love	4	1
Four games love	10	1
Five games love	21	1
When two games to one	8	5
Three games to one	5	2
Four games to one	5	1
Five games to one	15	1
When three games to two	7	4
Four games to two	4	1
Five games to two	10	1
When four games to three	2	1
Five games to three	5	1
The odds of an advantage set when the first game is won, are	5	4
When two games love	7	4
Three games love	3	1
Four games love	5	1
Five games love	15	1
When two games to one	4	3
Three games to one	2	1
Four games to one	7	2
Five games to one	10	1
When three games to two	3	2
Four games to two	3	1
Five games to two	8	1
When four games to three	8	5
Five games to three	3	1
When five games to four	2	1
When six games to five	5	2

The foregoing odds, as beforesaid, are generally laid, but the chaces interfering makes the odds very precarious; for example, when there is a chace at half a yard, and a set is five games all, and in every other respect equal, the odds are a good five to four; and if it were six games to five, and forty thirty with the same chace, the odds then would be a guinea to a shilling; so that it is plain that the odds at this game differ from those of any other: for one stroke will reduce a set, supposing the players to be five games all, from an even wager to three to two, and so on in proportion to the stage of the set.

There are various methods of giving odds at tennis, in order to make a match equal; and that they may be understood, we shall give the following list of them, with their meanings, so that any person may form a judgment of the advantage received or given.

The lowest odds that can be given, excepting the choice of the sides, is what they call a *bisque*, that is, a stroke to be taken or scored whenever the player, who receives the advantage, thinks proper: for instance, suppose a critical game of the set to be forty thirty, by taking the *bisque*, he who is forty becomes game, and so in respect of two *bisques*, &c.

The next greater odds are *fifteen*, that is, a certain stroke given at the beginning of each game.

After these, *half thirty*, that is, fifteen one game, and thirty the next. Then follow the whole *thirty*, *forty*, &c.

There are also the following kind of odds which are given, viz.

Round services; those are services given round the penthouse, so as to render it easy for the *striker-out* (the player who is on the hazard side) to return the ball.

Half court, that is, being obliged or confined to play into the adversary's half-court; sometimes it is played straightwise, and at other times across; both which are great advantages given by him so confined, but the strait half-court is the greatest.

Touch-no-wall, that is, being obliged to play within the compass of the walls, or sides of the court. This is a considerable advantage to him who receives it; as all the balls must be played gently, and consequently they are much easier to take than those which are played hard, or according to the usual method of play.

Barring the hazards, that is, barring the dedans, tambour, grill, or the last gallery on the hazard-side, or any particular one or more of them.

These are the common kind of odds or advantages given; but there are many others, which are according to what is agreed by the players: such as playing with *board* against *racket*, *cricket-bat* against *racket*, &c.

The game of tennis is also played by four persons, two partners on each side. In this case, they are generally confined to their particular quarters, and one of each side appointed to serve and strike out; in every other respect, the game is played in the same manner as when two only play.

Any thing more to be said upon this subject would be needless, as nothing can be recommended, after reading this short account of tennis, but practice and attention, without which no one can become a proficient at the game.

TENOR, or TENOUR, the purport or content of a writing or instrument in law, &c.

TENOR, in music, the first mean, or middle part, or that which is the ordinary pitch of the voice, when neither raised to a treble nor lowered to a bass.

TENSE, in grammar, an inflection of verbs, whereby they are made to signify or distinguish the circumstance of time in what they affirm. See GRAMMAR.

TENT, in war, a pavilion or portable house. Tents are made of canvas, for officers and soldiers to lie under when in the field. The size of the officers tents is not fixed; some regiments have them of one size and some of another: a captain's tent and marquee is generally 10¼ feet broad, 14 deep, and 8 high: the subalterns are a foot less; the major's and lieutenant-colonel's a foot larger; and the colonel's two feet larger. The subalterns of foot lie two in a tent, and those of horse but one. The tents of private men are 6¼ feet square, and 5 feet high, and hold five soldiers each. The tents for horse are 7 feet broad and 9 feet deep: they hold likewise five men and their horse accoutrements.— The word is formed from the Latin *tentorium*, of *tendo* "I stretch," because tents are usually made of canvas stretched out, and sustained by poles, with cords and pegs.

TENT, in surgery, a roll of lint made into the shape of a nail with a broad flat head; chiefly used in deep wounds and ulcers. They are of service, not only in conveying medicines to the most intimate recesses and sinuses of the wound, but to prevent the lips of the wound from uniting before it

Table of odds from the Encyclopaedia Britannica *of 1797.*

The eighteenth century was an age of gambling, and betting on Tennis was as normal as it had been in Scaino's day. Calculating odds during the course of a game was carried to extreme lengths by the Swiss mathematician Jakob Bernoulli who wrote *Lettre a un amy sur les parties du jeu de paume* in 1713. Joseph Fenn in 1772 wrote a forty-five-page booklet on the odds involved in a game. They were rather more simply listed in the *Encyclopaedia Britannica* of 1797. The *Annals of Gaming*, written in 1775 by 'a Connoisseur', warns against the risks run by the innocent Tennis punter:

> So various are the deceptions of this game, that it is almost impossible for a stranger to go into a tennis-court, and bett without losing his money – so prostituted is this noble game to what it used to be, that instead of seeing only persons of the first rank in England, as formerly, we see the Dedans now thronged with some of the most notorious sharpers in London.

Another royal patron of the game in the eighteenth century was Philip V of Spain, a grandson of Louis XIV, whose hands are said to have been calloused from riding and playing Tennis. Louis I is reported by the French Ambassador, Maréchal de Tessé, to have played Tennis as soon as he had dined, and during the reign of Charles III the post of 'Judge of Ball and Racket Games' was created.

Certainly Tennis continued to be played in Italy, for Marchisio, the French professional of the early nineteenth century, was the son of the master of the Tennis court to the Court of Turin. An interesting picture by Bella shows a form of Tennis in Italy. It is very much closer to modern lawn tennis than to the traditional game with its four walls.

Tennis declined in popularity not only in France and England during the eighteenth century, but throughout the continent of Europe, and probably also in America, where it nevertheless continued to be played. An advertisement of 1763 in the *New York Gazette* offers for sale a tavern with 'a very fine Tennis-Court, or Five-Alley' and three years later a certain James Rivington was importing 'battledores and shuttlecocks, cricket-balls, pillets, best racquets for tennis and fives'.

About this time the first glimmerings of lawn tennis appear, in the form of Field Tennis, described by William Hickey in 1767.

> In the summer we had another Club which met at the Red House in Battersea Fields, nearly opposite Ranelagh, a retired and pretty spot... This club consisted of some very respectable persons, amongst them were Mr Powell of the pay office, Mr Jupp, the East India Company's architect, Mr Whitehead, a gentleman of independent fortune, King, the celebrated actor, Major Sturt of the Engineers and others. The game we played was an invention of our own and called Field Tennis, which afforded noble exercise... Our regular meetings were two days in each week, when we assembled at one o'clock, at two sat down to dinner, consisting of capital stewed grigs...a large joint of roast or boiled meat, with proper vegetables and a good sized pudding or pie; our drink consisting of malt liquors, cyder, port wine and punch. At four our sport commenced, continuing until dusk; during the exercise we refreshed ourselves with draughts of cool tankard, and other pleasant beverages. The field, which was of sixteen acres in extent, was kept in as high order and smooth as a bowling green... Besides our regular days some of the members met every evening during the summer months to have a little Field Tennis.

The Graf von Wildenstein in a German court with curious chase markings.

Evidently the popularity of Field Tennis soon grew, perhaps owing to the liberal refreshment, which seems to have been an indispensable part of the game. At any rate, in 1793 the *Sporting Magazine* reported that,

> *Field Tennis threatens ere long to bowl out cricket. The former game is now patronized by Sir Peter Burrell; the latter has for some time back been given up by Sir Horace Mann.*

One player of the first rank still played Tennis in the James Street court in 1797 – Lord Lorne, later Duke of Argyll – and gave *The Times* an opportunity to record:

> *The once fashionable game of tennis is very much upon the decline. The court in the Haymarket seems to be now entirely forlorn.*

A game of Tennis in the eighteenth century.

NINETEENTH-CENTURY TENNIS

TENNIS IN ITS NATIVE LAND never recovered from the French Revolution. Napoleon played at Fontainebleau occasionally, as did Wellington, but neither had much talent. However, Napoleon kept this court and the one at Compiègne in good repair.

One court remained in Paris in the rue Mazarine until 1839, when it was replaced by another in the Passage Sandrié. This in turn was demolished in 1861 to make way for a new Opera House but, thanks to Napoleon III, Tennis continued in a new court in the Tuileries, opened in 1862 (with a match between Barre and Biboche) to which a second was added in 1882. Others were built in Deauville, Cannes and Pau, but most significant of all, the old court at Bordeaux was restored to use in 1878.

The court at Versailles had been neglected during the Empire and the Restoration, but took new life with the arrival of the 1848 Republic. The following year the meeting of the Congress of Peacelovers took place in Paris under the presidency of Victor Hugo. Afterwards the British delegation gave a banquet for the American delegation in the Tennis court at Versailles.

In 1855 it was actually re-opened for play with an exhibition match by the two leading players of the day, Barre and Biboche, but this revival didn't last long and on 20 June 1883, having been thoroughly restored at public expense, it was officially inaugurated as a museum of the Revolution.

In England, though, there was a distinct revival among the Victorian élite. Dukes, Marquesses and Earls, not to mention mere Barons, vied with each other to build courts on their country estates. The Duke of Wellington at Stratfield Saye; the Duke of Richmond at Goodwood; the Duke of Fife at East Sheen; the Marquess of Salisbury at Hatfield; the Earl of Craven at Coombe Abbey; the Earl of Plymouth at Hewell Grange; Lord Leconfield at Petworth; Lord Brougham and Vaux at Brougham Hall; Sir Edward Guinness at St Stephen's Green, Dublin; Sir George Prescott at Theobald's Park; Sir Thomas Fermor-Hesketh at Easton Neston; Sir Ivor Guest at Canford; Sir Andrew Noble at Jesmond Dene; Sir Charles Rose at Hardwick; Mr Albert Brassey at Heythrop House; Mr Edward Cazalet at Fairlawne; Mr J.P.F. Gundry at The Hyde; Mr Samuel Heilbut at Holyport Grange – all built courts at their stately homes during the course of the century.

All this was crowned by something of a revival of royal interest in the game.

In 1841, the year after their marriage, Queen Victoria and the Prince Consort visited Woburn Abbey as guests of Francis, seventh Duke of Bedford and his Duchess. On 28 July they inspected the Tennis court, where, according to Queen Victoria's diary, 'Albert tried to play at tennis.'

Evidently he enjoyed the experience for we find him playing again in the Duke of Wellington's court at Stratfield Saye in January 1845. Queen Victoria records in her diary:

> Jan. 22. *A cold morning ... We sang Albert's Duet & then walked to the Tennis Court, where we watched the markers playing, & Albert tried it also a little. He afterwards, in spite of rain, went out shooting. – We lunched the same as yesterday, only that the Duke of Devonshire was also at our table. We then all went over to the Tennis Court & saw a fat man called Philips, the Duke's butler, who plays beautifully, – as well as the marker from Hampton Court & his son. When a great deal of the company had gone, Albert tried to play a little...*
> Jan. 23. *I accompanied Albert down to the Tennis Court & watched him playing for a while. – At 11 we set off, just as we came, the good old Duke riding before us with Ld. Douro, etc, as before, on our arrival.*

The Prince Consort also announced his intention of playing at Hampton Court. A locker bearing his name is still in the dressing room there, but he played once

The court at the Tuileries in 1862.

only. The Prince of Wales (later Edward VII) played at Oxford and Cambridge and later at Hampton Court and Prince's Club.

For those not possessing their own court, several club courts were available. First in importance, until its closure in 1866, was the James Street court, off the Haymarket.

About 1820, Mr Robert Lukin became secretary of a club based on the court at James Street. A Silver Racquet was competed for annually, and, to all intents and purposes, this was the British amateur championship. The first University match was played here in 1859.

In 1822 Mr Lukin published a *Treatise on Tennis*, dedicated to George William, Duke of Argyll, 'an ardent admirer and patron of the game of tennis'. This contains the rules of Tennis at the time and hints on playing, and it is interesting to see that these rules differ very little from those of the modern game. There are one or two oddities, of course. The 'match of three' for instance, in which one player opposed two, was not unusual and he devotes a couple of pages to it. Certainly the great Barre often played against two others because he was so much better than anyone else. He played Peter Tompkins and W.J. Cox at Brighton in 1843; and Peter Tompkins and his son, Edmund, at Brighton in 1849.

Not only were the French still the best players but they also made the best racquets. 'The French Racket is far superior to any other, the preparation or seasoning of the wood being well understood in that country; those that have hitherto been made in England are but little admired,' says Lukin.

Clearly, betting in the course of the game was still commonplace, as he includes a table of 'Odds, as usually betted'.

In 1818, the Prince Regent gave orders that the court at Hampton Court should be put in order, and play continued there throughout the rest of the century. Near the court were rooms allotted to the Master of the Tennis Court and these were occupied by the last holder of that title, the Rt Hon. Major William Beresford, whose tenure of office was from 1815 until his death in 1883.

New courts were built at Brighton (1836) and Leamington (1846). In 1893, Prince's formed a link

The James Street court.

with the Brighton court which became known as Prince's Club, Brighton. For the next twenty years or so, it was the main court for world championships.

On 15 October 1838, Mr Aislabie, then secretary of the MCC, laid the foundation stone of a Tennis court at Lord's, situated on the east side of the ground. It cost Mr J.H. Dark, the lessee of the ground, over £4000, but it resulted in a very considerable increase in membership.

'Patrons can be furnished with as many as 100 warm and 100 cold baths per diem, with dressing rooms; couches have also been provided for their temporary use after a heavy practice, and there are two of the best billiard-tables that can be manufactured.' The interior dimensions of the court were 96 ft $\frac{1}{2}$ in x 31 ft 8 ins. A Rackets court was added in 1844.

When the James Street court closed in 1866, the MCC decided to make the court at Lord's the best in London. They re-paved the floor, but a plan for lighting the court from the roof was abandoned as too expensive. They also decided that it was necessary to glaze one side of the roof only. New blinds had been installed in 1865, which shows that the top of the side walls had been open – as was the case with most courts – and covered with blinds. At the same time, £250 was spent on the Rackets court. The roof and front wall were badly in need of repair.

It soon became apparent that Biggs, the head professional, was not up to the job. Several players could give him odds and there were complaints of his untidy habits. He was dismissed and replaced by George Lambert, from Hampton Court, assisted by his brother William.

The court was re-opened on 12 March 1867 and became the home of the MCC prizes competition, which superseded the James Street Silver Racquet. The MCC Gold Racquet was won by J.M. Heathcote every year from 1867 to 1881 and again in 1883 and 1886. For fifteen years, Heathcote never lost a set to an amateur on level terms. His main rival in later years was the Hon. Alfred Lyttelton, who defeated him in 1882, 1884, 1885, 1887 and then retained the Gold Racquet every year until 1895.

The University match was transferred from James Street to Lord's in 1867.

J.M. Heathcote.

Some indication of the staff and wages at this time is given by the 1883 staff list:

George Lambert (head pro)	£2 a week
William Lambert	£1 10s a week
James Fennell	£1 5s a week
John Fennell (a boy presumably)	15d a week
B. Peggs (Rackets marker)	£1 5s a week
R. Gaby (lawn tennis)	£1 1s a week

Charges were 5d for 2 hours' singles (4d for 1½ hours), 6d for 2 hours' doubles (5d for 1½ hours), 2d extra for non-members.

Gaby was the father of Richard Gaby, the Club Superintendent. The MCC presented a silver salver to father and son to mark the centenary of their fifty years of service to the Club.

Lambert's career at Lord's came to a sad end in 1889, when he retired, suffering from gout and bankruptcy, owing money to Alfred Tompkins for balls and to Biboche for racquets. Fortunately, he found another post at the East Road court at Cambridge and was succeeded at Lord's by James Fennell.

The MCC published their *Rules of Tennis* in 1872 and they differ little from modern rules. In the old court at Lord's there were 'fly nets' at the top four corners of the court and a ball that rebounded off them was in play. A pass neutralised a previous fault, but the rule that striker-out could take a pass was expunged in 1875.

In 1854 Prince's Club was opened on a site where Hans Place now stands. In addition to spacious club rooms, it contained two Tennis courts, seven Rackets courts, a cricket ground and, later, a skating rink, when roller-skating became fashionable.

An account of the club in 1872 is given in *Clubs and Club Life in London* by John Timbs.

> *The Club, established in 1854, is built upon the Pavilion estate, in the rear of the north side of Sloane-street, the principal entrance being from Hans-place. The grounds are of considerable extent, and were originally laid out by Capability Brown. They were almost environed with lofty timber-trees; and the genius of landscape gardening fostered by wealth, rendered this glade in the Brompton groves of old a sort of rural elysium.*
>
> *The Pavilion estate was once the property of Holland, the well-known architect, who planned Sloane-street and Hans Place, as a building speculation; and, in the grounds nearly between them, built himself what was then considered a handsome villa, the front of which was originally designed by Holland as a model for the Prince of Wales estate. In the grounds, among the remains of Brown's ornamental work, was an icehouse, amidst the imitative ruins of a priory. Here, also, were the Ionic Columns (isolated) which were formerly in the screen of Carlton House.*
>
> *The Club buildings comprise seven closed courts; a tennis court; gallery and refreshment rooms; baths, and a Turkish bath.*
>
> *Prince's Club is a subscription establishment; and its government is vested in a committee. Gentlemen desirous of becoming members of the Club must be proposed and seconded by two of its members. Two of the rules enact – that members have the privilege of introducing two friends, but that such visitors, if they play, be charged double the rate charged to members; and that no hazard, dice, or game of chance be allowed in the Club. Their Royal Highnesses the Prince of Wales and the Duke of Cambridge are members.*

It was a most popular club until property development caused it to close down in 1886. Immediately plans

The Rackets court at the original Prince's Club.

for a new Prince's were put in hand and the new club opened in 1888, just off Knightsbridge on a site once occupied by the Japanese village of the Great Exhibition of 1851.

The new club comprised two Tennis and two Rackets courts, two bowling alleys, a Turkish bath and various club rooms, including a pleasant sitting room, the Oak Room. It flourished for the next twenty years. The Prince of Wales (later Edward VII) was present at the opening of the first Tennis court when the Hon. Alfred Lyttelton played a match against Charles Saunders; the next Prince of Wales (later George V) was often in the club, sometimes accompanied by one or more of his sons. Two of them, Edward (later the Duke of Windsor) and George (later George VI), played many games of squash there.

Many officers of the Household Brigade found it convenient to be members, especially those quartered at Knightsbridge Barracks just across the road. In fact, the Orderly Officer at Knightsbridge was specifically allowed out of barracks to visit the club.

Rackets had been played in Manchester since 1876, but the Racquet Club's premises, including the two Rackets courts, were compulsorily acquired by the London and North-Western Railway Company little more than a year later. A new site was found in Blackfriars Road, Salford, and there the club reopened in December 1880, under the title of the Manchester Tennis & Racquet Club with one Tennis and one Rackets court. It remains the foremost club in the North of England.

In January 1888 two new courts were opened in London at the Queen's Club, West Kensington, where two Rackets courts had been opened the previous year. The Queen's Club Open tournament, instituted in 1888, became the British Amateur championship the following year and has continued to be held on the east court ever since, apart from occasional visits to other courts.

Tennis continued to be played at Oxford and Cambridge. When Peter Tompkins left Merton Street for the Brighton court in 1836, Thomas Sabin took over the management and ran the court with great success for thirty years. He instituted the Oxford Prize Racquet in 1850 and was responsible for training several first-class apprentices: E. (Ted) Hunt, who later went to Boston and taught Tom Pettitt, Thomas Lambert, and his younger brother George.

In 1866 the court reverted to Tompkins's management when the James Street court was closed, and Edmund Tompkins went to Merton Street. There he remained until 1887 when he was succeeded by his son-in-law J.H. Dickinson.

At the other Oxford court in Oriel Street, James Russell was in charge, with an assistant called Foulkes, until the court was converted into billiard rooms in 1860. Russell had club feet and was nicknamed 'Duck-legged Jim'. He would sometimes play with a ginger-beer bottle with a wooden peg stuck in the mouth for a handle. He was greatly respected as a teacher.

The Prince of Wales (later Edward VII) used to play in both Oxford courts and when Oriel Street was closed in 1860, he attended a benefit match for Duck-legged Jim in the Merton Street court.

At Cambridge, the Pembroke court had been rebuilt in 1734 and continued to be much used. J.M. Heathcote, the dominant amateur from 1867 to 1888, learnt to play there. As with so many courts at that time, the side windows were not glazed and he recalled how snow (and presumably rain) would come gusting in. There was no net in the dedans, to the great peril of any spectators. Nevertheless, Heathcote described it as 'a charming court, rather small and rather fast'. The Prince of Wales used to play in this court, too, which was then managed by Charles Phillips, with Henry Harradine as marker. When it was demolished in about 1880 the flagstones were used for the new court at Hewell Grange.

Meantime, two new courts had been built. When Phillips, the professional at Stratfield Saye and father of Charles and James Phillips, retired, the Duke of Wellington built a court for him at Parker's Piece, East Road, with a Rackets court as well. It was opened in 1853/54. The floor was of slate and rather slow according to J.M. Heathcote. On Phillips's death the court was managed by a Mr Chawner, a don at Emmanuel College, with Henry Harradine and John Bracher as markers. Bracher took over as manager in 1887, and George Lambert leased the court from 1889 to 1891 when it was closed.

Another court was built in 1866 at the top of Burrell's Walk, known as the Clare & Trinity court. The first manager was James Phillips, brother of Charles, who had two assistants, sons of Henry Harradine of the Pembroke court. The elder left after two or three years to become a non-conformist writer, but the younger, James, carried on and eventually took over from James Phillips in 1882. He remained in charge until 1910, when he handed over to his nephew, Arthur Twinn.

J.J. Russell.

A second court was built on the same site in 1890 and opened with a prestigious match between Peter Latham and Charles Saunders. About 1900 a curious match was played in one of these courts between Edgar Baerlein and Lord Howick – both mounted on bicycles.

This surge of court-building in England spread to the United States and Australia.

In 1876 Hollis Hunnewell and Nathaniel Thayer built a private court in Buckingham Street, Boston. They brought Ted Hunt over from Oxford to run it, and to assist him they engaged a twelve-year-old English boy, Tom Pettitt, who was later to achieve great things.

In 1879 another court was built at the Newport Casino on Rhode Island. The story of its origin is remarkable.

James Gordon Bennett, the publisher of the *New York Herald* and a world-wide traveller and explorer, thought it would be a great joke to have one of his polo ponies ridden into the club, the Newport Reading Room, by one of his young English friends, Captain Candy.

Alfred Tompkins.

The result was not received with any enthusiasm – in fact there was quite a row. It seems that the horse was not on its best behaviour. Bennett resigned from the Reading Room and left the club.

On thinking it over he decided that he had been rash and went back early next morning to retrieve his letter of resignation. To his dismay, he found that the committee had already met and that his resignation had been accepted.

To retrieve the situation he engaged the firm of McKim, Mead and White to build, opposite his own house on Bellevue Avenue, the Casino Club, with twenty-two lawn-tennis courts, a Tennis court, a theatre, a squash tennis court, and club rooms above.

This complex was completed in time for the national lawn-tennis tournament to be held there in 1880. As head professional, Tom Pettitt was engaged from Boston's Buckingham Street court. He forged a link with the Boston Tennis & Racquet Club in 1904, which he maintained until his retirement in 1927. At the Casino he was a legendary figure, continuing to serve it every summer until his death in 1946 at the age of eighty-seven.

The Tennis court was never much used owing to the humidity in the summer, and in 1945 the roof was destroyed by fire. In 1979 it was restored at a cost of over $250,000.

Another court was opened in Boston in December 1888 by the Boston Athletic Association, and Tennis grew steadily in popularity.

New York followed suit in 1891. The Racquet Court Club, opened in 1876 at 55 West 26th Street, moved to 27 West 43rd Street and built a Tennis court as well as two Rackets courts. The club wrote to Frederick Tompkins, then professional at the Duke of Wellington's court at Stratfield Saye, to offer him the post of Tennis professional. Tompkins went to see his eldest brother, Alfred, then running a hotel in Notting Hill, to borrow money for his passage to the United States, but Alfred decided to go himself and it was he, not Frederick, who took over the Tennis court. Before his arrival Robert Moore ran both the Tennis and Rackets courts, assisted by Stanley Lambert. In 1892, when Moore returned to England, George Standing took over the Rackets courts.

In 1893 the Chicago Athletic Association built a Tennis court, two Rackets courts and a squash tennis court. Harry Boakes from Quebec was put in charge with Eddie Rodgers, William Joyce and Jim Fellman to assist him, but the venture was not a success and the Tennis court was converted into bowling alleys in 1901.

The first court in Australia was built by Samuel Smith Travers in 1875 in Hobart, Tasmania, modelled on the famous James Street court. Smith Travers took with him as professional to the new court Thomas Stone, who had learnt his trade at Hampton Court, James Street and Oxford.

But in 1882 Stone was lured away to take over a new court in Melbourne, at a salary of £250 p.a. plus 10 per cent of the gross receipts from play. He gave wonderful service to this club for over forty years. At a crisis in the club's finances in 1916 he even offered to forego his salary until things improved, and was grateful when it was decided merely to reduce his salary to £150 p.a. He remained secretary of the Melbourne club until the year of his death at the age of eighty-five in 1924.

Elsewhere, in Europe, as in France, the game was on the decline. There was spasmodic play in Vienna and a court at St Petersburg remained open until 1866. Otherwise there is little evidence of activity.

Yet despite the swing in popularity from France to the English-speaking world, the first half of the century continued to be dominated by great French players.

The court at St Petersburg.

Joseph Barcellon, son of Guillaume, was a frequent visitor to England. He played a match on 1 May 1802 against Philip Cox (later known as 'Old' Cox, but at that time aged twenty-three).

Philip Cox was born in Oxford in 1779. He trained as a marker in the Oxford court and came to the James Street court in 1798 as assistant to John Mucklow. A contemporary report records:

> On Saturday, May 1st, at one o'clock at the Royal Tennis Court, St James's Street, was played a very famous match between the two best players in Europe, Monsieur Barcellon, a Parisian, and Mr Cox, junior, of London, a youth of about twenty years of age. The superior skill and knowledge of the former, obliged him to give fifteen for two bisques. The party was made for One Hundred Guineas, the best in five sets… The match was won by Monsieur Barcellon.

It seems likely that Barcellon was the best player of his day.

In 1813, Old Cox took a lease on the James Street court from John Mucklow and his mortgagees, paying £250 a year. The lease expired in 1832 when it was extended for a further forty years.

In 1816, Cox played a match for the world championship against Marchisio of Paris, son of the professional in charge of the Turin court and presumably by then the champion of France. The match was for 100 guineas and played over three days; Marchisio won. Three years later Amédée Charrier was champion of France and Cox had another chance at the world title. This time he won the match, played over two days, and was recognised as world champion for the next ten years.

It was remarkable that all these matches were played at James Street, Cox's home court, which must have given him a considerable advantage. Charrier's supporters offered to back him for £300 against Cox in Paris, but there is no record of that match being played.

But these ten years of an Englishman's superiority

Edmond Barre.

Charles Delahaye, nicknamed 'Biboche'.

were only a brief interlude, for there then arrived on the scene one of the great players of all time, J. Edmond Barre, who played and defeated Cox for the world title at James Street in 1829, and dominated the game for the next thirty years.

Barre was born in Grenoble in 1802. His father was a *paumier* of the second rank who moved to Paris and ran a court in the rue Mazarine. Here Barre learnt to play and soon made such an impression that in 1827 he played a match against Marchisio and Amédée Charrier at Fontainebleau in the presence of the King and his son, the Duc de Berry. His performance was so outstanding that he was appointed *paumier du roi*.

At the height of his powers in 1839 he could give Peter Tompkins, the best English player, half 30 and a bisque. In 1845 he played against Peter Tompkins and W.J. Cox (son of Philip Cox) and gave them half 15 and a bisque (reported in *Bell's Life* as 'seven and a half and a bisque').

Familiarly known in England as 'Papa' Barre, he was as much respected for his warm and friendly personality as for his outstanding prowess. He enjoyed playing for eccentric bets and there are many stories of these. On one occasion he played a match against the Comte de Reignac at Fontainebleau giving him 'all the walls' and having walked to the court from Paris. He left at dawn and arrived about 3 p.m., having covered the forty-three miles in ten hours. After an hour's rest he played and won the match. The next morning he walked back to Paris, accompanied by his colleague Louis Labbé who greatly enlivened the return journey by his antics. The latter on one occasion also played a freak match, carrying a marker on his back.

Barre was also known to play the ball between his legs (a dangerous shot for the novice) or with the handle of the racquet.

In 1855, he was appointed *paumier de l'Empereur* and he held the world title undefeated until 1862.

Such was Barre's pre-eminence that another great French player never even contested the world championship: Charles Delahaye, known as 'Biboche'. Born in 1825 of an old family of Tennis professionals, he was attached to the court in the Passage Sandrié in 1840. There he had the opportunity of playing with Barre and with an outstanding amateur, M. Mosneron, and soon he was second in prowess only to Barre himself. He defeated Peter Tompkins at Hampton Court in 1848, and in 1851 defeated his son, Edmund, at Oxford and at James Street. In 1860, he added another victory in Paris by 5 sets to 2 in a three-day match. He played a famous match against Barre to mark the re-opening of the Versailles court in 1856.

Biboche eventually became manager of the Passage Sandrié court until its demolition in 1861 when he took over the new court at the Tuileries. Again, Biboche played a match against Barre to mark the court's opening.

Biboche, too, was fond of bizarre handicaps and once played a match wearing the full dress uniform of the National Guard, even carrying a musket with fixed bayonet in his left hand.

Biographies and pictures of some of these great players are included in a book by Eugène Chapus published in 1862 under the title *Le Jeu de Paume – son Histoire et sa Déscription*. Biboche and his father, Henri Delahaye, Barre, Peter Tompkins and Masson are included. This was the year of the opening of the new court at the Tuileries, and the book has a chapter on it, together with an illustration.

The book also contains an extract from the club rules. Evidently, three professionals were always on duty and, if the court was empty, a member had the right to ask the professionals to play a match for which he would pay them.

As well as much other information on the history and playing of Tennis, there are also details of *longue paume* as played in the Luxembourg Gardens in Paris.

Barre finally yielded the championship to Edmund Tompkins in a great match at the James Street court in 1862. Barre was sixty, Tompkins thirty-six and at his peak; yet it was a tremendous struggle and officially declared a draw. The match was to be the best of fifteen sets. The rules required advantage sets to be played (i.e., after 5-all one player had to achieve a lead of two games to win the set) so only two or three sets could be played each day. It seems that if the set continued too long it could be treated as a draw – no tie-breaks then to suit television schedules.

On the first day, 16 May, the first set was drawn, the second won by Barre. On 20 May, Barre won two sets, Tompkins one. On 25 May, Tompkins won two sets, Barre one. On 28 May, the first set was drawn and the next two won by Tompkins. On 10 June, the first and third sets were drawn and the second won by Tompkins. By then of fourteen sets played, four had

Edmund Tompkins.

been drawn, six won by Tompkins, four by Barre. It was a tremendous performance by Barre, but he could do no more and although the match was declared a draw, Edmund Tompkins was regarded as champion of the world from then on, and the era of great French players came to an end.

The Tompkins were one of the great families of English Tennis. Originally from Waterperry in Oxfordshire, Peter Tompkins's grandfather took over the lease of the Merton Street court, Oxford in 1758, but his father moved to London to manage the court at Windmill Street. Peter himself (1802–63) – his real name was Edmund – started at Windmill Street, then returned to Oxford to the Merton Street court and finally, in 1836, took over the newly opened court in Brighton, where he remained until his death in 1863.

Peter had three sons. Edmund (1826–1905), world champion 1862–71, started at Leamington in 1846, took charge at the James Street court in 1849 and, when that court closed in 1866, returned to the family home in Oxford as lessee of the Merton Street court. Alfred

George Lambert.

Tom Pettitt.

(1832–1913) was assistant to his brother at James Street from 1849 to 1864, then moved to Brighton, where he ran a Rackets court in Middle Street. He became the principal maker of balls at Upper Lewes Road, Brighton, until his death. John (1836–1903) spent his whole career at Brighton, first as assistant to his father until his death, and then as manager until 1893.

In the next generation, Edmund's daughter married J.H. Dickinson, and he took on the Merton Street lease from his father-in-law. Their son, R.C.E. Dickinson, became head professional at Prince's Club from 1910 to 1923, when he returned to the Merton Street court as lessee on his father's death.

John Tompkins had seventeen children, of whom two sons followed the family tradition. J. Alfred became senior professional at Manchester from 1880 to 1887 and later went to New York. Frederick had experience at Prince's, Stratfield Saye and Malta (Rackets) before becoming Rackets professional to the Walnut Street Racquet Club, Philadelphia, in 1904. When, in 1907, the Walnut Street Club moved to new premises on 16th Street with the addition of a Tennis court, Frederick became manager of Tennis and Rackets.

But the supremacy of the Tompkins family came to be challenged by another great family of Tennis players, the Lamberts. Joseph Lambert (1814–1905), head professional at Hatfield from 1849 to 1905, played until he was over eighty years of age. His son George (1842–1915) trained with Thomas Sabin at the Merton Street court, Oxford (1859–66), managed Hampton Court (1866–69), Lord's (1869–89) and East Road, Cambridge (1889–1891).

In 1871, aged twenty-nine, George Lambert challenged Edmund Tompkins for the world title and Tompkins yielded it without a match. Such was Lambert's dominance of the Tennis scene for the next fourteen years that no one challenged him for the title and, when a challenger finally appeared in 1885, he was from the United States: Thomas Pettitt.

Pettitt had visited England in 1883, returning the following year, and had made a great impression with his aggressive play. One writer described his style as 'strange, wild, barbaric, untutored and apparently developed out of an inner consciousness'. He shocked the critics, used to a more delicate style of play, but he also shocked the leading players. Neville Lytton wrote: 'Then Pettitt appeared on the scene. He had quite different principles. He was revolutionary, almost a Bolshevist. He used to say: "When I get a fair sight of the ball I hit it, and I hit it d—d hard."'

Eustace Miles gave him high praise:

Tom Pettitt is famous for his strength and agility. It is said that he can take up a man and throw him as he would throw a ball. The best of his strokes have never been equalled, and can only be realised by those who stand up against him on a dark day. His resource is incalculable. No ball is ever dead while Pettitt is in the Court. Last, but not least, he conceals the direction of his strokes in a way which I can never imagine to be rivalled. He has done more than any one else to change ancient into modern Tennis; having once shown that the modern game was more paying than the ancient game, he was bound to have his followers. He forced hard where others would have played with a heavy cut for the corners. But the great point of his game is not his sheer Force. I have always considered one of his finest strokes to be his stroke for the length of the Court: he hits the ball into the Nick time after time. This stroke is among his most effective, and I have never met a critic who recognised the skill which it implies.

The championship match was played in 1885 at Hampton Court and was to be the best of thirteen sets, with no advantage sets. On the first day, 11 May, Lambert won three sets, Pettitt one. On 13 May, each player won two sets. On 15 May, Pettitt won all four sets and the match, although the final set was a tremendous struggle before Lambert lost it 5–6. In the end Lambert's age told against him in this gruelling encounter; he was forty-five to Pettitt's twenty-five.

But although the reign of the Lamberts was at an end, the family continued to give service to the game. George's elder brother, Thomas, served with Thomas Sabin at Oxford; his younger brother, William, at Hampton Court, Lord's and Hewell Grange; his next brother, Alfred, at Prince's Club; and his youngest brother, Charles, at Hatfield. George's son, Henry Charles, served at Lord's and Petworth; William's son, Stanley, at Hampton Court and Oxford; and Charles's son, Edgar, at Hatfield, Queen's and Jesmond Dene, which he managed from 1894.

Charles Saunders.

The next world championship match took place in 1890. Charles Saunders, a great stylist from Prince's Club, had established himself as the top British player by defeating George Lambert in a home-and-home match at Prince's and Lord's in 1886. He then challenged Pettitt and, in a bid for complete fairness, a most extraordinary match was arranged. It was to be played on Sir Edward Guinness's court – which had marble walls – at St Stephen's Green, Dublin. French balls were to be used and no practice was allowed on the court beforehand.

In these curious conditions, Saunders gained an early lead. On the first day, 26 May, Saunders led by 3 sets to 1. On 28 May, Pettitt squared the match at 4 sets all. On 30 May, Pettitt won by 3 sets to 1, thus retaining his title. But in September of the same year Pettitt decided he had had enough of competitive play and resigned, leaving Saunders as champion in name.

By now a new star had started to rise, one of the all-time greats of Tennis – and equally great at Rackets – Peter Latham. His early career and his great achievements in the Rackets court are described on pages 140–141.

Peter Latham.

In 1888 he became head professional at the newly opened Queen's Club, where he remained for the next ten years. In 1895, already Rackets world champion, he played Charles Saunders at Brighton for the Tennis world championship. On the first day he dominated the match, winning all four sets and losing only seven games. On the second day the sets were shared, two each, and on the third Latham won the first set to gain the title and become the only man to hold the world championships of Tennis and Rackets simultaneously.

In 1898 he defended his title against the former champion from America, Tom Pettitt, but the match, played at Brighton for £500 a side, was very one-sided, with Latham winning by 7 sets to 0, despite Pettitt's newly invented railroad service.

At the turn of the century, Latham was dominant in Tennis and Rackets as no man has been before or since.

In America, the growth of amateur interest in the game was marked by holding national competitions.

The Tennis singles championship of America was first played in 1892 and won by R.D. Sears of Boston. Apart from two victories in 1894 and 1895 by B.S. de Garmendia of New York, it was won by players from Boston until the year 1900, when E.H. Miles became the first Englishman to win it.

Our knowledge of the game in this century is extensive thanks largely to *The Annals of Tennis* by Julian Marshall, published in 1878. It is a scholarly book on every aspect of the game – its history, its equipment, its laws, its method of play. The research involved in its production must have been prodigious. Certainly every subsequent author on this subject, including this one, is indebted to Julian Marshall for his comprehensive and authoritative work.

Also of interest are the chapters on Tennis in the Badminton Library, written by J.M. Heathcote and published in 1890. They add nothing historically to Julian Marshall's book but provide a background to the contemporary game and its leading players.

On 19 May 1891, a poem entitled 'Parker's Piece' by J.K. Stephen was published in the *Cambridge Review*. Stephen died nine months later at the early age of thirty-three, but the poem is of interest in mentioning some of the great players of the age – three world champions (Lambert, Saunders and Pettitt), two leading amateurs (Alfred Lyttelton and J.M. Heathcote) and the leading professional at Cambridge (James Harradine).

Julian Marshall.

To see good Tennis! What diviner joy
Can fill our leisure, or our minds employ?
Not Sylvia's self is more supremely fair
Than balls that hurtle through the conscious air.
Not Stella's form instinct with truer grace
Than Lambert's racket poised to win the Chase.
Not Chloe's harp more native to the ear
Than the tense strings which smite the flying sphere.
    When Lambert boasts the super-human Force,
Or splits the echoing Grille *without remorse:*
When Harradine, as graceful as of yore,
Wins 'Better-than-a-yard,' upon the floor;
When Alfred's ringing cheer proclaims success,
Or Saunders' volleys in resistlessness;
When Heathcote's Service *makes the Dedans ring*
With just applause, and own its honoured king;
When Pettitt's prowess all our zeal awoke
Till high Olympus shuddered at the stroke;
Or when receiving 'Thirty and the floor'
The novice serves a dozen Faults *or more;*

Or some plump don, perspiring and profane,
Assails the roof and breaks the exalted pane;
When 'Vantage, five games all, the Door' is called,
And Europe pauses, breathless and appalled,
Till lo! the ball by cunning hands caressed
Finds in the Winning Gallery *a nest;*
These are the moments, this the bliss supreme,
Which make the artist's joy, the poet's dream.
    Let Cricketers await the tardy sun,
Break one another's shins and call it fun;
Let Scotia's Golfers through the affrighted land
With crooked knee and glaring eyeball stand;
Let Football rowdies show their straining thews,
And tell their triumphs to a mud-stained Muse;
Let india-rubber pellets dance on grass,
Where female arts the ruder sex surpass;
Let other people play at other things;
The King of Games is still the Game of Kings.

TWENTIETH-CENTURY TENNIS

1900–80

New Courts

IN PARIS THE TWO COURTS at the Tuileries did not survive long into the twentieth century. In 1907, they were converted into picture galleries, now well-known for their collection of Impressionist paintings. But thanks to the efforts of J. Jameson, W. Bazin and their supporters, two new courts were built on the second floor of 74ter, rue Lauriston, and opened in 1909. The master professional was Charles Lesueur, assisted by Ferdinand Garcin and Georges Cott, a grandson of Barre.

In 1899 the Raquette d'Or had been instituted in the Tuileries courts. This was confined to French residents and was, in effect, the French amateur championship. The competition was transferred to the rue Lauriston in 1910 and, at the same time, a new competition was introduced, the Coupe de Paris, open to all amateurs.

The only other French courts to survive were those at Bordeaux and Pau.

In Britain the boom continued until the outbreak of war in 1914. At Lord's the old court was demolished in 1898 to provide better seating accommodation and a new one built in 1900 in its present position behind the Pavilion. The paving stones of the old court were transferred to the new.

Sir Charles Rose, in addition to his court at Hardwick, built another at Suffolk House, Newmarket. It was opened in 1901 with a match between Peter Latham and Cecil 'Punch' Fairs. Finding his original court at Hardwick slightly further from his house than he wished, he built a second there in 1907, allegedly on his wife's rose garden while she was abroad on holiday!

In 1905 J.O.M. Clark built a new court at Troon in Ayrshire, the first in Scotland since Falkland Palace. In 1906 C.T. Garland opened his magnificent court at Moreton Morrell, Warwickshire, still one of the best in England. In 1907 Lady Wentworth opened her court at Crabbet Park, Sussex, with G.F. Covey as head professional. Lady Wentworth was undoubtedly one of the best lady players ever to have played the game. She described herself in *Who's Who* as World's Lady Tennis Champion – a title she assumed without challenge. In 1899 she had married the Hon. N.S. Lytton, a distinguished amateur player, who twice defeated Edgar Baerlein, in 1911 and 1913, to win the amateur championship.

In 1909 Alderson Horne opened a curious miniature court at Ditton Place, Balcombe, Sussex – later the headquarters of the Penthouse Club; the floor measured 78 ft x 28½ ft. Another miniature court came into play in the 1970s when Ted Allerman converted the chapel of his house at Tuxedo into a half-size Tennis court.

In 1912 J.F. Marshall opened his court at Seacourt, Hayling Island, with another Latham v. Fairs exhibition match. This latter court had a dramatic history according to Marshall's daughter, Mrs Joan Grant, in her book *Time out of Mind*.

At the end of what was going to be the garden Father had built a real tennis court and a billiard room. One morning I was in the tennis court with Father watching the walls being covered with a special kind of cement. Thirty men were working up ladders and the man who had invented the cement, who was called Mr Bickley, was there too. Suddenly Mother rushed in and shouted, 'Out, all of you! The roof is going to fall in!'

Everyone stared at her and then looked up at the roof – a glass roof with iron girders that had been put in by a firm which roofed railway stations. It looked perfectly solid, but Mother became so angry at not being obeyed that Father ordered the men to stop work; so they climbed down the ladders and filed out of the building. For about five minutes they stood about, trying not to show that they thought Mother was being ridiculous. Mr Bickley was saying to Father that if the walls cracked because the work had been interrupted he

The opening of the Tennis court at Suffolk House, Newmarket in 1901. Front row (left to right): *J. Bickley, E. Dealtry, E. Nusser, F. Covey, A. Dooley, E. Gray, P. Latham, C. Fairs, J. Fennell, W. Stevens, J. Harradine, G. Lambert, F. Tompkins, W. Payne, W. Webb.* Second row (left to right): *E.F. Newton, A. White, G.W. Smale, G.E.A. Ross, C. Saunders, T. White, P. Ashworth, J.F. Marshall.* Back row (left to right): *W.H. Cohen, S. Heilbut, C.D. Rose, Baron E. d'Erlanger, Maj. E.W. Baird, E. Crawley.*

could not be held responsible. Mother was holding me by the arm in case I tried to run back into the court, which I had no intention of doing. Suddenly there was a grinding noise and an enormous crash. Clouds of dust belched out of the openings where the side-gallery windows were going to be. 'My God, it has *fallen!' said Father. Mr Bickley looked as though he was going to be sick. Some of the workmen swore under their breath, and I saw three of them take off their caps and cross themselves. The only person quite unmoved was Mother, who said calmly, 'What did I tell you, Jack? You must admit there are advantages in being married to a witch.'*

Joseph Bickley was a famous figure in the Tennis world as a builder of courts, and his patent methods had a great influence on the development of the modern game. He built the two courts opened at Queen's Club in 1888 and the Tuxedo Club court in New York opened in 1900. From then on, most courts in England and America were built by him or in his manner, and some existing courts treated by his process, here described by Allison Danzig:

The walls and floor are made of a concrete material that has a base of atlas cement mixed with sand that is screened through a sieve that has 2000 squares to the square inch. This base is soaked every twelve hours for a period of thirty days. When work is started on the finishing coat, which looks like lamp black, and whose composition remains a secret, it must be continued day and night to obtain the uniformly smooth, even surface. Both the material and the laborers are sent out by the company from London to America, France, Australia or wherever the court is to be built.

This Bickley process enabled the floor to be laid in six large slabs rather than with paving stones, thus obviating false bounces at the joints, but it would be alarmingly expensive in overtime today. Joseph Bickley died in 1923 at the age of eighty-eight.

Mrs Grant, in *Time Out of Mind*, also writes of the professional at Seacourt.

Duncan Duncan Wilson, our tennis professional, came into my life when I was four. He had been christened Duncan Duncan because he had a paternal and a maternal uncle with the same name, and his parents wanted to make sure that neither of them was offended. Long before he started teaching me to play the game, which was not until I was seven, I used to watch him stringing rackets or re-covering tennis balls, nine dozen to each basket of them, in his room at the end of the court while he talked about tennis. He told me there were grossly ignorant people who confused it with lawn tennis, a very inferior game played outdoors which should be referred to by the well instructed as pat-ball or lawners. It was, of course, our tennis that was the Game of Kings. Henry V might not have beaten the French so thoroughly at Agincourt, after the Dauphin had started the war by sending him a basket of tennis balls as an insult, unless he had been determined to prove that he could win as easily on the battlefield as he could in the court. Anne Boleyn might have kept her head if she had taken the trouble to appreciate the game. 'She probably annoyed the king by clapping when he lost a chase, or by forgetting to clap when he put a nice shot into the winning gallery,' said Wilson.

At about the same time several old courts were renovated, including Petworth, Canford, Hatfield, Hewell Grange and Fairlawne. But the outbreak of war in 1914 cast a deep shadow over the game of Tennis.

After the war, only two new courts were built. One, constructed in 1922, was an open court with a penthouse along both sides on Lambay Island, Co. Dublin. It belonged to the Hon. Cecil Baring, later Lord Revelstoke. The other, opened in 1924, was converted by W.N. McClean from an 1886 long fives court at Rusthall House, Tunbridge Wells.

In the United States a very fine court, built with the aid of Bickley, was opened at the Tuxedo Club, Tuxedo Park in 1900. Robert Moore returned from England to take over as head professional and was later joined by Arthur Forester as Tennis professional. Forester took charge when Moore left in 1920. The Gold Racquet competition was first played in 1903.

In the same year, George Gould opened a private court at Georgian Court, Lakewood, New Jersey, together with a Rackets court, which became the 'nursery' of his son Jay Gould. To coach his two sons, Gould engaged Frank Forester, trained at Prince's, who had been in New York since 1898. When Forester left in 1914, Alfred White took over for a couple of years and after that there was no further play. The court was resurfaced by Bickley in 1906. It became a girls' seminary, but in 1966 was re-opened for an exhibition match between Jimmy Dunn and Tommy Greevy.

In 1902, the Myopia Hunt Club opened a court at Hamilton, Massachusetts with Alfred Kirton as professional, and in the same year William C. Whitney sponsored a new court at Aiken, South Carolina. This was especially popular during the winter polo season when an outside professional was engaged. At one time this was Jack White from New York, later David Kenney from Newport and then Pierre Etchebaster.

In 1904 a second court was added at the New York Racquet and Tennis Club, and the Boston Tennis and Racquet Club opened a magnificent new building at the corner of Boylston and Hereford Streets with a Tennis court, a Rackets court, and squash courts. Tom Pettitt came to take charge and remained with the club until his retirement in 1927.

Philadelphia followed in 1907 when a Tennis court was built in the new Racquet Club building on 16th Street. This time Frederick Tompkins, supplanted in an earlier appointment by his brother, successfully arrived to take charge of both games. He brought over Jock Soutar to assist him. The national doubles championship was first played here in 1909.

In 1908, the first American University court was opened at Harvard, principally thanks to the efforts of H.J. Coolidge, together with a Rackets court and two squash courts, known as the Randolph Tennis and Racquet Courts. The first professional, a man by the name of Clark, was later succeeded by Alfred Kirton. In 1916 these courts were converted into squash courts.

The following year, Clarence Mackay opened a magnificent new private court at Roslyn, Long Island and put Robert Moore Jr in charge. He was succeeded in 1915 by the former world champion Punch Fairs.

An equally luxurious private court was built in 1915 by Payne Whitney at Greentree, Manhasset, Long Island, with Frank Forester from Lakewood as the resident professional. On Forester's retirement, William 'Blondy' Standing, nephew of George Standing, took over.

In 1918, the New York Racquet and Tennis Club moved to its present site at 370 Park Avenue with two Tennis courts and a Rackets court.

The last court to be built in America was in Chicago by the Chicago Racquet Club in 1923. Charles Williams took charge and Rackets still flourishes there. The Tennis court has unfortunately been adapted for use as an indoor lawn-tennis court.

In Melbourne in 1971, an event took place that turned out to be of enormous significance to Tennis generally. At the eighty-ninth Annual General Meeting of the club in June of that year, the President, Richard Allen, won approval for the sale of the property in Exhibition Street for a sum of A$675,000 on the understanding that a new club would be built within a few miles on less expensive land. A new site was bought in Sherwood Street, Richmond for A$131,000 and the design of the new buildings entrusted to architect Daryl Jackson. After careful research in Britain, he built two magnificent new courts, remarkable not only for the excellence of their playing properties but also for the wonderful natural lighting.

The floor is red-coloured granolithic paving laid over concrete. The walls are of reinforced concrete, coloured

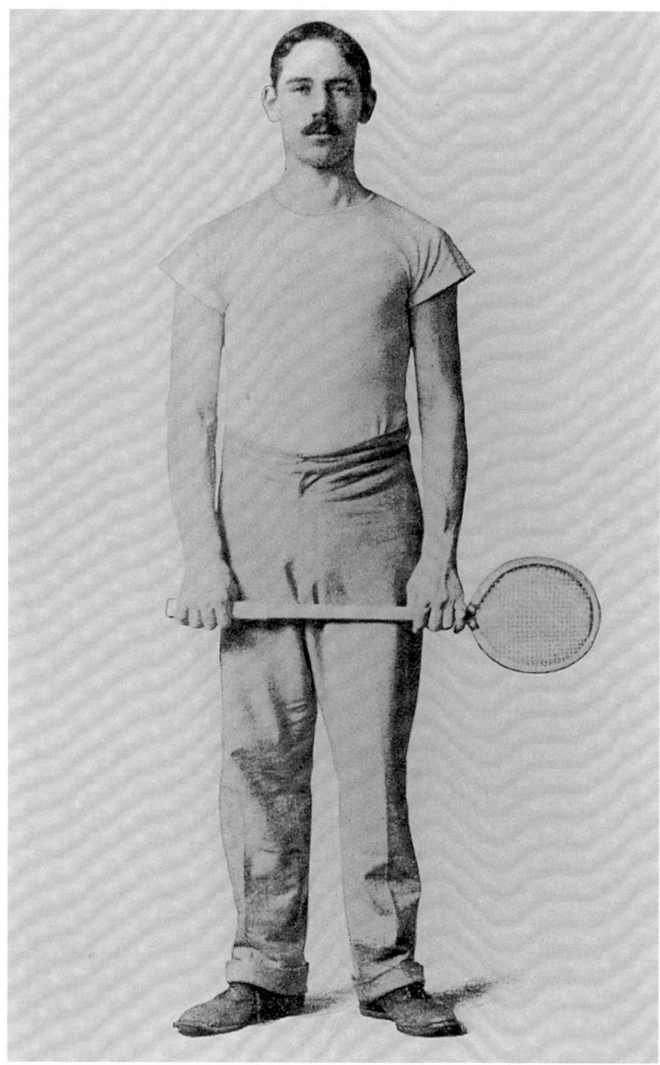

Payne Whitney.

olive green. The penthouse roof is of hardwood boards (Eucalyptus Regnans), sanded and left as natural wood. Sections of the roof are covered with perspex acrylic sheeting to admit diffused light. Behind a small dedans runs a glass partition through which spectators may watch play without distracting the players. There is also a large spectator gallery running the whole length of the north court high above the penthouse and this is able to accommodate at least 100 people.

In addition to the two Tennis courts, there were two squash courts, changing rooms, a children's pool and a flat for a resident professional.

The first to occupy the flat were Chris Ronaldson and his wife, Lesley, who arrived from Oxford early in December 1973. Ronaldson played many fine matches against his rival professional from Hobart, Barry Toates, and was responsible for a considerable raising of the standard of play in Melbourne. His wife gained a worthy reputation as a modern successor to Margot, the renowned early fifteen-century player.

The new courts were ready in 1974 and the official opening by the author, as President of the British Tennis and Rackets Association, took place on 23 March 1975. It was attended by numerous distinguished visitors from overseas, including two former world champions, Pierre Etchebaster, then retired and living in St Jean-de-Luz, and Northrup Knox. Unfortunately, an injury prevented Knox from playing. The full Bathurst Cup was played for the first time in Australia and was won by Britain (Alan Lovell and Andrew Windham), who beat both Australia and the USA by 5 matches to 0. Other visitors were invited to participate in various competitions as well as to partake in the lavish hospitality.

All those who had played in Melbourne moved on south to celebrate the centenary of the old court in Hobart. To mark the occasion a magnificent new trophy, the Governor's Cup, had been presented by the Governor of Tasmania, Sir Stanley Burbury, for an open competition to be held regularly from then on. It was won on this first occasion by Frank Willis from Manchester, who beat Barry Toates in the final by 3 sets to 2.

Where Australia had shown the way, France soon followed and in 1978 a magnificent new court was opened in the Avenue de Verdun, Mérignac, Bordeaux. The initiative for selling the old court in the rue Rolland and re-building in the Avenue de Verdun came from a senior civil servant, Claude Quancard. His enthusiasm, charm and ability overcame all difficulties. Unfortunately, soon after the court was completed he died suddenly.

The old premises were sold for 2,100,000 francs and for almost exactly the same sum the new buildings were erected – the Tennis court, four squash courts and excellent club accommodation. In addition, there were site costs of 345,000 francs and other expenses, but with the aid of a bank loan on favourable terms and a Government grant towards the squash courts (the first ever to be built in Bordeaux) the project was made possible.

The architect was Francisque Perrier, assisted by Lechêne. The first professional, Henri St Germain, had been coaching lawn tennis since his defeat by Jim Dear at Holyport in 1954.

The Tennis court was named after the greatest French player of the twentieth century, Pierre Etchebaster. An international competition was held there in April 1979 to mark the opening, and Etchebaster was presented with the medal of *L'Ordre du Mérite National* by M. Chaban-Delmas, President of the National Assembly,

Mayor of Bordeaux and a talented player of many games, including Tennis.

The four squash courts were named after de Suduiraut, de Luze, Biboche and Talbot.

Manchester, which had established particularly close links with Bordeaux, gave the club a stained glass window with a Tennis design, and Hayling Island provided the grille. The Tennis & Rackets Association presented them with a cabinet, and Petworth gave them two ancient racquets. The Knox brothers (Norty and Seymour) donated a challenge cup to be named after Etchebaster. Other clubs from Australia and Britain presented various books and prints in honour of the occasion.

Sadly, after thirty-five years of great activity the court was closed in 2013.

Champions of the Early Twentieth Century

In 1901, Latham left Queen's Club to work for Sir Charles Rose, one of his greatest patrons. He went first to Sir Charles's court at Newmarket (1901–7), then to his second court at Hardwick (1907–13).

In 1904, he was challenged by Punch Fairs for the world title. The match was played at Brighton on 16, 18 and 20 May. It was clear from the start that Latham was not quite as formidable as he had been in the last championship match against Pettitt, and that Fairs was a greatly improved player.

The first day's play was even and hard fought; Latham emerged the winner 6–5, 6–3, 6–4, 3–6 – 21 games to 18. Fairs got off to a flying start to lead by 5 games to 1 in the first set, but then Latham established his mastery to win that set and the next two. He played very severely and accurately, and volleyed most effectively, but Fairs had the better service.

On the second day, Latham was at his best. After two close sets shared 6–3, 4–6, he dominated the match and won the remaining two sets 6–1, 6–1. His return was outstanding, his accuracy in finding the winning openings was remarkable and again he volleyed powerfully. Fairs' service was still the better and won him the second set of the day.

That left Latham with one set to win on the final day to retain the championship, but Fairs did not give up without a fight. He had little to lose and, although Latham was not at his best and less accurate than previously, Fairs played outstandingly well. It was he who dominated the play in the first two sets, winning them 6–3, 6–3. The third set was a great struggle. In one game, Fairs hit the grille three times in succession before finally winning 6–5. He was now just one set behind in the match.

All seemed over when Latham led by 5 games to 1 in the fourth set, but again Fairs hit back and levelled the score at 5 all. Latham won the final game, however, to achieve the set he needed for victory.

Clearly Fairs had every right to challenge again and this he did the following year. A rather curious match was arranged on a home-and-home basis at Queen's and Prince's, four sets at each and, in the event of an equality, a final five sets at Brighton to settle the match.

The first leg was played on 7 October 1905 at Queen's, Latham's home court, and he made a disastrous start, losing the first three sets 0–6, 3–6, 4–6. Fairs was certainly playing well, but Latham had an off day. He made a lot of mistakes and missed too many easy shots, although every so often producing one of his great forces or making a superb retrieval. He managed to salvage the last set, winning it 6–1.

He faced a hard task, therefore, in the second leg on Fairs' home court at Prince's, and it proved too much for him. He was playing much better, but Fairs, too, was on top form. There was some excellent classical play on the floor. However, Fairs won the first set 6–2 and the second 6–5 (after Latham had led 4–2) to win the championship.

Next came a challenge from the leading French player, Ferdinand Garcin, who played Fairs at Brighton in 1906. On the first day, 21 April, he gave the champion a shock by winning 3 sets to 1. But Fairs reversed the score on 24 April to square the match at 4 sets all. On the third day, 28 April, Fairs crushed his opponent, winning the three sets required to retain the title by 7 sets to 4.

But his dominance didn't last for long. Latham

Jock Soutar and Cecil 'Punch' Fairs.

had been licking his wounds and was ready to make a come-back. He challenged Fairs and a match was arranged at Brighton.

On the first day, 6 May 1907, it became obvious that the old champion was back to form. He set a very fast pace all through the match, boasting and forcing marvellously and showing all his old powers of return. The first two sets were a magnificent display of Tennis, with many long and brilliant rests. At critical points Latham brought out his best and he won both sets, 6–5, 6–5.

He dominated Fairs in the third set, winning it 6–3, but, tiring, he lost the fourth 3–6, so ending the day leading by 3 sets to 1. He started the second day, 8 May, as if he intended to sweep Fairs off the court, leading 4–0 and 5–1, but Fairs fought back to 5 all before finally losing the set 5–6. Latham continued to dominate the play, taking the next set 6–3 and going on to lead 5–3 in the third. Unfortunately, at this point the light deteriorated to such an extent that play almost had to be abandoned. After a great struggle, Fairs won the set 6–5 and, with Latham tiring and suffering from cramp, took the next set 6–1, leaving the overall score 5–3 in Latham's favour.

On the final day, 11 May, Latham made certain of regaining his title by winning both sets played, the first easily 6–2, the second after a tremendous struggle 6–5. The strain had told on both players and the quality on this final day was less good, but nevertheless it was a magnificent achievement by Latham – one day after his forty-second birthday.

Immediately afterwards he resigned the title, which was re-assumed by Fairs. Latham continued to play in exhibition matches and handicap events for many years, however, and was especially highly regarded as a teacher. He returned to Queen's Club in 1916 and was there able to play a part in the post-war revival of Tennis. In 1919 he played two fine matches against the redoubtable Edgar Baerlein, the amateur champion, giving him odds of half 15.

When Latham died at the age of eighty-eight, Edgar Baerlein wrote of him:

One Tennis and two Rackets players are mentioned as possibly his equals. I cannot believe it. His ability was of a character that was not fully evident to a spectator. If an opponent had any effective attack, Peter would seem to say to himself 'we're not having that to-day' – and we didn't. He found a way of stopping it.

He was said not to have a very good service. It did not look remarkable but if you had a favourite return he saw to it that you had few opportunities of using it. His service at either game might win few aces but it gave him the attack and put handout on the defensive.

He was very quick to start and to move, so was able to wait, balanced, near the centre line until his opponent could no longer alter the direction in which his shot would go. The result was that it looked as if the ball was always being hit to him.

In fact, magnificent though he appeared to be as a player, he was an outstanding example of one who was 'better than he looked'.

Further, he was an artist, ever seeking perfection. For him it was not enough that a stroke should be a winner. It had to be that and more, the more being that even he could not improve it.

Finally he was a delightful opponent. Everything he did in the court made it a pleasure to play against him, and out of court his experience, intelligence, and natural courtesy, made him a popular figure wherever tennis and rackets were played.

Fairs was soon challenged again by Edward (Ted) Johnson, then the professional at Moreton Morrell, but he retained the title fairly easily at Brighton in June/July 1908 by 7 sets to 2. Two years later, he was called upon to defend the championship against Fred Covey, Lady Wentworth's professional at Crabbet Park.

The match again took place at Brighton and was extremely close. On 4 May the sets were shared two each. On 6 May Fairs, making good use of his high drop service, secured a lead of 5 sets to 3. On the final day, 9 May, Covey won the first set, Fairs the second to make it 6 sets to 4. Fairs made a tremendous effort to clinch the match in the next set, but lost it 5–6. The older man, he had taken a lot out of himself in the attempt and lost the next set 1–6, making the score 6 sets all. But in the end Fairs was the fitter of the two and, playing beautifully, he won the final set 6–1 to retain his title.

A return match was played in 1912 at Prince's Club, where the court had been recently renovated. It began on 29 April and seemed likely to be another very close contest, the day ending at 2 sets all. But when they met again on 1 May, Fairs was suffering from rheumatism, and Covey ran away with all four sets to lead 6 sets to 2. On 4 May, Fairs won the first set, but Covey easily won the next to win the match and become the new world champion.

This same year a somewhat curious situation arose over a challenge to Covey by Ted Johnson of Moreton Morrell. The Tennis, Racket (sic) and Fives Association

Gould clinched victory on the third day (6–3, 3–6, 6–2). Nevertheless, it was Kinsella who played Covey for the world title.

The match was played in 1922 at Prince's Club. On 15 May, Covey led 3–1; on 17 May, 6–2, and by winning the second set on 20 May he secured the championship by an overall margin of 7 sets to 3.

Lord Revelstoke recalls asking both players for their autographs.

Kinsella wrote: 'I am now returning to the States to learn how to "cut" the ball.' He did just that, and in a return match the following year he made an early breakthrough, winning the first three sets, but Covey struck back to take the next seven sets and the match, again by 7 sets to 3.

There now appeared on the scene another of the all-time greats of Tennis – not for the first time, a Frenchman. Pierre Etchebaster, born on 8 December 1893, was brought up in the Basque traditional games of *pelota*. He excelled at them, but his sporting career seemed thwarted when he was apprenticed to an uncle in Chile in 1909 and then called up for military service in 1914. However, demobilised in 1919, he resumed the Basque games and was soon champion of them all.

His recruitment to Tennis was due to Jacques Worth, couturier, brother-in-law of Cartier, winner of the Raquette d'Or in 1921 and 1922, and President of the club at rue Lauriston. He was on the look-out for a replacement for Ferdinand Garcin, who wished to retire, and he engaged Etchebaster in 1922. Although Pierre had never played the game before, he was soon the best in Paris. After two years he visited England and won the professional handicap competition at Manchester. In 1927 he challenged Covey for the world title.

The match was played at Prince's in May, and Etchebaster made a brilliant start by winning the first set 6–0, playing the traditional French game on the floor. Covey was too experienced to panic, and he fought back to win the second set 6–4. He went on to take the next set 6–4, to lead by 2 sets to 1. Now it was Etchebaster's turn to react, and he swept ahead to lead by 4 games to 0 and 40-love. It looked as if he was likely to win the first and final sets of the day's play to love.

But it is a great tribute to the champion's determination and skill that he fought back in masterly fashion to square the score at 4 all in about five minutes, and to win the next two games and the set at 6–4. Thus he led, somewhat unexpectedly, by 3 sets to 1 at the end of the first day's play.

The Times correspondent was so impressed with Etchebaster's talent in this match that he accurately predicted that he would 'one day be so good a player that later followers of Tennis will know him as "Pierre" only.' The correspondent paid tribute to both players, stating that the packed dedans considered the match to be the best exhibition of pure Tennis since the time of Peter Latham.

There was bound to be a reaction to the brilliance of the first day's play and although the game was closely contested on the second day, its quality was lower. Covey again emerged the winner by 3 sets to 1 (6–3, 5–6, 6–3, 6–5). Experience had given him a lead of 6 sets to 2 and he required one more set on the final day to retain his championship. It looked as if the match was over.

But not in Etchebaster's view. He started brilliantly on the third day, winning the first two sets 6–3, 6–4, and leading 3–1 in the third. Covey caught up to make it 4 all, then 5 all. Etchebaster led 40–15 in the final game but failed to hold his advantage and Covey won the set to retain his title by 7 sets to 4.

Etchebaster had proved that he was a worthy contender, but another rival had emerged in America, Jock Soutar, professional at Philadelphia. It was agreed that Etchebaster and Soutar should play a match to decide who should challenge Covey, and Etchebaster paid his first visit to the USA. The match was played in Philadelphia in February 1928 and easily won by Etchebaster, by 7 sets to 1. He had established his right to have another go at Covey.

The match took place at Prince's Club on 7, 9 and 12 May 1928. This time Etchebaster had improved considerably in all departments – he served more accurately, volleyed better and played a more severe stroke. Covey was now forty-seven, and his game had lost some of its edge.

Etchebaster swept to a 3–1 lead on the first day, winning both the first and last sets to love, 6–0, 2–6, 6–1, 6–0. Play on the second day started with a set of the highest quality, in which Covey showed his old skill against a younger opponent who was cutting the ball down and rarely making a chase worse than 2. At 5 all there was a tremendous battle for the final game. Covey led 15–0 and served a double fault; he led 30–15 and 40–30; he had advantage four times to Etchebaster's twice, before finally securing the two consecutive points and the set.

But the effort tired him. Etchebaster went on to seize the next three sets 6–3, 6–0, 6–1 to lead by 6 sets to 2, leaving him one set to win on the third day for the title. He started nervously and it was Covey

Pierre Etchebaster.

who took the first set, but Etchebaster made sure of the next, 6–2. He had begun his unbroken reign of twenty-six years. Soon after his victory, he joined the New York Racquet Club as senior Tennis professional.

His first challenger was Walter Kinsella, in 1930, and the match was again played at Prince's Club, on 26 and 28 May. Kinsella played a hard-hitting game of boast and force, but Etchebaster showed his supreme skill in controlling the ball and dominated the first day's play, winning all four sets 6–3, 6–1, 6–3, 6–2. On the second day he went on to take the fifth set 6–3, but in the sixth Kinsella, now desperate, started a wholesale bombardment of dedans and grille, which for a time was effective and took him to a lead of 5–2. Etchebaster regained control and caught him at 5–5, but Kinsella won the set. It was his only set, for Etchebaster went on to win the next two 6–2, 6–4 and the match by 7 sets to 1.

In 1937 Etchebaster faced a challenge from the outstanding American amateur Ogden Phipps, who won the amateur championship every year from 1934 to 1939 – except 1938, when he lost to his principal rival, Jimmy Van Alen, in the semi-final. Phipps had established his right to challenge Etchebaster in 1936, with an easy victory over Kinsella at Greentree in a challenge match for the American Open championship. Phipps won by 3 sets to 0. He was twenty-eight at the time, Kinsella fifty-one.

The match took place at Tuxedo in December 1937. Etchebaster soon established his superiority with beautiful strokes on the floor and deadly marksmanship for the winning openings, although Phipps had the more heavily cut stroke. Etchebaster served better and was effective in volleying Phipps's railroad service. He won the first two sets 6–3, 6–2. Phipps took the third 6–4, but Etchebaster won the fourth 6–1. Unfortunately, in the penultimate game of the last set Phipps, chasing a ball that had hit the wall above the dedans, slipped and fell into the gully under the net, twisting his ankle. This injury forced him to retire from the match, and not long afterwards the war intervened.

The competition for the British Open championship (Prince's Club Shield) was first played in 1931. In a remarkable first-round match lasting three hours and twenty-four minutes, Lord Aberdare beat Ted Johnson 5–6, 5–6, 6–5, 6–5, 6–5. The match took a lot out of both players and Aberdare fell an easy victim to Jack Groom in the semi-final. In the other semi-final, Edgar Baerlein beat E. Ratcliff. The final was another remarkable match. Groom was leading by 2 sets to 1 and 5–1. Twice he had a match point at 40–30 and advantage. But in the end, Baerlein took the set 6–5 and went on to win the final set and the championship 6–1 – a very fine achievement at the age of fifty-one.

Literature between the Wars

The years between the two world wars were rich in books on Tennis, regrettably less so on Rackets. First came the two volumes of *A History of Tennis* by E.B. Noel and J.O.M. Clark, published in 1924. Julian Marshall had done so thorough a job of research into Tennis history that there was not much to add, but in every other way these two volumes are a treasure trove of information about the game and its personalities.

In the first volume, the game's history is carried on from where Julian Marshall left off in 1878. The great championship matches are described, as are the characters of the champions, not only professional but also amateur, and not only in Britain, but in France, the USA and Australia. The final five chapters detail the history of the University matches.

The second volume contains chapters on the literature of Tennis, the laws of Tennis, racquets, balls and courts, hints on play and handicapping. At the end are a number of appendices containing invaluable information on courts and their dimensions, winners of events, professional and amateur players.

In the pages of these two books is everything anyone could wish to know about Tennis in the post-Marshall period up to 1924. It is a remarkable record on which this present work has drawn heavily and gratefully.

Not content with his book on Tennis, E.B. Noel collaborated with C.N. Bruce (later Lord Aberdare) to publish *First Steps to Rackets* in 1926. This is a very slim volume by contrast, and is mainly devoted to practical instruction as its title implies, but it has a useful chapter on the history of Rackets, as well as details of the more important championships as an appendix.

The Thirties were even more prolific, with two especially valuable books, *La Magnifique Histoire du Jeu de Paume* by Albert de Luze, published in 1933, and *The Racquet Game* by Allison Danzig, published in 1930. The former is one of those great works of scholarship in the Marshall tradition.

What Marshall did by patient research for the history of the game in England, de Luze did for it in France. After describing its history century by century, he writes of courts in the different *départements* of France – a tremendous task – as well as of courts abroad. In the second part, he gives details of courts, balls, racquets, professionals, championships and even of *parties excentriques* and *coups extraordinaires*. An excellent English translation by Sir Richard Hamilton, Bt. was published in 1979.

Once again the author of this present book unashamedly acknowledges his indebtedness to de Luze on all matters concerning the game in France. Equally, for its history in the United States there is no more authoritative account than that contained in Allison Danzig's book. It is all the more valuable in that it covers Rackets as well – not to mention squash rackets and squash tennis.

Another intriguing title appeared in 1932: *Tennis Origins and Mysteries* by Malcolm D. Whitman. This is a fascinating series of essays on all the unsolved problems, philological and historical, of Tennis, and some useful accounts of the origins of both Tennis and lawn tennis in the USA. It also contains (as an appendix) an invaluable bibliography of Tennis, compiled by Robert W. Henderson. As well as his own book, *Ball, Bat and Bishop*, Henderson wrote many articles on Tennis and Rackets.

Also in the Thirties, a volume on Rackets, squash, Tennis, fives and badminton was published in the Lonsdale Library series. It includes a most interesting section on the history of ball games by John Armitage, and some chapters on the playing of Tennis and Rackets by Edgar Baerlein.

POST-WAR CHAMPIONS

In 1948 Ogden Phipps once again won the US amateur singles, having been absent on active service in the Navy since 1939. In the final he overwhelmed Alastair B. Martin, who had a blistered hand, 6–0, 6–0, 6–2, and challenged Etchebaster, then aged fifty-four, for his world title. The match was played in New York in April.

On the first day Etchebaster was in command. Phipps played his usual strong floor game, cutting the ball heavily, but Etchebaster had an answer to his every stroke and kept returning the ball remorselessly to a perfect length. He served better, too, varying from sidewall to underhand twist, whereas Phipps exclusively served the railroad which Etchebaster took well. The result was a 3–1 lead for the champion, 6–3, 5–6, 6–0, 6–2.

Phipps played much better on the second day and only Etchebaster's skill at critical moments secured him the first three sets. After winning the first set 6–4, he was 0–4 and 2–5 down in the second before capturing it 6–5. He snatched the third, too, 6–5, and Phipps must have been very disheartened. He was also suffering from cramp, but went gamely on until Etchebaster showed signs of fatigue. Phipps deservedly took the fourth set 6–5. This left Etchebaster with one more set to win, and he accomplished this on the third day by 6–2 to retain his title.

Later the same year, Etchebaster faced another challenge, this time from the other side of the Atlantic, from Jim Dear.

Dear was a pupil of Peter Latham's and an outstanding player of both Tennis and Rackets, and also of squash. For three years in succession (1935–37), he had been narrowly defeated for the British

Open squash championship by the outstanding Amr Bey; in 1938 he was a worthy winner. At Rackets, he was British Open champion from 1946 to 1954 and again in 1960; he was world champion from 1947 to 1954. At Tennis, he was British Open champion from 1938 to 1950 and again from 1951 to 1962. He fully deserved the award of the MBE bestowed on him in 1960 for his unique services to Rackets, Tennis and squash.

His Tennis was marked by the same all-round ability as his Rackets. His eye and swiftness of foot gave him great power of return in defence, and in attack he was very accurate on the winning openings, particularly the dedans, often off the main wall. He played a very effective volley, an attacking rather than a purely defensive stroke. Not a railroad server, he had a wide range of different services for different occasions, including the high drop and the underhand twist.

Dear found conditions in New York very different from London. The balls were lighter and very difficult to cut; Etchebaster had perfected the type of game best suited to the conditions, using his outstanding ability to control the ball superbly and stroke it into the corners. Dear could only seek to mirror this game and to retrieve all he could with an occasional blast for one of the winning openings.

Etchebaster got off to a good start by winning three of the four sets on the first day, although Dear was unlucky not to win the second. The score was 6–1, 6–5, 6–3, 3–6. On the second day the sets were shared 2 all, 6–2, 1–6, 3–6, 6–3, and despite being almost seventeen years younger, it was Dear who appeared tired at the end. On the third day, Etchebaster started nervously to lose the first set 4–6, but at that point, in Dear's own words, 'my legs just died on me' and Etchebaster ran away to victory 6–0, 6–1. Dear believes that his leg failure may have been caused by electrical treatment which he received for a muscle strain.

As holder of the championship, Etchebaster had to be beaten on his own court. Had Dear been able to play him home-and-home, as he did Johnson in 1955, there might have been a different result.

In December 1949, Ogden Phipps had another go at the then fifty-six-year-old master. Phipps was at the height of his powers, having won the US Amateur singles for the seventh time and the British Amateur championship. Etchebaster had conceded four sets to Dear and might be thought to have passed his peak; but he proved it to be quite otherwise. Playing with flawless accuracy, he completely dominated the first day's play and allowed Phipps just four games in all.

Pierre Etchebaster serving his familiar railroad.

Sadly for Phipps, he found the champion on one of his greatest days, when all the magic of his Basque origin came to his aid and he was invincible. He won 6–0, 6–2, 6–0, 6–2.

It was an overwhelming lead for Phipps to face on the second day's play, but he was a fighter and surely Etchebaster could not again find such a sure touch. So it seemed when Phipps won the first set 6–4 and led 4–1 in the second. Then the master re-asserted his authority. He won the next five games to take the second set 6–4, and went on to win the next two sets 6–2, 6–3, retaining his world title by a superb exhibition of mastery and skill.

More evidence of his outstanding brilliance was yet to come. The following year an even younger opponent challenged him. Alastair Martin was the new US Amateur champion, and like his predecessor, he had added the British Amateur championship to his laurels. He was twenty years younger than Etchebaster, but he could do little better than Phipps against the superb authority of the champion. Etchebaster won the first set 6–2 and led 5–3 in the second. Then Martin made a great effort, drew level at 5–5, saving several set points in the process, and had a set point for 6–5. But Etchebaster won the set and effectively the match. He went on to win the next two sets 6–1, 6–0.

On the second day Martin fought back courageously, but however hard he tried he could not shake the uncanny control of the champion, who took the first two sets 6–4, 6–1 and went on to lead 4–2 in the third. Martin again made a tremendous effort to come back and squared the set at 5 all, but the pressure was too great and Etchebaster won the final game and the set to retain his title by 7 sets to 0.

Alastair Martin had a second challenge match against the champion, now aged fifty-eight, in November 1952. He fared little better. Etchebaster won on the first day by 3 sets to 1 (6–1, 5–6, 6–1, 6–0) and by the same margin on the second day (6–3, 6–3, 6–3, 5–6). He had to win just one set on the third, and despite a brave effort by Martin, he won the first set 6–5 to retain the championship.

Early in 1955, aged over sixty-one, Pierre Etchebaster resigned and a great reign came to an end. If he had started playing Tennis as young as some of his great predecessors, that reign might have been ten years longer, but his early preoccupation with Basque games and the intervention of the First World War prevented that. It is impossible to compare champions of one age with those of another, if only because playing conditions differ, but it is certain that Etchebaster has to be reckoned one of the great Tennis players of all time.

Not only was his greatness registered in his unbeaten record of victories up to the age of sixty, but he was also a great master of the science of ball games. He didn't play the game just by instinct; he thought deeply about technique and he was for that reason an outstanding teacher. Always make use of the spin already on the ball, he would explain; never try to impart the opposite spin. Always make use of the lower part of the net in the centre – don't try to be too clever and hit your ball over the high part. He would spend hours in the court, practising one particular stroke until it

The Van Alen Trophy match of 1956 at Lord's. Standing (left to right): *S.A.M. Collins (Oxford), G. Reindel (Princeton), M.R.M. Love (Cambridge), E. Harding (Harvard), H. Johns (MCC Head Professional), G. Unhoch (Yale), O.J. Colman (Cambridge), R. Hackett (Harvard), N.F. Robinson (Cambridge).* Sitting (left to right): *R.B. Bloomfield (Oxford), J. Van Alen II (Yale), M.H. Searby (Cambridge), James Van Alen, R. Aird (Secretary MCC), N. Ludington (Harvard), M. Coulman (Oxford), W. Van Alen Jr (Pennsylvania).*

Jim Dear and Albert (Jack) Johnson.

was to his satisfaction. Sufficient to quote the words of Allison Danzig:

> *No athlete I saw in nearly half a century of reporting Tennis, football, the Olympic Games, rowing, golf, baseball made winning seem so easy, perfection so commonplace, as did Pierre in Court Tennis.*

And Jim Dear:

> *His game is his own. There can only be one Pierre. No-one will ever study the game as he did in order to be such an artist at it.*

Etchebaster's retirement left the world championship vacant and it was necessary to arrange a home-and-home contest between the two best players on either side of the Atlantic. In Europe, Jim Dear first played a match at Holyport against the leading French professional, Henri St Germain from Bordeaux, and won comfortably. He then played Ronald Hughes for the Open championship.

Surprisingly, he had much greater difficulty in winning on his home court, Queen's, where the first leg was played. Having won the first two sets narrowly 6–5, 6–5, he went on to lead 4–2 in the third. Hughes fought back to win that set 6–4 and the fourth set 6–4 to square the match.

This encounter provided some of the best Tennis seen in Britain since the war. The pace and elegance of Hughes's ground strokes were met by Dear's brilliance and variation of attack.

Five days later at Manchester, Dear ran out an easy winner 6–4, 6–2, 6–1, Hughes making too many mistakes.

In America, Albert (Jack) Johnson, son of Ted Johnson of Moreton Morrell, who had joined the professional staff of the New York Racquet Club, first beat Jimmy Dunn of Philadelphia for the Professional championship (in Philadelphia 6–2, 6–2, 7–5; in New York 6–3, 7–5, 6–3) and then beat Alastair Martin for the Open championship in New York (6–5, 5–6, 6–1, 6–4, 6–4, 6–3, 6–2, 6–3).

The Dear v. Johnson match was played in New York and London in 1955. This time Dear was the older and Johnson had shown considerable improvement since his arrival in New York. On 25 February, they finished 2 sets all. On 28 February, Johnson dominated the play and looked like winning all four sets, but Dear made a tremendous effort and won the last set to make the score 5 sets to 3 in Johnson's favour. On 2 March, Dear won the first set, but Johnson narrowly won the next two 6–5, 6–5 to give him an overall lead of 7 sets to 4.

On 25 April the match was continued at Queen's Club. It began with Johnson looking a likely winner. He took the first set 6–3 and a terrific struggle ensued for the second set, clinched by Dear 6–5. By now Johnson was tiring and Dear was on top – he won the next two sets 6–3, 6–2 to lead by 3 sets to 1. On 27 April the situation was reversed. Dear started at a great pace to take the first set 6–0, but Johnson rallied and, after Dear had won the second set 6–5, went on to take the remaining two sets 6–5, 6–5 to leave the match 5 sets to 3 in Dear's favour.

On the final day, 30 April, it was necessary for Dear to win the first two sets to give himself a margin of 7 sets to 3 over Johnson's 7 sets to 4 in New York.

A pulled leg muscle made it look an impossible task. He consulted Dr Stephen Ward, who asked him how long he needed to play and Dear told him about an hour. It was enough – he won the two sets necessary in convincing fashion, 6–3, 6–1, to add the Tennis world championship to that of Rackets and, to all intents and purposes, of squash. He had very narrowly failed to equal Peter Latham's record of holding both Tennis and Rackets world championships at the same time, for he had lost the Rackets title to Geoffrey Atkins the previous year.

Johnson had his revenge two years later. A return match was played at Queen's on 25 and 29 May and 1 June 1957. On the first day Johnson won the first set 6–3, but Dear then struck his best form. In a brilliant burst he won the second set 6–1 and went to 3–1 in the third. But Johnson was very fit and full of return, while Dear was now forty-eight and as Rackets professional at Wellington had not had a great deal of match practice. Johnson took the next two sets to lead on the day by 3 sets to 1.

On the second day it was essential for Dear to get a good start and he led all the way through the first set to 5–4, but Johnson's return was sure and he never let go. It was he who eventually won the set 6–5. Dear managed to capture the next 6–4, but Johnson took the last two 6–4, 6–3 to gain a formidable lead of 6 sets to 2.

Northrup Knox and Alastair Martin.

On the third day, therefore, Johnson needed one set for victory and it seemed to be all over when he raced to a 4–1 lead in the first set. But Dear struck what *The Times* correspondent called 'a patch of pure purple' and, playing magnificent attacking Tennis, won the next five games for the set. He couldn't keep it up. Johnson re-established his smooth, fast game to win the second set 6–2 and the match. There had been much fine retrieving by both players during the match; Dear was the more adventurous in attack, but Johnson played a sound, steady game which in the end prevailed and the title went back to America.

In 1959 an amateur won the world championship for the second time – Northrup R. Knox, winner of the US Amateur singles in 1957 and 1958. He challenged Johnson for the world title and the match was played in New York in February 1959. Knox led after the first day's play by 3 sets to 1, but it could have been very different. Johnson started well, winning the first set 6–3 and leading 4–1 in the second. Knox hit back to win the second set 6–5 and the third 6–0. In the fourth, Johnson led 4–2 and 5–3, but it was Knox who eventually won it 6–5.

The pattern was reversed at the start of the second day's play. Knox began better, took the first set 6–3 and led 3–1 in the second. Johnson rallied to win the second set 6–4 and to lead 3–2 in the third. The pendulum swung again and Knox won the third 6–4. The all-important fourth set was a bitter struggle with Johnson playing well on the floor, but Knox the more accurate on the winning openings. At 5 all Knox led 40–15 with two set points, but Johnson put two successive balls into the grille and a third on to the tambour to stand at set point. Two good services by Knox gave him set point again and this time he took it to lead by 6 sets to 2.

He now needed one more set for the championship, and he won this 6–2 on the third day.

His first challenger in 1966 was a new British Open champion, Ronald Hughes. Hughes played hard and well, but in unfamiliar conditions Knox was too good for him and won overwhelmingly by 7 sets to 0.

Then two remarkable brothers, talented at all ball games, came on the American scene – G.H. (Pete) and J.F.C. (Jimmy) Bostwick of New York. Jimmy, the younger, was in fact the first to win the Amateur singles in 1959 at the age of twenty-two, defeating Knox by 3 sets to 1 in the final (6–3, 5–6, 6–3, 6–3) and even leading 5–2 in the second set. He played with great brilliance, but it must be remembered that Knox had only just emerged from an exhausting world title match with Johnson.

Knox re-established his superiority by winning the Amateur singles from 1960 to 1963. Meantime, Jimmy Bostwick won the Open championship, first in 1960, again in 1961, and then in 1962 with a convincing victory by 3 sets to 0 over his elder brother, Pete. In 1964, Knox did not defend his Amateur title and in a very close match Jimmy repeated his victory over Pete by 3 sets to 2 (25 games to 23).

In 1965 it was Pete's turn. He won the Amateur championship, which he held until 1969 and won again in 1971. In 1966 he added the American Open championship at Tuxedo, but lost it again the following year to brother Jimmy. In partnership, they won the Amateur doubles in 1969 and 1973.

In 1967, Pete challenged Knox for his world title and the match took place in New York in February 1968. Knox won by 7 sets to 3, but the match was a great deal closer than the score in sets suggests.

On the first day, Knox was dominant, serving better than Bostwick and finding more winning openings. He won by 3 sets to 1 (6–5, 2–6, 6–3, 6–3). He won again on the second day by the same margin, playing with beautiful control and great accuracy. The last two sets were of high quality, but in the end Knox took both (2–6, 6–3, 6–4, 6–4). On the third day, Bostwick at his most brilliant outplayed Knox in the first set, which he won 6–2, and went on to lead 4–2. Knox fought back to level the score at 5 all and won it 6–5 after Bostwick had had a point for the set. He retained his title, therefore, by 7 sets to 3, but in games the margin was narrow – 48 to 45.

On 10 February, Knox retired and again the championship was vacant. A match was arranged home-and-home between the US and British Open champions of the day, Pete Bostwick and Frank Willis, a professional from Manchester. The first leg was played at the New York Racquet Club on 28 and 30 April and 2 May 1969.

On the first day Willis made a good start, leading 3–0 and almost 4–0 in the first set, but Bostwick started to play well and Willis found the strange conditions difficult. The result was a 4–0 lead for Bostwick (6–4, 6–3, 6–2, 6–2). The second day's play was much closer and Willis did well to halve the four sets played after Bostwick had won the first two (6–3, 6–3, 4–6, 4–6). On the third day, Willis won the first set 6–5, but lost the next 2–6 to give Bostwick an overall lead in New York of 7 sets to 3.

Willis, therefore, seemed to have an evens chance at least, playing on his home court at Manchester and, indeed, he started well by winning the first set 6–3. But then Bostwick began to play superb Tennis and swept to victory in the next three sets 6–4, 6–3, 6–3, for an overall lead of 10 sets to 4. His supporters' hopes, dashed by the first day's play, rose rapidly when on the second day Willis won all four sets 6–3, 6–5, 6–1, 6–3. But on the final day he lost the first set 3–6 and Bostwick took the title by an overall 11 sets to 8.

Bostwick's first challenger was none other than his younger brother Jimmy. The match was played at the New York Racquet Club on 16 and 19 October 1970. Jimmy began in brilliant style to win the first set 6–4, but Pete, after a slow start, began to show his true form and won the next three sets 6–4, 6–5, 6–2. On the second day he continued where he had left off and won all four sets 6–5, 6–5, 6–2, 6–0 to retain his title.

As the score in the first two sets of the second day indicates, however, his victory was by no means easy. The match was spectacular, with long rallies. Both players covered the court magnificently and returned balls that seemed irretrievable. But Pete was slightly the more severe in stroke and deserved to win.

In 1972, again in New York, Jimmy turned the tables and won the title by 7 sets to 2. The full score was 6–3, 2–6, 6–5, 6–4, 6–2, 5–6, 6–5, 6–4, 6–2.

Above *Jimmy Bostwick in 1975.*

Below *Jimmy Bostwick and Howard Angus.*

At this point another remarkable all-round games player appeared: Howard Angus. Angus won the Amateur Rackets title from 1972 to 1975 and was Open champion from 1971 to 1973 and 1975–6. He won the Amateur Tennis singles and the MCC Gold Racquet from 1966 to 1980, the Cutty Sark championship in 1974, 1976 and 1977, and was Open Tennis champion from 1970 to 1979, despite four challenges by Frank Willis.

In 1973, Angus crowned his Rackets career with a decisive victory over Willie Surtees to become Rackets world champion. He sought to add the Tennis world championship and thus equal Peter Latham's record. It was agreed that before he should have the right to challenge Jimmy Bostwick for the title, there should be an eliminator between him and the US Open champion, Eugene Scott. This took place at Queen's Club on 29 and 31 March, and in New York on 8 and 10 April 1974.

Angus started badly, losing by 1 set to 3 at Queen's on the first day, and losing the first set on the second day to go 1–4 down. However, he fought back remorselessly, slowing down the pace intelligently, and won the next four sets. He thus finished the London leg leading by 5 sets to 4, not a very satisfactory lead on his home court. But by now Angus had sized up

Hampton Court, June 1977 – Howard Angus (centre) successfully defends his world title against Gene Scott (third from right). Also in the group are (left to right) Alastair Martin, David Warburg, Pat Barker, Jimmy Van Alen and Alan Lovell.

his opponent and he played with great skill in New York to win by 5 sets to 1 and prove his right to challenge for the world title.

The world championship match that followed was one of the most curious in the history of this event and Angus was desperately unlucky. It is typical of his good sportsmanship that he has never grumbled about events that might have sent others to seek the help of the Samaritans.

The match was scheduled for 16, 18 and 20 April in New York and, although feeling unwell, Angus won all four sets on the first day. He was examined by a doctor that evening, who recorded a temperature of 102 and diagnosed a respiratory infection. Angus asked for a postponement of the second day's play.

The USCTA, who had overall control of the challenge, did not come back to Angus with a decision on whether the postponement was granted or not, but he read in the *New York Times* that the first day's play had been declared null and void. A completely new match was proposed. Angus felt passionately that he should have been given the option, if no postponement was offered, of forfeiting the second day's play and playing from 4 sets all on the third day. The doctor had stipulated that Angus should not consider playing until his temperature had been normal for thirty-six hours. Angus turned up on 20 April and played one set against his trainer, Norwood Cripps, just to show he could have played on the third day, but it was a futile gesture.

In the intense negotiations to get the match re-scheduled, Angus was adamant that he wanted to play straightaway and not have to come back to New York at some future date. Luckily, David Norman happened to fly into New York at that moment and took up the negotiations on behalf of Angus and the Tennis & Rackets Association. Eventually, he reached agreement with the USCTA and Jimmy Bostwick to re-start the match on 1 May, with Angus undertaking to switch to Bancroft racquets since his 'frying-pan' church-type Grays racquet, although three-quarters of an inch inside the USCTA's 1973 ruling on racquet size, had attracted some criticism for being 'too wide'.

On the first day the sets were shared two all, Angus winning 20 games to Bostwick's 19. On the second day, however, Bostwick produced some of his most brilliant Tennis and won all four sets to attain a commanding lead of 6 sets to 2. Angus needed to win 5 sets on the last day to beat the champion. He nearly accomplished this seemingly impossible task. He won the first three sets 6–4, 6–3, 6–2, to make the score 5 sets to 6. The next set was a real cliff-hanger. Angus had a set point at 5 games to 4, but Bostwick made it 5 all. Angus had three more set points to square the match, but finally Bostwick won this all-important set to retain his title by a total of 7 sets to 5.

The next year Jimmy Bostwick retired and the world championship was once again vacant. The two obvious contenders were Howard Angus and Eugene Scott. A match was arranged in New York on 29 and 31 March and 1 April, and in London on 11 and 13 April 1976. Scott made a good start on the first day in New York, winning the first three sets and ending the day 3 sets to 1 up. On the second day, Angus repeated his achievement in the eliminator match two years previously and won four sets in succession to lead by 5 sets to 3. On the third day, there was only one man in it and Angus easily took the first two sets and the New York leg by 7 sets to 3. Having lost the first three sets, this was a remarkable achievement and made Scott's task on a foreign court look very daunting.

Indeed it was. On the first day at Queen's, Angus established a 3–1 lead. On the second he won the first set to make sure of the title. Although he had narrowly missed Peter Latham's record of holding both Rackets and Tennis world titles simultaneously, he had equalled Jim Dear's record of holding the titles individually and he was the first amateur ever to do so, and the first left-hander.

The next year a return contest took place on 8, 10 and 12 June – this time on the royal court at Hampton Court Palace, the first time that a world championship match had been played on this historic court since 1885. In that year, in another Anglo-American encounter, Tom Pettitt had beaten George Lambert. On this occasion the tables were turned and the British holder emerged the victor.

On the first day honours were even at 2 sets all. On the second there was a hard battle for the first two sets, which Angus eventually won 6–5, 6–4. Scott, showing signs of weariness in the face of Angus's determined retrieving of the most difficult shots, lost the next two sets outright, giving Angus a commanding 6 sets to 2 lead overall. On the third day, Angus won the first set to clinch his victory and retain his title.

Up to this date there had been no trophy for the Tennis world championship, but the omission was made good on this occasion with the presentation by the Tennis & Rackets Association of a silver salver engraved with the names of all previous holders, and with the outline of the four Tennis-playing countries and the names of their courts.

Howard Angus agreed to defend his title again in 1979, and challenges were received from leading players in Britain and the United States. To establish a British challenger, a match was played between Chris Ronaldson (Troon) and Norwood Cripps (Queen's), won by Ronaldson 5 sets to 1. In the United States, Jimmy Burke (Philadelphia) beat Eugene Scott (New York) by 5 sets to 3.

In the final eliminator, Chris Ronaldson beat Jimmy Burke by 7 sets to 1 at Hampton Court in April 1979. Burke began nervously, having not had more than a few days to get used to the strange conditions, and lost the first two sets 3–6, 3–6. He fought hard to win the third set 6–4, but lost the next 4–6 to leave Ronaldson with a lead of 3 sets to 1.

The second day's play produced some marvellous Tennis and Burke was unlucky not to win either of the first two sets. In the first he led at 5–4, 40-love, but Ronaldson was never better than when he had his back to the wall and he rallied to win it 6–5. He went on to take the next two sets 6–5, 6–0. In the fourth set he was 4–5 down again, but once more came from behind to win it and the match 6–5.

Both players had produced some lovely shots and Burke's return of Ronaldson's heavily cut stroke in the forehand corner was remarkable. Ronaldson was much the stronger at service and on the volley.

The challenge match for the world and British Open championship took place at Hampton Court in April 1979. Ronaldson had the advantage of youth, of having had to play several top-class matches to reach the challenge stage, and of having defeated Angus in the final of the 1978 Cutty Sark competition. Angus had had trouble with his back. Few people would have guessed that the champion would retain his title by 7 sets to 0, perhaps least of all Howard Angus himself.

The first day's play on 17 April produced an excellent match. There were many fine rallies and some quite extraordinary returns. Angus set a very fierce pace and his service was always aggressive. Despite this, Ronaldson certainly deserved to win one set – particularly the fourth in which he led at one point by 5 games to 4. Nevertheless, the final score to Angus was 6–4, 6–4, 6–5, 6–5.

That was a formidable lead for Ronaldson to face on the second day and it proved too great for him. He failed to produce the form he had shown previously, made too many mistakes and allowed Angus to win 6–3, 6–2, 6–3 and easily and worthily retain his world championship title.

Angus's record compares with the greatest players of all time. Apart from his domestic achievements (noted on page 102), he was Tennis world champion from 1976 to 1979. Few indeed are those players who can claim to have recorded a victory over him in a major championship. His Rackets achievements are recorded elsewhere (pages 155–157) and as a player of both games his record is quite outstanding.

Prominent Players

Apart from those few distinguished players involved at world championship level, there were many fine players of the game. Outstanding among English amateurs in the early years of the century was E.H. Miles, winner of the Amateur championship from 1899 to 1903, 1905–6 and 1909–10; winner of the Gold Prize 1897–99, 1901–06 and 1908–13.

An even more dominating figure came to prominence in 1912 – Edgar Baerlein, already established as a leading Rackets player and then aged thirty-nine. He first won the Amateur championship in that year, lost narrowly to the Hon. N.S. Lytton in 1913, and won again in 1914. After the war he won it every year from 1919 to 1927 and again in 1929 and 1930. He won the MCC Gold Prize every year from 1921 to 1929 and again in 1931.

As at Rackets, one of his chief rivals was the Hon. C.N. Bruce (later Lord Aberdare) but only once did Bruce beat him in a major championship. That was for the MCC Gold Prize in 1930.

Baerlein became the first winner of the Prince's Club Shield for the Open championship, when he

Edgar Baerlein.

beat W.A. (Jack) Groom 3–2 in 1931 at the age of fifty-one. His other great achievement was to defeat Jay Gould in Paris in 1923 in the course of the Bathurst Cup.

The mantle of Baerlein fell upon the shoulders of Lowther Lees, a fellow Mancunian of powerful physique. Lees won the Amateur singles in 1928, 1931 (when he beat Baerlein 3–0 at Manchester), 1933 to 1937 and 1946, when it was played at Lord's because of war damage to the roof of the Queen's court. He also won the Open championship by beating Jack Groom 7–1 in 1934 and 7–2 in 1935. He lost it in 1938 to Jim Dear, who won 5–1.

Among the professionals, Jack Groom of Lord's, Willy Ratcliff of Queen's and E.J.G. Johnson, son of Ted Johnson, were pre-eminent.

Ratcliff defeated Johnson 3–1 for the British Open in 1931 and Groom defeated Ratcliff 7–1 in 1932. Just before the Second World War, Dear started to make his presence felt, winning the Professional championship in 1937 and the Open in 1938. Had the war not intervened, Dear's record might have been even more astonishing than it was, but in 1939 he joined the RAF and Tennis and Rackets were out for the duration. All he managed was an occasional game of squash when the opportunity arose.

After the war, Dear did not defend his Open championship, being too busy with Rackets, and a match took place in 1950 in which Ronald Hughes, the Rackets professional at Malvern, beat Henry Johns of Lord's 5–3. Dear, however, returned to the fray in 1951 to regain his title by beating Hughes.

When Dear resigned as Open champion in 1962, Hughes regained the title by beating David Warburg 5–1. He in turn lost to Frank Willis of Manchester in 1967. Willis was potentially one of the great players of the day, but he was of too easygoing a nature to win as often as he might. He managed to stave off a challenge from Howard Angus in 1968, but he lost to Angus in 1970 and the latter held the title for the following four years.

In 1965, *The Field* gave a magnificent trophy for an annual open competition. Mostly this was won by Hughes, Willis and Angus, but three other names appear among the list of victors – Norwood Cripps, then at Queen's and now Rackets professional at Eton, had two fine victories over Willis in 1971 and 1973, and played in the final on six other occasions; Chris Ennis, who defeated Cripps in 1975; and Chris Ronaldson, who beat Angus in 1978.

Among post-war amateurs none was dominant before Angus in 1966, but competition was keen. Dugald Macpherson, who had won both the Amateur championship and the MCC Gold Prize in 1939, won the Gold Prize from 1947 to 1949 and in 1951 and 1952. The Hon. Morys Bruce (later Lord Aberdare) won the Amateur championship in 1953 and 1954, and 1956 and 1957, and the Gold Prize from 1954 to 1958.

Beating Macpherson for the Gold Prize in 1950, and then defeating Bruce in the semi-final and Peter Kershaw in the final of the Amateur in 1955, Robert Riseley showed what a fine player he was. Unfortunately, ill-health never allowed him to attain the heights of success that he deserved. Lord Cullen, who had previously won the Amateur in 1947 when he defeated Kershaw on his home court at Manchester, played brilliantly to beat Riseley in the final of 1952 by 3 sets to 2.

David Warburg had a successful record over a considerable period. He first won the Amateur championship in 1959 and repeated this success in 1961 and 1965. He was even more successful in the MCC prizes, winning the Gold Prize in 1953 and 1960–65.

Another outstanding player of beautiful style was Rackets champion Geoffrey Atkins. He won the Amateur in 1960 and 1962–63. In 1960 and 1963 he had the distinction of winning the Amateur singles title at both Tennis and Rackets. Anthony Tufton was a worthy winner in 1964 and Alan Lovell featured in five finals against Angus, taking him to five sets in 1977.

A great contributor to both Tennis and Rackets in the post-war years was Michael Pugh. Although never in the top flight as a player, he devoted his energies to spreading enthusiasm for both games and encouraging young players. His greatest playing achievement was to win the Bailey Cup (now the Tennis Amateur doubles, then an inter-club competition) for Manchester in 1951 in partnership with Peter Kershaw. He also played third string in the victorious Old Rugbeian Henry Leaf Cup teams in 1949, 1959, 1953–57 and 1959–60.

American Champions

In America in the early years of the century, Boston players enjoyed continuing success in the singles championship, in particular J. Crane Jr who won it from 1901 to 1904. There then arose that new champion of world class, Jay Gould, who won without defeat from 1906 to 1925 – except for 1918 and 1919 when no championship took place.

With the retirement of Jay Gould the competition became more open and a number of other players

Jay Gould.

won it: C. Suydam Cutting, Hewitt Morgan, William C. Wright and two British visitors, George Huband and Lord Aberdare.

In 1934 another player of world class took the title for the first time – Ogden Phipps, who won it five times in six years and again (twice) after an interruption caused by the Second World War. His principal rival in the early days was Jimmy Van Alen and they had some terrific struggles. In 1933 the singles were played for the first time in Philadelphia and Van Alen beat Phipps 3–0 in the semi-final, going on to beat W.C. Wright in the final and win the championship.

The following year Phipps turned the tables to take the title for the first time, but Van Alen still managed to beat him in the Tuxedo Gold Racquet in a closely contested five-set match. In 1936 Van Alen came very near to victory again in the Amateur singles, but eventually Phipps won by 6–0, 5–6, 5–6, 6–4, 8–6, after Van Alen had led 6–5 and advantage in the final set. He went on to win the Open championship in a challenge match against Walter Kinsella at Greentree. Kinsella was aged fifty-one to Phipps's twenty-eight and Phipps won easily 6–2, 6–1, 7–5.

Thereafter, Phipps dominated the Tennis scene, although Van Alen twice won the singles again in 1938 and 1940, when Phipps did not compete. Phipps's matches with Pierre Etchebaster have been mentioned earlier.

After Phipps came Alastair Martin, winner in 1941 and every year from 1950 to 1956. He, too, twice challenged Etchebaster for the world title without success. In 1954, playing brilliantly, he defeated a much younger opponent, Northrup R. Knox, in the final conceding just three games, but Knox, a favourite pupil of Etchebaster, could not be held down for long. The following year he took a set off Martin; in 1956 a knee injured playing polo prevented him from playing; in 1957 Knox won, and held the title for six out of seven years.

Knox successfully challenged Jack Johnson for the world title in 1959 and no doubt in reaction to that splendid effort lost his Amateur title to another rising star, twenty-two-year-old Jimmy Bostwick. The younger man played brilliantly to win 6–3, 5–6, 6–3, 6–3 – having also led 5–2 in the second set.

Knox did not defend his world title in 1964 and from then until 1972 it was shared by the two Bostwick brothers, Pete and Jimmy, both of them in turn world champions. In 1973 Howard Angus visited the United States and won the title. Until 1980 it was won consistently by Gene Scott except for 1979 when he was beaten by R.E. Howe.

A doubles championship was started in 1909 and many of the same players came to dominate it with various partners. Jay Gould won it in all nineteen times with three different partners.

A notable victory was that of the Van Alen brothers, J.H. (Jimmy) and W.L. (Sammy) in 1940. Even more remarkable, two more Van Alen brothers, J.L. and W.L. Jr (sons of Sammy), won the championship in 1967. The Van Alen family have been great supporters of Tennis in the United States. Jimmy originated the biennial match between undergraduates from Britain and America for the trophy which bears his name. Sammy was the first President of the US Court Tennis Association from 1955 to 1970, and is highly respected on both sides of the Atlantic.

Three sets of victorious brothers: (left to right) *W.L. Van Alen, J.H. Van Alen, N.R. Knox, S.H. Knox III, G.H. Bostwick Jr, J.F.C. Bostwick.*

It is remarkable that the doubles championship has been won by seven sets of brothers. Apart from the Van Alens, there were the Cuttings (1925), the Martin twins (1951), the Knox brothers (1958–59 and 1961), the Bostwicks (1969 and 1973) and the Howes (1974).

In 1956 the US Open championship was revived. The first player to have been recognised as Open champion was Jay Gould in 1921 when he beat Jock Soutar, but on his retirement the title was dropped. In fact, if not in title, his successors were Kinsella, Soutar and Etchebaster.

Etchebaster's retirement in 1954, and the founding of the US Court Tennis Association in 1955, were the main reasons for the institution of an Open championship. At first the professionals continued to prevail; for the first four years Albert (Jack) Johnson, then at New York, defeated Jimmy Dunn of Philadelphia in the final. But from 1960 to 1972 the championship was dominated by the Bostwick brothers; in those thirteen years Jimmy Bostwick won the title seven times and Pete Bostwick three times. Only Johnson, who won again in 1963 and 1965, and Ronald Hughes from England, who won in 1964, interrupted their monopoly.

From 1972 to 1977 the championship was dominated by another amateur, Gene Scott, but from 1978 professionals won again: J.J. Burke Jr of Philadelphia in 1978, Barry Toates of Boston in 1979 and Chris Ronaldson of Hampton Court in 1980.

In 1960 an Open doubles championship was first played. In its early years Jimmy Dunn was the most successful player, winning in 1960 and 1962 with W.I. Forbes Jr and from 1964 to 1967 with W.T. Vogt. The brothers Bostwick won in 1961 (when Dunn and Forbes had to scratch in the final owing to an injury to Dunn's leg), and from 1968 to 1970. The only non-American winners of the championship up until 1980 were Norwood Cripps, then at Queen's Club, and Chris Ronaldson, then at Melbourne, in 1977.

1980–2000

The explosion of interest in Tennis that occurred in the last decade of the twentieth century was built on a slow revival in the 1980s. In May 1981, the Jesmond Dene Tennis Court in Newcastle was reopened, followed in 1989 by the restoration of the court at Holyport. No new Tennis court had been built in Britain since 1912 until The Oratory School did so in 1990, largely due to the initiative of its headmaster, Adrian Snow. Then, in 1993, the Harbour Club court opened in London, its location in the basement involving a lower ceiling than normal. The Newmarket court was restored in 1995 thanks to the efforts of John Shneerson and Anthony Coles. In 1997 a new court was built for the Bristol and Bath Club in the grounds of Clifton College with the aid of a lottery grant, and the previous court at The Hyde, Bridport, was restored, also with a grant from the National Lottery. Both these last two courts were officially opened in 1998 by HRH the Earl of Wessex, who had performed the same service for the Harbour Club five years earlier. In 1999 two new courts, one of which has a glass grille wall, were built at the Prested Hall Racket Club near Chelmsford in Essex, as part of a sports centre planned by Mike Carter. The second court at Cambridge was restored and a magnificent new court at Middlesex University built with the aid of a very generous grant from Mr and Mrs Peter Luck-Hille. The latter was also opened by The Earl of Wessex, on 19 January 2000. So although the court at Troon was closed in 1991, by 2000 there was a net increase of ten courts in the United Kingdom.

In the United States, a new court – Prince's Court – was opened in McLean, Virginia, a suburb of Washington DC, and courts were reopened at Lakewood, New Jersey (the Georgian Court) and Newport, Rhode Island (the National Tennis Club). In Australia, new courts were built at Ballarat in 1984 with invaluable support from John Gilbert; in Sydney in 1997 at Macquarie University, thanks to the determination of the university's Executive Officer Robert Lawton and the generous financial support of Wayne Davies; and at Romsey in 1999, where Gordon Cope-Williams was the driving force. In harmony with this new-found interest in Royal Tennis, Australia produced some of the world's top players. Australia won the Bathurst Cup in 1982, for the first time ever, and the following year the Australian Royal Tennis Association was formed under the chairmanship of Bill Hepworth, largely made possible by generous sponsorship.

A new world champion emerged in 1981 when Chris Ronaldson, then senior professional at Hampton Court, defeated the holder, Howard Angus. In the British eliminator, Ronaldson had beaten Frank Willis by 7 sets to 0 and in the final eliminator beat Barry Toates 7 sets to 4. In the championship match, Ronaldson won all four sets in the first leg 6–5, 6–5, 6–5, 6–2. In the second leg, Angus won the first set 6–2 and Ronaldson the second 6–2. Ronaldson was leading 5–4 in the third when Angus tore a calf muscle and had to retire, conceding the match to a very worthy new champion.

Chris Ronaldson's interest in Tennis began in 1971 when he joined the Oxford court as assistant to Peter Dawes and later became senior professional. On the opening of the two new courts in Melbourne in 1974, he was appointed senior professional and made a major contribution to their success. In 1978, he moved to Troon in Scotland and in 1979 to Hampton Court. He then became the first head professional at Radley upon the opening of its new court in 2008. He wrote several books on the game including *Tennis: A Cut above the Rest*, which has an

Chris Ronaldson: among the cream of the world's professionals.

Chris Ronaldson (second left) *retained his world Tennis title at Hampton Court in 1983, beating Wayne Davies 7–4. Others pictured: Lord Aberdare* (left)*, Sir Clifford Chetwood and David Norman.*

accompanying video, and made a considerable contribution in the realms of administration and coaching. He was also called in to help at Bordeaux, Fairlawne and Holyport.

Chris Ronaldson first defended his title in 1983. Wayne Davies, a young Australian professional working at the New York Racquet and Tennis Club, had defeated a fellow Australian, Colin Lumley, in the eliminator. Ronaldson defeated Davies at Hampton Court by 7 sets to 4 to retain his title. In 1984, Ronaldson became the first player to take the Grand Slam in one calendar year, winning all four Open championships – British, French, US and Australian. In 1985, he rebuffed Davies in a second challenge by 7 sets to 1 at the Queen's Club to establish his complete supremacy at the time.

In 1987, he faced a third challenge. In the eliminators, Lachlan Deuchar beat Graham Hyland and Wayne Davies beat Deuchar to emerge once again as the challenger to Ronaldson. In the challenge match at the Queen's Club, Davies beat Ronaldson by 7 sets to 4 and became the new world champion. He faced a challenge from Lachlan Deuchar in 1988, but won without difficulty by 7 sets to 1 on his home court in New York. Lachlan Deuchar challenged again in 1991, having defeated Graham Hyland by 7 sets to love to qualify. Deuchar had a remarkable record. He had not lost a single match for almost two years and had won all four Open championships in the 1990–91 season. Davies, on the other hand, had had recurring injury problems, including operations on both knees. The challenge match was played at the New York Racquet Club over three days in 1991 and, after some closely fought sets, Davies retained his title by 7 sets to 4.

Deuchar launched yet another challenge to Davies in 1993, having first defeated the leading amateur player, Julian Snow, in an eliminator in Melbourne. The challenge match was dramatic and the score towards the end of the final day was 6 sets all. Deuchar's giraffe service had proved very effective. However, Davies rallied and finally won the deciding set by 6 games to 1 to retain his title. This was a sad result for Deuchar, whose record includes winning the British Open championship for six consecutive years, equalling the achievement of Chris Ronaldson.

Davies faced another challenge in 1994, on a home-and-away basis, this time from Robert Fahey, an Australian based at Hobart who had won the US, Australian and French Open championships in 1993.

Wayne Davies: the first Australian to become world champion.

The following year, 1996, brought forth a number of potential challengers. Davies was the US Open champion, Frank Filippelli the Australian and Mike Gooding the French. Fahey had beaten Deuchar in the final of the British. In the eliminator matches, Gooding beat Filippelli and Davies beat Gooding. The final challenge match was played in Melbourne when Fahey soundly defeated Davies by 7 sets to 1.

Julian Snow dominated the British Amateur championship, winning for thirteen years out of fourteen. He won the British Open in 1992, 1993, 1994 and 1998, when he beat Steve Virgona, an up-and-coming young Australian player, in the final. In 1998 he also won the Open doubles with James Male. By winning the 1997 US Open he qualified to challenge for the world championship in 1998. He defeated Chris Bray at Lord's by 5 sets to 2, Mike Gooding in Melbourne by 7 sets to 2 and challenged Fahey for the crown. He made a very gallant attempt to dethrone the champion – the match stood at 3 sets all and 5 games all at one point – but eventually lost by 4 sets to 7.

The candidates for the 2000 challenge were Chris Bray, who won the British Open in 1997, the US Open in 1998 and the Australian Open in August 1999, beating Fahey in 4 sets in the final; and Wayne Davies, winner of the US Open of 1999 at the age of forty-three. A preliminary eliminator took place at Hobart in February 2000. Bray led by 3 sets to 1 on the first day and, after the second day, by 5 sets to 3. On the final day some magnificent Tennis was played as Davies fought back to level the score at 5

He was injured when leading by 1 set to 0 in the final of the British against Julian Snow, but went on to eliminate Snow as a world championship challenger by 12 sets to 7, in a home-and-away match. The first leg of the championship match was played at Hobart where, on his home court, Fahey won by 7 sets to 1. The second leg took place in New York. Davies made a huge effort to offset Fahey's lead, winning the first three sets, but Fahey won the fourth. Fahey needed just one more set to win the match on the second day. Davies won the first set, but Fahey took the second and with it the match and the world title.

Fahey's first challenger emerged in 1995 after three elimination matches. In the first, Chris Bray, the professional at Petworth, beat Julian Snow at Hampton Court. In the second, Bray played Deuchar at Hobart and was leading by 6 sets to 1 when Deuchar had to retire with an ankle injury. Bray then played Davies in the third eliminator and lost to him by 7 sets to 1, leaving a repeat match, Davies v. Fahey, for the championship. Once again a splendid match was spoilt by injury. Fahey was leading by 6 sets to 2 after the second day's play when Davies retired with a back injury and Fahey remained champion.

Robert Fahey, the finest player of our time, took the world championship in 1994 at the age of 23.

Twentieth-century Tennis

Julian Snow dominated amateur tennis from 1987 into the 21st century.

sets all and to win the last two sets and the match by 7 sets to 5. It was a famous victory, entitling Davies to challenge Fahey for the championship, his tenth appearance in the final of this great event.

The championship match was played at Hobart later in February and was dominated by Fahey, who won by 7 sets to love. Davies never gave up and was unlucky not to win the sixth set after being 5 games all, but he found the champion in overpowering form. On 20 November 2000, Fahey defeated Chris Bray in the final of the British Open championship at the Queen's Club to achieve the Grand Slam of winning all four national championships in the same calendar year. The only previous occasion when this was achieved was in 1984 by Chris Ronaldson.

Lord Aberdare, with one of the game's major sponsors at that time, Sir John Ritblat.

Twenty-First Century Tennis

Thanks to the efforts of Real Tennis aficionados around the world, a number of courts have recently been revived. In southwest France there has been an astonishing renaissance, which includes the Beaumont court in Pau in 2005, the Hapette Court in La Bastide-Clairence in 2010 and Sainte André in Bayonne in 2011. The courts vary in size and attributes but the Beaumont court is the most similar to a normal Real Tennis court. In addition, many other modern trinquet courts are used occasionally for Real Tennis.

In the United States, a full-scale refurbishment of the Georgian court in Lakewood, New Jersey culminated in active play resuming in 2009. The Chicago Tennis Court – which had been adapted to function as a lawn tennis court in 1936 – was reopened, restored to its original purpose, in 2012.

The most significant achievement of court building in the last decade, and one which will undoubtedly serve to encourage development at the younger level of the game, was the construction of a new Tennis court at Radley. Building work commenced in October 2007 and the court was officially opened a year later, on 12 October 2008, by HRH the Earl of Wessex.

Along with the realisation of improved and new locations in which to enjoy Tennis has come the disappointing news of court closures. Greentree, once a private court on the Whitney family estate in Long Island, underwent renovations in the 1990s to encourage active play at the court. Unfortunately it became inactive in 2001 as a result of becoming part of a United Nations facility, so only limited use is now possible.

Romsey Tennis Court, although still in situ, became inactive in 2002. Another Australian casualty was the Tennis court at Macquarie University, Sydney, which closed in December 2005. However, an extensive search is proceeding for an ideal location for a replacement court. There are a number of excellent prospects which are being pursued.

Despite opening just fourteen years previously in 1993, the court at London's Harbour Club failed to escape closure, shutting in 2007. Players of the game who favour the lob might have been marginally less disappointed to witness the demise of this basement court, with its notoriously low ceiling!

In France, the Bordeaux Tennis Club's Mérignac court – host of the French Open on six separate occasions between 2003 and 2012 – was closed in March 2013. The club intends to rebuild in a new location.

Such disappointments have been allayed to some extent by plans to repair existing, and create new, Tennis courts. The Irish Real Tennis Association has affirmed its commitment to restoring the Dublin Court, which remained in use until 1939.

The Lambay Court, one of only two open-air courts in the world, and situated on an island in the Irish Sea, had weathered the elements since its construction in the early 1920s. After the court was declared in danger of collapse, repair work was initially undertaken in 2005. Plans to implement a full restoration were mooted in 2012.

There are further exciting plans afoot to restore the *kaatsbaan* (Dutch for Real Tennis court) in Haarlem, Holland. The club needs to secure the €1.4 million necessary to finance major restoration work of a Tennis court that is recognised as being amongst the oldest covered courts in the world.

In terms of potential *new* courts, Charleston Tennis Club, newly formed in 2008, aims to develop a demonstration court and Real Tennis complex in South Carolina. In Jersey there are hopes to build two Real Tennis courts, as well as one Rackets court, as part of a development programme at the University of Jersey which opened in 2014.

Meanwhile, Wellington have publicised a highly anticipated project to build a landmark Real Tennis court. Supporters of the initiative include HRH The Earl of Wessex, current world Real Tennis champions Rob Fahey and Claire Vigrass, as well as Chris Ronaldson, world Real Tennis champion 1981–87. Construction at Wellington is expected to go ahead once finance for the project, estimated at over £1 million, is in place.

The men's world championship remains the pinnacle of international competition. It is still contested on a challenge basis and is the best of 13 sets over three days. The challenger emerges from an eliminator, pitting the four highest-ranking players in the world (excluding the champion) against each other. The eliminator comprises a semi-final requiring the best of three 5-set matches over three days on a 'home and away' basis, and a final which is the best of 13 sets over three days.

In recent times, the world championship has been undeniably monopolised by Australian Rob Fahey. Over his twenty-one-year reign as world champion, Fahey has smashed all known records for the number of wins (twelve consecutive occasions, compared with eight for Pierre Etchebaster) and successfully dispatched many a worthy challenger.

Fahey's achievements in Real Tennis are nothing short of extraordinary. Having successfully challenged for the world singles title in 1994, aged twenty-three, Fahey has since remained an almost invincible force in the highest echelons of the game. During this time he has won a colossal number of Opens in either Britain, USA, France or Australia. He won the European Open back-to-back four times from 2004 to 2007. He dominated the Professional singles championship 2001–04 and again 2006–10, suffering only a rare defeat to Virgona in the 2005 final, when he was forced to retire from the match in the fifth set. Ever the consummate professional, Fahey combines intelligence of play with the determination of a champion and seldom fails to make the crucial points of a match count. Fahey's rivals have characteristically found him, when on form, near impossible to beat. However, young rivals have begun to pose problems for him. In 2013, Camden Riviere beat Fahey in the final of the European Open, UK and US Professional singles, and in 2012, Bryn Sayers beat him in the final of the British Open.

Riviere and Sayers' victories over Fahey in 2013 and 2012 respectively suggest the beginning of a new era in the sport. Riviere has dominated the European Open in recent years, winning it four out of five times since 2008, three of which were against Fahey. Having proved a troublesome opponent for Fahey in a tight-fought 2011 European Open final, staying in the match until Fahey's ninth match point, and in the marathon 2011 British Open final, in which Fahey eventually converted his eleventh match point, Sayers proved it was his time of reckoning in 2012. Sayers came through the match to win from behind in four sets, 2–6 6–5 6–1 6–5, and break Fahey's run of nine consecutive British Open championships. The following year, Sayers

Camden Riviere has dominated the European Open in recent years, winning it four out of five times since 2008. Pictured here with Bryn Sayers at the 2012 Event.

again defeated Fahey, but this time in the semi-finals, where he staged a Houdini-like recovery from two sets and 5–0 down in the third set, saving a handful of match points in the process. However, Steve Virgona was too great a challenge for him in the final, in the process gaining his first-ever British Open victory. In 2014 Riviere similarly gained his first-ever British Open victory, over-coming Virgona in the final.

In the inaugural world doubles championship in 2001, Tim Chisholm and Julian Snow emerged victorious over Steve Virgona and Ruaraidh Gunn. Thereafter, the tournament has belonged to the combined forces of Rob Fahey and rival Steve Virgona, a player considered by many as the world's premier doubles player. The Australian partnership has comprehensively dominated the world title on six consecutive occasions since their first in 2003.

Until losing to Bryn Sayers and Tim Chisholm in 2013, it has been a similar success story for Fahey and Virgona in the Open doubles. Reuniting after their initial back-to-back victories in 2001 and 2002, they achieved a further three consecutive Open doubles titles in 2010, 2011 and 2012. Fahey enjoyed additional success in the Open doubles with Rackets champion James Male in 2008 and also partnered by Ruaraidh Gunn – recording their first victory together in 2003, before a run of consecutive victories 2005–07. In 2014 Riviere and Chisholm, having recently dominated both the US and French Open doubles, won the British Open doubles for the first time, defeating Fahey and Sayers in the final.

The Amateur singles championship has been a tale

Rob Fahey and Steve Virgona won the 2013 world doubles championship in Paris.

singles champion David Woodman in 2007 and 2008, with Neil Roxburgh and Jamie Douglas respectively, Peter Wright and Jamie Douglas claimed the title 2009–11, and again in 2014. In both 2012 and 2013, a winning combination of youth and experience, in the form of Conor Medlow partnered by Julian Snow, once again saw Snow get his hands on the doubles title.

Apart from the world championship and the National Open championships, singles and doubles, many other competitions are held regularly. The Bathurst Cup attracts entrants from the four main Tennis-playing countries and rotates every two years between them. The UK annual fixture list includes championships for amateur and professional players of all ages and standards, both men and ladies. In addition to the well-established championships for the leading players, i.e. the Professional and Amateur singles and doubles, there are championships for every age group from the Under-12s to the Over-70s – and for every handicap group. The inter-club Amateur championships are run in two divisions for the Pol Roger and Field Trophy, plus the Brodie Cup for people with higher handicaps; and the National League, which is run by the Real Tennis Professionals Association (RTPA), involves approximately 200 players in nine divisions. Apart from the major competitions run by the Tennis & Rackets Association, there are innumerable club competitions played in every court, catering to the strong core of Tennis enthusiasts worldwide.

of Julian Snow: Snow has won the tournament a record-breaking nineteen times. On top of surpassing Howard Angus's record of sixteen Amateur titles, Snow achieved fifteen consecutive victories in the competition from 1991 to 2005. Snow did not compete during 2006 to 2011, but returned to retake the title in a nail-biting three-and-a-half-hour affair against Matthieu Sarlangue in 2012. More recently up-and-coming young players such as Jamie Douglas and Matthieu Sarlangue have clinched the title in 2013 and 2014 respectively.

Snow's principal rival in the Amateur singles for a number of years, Spike Willcocks, fared better in the doubles championship. Willcocks achieved some measure of revenge for his string of losses in the singles when he first seized the title from Snow and his specialist doubles partner James Acheson-Gray in 2001. Willcocks retained the championship from 2001 to 2003 with Alexis Hombrecher, before teaming up with Acheson-Gray himself to win the 2004 tournament. Snow and Acheson-Gray regained the title in 2005, which then passed to cousins Charles and Luke Danby in 2006. After back-to-back wins for 2006 and 2008 Amateur

Matthieu Sarlangue with Rob Fahey after winning the 2009 British Junior Open. Sarlangue went on to win the 2014 British Amateur singles.

P. Wright and J. Douglas beat M. Sarlangue and A. Lumsden in the 2014 Amateur doubles.

Long-serving club professionals still in harness include Chris Ronaldson (Radley), Lesley Ronaldson (Hampton Court), Kevin King (Bristol), Kees Ludekens (Cambridge), Kevin Sheldon (Leamington) and Steve Ronaldson (Canford).

New Media

Media operations have been transformed in the last fifteen to twenty years. The traditional freelance journalist is a thing of the past and this has sounded a death knell for reporting in the broadsheets, whose circulation had been declining throughout the latter part of the twentieth century. As less is available in the newspapers, the rise of the World Wide Web has created other, more dynamic, media opportunities. Results, reports and even photographs can now be online in a matter of minutes from the end of a tournament, providing a much more interactive solution. They can also be published from a number of sources, all of which are interrelated, so providing a more coherent and inclusive solution.

The latest progression is the utility of social media. This has swept the globe in the last five to ten years and is even more popular among younger generations than the Internet. Instant messaging using Facebook and Twitter allows for real-time, shot-by-shot exchange of information. It is now more common for young people to follow live Facebook feeds rather than a standard website update. Social media can also be used successfully to advertise events and encourage participation.

Another remarkable addition arising from the web is the phenomenon of web streaming, which for the first time ever has made live broadcasting of a minority sport economically viable. Web streaming is quickly developing to show on-court action in a compelling manner. Using anything from a basic video camera to the more sophisticated equipment seen recently in Melbourne for the world championship singles, a variety of sites such as YouTube can be employed to host the live streaming. There is, however, a balance to negotiate: better cameras produce better-quality footage, but this creates its own problems regarding bandwidth and upload capability at the supporting club. A cheap camera produces much poorer-quality imagery, but is far easier to upload; hence a balance needs to be struck (unless the club has exceptional bandwidth, for example, Lord's). High-quality production demands a minimum of 2 megabyte upload broadband speed, as well as specialist equipment and professional know-how – but the costs are getting cheaper each year.

For the world championships at The Oratory in 2006 (and Queen's in 2012), Horizon (247.tv) was the first company to broadcast live on the web. In 2010, Tiger Riviere (father of Camden) streamed the final eliminator for the first time at Tuxedo, followed by the world championship in Melbourne. Free websites such as Ustream and YouTube are the easiest way for anyone to start broadcasting, requiring only the simple set-up of a laptop and webcam. A number of enthusiastic players, for example Ryan Carey in the US, Frederika Adam in the UK and the members of the Hobart Club, utilise web streaming regularly. Their loyal grass-roots audiences are grateful for the opportunity to watch and keep in touch with the Tennis community online.

A conscious decision to develop high-quality web streaming led to the creation of Realtennis.tv by Frederika Adam and Paul Brown in 2010. They created a one-off event, with Rob Fahey and Claire Vigrass playing a singles match to showcase the sport, whilst demonstrating web streaming to an audience watching in the Old Library at Lord's. The broadcast, on a custom-built website by Media on Demand, exhibited live mixing, guest commentary and interaction with the online audience. Realtennis.tv has

Rob Fahey and Claire Vigrass demonstrate web streaming at Lord's 2010.

benefits of providing good content to a ready online audience are: to market the sport, to raise the profile of the clubs, to discover new players and to play an integral part in the success of an event. This is how the world communicates today, and Tennis and Rackets can afford to join the online revolution.

The next step for web streaming is to establish regular online coverage, in the form of a coordinated annual schedule consisting of all international, national and important club tournaments. In addition, there is a substantial online audience for alternative and special events which has yet to be realised. Together, all of these events should include web streaming as part of their sponsorship and marketing packages. Web streaming can be sponsored outright or set up as a pay-on-demand, but first clubs need to invest in the infrastructure (broadband and hardware) and put together their own team of local enthusiasts willing to run the equipment and put on a good show. It should be the case that all Tennis and Rackets events, shown in a compelling and exciting way, contribute to marketing and promoting the sports for a growing online fan base. Above all, a successful online presence will ensure the recruitment of the next generation of players.

since covered a number of Tennis and Rackets events at Lord's (European Open and Varsity match 2011), Queen's (Rackets world doubles 2011 and 2013 and Manchester (UK Professional singles 2011), Prested Hall (eliminator 2012) and Chicago (final eliminator 2014). The aim is to always improve with each broadcast, while encouraging more events organisers to consider high-quality web streaming.

The coverage of the 2014 world championship held in Melbourne was a major break-through for a professional broadcast in high quality. This was made possible by the fact that the event organisers worked together with the Fuzzy TV broadcast team on the production. Their key innovation was to replace the right side dedans netting with a Plexiglass sheet, allowing a camera, with cameraman, to follow the action without obstruction. The effect was to finally 'get inside the box', as if on court with the players. The broadcast flowed beautifully, with on-cue graphics and entertaining commentary, the result being that online audience numbers were high and constant.

It has taken many years to develop serious coverage of Tennis and Rackets. It was once said that these sports were impossible to film, and we now know that it is not only possible, but it can be done well. The

John Lumley warming up in Manchester ahead of the UK Professional singles 2011.

In an outcome reminiscent of Andre Agassi and Steffi Graf, Rob Fahey and Claire Vigrass were married on 25 July 2014.

LADIES' TENNIS

In May 1981, at Moreton Morrell Tennis Club, a men's world tournament was taking place. Chris Ronaldson, who two weeks earlier had wrested the world championship from Howard Angus at Queen's Club, was playing. Outside the rain-sodden marquee, Alan Lovell, then chairman of the Tennis Committee of the Tennis & Rackets Association, turned to Chris's wife Lesley and said, 'Have you thought of starting a ladies' association? You would have the blessing of the Tennis & Rackets Association.' Lesley, British Ladies' champion in 1979, 1980, 1981 and 1987, needed no further encouragement.

With Chris's help, a draft constitution was prepared for discussion at a meeting arranged for 31 October 1981 at Moreton Morrell, during the British Ladies' singles handicap tournament. The constitution was approved unanimously and the Ladies' Real Tennis Association (LRTA) was on its way. Nominations for a chairman, honorary secretary and honorary treasurer were requested to arrive before the next meeting, to be held on 16 January 1982 at Hampton Court during the first British Ladies' Open doubles championship. Lesley Ronaldson was elected chairman, Viv Dawes honorary secretary and Alex Warren-Piper (now Garside) honorary treasurer. A lady member was invited to sit on the Tennis & Rackets Association's Tennis Committee, and Sheila Macintosh joined it and served on the committee for sixteen years. Thus, ever since 1982, the LRTA has had a representative by right on the Tennis Committee. At the tournament, Sheila Macintosh and Jill Cottrell became the Ladies' doubles champions, beating Evelyn David and Lesley Ronaldson.

Lesley led the LRTA diligently and with great enthusiasm for its first ten years. In this period it became responsible for running the British Open singles and doubles and the ladies' handicap tournaments, set up the Ladies' Masters and, in conjunction with the Tennis & Rackets Association, set up and took on the running of the Billy Ross-Skinner British Invitation mixed doubles tournament. For much of this time, Lesley, whose game was based on classic shot play and a superb serve, continued to play Tennis at the highest level, including winning the world championship doubles and the British Open singles in 1987, as well as becoming the first lady professional in Britain.

Sheila Macintosh, a former captain of the Great Britain Ladies' squash team, took over the chairmanship in 1991, quietly asserting her authority as the LRTA expanded both in terms of membership and the number of regular tournaments and matches. She encouraged Lucy Davies to set up the ever popular Mothers and Daughters tournament and the Tennis & Golf Day and initiated the LRTA International Invitation, a tournament held every two years, alternating with the world championships, to give the top eight available players from around the world the opportunity to compete against those they might not otherwise play.

In 1998, she handed over to Sarah McGivern, ably qualified professionally to steer the LRTA in an increasingly technological world. Sarah had, during Sheila's chairmanship, worked to enable the LRTA to become financially independent of the Tennis & Rackets Association by finding its own sponsors, and has continued to strongly support this position, enabling prize money to be paid to lady professionals in ladies' tournaments. Under Sarah's guidance the LRTA improved its communications, establishing its own website, producing a more attractive newsletter and by extensive use of email. The LRTA was greatly assisted by Caroline and Jeremy Gilmore over many years in these technical areas, including the website, newsletters and tournament programmes and photographs. One of the main events early in Sarah's period of chairmanship was the 1999 world championships, held at Hampton Court. The following year the LRTA introduced its bursary scheme, which provides a number of free lessons to young players with a view to nurturing their talent. An Under-25 tournament and a handicap mixed doubles tournament were also introduced to the annual calendar.

Sarah introduced more formal procedures for the running of LRTA tournaments and spent many months

Ladies' tennis

The LRTA Chairmen (left to right) *Lucy Davies, Sarah McGivern, Alex Garside, Lesley Ronaldson, Sheila Macintosh at Hampton Court in 2011.*

liaising with overseas national associations to agree necessary changes to the ladies' world championship rules. She was chairman until 2004 and again from 2007–09. During this second time as chairman, agreement was reached to ensure that ladies are not penalised financially if they choose to be members of both the LRTA and the Tennis & Rackets Association, thus encouraging more ladies to support the Tennis & Rackets Association. Leamington opened its doors to ladies and Sarah introduced and organised an annual ladies' handicap tournament there. Serious work on preserving LRTA archive material was also begun.

Lucy Davies was chairman from 2004 to 2007, during which period the world championships were again held in Britain, this time in Manchester in 2007. In 2009, after her second period of office, Sarah McGivern exchanged roles with Alex Garside (nee Warren-Piper), so the LRTA retained Sarah's organisational and other skills as she became hon. treasurer.

With Alex the LRTA once again has one of the top players as chairman. One of her main focuses is junior development. The establishment of a Junior tournament for girls under the age of twenty-one is consistent with this focus, as well as the organisation of junior coaching clinics around the clubs. In addition, a junior squad has been established, and in 2013 the Incentive Scheme was set up to encourage already good young amateur players to improve their singles handicaps even more. Encouraging youngsters to play is paramount to the future, ensuring continuity and improvement in the profile of ladies' Tennis.

The LRTA seeks to encourage the ladies' game at all levels. In addition to running the tournaments for the top players, including the world championships when they are held in Britain, it runs tournaments for players of all levels. It also has a number of annual matches against individual clubs and associations, which are known for being very social occasions as well as full of enjoyable Tennis. It has a representative at each club and works with the Tennis & Rackets Association. Sheila Macintosh was co-opted onto the Council in 1984. Subsequently, in 1998, after some structural change, the Council decided to invite the LRTA chairman to be a member of the Council (which later became the Board) by right. The LRTA also has a representative on the Tennis & Rackets Association's Tournaments & Fixtures and Handicaps & Rankings sub-committees. Although it does not have its own court, the LRTA regards Seacourt as its 'home'. The British Open has been held there for most of its existence; it began life

Front row (left to right): *Maggie Wright, Jane Lippincott (US), Charlotte Cornwallis, Clare Southwell, Sally Jones, Susie Falkner, Jill Newby.* Back row (left to right): *Sheilagh Owens, Brenda Sabbag (US), Anne Balcerkiewicz, Gitte Dunkley, Catherine Walker, Christine Anies (France), Alex Garside, Evelyn David (US), Melvyn Pignon, Sarah McGivern, Ros Lake, Caroline Harding, Jane Vaughan, Sheila Macintosh, Viv Dawes, Lesley Ronaldson, Carolyn Armstrong-Smith, Kate Leeming (Aus), Sue Haswell, Fiona Deuchar (Aus) at the World Championships at Hampton Court in 1999.*

in 1978, when Viv Dawes's husband Peter, along with Paul Danby, suggested the first British Ladies' Open be held at Seacourt. The dinner to celebrate the LRTA's thirtieth birthday was held there during the 2011 British Open, when a new tournament was established, a handicap doubles tournament played at the same time as the British Open, to enable the not-so-good players to compete alongside – though not necessarily against – the top players. The Seacourt duo of Alex Garside and Viv Dawes, along with Sheila Macintosh, in their various roles on the committee, have provided invaluable stability over the years with their continued hard work and loyalty.

The LRTA also has strong links with Hardwick, where it plays a number of its matches, including the Gentlemen's Social Match, where lady members and gentlemen members play in a mixed tournament – the Ladies' Real Tennis Association is not just for ladies!

The ladies' game has produced some excellent players. The first world championship – played as a tournament and not a challenge – took place in 1985 in Melbourne. Talented Australian Judy Clarke beat Lesley Ronaldson in the closest of finals 6–3, 5–6, 6–5. Judy also won the second world championship in 1987 (it is held every two years), beating Katrina Allen at Seacourt.

Katrina Allen had already made her name as British champion from 1983–86. A player of great natural talent and strength, her flamboyance at times gave the impression that even she did not know what stroke she would play next! During her career she was world doubles champion (1987), French Open champion (singles 1986 and 1992) and doubles (1992) and US Open champion in 1995 (singles and doubles).

Then came the phenomenal career of Penny Lumley (previously Fellows, née Bland). The ladies' game was extremely lucky when in 1985 Penny became bored with lawn tennis and took up Real Tennis. Within four years she was the world champion, beating Sally Jones (now Grant) 6–4, 5–6, 6–3 in Philadelphia. She dominated the game for the next fifteen years; from 1989 to 2003 she won six (out of eight) world championships (singles) and was runner-up once. In that period she played in every world championship doubles final, winning six times. She did not enter in 2005 but played in the 2007 world championships in Manchester, winning the doubles with Charlotte Cornwallis and being runner-up to Charlotte in the singles. She won the inaugural International Invitation tournament in 1998 and took the title at the next three tournaments. Penny was the British Open singles champion twelve times between 1989 and 2004, including an unbeaten run of eight victories from 1995 to 2002; she won the doubles title ten times between 1991 and 2008. She was also successful abroad, winning the US Open (both singles and doubles) six times, the French Open singles seven times and the doubles ten times, and the Australian Open singles three times. In 1996–97 she achieved the ultimate when she won the Grand Slam, taking the British, French, American and Australian Opens, as well as the world singles and doubles titles. But life was not all Tennis for Penny: as well as winning an unprecedented number of titles, she also managed the small matter of having two children! Penny's elegant style of play combined an ability to retrieve anything and everything for as long as was needed with that of hitting an unbeatable length shot on the floor; all this accompanied by a very calm, controlled temperament.

Penny was undoubtedly one of the outstanding sportswomen of her time. In addition to her many titles she received numerous other accolades. The Tennis & Rackets Association awarded her the Baerlein Cup – for the best Tennis performance by an amateur – six times, and the Greenwood Trophy in 1989 for the most improved Tennis player of the year. She was the first lady to be given these awards. In 1999 she was presented with the Medal of the French Republic for her achievements in Tennis and in particular for her seven French Open singles titles. In 2000 she won the Unsung Hero/Heroine category and the overall Grand Prix Prize at the Best of British Awards for Great Sporting Achievement. She was awarded the MBE in 2004. In 2011 Penny was inducted into the International Hall of Fame of the US Court Tennis Association, only the second lady ever to receive this award. Having taken some time out of competitive Tennis, Penny started playing in tournaments again. In 2013 she was a finalist in the world championship

World Championship doubles finalists (left to right) *Sue Haswell, Kate Leeming, Penny Lumley and Charlotte Cornwallis, Manchester 2007.*

doubles with her daughter, Tara, and a finalist in the French Open singles and doubles (again with Tara) and was a finalist in the LRTA International Invitation tournament in 2014, proving that she is still playing at the top level despite her years! With a marvellous temperament and elegance on and off the court, Penny was and is a wonderful ambassador for the game.

By the end of the century, a small but established nucleus of world-class players had formed. Headed by Penny, they included Sue Haswell, Katrina Allen, Sally Jones, Alex Garside, Charlotte Cornwallis and Kate Leeming, the last two having turned professional.

Sue Haswell came to Tennis from lawn tennis at a relatively late age (she was in her late thirties) but took to it with a vengeance, being awarded the Greenwood Trophy for the most improved Tennis player in 1995 after only a few years in the game. She was the world singles number two for many years and won the world championship doubles three times (with Penny Lumley). Sue continues to play in top tournaments at home and abroad.

Sally Jones was twice runner-up to Penny Lumley in the world championship (1989 and 1991), each time taking the match to three sets; she was world champion in 1993 beating Charlotte Cornwallis in Bordeaux; and she and her regular partner Alex Garside took the world doubles title twice. She was twice British Open singles champion (1988 and 1990), and British Open doubles champion seven times, six of those with Alex Garside. Strong and athletic, and a talented all-round sportswoman, Sally was a British schoolgirl lawn tennis champion, played lawn tennis for Warwickshire, squash for South Wales, and managed five blues at Oxford. As a sports journalist, she has made a valuable contribution to the growth of the ladies' game.

Alex Garside has always found time to play at the top level, despite her duties with the LRTA, her family and work commitments. Often partnering Sally Jones, but also playing with others such as Penny Lumley and Charlotte Cornwallis, she has been particularly successful on the doubles court, her top-class cut shot standing her in good stead, winning the world championship doubles twice and being runner-up three times. In the seventeen years from 1987 to 2003, Alex reached the final of the British Open doubles sixteen times, winning the title nine times. Pregnancy prevented her from entering in 1995; like Penny, she fitted in having two children whilst playing at the top level! She also won Open doubles titles in the US (twice) and France (six times). But it is not only doubles where Alex has had success; in 1994 she won the British and the French Open singles championships, the latter when

Charlotte Cornwallis with the World Championship singles salver, Manchester 2007.

four months pregnant. She continues to play in major tournaments.

Despite their successes, neither Sue, Sally nor Alex was able to replace Penny as the dominant force in the game. But then came Charlotte Cornwallis. She developed an aggressive style of play, hitting the ball hard and making strong cut shots with ease. Her strong, physical style of play contrasted with Penny's style, though they complemented each other when they played doubles together. Charlotte became the dominant player in the ladies' game in the mid-2000s and was the first lady to achieve a single-figure handicap: her best was eight. She turned professional and found time to coach and generally promote the game (including appearing on television), as well as being unbeatable on court when she was at the height of her powers. She won the world championships singles and doubles four times, including a run of three in 2005, 2007 and 2009, and the LRTA International Invitation tournament in 2006 and 2008. She was British Open singles and doubles champion seven and four times respectively, she won the US Open singles six times and the doubles four times, the French Open singles seven times and the doubles six times and the Australian Open singles twice and the doubles three times. Charlotte achieved the singles and doubles Grand Slam in 2008–09. She won the Browning Cup in 2005, the only lady ever to win this professional handicap tournament. The Tennis & Rackets Association awarded her the Warburg Salver for the best performance by a professional three times; she is the only lady ever to be given this award. It was a huge blow to Charlotte and a great loss to the game when she was forced to retire through injury in 2009. She was playing wonderful Tennis and was an inspiration to the next generation of up-and-coming players. It would have been very good to see Charlotte on court with them.

That next generation includes the Vigrass sisters, Claire and Sarah, Karen Hird and Tara Lumley, young stars of the game in this country and worldwide. They have all played at the top level at a young age and all benefited from the LRTA's bursary scheme.

Claire Vigrass has taken over Charlotte Cornwallis's mantle as the dominant force in the ladies' game and has taken it to a new level. Hitting the ball harder than any other lady, she has all the shots; serves, volleys and retrieves well, and cuts the ball in a much more dramatic way. In 2011 she became the youngest-ever world champion at the age of nineteen, winning the singles and also the doubles with Sarah, and she repeated these successes in 2013. To date, Claire has won the British Open singles five times (2010–14) and the doubles four times (2010 and 2012–14). She has won the US Open singles five times (2008, 2010–12 and 2014) and the doubles four times (2010–12 and 2014), the Australian Open singles and doubles four times (2010–12 and 2014) and the French Open singles five times (2010–14) and the doubles six times (2009–14). In 2010 the Tennis & Rackets Association awarded Claire the Baerlein Cup for the best Tennis

(left to right) Sarah Vigrass and Karen Hird at the 2012 LRTA International Invitation tournament at Holyport.

performance by an amateur and she is the first lady to be selected for the Van Alen Cup team. Claire's best handicap to date is an amazing 2.4, and she has the ability and determination to improve on that. She turned professional in 2011. She managed all of this top-class Tennis despite breaking her ankle on a Welsh mountain in late 2010! Claire is a prodigious talent and it must be hard for the other players to envisage toppling her.

Karen's main sport was badminton until she was seventeen, when she turned her focus to Tennis. She won the world championship doubles with Charlotte Cornwallis in 2009, reached the singles final in 2009 and 2011 and the doubles final in 2011. Karen won the French Open singles in 2009 and has won a number of Open doubles titles, namely the US thrice, the British twice and the French once. Karen is a tenacious competitor, plays a classic game and is a particularly strong volleyer. However, since 2013 she has concentrated on fives, which is a loss to Real Tennis.

Sarah Vigrass is a strong player who hits the ball hard, though not quite as hard as her sister. She has reached the finals of the Open singles in Britain, France and Australia, but her main success has come in doubles, where she usually partners Claire. They won the world championship doubles in 2011 and 2013, the Australian Open doubles three times (2010–12), the French Open doubles in 2011 and the British Open doubles in 2012–14. She won the LRTA International Invitation tournament in 2014. Sarah is a huge talent and is currently Claire's main rival, but with a full-time

Claire Vigrass with the World Championship singles and doubles salvers, Melbourne 2011.

(left to right) *Charlotte Cornwallis, Penny Lumley, Alex Garside and Sally Jones before the World Championship doubles final in Bordeaux in 1993.*

job she does not have the time to devote to reducing her handicap.

An emerging talent and potential rival to Claire is the ever-improving Tara Lumley, daughter of Penny, with whom she reached the finals of the 2013 world championships and 2013 and 2014 French Open doubles. In the 2013 US Open she won the singles title, her first 'major'. She is clearly one to watch.

Ladies' Tennis has come a long way since those early days in the 1960s when just a handful of ladies knew the game and most of those would be playing at Queen's, Seacourt or Hampton Court. That first British Open in 1978 was won by Anna Moore, a lawn tennis player who had been playing Real Tennis with men at Seacourt since the club was formed in 1965. Entrants for the Open numbered ten – six from Seacourt and four others. Especially in recent years, with Charlotte Cornwallis and Claire Vigrass, the ladies' game has progressed, like the men's, to a harder, faster way of playing.

Another change has been in the area of professionals. The idea of a lady professional is no longer unusual; indeed, in 2006, Susan Castley, whilst working in the UK, was the first lady to be awarded the Henry Johns Cup by the Tennis & Rackets Association for the best all-round performance by a young Tennis professional.

In the UK, lady players are now eligible for selection for their club teams and to compete in the National League, the Pol Roger Trophy, the Field Trophy and the Brodie Cup, the Bridgeman Cup, the Seacourt Silver Racquet and the Henry Leaf Cup. Annual category tournaments are open to men and ladies, and matches with mixed teams are common, giving those lady players with equal handicaps the chance to play against men of similar standards in everything but strength. In 2011 the Tennis & Rackets Association decided that it could, should it so wish, invite ladies with suitable handicaps to enter its tournaments. If more ladies can achieve the level of handicap reached by Charlotte Cornwallis and Claire Vigrass, the ladies will be on court with the men more in the future.

There has been a healthy increase in the number of promising lady juniors entering both LRTA and Tennis & Rackets Association tournaments, which bodes well for the future.

HISTORIC TENNIS PHOTOGRAPHS

Right: *Very recently excavations at Woking Palace have revealed what is thought to be another Tennis court built by Henry VII. If so, it is the oldest surviving court in the British Isles of which anything remains (see* 16th Century Tennis*)*

Below: *Tennis emblem from* Teatro d'imprese *by Giovanni Ferro de' Rotari, 1623. Ferro dedicated the book to Maffeo Barberini who became Pope in 1623 and whose family were keen Tennis players. Ferro includes an essential feature of aristocratic tennis in the image: a small hole at the bottom of the main wall, in which the players used to place the money they had wagered on the outcome of the match. (see* 17th Century Tennis*)*

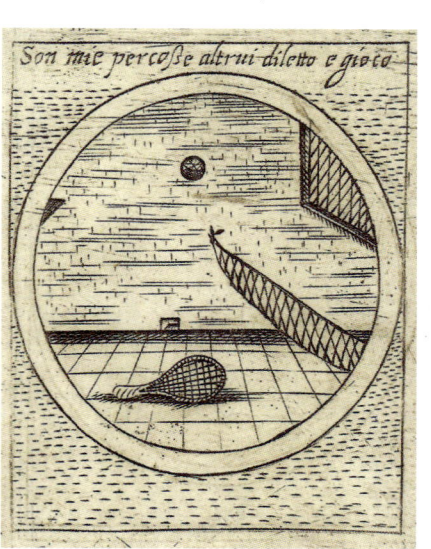

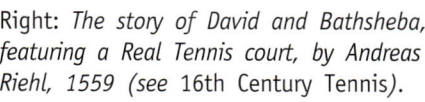

Right: *The story of David and Bathsheba, featuring a Real Tennis court, by Andreas Riehl, 1559 (see* 16th Century Tennis*).*

125

Guillaume Barcellon by Etienne Loys, 1753 (see 18th Century Tennis)

Portrait of family of Janvier-Jacques Charrier, 1780, father of Amedee, who were both famous professionals (see 19th Century Tennis).

The Death of Hyacinth, circa 1618–20, by Caravaggist painter (see 16th Century Tennis).

Putti playing Pallone, by follower of Perino del Vaga, early 16th Century (see 16th Century Tennis).

A game of paume being played alongside a penthouse in the street, from the Book of Hours of the Duchess of Burgundy, circa 1460 (see How Tennis Began*).*

Longue-paume is still being played in the Luxembourg Gardens in Paris (see The Medieval Game*).*

Part II
Rackets

The King's Bench prison in 1822 showing the Rackets courts in the background.

How Rackets Began

Tracing the history of Tennis from its early beginnings in about the twelfth century, it clearly emerges that a number of different games were played under the general umbrella of what Scaino called *giuoco della palla*. There was *pallone* (balloon ball), *jeu quarré*, *jeu à dedans*, *longue paume* and other variations played with various implements, or none at all. But the theme running through them all is that of two sides engaged in combat across a dividing line. Scaino calls it a battle.

Rackets is quite different from this family of ball games in being played against a wall and not across a net. The only game that resembles it is pelota in its various forms. Pelota is of Basque origin and *frontons* are to be found in many a Basque village and town, but they never spread to Northern Europe. Joseph Strutt, in his *Sports and Pastimes of the People of England*, makes no mention of a game of Rackets. The truth is that Rackets started in the debtors' prisons, the Fleet and the King's Bench, in the mid-eighteenth century.

Many a gentleman confined for debt was able to lead a reasonable life if he had friends to support him and many of them, familiar with the game of Tennis, brought their racquets into the prison to while away the tedious hours. They found the high prison walls ideal for this purpose.

Rackets was certainly played at the Fleet in 1749. A humorous poem of that date, written by 'a Gentleman of the College' contains these lines:

Within whose ample Oval is a Court,
Where the more active and robust resort,
And glowing, exercise a manly Sport
(Strong exercise with mod'rate Food is good,
It drives in sprightful streams the circling Blood;)
While those with Rackets struck the flying Ball,
Some play at Nine Pins, Wrestlers take a Fall;
Beneath a Tent some drink, and some above
Are slily in their Chambers making Love;
Venus and Bacchus each keeps here a Shrine,
And many Vot'ries have to Love and Wine.

An illustration accompanying this poem shows a new arrival being introduced to the cook by the chamberlain; he has evidently already met the tapster and the gaoler. In the background a game of Rackets is in progress, from which it is quite clear that Tennis racquets were being used at this early period in the game's history.

In 1780 John Howard published a report on *The State of the Prisons in England and Wales*. He had visited the Fleet in 1776, and writes at one point in his report: 'I mentioned the billiard table. They also play in the yard at skittles, mississippi*, fives, tennis, etc.'

The situation was similar at another debtors' prison, the King's Bench in Southwark. John Howard wrote of the King's Bench: 'One can scarcely even enter the walls without seeing parties of skittles, mississippi, portobello, tennis, fives, etc.'; and later James Neild recorded: 'Part of the ground next the wall is appropriated for playing at rackets and fives.'

In 1780 the old Fleet Prison was destroyed during the Gordon Riots, but it was soon rebuilt, and reopened in 1782. Rackets continued to be popular there and a good view of 'the Bare' or Rackets ground in 1808 is contained in Pugin and Rowlandson's *Microcosm of London*. Rackets at the King's Bench is also illustrated in the *Microcosm of London* and in a print drawn by Theo. Lane, engraved by Geo. Hunt and published by Charles Hunt of Covent Garden.

James Neild wrote on the general state of prisons in England, Scotland and Wales in 1812. He notes that at the Fleet there was:

---

*A form of bagatelle, normally played on a board, but in this case no doubt on the ground.

Surgeon, none. No medical assistance in case of sickness [but] a spacious yard behind the Prison, in which the Prisoners play at skittles, fives, and tennis, etc.

Fives was sometimes confused with Rackets, as appears in a print of 1788 in the Crace collection entitled 'Fives, Played at the Tennis Court, Leicester Fields'. Here again the game involved is clearly Rackets and the print provides the first evidence of the game being played outside prison walls.

A game of Rackets at the Fleet is described in *Finish to Life in London*, by Pierce Egan in 1829.

The fat Knight, it appears, had flattered himself that having received lessons from the late celebrated players at racket, Messrs Davies and Powel, and also some instructions as to the game of fives, under that phenomenon, the late Pat Cavanagh, he laughed outright at the efforts of the 'Young One' and the Corinthian, as mere commoners; and, over his wine, offered to make a match with our heroes, for a 'rump and a dozen!' The proposition was immediately accepted by Tom and Jerry; and Logic was quite pleased that it would afford him a fine opportunity of visiting his old acquaintances and friends on board the 'Fleet'! But the 'uncommonly big gentleman' soon found out his mistake, to his cost and ridicule; also, that talking and doing were widely different; and the loud laugh was now turned against the fat Knight, on his being floored by a false step, in his eagerness to strike the ball. 'Well, my friend,' said Old Mordecai, who was 'blowing his cloud', and watching the movements of the game, with a grin upon his countenance, 'Vere's your rump now? Vat, you have dropped down upon your knees! I

A new arrival at the Fleet Prison.

vill bet de synagogue to a vatch-box, that Young Lambert does not get upon his legs again, vidout some help. Vy, you have made de valls of de Fleet shake again!' The whole of the spectators joined in the laugh at the ridiculous situation of Sir John Blubber; and several of them offered to run for a doctor, 'as they were sure his latter end must have been very much injured by so severe a fall'. Logic and Jerry immediately offered the 'fat Knight' their assistance, who, upon obtaining the use of his legs, was quite out of temper at the satirical remarks and jests levelled against his bulky frame, but more especially with Old Mordecai, and immediately Sir John gave up the match in favour of his opponents.

In 1832 Pierce Egan published his *Book of Sports and Mirror of Life* in periodic issues at threepence each. Number XV was entitled 'The Game of Rackets'.

It includes William Hazlitt's magnificent obituary of John Cavanagh, the fives player, from his essay, 'The Indian Jugglers'. No greater tribute has ever been paid to any sportsman than this eloquent piece of prose.

The full text of Pierce Egan's article is as follows:

THE GAME OF RACKETS is a truly pleasing Sport; not only for the spirit and amusement which it affords to the mind, but the good results which the constitution derives from such active exercise; there is no game, perhaps, not even cricket itself, which combines so well skill with so much bustle, that even an indolent man must be alive to all the movements of the game, while the bat is in his hand. The racket player is always on the move; standing still is entirely out of the question; and two or three games at rackets are calculated to do more good towards the restoration of health, and keep the frame clear from the effects of gout and rheumatism, than the whole contents of Apothecary's Hall. In an enclosed court it may be played all the year round; while in an open court it can only be played in the summer.

It is now eight or ten years since old one-eyed Powell's establishment (so designated from having lost one of his eyes by a ball, while playing a game at rackets) was broken up by his Court being broken down. All who have any acquaintance with rackets recollect him, in his day, a first-rate player, and, after his day, competent to cool the consequence of many who fancied themselves good performers.

The game of rackets is not like tennis, which is played by dropping a ball over a central net, on each side of which the players stand; but, at rackets, the ball is struck against what is called a head-wall, and returned at the bound to the same wall, each player endeavouring so to strike it against the wall that his adversary may not be able to return it; he who does not return it, either loses a point (or, as it is technically termed, 'an ace') or has his 'hand out' that is to say, forfeits the situation in which he would be able to add to his score of the game. People, in general, are not aware of the skill required to play the game well, and the fact is, the better it is played the more easy it appears.

There are several open Racket Courts, independent of the King's Bench and the Fleet Prisons, where gentlemen seldom go voluntarily for the sake of playing, although they take it now and then 'upon compulsion'. There is a good open Court at the Belvidere, Pentonville; another at the Eagle Tavern, in the City Road; and the proprietor of White Conduit House a third; but the fault of these places is that the company is not sufficiently select, and that a gentleman who is fond of the game (and all are fond of it who can play at all) are there compelled to join a miscellany of very respectable persons no doubt, but not of the highest grade in society. As it is, the ardour of some individuals of rank and education in pursuit of the game induces them to overlook the inconvenience to which we have alluded, and we must do the proprietors of the Courts we have named the justice to say that they contrive to keep persons of really questionable character and appearance at a distance.

Independent of 'the old school', there are many first-rate players at present in the height of their performances. There can be no objection to naming and describing the qualifications of a few of the professors, who, generally speaking, have other and very reputable employment besides being racket players. There is no question that Pittman is the best player in England – we do not mean Thomas Pittman, who some years ago held this envied station, but his younger brother John, who is most accomplished at all points – the volley, that is, returning a ball before it touches the ground; the cut, a sharp hit which strikes the ball so low against the wall, and so swiftly, that on its return, there is little or no hop to enable the adversary to strike it; and the twisting drop, given gently and quietly from the racquet, in consequence of which, the ball, after it reaches the head-wall, falls dead at once, and a return is almost impossible. In these respects, and more, John Pittman is perhaps the most perfect player that ever existed, and probably better than his brother Tom, in his best day.

We know that Tom has some old friends who will deny this position, but our opinion is formed after seeing both perform, the one ten years, and the other a short time since. Tom Pittman is still capital, and superior to

John in cramp matches, where he plays under certain disadvantages, in order to make the contest with an inferior player more equal. With his back-hand he can beat nearly all the amateurs, and there are few that can compete with him when his hands are tied together at the wrist, and he is consequently obliged to hold the racket with both; he has beaten tolerable players in this way, and with the addition of a couple of flat irons fastened to his ankles on the inside. If we mistake not, it was he who, some years ago, played with a rolling pin instead of a racket, and won his match. Matthew Pittman may also be reckoned a good player, but he is not to be named in the same century with his two brothers. John Pittman's principal rival is a person called 'Tawney Sam', a small but active little man, who hits with the greatest nicety and precision, and who last year carried away the prize-racket from some excellent competitors, among them a person named Morris, who in some points of the game is superior to Sam, but who is by no means so certain.

Morris has a fine free hit, perhaps the severest in England, and is a fine partner in a four match. His play and that of 'Tawney Sam' are in some respects contrasted, for Sam is all delicacy and finesse, and Morris all force and vigour. Morris has a one-eyed friend, whose name we do not know, who is celebrated for playing under his leg, and who in this manner will contend against any man in England, although, in other points, he is inferior to several. Sowden has been a player quite from his childhood, and, on the whole, is perhaps only inferior to one or two, while, in some particulars, he exceeds them; he would unquestionably be first-rate, and on a level with John Pittman, if he had a good back-hand; but there he fails, and is often put to a difficulty in order to get at a ball with his front-hand, that ought to be returned with his back-hand. He is a capital player to give odds, for then he is perfectly confident; but he seems a little nervous when opposed to a man of equal or greater skill.

These are the prime players of London, and so good that any of them could give what is called 'the odd hand' to country performers: giving the odd hand is about equal to giving one-third of the game. Besides these, there are Lamb and Chapman, and half a score more second raters, besides the players who are in the habit of exhibiting in the King's Bench and Fleet, of whose merits we are not competent to speak. Many distinguished members of the Prize Ring have been good players at fives and rackets, and it may be remembered that the celebrated Jem Belcher lost his eye at the game.

The game of rackets in the Fleet and King's Bench Prisons, has often turned out a source of livelihood to a number of the prisoners who have been attached to the sport. The following anecdote of a man of the name of Hoskins, who was at one period of his confinement the *racket-master*, a capital player, and who altered the game from 11 to 15, may not altogether prove uninteresting to the reader: Hoskins made the Fives Court, which is so much played in during the summer time by the prisoners, and also visitors to the King's Bench Prison; he was an industrious and sober man, and also from his knowledge of the game continually in practice; and waiting upon gentlemen with the bats and balls, and frequently taking a hand in a match, he was enabled to support his family of seven children with credit to himself, and with variable success, until at length a disease settled in his legs, and totally incapacitated him for nearly the last twenty years of his life from following any employment.

Poor Hoskins might have exclaimed with Sterne's Starling – 'I can't get out!' In the year 1798, a material part of the King's Bench was consumed by fire, whether by accident or design was never ascertained; the arched chambers will show where the fire raged, they are the rebuilt part, and said to be fire-proof, so that a fire taking place in any one of these chambers cannot extend beyond it. Hoskins' life was one of continued vicissitudes, which even imprisonment could not abate; he was once the Post-master of the prison. Hoskins was a Cornish man, and of a very good family; his father was a respectable surgeon, and Hoskins was brought up a gentleman; he was here THIRTY-EIGHT years, at the suit of a single creditor, one whom he once called friend and benefactor, and for a disputed debt which he vowed he would never pay. He was a good-tempered, convivial, amiable and benevolent man.

Hoskins was one of the burnt out: he had been at the time so many years a prisoner that no connection remained to draw him back to the world he had quitted; the BENCH was *his* world! and he surveyed its ruins with a pensive and powerful feeling; as though the work of desolation had done its worst, and robbed him of his home. In this state of mind he reared himself a shed from the scattered fragments of the former pile, and lived amidst the ruins, seemingly content, sharing his meal with a poor mouse, who every morning visited him at the breakfast hour, and was fed. Hoskins and the mouse found a home amidst desolation, and they sojourned together in unabated friendship, until the builder's hand disturbed their good harmony and good fellowship.

It is, however, due to Mr Jones, the Marshall, to confess his kindness to this forlorn individual; he supported him for the last two years of his life, and buried him

A word of advice from an old professional in a debtors' prison.

promenade, almost every evening, until the cry of 'all out' occurred, was a complete picture of *le beau monde*. It exhibited some of the most elegant dressed females in the kingdom; the finest, nay, fashionable women who felt not the slightest reproach by visiting their unfortunate friends in 'durance vile'.

In truth, in this 'place of retirement' from the eye of the public, a number of men of fortune, who had 'outrun the constable', had taken up their abode in order to avoid the bore, threatenings, and a thousand other 'little disagreeables' from those persons who 'only ask for their own', to enjoy a bit of *quiet* life, and join in the well-known *chant* –

Welcome, welcome, brother debtor,
  To this poor, but merry place;
Where no Bailiff, Dun, or Setter,
  Dares to shew his measly *face!*

The game of rackets was carried on with great spirit under the patronage of the above fashionable leaders; and the ground was frequently covered with visitors of the most elegant description to witness the trials of skill, and great matches between those celebrated players of the game, Messrs Lewis, Mackey, and Smith.

Since the above period, indeed, almost to a very recent date, the brave Major Campbell has been the principal hero in the field respecting his superiority at the game of rackets. It is too true that the Major had rather a 'long innings', nearly fourteen years in the situation of a lodger to Mr Jones. The high spirit of the Major – his fine stamina – his great activity – and his attachment to rackets – united with considerable experience, and his 'long practice' in the Racket Court, rendered him a first-rate player in every point of view. As a 'gentleman' he had scarcely any thing like a competitor; and with the very best professed players of the day, the Major always proved himself a most powerful opponent. But he is now restored to the society of his friends and enjoying the 'Sweets of Liberty'; and should his king and his country demand his services he is quite ready to make use of *balls* of another description.

Ireland has also given birth to some celebrated racket players – Mr Carney, a gentleman well known in the sporting circles at the West end of the Town, distinguished himself in a number of great matches, not only as a first-rate player, but with eminent success, under the patronage of the late Duke of Richmond: indeed, Mr Carney was viewed by his countrymen as the *crack* player in Ireland. He is also a capital wrestler. Mr Carney won a double match in March 1825, for 300*l* made on the spur of the moment between him

on his decease, in the month of December 1823, after an *uninterrupted imprisonment of* THIRTY-EIGHT *years!!!*

During the *Swellish* times, as they have been since termed by those persons who were in the habit of 'making money' by the rich debtors, when those high-bred ones the late Honorable *Tom* Coventry, and the late Captain *Tom* Best (whose memorable but unfortunate duel with Lord Camelford, gave him great notoriety in the fashionable and sporting world), *sojourned* within the walls of BANCO REGIS, or were otherwise lodged within its *Rules* prescribed for the health of the patients of the Marshall – the GAME OF RACKETS was in high estimation, and very large sums of money were lost and won upon it.

The King's Bench Prison at that period was one continued scene of *gaiety* and *dash* – indeed, it was like any thing else but a place of confinement. The

and the celebrated Mr Hayne, by defeating the '*great gun*' of Windsor, Tom Cannon, in a trial of skill at wrestling, at Ireland's garden, Brighton. Mr Carney likewise won the billiard match with Jonathan Kempfield, on his own table, and also acknowledged the first player in the world; but it is only justice to state that Jonathan gave *seventy* points out of one hundred to Mr Carney. The latter person is also distinguished for throwing a heavy weight to a much greater distance than any other man in the kingdom.

We flatter ourselves that the following sketch of the late *Pat Cavanagh*, so truly celebrated as a Fives player, and also a 'good one' at rackets, will prove highly interesting to the readers of the BOOK OF SPORTS:–

'When a person dies,* who does any thing better than any one else in the world, which so many others are trying to do well, it leaves a gap in society. It is not likely that any one will now see the game of Fives played in its perfection for many years to come – for Cavanagh is dead, and has not left his peer behind him. It may be said there are things of more importance than striking a ball against a wall – there are things, indeed, that make more noise and do as little good, such as making war and peace, making speeches and answering them, making verses and blotting them, making money and throwing it away. But the Game of Fives is what no one despises who has ever played at it. It is the finest exercise for the body, and the best relaxation for the mind. The Roman poet said that "Care mounted behind the horseman and stuck to his skirts." But this remark would not have applied to the Fives player. He who takes to playing at Fives is twice young. He feels neither the past nor the future "in the instant". Debts, taxes, "domestic treason, foreign levy, nothing can touch him further". He has no other wish, no other thought, from the moment the game begins, but that of striking the ball, of placing it, of *making* it. This Cavanagh was sure to do. Whenever he touched the ball there was an end of the chase. His eye was certain, his hand fatal, his presence of mind complete. He could do what he pleased, and he always knew exactly what to do. He saw the whole game, and played it; took instant advantage of his adversary's weakness, and recovered balls, as if by a miracle and sudden thought, that every one gave for lost. He had equal power and skill, quickness and judgment. He could either outwit his antagonist by finesse, or beat him by main strength. Sometimes, when he seemed preparing to send the ball with the full swing of his arm, he would by a slight turn of his wrist drop it within an inch of the line. In general, the ball came from his hand, as if from a racket, in a straight horizontal line; so that it was in vain to attempt to overtake or stop it. As it was said of a great orator, that he never was at a loss for a word, and for the properest word, so Cavanagh always could tell the degree of force necessary to be given to a ball, and the precise direction in which it should be sent. He did his work with the greatest ease; never took more pains than was necessary, and while others were fagging themselves to death, was as cool and collected as if he had just entered the court. His style of play was as remarkable as his power of execution; he had no affectation, no trifling.

He did not throw away the game to show off an attitude or try an experiment. He was a fine, sensible, manly player, who did what he could, but that was more than any one could even affect to do. His blows were not undecided and ineffectual – lumbering like Mr Wordsworth's epic poetry, nor wavering like Mr Coleridge's lyric prose, nor short of the mark like Mr Brougham's speeches, nor wide of it like Mr Canning's wit, nor foul like the *Quarterly*, nor *let* balls like the *Edinburgh Review*. Cobbett and Junius together would have made a Cavanagh. He was the best *up-hill* player in the world; even when his adversary was fourteen, he would play on the same or better, and as he never flung away the game through carelessness and conceit, he never gave it up through laziness or want of heart. The only peculiarity of his play was that he never *volleyed*, but let the balls hop; but if they rose an inch from the ground he never missed having them. There was not only nobody equal, but nobody second to him. It is supposed that he could give any other player half the game, or beat them with his left hand. His service was tremendous. He once played Woodward and Meredith together (two of the best players in England) in the Fives Court, St Martin's Street, and made seven and twenty aces following, by services alone – a thing unheard of. He another time played Peru, who was considered a first-rate Fives player, a match of the best out of five games, and in the three first games, which of course decided the match, Peru got only one ace. Cavanagh was an Irishman by birth, and a house-painter by profession. He had once laid aside his working-dress, and walked up, in his smartest clothes, to the Rosemary Branch, to have an afternoon's pleasure. A person accosted him, and asked him if he would have a game. So they agreed to play for half-a-crown a game, and a bottle of cider. The first game began – it was seven, eight, ten, thirteen, fourteen, all. Cavanagh won it. The next was the same. They played on, and each game was hardly contested. 'There,' said

---

*John Cavanagh died in January 1810, in Burbage Street, St Giles's.

the unconscious Fives player, 'there was a stroke that Cavanagh could not take: I never played better in my life, and yet I can't win a game. I don't know how it is.' However, they played on, Cavanagh winning every game, and the by-standers drinking the cider, and laughing all the time. In the twelfth game, when Cavanagh was only four, and the stranger thirteen, a person came in and said, 'What! are you here, Cavanagh?' The words were no sooner pronounced than the astonished player let the ball drop from his hand, and saying, "What! have I been breaking my heart all this time to beat Cavanagh?" refused to make another effort. "And yet, I give you my word," said Cavanagh, telling the story with some triumph, "I played all the while with my clenched fist." He used frequently to play matches at Copenhagen-house for wagers and dinners. The wall against which they play is the same that supports the kitchen-chimney, and when the wall resounded louder than usual, the cooks exclaimed, "Those are the Irishman's balls," and the joints trembled on the spit!

Goldsmith consoled himself that there were places where he too was admired; and Cavanagh was the admiration of all the Fives Courts where he ever played. Mr Powell, when he played matches in the Court in St Martin's Street, used to fill his gallery at half-a-crown a head, with amateurs and admirers of talent in whatever department it is shown. He could not have shown himself in any ground in England, but he would have been immediately surrounded with inquisitive gazers, trying to find out in what part of his frame his unrivalled skill lay, as politicians wonder to see the balance of Europe suspended in Lord Castle-reagh's face, and admire the trophies of the British Navy lurking under Mr Croker's hanging brow. Now Cavanagh was as good looking a man as the Noble Lord, and much better looking than the Right Honorable Secretary. He had a clear, open countenance, and did not look sideways, or down, like Mr Murray the book-seller. He was a young fellow of sense, humour, and courage. He once had a quarrel with a waterman at Hungerford-stairs, and, they say, served him out in great style. In a word, there are hundreds at this day who cannot mention his name without admiration, as the best fives-player that perhaps ever lived (the greatest excellence of which they have any notion), and the noisy shout of the ring happily stood him instead of the unheard voice of posterity! The only person who seems to have excelled as much in another way as Cavanagh did in his, was the late John Davies, the racket-player. It was remarked of him that he did not seem to follow the ball, but the ball seemed to follow him. Give him a foot of wall, and he was sure to make the ball. The four best racket-players of that day, were Jack Spines, Jem Harding, Armitage and Church. Davies could give any one of these two hands a time, that is, half the game, and each of these, at their best, could give the best player now in London, the same odds.

Such are the gradations in all exertions of human skill and art. He once played four capital players together and beat them. He was also a first-rate tennis player, and an excellent fives player. In the Fleet or King's Bench he would have stood against Powell, who was reckoned the best open-ground player of his time. This last-mentioned player, till lately, was keeper of the Fives Court, and might have used for a motto over his door – '*Who enters here forgets himself, his country, and his friends.*' And the best of it is that by the calculation of the odds, none of the three are worth remembering! Cavanagh died from the bursting of a blood-vessel, which prevented him from playing for the last two or three years. This, he was often heard to say, he thought hard upon him. He was fast recovering, however, when he was suddenly carried off, to the regret of all who knew him. As Mr Peel made it a qualification of the present Speaker, Mr Manners Sutton, that he was an excellent moral character, so Jack Cavanagh was a zealous Catholic, and could not be persuaded to eat meat on a Friday, the day on which he died. We have paid this willing tribute to his memory:

*Let no rude hand deface it,
And his forlorn* – Hic jacet.'

Cavanagh must have been a wonderful player to evoke such a paean of praise from Hazlitt.

Charles Dickens was familiar with Rackets at the Fleet and mentions it on several occasions when Mr Pickwick was unfortunate enough to find himself in that prison. For example:

The area formed by the wall in that part of Fleet in which Mr Pickwick stood was just wide enough to make a good racket court, one side being formed, of course, by the wall itself, and the other by that portion of the prison which looked (or rather would have looked, but for the wall) towards St Paul's Cathedral. Sauntering or sitting about, in every possible attitude of listless idleness, were a great number of debtors... Some were shabby, some smart, many dirty, a few clean... Lolling from the windows which commanded a view of the promenade were a number of persons, some in noisy conversation with their acquaintance below, others playing at ball with some adventurous throwers outside; and others looking on at the racket players, or watching the boys as they cried the game.

The popularity of Rackets at the debtors' prisons made the post of Racket master one that was highly prized. In 1814 there were six Racket masters at the King's Bench prison, administering four courts. They would provide racquets, balls and a ball-boy for a fee. A new racquet cost a guinea and the court fee was sixpence. Out of this the Racket master paid fourpence for two new balls and a halfpenny to the ball-boy, retaining three-halfpence for himself. Extra balls were charged for, and some strong players, we are told, used four balls in a game.

At the King's Bench the appointment of Racket master was made by the authorities, but at the Fleet he was elected twice a year by the prisoners themselves.

The situation drew comment from the Committee of the House of Commons on the King's Bench, Fleet and Marshalsea prisons in respect of the King's Bench:

There is however a practice, which, though it would be injudicious altogether to prevent, might still be put under regulation. The practice alluded to arises out of the racket-grounds. For a long period, a portion of the court has been divided into four racket-grounds, which are held by six masters; the successor to each ground pays something to the first occupant, on his quitting the prison, partly for the purchase of rackets, and partly for the goodwill. One of the present racket-masters paid as large a sum as six guineas. A small fee is paid by the players: and though it be said that any one may play there who chuses, whether he pays or not, yet it is also said that this circumstance hardly ever happens, there being a point of honor felt by the prisoners upon this subject. The objection seems to be, the permission given to strangers to play there; it is an open place, where any one may play, and as such it may become the resort of the idle and the dissolute. As an exercise and amusement to the prisoners it is unobjectionable; as a place of resort, from the opportunity it may furnish to gambling, it is fitting that some regulation should be adopted to limit the practice as at present existing.

And of the Fleet the Committee concluded:

The system of letting the Racket-grounds within the prison exists here as in the King's bench; but from the situation of the Fleet, they are more frequented by strangers. Mr Nixon says that the profit to the holder of each racket-ground may amount to one guinea per week. Your Committee are of the opinion, that this practice requires the same regulations as that which they have pointed out, when reporting on a similar usage existing in the King's Bench prison.

The following is an example of a Racket master's election address of 1841 – interestingly, seeking support from ladies as well as gentlemen:

Ladies and Gentlemen,
The time having now arrived when, in conformity with the established rules of the place of which we are at present inmates, it is customary for such persons as are desirous of becoming elected as Masters of the Racquet Grounds, to canvass your votes, I do myself the honour of addressing you, to request a continuance of the support that on a former occasion procured me that appointment.

I hope I may say my past conduct has been such as to render any protestations for the future, save that it shall be the same, unnecessary.

I feel the situation is one that requires attention and unceasing exertion – not so much from the individual position, as from the circumstance that the amusement and (what is still more vitally important), the health of my fellow inmates is in some measure placed in the hands of the person appointed; and I beg to assure such as may kindly favour me with their votes, and the members of our community in general, that no attention on my part shall be wanted to render the Racquet Court as eligible as possible, and the necessary 'materiel' such as to ensure the approbation of the players.

I believe my application is somewhat late, but I feel confident, by your kind support, of finding myself appointed to the office I now respectfully solicit. I shall do myself the pleasure of waiting on you, for an answer; and have the honor to be,
Ladies and Gentlemen,
Yours obediently,
JOHN ALDRIDGE

2 Coffee Gallery
Fleet Prison
Dec. 11th 1841

Until 1 August 1850 the Racket master was one of the prisoners, and it was not unknown for him to make enough money to pay off his debts and regain his freedom. From that date, however, visitors were barred from the prison courts and the master had to be appointed from outside.

We are given some idea of the amount of play at these courts – and possibly the lack of skill of at least some of the players – by the fact that at the annual restoration of the four courts at the King's Bench, some 250 dozen balls were recovered from neighbouring roofs and gutters.

From the prisons Rackets spread to the taverns, where it was first played in an open court, consisting of little more than a front wall.

A description and rules of the open game are given in Donald Walker's *Games and Sports*, published in 1837.

The Racket-ground presents, in the first place, a very high wall of about forty or more feet in width; and at the top of the wall is a net-work of about five feet in height to prevent those balls going over that happen to be struck above the coping of the wall... The player who commences, or the server, stands in the centre of the ground, in a space marked out for the purpose... If he fail to serve it above the red line, it is called a 'cut' ball; and if it falls inside the line, it is called a short ball, and his opponent may accept it or not, as he chooses... The in-player or server is out if he serves three cut balls, if he strikes the wood which runs along the wall at about eighteen inches from the bottom, if he misses the ball twice with his racket in attempting to serve it, if the ball fall out of bounds, or if he wilfully obstruct his opponent's stroke... If a ball falls on the line, it is called a line ball, and is played again... A marker is always required at this game. His duty is to keep the balls well covered with chalk, so that they may leave a mark upon the wall, to watch carefully whether the ball falls in or out of bounds, to call the game as each stroke is made, and to be ready to be referred to, if necessary, by the players.

From this account it appears that the server had three chances to produce a good service so far as the service line on the front wall was concerned, but seemingly he could serve any number of short services; hand-out could take a short service, but not a 'cut'.

We learn more about the early game of Rackets from J.R. Atkins, a civil servant, whose *Book of Racquets* was published in 1872. It is of very great interest not only in its description of how the game was played, but especially for its illustrations of various types of court and some basic shots.

He, too, in his historical introduction, refers to the game in the singular as 'the game of Racquet'. He ascribes the growth in its popularity to the general spread of 'muscular Christianity' in Britain, and blames the French defeat by the Germans in 1870 'in some measure to the neglect and decay of active recreations in the school life of the French youth of our time'.

Atkins gives a full and illustrated account of all the various types of court that existed in this transitional period – and some that didn't exist which he thought should.

The open court is the same as that previously described by Walker but with the added information that the front wall is about 45ft high. One refinement is that the wood or tiles on the floor marking the boundaries of the court are now coloured with ochre, so that a ball that bounces on them will show a red mark. By this time, too, the server was allowed two attempts at a good service, not three as previously. Game was 11 points in the open court game, 15 in the covered court. Two of the markers' cries unfamiliar to modern ears were 'Over' (beyond the back line) and 'Gone away' (out of court).

In doubles it was necessary to serve alternately into either side of the court. Having done so, the server was responsible for taking balls at the back of the court, while his partner looked after the short balls. Walker notes the vulnerability of an open court to weather, but stresses its great advantage in allowing ample space for spectators.

He describes the covered court, which is identical to those in use today, and the semi-open court, which was popular in Ireland. This was the same as the open court except that it had two side walls sloping gradually downwards from the top of the front wall to a height of about 10 to 15ft at the back. He also describes a small wooden court suitable for a garden and allegedly used in the United States.

He puts forward his own ideas for new types of court. The Great Match Gallery Court is covered, with no back wall, so that large numbers of spectators can be accommodated in galleries at the back of the court. The Tent Court and the Covered Open Court are essentially open with either a temporary or a permanent roof. The Gaslight Close Court is a covered court artificially lit, possibly, he suggests, using white walls and a somewhat larger-than-usual black ball. 'The fact that racquet could be played by gaslight would mark a decided era in the history of the game.'

Atkins offers his readers some advice on playing the game. 'A graceful attitude and mode of delivery and return should also be studied from the outset. A loose and awkward manner of hitting a ball on the part of the player detracts greatly from the pleasure of the spectator.' As for clothes:

Diagram of the open court.

...*a racquet suit can scarcely be too thin. A pair of trousers of white flannel, with a fancy flannel shirt and belt is the costume most in vogue, at least in close courts; but in open and close courts alike a Jersey or vest of some light material – silk, cotton, or merino – is frequently adopted, instead of the shirt, open at the throat. In all cases India-rubber-soled canvas shoes should be worn, to insure firmness of tread and immunity from slipping on the court. Some players (especially in open courts, where there is a danger of a draught) always wear a thin white kerchief round the neck, to avoid cold, and also a light cricket cap. But those appendages are seldom adopted by close-court players.*

He has some sound advice for the young on drinking.

Some young players are apt to indulge too freely in copious draughts of bitter beer and other drinks in the course of a morning rubber. This is unwise, for the result is profuse and excessive perspiration, which is weakening. No doubt a novice, at the outset of his career, is apt to feel rather dry in the mouth, with a parching sensation about the tongue and lips, and he is sorely tempted to 'moisten his clay' as often as he can. Well, this he may do, if 'moistening' is to be taken in the literal sense of the term. The best plan is to wash the mouth out

A well-dressed player, illustrated by J.R. Atkins.

Diagram of the covered court.

Atkins' idea for a Great Match gallery court.

occasionally with a little mild brandy and water, or water pure and simple – retaining it in the mouth for a few seconds before ejecting it... After the play is over, however, we recommend a little brandy and water, or sherry and water, to keep the body from cooling too rapidly. Pale ale or claret at this time, however tempting, is apt with some persons to produce a chilling sensation inwardly – but if the constitution be robust, and the circulation powerful, these drinks may be taken with impunity.

At the end of the book there is an account of the cost of the game: full-sized racquets were from 7s 6d each, boys' racquets from 6s and balls 14s a gross.

The names of some of the taverns where Rackets was popular are known. The most famous, where open court championships were frequently played, was the Belvedere (sometimes spelt Belvidere), Pentonville.

Other courts were to be found in London at the Eagle, City Road; the Yorkshire Stingo, Marylebone Road; the Oxford & Cambridge, Chalk Farm Road; White Conduit House; the White Bear, Kennington; the Rosemary Branch, Peckham; and the Boileau Arms, Castelnau, Hammersmith. Outside London there were courts at the Eglinton Arms, Bristol; the Griffin and Porter Butt, Bath; and the Three Blackbirds, Bristol, as well as at taverns in Cork, Belfast and Birmingham. The Earl of Eglinton and Winton had a court at Eglinton Castle in Scotland.

A contributor to *Baily's Magazine of Sports and Pastimes* wrote that 'it was very much a public house game, and savoured of drinking boxes, long pipes, and beer; but in itself it really was a fine manly game.'

When Disraeli, then aged twenty-six, visited Malta in 1830 as part of a Grand Tour of the Mediterranean and Near East, he wrote of the occasion:

Affection tells here even better than art. Yesterday at the racket court sitting in the gallery among strangers, the ball entered, and lightly struck me, and fell at my feet. I picked it up, and observing a young rifleman excessively stiff, I humbly requested him to forward its passage into the court, as I had really never thrown a ball in my life. This incident has been the general subject of conversation at all the messes today!

The earliest known racquet-maker was Pittman in 1834 – no doubt one of the early champions, Thomas or John, or at least a member of that family. He was succeeded by Jefferies of Woolwich, P. Wilson, E. Bluck, T.H. Prosser of Pentonville Road, F.H. Ayres, Buchanan and Malings, the successor to Jefferies in Woolwich. Pittman also made balls, and after his death the father of John Mitchell, champion in 1846, took over making balls. Later they too were made by Malings. Today the predominant firm making racquets is Grays of Cambridge.

The design has altered little over the last half century, though Grays have managed, to some extent,

The Belvedere Rackets court.

to follow the trend in other racquet sports for lighter frames, even whilst adhering to the use of wood for Rackets racquets. Nowadays, in addition to the standard blue-painted frames, and lighter white-painted frames, Grays also produce a silver-painted *Semi-tec* frame, which has grey reinforcing material bonded to the inside of the racquet-head, similar in concept to their *Semi-tec* Real Tennis frames. Most Clubs and Schools also order frames painted in their own colours, with logos added, but underneath the cosmetics it is a standard Grays frame.

Harrow Sports, a major sporting goods company in North America, have been developing some prototype and production Rackets racquets and working on a drill press to improve the consistency of the stringing holes. Time will tell whether Harrow can challenge the playing qualities of the Grays frame, but Mark Hayden from Harrow Sports is very committed to both Real Tennis and Rackets, and remains undaunted by the difficulties of manufacture encountered so far.

Rackets at the White Bear, Kennington, in 1846.

Nineteenth-Century Rackets

The popular spectator sport of the taverns was destined for a different future in the exclusive circles of public schools and private clubs.

Harrow can claim to have been the first public school to play Rackets, developed in the school yard when that was enlarged in 1821. The sixth and fifth forms used the west wall of the Old Schools, with the east wall of the Milling Ground as a back wall; the rest of the school used the high south boundary wall, which was pulled down in 1889. These 'courts' were full of natural hazards such as chimneys, wire-covered windows, drain-pipes and other architectural features, necessitating an elaborate code of rules.

The game was played with leather-covered balls called 'best fives' and old Tennis racquets, cut down and lightened. Balls and racquets were originally sold by an old lady called Arnold, commonly known as 'Old Polly'; later by Sam Hoare, the Custos (head porter).

Two new courts were built at Harrow in 1850 just west of the Milling Ground, known as the Shell and Fifth Form courts. Both were open and the Fifth Form court had only one side wall.

The earliest covered court was built by the Royal Military Academy at their Woolwich Depot. The MCC built a court at Lord's next to the old Tennis court in 1844, and Prince's Club opened its doors in Hans Place in 1853 with several Rackets courts, two Tennis courts and later a cricket ground.

The main Rackets court measured 60ft x 30ft and set the standard measurements for the future. Before that it had been the practice in open courts to play doubles in a larger version (80ft x 40ft) in which two players would cover the front of the court and two the back. The popularity of the game grew rapidly and at one time there were seven courts at Prince's, but one sad result of the vogue for the covered court was the gradual disappearance of public courts attached to taverns. Rackets lost its popular appeal and became a game for the well-to-do.

A court was built in 1857 by Colonel Lord West at Buckhurst Park, in Sussex, to commemorate the capture of Sebastopol, where he had commanded the 21st Royal North British Fusiliers. About the turn of the century Joseph Bickley re-faced the walls. During the Second World War the court was requisitioned by the Army, but little harm was done.

Thanks to the support of Earl de la Warr it remains the only private court in the country.

Both Oxford and Cambridge had courts and this led to the first University match in 1855. This was limited to doubles, but in 1858 a singles match was also played between the first strings. This remained the pattern until 1921 when two singles matches were played, although the second did not count towards the result until 1937. The first match in 1855 was played at Oxford, but subsequent matches took place at Prince's until that club was demolished in 1886. The match was played at Manchester in 1887 and thereafter at Queen's.

The Victoria Club, Torquay was built at 23 Victoria Parade by Henry Day, in 1859. It included a Rackets court as well as billiard and reading rooms. Rackets was popular at first, but interest waned in the Eighties and by the end of the century the court was being used for badminton. It also served as an overflow dormitory for the adjacent Sailors' Rest when the Fleet was in Torbay. It was reported that 'its sepulchral qualities were occasionally used to good effect in reducing bibulous sailors to awe-struck silence.'

There was a court in Rose Street in Edinburgh. In 1864 Prince Alfred, second son of Queen Victoria, was struck in the eye while playing there.

The first covered court at Harrow was opened in 1865 immediately adjoining the Fifth Form court to the west. It is slightly larger than standard and remains in use today.

The Public Schools Rackets championship began in 1868 at Prince's, was played at Lord's in 1887 and thereafter at Queen's, except for 1941 when the final was played at Wellington.

An interesting former Rackets court still stands in Eastbourne at the Winter Gardens, although it has been partly walled up for other purposes and is now mainly used for storage by Eastbourne Theatres. The walls are intact, however, the glass roof only partly replaced with corrugated iron and above the entrance are still the words 'Racquet Court'.

It was built about 1870 as part of the recreational area known as Devonshire Park, which also comprised two swimming pools (male and female), lawn-tennis courts, Turkish baths, athletic facilities and later, squash courts. Teas and concerts were organised at the Winter Garden. The game also spread rapidly to Army posts in India, Pakistan, St Lucia, Jamaica, Canada, Malta, Gibraltar, Hong Kong, Shanghai, Canton, Burma and Yokohama.

The growing popularity of Rackets led to the building of several club courts: in 1876 two courts at Manchester and in 1888 two others at the new Prince's Club, Knightsbridge, and two at the Queen's Club, West Kensington.

In 1877 the Liverpool Racquet Club was opened, with two Rackets courts and a bowling alley, at a cost of £7000. In 1894 the bowling alley was converted into two courts, for Eton fives and Rugby fives, although not long afterwards the latter came to be used for squash. In 1912 one of the Rackets courts became a small squash court with adjoining squash tennis court, and in 1928 the second was converted into a standard squash court.

In 1919 Archie Hathrill joined the club as Rackets professional. He had been trained at Marlborough and was badly wounded on the Somme during the First World War. When the last Rackets court disappeared he took up the coaching of squash, lawn tennis and fives, and after the club courts were destroyed by enemy action in the Second World War he became Steward. In 1969 he completed fifty years' service with the club.

In Oxford there were two covered courts near St John's College and two more were built about mid century in St Aldate's, close to Christ Church.

Sir William Hart-Dyke, who was at Oxford from 1856 to 1861, recalls that at that time the service line was higher and a high drop service falling awkwardly into the corner was demanded. This was usually returned on the volley. Great use was made of drop shots and it was common in doubles for two players to guard the front of the court in order to get back drop shots, and two the back. There were often long rallies. The game in general was much slower than the modern game.

In Cambridge, Rackets began, as elsewhere, in open courts attached to public houses. One of these, at the University Arms, was kept by H.J. Gray for eleven years before he went to the East Road or Wellington court at the invitation of its owner, Phillips.

In 1858 St John's College opened two new courts (one open and one closed) built at a cost of £1689 5s 9½d and owned by shareholders. H.J. Gray was approached to run both. At first he demurred, having been not long with Phillips at the Wellington court, and suggested his younger brother, William. But William was only twelve at the time and considered too young, so in the end Harry Gray accepted.

The rules of these courts allowed shareholders to book them after 9.00 a.m. and members of the College after 10.00 a.m. The subscription was half-a-guinea a quarter and court charges were:

	Subscribers	Non-Subscribers
Single-wall game	2s	3s
Four-wall game	3s	4s
Each ball	2d	3d

No play was allowed except in slippers.*

In 1864 new shares were issued to cover the cost of roofing over the open court for about £330. In 1883 the shareholders were repaid at par and a fourteen-year lease was granted to Harry Gray at a rent of £100 p.a. Gray surrendered the lease in 1895 and soon afterwards the courts were demolished.

Meanwhile, in 1892, St John's leased a plot of land in Portugal Street to the Rev. R. St John Parry and others, for ninety-nine years from 29 September 1887 at a rent of £18 6s 8d p.a., on which were built two Rackets courts and fives courts. Latterly, the Rackets courts were used for badminton, one even had a wooden floor, and there were also two Eton and two Rugby fives courts and three squash courts; but the whole complex has now been demolished.

The St John's College Archives contain various accounts relating to the Rackets courts, which are interesting in throwing light on the suppliers of balls. The earliest were supplied from 1858 to 1860 by George Erwood, once master of the Royal Artillery court at Woolwich. He charged sixteen shillings a gross for new balls and ten shillings a gross for re-covered balls; and he charged £10 in December 1858 for supervising the protection of the roof windows of the closed court with wire-netting and the staining of the floor.

From 1859 to 1870 balls were supplied by the firm of Jefferies and Malings of Woolwich, who also

---

*St John's College Archives.

charged sixteen shillings a gross and allowed a rebate of six shillings a gross returned.

In 1862, T.H. Prosser, later well-known as makers of Tennis racquets, entered the scene. Evidently, Prosser had trained at Jefferies and Malings, as he proudly claimed on his invoice, together with the fact that he was 'patronized by the Princes' Club'. By 1866 he had moved to Pentonville Road, and in 1882 claimed the patronage not only of Prince's Club, but also of Oxford and Cambridge Universities, Harrow, Eton, Rugby, Cheltenham, Marlborough, Winchester and 'Hailesbury' Schools. He, too, originally charged sixteen shillings a gross for new balls, but by 1882 this had risen to one guinea. For re-covering old balls he charged fifteen shillings a gross, and gave a rebate of six shillings a gross for balls returned.

H. Day of Lisson Grove near Lord's supplied one batch of ten gross of balls at eighteen shillings a gross in 1866, and it seems balls must have been in short supply, for the next year a batch was ordered from T. Watters of Dublin and he continued to supply them for several years. His charge was one pound a gross for new balls, allowing a rebate of four shillings and sixpence for balls returned.

In 1873, Henry Malings of Woolwich appears, describing himself as 'late of the Firm of Jefferies & Malings' and 'By Special Appointment to the Marylebone Club (Lord's)'. He charged eighteen shillings a gross and gave a rebate of five shillings.

H.J. Gray first sent in an account in 1878, describing himself as 'Racquet Manufacturer'. By 1882 he had become H.J. Gray & Sons, 'Racquet & Lawn Tennis Manufacturers'. He charged eighteen shillings and sixpence a gross for Rackets balls and forty-eight shillings a gross for fives balls.

In 1860, members of University Hall, London raised money to build a Rackets court on their premises. This project failed after three years of negotiation with the freeholders, but in 1864 an agreement was reached with the council of University College, London, that they would provide a site, on condition that it was primarily for the use of students of the College and the Hall.

Construction began in August 1864 and the court was completed in November 1865. The architect was Horace Field and the main subscriber, anonymous at the time, Henry Crabb-Robinson. In 1868, Edward Enfield gave a silver cup for the best student of the session, first won by E.B. Hume. A Racquet Club was formed in 1892, controlled by a committee, and an annual dinner inaugurated. In 1895, extensive repairs were carried out to the floor and to front and back walls. A single door was installed to replace the previous double doors in the back wall.

The first home match took place in November 1896 against two Oxford University players, B.N. Bosworth-Smith and H.D.G. Leveson-Gower, University College being represented by C.E. Marriott and G.J.E. Pittman. The same year the court acquired its first professional, N. Naylor, who had recently retired from Clifton College. He was allowed to use the court for practice and to give lessons at one shilling an hour.

In 1898, a silver cup was purchased for the singles championship, and in 1907 it was agreed to present the winner with an inscribed medal. The court was closed during the 1914–18 war but returned to use afterwards. It was still in play in 1930, but shortly thereafter was converted to provide two squash courts and accommodation for the dramatic society and the presidents of the two union societies.

In 1888 Antony Gibbs, grandfather of Lord Wraxall, moved into Tyntesfield near Bristol. He had been a keen Rackets player at Exeter College, Oxford, and decided to build himself a court.

Not far from Tyntesfield he owned another house, Belmont, built in 1780 by William Turner in the shape of a centre block and two wings. The centre block was gutted to provide a Rackets court and the library converted into a boiler house and changing rooms. A complete glass roof was built over the court to give maximum light.

In 1920, Belmont House was required as accommodation for the estate's agent and considerable rebuilding took place. A squash court was built across the middle of the Rackets court, rooms were rebuilt on the ground and first floors and a garage was constructed. The 1920 alterations have since been largely removed.

Another court was built in the nineteenth century at Elvaston Castle near Derby, once the home of the Earls of Harrington.

A most noteworthy event was the building of a court in Melbourne in 1876 by the Melbourne Club. The idea was first mooted in 1868, but other improvements in club facilities, such as a new billiard room, took priority over the Racket court. However, a meeting of forty-five members on 11 February 1876 unanimously passed a resolution proposed by Molesworth Greene and seconded by Captain Standish to erect a court on the Little Collins Street frontage.

The contract went to G.W.T. Freeman and by the end of August the building was virtually complete at a total cost of some £1600. In September a marker was engaged at £1 per week, including clothes and board.

Balls cost twenty-four shillings a gross, shoes eighteen shillings a pair and racquets £1 each.

But its success was short-lived and by 1890 it was being used as a servants' dormitory. In 1891, new quarters were built for the servants and the court restored to use at a cost of £30. There were bursts of activity in the court in 1901 and 1911 but in 1912 the committee accepted a proposal in the suggestion book that the court should be converted to two squash courts. By May 1913, the work had been carried out at a total cost of £120, including a bath and hot shower. Later the site became used as a store-room and then a garage. Recently it has been completely refurbished for use as an art gallery.

Nineteenth-century Champions

All the early champions up to 1862 were trained at the Fleet or King's Bench prisons in the open courts that existed there. The first names known to us are those mentioned by Pierce Egan, and it is difficult to distinguish a true champion with any certainty until Thomas Pittman in 1825. Before him, William Hazlitt refers to John Davies as the outstanding player of his day and to Powell, 'who was reckoned the best open-ground player of his time'. The same two names are mentioned by Pierce Egan, who tells us that the 'fat knight' prided himself on having had lessons from them.

However, Robert Mackay (or Mackey) is usually recognised as the first champion, as he was the first to claim the title in 1820, having defeated James Lewis at the King's Bench. His claim cannot be considered very good, as Pierce Egan makes no mention of it and merely refers to 'those celebrated players of the game [at the King's Bench] Messrs Lewis, Mackey, and Smith'. It seems likely that there was little competition between players in the two prisons, and that Mackay should more realistically be considered champion of the King's Bench.

Another outstanding player of those early days was Matthew Pittman, father of Thomas, John and Matthew junior. It was to Thomas Pittman that Robert Mackay resigned his championship claim when ill-health forced him to relinquish it. Thomas Pittman issued a challenge to all-comers to play him on 26 June 1825 at the Belvedere Gardens, Pentonville, for any sum between £5 and £500. Bad weather prevented play and the match was postponed, but even so no challenger came forward. From that date, therefore, Thomas Pittman can clearly be considered the champion, as Pierce Egan acknowledges.

His first challenger was Thomas Butler of Birmingham. Rackets had been introduced there by a Mr Atkins at the Islington near Pie Bridge, where Butler had learnt to play.

The match took place in the Birmingham court on 21 July 1828, and Pittman won the best of nine games to retain his title.

In November 1834, Thomas Pittman resigned in favour of his younger brother John, who was renowned not only as a great player of volley, drop and cut, but also introduced a new shot, the twist. In 1837, John Pittman played an informal match with John Lamb at what was now the Queen's Bench prison. Lamb won the match, which was thus described in the *New Sporting Magazine*:

> ...*a hasty, unprepared, crude match, knocked up and knocked off – brilliant, but unsatisfactory – smartness, judgment and energy mixed up with those sad antidotes to such qualities – viz. fatness, and previous long and pampered inactivity on one side, and bodily malady and uncultured strength on the other.*

This led to a formal challenge, and a match was arranged to take place on 11 June 1838 at the Belvedere court for £100-a-side, the best of fifteen games, each game then being of 11 points. The players were to be allowed a half-minute rest between rallies and two minutes between games. A special box was built for the referee and umpires. Pittman trained for the match under J. Sowden, one of the players mentioned by Pierce Egan and later the Racket master at the Boileau Arms court. Unfortunately, a thunderstorm prevented play and the match had to be postponed.

It took place on 19 June, and was described by the *New Sporting Magazine* of October 1838:

> *The great struggle for superiority in the art of racquet-playing, was brought to a focus by a match being at length made upon the fairest possible terms, for Lamb to play John Pitman the best of fifteen games, for 100l. a-side, at the Belvedere Court, near Islington, and we attended, with a sincere anxiety for a true game, truly played, and success to the best. The ground was in perfect order, having been attended to with unceasing care by Thomas Pitman, the owner of it, and the well-known brother of the player in the match. The chalking the lines of the court, and other preliminaries were carefully completed. The first of the players we saw, was John Pitman. He was wrapped in a large beaver great-coat; but the neat and powerful shoes carefully put on, clean white cottoned ankles just seen expanding into muscle, under the skirts*

of the coat, met at the other extremity by the light and quiet eye, clear complexion, firm neck, and pale forehead; no man could look better to enter a ring for any athletic sport:— He reminded us strongly of poor honest Tom Shelton, in his palmy days! We shortly afterwards saw Lamb, as quiet and unassuming as his namesake. He looked slim and pale, but there was a good-heartedness about his confidence, and an unaffectedness attending his attire, that could not but pleasantly strike the looker-on.

John Pitman is by very far a more athletic man than Lamb; he has, perhaps, a harder face; a more resolute carriage; but no one could act, on this occasion, with a more controlled temper, or submit with finer moderation to adverse decisions (during the match) than this admirable player. The hour of play, however, arrived; and the coats were thrown aside – the umpires taking their places on an elevated platform in front of the stage. It was an anxious moment!

Pitman first appeared in the court, and showed through his flannel shirt and tight lower white clothing, great muscular symmetry and power. He flashed, or idled, a ball against the court-wall as a race-horse canters before the stand, to give a glimpse of his condition, his action, and his confidence. Lamb was slower to appear; and when he did, there was a lathiness *about his figure which bore not a favourable contrast with the iron frame of his competitor. He was dressed in trousers (always "a questionable shape" with those who come forth as the* Athletae*), and there looked a painful inwardness of the points of the shoulders which promised unfavourably for* lasting.

The Two shook hands. The racquet was tossed up, and Pitman won the hand. *And from this moment nothing could be more cool, precise, or energetic than the exertions of each. Pitman played with the greater strength; Lamb with the finer niceties of the science.*

There can be no doubt in an unprejudiced mind, that the result of this match exhibited the best player. Pitman played with infinite resolution up to the last game, but one; and there the jading of an up-hill journey told upon his harassed spirits, and baffled skill. His temper, however, was maintained with admirable evenness to the last. His early strength, however, was lavished and wasted upon the calm science of Lamb; and (to descend for an instant to minutiae*), we thought he too regularly served Lamb in his favourite corner.*

The match lasted for two hours and twenty minutes, and was won by John Lamb by 8 games to 4. The full score was 11–7, 7–11, 11–6, 7–11, 11–8, 11–7, 11–9, 11–7, 10–11, 9–11, 11–6, 11–5. While his delighted backers collected their debts, Lamb was rewarded with £10. T.J. Gem described Lamb as a 'fair-haired, muscular, little man, very quick upon his legs, with an imperturbable temper, and a head that never lost a chance'.

In September the same year, Lamb was so confident of his prowess that he offered to play anyone, giving them two points in a 15-point game for £100-a-side, but no challenger came forward. Two years later he died of consumption. The championship was now vacant and three claimants appeared. All of them issued challenges to meet anyone on their own court, but none was accepted and during that six-year stalemate the championship must be considered to have been in abeyance. The three contenders were George Erwood, a left-hander trained in the Fleet and then master of the Royal Artillery court at Woolwich; John Pittman, the former champion

John Mitchell.

from the Belvedere court; and Samuel Young from Birmingham.

Eventually, in 1846, John Charles Mitchell, trained at the Queen's Bench and later Lord Eglinton's marker in Scotland, took up Young's challenge. At the time, Mitchell was landlord of the Sea-Horse, Maudlin Street, Bristol (re-named the Eglinton Arms in 1853) where there was a court; he also played at the Three Blackbirds, Ellbroad Street, Bristol, and at the Griffin and the Porter Butt in Bath. Mitchell was another who enjoyed playing at unusual odds. He would often take on a lesser opponent using a kitchen brush, the handle of a racquet or a soda-water bottle. On one occasion, he won a match against a certain member of the peerage, giving him 99 points in 100.

The match, the best of nine games, took place at a recently built close court in Bath Street, Birmingham, and Mitchell won by five games to love. This was the first championship played in a close court and for some time afterwards there were separate championships for close and open courts. However, the main interest gradually shifted to the close-court game of which Mitchell remained champion for the next fourteen years.

T.J. Gem, one of the founders of lawn tennis at Leamington, was among those who regretted the change. He wrote in 1873:

It was the old open-court rackets, the London game, as played in the Queen's Bench and the Fleet, and at the Belvidere ground, Pentonville, that taught men to hit. The play-ground being indicated by white lines, and there being no back or side walls, a man must use his head, as well as his hand, and hit to points, or be out of bounds. There was no hitting with outstretched arm, and trusting to the chapter of accidents there. Those who remember the 'drops' of old John Lamb and George Erwood will know the accuracy that was attained, or have seen the Pitmans, John and Tom, and John Mitchell, with the arm close to the side, swing the racket down below the calf of the leg and give a 'crusher' that took all 'rise' out of the ball, can testify the hits that could be made. It is not contended that nobody can do this now; but certainly the pleasant mode of playing this excellent game does not make it a necessity.

Exterior of the court at Eglinton in 1980.

Mitchell's successor at Eglinton Castle was Patrick Devitt. Lord Eglinton had great faith in his prowess, especially as he had defeated Francis Erwood by 3 games to love in January 1847 and Billy Magrath, from the Kildare court in Dublin, by the same score in January 1848. After this match, a letter appeared in *Bell's Life*, alleging that Devitt was invincible in his own court. This led to an immediate response from Mitchell and Young.

Matches were soon arranged for £100-a-side to be played at Eglinton and Birmingham. On 22 March at Eglinton, Young beat Devitt by 4 games to 2, and on 24 March Mitchell did likewise by 4 games to 3 after a match lasting two hours and twenty-four minutes. At Birmingham in April, Devitt again lost both matches: to Young 0–4 and to Mitchell 2–4.

These details come from the match book of the Racket Court at Eglinton Castle covering the period December 1846 to January 1849 (kindly lent by the Earl of Eglinton). It records matches played between members of the leading families of Ayrshire, Lord Eglinton himself playing in many of them.

The Rackets Court at Eglinton was built shortly after 1839 and is the oldest surviving covered court in the World. The building has been restored to a very high standard, but not as a court. These days it is used for art shows, meetings, conferences and parties. The viewing gallery houses the Eglinton archive.

In 1859, Francis Erwood – originally trained at Lord's and then at Woolwich with his brother George – challenged Mitchell for the championship. The match was to be home-and-home, the best of seven games at each court, for £200 each match. The first match was played at Woolwich on 6 March 1860, the referee being Mr George Prince, founder of Prince's Club, and was won by Erwood, 15–11, 15–2, 15–8, 15–6.

This was a daunting lead for Erwood before the next match at the Eglinton Arms, Bristol, but the courts varied considerably and Mitchell's backers were still confident that he would turn the tables. A packed gallery cheered both players on to the court on 27 March. Erwood won the first two games 15–6, 15–6; Mitchell the third 15–11. The fourth game was vital to any hope that Mitchell had of winning this leg and saving his backers a further £200. It lasted more than half-an-hour and was of very high quality. At 14–14 Erwood was serving at game ball – evidently there was no rule about 'setting' at the time. He won the rally despite a protest that the ball was 'foul' (presumably 'not up') and went on to win the next game 15–9. So the match was his, and the championship. Mitchell was the last great exponent of both the close and open court game.

Francis Erwood was now champion of the close court and his brother George of the open court game. The latter had issued several challenges to all-comers, but no one had come forward. A Mr Ede had on occasion taken up the challenge but on the day no one appeared and he lost his deposit. It was suggested by some that these were ploys to allow Erwood to retain his championship without having to defend it, so when Mr Ede once again took up the challenge for a match on 27 June 1863 no one paid much attention, least of all Erwood who had put on weight and was in poor training.

However, on this occasion Mr Ede's dark horse appeared at the last moment in the shape of Edmund Bailey. Erwood took the lead (11–10, 11–7) with the odds 5–2 in his favour. But his lack of training became apparent and he lost the next two games (7–11, 6–11) to square the match at 2 games all. The final game took place amid tremendous excitement and uproarious cheering; Bailey finally emerged the victor by 11–10.

About this period, the influence of public school and university Rackets began to be felt – particularly

Sir William Hart-Dyke.

in the person of Sir William Hart-Dyke, who learnt the game at Harrow School.

Sir William won the first Oxford v. Cambridge singles for Oxford in 1858 and repeated his victory in 1859 and 1860. In those three years he also won the University doubles match in partnership with J.P.F. Gundry.

In 1862, he challenged Francis Erwood for the championship and the match was played at Woolwich and Prince's for £50-a-side. He won at Woolwich 5–15, 15–7, 15–11, 15–5, 17–18, 15–2, and at Prince's, 14–17, 15–6, 15–3, 15–12, 15–14, to become the first amateur to win the championship – and the first player not to have had his initial training in a debtors' prison! Unluckily, not long afterwards Erwood was struck in the face by a ball while playing against an officer at Woolwich. The injury affected his left eye and he was obliged thereafter to give up match play, so that when Sir William resigned the title the following year he was unable to contest it. Sir William's resignation was to allow him to pursue his political career. He was an MP for forty-one years and among other offices was Chief Whip in Disraeli's government of 1874. He died in 1931 at the age of ninety-three.

Although Sir William himself triumphed in the covered court, he retained a considerable respect for the earlier open-air game that he had known in his youth. 'The close-court game has no doubt wrought changes for the worse so far as the best features of Rackets are concerned,' he wrote. 'The game as played in open courts against a single wall was a severe test of skill and judgment in placing the ball, and accuracy as regards strength and measuring distance.'

The resignation of Sir William heralded the reign of the eldest of the famous five Gray brothers of Cambridge, who laid the foundations of the firm of Gray's of Cambridge, which has served court games so well by the provision of first-class racquets and equipment for so long.

The eldest was Henry John Gray, born in 1837 and introduced to Rackets at the age of ten at the open court of the University Arms. In 1855, he founded the firm, making racquets at the St John's College courts, where he was then the professional. He remained there for many years and taught the game to his four brothers. He challenged Erwood, whose injury prevented him from playing, and H.J. Gray assumed the title in 1863.

In 1866 he resigned in favour of the second brother, William, born in 1846. At the age of sixteen, William had become champion of Ireland by beating Dalton, the marker at the Vice-Regal Lodge court in Dublin.

He was soon called on to defend the title when a challenge came from Joseph Foy of Aldershot.

The match took place for £200-a-side in 1866. William won the first leg 4–0 on 26 February at the University Club court in Dublin and the second 4–2 on 19 March at Aldershot.

William is generally regarded as one of the outstanding players of all time for skill and grace. Alfred Lyttelton wrote of him:

When the greatest masters of various games are passed in review, none seem to have quite equalled Gray in the combination of absolute success with absolute gracefulness... But if perfection in a game be attained by combining success in results with beauty of style...no one to my mind, has brought any game to such perfection as that to which William Gray raised the game of Rackets.

Present at this match was Auguste La Montagne, a Canadian, who with the support of friends had built a court on 13th Street, New York, near Sixth Avenue, called the Gymnasium Club.

La Montagne offered to match the American champion Fred Foulkes against Gray in a home-and-home match. Gray at once accepted this challenge for £1000-a-side, but La Montagne considered this too high and the match was eventually made at £500-a-side.

Gray, accompanied by his sixteen-year-old brother Joseph and his trainer, Walters, arrived in New York aboard the steamer *City of Washington* on Monday, 25 March 1867 and took up residence at the Buck's Head Hotel, 15/17, Crosby Street. He immediately started to practise at 53/55, West 13th Street, finding the court strange as it was 10 ft longer than an English court, with a wooden floor.

The *New York Clipper* described him as 'a handsome, intelligent, young fellow, twenty-one years of age, about 5 ft 8 ins in height and of a slender, well-knit frame, combining strength and activity in admirable proportions'.

Frederick Foulkes was an Englishman by birth, from Leamington. He had trained in Rackets at Oxford before emigrating to Canada in 1858. From there he won the American championship in a match against Billy Devoe. In 1865 he again defeated Devoe and was engaged by the New York Gymnasium Club. The *New York Clipper* described him as 'about thirty-four years of age, stands 5 ft 6 ins and is light and active in build'.

The first leg of the contest began on Monday, 22 April and the gallery was crowded to capacity, not only by members but also by 'the élite of the sporting and turf men of the city'. Betting was fierce and, having started at 100–80 on, Foulkes, by the start of the match, was at evens.

Gray started brilliantly, won the first game 15–5 and the betting on him went to 100–60. But Foulkes evened the match by winning the next game 15–5. Gray won the third game 15–6 and a very close fourth game followed which after 13 all and set 5 Foulkes won 18–15 to even the score again. Gray came back strongly in the fifth game and led by 14–8, looking a certain winner, when he broke his racquet. Foulkes scored six points in succession to make it 14 all and went on to win the next three points and the game 17–14. By now the betting was 500–400 on Foulkes, but with the score 6–5 in Gray's favour, a storm broke and the light deteriorated to such an extent that further play had to be postponed until the following day.

On resumption, Gray was in top form. He won the unfinished game 15–8 and the final game 15–0. 'This decided the American half of the game and amid loud cheers Gray tossed up his Racquet.'

The second leg was played at the Ulster Club in Belfast on 6 July 1867. There the match was reported by the *Belfast News*, which described Gray as 'exceedingly graceful, presenting an open, expressive and intelligent countenance. Like his opponent Foulkes, he is very quiet and gentlemanly in his manner, and possesses a frame combining strength, activity and symmetry in an unusual degree.' Gray's practice was somewhat hindered by an injury to his thumb, sustained on the passage from America in the *City of New York*.

This second match began as closely as the first. Foulkes won a hard-fought first game 15–8. Gray made sure of the second 15–3. Another close game was won by Foulkes 15–10, followed by another game to Gray 15–12. Then Gray broke away to win the next two games and the championship 15–5, 15–9.

The *Belfast News* concluded its account: 'The game was carefully marked and most audibly too by Richard Armstrong.' How rarely do we give praise to all those markers who give such wonderful service to the game of Rackets.

Gray was now undisputed world champion, but alas, in 1875, at the early age of twenty-nine, he died at Eton College, where he was in charge of Rackets.

A match was arranged for the vacant title between Joseph Gray, another brother, then the Rackets professional at Rugby School, and H.B. Fairs. Fairs and Stevens were Rackets professionals at Prince's Club, known to the members as 'Punch' and 'Judy'. The nickname 'Punch' passed from father to son and 'Punch' Fairs Junior was later to become Tennis world champion. 'Judy' Stevens was for many years the Rackets professional at Harrow.

The match was played in January 1876 at Prince's and Rugby; each player was allowed four days' practice in his opponent's court. The stake was £250-a-side and, as in prize-fighting, the players were weighed in. Fairs, almost twenty-seven, scaled 8 st 10 lbs in playing costume, and Gray, aged twenty-five, 9 st 12 lbs.

After a nervous start by both players, Fairs won the first leg at Prince's 15–7, 15–1, 15–9, 6–15, 15–12. Gray put up greater resistance at Rugby, where the court was 5ft longer and 2ft wider than that at Prince's with a paved floor and poor light. Nevertheless, Fairs was victorious again 15–3, 18–14, 8–15, 15–11, 3–15, 17–14, and became the new champion. E.O. Pleydell-Bouverie wrote of this match in the Badminton Library:

The 1876 match presented great differences of style, Gray's self-contained neatness being in marked contrast to 'Punch's' slashing sweep. 'Punch' was a little man, standing somewhere about 5 ft. 4 ins., but the manner in which he reached the ball would lead one to suppose that he had the length of arm of a six-foot man. That arm too was extraordinarily loose. To see him hit gave rather the impression of a racket being slung at the end of a rope, so flexible were his joints. As he played it seemed as though H. Fairs was an arm and a racket, the rest of him being a mere appendage.

Once again tragedy intervened and Fairs died two years later. Joseph Gray became the third brother to hold the championship and he did so unchallenged for nine years.

Joseph Gray went to New York in 1881 to play a match for $1000 against the American champion, Harry Boakes, professional in charge of the Quebec court. Joseph was accompanied by his brother Walter, and Boakes practised with the New York professional, Robert Moore. In a preliminary to the challenge match, Walter Gray easily defeated Robert Moore. In the words of the *New York Herald* reporter: 'he played with Moore as a cat would do with a mouse…Moore was simply a novice in the hands of Gray.'

Reporting on the challenge match itself, he writes:

The grandest exhibition of scientific manipulation of the racket ball that has ever been witnessed in this city was the great championship match yesterday afternoon at the New York Racket Club.

Joseph Gray started a clear favourite, but Boakes played brilliantly to win the first game 15–12. The second game was fiercely fought, Boakes making much use

Harry Boakes and Joseph Gray.

of the drop shot, while Gray played a more orthodox straight up-and-down game. Eventually Boakes won it 18–15 and went on to take the third game easily 15–7. Gray appeared exhausted by his efforts in the second game and Boakes relaxed. It was a costly mistake. Gray won the fourth game 15–4, the fifth game 15–5, and the sixth game 15–5, to square the match at 3 games all.

Boakes seemed thoroughly rattled and Gray was completely on top. The last game was a cliff-hanger, as Boakes pulled himself together and made a final effort. The score reached 7 all, 12 all, 13 all, set 5. Amid intense excitement Gray just won it at 18–15.

'Never has such a thrillingly exciting contest been played in racket circles in this city,' proclaimed the *New York Herald*. 'The play was of the sharpest nature, and of a rarer description than the lovers of the game here have been accustomed to seeing.'

The first challenge to Gray's title came from Peter Latham of Manchester.

Latham was born in Manchester on 10 May 1865. He started his career as a boy, aged eleven, at the opening of the Manchester Racquet Club in 1876. When that club was compulsorily acquired by the London and North Western Railway Company for their Exchange Station, he moved with the club to their new premises in Blackfriars Road, Salford.

There he prospered and gave notice to the champion of his ability when in 1886 he defeated Walter Gray by 4 games to 2.

The challenge match was played on 20 April 1887 in the new court at Rugby and on 27 April at Manchester. Immediately under the announcement of the match in *The Field* appears an interesting advertisement for 'Naylor's Racquet Court Wall Black'.

Gray was considerably the elder of the two players – he was thirty-seven, Latham twenty-two. He put up a tremendous struggle in his home court and after a very close match with many long rallies emerged the victor by 4 games to 3, (15–7, 10–15, 9–15, 15–10, 15–9, 8–15, 15–8; 87 points to 79).

But at Manchester, Latham had it all his own way, largely thanks to his service, and won 4–0 (15–2, 15–4, 15–11, 15–9). The account of the match in *The Field* is of interest in mentioning that balls of excellent quality were supplied by Gradedge (*sic.*) of Woolwich, H. Gray of Cambridge, and Prosser of London.

This was too much for the Grays to tolerate, and the following year Latham was challenged by brother Walter, the Rackets professional at Harrow from 1873 to 1878 and after that at Charterhouse. Again, largely thanks to his dominating service, Latham swept ahead in the first leg played on 25 April 1888 in the recently opened court at Queen's Club, where he was in charge of Rackets. He won 2–15, 15–12, 15–7, 16–14, 15–6. In the second leg, played on 2 May at Charterhouse, he faced a partisan gallery, who cheered Gray's every stroke and largely ignored Latham's. The match was close but he won the two games necessary for overall victory out of four games played, the score being 8–15, 15–4, 12–15, 15–9.

This was the last time that one of the Gray brothers competed in a world title match. Four out of five brothers had contested the title over twenty-five years and three of them had held it for twenty-one – an astonishing performance. The fifth brother, George, born in 1852, was also an accomplished player and was in charge of Rackets at Haileybury.

Another American challenge was received in 1891 for a stake of $5000 from George Standing, originally trained at Prince's Club but then Rackets professional at the New York Racquet Club and the outstanding player in the USA. The match was played on 25 April at Prince's Club and on 2 May at Queen's Club, Latham winning with great ease by 5 games to 0.

At Prince's the score was 15–6, 15–12, 15–9, 15–5. Latham required one more game at Queen's to assure himself of overall victory and this he won 15–6.

Latham's predominance at Rackets enabled him to turn his attention to Tennis with an ambition to win the world championship of that game too – a feat he accomplished in 1895.

He was challenged again for his Rackets title by George Standing in 1897 and this time the match was to be played in England and America, for a stake of £2000. Standing practised with Walter Gray at Charterhouse; Latham retired to the salubrious air of Blackpool and practised at Manchester and Liverpool.

The first leg was played at Queen's on 16 October 1897. The marker was André of Winchester. Latham had played very little Rackets since his victory over Standing in 1891, as he had been preoccupied with winning the Tennis world championship. He started the match in fine form, however, serving well, showing his old power of return and mercilessly killing the easy ball. He won the first game 15–11, the second 15–13 after being 0–9 down, the third 15–10 and went on to lead 9–3 in the fourth. Standing rallied at this point, caught up at 13 all and won the game 18–15, but Latham took the next 15–4 to lead by 4 games to 1.

The second leg was played in New York on 27 November. 'Reporters were not admitted,' wrote *The Times* correspondent, so that the exact score of the match is not easily determined, although Latham certainly won it by 4 games to 3. He started well to take the first game 15–2. The second was a particularly brilliant game, just clinched by Standing 18–16. Standing went on to win the third game 15–3, but the tremendous pace had told on him and he could not prevent Latham from seizing the fourth game and so retaining his title. The match was played out, the score of the last three games from Latham's viewpoint being 9–15, 16–15 (or 17–16), 15–1.

Latham's last defence of his title was in April 1902, against Gilbert Browne of Prince's Club. This match evoked very little interest and the gallery was at half capacity to see the champion retain his title with the greatest of ease, by 4 games to love at the Queen's Club – 16–13, 15–10, 15–0, 15–2 – and 1 game to love at Prince's, 15–11.

After this match Latham resigned the title, undefeated. He was undoubtedly one of the outstanding Rackets players of all time. He dominated the world scene for fifteen years and was Tennis world champion for ten. When he died in November 1953, at the age of eighty-eight, *The Times* obituary was headed 'A Peerless Player of Rackets and Tennis', and of his Rackets play recorded that his 'wonderful wrist, balance, and footwork gave him a grace and perfection of style and movement, and there was no weak point in his armour.'

George Standing v. *Peter Latham in New York 1899.*

TWENTIETH-CENTURY RACKETS

1900–80

IN AN ARTICLE in the *National Review*, E.B. Noel gives some interesting facts about Rackets courts at the beginning of the century. Those that had gone out of play between 1900 and 1919 were at Eastbourne, Oxford, Torquay, Newcastle, Liverpool, Leamington and some private courts. Existing in 1914, in addition to those at public schools, were courts at Queen's (two), Prince's, Lord's, University College London, Manchester, Cardiff, Cambridge, RA Woolwich, RMA Woolwich, RE Chatham, RMC Sandhurst, Aldershot, Colchester and Shorncliffe.

Abroad there were courts in Malta, Gibraltar, Hong Kong, and at the Hurlingham Club, Buenos Aires, where the Argentinian championship was played.

Thanks to the South Glamorgan Library, the story of the Rackets court in Cardiff is known. It was built in 1878 for £2300 by the 'Cardiff Racquet and Fives Court' Company in Westgate Street, adjoining Cardiff Arms Park. At that time it was the only building on the west side of Westgate Street. In 1880 lawn tennis courts were added.

The premises, known as Jackson's Hall, were later used as offices.

WORLD CHAMPIONS UP TO 1939

When Peter Latham resigned as world champion, a match was arranged to decide his successor between Gilbert Browne, Latham's last unsuccessful challenger in 1902, and J. Jamsetji, a professional from Bombay and the best player in India. Despite the very different playing conditions in England, where the game was somewhat faster, Jamsetji was victorious by 6 games to 2 in a match played at Queen's Club and Prince's Club in May 1903. This was a dull and disappointing match and a considerable anti-climax after the great days of Latham. At Queen's Club, Jamsetji won 15–11, 18–16, 13–16, 15–8, 15–4, and he won the necessary

The Rackets court in Cardiff.

two games at Prince's, 15–5, 11–15, 15–5, to become the first overseas player to hold the championship – and as yet the only player not to come from Britain or America. Perhaps sadly for Rackets, his very talented countrymen from the Indian continent have taken to squash rackets.

A unique event took place in 1908 when Rackets for the first and last time was included in the Olympic Games, held that year in London. The competition was played at Queen's and comprised both singles and doubles. It was hardly an Olympic event – indeed it was a bit of a farce.

Only English players entered and the Amateur champion and likely winner, E.M. Baerlein, retired before playing a match. In the second round, just one match was played as three players retired. Worse still, in the final, H.M. Leaf scratched as a result of an injured hand and the Gold Medal was won by E.B. Noel. Noel had won the Amateur championship in 1907 and was runner-up to Edgar Baerlein in 1908, but his Gold Medal should more deservedly have been awarded to him for his service to Tennis and Rackets as historian and Queen's Club secretary.

The doubles, a similar fiasco, was won by V.H. Pennell and J.J. Astor.

Jamsetji was challenged in 1911 by Charles Williams, a brilliant young professional who at the time had just gone to Harrow. Williams, when at Prince's, had defeated T. Jennings of Aldershot in a home-and-home match in April 1909. He had then challenged Walter Hawes of Wellington for the Professional championship and beaten him too, in a match played at Queen's and Princes's in June 1909.

A match for the British Open championship was arranged between Williams and Edgar Baerlein, but had to be postponed (owing to an accident involving Baerlein). It took place eventually in January 1911 and provided a marvellous match for spectators. Williams was one of the hardest hitters of the ball, with a wonderful backhand; Baerlein was full of skill and determination. In the first leg at Queen's, Williams easily won the first game 15–2, but Baerlein took the next two 18–15, 15–6. Unfortunately, he was hit on the elbow at the end of the third game, and this caused him difficulty in throwing up the ball for service. He fought hard but just lost the fourth game 10–15. Thereafter Williams, hitting harder than ever, swept away to win the last two games 15–3, 15–3.

The second leg at Manchester also provided a magnificent match, but Williams was at his best, making few mistakes, and Baerlein was mainly on the defensive. Williams again won 4–2 (15–8, 7–15, 15–2, 18–16, 8–15, 15–2).

It was hardly surprising, therefore, that when he played Jamsetji for the world title he overwhelmed him. On 25 April at Queen's he won 4–0 (18–15, 15–2, 15–9, 15–8) and on 13 May at Prince's he won the necessary game for the match (15–7). Jamsetji at the time was thirty-nine, Williams twenty-two.

Charles Williams was a remarkable player and a terrific hitter of the ball. Practising for a championship match, he would play single-handed against a formidable amateur pair, Cyril Simpson and Roddy Williams, and beat them. As a young man he had the alternative of becoming a Rackets professional or a welterweight boxer. He used to say that he regretted his choice as he'd have 'murdered' his pugilistic opponents as he did his Rackets ones.

Charles Williams and Jock Soutar.

The next twenty-five years were dominated by two great rivals, Charles Williams and Jock Soutar, who had trained together as junior professionals at Prince's Club. Soutar was a Scotsman, brought over to Philadelphia in 1907 by Frederick Tompkins to assist him at Rackets. He was also no mean Tennis player, and held the US Professional Tennis championship from 1925 to 1928 until the arrival of Pierre Etchebaster. He also dominated the American squash rackets scene from 1916 to 1925.

However, in 1912 George Standing was still American Open champion and it was he who challenged Williams for the world title. Williams was on his way to America to play this match on the maiden voyage of the *Titanic* when she struck an iceberg and sank on 14/15 April 1912, with the loss of 1513 lives. He spent nine hours adrift in a small boat before being rescued, and naturally the match was called off. By 1913, Standing had retired and Williams agreed to meet Soutar in a home-and-away match.

The first leg, played at Queen's Club, was distinguished by hard and accurate hitting and by Soutar's heavily cut service, which never rose from the back wall. Williams

World Rackets championship, 1914. Standing (left to right): G. Standing, F.C. Tompkins, Jay Gould, Tom Pettitt, W. Wilson Potter, Edgar Scott, Milton Berger. Seated (left to right): Peter Latham, Foxhall Keene, James Potter, Charles Williams, W.H.T. Huhn, Jock Soutar, Percy Houghton, George H. Brooke.

took this formidable service on the volley and his brilliant backhand and speed about the court brought him victory by 4 games to 2 (6–15, 15–12, 15–11, 15–10, 9–15, 15–6).

Soutar won the second leg in Philadelphia with great ease by 4 games to 0 (15–2, 15–8, 15–4, 15–3). The day was extremely hot and Williams never showed his true form in the conditions. His hard hitting broke all his best racquets, but he refused to accept the offer of one of Soutar's – indeed every encounter of these two friends was marked by good sportsmanship. Soutar thus became the first American world champion.

The war years prevented any further matches between them until 1922, when a return match was played in Philadelphia and New York. Williams gained a modest lead in Philadelphia by 4 games to 3, but in New York, Soutar again won four games in succession to retain his title by 7 games to 4.

Soutar's next challenger in 1927 was a fellow-American, William 'Blondy' Standing, nephew of George Standing. But Standing was unable to cope with Soutar's mighty service and lost by 8 games to 1 in a match played in New York and Philadelphia.

In 1923, Charles Williams went to America to join the Chicago Racquet Club as senior professional. In 1929 he made a third effort to defeat Jock Soutar, this time successfully. Once again he started well, winning the first leg in Philadelphia by 4 games to 2, but this time he made no mistake in the second leg in Chicago, winning by 3 games to 1 – an overall victory of 7 games to 3. He was champion again, eighteen years after he first won the title and sixteen years after losing it to Soutar. He was now undisputed master of the game.

Charles Williams's death in 1935 left the world title vacant, and an Anglo-American home-and-home match was arranged to fill it. From Britain came David Milford.

Milford was a remarkable master of the game; not a hard hitter but with perfect control which enabled him to place the ball with consummate skill and bring off an unexpected winner from a difficult position. He had an astonishing record, which would have been even better but for the intervention of Hitler.

He first distinguished himself at Rugby, winning the Public Schools championship in 1923 and 1924. At Oxford he represented the University for four consecutive years (1925 to 1928), winning all four doubles matches against Cambridge and two out of the three singles played. His only defeat was in 1927 at the hands of Peter Kemp-Welch.

He first won the Amateur singles in 1930. That same year he won his first hockey cap and gave up Rackets to concentrate on hockey. He did not enter for the

Amateur Rackets again until 1935, when he won it, beating Ian Akers-Douglas in the final. The following year he won the final by 3 games to 1 against John Pawle. The match was very close at 1 game all and 9 all in the third when Milford was hit on the back of the head by a ball off the back wall. After a short break the match was resumed and Milford never lost another point.

The same year he challenged Albert Cooper for the British Open championship and beat him by 8 games to 3. Milford rates the first leg of this match as the best Rackets he ever played. After losing the first game 17–18, he went on to win by 4 games to 2. This victory gave him his chance to win the world championship in 1937. Quite unexpectedly, Norbert Setzler had beaten Bobby Grant for the North American Open, so it was Setzler not Grant who opposed him. Had it been Grant, Milford modestly doubts the outcome, for in three matches he played against him (admittedly two of them 'friendly'), he never won a game.

The first leg was played at the New York Racquet Club on 16 January 1937 and provided a thrilling match. The first four games were exactly divided, the score being, from Setzler's viewpoint, 9–15, 15–9, 10–15, 15–10. Setzler won the fifth game 15–8, but lost the sixth 12–15 to make the score 3 games all. In the final game, Milford led most of the way up to 11–9, but Setzler made a great effort, overtook him and went on to win the game 15–12 and the match by 4 games to 3.

Setzler played some magnificent, hard-hitting Rackets, but Milford showed how good he was at varying the pace and length of his shots. He did well to hold Setzler to so close a score on the New York court.

The second leg was played at Queen's Club on 10 April 1937 immediately following Milford's fourth (and third consecutive) win in the Amateur singles. This time the match was one-sided and Milford ran out an easy winner by 4 games to 0 (15–4, 15–4, 15–9, 15–12). He was amazingly quick about the court, with a wonderful eye and wrist, and at times played strokes of sheer genius when caught on the wrong foot. He also served much better than Setzler.

Milford was a very worthy world champion and the first amateur to hold the title since Sir William Hart-Dyke in 1862. He retained his Amateur title in 1937 and 1938, beating Robert Riseley and Ian Akers-Douglas in the finals, but did not enter in 1939. The doubles took place in term-time and Milford was a master at Marlborough, so he entered just once, in 1938, partnered by Peter Whitehouse – and won.

OTHER CHAMPIONS UP TO 1939

Between the wars many fine matches were played for the British Open championship. Until he left for Chicago in 1925, Charles Williams was the dominant player and was recognised as such without challenge. Cosmo Crawley recalls asking Walter Hawes why no Professional championship was held between 1918 and 1925 and receiving the reply: 'What's the good of having a Professional championship with Charlie here? He could give any of us at least 10.'

On his departure, however, a Professional championship was held at Queen's in January 1925 and won by Charles Read without conceding a game. This made him Professional champion of Rackets and squash; he had previously been Professional champion of lawn tennis too.

In April 1929, the first match was played at Queen's for the Open championship between Read and J.C.F. (Cyril) Simpson, the brilliant left-hander who had won the Amateur championship in 1926, 1927 and 1928. Simpson set a fast pace and won the first leg by 4 games to 1. On the second day he won the first two games to secure the championship.

A return match was played in April/May of the following year, again at Queen's. Simpson was recovering from a bad cold and knew he could not last a long match. He threw everything into one great effort to win by 4 games to 0, but the last game was very close with Read starting to play well.

In the second leg, Simpson needed one game for the match and this he won 15–10. Read was no mean opponent, as the score might suggest. The match was played out on the second day and he won all four of the next games.

Cyril Simpson was an attractive personality and player. He was none too good in the morning, and he was apt to do most of his training at the Café de Paris. On one occasion, however, he recalls arriving at Queen's in this pyjamas for a 10 a.m. match and winning. It was a great loss to the game when he broke both wrists in an accident and was unable to play again.

He had a wonderful doubles partner in R.C.O. (Roddy) Williams, and together they toured Canada and the USA in 1925. They met the redoubtable C.C. Pell and S.G. Mortimer in the Canadian final and scored a remarkable victory after trailing by 1 game to 3 and 7–14. However, the tables were turned in New York when Pell and Mortimer won by 4 games to 2.

Simpson recalls that in those days in the United States, instead of the receiver asking for a let if he was in danger of hitting the server, he would shout

out 'turning' and strike the ball as he pleased. This was a terrifying situation for the server, and Jay Gould recalled two occasions when a player lost an eye as a result of turning.

Simpson also noticed that American players laid their spare racquets in the court under the board. He was told by Peter Latham that there was a good reason for this. When he played George Standing for the world championship in 1897, he broke a string and went out for a new racquet to find that the strings of all his racquets had been 'nicked'!

In 1931 Lord Aberdare had won the Amateur championship and beaten Simpson in the process. He challenged him for the Open, and the match was played at Queen's in January 1932. Aberdare was forty-six, and there was some doubt about whether he could last a long match against a younger opponent. But in the event he won by 6 games to 2, mainly thanks to his murderous service – 'probably the best in the world', wrote *The Times* reporter. However, even his service could not prevent him losing the title the following year to Ian Akers-Douglas, Amateur champion from 1932 to 1934. Akers-Douglas easily won the first leg in March 1933 (4–0) and Aberdare retired.

In 1934 Akers-Douglas was challenged by Albert Cooper, then Professional champion. It is remarkable that in 1932 Charles Read, then aged forty-two, had been able to beat Cooper in the final of the Professional championship (3–2), but in a challenge match the following year Cooper had his revenge, winning (6–3).

The match took place at Queen's in February 1934. Cooper won the first leg 4–2 (15–4, 15–12, 15–9, 8–15, 9–15, 18–13). His victory was due almost entirely to service and he made fifty-two service aces in the course of this leg of the match. This enabled him to sweep ahead and lead by 3 games to 0. He appeared to tire, however, and Akers-Douglas played brilliantly to win the fourth game, his last stroke being a wonderful 'get' off the back wall, played between his legs. He continued to dominate in the next game and when he went to 9–1 in the sixth it looked as if he might well square the match. Cooper fought back hard, caught him at 13 all and went on to clinch the match by winning the set to 5.

On the second day, Cooper needed three games to win the title, but the match was far from over when Akers-Douglas, very fast about the court and serving well, won the first two games 17–15, 15–13 and went on to lead 8–0 and 12–4 in the third. This was the vital game. Cooper, making a great effort, levelled the score at 13 all and won it 18–14. In the fourth game, Akers-Douglas began to slow up as the terrific pace of the match began to tell, and Cooper won it 15–10 to make the score 2 games all.

The final game was all Cooper's. He raced ahead to 12–0, then served his hand out. Akers-Douglas managed to take 2 points, but Cooper got back in and went to 14–2. At match point, there was an accident. Akers-Douglas, in his anxiety to win the point, ran right across in front of Cooper as the latter was about to make a forehand kill. Cooper checked his stroke but the ball hit Akers-Douglas on the back of the head. He reeled and collapsed in the corner. After a five-minute interval, although still dizzy from the blow, he gallantly insisted on resuming the match. One service from Cooper won him the game 15–2 and the Open championship.

In 1936 Cooper lost the Open title to David Milford. The first leg was played at Queen's in April and produced a gem of a match. The first game, won by Cooper 18–17, was a wonderful exhibition of Rackets. Cooper's glorious hitting was matched by Milford's speed of foot and wonderful ball control. Milford emerged the winner by 4 games to 2. The second leg was inevitably disappointing by comparison. Milford's persistence of return wore the edge off Cooper's powerful hitting and he won by 4 games to 1.

The first international Rackets match between Great Britain and the United States took place in America in 1928, when a cup was presented recording an American victory by 3 matches to 2. The United States team comprised Clarence C. Pell, Stanley G. Mortimer, Hewitt Morgan and Charles J. Coulter; the British team was Cyril Simpson, the Hon. Clarence Bruce, Peter Kemp-Welch and George Huband. During the visit Bruce won the Canadian singles and Bruce and Simpson won the US doubles.

A second match, in 1930, resulted in another American victory by 5 matches to 1. The American team was largely the same: Pell, Mortimer, Morgan and Coulter, with the addition of E.M. Edwards; for Britain, Bruce (then Lord Aberdare) and Kemp-Welch returned and were accompanied by Dr H.W. Leatham and L.D. Cambridge.

The Prince's Club

Many players had happy memories of the Prince's Club in Knightsbridge, and its atmosphere of sportsmanship and good company. It enjoyed royal patronage – Edward VII, then Prince of Wales, was present at a match to open the first Tennis court between the Hon. Alfred

Lyttelton and Charles Saunders; George V was often in the club and his sons, later George VI and Duke of Windsor, played many games of squash there. It was particularly convenient for officers stationed at Knightsbridge Barracks and, in fact, by special dispensation the orderly officer was allowed out of barracks to use its facilities.

Originally it contained two Tennis courts, two Rackets courts, two bowling alleys, a billiards and card room, a Turkish bath and club rooms, including a luncheon room and the famous Oak Room. It was very much a male preserve except for Miss Shepherd, who sat in a box by the main door and presented members with their bills for games, meals, baths, and suchlike before they left the building. But in its last few years, ladies were admitted to play squash and to dine.

Soon after the First World War, one of the Rackets courts was converted into three squash courts, none of them standard size, all with a stone floor and all with one wooden side wall formed by the partition – except for the centre court which had two wooden side walls.

Two games were played in the bowling alleys: American nine-pin bowls with 14lb balls (with no finger holes) and 'cocked hat', played with three pins and a small ball. The boys would get sixpence an hour for replacing the pins, apparently an enjoyable task except when the Earl of Stair was playing. He was 6ft 8ins tall, immensely strong, and would pick up the largest ball as if it were a mere golf ball and hurl it furiously down the hog-backed alley, to the terror of everyone in the vicinity, while at the same time instructing the pins in stentorian tones what to do. They usually did.

Many of these boys were later to become great names in Tennis or Rackets or both. Henry Johns had been a ball-boy at Queen's before going to Prince's in 1925; Jim Dear followed him there in 1927, when E.J.G. Johnson, Ted's eldest son, went to Brighton. At that time R.C. Dickinson was the head professional, with William Webb and Alfred Dooley to assist him. Other boys were Bill Tutt and Geoffrey Dawson.

The courts were the scene of many famous matches – seven Tennis world matches and four Rackets world matches. Here, too, the Army and Navy Rackets championships were regularly played and the inter-regimental doubles. Despite its popularity, the club was often facing financial crises.

One such, in the early Thirties, led to the appointment of a new board of directors of Prince's Club Limited, with Max Heilbut as chairman. This did not affect the club committee, which continued under the chairmanship of Douglas Barry. A deputation from the board, led by Max Heilbut, visited the landlords – the Prudential Assurance Company Limited – who always treated the club most generously. As a result of this meeting the rent was reduced, and four standard squash courts were built in one of the Tennis courts. A small end of the Tennis court was left over, and much thought and ingenuity went into ideas for a new game – without success. Other improvements were made. The club was now to remain open for dinner, having previously closed at 6 p.m., and periodically club dinners were held, followed by exhibitions of Tennis and Rackets by leading players. Some remarkable – and uninhibited – matches were played.

A proposal to redevelop the site and reconstruct the club on the top floor was abandoned because of the weight factor. During the Second World War, the premises were taken over by the Army Post Office and afterwards were demolished to make way for flats.

Post-war Revival

The end of the war led to a burst of Rackets activity everywhere and the start of two new competitions. The Army Open Rackets (Victory) competition was first played in 1946 when the old-timers, Cosmo Crawley and Peter Cazalet, won a remarkable victory over the much younger Geoffrey Atkins and Ronnie Taylor. The following year, Crawley won again, in partnership with Kenneth Wagg, and in 1948, the last year it was played, the winners were R.A.A. 'Bimby' Holt and Kenneth Wagg.

More enduring were the Combined Services (past and present) competitions, first played in 1949, when Geoffrey Atkins won the singles, and the doubles in partnership with Ronnie Taylor. The singles were last played in 1967, but the doubles have continued and have been won by many different pairs. The brothers Pugh (Tim and Tom) have won it on three occasions.

To mark the end of the Second World War and the revival of Rackets, Cosmo Crawley and Clarry Pell planned a British Rackets team tour of North America to take place in January/February 1947. The British team consisted of Cosmo Crawley (captain), Ian Akers-Douglas, Bimby Holt, John Pawle, Ronnie Taylor and Kenneth Wagg. They were accompanied by Jim Dear, who was on his way to play for the world championship and able to give them invaluable practice, beginning with some keep-fit squash on the *Mauritania* at sea.

The hospitality extended to the team wherever they went was beyond praise – in fact, it was remarkable that they managed to achieve such excellent results in

A toast to conclude the 1947 tour of America – standing (left to right, those in full view): *Jim Dear, Eddie Rogers (drinking), Clarry Pell, Bobby Grant, Malcolm Kirkbride, Cosmo Crawley, Ronnie Taylor.* Seated: *Bimby Holt, Ian Akers-Douglas, John Pawle.*

the circumstances! Their position was made the more embarrassing by the strict financial controls of the immediate post-war years, but American generosity and some assistance from Lord Astor of Hever overcame all difficulties. In the Rackets world at least, the tour was a practical expression of Anglo-American solidarity in defence of freedom, individual achievement and good sportsmanship.

The tour began in Chicago with the Western Amateur championships. This was a tuning-up affair in the absence of the best American players and resulted in all-British finals. Bimby Holt won the singles, defeating his doubles partner, Ronnie Taylor, in the final by 3 games to 2, and Cosmo Crawley and John Pawle won the doubles, beating Holt and Taylor 4–2 in the final.

Next port of call was Montreal, for the Canadian Amateur championships. This visit produced the best singles match of the whole tour when, in the final, Bobby Grant beat John Pawle by 3 games to 2 (13–18, 12–15, 15–9, 15–8, 15–10). It was an outstanding match between two brilliant players, both of whom believed in classical Rackets, hitting the ball hard and low, going out for the kill at every stroke. The score indicates how close the match was, but not the tension of the final game when Pawle led 9–3. This magnificent match was witnessed by the Governor-General of Canada, Earl Alexander of Tunis, who presented the trophy.

In the doubles, Crawley and Pawle were again victorious, this time beating the best American pair, Grant and Pell, by 3 games to 1.

Next stop on the tour was Tuxedo, for the Gold Racquet, where the team failed to distinguish itself and left Grant to win it in a final against fellow American F.F. de Rham.

They moved on to New York, for the US singles championship. In the semi-finals, Holt had an unexpectedly easy victory over Grant by 3 games to 0 (16–14, 15–8, 15–8) and Dick Leonard beat Pell by 3 games to 2. In the final, Holt easily won the first two games (15–8, 15–2) but Leonard took the

Anthony Ward and Richard Greenwood, the Eton pair in 1944.

next three (15–11, 15–12, 15–7) to win the championship. Holt, however, had his revenge in the Pell Cup, beating Leonard by 4 games to 0 (15–2, 15–5, 15–7, 15–6).

The US doubles championship was played in Philadelphia and won by Holt and Taylor, who beat Leonard and M. Kirkbride 3–0 in the final.

The highlight of the tour was the international match played at the New York Racquet Club on 31 January and 1 February and won by Great Britain by 5 matches to 2. Three doubles matches were played on the first day: Crawley and Pawle beat Grant and Pell by 3 games to 1; Holt and Taylor beat Leonard and M. Kirkbride by 3 games to 1; Akers-Douglas and Wagg lost to R.L. Gerry and F.F. de Rham by 3 games to 1. Great Britain thus had a 2–1 lead.

In the singles Pawle lost to Grant by 0 games to 3; Holt beat Leonard by 3 games to 0; Taylor beat de Rham by 3 very close games to 0 (16–15, 17–15, 15–12); Crawley beat Pell after a real cliff-hanger match by 3 games to 2 (15–12, 5–15, 8–15, 15–6, 18–17).

THE WORLD CHAMPIONSHIP AFTER 1946

In 1946, Milford resigned his world and Open titles, but continued to play in the Amateur, appearing in eight finals between 1947 and 1955, of which he won two, in 1950 and 1951. He was narrowly defeated by John Pawle (3–2) in the finals of 1947, 1948 and 1949. In the 1948 final, he actually had two match points in the fourth game and in the fifth led 10–0. Pawle, with a badly blistered hand, was forced to change his grip and served a stream of aces to win the match.

In the doubles he found a magnificent partner in his Marlborough colleague, John Thompson. They won ten times – 1948, 1950–52 and 1954–59.

Milford's resignation meant a vacancy for world champion; moreover, Cooper decided not to defend his Professional championship, and there was no North American champion. To fill these gaps, a considerable programme of matches was organised in 1946.

First, the Amateur championship was revived, and in the event was won by John Pawle. Then a match was arranged at Rugby and Queen's Club between Peter Gray and Jim Dear for the Professional championship – won by Dear 8–0. Then Dear, rather unfairly it seems in retrospect, was to play first John Pawle, then Peter Kershaw, Amateur champion in 1939, for the Open championship.

Dear won both these matches. On the first day at Queen's against Pawle, he won 4–2. This was a very closely fought match for the first four games, but then Pawle faded and lost the last two games, 0–15, 1–15. Dear took the second leg at Queen's 4–1. He went on to play Kershaw at Manchester where he won 4–0, although Kershaw put up stiff resistance in the last game, leading by 14–8 and eventually losing it 15–17. In the second leg at Queen's, Dear won 4–1, but only after Kershaw had put up a fierce fight for the first three games.

Bobby Grant, the brilliant American amateur from New York, was expected to beat Kenneth Chantler, the Montreal professional, for the North American Open, so Dear went off to start practising in New York. Unexpectedly, Chantler beat Grant in a very close match 15–6, 16–18, 13–16, 15–9, 15–1, 11–15, 18–15 after Grant had led 10–4 in the final game.

Dear had to play in Montreal with only a few days' practice. However, he won a convincing victory (15–9, 16–17, 15–10, 15–11, 15–11). Chantler put up a good fight. There were many long rallies and plenty of hard hitting, but it was Dear who, every so often, played a very effective drop shot to win a valuable point.

In his own court Dear swept to victory by 4 games to 0, having in reality won the championship when

Jim Dear and Jack Johnson.

he won the second game. But great praise is due to Chantler. He was the first Canadian to dispute the world championship and he did not have the advantage of close competition in Montreal. The game of Rackets, particularly in Canada, is greatly indebted to him. His enthusiasm and encouragement have introduced many a young player to the game and his friends are to be found wherever there is a Rackets court.

Jim Dear was born in Fulham in 1910, two years after his brother William. Both started work as ball-boys at Queen's, aged fourteen. William was very good at lawn tennis; Jim hated games and was nearly sacked when he was seventeen for showing no promise. In 1927, he was offered an apprentice post at Prince's, when E.J.G. Johnson left for Brighton; he accepted it reluctantly and joined Bill Tutt, Bill Webb, Alfred Dooley and Henry Johns.

At Prince's he was the only Rackets and squash professional, playing squash on the sub-standard courts converted from the second Rackets court. On one of these courts he beat Amr Bey, who was practising for a Bath Club Cup match against Sir John Child, and from that day on Amr Bey would take him to other courts in London to practise with him. Dear won the Professional Squash championship in 1935, beating Donald Butcher at the Conservative Club and Prince's, but he lost the Open to Amr Bey in 1935, 1936 and 1937. Finally he won the Open championship he so richly deserved in 1938, defeating A.E. Biddle.

He gained some Tennis experience by playing Tutt from time to time for a glass of beer.

During the Second World War, Dear was in the RAF, grounded by a perforated ear-drum, and able to play just the occasional game of squash. Prince's closed during the war and he returned to Queen's in 1946.

As a player, Dear was outstanding for his all-round ability on the court and his wonderful ball control. Not an especially hard hitter, he was a master of the angles and of change of pace. He could produce a beautifully timed drop shot even from a volley, which earned him many an important point. He was vulnerable, perhaps, against a really hard hitter such as Bobby Grant, but in general his accurate eye and swift footwork made him difficult to beat.

After Chantler, Dear faced a sterner task. John Pawle had emerged as the outstanding amateur of the post-war years. He won the Amateur championship in 1946, defeating Ian Akers-Douglas in the final, and in 1947, defeating David Milford, albeit narrowly, in the final. Now he challenged Dear for his world title.

The match took place at Queen's Club on 21 and 28 January 1948. The first day's play was of the highest quality and must be considered one of the greatest matches ever played at this level. Dear won the first game 15–5, and no one can have given Pawle much hope at this stage. But in the second game, he started to serve well and play brilliantly in the rallies. Full of confidence, he surged ahead to take the next three games, 15–6, 15–12, 15–9. Unfortunately in so doing he injured his back, and Dear, playing consistently well, fought back to win the next two games, 15–9, 15–5, and square the match at 3 games all. The final game was a tremendous struggle with Dear always slightly ahead. He reached 13–9; Pawle crept up to make it 12–13, but after several changes in hand Dear finished it off at 15–12 to lead by 4 games to 3 on the first leg.

After the brilliance of this first leg, the second was almost inevitably an anti-climax. It started well, Pawle winning a very close first game 18–15 and Dear the second 15–10. But in the third game Pawle's back again handicapped him greatly. Dear won that game 15–1 and the next 15–7. Pawle put up a courageous fight for the fifth game, but Dear emerged the winner 16–13 to retain his title.

John Pawle had another go at Dear in 1951, the match taking place at Queen's on 24 February and 3 March. Dear won the first game 15–6. Pawle fought back to win the next two games 15–7, 15–12, and lead by 2 games to 1. But from then on Dear was in control, covering the court with amazing speed and winning the next three games 15–2, 15–7, 15–6. In the second match, Dear was even more dominant and won the three games necessary for overall victory 15–9, 15–9, 15–6, as well as the fourth game 15–8.

His next challenger was Geoffrey Atkins, who had learnt to play Rackets at Rugby and was to be the

Geoffrey Atkins.

outstanding player of the next fifteen years. He had won the British Amateur singles in 1952 and 1953 and also held the American and Canadian Amateur singles titles when he challenged Dear for the world and British Open championships.

The match was played at Queen's Club on 15 and 22 April 1954. In the first leg, Atkins took an early lead and Dear, who was somewhat out of match practice, was having great difficulty taking his underhand twist service. Atkins won the first three games 15–9, 15–1, 15–8, playing brilliantly and seemingly invincible. But Dear's experience as a match player and his fighting qualities came to his rescue. From 2–5 down in the fourth game he won 13 consecutive points to take the game 15–5 and went on to lead 14–10 in the next. But Atkins caught up at 14 all and Dear set 3. This was the crucial moment of the whole match and the pendulum swung this way and that in an agony of suspense for the players and spectators.

Atkins went to 1–0. Dear put him out and went to 2–1. The game seesawed and Dear had three game points. Finally, luck took a turn, and Atkins put him out with a winner off the wood. He went on to win the next two points and the game to lead 4–1.

Dear, however, was not down-hearted and started the second leg of the match in overwhelming fashion. He won the first game 15–10 and, after a fierce struggle, the second 18–17. He took the third game 15–6 to lead by 3 games to 0.

Atkins rallied splendidly in the fourth game and won it 15–10. Now came the vital game. If Dear could seize it, he would win the second leg 4 games to 1 and the match would have to be decided on points. Such was the points situation that he had to prevent Atkins from getting more than 7 points. In the event, Atkins was now in full flood and forged ahead to 7–3. One magnificent service and he had won the championship. In fact, he went on to win the game 15–10 and lose the final game 16–18.

Another great champion had arrived. He had shown his mettle in this splendid match, and a sporting temperament that refused to be panicked. Whenever and wherever he played, Geoffrey Atkins was always a shining example to all of perfect court manners.

His style of play was not unlike that of Dear, relying more on accuracy and consistency than big hitting. He seldom put the ball on the back wall and at his best seemed never to make a mistake. His footwork was phenomenal and he covered the court seemingly without effort. His forehand was particularly good and his service very effective. These qualities enabled him to take Willie Surtees to five games in the US Open in New York and the US Amateur in Chicago in 1971 at the age of forty-four.

With this match, Dear lost the British Open championship as well, but it was typical of his fighting spirit that in 1960, at the age of fifty, he regained it, defeating John Thompson by 7 games to 4.

The same year, Atkins went to work in Chicago and his name was engraved often on the board of winners of the American and Canadian national championships. He won the US singles in 1954, 1955 and 1956, when he also won the British singles, and in 1959 and 1960. In that year he returned to Britain and again won the singles.

His first challenger for the world title was J.W. (James) Leonard, who had won the Amateur championship in 1961 and repeated his success in 1962, narrowly defeating Atkins in the final by 3 games to 2. This established his right to challenge, and the match took place at Queen's Club on 19 and 26 January 1963. Atkins won the first two closely contested games (17–15, 15–12), lost the third (8–15) but won the next two (15–11, 15–6) to lead by 4 games to 1 at the end of the first day's play. On the second day, he won the first two games (15–8, 15–6) and thus retained his title by 6 games to 1.

Leonard was an intellectual player, concentrating on length and placing the ball. His very heavily cut service was awkward to take and he made few errors in the rallies. He was calm and intelligent, never easy to beat.

The next challenger was Charles Swallow, who had narrowly beaten Atkins by 3 games to 2 in the final of the 1964 Amateur championship. The match was played at Queen's on 31 March and 4 April 1964. Swallow started well and was leading by 2 games to 1 when he had to stop for a while, suffering from cramp in his right hand. On play being resumed, Atkins narrowly won the next game (18–14) but took the last two games with ease (15–6, 15–2) to end the day 4 games to 2 up.

On the second day, Swallow again started in great form. He won the first two games (15–9, 15–11) and led 13–12 in the third. This was a vital turning point; Swallow could have won the championship had he won this game. But Atkins, always at his best in a crisis and showing no emotion, went coolly on his way to win that game (18–14) and the next (15–12), squaring the match at 2 games all. Swallow was still in with a chance when he took the fifth game (15–12), but Atkins made sure of overall victory by winning the sixth game (15–8). The second day's play provided a

James Leonard.

Chicago, 30 March 1967. Geoffrey Atkins (seated second from the right) still unruffled after his 4–2 win in the first leg of his world title defence against James Leonard *(racquet in hand).*

crowded gallery with a magnificent spectacle. Swallow at his peak was one of the finest strikers of the ball in the classical tradition and seemed at times invincible. Only Atkins's calm temperament, speed of foot and power of return enabled him to weather the storm and emerge victorious.

Swallow came very near to being the greatest player of his day and his matches with Atkins were great demonstrations of Rackets at its best.

From 1964 to 1966 Atkins was working in Japan and played no Rackets. When he returned to Chicago, he decided to resign the British Open championship. A match was arranged for the vacant title between the two best players of the day, Leonard and Swallow, and was won by the former, by 7 games to 4. Leonard then challenged Atkins again for the world title. The first leg of the match took place at the Chicago Racquet Club on 30 March 1967, the second at Queen's Club a week later.

In Chicago, Atkins established a lead of 4 games to 2. In London, he dominated play, winning the first three games and conceding just 18 points.

Three years later, it was Swallow's turn again to have a go at the champion, having clearly proved his right to do so by winning the Amateur championship in 1968 and 1969 and the British Open championship in January 1970, defeating Leonard by 7 games to 4.

The match was played in Chicago and London in April 1970. In Chicago, Swallow had shown excellent form in practice with Mark Faber and looked a likely winner; but pre-match nerves and a sleepless night when opposed to the almost casual confidence of Atkins got him off to a bad start. He rallied towards the end and the last two games were hard-fought, but Atkins emerged the winner by 4 games to 1.

This was a heavy handicap with which to start the London leg, played as usual at Queen's Club.

H.R.H. the Duke of Edinburgh and Lord Aberdare at the 1968 T&RA dinner.

Nevertheless, Swallow made a tremendous effort. The first game produced Rackets of the highest quality and was just won by Swallow 18–16. He swept on to take the second game 15–4, but he could do no more. Inexorably, Atkins fought back to win the next two games 15–7, 15–5 and retain his title.

The following year Geoffrey Atkins, now aged forty-four, resigned the world championship after a record reign of seventeen years, a tremendous achievement amid fierce competition from many younger players.

It was agreed to arrange an Anglo-American match to decide the next holder of the title. The North American Racquets Association nominated Willie Surtees, an Englishman resident in the United States. Surtees had learnt his Rackets at Rugby, too, and was first string in the pair that won the Public Schools Rackets championship in 1965.

It was not easy for the British Tennis & Rackets Association to nominate anyone. The year before, Swallow had decided to resign as British Open champion and the title had become vacant. It was agreed that a preliminary competition should be held between Charles Hue Williams, Tom Pugh, Richard Gracey and James Leonard to decide who should have the right to play the Amateur champion, Martin Smith, for the vacant title.

In the event, Pugh won the eliminator, but unfortunately contracted a virus infection that prevented him from playing Smith, who was recognised as British Open champion. When the world title fell vacant in 1971, Howard Angus had not yet won the Amateur championship. He was narrowly defeated by Smith in the final, but reversed this in 1972. Nevertheless, it was agreed that Angus would meet Pugh in a play-off to find the world championship challenger – the winner of that match would play Smith for the British Open title and the right to play Surtees for the world title.

Angus never dominated the Rackets scene as he did Tennis, but his great speed and wonderful footwork made him a formidable player. He had a good, accurate service, but it was his power of retrieval, backed with his physical fitness, that won him many matches. He had shown Rackets talent since his time at Winchester, where he was in the pairs reaching the final of the Public Schools championship in 1962 and 1963. In 1965 and 1966, he played Rackets for Cambridge and thereafter embarked upon his outstandingly successful Tennis career with victory in the Amateur championship and the MCC Gold Prize in 1966.

In the play-off, Angus beat Pugh 4–0 and Smith 6–2. He played Surtees for the world title in two legs, at Queen's Club on 7 January and in Chicago on 15 January 1972. Angus romped home at Queen's Club, winning by 4 games to 1. Surtees was unlucky not to win the last game, having led by 13–6 and 14–10, but eventually lost it 14–17.

Surtees started with that considerable disadvantage in the second leg in Chicago. However, Angus too suffered from disadvantages. He was not familiar with the court and, because of central heating, necessary when the outside temperature was 50 degrees below freezing, the gut strings of his racquets had to be replaced with nylon. This had a considerable effect on his service, not helped by the one-service rule. In the first game, Surtees raced ahead to 13–7, serving well; Angus caught him at 14 all, but lost the game 16–17. Surtees won the second game 15–10 and swept on to an easy win in the third. The tension during the fourth game was even greater than in the first, with the championship at stake.

Angus fought gamely to lead 6–1, 12–8 and 13–11, but Surtees levelled the game at 13 all and went on to win the next five points and the world championship.

The following year, 1973, Angus turned the tables in no uncertain fashion. He had already retained his Amateur singles title when he went to the USA with a Jesters team. In the course of this visit, he began with Tennis, winning the Tuxedo Gold Racquet, beating Eugene Scott in the Bathurst Cup and winning the US Amateur Tennis title with victories over both brothers Bostwick. He then turned to Rackets and was due to play Surtees in the final of the US Amateur Rackets championship in Boston. Unfortunately, following an accident, Surtees had to have six stitches in his right eyelid, and the match was postponed. Nevertheless, the world title match went ahead as planned. It was played at the Chicago Racquet Club on 17 March during the Club's fiftieth anniversary celebrations.

Surtees started the first game in fine form and led 14–9, but Angus fought back to equalise at 14 all and won the game 17–15.

Angus went from strength to strength and, although Surtees had a chance in the third game, Angus won the next three games to lead 4–0 in the first leg. This match was also counted as the postponed final of the US Amateur championship, and as a consequence Angus achieved the feat of being Amateur champion of Rackets and Tennis on both sides of the Atlantic. The next day they played again for the North American Open Rackets title and this time Surtees had his revenge after a fine match, by 3 games to 2.

The second leg took place on 24 March, as usual at Queen's Club. After losing the first game 8–15, Angus won the second 15–3 to become the first left-handed world champion. He went on to crown this fantastic year of success by winning the British Amateur Tennis championship and the MCC Gold Racquet – both for the eighth year running. His ambition was now set on the Tennis world championship, so as to hold both

Willie Surtees in play against Howard Angus.

Rackets and Tennis titles simultaneously and equal the achievement of Peter Latham.

However, Angus retained his Rackets amateur title in 1974 and 1975 and played another match with Surtees for the world title in March 1975. This time the position was reversed. Surtees won the first leg in Chicago by 4 games to 0 and came to Queen's Club requiring one game to give him back the title. The first game was very hard fought and Angus emerged the victor at 15–12. He now seemed to be in with a chance, reaching 11–1 in the second game. At this point, Surtees struck his best form, but Angus struggled on to reach 13–8. Surtees took the next three points to trail 11–13, but then Angus served an ace to reach game-ball at 14–11. He failed to clinch the game and, although he had another point for the game, Surtees finally won it 17–14, to reclaim his title.

The following year, Angus triumphed over Eugene Scott to win the Tennis world championship and needed to win back the Rackets title if he was to hold both at the same time. He challenged Surtees once again and a fourth match was arranged between the two rivals.

The first leg was played at Chicago on 5 March 1977 and resulted in an overwhelming victory for Surtees by 4 games to 0. Angus fought hard in the final game and lost it by the barest margin 16–17, but in the other three games he could manage no more than 18 points against a champion in top form.

When the second leg was played at Queen's on 12 March, Surtees required one game to retain the championship; he won the first game 15–11 in less than a quarter of an hour.

Surtees's style of play was good to watch. He had few weaknesses, an outstanding backhand, and he hit the ball hard and low. He was very fit and had plenty of stamina for a long match. He had many of those match-winning qualities that distinguished Geoffrey Atkins in his day as world champion.

OTHER PROMINENT PLAYERS, 1900–1980

One outstanding amateur player of Rackets and Tennis was Edgar Baerlein, beaten by Charles Williams in an eliminating contest for the world Rackets championship. He was also a brilliant all-round games player. He considered himself the best at the Eton field game and certainly expected to get a Blue for either rugger or soccer at Cambridge until he broke a knee playing Rackets in his first term. He played golf, lawn tennis and ice-hockey for Lancashire.

At Rackets, he first came to prominence in the Oxford and Cambridge match, winning all four of his

Edgar Baerlein.

singles matches from 1899 to 1902 and the doubles in 1899, 1901 and 1902 with E.B. Noel and F.B. Wilson as his partners. In his first year after leaving university, he won the Amateur singles, lost in the final of 1904 to the great H.K. Foster, but won again in 1905, 1908 to 1911, 1920–21 and 1923. He won the doubles while still at university in 1902, from 1904 to 1905 with E.H. Miles, in 1909 with Percy Ashworth, and in 1914 and 1920 with G.G. Kershaw.

But even he would admit that when he was Amateur champion Peter Latham could give him 7.

Ronny Aird recalls playing as Baerlein's partner in the Amateur Rackets doubles in the 1920s. During a long rally he took a ball just inside Baerlein's half of the court. The next shot went straight to Baerlein, who left it and lost the point. To an astonished Aird he explained, 'After you took the last one, I thought there was no need for the further play on my part.' Aird also recalls Baerlein's wise advice when hand-in to try to hit the ball between one and two feet above the board, but when hand-out between one and two inches.

His achievements at Tennis are listed elsewhere and, although he never played much lawn tennis, it was the general opinion that he would have been among the top flight of players.

James Agate, the well-known critic, was an admirer of Baerlein's ball-playing skill and makes mention of him in his writing. Of his character he writes that his passion was an ice-cold demonstration of superiority and the quickest, most exact brain he had ever known. He reports that Baerlein told him he would have been Rackets world champion but for his extraordinarily long wrist, which got him out of difficulties into which, without it, he wouldn't have dared to get; and also that he had calculated the odds against an after-life at a shade worse than 5–2.

One of his great rivals at both Rackets and Tennis was the Hon. C.N. Bruce, later Lord Aberdare, a brilliant player of all ball games and an especially attractive batsman for Middlesex.

Bruce had won the Public Schools Rackets championship for Winchester in 1904, the University singles for Oxford in 1908 and the University doubles the same year with H. Brougham. Four years in succession (1920–23) he played Baerlein in the final

Charles Read and Jim Dear.

The Hon. C.N. Bruce (later Lord Aberdare) and Dr H.W. Leatham.

of the Amateur singles, but on only one occasion did he win, in 1922. He reached the final again in 1927 and 1928, when Cyril Simpson was at the top of his form, and Simpson won on both occasions.

Bruce was a very fit man, however, and seemingly ageless. In 1931, at the age of forty-five, he defeated a much younger Ian Akers-Douglas to win the Amateur singles, and the following year defeated Cyril Simpson by 9 games to 2 for the Open championship.

Undoubtedly his greatest achievements were as a doubles player. He won the Amateur doubles ten times between 1910 and 1934 with four different partners, mostly H.W. Leatham, the Charterhouse doctor. They won on six occasions. Bruce also won the US doubles with Cyril Simpson in 1928, and the US and the Canadian doubles with Leatham in 1930.

In 1939, at the age of fifty-three, he entered the Amateur doubles with yet another partner, his eldest son, Morys, then aged nineteen. This ill-sorted pair managed to reach the final, where they were beaten by Cosmo Crawley and John Pawle by 4 games to 3. The Second World War put an end to any second attempt.

Cyril Simpson was a brilliant left-hander, whose half-volley left his opponent standing and the spectators gasping. He won the Amateur singles from 1926 to 28, and was the first holder of the Sheppard Cup for the Open championship, beating Charles Read in 1929 and

1930. He lost this in 1932 to Lord Aberdare, who in turn lost to Ian Akers-Douglas in 1933. Akers-Douglas was Amateur champion from 1932 to 1934 and with Kenneth Wagg made up a formidable doubles pair, winning in 1932–33 and 1935.

Another outstanding doubles player of this period was Cosmo Crawley, Simpson's partner in the winning team of 1931, 1936 and 1937, and partner of John Pawle in the winning team of 1939 and 1946. He also won the Amateur singles in 1929.

The only professional of this era able to hold his own with this galaxy of talent – other than world champion Charles Williams, who had left Harrow for Chicago in 1923 – was Albert Cooper, who had learnt to play at Wellington under Walter Hawes. He was a mighty left-handed hitter. He won the Scott-Chad Cup for the Professional championship of the British Isles in 1932, and in 1934 he defeated Akers-Douglas for the British Open championship. Two years later he was defeated by David Milford, who went on to win the world title. Shortly before the war, he went as Rackets professional to Eton, where he kept the game alive in very difficult circumstances.

A professional of a slightly older generation who certainly deserves a mention is Charles Read of Queen's Club, where he started as a ball-boy at the age of thirteen in 1902. A year later he joined his uncle 'Judy' Stevens at Harrow, and here he learnt to play Rackets and squash rackets. At seventeen, he returned to Queen's Club as head Rackets professional, replacing Walter Hawes who had gone to Wellington.

He was successful at all three games he played. At Rackets, he was Professional champion from 1925 to 1932. In 1931 a competition was held for the professional title in which he beat C. Atherton of Cheltenham to reach the final. His opponent was Albert Cooper, who had beaten Jim Dear. In the final Read won by 3 games to 2. At squash, he was Professional champion from 1920 to 1929 and at lawn tennis from 1921 to 1928.

Arthur Whetton of Haileybury might well have been in the top rank of players had he not been killed in the Second World War. After the war, a new generation of talented Rackets players emerged. Competing for the world title were such amateur players as John Pawle, Geoffrey Atkins, James Leonard, Charles Swallow, Willie Surtees and Howard Angus. At British Open championship level were players such as Peter Kershaw, John Thompson, Richard Gracey and Martin Smith. These were the players who won the Amateur singles from 1946 to 1975, apart from 1950 and 1951, when Milford returned to show what an old dog could do. Most of them were also winners of the Amateur doubles,

Left to right: *David Milford, John Thompson, Peter Kershaw, Geoffrey Atkins*.

in such fine company as Bimby Holt, Ronnie Taylor, Tom Pugh and Charles Hue Williams.

Milford and Thompson had an outstanding record in the Amateur doubles, winning ten times between 1948 and 1959. Their nearest rivals were Bimby Holt and Ronnie Taylor, winners in 1947 and 1949, who ran them very close in five finals. In 1951, the match was so even that both sides ended up winning 84 points, although Milford and Thompson won by 4 games to 3.

John Thompson won the Amateur singles in 1954–55 and 1957–59, and won the doubles again in 1966 with Tom Pugh as his partner.

Thompson's fighting spirit – the mark of a champion – was called upon in two exciting finals of the Amateur championship. In 1957, he lost the first two games to Mike Coulman, won the next two and led 12–3 in the fifth. Coulman caught him and led 13–12; Thompson made it 13 all. Coulman again led 2–0 in the set to 3, but Thompson finally won the game 16–15, and with it the match and the championship, with a timely drop shot.

He endured an even worse situation in 1959 against J.M.G. Tildesley, who won the first two games 15–11, 15–0 and led 14–8 in the third. All seemed to be over to everyone except John Thompson. He fought back to win the third game 17–16, the fourth game 15–13 and the final game 15–8. This is without doubt one

Silver statuette made by David Wynne for Lord Aberdare.

of the best examples of the saying that a match is not lost until the last ball is played.

Michael Pugh was known and admired throughout the Public Schools for his energetic organisation of a 'Circus' – a group of his friends with whom he would tour the schools and give invaluable match practice to young players. He took the idea from Peter Eckersley, who had played against a few school second pairs before the Second World War. His first regular partner was C.G. (Tim) Toppin, and later Malcolm Burr. Other members of the Circus were his two sons, Tim and Tom, Roger Eckersley and Charles Cullen. Nothing gave him greater pleasure than the success of his two sons at Tennis and Rackets.

He was a man of taste – in claret as well as art. He was an early sponsor of the sculpture of David Wynne, also a useful Tennis player, and commissioned a head of Peter Latham. In 1960, David Wynne made a figure of a Rackets player for Lord Aberdare out of silver from his father's trophies; the model was Tom Pugh.

Two other outstanding pairs were Geoffrey Atkins and Peter Kershaw (1953, 1961–62), and Richard Gracey and Martin Smith (1964–65, 1969–71).

Another remarkable doubles player was Charles Hue Williams, with five victories to his credit with three different partners – James Leonard (1967–68), Howard Angus (1972–73) and Geoffrey Atkins (1974). He also earned a well-deserved victory in the Amateur singles in 1977.

Two players to emerge at this time were later to develop into world-class competitors. Willie Boone and John Prenn were in the winning pair for their respective schools, Boone for Eton with Mark Faber in 1968, Prenn for Harrow with Mark Thatcher in 1971. Prenn went on to win the Swallow Trophy for three successive years, 1974–76.

They first clashed in a major competition in the final of the Amateur singles in 1976 when Boone won a very close match by 3 games to 2. In the final game Prenn had a match point at 14–10 and three more at 14–13 before Boone clinched it at 17–14. The following year, Boone beat Prenn again in the semi-final by 3 games to 0, but in the final of the Louis Roederer Open, it was Prenn who beat Boone, by 4 games to 1.

They met yet again in the final of the Amateur singles in 1978, when Boone won another close match by 3 games to 2. They played off in April to decide who should be recognised as challenger to Surtees for the world championship. Prenn took the first leg 4–2; Boone won the first two games of the second leg easily, to level the match. The next two games were extremely close, but were eventually won by Boone, 17–14, 17–16. In the match, Boone won 113 points to Prenn's 110.

Prenn won the Amateur singles for the first time in 1979, beating Boone in the final, but Boone had his revenge in the Louis Roederer by 4 games to 1.

Prenn retained his Amateur title in 1980, beating Boone convincingly by 4 games to love in the final, and went on to win the Open championship again beating Boone, but more narrowly by 4 games to 2.

These two leading players presented a contrast in style. Boone was the mighty hitter with a formidably fast service. He was quite capable of overwhelming an opponent with the violence of his attack, and was a dogged fighter in adversity. Prenn, an outstanding stroke-player in the classical mould, hit the ball hard and low, and he had the ability to vary his service, which was a highly effective tactic. He invented a service of his own, the equivalent of the American twist lawn-tennis service, which won him many important points.

Rackets Tours

Following the very successful American tour of 1947, several more tours took place up to 1980. In 1953, Great Britain fielded a very strong side, comprising Kenneth Wagg (captain), David Milford, John Thompson and Geoffrey Atkins.

Before the international match, Milford and Thompson won the US Amateur doubles in Detroit and the Canadian doubles in Montreal, but Bobby Grant had shown what a formidable competitor he still was at the age of forty-one by beating Milford (3–0), Thompson (3–0) and Atkins (3–2) on successive days to win the Canadian singles. In the final, he had a great struggle with Atkins, who looked the likely winner when leading 10–8 in the final game. Atkins overall won 67 points to Grant's 64.

In the US singles, Grant continued on his triumphant path, beating Thompson (3–0) in the semi-final and Milford (3–0) in the final.

In the international match, Britain had a convincing victory over the USA by 5 matches to nil. Atkins, playing brilliantly, had a surprisingly easy revenge on Grant (3–0); Milford beat Stan Pearson (3–1); and Thompson beat Clarry Pell (3–1). In the doubles, Milford and Thompson beat Grant and Pearson; Atkins and Wagg beat Dick Leonard and F.F. de Rham.

Atkins stayed on to compete in the Tuxedo Gold Racquet and had the satisfaction of a fourth victory over Grant (3–1).

In 1956, the international trophy was contested at Queen's Club, London. A powerful British team retained the trophy, winning by 4 matches to 1. Atkins was by that time resident in Chicago and played for the USA. He duly won the top singles honours, beating Thompson after a close match (3–2). Milford beat Charles 'Babe' Pearson (3–1), Mike Coulman beat Stephen Colhoun (3–0). Milford and Thompson beat Atkins and W. Wood Prince (4–1) and Bimby Holt and Ronnie Taylor beat Pearson and Wagg (4–1).

The 1960 tour was led by Dick Bridgeman, who unfortunately fell ill. The British team were further handicapped by the absence of David Norman as the result of a leg injury incurred in the final of the Canadian doubles. America won the international match by 5 matches to 2. The American team made an impressive start, winning the first three matches. Grant beat Mac Bailey (3–0), Peter Read beat Robin Allen (3–1) and

The international match of 1956. Standing (left to right): *Charles Pearson, Steve Colhoun, John Thompson, Bimby Holt, Kenneth Wagg, David Milford, Ronnie Taylor.* Seated: *Mike Coulman, Geoffrey Atkins.*

Atkins and Babe Pearson beat Tom Pugh and Bailey (3–0). Roddy Bloomfield gave Britain her first victory, beating Babe Pearson (3–2), but Atkins secured the match by beating Tom Pugh (3–0), giving the US a decisive 4–1 lead. In the two doubles matches that followed, Clarry Pell and Read beat David Scholey and Malcolm Burr (3–0), and Stephen Colhoun and Pearson were leading 2–1 against Bloomfield and Allen when they were forced to retire after Colhoun sustained an injury over his left eye from a ball that flew off his racquet.

During the course of this visit, Tom Pugh won the Western American singles and, in partnership with Mac Bailey, the US and Western American doubles.

In 1962, another British assault again failed to reclaim the trophy, the USA winning by 5 matches to 2. On the first day, the US won two out of the three doubles matches, the only winning British pair being Kenneth Wagg and Dick Bridgeman, who beat Clarry Pell and Babe Pearson 3–1 after a fast and furious contest. In the singles, Bridgeman beat Pearson (3–1), but Peter Read beat Tim Pugh (3–1), Jimmy Bostwick beat Roger Eckersley (3–0) and Clarry Pell beat Julian Bevan (3–0).

In 1963, a Jesters Rackets team toured the USA. Miles Connell was captain, and his powerful team included Charles Swallow, Mike Coulman, Dick Bridgeman, Jeremy Hogben, Maurice Baring, M.S. Ross-Collins and Oliver Case. They won the international match by 8 matches to 1.

There was a visit to Canada in May 1967 to celebrate the centenary of the Montreal Racket Club. Eight leading British players were invited and all expenses were paid by their generous Canadian hosts. Pete Bostwick from New York won the singles, defeating James Leonard, Jeremy Hogben and Charles Hue Williams in so doing

Dick Bridgeman.

– a notable performance. The doubles were won by Richard Gracey and Martin Smith.

Another Jesters team toured America in 1973 and retained the trophy. Howard Angus was a member of the team but could not play in the international match, which clashed with the US Tennis singles. The Jesters team consisted of Charles Hue Williams, J.K. Rogers, P.D. Rylands, A.C.S. Tufton, T.P. Halford, J.G.M. Walsh and J.N. Travis.

1980–2000

Although Rackets did not quite match Tennis for the number of new courts opened in these twenty years, there was a considerable increase in the number of people continuing to play after leaving school. Under the guidance of the Rackets Committee, chaired successively by Garth Milne, Paul Nicholls, Charles Hue Williams and Sir Mervyn Dunnington-Jefferson, several new tournaments were introduced, there was a significant increase in the levels of sponsorship, and evening clubs thrived on school courts. This process was accelerated in 1989 by the appointment of Brigadier Andrew Myrtle as the first full-time administrator of the Tennis & Rackets Association. In addition, a National League, the brainchild of Mick Dean, meant that competitive matches, latterly under a handicap system, became a regular feature of the evening clubs. Rackets was consistently sponsored by Celestion Loudspeakers and Lacoste, thanks to Dan and John Prenn, while other major supporters included Rank Xerox, Peel Hunt and Henderson Private Investors. A number of specific events were sponsored by other individuals and firms.

In 1980, there were twelve schools with courts, six of them with two courts. A further six clubs made a total of twenty-four courts. Since then, four courts have been restored at Marlborough, Cheltenham, Newcastle and Queen's Club, and a new court built at St Paul's School, thanks to the generosity of an Old Pauline benefactor. Sadly, St John's College, Cambridge, decided to demolish the Portugal Place complex, so that neither of the ancient universities has a Rackets court, and players depend for practice on the hospitality of Haileybury and Radley. Thus in 2000 there were twenty-eight courts in action in the UK.

The resurrection of the second court at Queen's Club was achieved due to the determination and drive of David Norman, and with generous financial help from many devoted enthusiasts. It was named the Bridgeman Court to mark the dedication of Dick Bridgeman, who did so much to promote Rackets post-war. The additional court meant that there were much better facilities than there were before at the headquarters of the game. It was also used by Westminster School.

In the world championship, the years from 1980 to 1987 were dominated by the continued rivalry of John Prenn and Willie Boone. John Prenn defeated the holder, Willie Surtees, in 1981, by 6 games to 4 in a match played in New York and at Queen's Club. In 1984, he lost the title to Boone by 2 games to

David Norman was an effective chairman of the T&RA.

7 in Montreal and at Queen's Club. Prenn had his revenge in 1986, winning by 8 games to 6 in New York and at Queen's Club.

In 1988, a new star arose in the Rackets court – James Male, the first ambidextrous and double-handed player in the game. John Prenn had decided to resign the world title for business reasons and a

British world champions invited to a Garden Party at Buckingham Palace in 1992 to celebrate 40 Years of Her Majesty's Champions (left to right) James Male, Howard Angus, Geoffrey Atkins, Willie Surtees, John Prenn and Willie Boone.

Neil Smith, the elegant challenger, beat world champion James Male 4–2 in Chicago in 1999.

match was arranged between Male and Boone for the vacant title. Male won the first leg, played in Chicago, by 4 games to 1. He narrowly won the first two games of the second leg at Queen's Club and, aged twenty-three, became the youngest world Rackets champion since Peter Latham, who won in 1887 aged twenty-two.

Male successfully defended his title in 1991 in Chicago and at Queen's Club, defeating Shannon Hazell by 6 games to 2; in 1993 in Philadelphia and at Queen's Club, defeating Neil Smith by 6 games to 5; and in 1995 in Chicago and at Queen's Club, defeating Neil Smith again, this time by 6 games to 2.

In 1999, a further challenge was arranged between the same two outstanding players in Chicago and at Queen's Club. Smith led by 4 games to 2 in Chicago, but unfortunately injury prevented Male from playing the second leg and Smith became the new world champion.

The outstanding new Rackets court at St Paul's was officially opened by Lord Aberdare on 20 January 2001. This coincided with the second leg of the world singles championship. James Male, the challenger, had defeated the holder, Neil Smith, by 4–1 in New York the previous week, and by winning the two games required for outright victory he regained the title he had held between 1988 and 1999. The length of time it took to play these two games and the quality of play were a fitting tribute to the condition of the new court.

The Open singles was dominated, not surprisingly, by the same players as the world championship.

Between 1977 and 1986, Willie Boone and John Prenn contested the final eight times, Prenn winning on six occasions. Prenn was a fine tactician with an ideal match temperament. He never seemed to be under pressure, and his wide range of strokes made full use of the geometry of the court. There followed three epic victories by James Male over Neil Smith, repeated again in 1991 and 1996, but Smith had some consolation in winning against Shannon Hazell, Rupert Owen-Browne and Boone (twice) in the 1990s. Boone, who won on six occasions between 1979 and 1998, was narrowly beaten by Smith by 4 games to 3 in 1999. Boone's long run of successes was a tribute to his supreme fitness and his match temperament, although his ebullience led to difficult moments for the referee. Male won again in 2000 when he beat Peter Brake, the Queen's Club professional, by 4 games to 2.

Willie Boone's first appearance in an Amateur singles final was in 1976. Up to 1996 he appeared in twenty-two consecutive finals, two competitions having been held in 1985 and 1988, in January and December. The sequence must surely be a record for a national final in any sport, and he returned in 1998, winning on eight occasions in all. In the same period, John Prenn won five of his twelve finals, and James Male won on all eleven occasions in which he was a finalist. The world doubles championship was inaugurated in 1990, with the expectation that challenges would occur every two years, alternating with the world singles challenge. John Prenn and James Male were the first winners, beating Neil Smith and Shannon Hazell by 8 games to 5 at Manchester and Queen's Club. Then, in 1992, Smith and Hazell beat Prenn and Willie Boone by 7 games to 3 at Clifton College and at Queen's Club. They defended their title successfully on three occasions, Smith having moved from Queen's to New York, and despite the fact that Hazell had left Rackets to be a squash professional in the US. In 1993, they beat Prenn and Male by the narrowest of margins, the games being 7 all, 166 points to 160. In 1996, they beat the same opponents by the emphatic score of 5 games to love, but were hard pressed by Boone and Peter Brake in 1998, winning by 7 games to 6. Their success came from the combination of Smith's elegant stroke play down the side walls, and Hazell's fleetness of foot in retrieving and volleying up the front of the court.

The Open doubles began in 1981, and for the first five years was dominated by Willie Boone and Randall Crawley, whose persistence in return made him an ideal partner for Boone. John Prenn and James Male were equally dominant from 1986 to 1990, beating Boone and Crawley three times and Neil Smith and Shannon Hazell twice. Boone characteristically bounced back to win from 1995 to 1997, twice with Tim Cockroft and once with Peter Brake. The most remarkable result was in 1998 when Male, with a much younger partner, the left-hander Mark Hue Williams, beat the world champions Smith and Hazell by 4 games to 1. The success of this new partnership was confirmed in 1999 when they beat Jonathan Larken and Toby Sawrey-Cookson, the Clifton professional, in straight games; and in 2000, they beat Guy Barker and Alister Robinson by 4 games to 2, a repetition of the result in the Amateur doubles.

The pattern was similar in the Amateur doubles, with Willie Boone and Randall Crawley successful from 1980 to 1984 and again in 1986, and John Prenn and James Male winning from 1988 to 1991 and in 1993 and 1995. Tim Cockroft was successful four times in the 1990s, three times with Boone and once with Rupert Owen-Browne, a mighty but somewhat erratic striker of the ball. A significant breakthrough for the younger generation of players came in 1999 when Guy Barker and Alister Robinson, who had won the Public Schools championship in 1983 for Marlborough, beat Boone and Mark Hue Williams by 4 games to 2; but in 2000 they lost by the same score to Male and Hue Williams, who had entered this competition together for the first time. During these twenty years, faster balls, more tightly strung racquets and warmer courts meant that doubles at the highest level became a breathtaking spectacle. There have undoubtedly been moments of danger when all four players have tried to seize the initiative by advancing up court to volley, but there have been no serious incidents, probably due to disciplined training at school. The role of the referee has become more difficult as the quicker players are able to retrieve shots that have passed their partner's attempts to volley, or to claim a let at the back of the court.

In the Public Schools doubles championship, Tonbridge was the dominant force, playing in nine of the twenty-one finals and winning six. Otherwise honours were well spread, with Harrow winning three times, Marlborough, Clifton, Rugby and Eton twice, and Wellington, Radley, Winchester and Haileybury once. In the same period, Tonbridge and Eton were the most successful schools in the Colts and Junior

Play in the Open doubles at Queen's, which was won by James Male (bottom) *and Mark Hue Williams* (top left). *Their opponents were Toby Sawrey-Cookson and Jonathan Larken* (far right).

Andrew Myrtle, retiring Chief Executive of the T&RA, and Norman Rosser, chronicler of the game at that time.

Colts doubles, a tribute to their professionals, David Makey and Norwood Cripps, respectively.

In the Foster Cup for singles, success was confined to seven schools, with Tonbridge and Harrow winning five times, Radley and Rugby three times, Clifton twice and Eton and Cheltenham once. Winners on two occasions were James Male (Radley), Johnny Longley (Tonbridge), who had the distinction of not losing a match at Queen's Club in singles or doubles at all ages, Matthew Windows (Clifton), Richard Carter (Rugby) and Alex Titchener-Barrett (Harrow). All of these had successes in the doubles, and another prominent player was Rupert Owen-Browne (Tonbridge) who won the doubles twice and the singles once. Particularly noteworthy was the success of Jamie Stout in the Foster Cup 2000, just twelve years after Cheltenham reopened their court. Professionals Ron Hughes (Malvern), Roger Crosby (Harrow) and Peter Ellis (Haileybury) retired after a lifetime of service to the game, while Mick Dean retired after over twenty years as Radley's professional.

Although the prestige of Rackets remained high in the schools, the opportunities for practice tended to diminish as demands for academic time increased and the major team games claimed more time both for matches and practices. Thus the role of the masters-in-charge, in support of the professionals, became more significant as they sought to protect the players, invariably good all-rounders, from excessive demands on their time. Among those who promoted the cause of Rackets, while assisting on court with enthusiasm and varying degrees of skill, were Mark Greenstock and Peter Warfield (Harrow), Norman Rosser, Andrew Rambridge and Andy Murtagh (Malvern), John Thompson (Marlborough), Ian Graham (Rugby), David Kemp and John Gibbs (Tonbridge), Chris Potter (Wellington) and Robert Turnbull (Haileybury). Karl Cook played a major part in the revival of Rackets at Cheltenham, firstly as professional and latterly as master-in-charge.

Twenty-First Century Rackets

It is certainly a happy occurrence to report that there have been no major closures of Rackets courts in the period. Indeed, use of the old courts at Dartmouth is under review, where enthusiasts hope to secure the courts' revival. Despite the building being disused for so long, it is structurally in good shape. Also, at Buckhurst Park the family are exploring ways of raising funds to restore the court and recommence play.

Even greater positive news for the future of the sport came when a second Rackets court opened amidst great enthusiasm at Tonbridge in March 2012. Steadily increasing interest in the game, combined with the initiative of Tonbridge professional David Makey, was the impetus to construct a court within the walls of the old school gymnasium. 'The Appeal Court' stands adjacent to the school's original Rackets court, built in 1897.

The 2003 retirement of world champion and Rackets great James Male, who held simultaneous singles and doubles world championships from 2001 to 2003, made way for the achievements of younger players. Male had reigned as world champion for all but two years of an extraordinary fifteen-year period, 1988–2003. The likes of Harry Foster, who followed up his world title win in 2005 by winning seven out of eight singles and doubles tournaments in a virtually unbeaten season in 2006–07 – only marred by defeat in the 2007 semi-finals of the Open doubles – then came to dominate the major championships. Foster's remarkable feat of collecting the Open, Amateur and Invitation singles in just one season was an achievement that had been completed only twice before him in the history of the sport.

James Stout's back-to-back Foster Cup titles for Cheltenham – his first in 2000 as a sixteen-year-old – were an early sign of the dominance he would go on to demonstrate in world Rackets. Stout completed an impressive Open singles double in 2008 and 2009. In 2008, Stout also became the youngest Rackets world champion in twenty years, after beating Harry Foster 6–1. He successfully defended his world title against challenger Alex Titchener-Barrett in 2010.

After James Male and Mark Hue Williams's consecutive world doubles victories in 2001 and 2003, the world title has since been hotly contested. In 2005, Guy Barker and Ali Robinson claimed the crown, building on a run of Amateur and Open doubles form in the 2003–04 season. Their 7–4 victory over Tim Cockroft and Guy Smith-Bingham was a more than palatable revenge for the ex-Marlborough team-mates, compensating for their Amateur doubles defeat earlier in the year. Pro pairing Neil Smith and Mark Hubbard, so often rivals in the Professional singles championship, united to win the 2007 world title. Then the trophy was Mark Hue Williams's again in 2009, which he won this time with Harry Foster. Tim Cockroft and Alex Titchener-Barrett were victorious in 2011, but then were defeated 6-2 by the youthful partnership of James Coyne and Will Hopton in April 2013.

James Coyne and Will Hopton win the 2013 world Rackets doubles.

Hoppy takes off – *Will Hopton winning the 2014 British Open singles.*

champion Foster in 2003, and beating Alex Titchener-Barrett in 2005. In between Smith-Bingham's brace of titles, Ali Robinson defeated Harry Foster in the 2004 Open. Alex Titchener-Barrett's record of three out of the last five Open championships, between 2010 and 2014, has only been marred by defeats to Will Hopton in 2012 and 2014. After Titchener-Barrett had eased comfortably past him in the 2011 Open final, winning by 4 games to love, Hopton made a successful title bid in his first season as a pro player in 2012. A steely and determined Titchener-Barrett reclaimed his crown in April 2013, defeating the hard-hitting James Coyne 4–1 in the final, but was again defeated by Will Hopton in an extraordinary match in 2014. Hopton clawed his way back from 3 games down to save a championship point and win 4–3.

Following on from Male's five British Open singles victories in the 1980s and 1990s, he won the Open title in both 2000 and 2001. Foster picked up a hat-trick of championships in 2002, 2006 and 2007. Guy Smith-Bingham won the title twice, defeating defending

In the Open doubles championship, James Male and Mark Hue Williams matched their world doubles success with consecutive Open titles in 2000 and 2001. Hue Williams subsequently went on to win the title three times with Harry Foster – in 2005, 2007 and 2008 – but not before an unbeaten run for Guy Barker and Ali Robinson, from 2002 to 2004. Then followed two sets of back-to-back victories: first for Tim Cockroft and Alex Titchener-Barrett, in 2009 and 2010, before James Coyne and Will Hopton – unsuccessful in the

Finalists of the 2014 British Open doubles (left to right) *James Coyne, Mike Bailey, Christian Portz, Alex Titchener-Barrett, together with Tim Cockroft.*

Finalists of the 2013 Amateur singles Alex Titchener-Barrett and James Coyne, with William Maltby.

2009 final against Cockroft and Titchener-Barrett – were triumphant in 2011 and 2012. The year 2013 heralded new Open champions, Cheltenham old boys Ben Snell and Nick James. Snell and James were tied at 3 games all in what had been a bruising encounter against Jamie Stout and Mike Gooding. Heading into a deciding seventh game, their opponents decided to withdraw – Stout was suffering from an ankle injury sustained early on in the match and felt unable to play on. Then, in 2014 Alex Titchener-Barrett and Christian Portz secured the title from James Coyne and Mike Bailey. Mention must also be made in relation to this tournament of Guy Smith-Bingham, for whom the Open doubles title proved elusive – in spite of reaching the final five times in six championships, 2001–06.

Smith-Bingham has enjoyed a more successful time of it in the Amateur singles, with triple back-to-back victories in 2002, 2003 and 2004. Either side of Smith-Bingham's wins, Ali Robinson recorded a narrow 3–2 victory against John Prenn in 2001, and dispatched Charles Danby 3–0 in 2005. Foster prevented Smith-Bingham from gaining a fourth singles title in 2006, in a close-fought 3–2 encounter, and himself retained the crown the following year against challenger Jonathan Larken. Since 2008, Alex Titchener-Barrett has been imperious in the tournament, with six consecutive victories to his name, only allowing his opponents two games throughout that period.

Between 2000 and 2013, Mark Hue Williams and Tim Cockroft have – individually – been the most successful players in the Amateur doubles. Hue Williams secured separate hat-trick victories, consecutively with world champion James Male (2000–02) and again with Harry Foster in 2006, 2007 and 2009. Cockroft has been victorious with three different partners in five championships, starting with a first win together with Rupert Owen-Browne in 2003, after injury to opponent Guy Barker – one half of the Open doubles-winning partnership with Ali Robinson – spelled their retirement from the match. Cockroft tasted success again with Guy Smith-Bingham in 2005, before teaming up with the most successful amateur of recent times, Alex Titchener-Barrett, to win doubles titles in 2008, 2012 and 2013.

Until Will Hopton's back-to-back victories in 2012 and 2013, the Professional singles championship was entirely dominated by rival professionals – and sometime doubles partners – Neil Smith of New York and Mark Hubbard of Radley. Neil Smith overcame defending champion Toby Sawrey-Cookson in 2001, before losing his crown to Hubbard the following year. Smith then settled into a three-year period of dominance from 2003 to 2005, each time achieving victory over Hubbard. Hubbard turned the tables on Smith to achieve his own three years of uninterrupted victories between 2006 and 2008, before Smith edged past his long-term rival once more in 2009 to take his tally of overall victories in the competition to fourteen. Hubbard rallied to secure further consecutive victories in 2010 and 2011, although the youthful might of Will Hopton proved too much for the Radley pro in 2012. Hopton was able to comfortably defend his championship against Ben Snell with another straight sets victory in January 2013.

Between 2000 and 2014, the Public Schools doubles championship has been principally dominated by Harrow and Cheltenham; the former having won the championship five times – firstly in 2000 and most recently in 2013 – and the latter four times, recording consecutive titles in 2001 and 2002, and again in 2006 and then 2012. Winchester also achieved three consecutive doubles championships, the first two through partnering Sean Knight and Christian Portz, who emerged victorious in 2008 – a final in which they upset Harrow top seeds Sam Northeast and Will Jones to become the first second pair ever to win the doubles championship. Christian Portz won his third final partnered by Ben Stevens.

In the Public Schools' singles, honours have been shared more equally: Cheltenham, Eton, Wellington and Harrow have each recorded three or four victories; whilst Winchester and Marlborough both achieved one. Christian Portz's win for Winchester in 2009 was their first since Howard Angus's victory in 1963. In 2011, Chris Stout emulated brother Jamie's earlier success for Cheltenham with victory over the tournament's top seed Jamie Giddins (Eton).

In 1993, the Faber family presented a cup in memory of Mark Faber, an outstanding games player, who had been in the winning Eton pair for three years from 1967 to 1969 and had played in three Foster Cup finals, winning twice. The cup is awarded each season to the school with the best combined results in the singles and doubles tournaments, played at Christmas and Easter, points being awarded to semi-finalists and finalists, with weighting in favour of the doubles and the senior events. Rugby won in 1993, Eton from 1994 to 1997, Tonbridge in 1998 and 1999, and Harrow in 2000. The last thirteen years have been dominated by Eton and Cheltenham, both winning five times, with single successes being achieved by Tonbridge, Wellington and Winchester.

The influence of long-serving professionals who remain in harness, such as Martin Crosby (Charterhouse), Steve Tulley (St Paul's), Tim Cawston (Winchester), Robert Wakely (Marlborough), Philip Rosser (Rugby), Peter Brake (Eton) and, of course, David Makey (Tonbridge), has been integral to the growth of schoolboy Rackets. Their devotion to the game has inspired increasing popularity and standards of play – a fact made evident in the increasing number of entrants in both the Public Schools' singles and doubles competitions year on year.

Several families have also made remarkable contributions to Rackets over the years and, for two of them, the Grays and the Crosbys, this has continued into the twenty-first century. The Gray family influence began with Henry, William and Joseph, world champions between 1863 and 1878, except for two years. It included three generations of professionals at Rugby, spanning over a century – Joseph (1868–94), Harry (1894–1937 and 1939–46) and Peter (1936–39 and 1946–71). Now Richard Gray's firm is the only UK manufacturer of Rackets' racquets. Equally remarkable is the Crosby family, with four generations of professionals. Jim Crosby was at Whale Island, Portsmouth, from about 1890 to 1895 and then at Marlborough (1895–1922). His sons Jim (Winchester 1910–39) and Fred (Harrow 1922–62) followed him into the profession, and Fred's descendants carried on the tradition. His son Roger was first assistant and then professional at Harrow from 1951 to 1996; grandson Martin was assistant at Harrow (1983–88) and is now the professional at Charterhouse. Surely no other game can boast such dedication from these and countless others.

In 1987, Bill Stephens, then Secretary of the Tennis & Rackets Association, and the late James Knott Jr, initiated a scheme whereby groups of players from the UK and the USA and Canada were to tour each other's country, visiting clubs and schools. The first tour took place in 1989 when a British team visited North America. Two years later there was a return tour from North America to Britain and this pattern has continued up to 2014 – thirteen tours so far. The first incoming tour in 1991 featured a vast NARA delegation including James Knott Jr, Denis Walsh, Tim Price (Montreal) and the legendary 'Fast Eddie' Matthews. The Knott Stephens is very much seen as the Rackets equivalent of the Real Tennis Van Alen. Although the Van Alen is much the older tour, going back to the 1950s, the Knott Stephens at Rackets and the Van Alen at Real Tennis now rank equally as the pre-eminent cross-Atlantic institutions for younger players of our two games, and it is regarded as a great opportunity to be invited onto one of the teams. Often they are the first chance players will have to travel 'over the pond' to play, and teams have been wonderfully entertained by their hosts in North America and Britain. It is hoped that the tradition will continue for many years to come.

James Stout, world champion since 2008.

LADIES' RACKETS

Although Rackets dates back to the eighteenth century, due to the nature of where the game was played – originally in debtors' prisons, later in taverns, followed by boys' public schools and the armed forces – it was rarely played by women. However, in more recent times, the game has opened up to girls as some of the boys' schools have become co-ed (even if just at sixth-form level), and is also played at private members' clubs such as Manchester, Queen's and Seacourt, Hayling Island. Some of the schools with Rackets courts also open them up to local players on certain evenings during the week, so the game can be more widely enjoyed. The more proactive the school pros are in getting more people involved in the game, the better, although they are often constrained by court availability, which makes it tricky with so many boys wanting to practise, particularly in the run-up to the major public schools' tournaments, and especially for schools with just one court. This applies also to the schools with girls, where court practice time is limited, which may discourage some girls from getting onto court.

However, girls are now starting to come through from the schools. This is largely down to two reasons: the introduction of the British Open Ladies' Rackets and, at the same time, the girls' Under-16 and Senior Girls' Events in the 2010–11 Rackets season; and so with that came a real motivation for the schools pros to get a few of their girls trained up to take on that challenge. It is really encouraging that the game is now more accessible to more girls than ever before, and so by learning the game from the start of their senior school days, it will give them the best chance possible to develop their games, just as the boys can do.

The ladies' game has really got going over the last few years and was greatly encouraged by Howard Angus, the previous head Rackets pro at The Queen's Club. Queen's has been lucky enough to have the ex-world Rackets and world Real Tennis champion as previous head Rackets pro, now retired, and he organised Rackets open days for all members – thereby opening the game up to other racquet-sports members of the club. Some ladies were introduced to the game from lawn tennis; Alex Brodie (née Kurkjian), though she mis-hit a lot of balls at her first attempt, straight away realised what a fantastic, adrenalin-fuelled game Rackets is.

Alex stuck with the game and spread the word, promoting the game to other lawn tennis, Real Tennis and squash members at the club. With Howard's help, she organised a ladies' Rackets open evening and attracted thirty new ladies to the game, to try it with a pro/top player and then enjoy watching a top-level exhibition doubles game featuring James Coyne and Alex Titchener-Barrett.

Following the high level of interest, Howard kindly put on free beginners' workshops for the keen ladies, so they could come and practise every week. Ladies' Rackets took off and, a few months later, Malvern College organised a ladies' exhibition doubles match during the reopening ceremonies in November 2010 for their refurbished Ron Hughes Courts, which was the first ever official ladies' Rackets event. On this significant occasion, Alex Garside and Alex Brodie overcame the strong pair of Sally Jones and Claire Vigrass.

Alex Kurkjian and Alex Garside win the first ever official Ladies Rackets event at Malvern in 2010.

Claire Vigrass, winner of the 2014 Ladies Open singles, with Howard Angus.

In the following year, there was enough interest for the first ever T&RA Ladies' British Open, organised by Alex Brodie and sponsored by Neptune Investment Management. There was a strong entry of nine ladies, which was encouraging. Claire Vigrass won, triumphing over South African squash player Barbara Vintcent and, in 2012, over Alex Brodie in a slightly closer-fought final. Claire repeated this result against Alex in 2013 and 2014, though the match play from both players, and across the whole tournament, substantially increased year on year, and it was encouraging to see a wider field entering each year with more young ladies taking up the game.

A challenge match took place in 2012 and Noel Brett from Malvern and Alex worked with the T&RA to turn this event into the official ladies' doubles tournament. So, in 2013, it became the British Amateur Ladies' Doubles tournament, which top Real Tennis player Karen Hird won with Alex Brodie, by defeating Ashley Lenihan and Ella Gaskell in 2013. They retained it in 2014 by defeating the strong home team of Shinan Zhang (top junior Rackets player) and sports teacher Chey West.

Ben Snell joined Howard as the Rackets assistant pro and subsequently took over as head pro upon Howard's retirement. He enthusiastically took up Howard's work by continuing the ladies' Rackets clinics. Gradually the game is being more widely played by girls and ladies, and all the encouragement along the way, from schoolboys, members at clubs, and club and schools' pros, is helping to further the reach of the game for girls. It is difficult with so few clubs and the limited number of co-ed schools with Rackets courts but, as more girls come through the schools playing Rackets, hopefully they will want to continue playing the game and keep playing wherever possible. It is encouraging to see the game being played more widely amongst the ladies and the future of the female Rackets game growing in popularity.

Alex Brodie and Karen Hird, winners of the 2014 Ladies Amateur doubles, with Howard Angus.

Rackets in the USA and Canada

USA

Rackets has been played in New York since the end of the eighteenth century. James Knox acquired property on Allen Street in 1793 and a few years later built a Rackets court. He had learnt to play in Halifax, where he had sought refuge during the Revolution. The court was 100ft long by 36ft wide, with no back wall but a line on the floor. There were two other lines across the court: one 30ft from the front wall with a circle in the centre, and another 80ft from the front wall. Service had to be delivered from the circle and had to fall between the 30ft and 80ft lines.

The balls were 'made of white woollen yarn dampened and wound over a piece of solid rubber about the size of a marble. They were covered with leather and sewed with different colors of silk, blue, yellow and scarlet' (G.M. Rushmore). Liquor was free, champagne $2 a bottle and Havana cigars 5¢ each.

In the 1830s another court was built at the corner of Bowery and Broome Streets, run by Alexander Fink and known as the Butchers Club. Their best player was Elias de Forrest, known as Uncle Elias, but the court did not last very long.

Meantime, the Allen Street club had become immensely popular. Robert Knox, son of James, was the local champion until the arrival of Edward La Montagne from Montreal in 1848.

In 1845 the Broadway Racquet Club was built, inspired by Robert Emmet and designed by Richard T. Carman. It lay on the east side of Broadway between Prince and Houston Streets and included bowling alleys and a billiard room. The Rackets court was of the same dimensions as that in Allen Street. The professional in charge was Billey De Voe, the first American professional of whom any record exists.

The game was very popular and the club had some 200 members. The players, though keen, were not of a very high standard; the best among them were Robert Edgar, Edgar Newbold, Beverley Robinson, John A. Post and William J. Emmet. None of them was a match for Edward La Montagne. La Montagne was the outstanding amateur player of the 1840s and 1850s. Like other well-known players of the game since then, he was a wine merchant, representing the celebrated Bordeaux firm of Barton et Guestier, whose directors have always taken a keen interest in Tennis.

Edward La Montagne.

In 1854, La Montagne built the first covered court on Thirteenth Street/Sixth Avenue, known as the Gymnasium Club. He was guaranteed a return of 7 per cent for four years on his investment. The court was 70ft x 30ft (10ft longer than standard) and had two galleries for spectators. The front wall was of polished stone, the side walls of cement and the floor of Georgia pine. The professional was Fred Foulkes, the American champion defeated by William Gray in 1867. The club was sold in 1868.

The popularity of Rackets soon spread to other American cities. On 25 November 1889 at 923 Walnut Street, the Racquet Club of Philadelphia was opened with two Rackets courts; and the Boston Athletic Association opened its doors in December of the same year with Tom Pettitt as head professional. In September 1893, the Chicago Athletic Association opened two courts on Michigan Boulevard and put Harry Boakes in charge.

In the winter of 1899/1900, the Tuxedo Club opened with a Tennis court and squash courts. The Rackets court, designed by Bickley, was not ready until 1902.

In 1903, a new court was opened at the Racquet and Curling Club of Detroit (now Detroit Racquet Club) with a match between George Standing and Harry Boakes. This was another Bickley court of standard size. The first professional was George Healey.

Rackets grew rapidly in popularity in Boston, where two courts were built at the Tennis and Racquet Club in 1904, and four years later a fourth was built at the Randolph Club at Harvard. In Chicago, a third court was opened at the Illinois Athletic Association in 1906. This was unique in that the players had to enter it through a trap-door in the floor.

In 1909, a court was opened in St Louis, with Dave Gardiner, trained by Standing in New York, in charge. Two years later he was replaced by Frank Lafforgue, another of Standing's pupils. It was mainly thanks to Lafforgue's coaching ability that Joseph Wear and Dwight Davis won the Amateur doubles title for St Louis in 1914.

In 1909, two more courts were built at the University Club of Chicago, as well as four squash courts. Harry Boakes was put in charge with his son, Harry Boakes Jr, to help him. In Philadelphia the Racquet Club moved to its present building on Sixteenth Street in 1907, with two Rackets courts, a Tennis court, five squash courts and an unused space that was converted within a few years into a doubles squash court, the first in the United States.

During this period, two private courts were built – one by Eugene Higgins at Morristown, New Jersey in the 1880s, and the other by George Gould at Georgian Court, Lakewood, New Jersey, about 1900. Frank Forester taught Jay Gould and his brother, Kingdon, to play Rackets at Lakewood.

Two post First World War events that took place in New York and Chicago are of great importance to the modern scene. Firstly, the New York Racquet and Tennis Club moved in 1918 to its present location at 370 Park Avenue, where it had two Rackets courts, two Tennis courts and five squash courts. Secondly, two courts were opened at the new Chicago Racquet Club on Schiller Street in 1924, and Charles Williams was invited over from England to take charge of them.

The last court built in the United States was at the University Club in Detroit in 1931. Sadly, it is also the most recent court to have been destroyed, when the entire clubhouse was demolished in 2013 after a devastating fire in the then empty building. Also, on a historical note, some time before 1920, through the generosity of Harold McCormick, a court was built under the football stands at the University of Chicago; on 2 December 1942, the first self-sustaining nuclear reaction occurred in the court.

During the early years of the game in the United States, many fine players emerged; most of the professionals were recruited from England, but the amateurs were all home-bred. The first-known American champion was Fred Foulkes of New York, who played and lost to William Gray for the world championship in 1867. By the 1880s, the two outstanding players were Englishmen: Harry Boakes, at Quebec and later at Chicago (1893), and Robert Moore, at New York and later at Tuxedo (1900). They met for the Professional championship in 1883 and Boakes won. Nominally, he held the title until defeated by George Standing in 1893, but had he been in the United States rather than in Canada, he might well have been defeated before then by Tom Pettitt, another Englishman, trained in Boston and holder of the world title at Tennis from 1885 to 1896.

George Standing had come to the New York Forty-Third Street Club in 1892, and after defeating Boakes established himself as the outstanding player in America. In 1897, he challenged Peter Latham for the world championship, but was defeated by 8 games to 4 in a match played at Queen's Club and the New York Racquet and Tennis Club.

In 1890 the American Amateur championship was inaugurated, and for the first eight years shared by two outstanding players, B.S. de Garmendia (six) and J.S. Tooker (two). In 1898, the sequence was broken by a great Canadian player, F.F. Rolland.

B.S. de Garmendia.

Stanley Mortimer and Clarry Pell.

The next great professional was a Scotsman, Jock Soutar, brought to Philadelphia by Frederick Tompkins in 1907. The story of his rivalry with Charles Williams has already been told. Soutar won in 1913 and 1922, but Williams had the last laugh in 1929.

In the meantime, some outstanding amateur players had emerged. In the 1890s Clarence Mackay of New York was in the forefront of amateur players and, shortly after him, Lawrence Waterbury and Reginald Fincke. The latter was considered by some to be potentially the greatest Rackets player of all time, and he was certainly able to defeat professionals as well as amateurs. Unfortunately, however, he had to give up after an accident in the court while still under thirty.

The years 1915 to 1933 were dominated by Clarence C. Pell and Stanley G. Mortimer. Their record speaks for itself – Pell was the Amateur singles champion twelve times and won the Tuxedo Gold Racquet fourteen times. Mortimer won the Amateur singles on four occasions and the Tuxedo Gold Racquet on three. Together they won the Amateur doubles nine times. Pell won the British Amateur singles in 1925, beating H.W. Leatham 3–0 in the final.

In the late 1930s, there emerged another outstanding amateur player, Bobby Grant III of New York, who had learnt to play Rackets at Eton. He won the American Amateur singles ten times, despite four lost years of war when no competition took place. With Clarence Pell Jr he won the doubles seven times. He won the Canadian singles on all eight occasions on which he competed. In 1953, he showed his tremendous ability against a strong team of British visitors, including David Milford, John Thompson and Geoffrey Atkins.

Grant was also a first-class Tennis player. In 1946 he achieved a double victory, winning the Amateur championships of both Rackets and Tennis, a feat accomplished previously only by B.S. de Garmendia in 1894 and Eustace Miles in 1900. He also won the Amateur doubles twice, in 1941 with Ogden Phipps and in 1960 with Alastair Martin.

Grant was the last great American player. Since then, the Amateur championship has been won mostly by British-born players, working in America or visiting. They have included Geoffrey Atkins (seven times), David Norman (five times), Willie Surtees and Willie Boone (nine times), Jonathan Larken (five times, the latest being in 2013), Rupert Owen-Browne (three times) and, most recently, young Tom Billings bested all of his seniors to win in 2014 at the age of twenty. Canadian David McLernon won four Amateurs, and

Bobby Grant and Clarry Pell.

recently Todd Meringoff became the first American to win the Amateur since 1965 (in 2010 and 2012).

In 1938, Ogden Phipps presented a cup for the Open championship of the United States in memory of Clarence Pell – the Clarence Pell Cup. The first winner was Bobby Grant, who won it again in 1941, 1948 and 1950. Ken Chantler of Montreal was the first professional to win it in 1940, and again in 1957 and 1960. Albert (Jack) Johnson won it in 1959 and 1964, Jim Dear in 1962 and 1963.

Several amateurs were multiple victors of the Open singles – Geoffrey Atkins (1958 and 1968), Tom Pugh (1966–67) and Pete Bostwick (1969–70) – and then Willie Surtees surpassed all before him by winning from 1971 to 1979. In the 1980s Willie Boone won five US Open singles titles and John Prenn two. In the last twenty-five years, James Male has won four US Open singles and Rupert Owen-Browne and Jonathan Larken have taken two each.

Among professionals, Neil Smith has accumulated more US Open singles victories than anyone: ten, including six straight from 1991 to 1996 (coupled with twelve US Open doubles victories from 1989 to 2012, to make a remarkable twenty-two total Open victories). His fellow professional, James Stout, has now won five Opens, the most recent being 2014.

CANADA

As in India, Rackets was first played in Canada in military garrisons. It started towards the end of the eighteenth century in Montreal, Toronto and Hamilton (Ontario), Quebec and Halifax, Nova Scotia.

It is believed that the Montreal Rackets Club was formed in about 1800. It certainly existed in 1825, when a military map shows a court on the east side of Sanguinet Street, north of Craig Street.

The next court in Montreal was built in 1836 at the corner of St Peter and Craig Street. It was an open court of wooden construction, measuring about 34ft x 80ft. It was much used by officers of the garrison as well as pupils from neighbouring schools. Here Edward La Montagne learnt to play, and held the club championship from 1839 until he left for New York in 1852. He later described the court as open to the sky, the walls and floor painted black. Small boys would gather around it to pick up the balls that now and then went over the walls.

A macabre story is told of this court. Major Erle, later General Erle of Majuba Hill fame, was struck in the eye and the eyeball fell at his feet. Clapping his hand to his face he turned to the gallery and said, with a smile, 'The ladies won't look at me now.'

One of the first champion players was Sir Hippolyte Lafontaine, who played with a Pittman racquet, shaped like a Tennis racquet.

In Quebec, an old open-air court is known to have existed in the Artillery Barracks, and a new one was built about 1851 at the rear of Palace Street. Here the governor-general, Sir Edmund Head, used to play. The marker was Mahon, who later went to Montreal. This court was burnt down in about 1861 and a new one built, originally near St Louis Gate but later moved to a site off Grande Allée. Here the marker was Harry Boakes, who later played such a magnificent match with Joseph Gray in New York.

The Toronto court was attached to Lamb's Hotel near the junction of King Street and Simcoe Street. It was built by A. Thornton Todd, founder of the Toronto

Club, some time before 1844. In 1860, Queen Victoria's eldest son, later King Edward VII, played there while on an official visit to North America. A year later, the court was destroyed by an arsonist. The Hamilton court was built in 1860 and initially much used by civilians and military alike. It went out of use in 1883.

Two more courts were built in Montreal before the Montreal Racket Club court was opened in 1862 between Craig Street and Fortification Lane. This was a covered court with good natural lighting and remained in use until sold to the Montreal Star in 1870.

Many curious activities took place in these early courts, including boxing and rat-killing. The club professional would obtain a sackful of rats from the harbour from time to time and release them in the court. Whereupon members would watch from the gallery as their pet fox terriers were let loose, wagering on which terrier would kill the most rats.

About 1875, the Montreal Racket Club moved to St George Street and engaged Mahon and his son from Quebec as markers until 1881, when Albert Bridger was invited over from England. This court was regulation size, 30ft x 60ft, but the back wall was not at right angles – the left receiving court was slightly obtuse, the right slightly acute. Exhibition matches were played here by Bridger and Boakes from Quebec. It was highly exclusive, with only thirty to thirty-five members. Prominent among them was F.M. David, a brilliant, if somewhat erratic, player, who had brought Bridger from England and who was responsible for raising the money and supervising the building of the present Concord Street court in 1889.

In a mistaken endeavour to improve the doubles game, this new court was originally about 4ft longer and 2ft wider than normal, but in 1909 this was remedied with the aid of Bickley, and the court reduced to regulation size.

The earliest outstanding Canadian Rackets player was F.F. Rolland, the first winner of the Canadian Amateur championship in 1896 and the winner on seven other occasions. In 1898 he won the American singles, played that year in Boston, becoming the first of only two Canadians to have won this event. Apart from his skill as a player, he set a fine example of good sportsmanship and was an inspiration to many young players.

The Canadian championship – and the renowned hospitality of Canadians – has attracted many foreign visitors. The first visitor to win was B.S. de Garmendia from New York in 1897, followed by Q.A. Shaw from Boston in 1898. Rolland came back into his own in 1899, but Eustace Miles from England took the title in 1900.

Between the two world wars, the best Canadian amateur was Angus Cassils, who won the Montreal club championship every year from 1919 to 1930, except for 1923. He won the Canadian championship in 1920 and 1929, but mostly this was won by American visitors, especially Clarry Pell (first in 1914 and subsequently seven times) and Bobby Grant III (three times).

Since the Second World War, the best Canadian amateurs have been J.A. Rolland (winner of the Canadian championship in 1964), David McLernon (winner of the Canadian championship 1970–72 and 1976) and recently Bart Sambrook (in 1993 and 2006). Otherwise, the Canadian Amateur championship has continued to be dominated by foreign visitors, mostly British. Bobby Grant added five more victories and the title has been won by Geoffrey Atkins (six times), David Norman (three), Willie Surtees (four), Willie Boone (three), John Prenn (eight), James Male (five), Jonathan Larken (six), Rupert Owen-Browne (four) and Tim Cockroft (three), among others.

There has been a tradition of rivalry between Montreal and Boston, and in 1936 a handsome trophy was given for an annual match between the two clubs.

Celebrated Canadian amateur, David McLernon.

THE RECENT YEARS

Rackets in North America was indeed lucky when the era of Grant, Pell and Atkins was succeeded by the arrival of Willie Surtees, who lived first in Chicago and then in New York. He became world champion in 1972, lost to Howard Angus in 1973, regained the title in 1975 and then defended twice, before losing to John Prenn in 1981. By bringing such great champions as Angus, Prenn and Willie Boone to the North American shores, Surtees firmly established the tradition started by Geoffrey Atkins of playing one leg of the world championship in the New World. David McLernon of Montreal was also a revelation during this period. He was the best North American-born player since Bobby Grant and duelled often with Surtees.

The leading English players of the era came for a crack at Surtees, lured also by the North American formula for a Rackets weekend – black-tie stag night on Thursday, ball on Saturday, Rackets from Thursday to Sunday, singles and doubles. In addition to the future world champions, including James Male, other English tourists (and sometime residents) were David Norman, Charles Hue Williams, Garth Milne, Christopher Greene, Richard Bonsor, Andrew Beeson, the brothers Crawley and Nichols, Simon Davies, Tim Cockroft, Victor Cazalet, Rupert Owen-Browne and William Maltby, among others. The effect of these visits was to raise the standards and excite the appetites of North Americans for top-class Rackets. Plenty of them caught the bug, and many – Rob Wood of Chicago, Michael McMaster, Bart Sambrook and McLernon of Montreal, Dick Turner and Murray Sales of Detroit, Devens Hamlen of Boston, Peter Read and Edward Ulmann (winner of eight Amateur and two Open doubles titles in three different decades) of New York and Peter de Svastich of New York and Tuxedo – all became homegrown winners of national titles, albeit often in doubles with English partners.

The international flavour of the game gave birth to the first Quadrathlon, held in Montreal in 1976 – Rackets, golf, lawn tennis and squash. It was a huge success and has been held roughly every ten years since then. The Queen's Club hosted the Quintathlon (with Tennis) jamboree, and its own Centenary, in 1986. In 1996, it was another Quintathlon (shooting replaced Tennis) in Chicago and Detroit, and the millennium ended with the Queen's Quintathlon in 2000, to which over seventy North American Rackets players travelled. Finally, in 2012, Queen's again hosted a Quintathlon to coincide with the London Olympics.

North American Rackets owes a great deal to the wonderful professionals who have nurtured the spirit and skill of the game in the clubs. The doyens were Ken Chantler (Montreal), Jack Johnson (Chicago) and Jimmy Dear (New York). Jimmy Dunn in Philadelphia recruited boys from the city neighbourhoods to learn discipline and new, unusual (to them) games – Rackets and Tennis. As a result, the next generation of professionals included Dunn's protégés Jimmy Burke (Boston), John Cashman (Chicago), Tom Greevy (Tuxedo) and Eddie and Mike Noll and Rob Whitehouse (Philadelphia). Other prominent professionals at the time, both homegrown and English, were Mark McDonald (Chicago), Steve Tulley (Montreal), Shannon Hazell and James Beaumont (New York) and Neil Smith (Chicago and New York).

The clubs themselves were lucky to have guiding spirits who fostered the game at home and continentally via the North American Rackets Association. These included Michael Huband, Ron Kaulbach, Rick Hart and Tim Price in Montreal; Rob Wood, Rick Durkes, Ted Tieken and Davis Anderson in Chicago; Kevin Broderick, Tom Howe and Bob Thibodeau in Detroit; Tom Elliott and Louis Habina in Philadelphia; Kurt Graetzer, Greg Van Schaack, Peter de Svastich and Edward Mathews in Tuxedo; Devens Hamlen and Denis Walsh in Boston; Edward Ulmann, Peter Read, Kevin MacGuire, Nick Gardiner, Kendrick de Koning (also Chicago), William Bristowe and Guy Devereux in New York.

The twenty-first century dawned with a fine prospect in Jonathan Larken, Old Etonian, resident in New York, who in 2001 swept the US and Canadian Amateur singles and the US and Western Opens with wins in formidable company, earning the right to challenge James Male for the world championship in 2003, losing 5–4. Larken has continued to be the most competitive amateur player based in North America, most recently winning the 2013 US Amateur and consistently holding a top five ranking in the World Ranking System. He has had great competition from the likes of his fellow New Yorker, Devereux, Bart Sambrook and Karel Nemec (Montreal), Todd Meringoff (Boston) and recently Jon Crowell (Philadelphia). Meringoff brought his considerable lawn tennis skills to the Rackets courts, taking Alex Titchener-Barrett to four match points in the 2009 US Open and then winning the Amateur in 2010 and 2012.

The North American game changed further when Bermudian and Cheltonian James Stout joined fellow

2011 Invitational Rackets Event in Chicago, front row (left to right) *Todd Meringoff, Will Hopton, Ben Bomford, James Stout, Alex Titchener-Barrett, James Coyne, Nick James, Christian Portz.*

professional Neil Smith in New York in 2006. Since Stout's arrival, he has been world champion (since November 2008) and uncontested number one player in the world. In 2012, Will Hopton, a young Etonian and winner of several events on both sides of the pond, including the 2011 US Open, joined the staff in Chicago.

In the mid-1990s Detroit, for many years without a full-time professional, started a programme of bringing to the city, typically in their gap year for a two- or three-month Fellowship, young Brits who had become accomplished Rackets players at school. The programme blossomed to all clubs over the years and has been especially active in Chicago and Montreal. The bond between Rackets players on both sides became stronger still, further increasing enthusiasm and the level of play in North America and interest in coming to North America amongst young Brits. And, importantly to the future of the game, some Fellows have come back to North America as professionals at the clubs. Ryan Tulley, who was a Fellow in Montreal, later became the professional in Montreal. When he went back to England, he was followed by James Rock, who had been a Fellow in Chicago, the site where Will Hopton was a Fellow in 2010.

Steve Toseland became full-time professional in Detroit in 2006, while Barney Tanfield became Rackets professional in Philadelphia in 2007. Tim Chisholm, an American with exceptional talent in Rackets and Tennis, assumed the Tuxedo position with the retirement (from full-time service) of Tom Greevy in 2010. With Greevy's retirement, John Cashman (Chicago) and Jimmy Burke (Boston) became the deans of North American professionals.

With great teaching and play, Rackets in North America continued to attract young players – and even a few older ones – who were infected by the great speed and excitement on court, as well as the camaraderie and hijinks off court. Keene Addington, Jeff Durkes, Tim Merrill and Colt Landreth (Chicago), Christopher Scott, Peter Pell and Addison West (New York), Michael McLernon and Glenn Chamandy (Montreal), Jeff Yager and Dick Tanfield (Philadelphia), Manny Tancer, David and Grant Lockhart and Norb Madison (Detroit) and Greg Gross (Tuxedo), with many others, kept the game alive and healthy in every venue.

The tradition of lively off-court events and entertainment to complement great play on court continued. Notably, in 2004 the Rackets world celebrated in Chicago the fiftieth anniversary of Geoffrey Atkins's first world championship. All living champions attended, and James Male, having recently announced his retirement as champion, won the US Open singles title. In 2007, also in Chicago, the North American Rackets Association celebrated its fiftieth Anniversary. Many Rackets notables have served NARA, and in 2009 they gathered in New

Eton Tour in 1988, including Jonathan Larken and professional Norwood Cripps.

York to honour and recognise singularly Denis Walsh and his impact on Rackets. Importantly, the tradition continued of having one world championship leg, in both the singles and doubles, in North America, with attendant celebratory events.

Important to the success of these events continue to be the tourists who travel from England and contribute their skills to events on and off court. The Mjolnirs, in particular, in recent years have ensured a large contingent of Brits at almost every North American event, with Mark Agate, James Coyne and Dom Wright leading always through example. Since, sadly, there were no Rackets or Tennis events scheduled at the 2012 Olympics in London, a large contingent from North America went the other way across the pond to join their English hosts, led by Captains John Prenn and James Coyne, for the 2012 Quintathlon, reported as a 'flawless' execution of Rackets-style fun and games.

Two other activities have furthered the cross-ocean Rackets connections. In 1988, a group from Eton College, led by Rackets professional Norwood Cripps, travelled to North America for a schoolboy tour of the North American clubs. Every year since, contingents of Rackets-playing boys from two or three schools have come across the ocean and been introduced to their older, wayward North American cousins. Acquaintances and friendships begun on these tours often last a lifetime. In 1989, Jimmy Knott in New York and Bill Stephens in London started a bi-annual tradition of organising a team of generally younger players who would travel across the Atlantic to visit many of the Rackets venues on the other side. One year, English players would visit North America, and two years later, North American players would visit England. Under the watchful and passionate eye of Bill Stephens, who has carried on after the untimely death of Jimmy in 1995, there have been twelve Knott Stephens tours across the Atlantic.

As this great game continues forward, a new wave of young enthusiasts is beginning to make its mark on the world of Rackets, including Lucas Walsh in Boston, Zach Sacks in New York, Baker Thompson, Chris Leffingwell, Mike Keiser and Marty Kinsella in Chicago, Jon Crowell and Gary Swantner in Philadelphia, Chris Deruchie, and Charles and Fred Vennat in Montreal. Their names, following behind Grant, Pell, McLernon, Surtees, Ulmann, Walsh and many others, will headline the next bright chapter of Rackets in North America.

Knott Stephens Tour 2005, including James Coyne, Mark Agate and founder Bill Stephens.

RACKETS IN INDIA

A SPLENDID BOOK, *Rackets in India* by Colonel A.R. Winsloe, CMG, DSO, late RE, was published in Bombay by the Times of India Press in 1930. This comprehensive account of the game in that country between the wars provides much information about contemporary racquets, balls, methods of building courts and running competitions; in the course of this, many interesting sidelights are revealed on the state of the game.

The book is dedicated to Major-General S.H. Sheppard, CB, CMG, DSO, who wrote a foreword. His knowledge dated back to 1892 when, he tells us, 'Polo, Cricket and Rackets were the leading games in India.' After the war of 1914–18, Rackets declined in popularity, partly because of the expense and partly through the rival attractions of lawn tennis, hockey and squash. He pays tribute to Colonel Winsloe for his great efforts to revive the game in India.

Colonel Winsloe devotes a chapter to the history of Rackets in India and how it had spread throughout the country in the wake of the British Army. He recalls that forty years earlier, 'the income of the average sportsman enabled him to play polo and Rackets in addition to going out pig-sticking and shooting.' When he wrote, costs had risen greatly, not least due to a 30 per cent customs duty on goods imported from England.

He writes of some seventy courts in total and a map showing their location is included as an appendix. These courts evidently varied tremendously in size and pace; some were considerably larger than standard; all were slower than their English counterparts. Some were covered, most open. The oldest were at Sangor (1821) and Madras (1831); the best at Bombay, Calcutta, Jubbulpore (all covered courts) and Rawalpindi (an open court). The Bombay court was slightly larger than usual (64ft x 32ft), the same size as the older of the two present courts at Harrow.

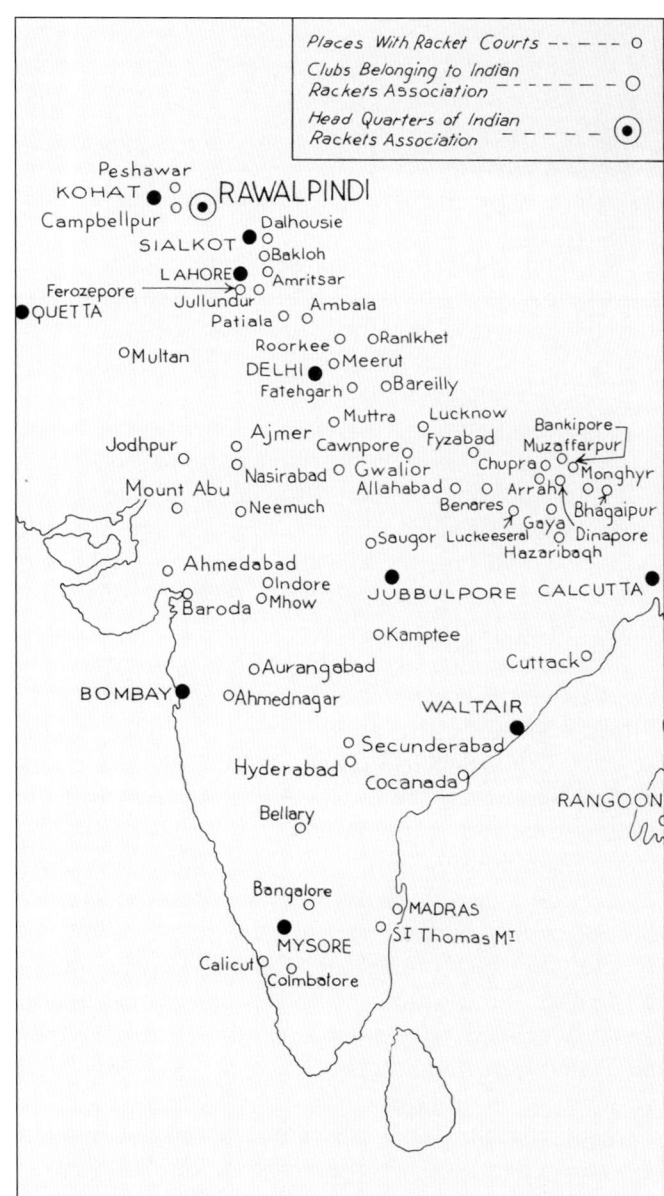

Rackets courts in India (from Rackets in India by Colonel A.R. Winsloe).

The court at Kohat (far left) *near Peshawar, Pakistan, in 1873.*

Several major tournaments were held, the first being the Bombay Gymkhana in 1885. The tournament in Rawalpindi started in 1901, the Northern Circars in 1903, Western India at Poona in 1904 and Central India at Jubbulpore in 1927.

Outstanding among players was Jamsetji, the Parsee marker at the Bombay court, who came to London in 1903 and defeated Gilbert Browne of Prince's Club for the world championship. In 1911, he lost the title to Charles Williams, the Harrow professional, who was sixteen years or so younger. Jamsetji was Professional champion of India from 1899 to 1917.

Of the amateurs, General Sheppard was outstanding, but Colonel Winsloe also mentions Colonel W.E. Wilson-Johnston, the aptly named Colonel A.J.H. Sloggett, Colonel J.G. Greig and R.J.O. Meyer. General Sheppard was the only Indian Army player to win the British Amateur championship and he also won the Army championship at Prince's in 1903, 1906 and 1921 – on this last occasion as a Major-General, at the age of fifty-one.

After the rules of Rackets, Colonel Winsloe writes of the balls and racquets, which he calls bats. Balls had evidently tended to get larger until standardised by the Tennis and Rackets Association some twenty years previously at about one inch in diameter and one ounce in weight. Balls in India were either covered with linen or leather, but both were affected by climatic factors, such as damp or excess heat. It is of interest that in England balls were apparently baked in the course of manufacture and had then to be allowed to cool down for twenty-four hours owing to the heat-retaining property of the wool in them. This wool content also made them appetising to the white ant, and the Colonel recommended keeping them in a linen bag.

It wasn't easy, he points out, to replace the woollen part of the core, since the old blue and red uniforms were no longer readily available and khaki was a poor substitute.

Racquets, too, deteriorated with climatic conditions in India. The Colonel recommends olive oil or linseed oil, and black rather than white gut. Attempts at producing a metal racquet with metal strings had not succeeded.

After a chapter on the construction of courts, he lists them all, indicating in each case their location, size, whether open or covered, their ownership, the material of the walls and any special remarks. Among the latter are ferro-concrete doors at Rawalpindi and Jubbulpore, a door in the side wall at Bakloh, and a note of the court's location in Residency grounds at Hyderabad.

As an appendix, he lists results of the various championships as well as detailed specifications for the construction of courts.

In 1975 Mr Muneer, Chairman of the Punjab Squash Club in Lahore, and Hashim Khan (Squash Champion) confirmed to Bill Stephens that only Rawalpindi and Peshawar still had Rackets courts standing in Pakistan.

History of the Rackets Ball

The earliest known *Book of Racquets* by J.R. Atkins, published in 1872, describes in detail the characteristics of the ball in use at that time. It was made by J. Wilson of 17 Roman Road, Victoria Park, London, who appears to have been the main manufacturer of both racquets and balls.

The 'Wilson' ball as used in the latter half of the nineteenth century was smaller than the present-day ball. It had a diameter of between 1in and $1\frac{1}{8}$ins and weighed less than 1 oz or 28 gms. There is, however, some evidence that in the 1850s the ball was both larger and heavier.

The Wilson ball was made of compressed cloth cut into strips and soaked in water. When saturated, the cloth was rolled into a ball and secured with several coils of strong hempen thread. It was placed in a 'cup' made of iron or hard wood consisting of two hemispheres, and compressed in a screw-press. The resulting core was further wound with damp worsted thread with further pressings until it had reached the proper dimensions. The finished core was placed on a square of sheepskin (smooth side out) which had been dampened and stretched. The four corners were pulled up and secured with stout thread. The overlapping pieces were cut off and the four seams were stitched together in a similar way to lacing a boot. The finished ball would undergo further pressing and baking to harden and dry it.

From early in the twentieth century, Rackets ball manufacture passed to Jeffrey Maling of Woolwich. Edward J. Bailey later became director of the business and became the main supplier of fives and Rackets balls until 1952.

The 'Bailey' ball was similar in construction to the old Wilson ball, but was somewhat larger and heavier. Although its characteristics were inconsistent, in general it measured about 1.56 ins in diameter and weighed about 35 gms.

Examination of old Bailey cores shows that the inner cloth was almost exclusively made from soldiers' uniform material and in one or two cases the piping from uniform trousers has been found. Maybe a supply of out-dated uniforms was purchased by Malings as suitable material for the inner cores of Rackets balls.

The performance of the Bailey ball was variable and often it would either lose its shape or the stitching would come adrift after a rally or two. A really good yellow, well-baked ball was much sought after by the players and was a delight to use. On the other hand, a 'stone' or heavy, poor-bouncing ball gave no pleasure, but was useful to the server.

Fifty or more balls were often used in a match and many were discarded after a single rally. At that time, any player could discard a ball at will and it was not until the late 1950s that the present rule was introduced, permitting only the receiver to claim a new ball. The balls were the property of the club professional who usually held a stock of two or three gross. He would bounce out a good set of balls for an important match and keep the throw-outs for the lesser players. In the 1930s, the cost of a ball to the player was about threepence and after use the balls were sent back to Bailey for reconditioning and re-covering.

Sadly, during the Second World War, Maling's premises suffered considerable bomb damage and Mrs Bailey was a casualty in the air raids. After the war, Bailey, then in his seventies, carried on limited business at 96 Wellington Street, Woolwich, but sheepskin covers were no longer available. White linen adhesive tape was introduced in lieu and this could be easily removed and replaced at the court after use. By 1950, there was a serious shortage of Bailey balls. Existing stock at the courts had run down and Bailey was no longer able to produce new cores. In addition, makeshift repair by inexperienced hands had damaged cores beyond the point of reconditioning. Some of the school courts which had closed during the war found it very difficult to obtain balls and, as so often happens, necessity became the mother of invention.

In the early 1950s, John Thompson, the Rackets

master-in-charge at Marlborough College, and Bill Gordon, who was appointed Marlborough Rackets professional in September 1951, began experimenting in making new Rackets balls. They were convinced that the secret of preventing loss of shape lay in finding a suitable material to make a solid inner core. They tried wood, ebonite and even glass marbles, but to no avail. The resulting worsted-wound balls neither had the correct bounce nor made the right sound.

In 1954, Dr J.C. Swallow (whose son Charles was at that time in the Charterhouse pair and in 1970 became British Open champion) provided some invaluable advice. He was a director and later chairman of the Plastics Division of ICI and he suggested that it might be worth trying polythene, a derivative of crude oil. During the war, Dr Swallow had headed a research team experimenting with polythene as an electrical insulator. The results of this work had figured in the development of RADAR equipment, which contributed so much to the UK war effort.

Polythene was produced after the war in 1¼in diameter spheres for medical use, to prevent the collapse of patients' lungs during surgery. Dr Swallow helped in procuring some of these spheres both for Marlborough and for Bill Hawes, the Charterhouse professional who was also experimenting with ball-making at the time. Hawes turned some polythene spheres on a lathe so that he could try cores of different sizes.

The first polythene balls were made at Marlborough and Charterhouse in 1954 with these 1¼in spheres. Adhesive tape covers were placed on the polythene core, which was then wound by hand with damp worsted, and two outer white tape covers were added. This produced a ball with encouraging characteristics. Unfortunately, the polythene cores tended to crack in play and the ball was too slow when cold and too fast when it warmed up with play.

The Tennis & Rackets Association had been kept informed of these experiments and they proposed that in due course each court in the country should be sent balls for trial. It was hoped to use the polythene ball for championships as soon as a suitable prototype was in production.

Bill Gordon ground down some cores to 1in diameter and these produced better playing characteristics and helped to reduce the pace of the ball when warmed up. Meanwhile, Dr Swallow suggested that injection moulded polythene would be stronger. Craxford Mouldings Limited were approached and they agreed to produce injection moulded polythene spheres of 1in diameter and the Tennis & Rackets Association agreed to purchase the matrix mould. The first supply of these cores arrived at Marlborough towards the end of 1954.

The first use of the polythene-centred ball in a championship was in January 1955 for the Noel-Bruce Cup at Queen's. John Thompson produced a set of balls with the new 1in spheres, which were called T2. These had six inner tape covers and were wound with worsted with two outer tape covers. The ball was about 1.5ins in diameter and weighed about 29gms.

After the championship (incidentally, won by Thompson and M.C. Cowdrey for Tonbridge) a questionnaire was completed by the eighteen leading players and elicited the following comments:

Question	Yes	No	Generally satisfactory
Do you like the T2 ball better than the Bailey ball?	13	2	3
Is the ball too fast?	3	10	5
Is the bounce too high?	6	2	10
Is there too much variation when the ball is hot and cold?	15	2	1
Is the ball an improvement on any other in use since the war?	17	1	
Would you be prepared to use the T2 ball in the Amateur championship?	15	1	2

These generally favourable comments were received with some relief. The two main criticisms were that there was too much variation in pace with temperature, and that when warm the bounce was too high. For a brief period a ball-heater, consisting of a small box containing a 60-watt electric lamp and a shelf for the balls, was tried. This was placed in the gallery by the marker and enabled the balls to be warmed up before use. This reduced the variation in pace, but did not solve the problem of the high bounce. Although the T2 ball was suitable for adult play at the top level, it was too fast for schoolboys and the Public Schools championship.

Bill Gordon found that by adding additional inner tape covers, the pace of the ball could be reduced, and from then onwards a polythene-cored ball could in theory be made to suit any court.

In February 1955, the Tennis & Rackets Association set up a ball-testing sub-committee comprising Harry Altham, the Winchester master-in-charge, and Jim Dear, the senior playing professional at Queen's, to whom all makers were invited to send samples for testing. The G6 ball made by Bill Gordon at Marlborough won the day, and the Tennis & Rackets Association decided that the G6 ball should be used for the Public Schools championships in 1956 and 1957.

The problem of producing the G6 in sufficient numbers still had to be solved. Each hand-wound ball took at least half an hour to make and was very hard on the hands. Gloves had to be worn to prevent the worsted thread cutting the fingers. Between May 1955 and January 1956, Bill Gordon made 1000 G6 balls – some 500 hours' work. This should go on record as an outstanding feat of patience and dedication which undoubtedly did much to save the game from extinction during this critical period.

Despite this magnificent effort, the problem of production remained if all courts were to have adequate supplies of the new G6 ball. In the summer of 1955, Marlborough began experimenting with a winding machine. John Thompson produced a Heath Robinson contraption made from old film spool-winding apparatus found in a science laboratory cupboard. With the aid of a foot clutch made from an old bicycle three-speed cable, he was able to wind a ball in fifteen minutes by turning the handle with his right hand, operating the clutch with his left foot and rotating the ball gradually with his left hand. This gave rise to thoughts of a mechanical power-driven winder, which would solve all problems.

At last help came from an unexpected quarter. Jim Hurn, captain of Wiltshire County Cricket Club at the time, was a talented mechanical inventor and he became interested in the notion of an automatic winding machine. Towards the end of 1955, he and a Melksham garage mechanic, Charlie Vines, produced the first prototype. There were initial problems in the timing of the rotation of the ball as winding proceeded, so that the thread did not build up on an axis. Eventually this was solved by trial and error and on 21 January 1956, Jim Hurn arrived at the Marlborough Rackets Court with the machine. Having set it up in Bill Gordon's room, Jim Hurn said, 'Right Bill, try that. If it works, let us have it back and we'll put in permanent bearings.'

Since then, this fantastic machine has wound some 50,000 Rackets balls. It can wind two balls in seven minutes and after fifty-eight years is still going strong. It has never been back for permanent bearings! The problem of supply was solved and Bill Gordon set to work in earnest.

In 1956, the G6 ball was officially adopted as the championship ball throughout Great Britain. In 1963, the North American Rackets Association also recognised it. The G6 was almost indestructible – it kept its shape indefinitely, the bounce was consistent and there was little variation with temperature.

In the late 1950s, terylene thread replaced worsted, as it was stronger and could be wound dry. Terylene was in turn superseded by nylon, which has similar properties. The original G6 had a diameter of 1.5 ins and a weight of 28 gms. Thus it was slightly smaller and lighter than the old Bailey ball and fewer racquets were broken. One ball lasted at least half a game, and this all-round economy greatly reduced costs.

However, although the G6 was such a success, there were some problems with the core, which eventually cracked. This, combined with the need to reduce production time, led Bill Gordon in the early 1980s to change from the 1in moulded core to a $1\frac{1}{8}$ins core turned on a lathe from an extruded rod of polythene. This increase in core size reduced the winding time considerably.

In 1992, Bill Gordon, at the age of seventy-nine, finally retired and his son Nigel took over production of the G6 ball. After thirty-seven years and over 32,000 balls, Rackets owes Bill Gordon an enormous debt of gratitude for his dedication to the game.

Since then, some minor, but important, changes have been made to the ball, mainly in the method of manufacture. Responding to requests for balls of different speeds, Nigel Gordon has introduced four balls of varying specification. These can be tailored to suit an individual court, primarily by altering the core size.

Allowing for the original winding machine's longevity, a new machine has been made which could replace it,

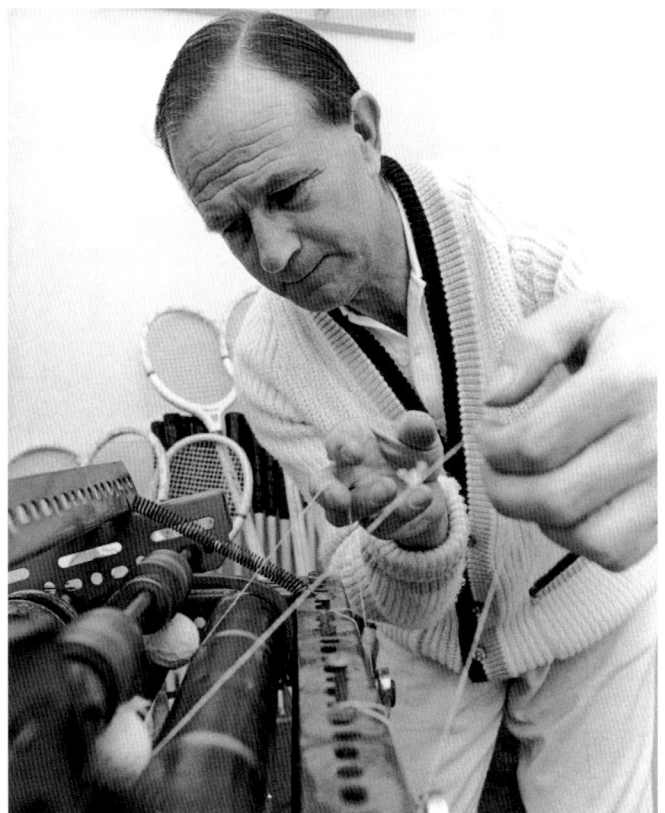

Bill Gordon making Rackets balls.

but at present Nigel uses the new machine for making Rugby Fives balls.

Over the last forty or so years, balls of a very high quality have been made by Peter Ashford, who started producing Rackets balls in the early 1970s. His ball is used for the Public Schools singles and doubles championships and has been adopted by many schools. He shapes the polythene cores himself, and then winds them by hand, so the balls are essentially fully handmade. Peter Ashford has been able to make at most five or six balls in an hour, but over a period of four decades the total number he has hand-produced may be 35,000. During the time in the early 1990s when Nigel Gordon was taking over manufacture from his father, there was a fifteen-month period when only Peter Ashford was supplying the Schools and Clubs, during which time he hand-made 3000 balls. A similar number of balls, perhaps up to 40,000, have been supplied in the last twenty-plus years by Nigel Gordon, notably for all the non-schoolboy events at Queen's and for some of the Schools in the UK and some of the Clubs in North America.

Over the last three years the T&RA, at the instigation of James Walton, have set in motion extensive research to find out how additional sources of Rackets balls could be established in order to protect the long-term future of the game. A Committee of Guy Smith-Bingham, Graham Tomkinson, Peter Brake, James Walton and Martin Crosby have found new sources of raw materials, clarified the most effective methods of manufacture and carried out frequent trials on samples. A Pelota-ball manufacturer in France called Punpa has produced samples that appear to be very encouraging and some of the Rackets Professionals in the UK are producing prototypes. A member of Queen's Club, Walter Thorpe, who has for three years been conscientiously investigating methods of producing good, consistent Rackets balls, submitted a batch to Ben Snell in January 2014 that Ben felt were worthy of being considered for use in the British Open championships. After being assessed by a number of top players, it was decided to play the Qualifiers with them, and then the Main Event as well. They were well liked by the competitors. It is hoped that balls from Punpa, Walter Thorpe, and maybe other sources, will be officially approved in due course, along with the two existing sources, Peter Ashford and Nigel Gordon, and that an up-dated Specification for Rackets balls can be agreed.

Right High stakes. The ball used at Manchester on 20 April 1887 in the match for £100 a side between Harry Gray and Peter Latham. Gray won 4 games to 2.

Below Old sewn Bailey balls and stages in the manufacture of the modern polythene-centred G6 ball.

Part III

Tennis and Rackets Courts around the World

Watercolour commissioned by Bobby Goodyear and painted by Phil Permar in 1990.

AIKEN TENNIS CLUB

A VERY LONG WAY from other US Tennis centres, the court at Aiken (near Augusta, on the Georgia/South Carolina border) was built in 1902 under the sponsorship of William C. Whitney. In 1937 it was sold to a local garage, but a group of Tennis enthusiasts refused to lie down and fortunately bought it back. Pierre Etchebaster was then engaged as part-time professional and had a profound influence on the game of Tennis there. He trained three students of the Aiken Preparatory School, each of whom later became world Tennis champion – Norty Knox and the brothers Bostwick, Pete and Jimmy.

More recently, Mark Devine took over as professional in 1995, having begun his career at Leamington. Under his watch, Camden Riviere won British Under-12 and Under-14 championships quite convincingly, and at the age of twelve had a handicap in the low 20s. Mark was succeeded by Gabe Kinzler in 2005 and continued until 2011 when Dacre Stoker took on the mantle.

Bobby Goodyear stepped down as president of the Aiken Tennis Club (ATC) in 2007 after serving with distinction for over thirty years, handing over the duties of president to Rick Preston. Rick is joined by Board members Paul Sauerborn, Lou Papouchado, Jim Geddes, Dacre Stoker, François Verglas and Michael Sullivan, in the running of the club. Bobby passed away in 2011 and, in his memory, the recently renovated bar area in the clubroom has been dedicated and named in his honour. His fellow club members, and also the hundreds of visitors to Aiken whom Bobby hosted as guests at the Augusta National Golf Club, will miss Bobby very much.

The current membership at the ATC is near capacity at about one hundred members, many of whom are active in either Tennis and/or bottle pool. Court usage

The court was built by Joseph Bickley under the sponsorship of William C. Whitney in 1902.

A promising future – Camden Riviere with Ginny Goodyear and Mark Devine.

ATC member Camden Riviere has risen through the professional ranks to win numerous national and international championships and contend twice for the world championship. ATC is very proud of his accomplishments.

Informal dinners have continued on Wednesday evenings at the club. These are held mostly outdoors on our patio, or indoors if the weather is too cold or rainy (which is not too often). Members rotate responsibilities to cook, or to bring prepared foods, to serve any number from eight to over twenty regulars, all of whom really enjoy this event.

The playing of bottle pool has once again become a regular event in the clubroom. The game has been revitalised through the efforts of the new pool committee, led by John Harte. The committee has organised clinics for novice players and has managed to get many new players involved in the game. The club singles handicap tournaments have been resurrected, and two tournaments were held this year. These tournaments attracted a record number of members and were hotly contested. Members also enjoyed reading fun commentaries that were written regularly describing the matches. The clubroom is now buzzing with activity most evenings and during the weekends.

is at an all-time high, aided by the new online court booking system. The doubles tournaments are well subscribed and more interest has begun to be seen in singles play, especially by younger members. League Tennis play has become a regular event and has had excellent participation levels.

Children of more than half a dozen members are now actively playing Real Tennis, including the Bostwicks, Goodyears, Harringtons, Kings, Rutherfurds, Stokers, and Voegeles.

Annually, the club hosts two signature Tennis events: The Calhoun Witham doubles tournament in early November, for players with handicaps over 30, and the Norty Knox doubles tournament in April, for players with handicaps under 30. Over the years, both these events have attracted fields of teams from other US and international clubs, who have enjoyed southern hospitality, nice weather, competitive play and social activities.

The club also hosts the Honeck Bisque, which is a team doubles tournament where handicap points are replaced with an appropriate number of bisques or half bisques, in memory of a departed club member Hank Honeck, who wrote a dissertation on the use of the bisque.

(left to right) Rick Preston, Woody Millen, Dacre Stoker.

Knox 2010 and 2011 winners (left to right) Gabe Kinzler marker, Ben Cook, Rick Preston, Rakesh Jasani, Dacre Stoker.

Honeck Team doubles 2005.

BALLARAT TENNIS CLUB

The Tennis court at Ballarat, a substantial city in Victoria, Australia, was built by John Gilbert in 1984. The first professional was Rob Bartlett, who had been born in the neighbouring town of Daylesford, training as a Tennis professional at Hampton Court Palace and Canford School before returning down under.

Almost from the word go, the court received accolades from many international players who had experienced the vagaries of other courts. This from Melbourne's Ted Cockram soon after the court opened:

The court – and penthouse in particular – reminds me of the New York court. The ball tends to pull up slightly on the penthouse, which is not as fast as the Melbourne penthouse. The walls are livelier than Melbourne and the floor surface is good, if a little rougher, and this tends to keep the ball lower . . . there is potential for experimenting with high serves such as the 'giraffe'.

The Ballarat court is of similar design and measurements as the Melbourne courts; however, the roof is

Court built in 1984, largely due to John Gilbert.

unencumbered by beams, the walls are a dark burgundy colour, the floor a light green and the lines and chase markings of white and yellow. The side galleries and penthouse ledges are slightly lower than at Melbourne, and the tambour has its own angle, which can only be 'read' after time spent on the court.

The Ballarat Silver Racket was inaugurated in the year that the club opened and, over the years, some of the best players in the world have competed in the event. Winners read like a *Who's Who* of tennis: Chris Ronaldson, Graham Hyland, Lachie Deuchar, Julian Snow, Frank Filippelli, Chris Bray, Brett McFarlane and Jonathan Howell. In recent times, the difficulty in raising sponsorship has seen the event suspended pending its new role as an 'Open handicap event'.

In 1988 Ballarat hosted the Bathurst Cup, which enabled the local members to witness the play of some of the finest amateur players in the world.

The court is under the control of professional Brett McFarlane, who started at the club in 1997. His arrival virtually coincided with the ladies' world championship at Ballarat, which saw England's Penny Lumley retain her title. Brett had studied at the University of Ballarat in the Physical Education faculty, and he played a high standard at squash before joining the Royal Melbourne Tennis Club as coach for both squash and Tennis.

In 2012 Ballarat staged an exhibition match featuring Rob Fahey and Claire Vigrass.

2012 exhibition match featuring Rob Fahey and Claire Vigrass, with Pro Brett McFarlane.

The Ballarat club has produced some fine players over the years, such as Steve Virgona and Andrew Fowler in the professional ranks, Wayne Spring, John Faull and David Parker in the amateur ranks, and Daniel Williams, Michael Williams and Laura Fowler in the junior ranks.

LE JEU DE PAUME DE BORDEAUX

This Tennis club has been in existence since 1788, when M. Peres Duvivier, a rich Martinican, built a court in the rue Rolland to satisfy the Duc d'Artois, who intended to spend some time in Bordeaux. The first known court in the town, however, existed in 1460 and bore the name of Talbot. John Talbot, Earl of Shrewsbury, was appointed Lieutenant of Aquitaine by Henry VI and in 1429 directed the siege of Orleans. He and his son were killed in battle when fighting on behalf of the barons of Aquitaine, faithful to the English King, against the forces of Charles VII of France. Talbot is buried in Winchester Cathedral. The French Revolution ruined the Duvivier family. The court was sold to a firm of carpet makers and had ceased to be used for Tennis by 1827. Fifty years later, after periods as a concert hall and then an auction room, it was bought for 53,000 francs by an enthusiast, M. Duroy de Suduiraut, who restored it. In so doing, he reversed the court so that the dedans was more conveniently situated at the end that had previously been the grille.

The Merignac court, which sadly closed down in 2013.

Camden Riviere wins the 2012 French Open.

from four Tennis-playing nations every year. There was also an unusual team competition (two singles and a double) for the Coupe de Noël, in which all entrants were listed by ability, and the worst paired with the best. The French Open was hosted at the club in 2003, 2005, 2008, 2009, 2010 and 2012 and was won in each case by Robert Fahey, apart from in 2003, when the title was claimed by Tim Chisholm, and 2012 when Camden Riviere won it for the first time.

In 2001 Gerard Eden took on the role of professional, until he was replaced by Julian Fox in 2003, who continued for three years. Simon Marshall took over in 2007 and remained at the club until its closure. He was assisted by Lucy Caulfield from September 2011 until the end. In January 2012 a vote was passed to sell the club and rebuild it somewhere else in Bordeaux. The club finally closed its doors in Merignac on 31 March 2013. When it closed there were fifty-five members, the highest number for the last twenty years.

This meant an alteration to the tambour, and may explain the curious construction of the wall at the top, which was retained when the old premises were sold and a new court was built in 1978.

The new court was situated in Merignac, a pleasant suburb of Bordeaux. Among the annual competitions were the Coupe Duroy de Suduiraut (the club championship), the Raquette d'Or and the Raquette d'Argent (for French players only), and the Coupe de Bordeaux, open to amateurs of any nationality. This was won by some distinguished foreign players, including Edgar Baerlein, Lord Aberdare and Howard Angus (five times). John Ward won in 1982 and 1985, before Julian Snow captured it in 1987 and held it for ten years. Alongside the Coupe de Bordeaux was the Edouard Kressmann Trophy tournament, an international handicap event for the Over-50s, played in memory of a remarkable connoisseur of the game and initiated by his son Roland. The Kressmann competition was very popular and there tended to be roughly forty entrants

Lucy Caulfield and Simon Marshall.

BOSTON
THE TENNIS AND RACQUET CLUB

Founded early in the 1900s, the Tennis and Racquet Club enjoyed great prominence through the first half of the twentieth century, no doubt partly due to the desirable location of its magnificent building. No expense was spared in its construction. The entrance hall was finished in Caen stone, and it had a staircase of marble and wrought iron, and a panelled ceiling.

During the latter part of the twentieth century, the club encountered major financial challenges, which continued into the first part of the twenty-first century. Declining membership numbers, a worsening financial picture, and unimproved facilities plagued it, while interest in the games, quizzically, increased. The Rackets programme witnessed a burst of activity with Mike McLernon, Jeff Yager, Alistair Gourlay, Rob McLane, Nelson Russell, Tom Bristowe, Dev Hamlen and Denis Walsh all contributing to an active Rackets court and travelling core to other clubs.

During this period, the club built two new international squash courts, which helped attract returning players. A good number of these players subsequently took up Real Tennis and Rackets and became hooked.

The clubhouse was designed in the early 1900s by J. Harleston Parker in the style of Louis XVI, and Joseph Bickley supervised the building of the courts.

(left to right) *Mike McLernon, Lucas Walsh, Todd Meringoff, Devens Hamlen.*

(left to right) *John Mears, John Bigelow, Pro Jimmy Burke, Dick Brickley.*

Rackets player Alan Rose took over as club president after Bob Hurley's term, and helped to see the squash court project through to completion. In the pro shop, Jimmy Burke remained steady at the helm as head Tennis and Rackets professional and introduced many members to both games. On the Tennis side, Rob McLane, Brian Hill, Sam Stevens, Will Thompson, Bradley Allen, Robert Sheppard, P.J. Yeatman, John Bigelow, Steve Poskanzer, Mark Slater, Jeremy Wintersteen and Dick Brickley were among the more active players.

Batons would be passed for leadership of the Tennis and Rackets Committees with Todd Meringoff, Lucas Walsh, Jeremy Wintersteen, Shawn Herlihy, Ken Forton and Arthur Drane taking on more responsibilities after many years of service to the games from Denis Walsh and Dick Brickley.

During this time, and it's hard to pinpoint exactly why, Tennis began to undergo an uptick. The club stepped up to the plate to host a variety of tournaments, including US Opens and other upper-level competitions. Court hours increased, more lessons ensued, players increasingly travelled to other clubs for tournaments, and overall play improved. What the club lacked in funds, it made up for with a welcoming, friendly and fun atmosphere for visiting players and tours.

The club managed to stay afloat and upgraded the men's and women's locker rooms and fitness centre. Christmas parties, exhibition matches, a host of tournaments and an increasingly lively athletics and bar scene became the staple of the club. A number of assistants and visiting players came through Boston and helped Jimmy. These included Camden Riviere, Jacques Faulise, Tim Chisholm, and several young Rackets players from the club's Rackets Fellows programme.

Arthur Drane, a long-time Tennis player and enthusiast (and current Tennis Committee chair), helped to revive the Patriot Cup, an annual inter-city competition between Boston and Newport. At the

Denis Walsh.   *Arthur Drane.*

same time, more club players continued to travel and post better tournament results. Top on this list would be Matt Porter, a Tasmanian transplant to Boston. A satellite tour lawn tennis player, Matt took up the game quickly and became both club (with Kip Curren) and US Amateur singles, doubles and mixed doubles champion, also gaining a Kendrick Cup Rackets title. For the US Amateur, Matt became Boston's first national singles champion since 1948 and, with Jeremy Wintersteen, first doubles champion since the early twentieth century. After years of being a doormat, and then several years of coming painstakingly close, the club – along with sister club Newport and together forming a 'New England' team – won the Whitney Cup two years in a row, followed by two finalist appearances. The club also hosted two world championship eliminator matches (featuring then-club member Tim Chisholm) and a successful world championship doubles tournament in 2007. In 2009, the Winter League was formed, and has since become a very popular weekly competition and social night.

Club Tennis players have posted wins in a number of USCTA tournaments including Level championships, Etchebaster, mixed doubles, Calhoun Witham, Norty Knox, Jimmy Dunn, NY Open handicap, Age Levels, World Overs, Lord Percival, Anne Boleyn, Newport handicap and Pell Cup. A number of players have made the USCTA's Top 25 lists, with Matt Porter often in the top spot. Suzy Schwartz, Helen Grassi and Nancy Multer have been among the more active women players. Other active players have included Breton Hornblower, Jeff Horine, Garrett Gates, Alex Spence, Phil Stockton, Eric Shabshelowitz, Nick Miller, Gary Multer, Dave Tedeschi, Ken Forton, Andy Roberts and Harsha Gopal. George Bell, who had been away from the game, moved back to Boston and quickly became a good addition to the Tennis programme. Lunchtime regulars include John Mears, Ed Wadsworth, John Bigelow, Kevin Clancy, Paul Bolster, Rick Gold and Larry McCray. John Mears has been one of the more active players and has also generously hosted a number of visiting tours at his apartment. Dan di Bartolomeo has also been a long-time player and supporter of Real Tennis in Boston.

Tony Hollins joined the pro shop in 2012 as senior professional, and has been a great addition to the club. He has organised Winter League, boosted play in both Tennis and Rackets, and has been an integral part of the Tennis and Rackets growth. The club's National League team ('New England' – Tony, Rich Smith of Newport and Camden Riviere out of Charleston) defended their title in 2013.

On the Rackets side, Todd Meringoff quickly picked up the game and became one of the top amateurs in the US. He has won several US Amateur singles and doubles titles and has a lot of paint on various club Rackets championship boards. In recent years, the Rackets programme has seen a rebound, with several new members taking up the game. These include Lucas Walsh, Matt Breuer (US Amateur doubles champion with Todd), Eike Satake, Josh Peck, David Kohn and Ryan Hayes. The Rackets Committee has also successfully hosted a number of tournaments, bringing more people to the Hub and helping to grow the game. The club also hosted a very successful US Open in 2014.

While the Tennis and Rackets programmes continued to grow, the club's roof finally reached breaking point. After several postponements due to weather, the USCTA pulled Tennis tournaments from the club until the roof was properly fixed. Club members were used to having to check the weather before heading over to play an indoor sport; lessons were repeatedly cancelled due to weather. After years of patching and hoping, the club and the building owner partnered on a successful effort to fix the roof (over the Tennis, Rackets, and one squash court). The Roof Project was led by Suzy Schwartz, who became the club's first female president in 2009. Suzy did an incredible job of pulling together a lot of pieces. With help from the USCTA, the US Court Tennis Preservation Foundation, and many generous donors, the club was finally able to fix the roof. As part of the Roof Project, building owner Devens Hamlen placed a deed restriction on the building, guaranteeing the permanent future of the Tennis court. In addition to the roof, new windows, gutters, downspouts, painting and other building improvements were made. A new floor was laid on the Tennis court and a sound system added. A successful Raise the Roof tournament weekend was held in 2013 to commemorate the new roof. The national Open was held in December and marked the return of tournament play to the club. No weather forecasting was needed!

With Tom Dobbins and Janice Pearson at the helm as club manager and finance manager, long-time member and Tennis and Rackets player Dick Brickley took over as club president at the end of 2013. With a repaired roof, new and younger players, and momentum gathering, Tennis and Rackets are in a good place in Boston and will continue on for many years in some of America's oldest courts.

BRISTOL REAL TENNIS CLUB

Although the Bristol Real Tennis Club was founded in December 1985 as the Bristol & Bath Tennis Club, it was another twelve years before it had a court of its own. During that time, competitive home fixtures were played at the Hardwick House court, the club having obtained a corporate membership by courtesy of Phoebe, Lady Rose. They also put on special events and coaching days at Hardwick in order to promote the game generally and to enhance membership. As a result of these activities, the club built up a total membership of over 200 from all over the country and abroad, before opening their own premises.

The club was founded on the desire of a few enthusiastic players in the Bristol area to restore the court in Bath, or alternatively to establish a new court in the locality. The inaugural meeting was held under the chairmanship of John Barford on 5 December 1985. It was clear that the Bath Court, probably the only surviving eighteenth-century court in the country, was not going to be available, because the Trust which ran an industrial museum in the building was unwilling to relinquish occupation. So the club concentrated on procuring a site in the Bristol area and efforts were focused on land owned by Clifton College.

After several years and a number of abortive investigations, Clifton College kindly offered a site at the Beggar Bush playing fields, about a mile west of the main campus over the Clifton suspension bridge. The site was occupied by some old workshops and the provision of land for the court was conditional on the club providing new workshops. John Bretten, chairman at the time and a member of the inaugural committee, and Michael Jones, the secretary, formulated detailed plans and a financial strategy. Planning permission was obtained, after a long battle, in autumn 1994, and at this stage the building costs of the court were estimated at £404,000. This was shortly before the National Lottery came into operation in January 1995, and Bristol were among the first applicants for a grant to submit detailed proposals.

In August of that year the club was told that its application had been agreed in principle, and the grant was formally confirmed in May 1996. The final costings amounted to £565,000 plus VAT; the lottery

The court was built on land belonging to Clifton College with National Lottery funding, and officially opened by The Earl of Wessex in 1998.

Kevin King hard at work.

contributed £353,000, and the balance was raised by the club, mainly through selling fully transferable twenty-year memberships.

The first ball was struck in December 1997 and the court was officially opened by The Earl of Wessex on 14 February 1998. There are extensive clubrooms, some of which overlook the court at first-floor level, providing an unusual viewing area.

The club secured Kevin King as the first professional, and such was the enthusiasm that, by the third week of November 1998, less than a year after play began, all ninety-eight hours of court time were filled. Over sixteen years later, Kevin continues to be the head professional; under his leadership a number of well-known full-time assistant pros have been employed, the first of whom was Charlotte Cornwallis in 1998. Andrew Fowler became assistant pro in 2011 before moving on to Queen's the following year. During this time he arranged a series of exhibition matches against Ben Matthews, Conor Medlow and John Lumley.

In 2003 the club hosted the inaugural championship of the Irish Real Tennis Association (IRTA). It was so successful that the IRTA have been back many times since, while they continue to try to get the court in Dublin back in play. That same year the club founded the Scholarship Trust as a charity to encourage children and young people to play Real Tennis. This initiative has led to a successful junior programme, including the Bristol Schools Medal, which is open to all-comers from all schools in the wider Bristol area. In addition to hosting matches against other schools for Clifton College, the club has a series of fixtures against other clubs for its young players. The club also encourages players from Bristol University to play matches against other university teams.

In May 2004, Rob Fahey treated the club to a coaching clinic and exhibition match against Nick Wood. This was followed by a doubles exhibition in March 2006 comprising Rob and Mark Eadle from The Oratory against Rod McNaughtan from Middlesex and Brad Dale from Hobart, who had temporarily exchanged jobs with Kevin. Then Claire Vigrass staged a clinic and exhibition match in 2010, followed by an exhibition match with Rob in 2013, which attracted radio and TV coverage.

In 2008 the club celebrated the tenth anniversary of the official opening of the court with a Festival of Tennis comprising two new competitions, the Brunel Cup – with teams of two doubles pairs – and the Anniversary doubles. The centrepiece of the festival was a dinner on SS *Great Britain*, the iron ship designed by Isambard Kingdom Brunel in 1843 and restored in the 1970s. Peter Probyn succeeded John Bretten as chairman in 2002, followed by David Pigott in 2006, Julian Hemming in 2010 and Denis Mullan in 2014. The club continues to grow, attracting the majority of its members from newcomers to the game, and thus meeting one of its principal aims of widening participation in Real Tennis in the West Country.

Andrew Fowler, seen here with former Chairman Julian Hemming, was assistant professional in 2011.

Brunel Cup Winners (left to right) *Nick Ponsford, James Dron, Ann Skelhorne, Judy Orme.*

CAMBRIDGE UNIVERSITY

By the end of the sixteenth century, most Cambridge colleges had their own Tennis courts, but they gradually fell out of use. By the beginning of the nineteenth century only Pembroke's survived, giving its name to Tennis Court Road. In 1853, the Wellington court was built in East Road, and both courts were used by the university until their demise at the end of the century. The annual match against Oxford began in 1859 – just three years after the establishment of a regular Boat Race.

The first of the two Clare and Trinity courts, modelled on the Tuileries court in Paris, was built in 1866 at a cost of nearly £3,000; the second was added in 1890 for £2,232, under the supervision of William C. Marshall, who was responsible for the Queen's Club courts. The roof of the second court was opened up in 1913, giving overhead light to supplement the customary side windows.

The outbreak of the First World War led to their temporary closure. Appeal funds saved them in 1919 and 1929, but in 1933 the 1890 Tennis court was converted into four squash courts. At the same time, electric lighting was installed in the old court, the walls and floor were painted white and orange balls were used in an attempt to improve visibility. The experiment was not a great success and the original colour was restored in 1960.

In 1998 the committee launched an appeal to fund the restoration of the 1890 court, which had previously been turned into four squash courts. The conversion of

The 1890 court was converted back from squash courts and reopened in 1999.

the squash courts back into a Real Tennis court was a major team effort – Club Treasurer Jeremy Fairbrother negotiated with the university to secure a contribution towards fixing the roof, and raised the rest of the money from various sources. Several club members, including Fairbrother and Simon Stokes, helped knock down the squash courts and Alexis Hombrecher painted the lines.

It was opened for play a year later and named the Blue Court. The reopening of this second court made a dramatic difference to the club. Since then, membership has more than doubled and the pros have been able to run an enhanced programme of tournaments and junior courses, as well as varsity and senior member development. The court was opened by the vice chancellor of the university, Alec Broers (now Lord Broers) in December 1999. Broers, upon an invitation from club stalwart Nigel Brown, managed to hit the grille at his first attempt (although he was standing in the hazard end at the time). Jimmy Carr, the oldest member of the club, played the first shot of the first match on the new court, an event later marked by a plaque in memory of Jimmy, who passed away in 2000.

In memory of Jimmy Carr (1916–2000), who hit the first ball on this restored court on December 2nd 1999, a high lob into the dedans.
He gave encouragement to everyone who met him and we can be proud to follow him on court.

In the last ten years the club building has seen a number of other renovations, including creating new viewing spaces at the dedans end of the Blue Court both upstairs and downstairs. The upstairs room now has a reinforced glass wall as well as a kitchen and dining facilities. The pros moved to the downstairs area of the dedans, and in 2012 the space was divided, to separate the pros' office from the spectators' area. Tennis Court House, home of the senior pro, was also upgraded, with a loft conversion giving the house an extra bedroom. More recently, the club also had a face-lift in preparation for the Corinthian Cup, an international tournament held by the Cambridge, Newmarket and Hatfield clubs to coincide with the 2012 Olympics.

Only six professionals have been in charge during more than a century, each an outstanding contributor to the success of the game at Cambridge. John Phillips, son of the Duke of Wellington's former professional at Stratfield Saye, was appointed manager in 1866 (at a salary of 25 shillings a week) and reigned until 1882. He was succeeded by his assistant, Jim Harradine, who took on his nephew, Arthur Twinn, as a boy assistant in 1893. Twinn took over in 1909 and in 1921 was joined by his son Eric, and they remained together until the outbreak of war in 1939.

Bill Tutt was in charge from 1945 to 1956, followed by Brian Church in 1958. He was responsible for training many of today's professionals, including Barry Toates (Hobart), Adam Phillips (Lord's) and Andrew Knibbs (Newmarket); but the outstanding trainee was Chris Bray (Holyport), who rose to be second in the world rankings. Church also trained a large number of first-class amateurs, the most eminent being Howard Angus, Amateur champion 1966–82 and world champion 1976–81 – the only amateur to have won the world titles at both Tennis and Rackets.

Peter Paterson joined as assistant professional in 1995, and Kees Ludekens became senior professional after Church retired in 1996, with assistance from Kate Leeming and Mark Hobbs. Ludekens encouraged the growth of the game in Cambridge to such an extent that the court was in use for fifteen hours a day almost every day of the week. Scott Blaber joined as trainee professional in 2003, having never played before, and was promoted to assistant professional in 2007.

The current team of Ludekens, Paterson and Blaber run a very busy competitive and social programme for members. Club handicap leagues, including an Over-60 category, and several other tournaments are held during the year. The Cambridge Singles League, held in the spring, now involves around a hundred members, and features dinners provided by the designated 'home' teams. The annual Cambridge Weekend has been a regular fixture since 2005, and sees the club welcome former and current members for a weekend of competitive handicap doubles and the annual club dinner, usually held in one of the Cambridge colleges. The Champagne

Kees Ludekens teaching an airborne stroke.

(left to right) *Pros Scott Blaber, Kees Ludekens, Peter Paterson.*

League, a summer tournament sponsored by Pol Roger since 2010, culminates in a knockout finals weekend.

The pros have also developed a busy junior programme, which runs early on weekdays and on Sundays and is supported not only by parents, but also by Cambridge University Press. In 2011, Cambridge junior Tatham Harper reached the British Under-12 final at Queen's, eventually being defeated by Nicholas Milton of Hyde.

Since 2000, Cambridge has had a fantastic showing in the National League, topping the honours board in 2002, 2005, 2007, 2008 and 2009, and being a finalist in 2003 and 2006. Rob Fahey, multiple world champion, represented the club from 2000 to 2007; other players who have represented Cambridge include Jamie Douglas (2009 UK Amateur singles champion and 2011 Amateur doubles champion), Alexis Hombrecher, Rod McNaughton, Neil Roxburgh and David Woodman. In 2012, the Cambridge Division 1 team of David Woodman (2007 UK Amateur doubles champion) and Andrew Fowler were defeated in the semi-finals by the Dedanists. James Watson (Varsity captain 2011–12) and Scott Blaber (assistant professional) won the National League Division 2 final that same year.

In 2007 George Pearson took over the reins as club president from Peter Raby and has worked with the pros to expand club activities on and off the courts. Club captain Duncan Colquhoun led the Cambridge team to victory in the Field Trophy in 2009, and a succession of fixtures secretaries have ensured that Cambridge teams travel not only to courts around the UK, but also overseas, particularly to the Boomerang Cup in Australia.

Varsity matches continue to provide exciting Tennis and develop a few exceptional players. The Cambridge ladies' team was dominant for the five years from 2005, with players including Karen Hird, Sarah Vigrass, Claire Watson, Julia Clarke and Marsali Grant. Several of the men's players have reached single-figure handicaps, including Alexis Hombrecher, David Woodman, Jamie Douglas, Neil Roxburgh and Burak Salgin. Giraffe membership, an initiative started in the early 2000s, gives university alumni and former CURTC members the opportunity to support the Varsity team. Their donations go towards coaching, travel to other clubs, and court and marking charges, as well as helping the Varsity teams to travel overseas in the summer to play, principally in the US and France. Despite the high number of playing members, there is still capacity for extra players on the two courts.

The next goal for CURTC is to push senior membership above 300 in the near future.

CANFORD SCHOOL

Canford's first Tennis court is mentioned in a 1541 document describing the 'Cituation of the house and manor of Canford':

The tenys playe: itm thar is a tenys playe buylded of tymbr and bords standing sowth and north and it jonyth to the sowth east corner of the forsaid bed chamber havyng a wyndow lowkyng owt of the chambr in to the tenys playe and the flore of the saime playe is of hard stone that came owt of purbeke and it contz in length xxiiijvj ffowt and in bredith xxiij ffowt but the bords and timbr warke is in great decay.

After 1776, the medieval buildings (apart from 'John o'Gaunt's kitchen', which still stands) were replaced by a mansion, and this was greatly enlarged after Sir John Josiah Guest bought the Dorset manor in 1845. It was the second baronet, Sir Ivor Bertie Guest, later Lord Wimborne, who in 1879 had both a Tennis and a Rackets court built in the grounds. *The Times* attended the opening:

The floor is of slabs of Yorkshire flag, each 7ft. by 4ft. and 4ins. thick, laid on dwarf walls, so as to secure ventilation and prevent sweating. There are no windows, but the court is beautifully lit from above by skylights 16ft. deep, running on either side of the ridge the whole length of the roof, and completely preventing the possibility of shadow. The distinguishing feature of the court, however, is due to the attention which has been paid to ventilation, which is secured by Louvre ventilators placed over the tie-rods of the roof at either end. Openings fitted in the same manner are made in the main wall above the play line. The result of the care and attention bestowed upon every detail of the court was seen in the admiration expressed by all the players on each day of a most trying week, and so far experience has shown that that admiration was not misplaced.

The Tennis court was renovated in 1913 and a new floor installed, but the Rackets court fell into

The court was built in 1879 by Sir Ivor Bertie Guest, later Lord Wimborne.

216

The pair who wanted to play with lawn tennis racquets..., Commissioned by Richard Greenwood and painted by H. M. Bateman after a visit to Canford in 1964.

disrepair (it was converted into two squash courts in 1962).

Canford School was founded in 1923, in the final years of the resident professional, Edward 'Ted' Johnson. His eldest son, Edward Junior, taught the game to a handful of boys, and they played their first match against a team from Queen's Club in November 1925.

During the 1930s, the fixture list was extended and the master-in-charge, W.S. Strain, devoted much time to taking boys in his car to play in other courts. G.H. Holman arrived as professional in 1933, and in 1935 W.D. Whiston became the first Canfordian to win a Tennis blue at Cambridge. No competitive play was possible during the war, as American servicemen occupied that part of the school near the Tennis court.

The roof, which had been restored in 1935 through the generosity of Lord Aberdare and others, was battered in the war, and severe gales continued to take their toll. Strain and, briefly, Holman worked on after the war to revive the game, and the court was much restored in 1952.

By then, J.T. Hankinson had taken over as master-in-charge, and Malcolm Taylor, the school's cricket professional, had been trained at Lord's to move into Tennis. He was replaced in 1969 by Hampshire's former Test cricketer Derek Shackleton, who, the records say, 'received some basic instruction at Lord's and soon became a competent marker.'

Darcy Steed, who had served Canford since his boyhood, spent his final ten years before retirement as master-in-charge. He gave way to John Boys in 1973, the golden jubilee of the school's foundation, which was marked by the complete redecoration and re-equipment of the dedans by the Old Canfordian Society. The centenary of the court, in 1979, was celebrated with exhibition matches between several leading players.

In 1980, Boys and his headmaster, M.M. Marriott, realised that the school could not support a full-time professional unless the court was opened to outside players. Rob Bartlett, trained by Chris Ronaldson at Hampton Court, was appointed with authority to make part of his living by forming a club for local enthusiasts, who would pay subscriptions and court fees. It was an immediate success, and membership now stands at 120. Bartlett left for the new court at Ballarat, Victoria, in 1982, but not before he and one of the boys, J.S.M. Trice, had been sponsored in a twenty-six-hour marathon to raise money for improved lighting.

He was succeeded at Canford by Steve Ronaldson, brother of Chris, under whose long tenure of office

A youthful Steve Ronaldson.

Over the years, the club has funded many improvements to the Tennis facilities, including comfortable furniture in the dedans, which is now partitioned from the court; a kitchen area with limited bar availability; heated changing rooms with showers, and a new roof and penthouse.

The school team, while inevitably varying in strength, has maintained a busy fixture list, which notably includes the Hatfield House weekend at Canford, for decades a major social event. When John Boys retired (after thirty-three years), his successor as master-in-charge, Rick Raumann, twice took boys to the United States, playing at New York, Philadelphia, Tuxedo and Washington. Several boys have won national Junior titles in various age groups and some have gone on to be full-time professionals. Outstanding among the Old Boys is James 'Spike' Willcocks, who at twenty-three became the second-ranked British amateur. He and B.J. Ronaldson brought the Henry Leaf Cup to Canford in 1998 and 1999. In 2007 Dave Harms won the British Amateur singles.

Canford School confidently expects its ninety-year-old reputation as a nursery for Tennis talent to extend far into the future.

both the club and the school have developed greatly, hosting several national events and establishing the annual ladies' doubles tournament. A series of assistants have given excellent support, including such talented players as Mike Gooding, Adam Phillips and Austin Snelgrove, who in 1997 went on to become the first professional at the new Prince's Club in Washington, with which the Canford Club is affiliated. The current assistant pro is Darren Long.

Daz protects the grille in spectacular fashion.

CHARTERHOUSE SCHOOL

Although the school's greatest days of Rackets lie largely in the past, Charterhouse retains an honoured place in the history of the game. One of the four entrants in the first Public Schools championship of 1868, they reached five finals in the eight years from 1887 to 1894, winning three, and won every one of their five finals from 1906 to 1914.

Their very earliest Rackets years were significantly disadvantaged. There was a court of some kind in the corner of their cricket ground in central London in the early nineteenth century, and two new open courts had been built by the 1860s – one possessed only one side wall, the other none at all. They drew Eton (the eventual winners) in the 1868 contest, lasted seventeen minutes and won seven points. They did not enter again until 1878, by which time the school had moved to Godalming, Surrey, and boasted (from 1877) two covered courts. The covering must have been on the scanty side, for a writer in the school magazine of 1881 deplored 'the occasions on which the court is so wet as to be worse than useless'. Nearly fifty years passed before it was decided to reroof the No. 1 court, but while the work was in progress, a storm flooded the court and ruined the floor. In 1939, extensive repairs were carried out and the floor partly re-laid, but not sufficiently far forward, resulting in the two-paced floor of today – a considerable advantage to the home team.

The first outstanding player at Charterhouse was probably F. Dames Longworth, who later won the UK Amateur singles three times. He was the school's first string in 1881, and must have watched a remarkable exhibition match played there in 1879 by four of the Gray brothers. Walter, the school's resident pro, who challenged for the world title in 1888, partnered Henry (Cambridge), who had been world champion 1863–66. They were beaten by Joseph (Rugby), the reigning world champion, and George (Haileybury) – the only one of five brothers not to be world champion. The fifth and greatest, William, had died at Eton four years earlier at the age of twenty-nine.

Dames Longworth returned to the school as a master in 1886, and had an electrifying effect on the game there, inspiring his pupils to the Public Schools final ten times in the next twenty-eight years. They won in 1888, 1893, 1894 (Vane Pennell and Edward Garnett in both 1893 and 1894), 1906, 1909, 1910 (H.W. Leatham and H.A. Denison, who two years later won the UK Amateur doubles), 1912 and 1914.

Leatham, who returned to Charterhouse as the school doctor, had a distinguished court record. He won the Amateur doubles six more times, mainly in partnership with the Hon. C.N. Bruce (later Lord Aberdare), and was Amateur singles champion in 1914 (beating Edgar Baerlein in the final) and 1924. At Cambridge, he played against Oxford for three years at Rackets and two years at Tennis, winning all his matches, singles and doubles, in both sports. His predecessor at Charterhouse, Vane Pennell, also became an excellent Tennis player, taking the Amateur singles title from Eustace Miles in 1904.

Dames Longworth retired from his post in 1921, and it was more than thirty years before the school had cause for serious Rackets celebration. Then came the greatest player in their history, and one of the greatest in the world, Charles Swallow. He was in the first Charterhouse pair for three years, winning the Foster Cup in 1955 and leading them to the championship in 1956. He won all his matches for Oxford against Cambridge from 1959 to 1961, and won the Amateur doubles with his university partner, J.M.G. Tyldesley, in 1960.

Swallow first won the Amateur singles in 1964, taking the title 3–2 from Geoffrey Atkins. In the same year he challenged him for the world championship, losing 5–7 at Queen's Club. Swallow went on to be Amateur champion in 1966, 1968 (the year in which he and J.J.M. Hooper secured the Old Carthusians' only victory in the Noel-Bruce Cup) and 1969. He lost the Open singles final to James Leonard in 1967, but beat him for the title in 1970. Then he attacked Atkins for the world again, going down 3–6 over the two legs in Chicago and at Queen's. In 1997, Charles Swallow succeeded David Norman as chairman of the Tennis & Rackets Association, which position he held till 2003.

Bill Hawes was the professional who coached Swallow through his school years. One of the famous Rackets-playing family (the son of Walter), Hawes

Martin Crosby and Marty Kinsella, from Chicago.

served Charterhouse with inspiring enthusiasm and untiring devotion for thirty-three years after the war. His predecessors included Walter Gray (twenty-five years), Gilbert Browne (twenty-two years) and Jack Giles (fourteen years). Steve Tulley stayed for eleven years after Hawes, and Martin Crosby (son of R.J., grandson of F.J.) has run the show since 1988.

Crosby's successful nurturing of the game is reflected in the healthy competition that exists in all age groups for places in the teams – despite the siting of the courts at the bottom of a steep hill. On his arrival, he also set up the Charterhouse Monks Rackets Club. It has flourished with regular fixtures against the school, Queen's Club, Harrow and Marlborough, as well as representation at various weekend events, undertaking a North American tour in 1995 and the hosting of touring clubs from the US.

In October 2012, eight senior members of the Charterhouse Rackets team embarked on a tour of North America. The tourists visited Tuxedo Park, which offered charming hospitality, Real Tennis and some most enthusiastic Rackets on a fast court, as well as the Racquet clubs of Philadelphia and Chicago. Martin Crosby had taken the Charterhouse Monks on tour in the past, but this was the first US tour for Carthusians. Martin was accompanied by Bob Noble, the director of Charterhouse sport. Unfortunately, Hurricane Sandy curtailed some of the play at Tuxedo as it took the

Touring the USA in 2012.

power out and left the Tennis House in darkness. Despite this, the trip was a huge success and enjoyed by all involved.

The year 2012 also started with renovation of the Rackets courts. Charterhouse, with the help of parents, Old Carthusians and The Monks evening club, set about raising funds for a refurbishment of the foyer, the gallery and the changing facilities. The result was a far nicer entrance to the building into the foyer, decorated changing rooms and the addition of a new room in the gallery with glass viewing panels and a kitchen. This has created a warm area where spectators can watch play and a meeting room with live action from court one fed through to a large television. To mark the generosity of the benefactors, an exhibition match between Will Hopton and Charlie Danby against Ben Snell and Ben Bomford was arranged. A large gallery watched a display of Rackets of the highest level, followed by a fine dinner in Brooke Hall.

As professional, Martin Crosby has been fortunate to have been assisted by a number of memorable masters-in-charge. Major Chignall will be remembered most fondly by many who knew him. Roy Woodcock took on the role for a short spell, going at it with magnificent aplomb. Martyn Lloyd charmed with engaging conversation and encyclopaedic knowledge, and now Andrew Johnson takes over the reins, looking to be a huge asset to Charterhouse Rackets.

A large number of Carthusians have also been introduced to the delights of Real Tennis by Martin Crosby. Trips to Petworth and Hampton Court have given players a grounding in the sport, opening up the possibility of playing a new game if there is no Rackets court near to their chosen university.

The OC Rackets is in a healthy state, with many playing at Queen's and entering the Noel-Bruce. Recent leavers have also supported the Fellows scheme, with five Old Carthusians going out to North America on their gap year to assist at clubs and improve their game.

The Charterhouse Monks Rackets Club continues to thrive as it passes its twentieth year, with new members learning the game and members who played at school providing stern competition for other school clubs.

2012 exhibition match with (left to right) *Ben Bomford, Charlie Danby, Will Hopton, Ben Snell.*

CHELTENHAM COLLEGE

Two open-air Rackets courts were built in 1852, on the site of the present English department and kitchens, and the first singles championship was held in 1858. Two covered courts were completed, on either side of the gymnasium, in 1864; and four years later the college was one of four schools contesting the first Public Schools doubles tournament at Prince's Club, London. George Gray, of the famous Rackets family, was appointed part-time professional in 1870, and Albert Wright took on the job with great success in 1896.

Soon after the First World War, K.S. Duleepsinhji, later to be known as one of England's great batsmen, briefly attended the college and proved to be a phenomenal Rackets player. He was the singles champion for each of his three years as well as the doubles champion (with different partners), and in 1922 the Cheltenham first pair won every school fixture.

The game declined thereafter, and in 1939 it expired. During the war the whole gymnasium block was requisitioned by the War Office, and subsequently one court became the maintenance department's workshop and the other was divided for various uses (including badminton).

Nearly fifty years later, thanks to the efforts of headmaster Richard Morgan, the east court was reopened for play, and it remains one of the fastest and truest courts in the world. Karl Cook, who had been trained by Shannon Hazell at Clifton College, was appointed the professional, the school came back on to the competitive circuit, and the Cheltenham Gold Racquet was instituted. As part of the school's 150th anniversary celebrations, the Professional championship was held there in 1991 – won, appropriately, by Shannon Hazell.

Eight of the club players toured North America in 1994, after which Karl Cook had to retire from the pro's job, as he was appointed a housemaster.

Former Worcestershire and Durham cricketer Mark Briers, then the cricket pro, got a taste for the game in 1994, and took over the following year. He and Karl Cook, as master-in-charge, formed an effective partnership – one eager to learn, the other reluctant to let go.

The season 1999–2000 proved to be a memorable one. The college hosted the British Professional championships; toured North America, notching up some impressive performances in New York, Tuxedo Park, Philadelphia and Montreal; boasted a Foster Cup finalist, Graeme Tyndall, and a Renny Cup winner, Michael Stout. Together these two were runners-up in the Public Schools doubles championship, whilst James Stout and Alex Coldicott won the Colts doubles.

An impressive start was made to the 2000–01 season, with an all-Cheltenham Foster Cup final – James Stout beating Alex Coldicott. Dan Hall was also successful in the 2000 U15 singles – and, indeed, went on to win the U16 singles the following year.

The dawn of the new millennium heralded great success for Cheltenham College Rackets, featuring appearances in the Public Schools doubles championship final in ten out of fifteen years. The year 2000 is also remembered at Cheltenham as having signalled the emergence of the surname 'Stout': indeed, all four Stout brothers have found their way into the winners'

The 4 Stouts at the 10th Old Cheltonian Gold Racquet Weekend: Jamie (world champion since 2008; Foster Cup winner 2000 & 2001; Public Schools doubles champion 2001 and 2002); Chris (Foster Cup winner 2011; Public Schools doubles champion 2012); Andrew (Renny Cup winner 2005); Michael (Public Schools doubles champion 2001).

2012 Public Schools doubles champions Chris Stout and Alex Duncliffe-Vines.

Mark Briers relaxes in Chicago.

enclosure at the Public Schools championships. In particular, Jamie Stout (1997–2002) was successful in securing the Foster Cup twice and the Public Schools doubles twice (once with brother Mike, and once with Alex Coldicott), before going on to winning the world championship in 2008 and retaining it in 2010. Graham Tyndall and Mike Stout were runners-up in the 2000 Public Schools doubles; Nick Abendanon and Dan Hall the same in 2004; Nick James and James Rock (current Montreal Rackets professional) won it in 2006; Dan Shiner and Charlie Wootton were runners-up in 2009; Richard Owen and Chris Stout the same in 2010 and 2011. Chris Stout and Alex Duncliffe-Vines won it in 2012.

In terms of singles silverware, Lily Owen became Cheltenham's first girls' national Rackets champion in 2012, joining Foster Cup winners Jamie Stout (2000–01) and Chris Stout (2011) as a senior singles title-holder.

The college toured the NARA Clubs in 2002, 2009 and 2011, which each time proved a success for both parties, and also hosted the Knott-Stephens tour party on every one of its ventures to the UK.

Since 2000, the Cheltenham Gold Racquet has been cemented as a respected doubles fixture in the T&RA calendar – an achievement that Richard Morgan, the headmaster responsible for the opening of the Rackets court, was particularly keen to see. The tournament's unique format of pairing up an Old Cheltonian with a non-Old Cheltonian has constituted an opportunity for more and more Rackets players to have the chance of playing on the court, which remains quick and true.

In the 2012–13 season, Cheltenham celebrated twenty-five years since the court's reopening (and thirty-three winners at the Public Schools championships during that time) with a doubles exhibition including the world singles champion and partner (Jamie Stout and Richard Owen), the British Open doubles champions (Nick James and Ben Snell) – all four OCs – and the world doubles champions (James Coyne and Will Hopton). Cheltenham can count a number of other achievements: there are close to sixty players playing regularly; in addition, a further staff of twelve have had

2011 tour to USA and Canada.

10th Old Cheltonian Gold Racquet 2010 including James Stout, Will Hopton, Alex Titchener-Barrett, James Coyne.

fixtures against Manchester and The Jesters and plan to tour the USA in 2015.

The OC Weekend, held annually in March, attracts a further 35–40 players and justly serves to celebrate the increasing successes of Old Cheltonians in the Rackets world, who have won Open and Amateur titles either side of the Atlantic.

Along with trainee Andrew Stout (2001–06), Mike Cawdron (1988–93), Ben Snell (1997–02), James Stout (1997–02) and James Rock (2001–06) are all head professionals at their respective clubs.

Mark Briers and Karl Cook are now in their twenty-first years as professional/master-in-charge. Talk of adding a second court at Cheltenham continues!

Cheltenham Masters Rackets Club (CMRC) at Manchester.

THE RACQUET CLUB OF CHICAGO

The last [Tennis] court to be built in America was in Chicago by the Chicago Racquet Club in 1923 . . . The Tennis court has unfortunately been adapted for use as an indoor lawn tennis court.
The Willis Faber and J.T. Faber *Book of Tennis and Rackets*, 1980 and 2001

On 31 July 2012, after more than seventy-five years, proper balls were struck with proper racquets on the Tennis court in Chicago, restored to its original and glorious purpose!

The Racquet Club of Chicago, founded in 1922, opened its clubhouse in 1924 with Tennis, two Rackets courts and singles and doubles squash courts. The founding members located the club in a residential neighbourhood of the city, north of the business centre, different from similar clubs both in Chicago and other US cities. (Including those at the Racquet Club, Chicago was once home to eight Rackets courts and two Tennis courts.) The robust social and athletic nature of the club was evident from the beginning and continues today.

In 1936, however, in response to the economic times, the gallery, penthouse and tambour walls of the Tennis court were removed to create an indoor, albeit irregular, lawn tennis court. Over time, usage dwindled, but several efforts to restore Tennis failed, due to opposition within the membership. In 2011, however, a group of young members led an organised effort to restore the court. Support from the general membership followed, and the Board of Governors decided unanimously to proceed with restoration. On 1 November 2011, the membership voted to ratify the decision of the Board, and the new age of Tennis in Chicago was born.

Three Racquet club individuals among many were instrumental in the restoration: Ally Bulley, president during the decision-making process, Bill Bickford, his successor, and John Cashman, head professional. The process might have had its difficult moments, but the due diligence was thorough. Given the historical nature of the game, both in general and at the club, and its growing popularity around the world, the proper course clearly was not only to restore the court, but also to recreate a world-class Tennis facility.

While the restoration was funded by the members, the entire Tennis world was enormously helpful in making sure that the club had the benefit of all recent court construction and restoration efforts. Chris Ronaldson, Peter Lucke-Hille and Colin Lumley were especially generous with their time, knowledge and counsel.

On 20 September 2012, the court was formally opened to the membership. Over three hundred people, many of whom had never seen the game before, watched Rob

Restoring the former Tennis court to its rightful status.

The restored court in all its glory.

Fahey and new club Tennis professional, Steve Virgona, in an exhibition match, followed by mixed doubles with Claire Vigrass and Frederika Adam. Earlier, John Prenn had become the first club Tennis champion to win on the club's court since 1932, and John and Rick Durkes became club doubles champions. Rackets, not to be outdone, had its own spirited exhibition between James Stout and Will Hopton.

Finally, on the weekend of 25–28 October, 150 out-of-town guests from Australia, England, France, Ireland and America came to Chicago for the international opening of the court. William Maltby, Henry Turnbull and Greg Van Schaack represented the respective Tennis associations they each chair, while former world champions Pete Bostwick, Howard Angus and Chris Ronaldson joined current world champion Rob Fahey for the event. A Saturday dinner-dance with welcoming speeches from around the world and a number of exciting Sunday matches put the perfect touches to the final christening of the newest (old) Tennis court in the world.

Over the past many decades, without Tennis, Rackets has sustained the spirit and defining character of the club. The world champion heritage, begun by Charles Williams in 1929, continued with members Atkins, Surtees, Angus, Prenn and Male all challenging or defending on the No. 1 court (and Foster becoming champion at other venues). Chicago players, led early by Billy Wood Prince and then by Wood, Tieken, Durkes and Anderson, followed by Peter Dunne and Will Fitzsimons, provided an important leadership role in the club. All club presidents have been active Rackets players and/or supporters, and the entire impetus for restoring Tennis came from playing Rackets at other clubs with Tennis courts – and then wondering why the Chicago court was gone. Recent club champions have included Keene Addington, Rowan Carroll, Tyler Mongerson and Marty Kinsella.

The club owes part of the uniqueness and strength of the Rackets programme to a historical nuance. Some founding members must have been familiar with a game, new at least to America, called doubles squash, introduced by Fred Thompkins in an unused space at the Racquet Club of Philadelphia, some time after the new clubhouse

The grand opening of the restored Tennis court 2012. in the forefront toward the left is Freddy Prince, just behind him and to the left is Ally Bulley, centre front is Denis Walsh, Ted Tieken and Bill Bickford and second on the far right is Rob Wood. Over Ally's left shoulder is Peter Van Nice, President of the club in 1985.

The Racquet Club of Chicago

Harry Foster and James Coyne, finalists of the 2007 US Open.

was built in 1907. Fortuitously, in the basement floor of the new building in Chicago, two doubles squash courts were included in the design. The Racquet Club of Chicago, therefore, is the only North American venue to have the luxury of two Rackets courts, the second court not having been converted to doubles squash.

In recent years, following a long tradition, Chicago has continued to host significant Rackets events. In 2004, an event to celebrate the fiftieth anniversary of Geoffrey Atkins's first world championship was held, attended by all living world Rackets champions. In 2007, Keene Addington, as president of the North American Racquets Association, welcomed the NARA community to celebrate NARA's fiftieth anniversary and also held the US Open. In 2013, Will Hopton and James Coyne became world doubles Rackets champions, defeating the defending champions, Alex Titchener-Barrett and Tim Cockroft, at the Racquet Club and at Queen's.

Head professional John Cashman, who arrived as an assistant in 1988 for a two-year stint, has followed in the footsteps of such legendary professionals as Charles Williams, Tony Bertolotti and Jack Johnson. With the opening of the Tennis court, Steve Virgona joined the staff as Tennis professional and Will Hopton as Rackets professional. In addition, Chicago is a strong supporter of the Rackets Fellows programme, having anywhere from two to five terrific young men from England at the club each season.

The Racquet Club of Chicago has come full circle back to the vision of its founders. On 9 November 2012, with multiple musical acts throughout the clubhouse and a French circus on the newly restored Tennis court, the Racquet Club celebrated its ninetieth year, having rejoined the ranks of great clubs around the world playing Rackets *and* Tennis.

Recreation and Restoration

Material specifications, penthouse details, court dimensions and angles were shared within a small group of architectural, construction and court experts. Although the penthouse and tambour walls had been removed in 1936, the original Bickley floor remained, beneath multiple layers of glue and sport-court flooring. The most important element to a successful project was to perfectly restore the original court floor, which was the last Tennis court floor ever installed by Joseph Bickley. The floor restoration was an intricate process of heating the dried glues and rubber flooring, careful scraping of excess materials and thorough cleaning of the Bickley surface. The ball trough was excavated, new lines were painted, and the results are well beyond any expectations. The gallery, dedans, tambour and penthouse were all reconstructed, following the original drawings for the court. Minor adjustments were made to the bandeau height, penthouse roof angle and dedans opening to ensure proper play at all levels of the game. All new play-wall surfaces were constructed of solid-core concrete block, finished in high-strength Armourcoat to provide the required density for ball impact. All court lighting was replaced, the gallery ball troughs were fabricated and installed (by Racquet Club staff), the unofficial Club mascot, Billy, the Celebrated Rat Killing Dog, was painted at the receiving wall, and the flags of each country participating in the sport of Tennis were hung above the upper play line on the main wall. Ready for play!

(left to right) Head Pro John Cashman, Chicago Fellow Alex Rozier-Pamplin, Tennis Pro Steve Virgona, Rackets Pro Will Hopton.

CLIFTON COLLEGE

The college has had a Rackets court since 1884, entered the Public Schools championship in 1886 and first reached the final in 1895. Among its most remarkable players were H.H. Lonquet-Higgins, who was in the school pair for four years before the First World War, and the gifted all-rounder R.C. Riseley. After playing for Clifton, he was first string for Oxford for four years, winning the Varsity singles in 1935, 1936 and 1937 (each time beating J.H. Pawle, later to be four times Amateur champion) and the doubles in 1934, 1935 and 1937. While still an undergraduate, Riseley reached the Amateur singles final, losing to David Milford, the world champion.

At Tennis, he won the Varsity singles in 1935 and 1936, and the doubles in 1934, 1935 and 1936. He won the MCC Gold Racquet in 1950, and twice reached the final of the Amateur singles, taking the title in 1955 against Peter Kershaw, his former Oxford Rackets partner.

The college next reached the Public Schools doubles final in 1936, and was there again in 1941, when the extraordinary Jeremy Potter was in the pair. This talented and enthusiastic games player (hockey, cricket, squash, lawn tennis as well as Rackets) was also head boy at Clifton and became a celebrated writer, historian and publisher. In 1994, he produced a scholarly historical work, *Tennis and Oxford*, inspired by the fact that by then he had become entranced by the game. He came to it late, but nevertheless had considerable success in veterans' tournaments in his sixties. Shortly before he died in 1997, at the age of seventy-five, he wrote a biography of Clifton's first headmaster, John Percival, whose son was in that first Rackets pair of 1886.

Towards the end of the twentieth century, Clifton's Rackets history was brilliantly embellished by the achievements of Matthew Windows, the most talented player of his generation. For four consecutive years he swept the Public Schools' mantelshelf of its trophies – in 1987 the Jim Dear Cup (Under-15), in 1988 the Incledon-Webber (Under-16), and in 1989 and 1990 the Foster Cup – only the second Cliftonian to win it, and only the seventh player to retain it.

Meanwhile, Windows and Justin Crane proved almost invincible doubles partners throughout their schooldays. In 1990, they brought the championship to Clifton for the first time – at the 101st attempt! – beating Eton in the final. For only the second time in history, the same four players contested the final in March 1991 (Alex Smith-Bingham and Jonathan Larken for Eton). By that time, Windows had beaten Smith-Bingham in two successive Foster finals, and it was no surprise that the Clifton pair triumphed again.

Not for the first time in the history of the game, cricket claimed a young man who might have gone on to be a great Rackets player. After reaching the semi-finals of both the Amateur and the Open championships in 1998, Windows devoted himself to batting for Gloucestershire.

Among the line of Clifton professionals, Bertie Barnes (1900–50) was outstanding as a player and a

Built in 1884, the court is similar to the one at Queen's.

character. To mark his retirement, he partnered R.P. Keigwin in a match against the school pair. Keigwin, coached by Barnes, had been in the Clifton pair in 1901 and 1902, and their combined ages amounted to 141 against the school pair's thirty-four, but experience carried the day.

In 1965, Terence Whatley took over, after the early death of George Ferguson, and considerable success ensued. J.P. Willcocks won the Incledon-Webber Cup in 1968, D.G. Parsons in 1969 and 1970, D.R. Gordon in 1971. Willcocks and Parsons lost the championship final of 1971 to Harrow (Mark Thatcher and John Prenn) and, in 1972, Parsons became the first Cliftonian to win the Foster Cup. Whatley himself did well enough, winning the Professional singles against Norwood Cripps in 1980; and his 1994 successor, Toby Sawrey-Cookson, a contemporary of Matthew Windows, won the same title in 1999 – and, incidentally, beat Windows in the Open semi-final of 1998, having in the previous round inflicted the first defeat for ten years on world champion James Male. Sawrey-Cookson's success as a professional at Clifton climaxed in 2001, when a talented pupil at the school, Sam Byron-Evans, won the Renny Cup, overcoming the favourite D. Jarvis.

Sawrey-Cookson was succeeded by Reg Williams in 2002; Williams acknowledges him as the one responsible for helping him to learn the game. In 2004 John Beale succeeded in getting into the Foster Cup but was unfortunately drawn against the number one seed Joe Bone. Since John Beale's departure from the school, he has played in many tournaments, toured with the Mjolnirs to America and in 2012 won the Varsity match playing for Oxford with A. Portz against Cambridge.

Ben McGeoch wins 2011 Renny Cup against Alex Goldie, with William Maltby.

Clifton provides both U18 Singles Finalists, Lucy Pigott and Emma Powell, in 2011, with Pro Reggie Williams.

A tenth anniversary of Clifton failing to achieve a trophy in any of the boys' competitions was averted by Ben McGeoch in December 2011. His great skill, determination and composure, as well as his desire to win all, enabled him to bring the Renny Cup back to Clifton. In the final he faced Alex Goldie from Eton and, after a tense match with fantastic rallies, McGeoch's ability to serve beautifully at crucial times and to keep his nerve throughout the match won him the prestigious trophy.

Girls' Rackets has been flourishing at Clifton. At the inaugural U18 Rackets singles in 2011, Clifton provided the winner, Lucy Pigott, and the runner-up, Emma Powell. Then, in 2014, Lea van der Zwalman won it again for Clifton.

In January 2006 the Professional singles championship was held at Clifton, thanks to support from the Old Boys and Clifton Boasters. The whole court had been revamped: the roof replaced with new wood and Perspex, the walls, viewing gallery and lines on the court redone to create an immaculate display. The court was reopened a couple of days before the competition with an exhibition match between John Inverdale and Matthew Windows. In the Professional singles, Old Radleian Mark Hubbard beat New Yorker Neil Smith with 50 to 60 boasters, and provided an amazing display of Rackets.

The Clifton Boasters evening club continues to thrive through the hard work of Sam Beale, who ensures that the court is used every night. Currently there are around eight university boys who play once or twice a week on a regular basis. Every year Sam, Elenor and John Beale also mastermind a great Clifton Boasters weekend, consisting of Rackets, Real Tennis and badminton.

DETROIT RACQUET CLUB

JOSEPH BICKLEY built the Detroit court in 1903, and it remained an open one until 1912, when it was glazed over, electric lighting installed, and the walls renovated by Bickley at a cost of $3,800. There is a notably splendid gallery capable of accommodating more than 100 spectators. The club also housed three squash tennis courts, later converted to standard squash courts in the 1920s, with a curling barn to the rear of the clubhouse holding two curling sheets. In fact, the original name of the club was the Detroit Racquet and Curling Club.

Rackets has always been the raison d'être of Detroit. The first national championship to be played in Detroit was the US Amateur singles championship in 1951 (the first time it was held outside New York, Boston or Philadelphia), followed by the Amateur doubles in 1953. Many top-class players competed in both, including Geoffrey Atkins, Bobby Grant and Clarry Pell. The 1951 Amateur singles was won by Bobby Grant and the 1953 Amateur doubles was won by David Milford and John Thompson.

Currently national championships are allocated to courts on a rotating basis by the North American Racquets Association, and the Detroit Club hosts either the Western Open, the Kendrick Cup, the Pell Cup (US Open singles), the Bertolotti Cup (US Open doubles) or the US Amateur singles and doubles championships. The Kendrick Cup for novices was presented in the mid-1950s by Charles Kendrick, a member of the club, and was first played in Detroit. A competition in memory of Murray W. Sales for singles and doubles for the Over-40 crowd was instituted in 1989.

In 1966, the US Amateur doubles was won by Detroiters Richard Turner and Murray Sales. The game had lain fallow for a while at Detroit, and was rejuvenated in the 1970s and 1980s, largely through the efforts of Sales and other members. They attracted a much-needed infusion of energy to the court, in the shape of players such as Patrick Duffy, Tom Muer, Gene O'Brien, Paul Sprinz, Olaf Holvick II, Robert Evans, Jr., Kevin Broderick, Chuck Caulkins and George Fern. Prompted by Sales, Broderick, initially – followed by Holvick, Evans and others – visited the Montreal Racket Club repeatedly in the early 1970s, returning with tales of good times, special camaraderie and top-level Rackets. They were followed in subsequent years by Joseph and John O'Brien, Bryan Melvin, Bruce Nichols, Thomas Shumaker, Edward Turner and Bruce MacFarlane. Since that time Montreal and Detroit have annually sent large contingents from their respective clubs to the other, reinforcing the special relationship between the two clubs.

The rejuvenation of the game in Detroit was capped off when the club hosted the 1985 United States Open, featuring such top players as world champion John Prenn, a young James Male on his first Rackets trip across the Atlantic, perennial Canadian champion David McLernon, brothers Randall and Andrew Crawley and Shannon Hazel. Prenn bested Male in the singles final, while Prenn and Male defeated Hazel and New Yorker Edward Ulmann in the doubles.

Players such as Thomas P. Howe, Robert Thibodeau Jr., William Goldsmith, Ronald Birgbauer, George Dambach and Michael Goodell joined the ranks in the 1980s. Howe was the best of these and won the club championship twenty times between 1984 and 2005, his string of victories twice interrupted by Birgbauer. Most recently, Christopher Jeffries, Manuel Tancer and Grant Lockhart have each held the singles crown.

The year of 1995 was the first of the Detroit Racquet Club's Amateur Rackets Fellowship, whereby a player trained at a UK public school plays as a guest of the club for three months during his gap year. Founded by Birgbauer, and subsequently shepherded by Goodell and Nichols, the programme continues to this day. Detroit has hosted nineteen Rackets Fellows and the practice has spread throughout NARA. Detroit hired Steve Toseland, formerly of Tonbridge School, as its Rackets professional in 2007. Toseland, David Lockhart and Christopher Manown were actively involved in an extensive repair and restoration of the court in 2009. Detroit continues to host schoolboy tours from the UK and considers it an honour to do so.

In recognition of the 100th anniversary of the founding of the club, a Centennial Celebration was staged in May 2002. Distinguished guests included senior representatives of every North American club and Queen's Club in London, with a five-day extravaganza of Rackets, golf, lawn tennis, shooting, squash and Chicago-style softball, culminating in a formal dinner on the court.

In 2009 the first floor of the clubhouse was renovated, adding a standard bar to the facility for the first time. Two small rooms were combined to create a large clubroom for the members and the changing facilities were renovated with wood panelling, new lighting and plumbing. A steam bath was added to assuage the members' aches and pains.

In 2012 Detroit celebrated its 110th anniversary with a gentlemen's dinner and a Rackets singles exhibition match featuring James Stout and Neil Smith. As Detroit moves beyond its 110th year, it is well positioned to continue as one of the strongest supporters of the game of Rackets in North America.

Exhibition match for the 110th Anniversary in 2012 (left to right) *James Stout, John Park (President), Pro Steve Toseland, Neil Smith.*

Celebrating the 110th Anniversary in 2012.

ETON COLLEGE

Eton launched themselves on the Rackets world in spectacular fashion. They won the first two Public Schools team championships in 1868 and 1869, though their first courts were not built until 1866. They were runners-up for the next three years, and in the first eighteen years of the championships failed to reach the final just four times. Those first courts, which were replaced in 1903, were said to be adequate, but slow, with the service line lower than it is today.

Great start though that was, the achievement was eclipsed more than a century later by an astonishing result in the Foster Cup, the Public Schools singles contest. All four entrants from Eton reached the 1998 quarter-finals, and all four won – a clean sweep for the cup that caused many an Old Etonian chest to swell with pride.

Their first outstanding player was C.J. Ottaway, who played in both the college's early triumphs. It is said that he never lost a match for Eton or Oxford, where he won the university singles three times and was in the winning doubles pair four times in successive years.

By the end of the century, Eton had produced one of the great names of these games, Edgar Baerlein, later to be Amateur champion of Rackets nine times, and of Tennis thirteen times.

The two 1902 courts are still regarded as among the best in the country, and helped the college win the Public Schools championship again in 1905. They were, incidentally, upgraded, when the Old Etonian Racquets and Tennis Club contributed to the installation of modern lighting in 1973, as well as improved changing facilities.

Eton's next golden period came in the 1920s, when they won three times and (up to 1931) played in nine finals. Among the successful players of that period were Ronny Aird, later to become secretary and then president of the MCC, and the formidable combination of Kenneth Wagg and Ian Akers-Douglas, who won the Amateur doubles three times. Akers-Douglas also played in eight Amateur singles finals, winning three of them, and in 1933 beat Lord Aberdare for the Open title.

The brilliant young American Bobby Grant III played first string in 1929 and 1930, later dominating the Rackets scene on the other side of the Atlantic for seventeen years. In 1947, he was surprisingly beaten in a match to decide who played Jim Dear for the world title.

Four Eton pairs reached the schools' final in the 1940s (only once during the war years was the competition not played), and in 1944 the pair were Anthony Ward and Richard Greenwood, both of whom subsequently gave unstinting service to Rackets and Tennis as administrators as well as players. Ward became chairman of Queen's Club, and Greenwood was for many years honorary treasurer and membership secretary of the Tennis & Rackets Association.

Twenty-seven years after their last Public Schools competition triumph, Eton hit the button again, winning seven times between 1955 and 1970, every one during the reign of the outstanding professional Ronnie Hawes, who established a wonderful rapport with the boys. His coaching and encouragement led to the development of some of the finest Rackets players of the era. They included Tom Pugh (1955), who won the Amateur doubles with John Thompson in 1966, and with Willie Boone from 1975 to 1977. Pugh twice won the US Open and the Tuxedo Gold Racquet (1966 and 1967), and he had victories in the US doubles (with Mac Bailey) and the Canadian doubles (twice with Boone), as well as the Canadian singles.

An even finer player led the Eton pair in 1958 – James Leonard. He later played Geoffrey Atkins for the world championship twice, was Open champion from 1967 to 1970, four times Amateur champion and three times won the Amateur doubles (once with Charles Swallow and twice with Charles Hue Williams). His partner in that Eton victory was David Norman, whose achievements were also spectacular. Norman was five times US Amateur and once US Open champion. He was champion of Canada three times in singles and four in doubles, and later he was an inspiring chairman of the Tennis & Rackets Association.

Garth Milne was another of Eton's successes, in 1960 becoming the first player to win the Foster Cup two years in succession, and the next year taking the doubles championship with Brian FitzGerald. Then came the three Faber brothers, a rare family whose father, Julian, led Winchester to the Public Schools trophy in 1935. Michael was in Eton's winning pair in 1963 and 1964, and the youngest, David, reached the final in 1979. Between them came the most remarkable Faber, Mark. He equalled the Public Schools record by being in the winning pair three times, 1967, 1968 and 1969, playing with Lord Richard Wellesley, Willie Boone and Andrew Milne. He won the Foster Cup in 1967 and 1968, and went on to take the university singles and doubles for Oxford three times from 1970. After his tragically early death, his family presented the association with the Mark Faber Cup, which rewards consistency and depth in school competition. In recent years, it has been won by Eton four times in succession.

Boone became one of the world's greatest players, and remained so for a remarkably long time. Between 1976 and 1986 he played in eleven consecutive Amateur singles finals, winning five of them. Eight years after that he won the Amateur singles and doubles and the Open doubles all in the same year, by then skipping lightly through his forties. He first won the British Open singles in 1979, and was heading for middle age when he won it again in 1995.

Following Mark Faber's three Public Schools doubles wins, Robin Drysdale (later to play Davis Cup tennis) led Eton to a fourth successive win in 1970, the year in which he also won the Foster Cup. It was twenty-five years before Eton won it again. That was the stunning year when the college made a clean sweep of the quarter-finals, and Neal Bailey, Patrick Wigan, Guy Smith-Bingham and Dominic Palmer-Tomkinson fought it out for the Foster Cup. This was the only singles trophy that had so far eluded the master-professional, Norwood Cripps, during his seventeen years at the school. Bailey took the prize, beating Smith-Bingham in the final. Smith-Bingham, whose elder brother Alex also reached the Foster final, won the Under-15 Public Schools singles in his first two years at Eton. In 1997, he and Hugo Loudon (unseeded) won the Public Schools final, losing only one game throughout the competition.

The long line of outstanding players who joined Eton as professionals must take much credit for the school's gilded history in the game. Ronnie Hawes and Norwood Cripps have been mentioned, but among the others were three world champions – William Gray, who began the line in 1868, Cecil 'Punch' Fairs in 1875, and Jim Dear twice, from 1951 to 1952 and from 1972 to 1979.

Present and past stalwart pros Peter Brake and Norwood Cripps.

In the summer of 2002, Rackets professional Norwood Cripps retired after twenty-three years' distinguished service to the school. Eton was extremely fortunate to be able to recruit Peter Brake as Norwood's successor from the Queen's Club. Peter is well known as one of the best Rackets coaches in the world, and has shown in his time at Eton a remarkable combination of patience, good humour and technical skill in his work. The many successes that Eton College has enjoyed at Queen's in the Public Schools championships in the past decade or so are due entirely to the skill with which boys across the ability range are coached and to the friendly, welcoming and relaxed atmosphere Peter engenders at the Rackets courts.

Eton also played a role in training two assistant professionals in recent years. Ben Snell was already a high-quality player when he joined us to complete his training. It was appropriate that, having lured an excellent Queen's Rackets professional away from London in 2002, Eton could return such a great replacement just a few years later. Dan Fisher was new to the sport when he arrived at Eton in 2012, although an experienced lawn tennis coach.

Eton celebrated the centenary of their Rackets courts in 2003, marking the occasion with an enjoyable tournament for both professionals and amateurs. The two 1903 courts remain regarded as among the best in the world. The new improved lighting on both courts has removed any excuses players might have had for missing the ball; as a by-product, it has also helped generations of Eton boys as they sit public exams in the Rackets courts every summer. Both courts have now also been fitted with cameras so that spectators can watch from the warmth of the professionals' office downstairs and matches can be recorded to help with

Tournament finalists at the 2003 Centenary of the Rackets courts (left to right) *Ainsley Barker, Alexander Smith-Bingham, Peter Brake, Neal Bailey.*

coaching. Although the changing rooms and shower facilities are still rather primitive, they are at least more reliable at generating hot water for visiting players than in the past.

Eton has enjoyed a most successful decade at the Public Schools championships, winning the Mark Faber Cup for best overall school on five occasions in the last decade. There have been many Etonian winners at Queen's in this time, but among the most noteworthy was certainly the first pair of Harry Franks and Matt Readman, who won the championship in 2004. They faced a tough draw against the Eton second pair in the first round and found themselves 3 games to 0 down and preparing for an early exit. Somehow they dragged themselves back into it to win 4–3; it was remarkable that they won by this score in every subsequent match in the tournament – including the final.

In 2006 Will Hopton won the Foster Cup in his final year at school, beating Sam Northeast from Harrow in a thrilling final. This was the first occasion in which Hopton reached a national final, and he has since gone on to develop into one of the top players in the world and a world doubles champion.

Harry Franks and Matt Readman win the Public Schools championship in 2004, shown with Peter Mallinson.

Toni Morales beats Robbie White (Harrow) in the 2013 Foster Cup, with Howard Angus.

The 2013–14 Rackets season was perhaps the most successful in the school's history. Toni Morales won the Foster Cup and his doubles partner Charlie Braham reached the semi-finals. They followed this performance at Christmas with victory in the first-pairs championship in 2014. Both boys returned to Queens as finalists in the Christmas 2014 Foster Cup, with Braham emerging victorious. The second-pairs championship has been won by Eton pairs for the past three seasons, and in 2013–14 the Colts singles and doubles titles also returned to the Eton courts.

One of the highlights of the past decade occurred when, due to the gallery developments at Queen's, Eton was able to host several major tournaments. The school courts were used for the first four days of the Public Schools singles in December 2011, before the quarter-finalists in all four competitions headed back to Queen's. Then, in January 2012, Eton hosted the Neptune British Open. The final was a tremendous occasion, with a packed gallery of over 120 boys, masters and other supporters, who watched Hopton win his first British Open title against an opponent who had beaten him on their twelve previous encounters. There was a great interest among the schoolboys in watching this tournament and the atmosphere in the gallery for the final showed the healthy state of the sport in Eton at the moment.

Eton was also honoured to host the 2014 Amateur doubles where Harry Foster and Mark Hue Williams were victorious.

Toni Morales and Charlie Braham win the 2014 Public Schools championship, shown with Pro Peter Brake.

Harry Foster and Mark Hue Williams win the 2014 Amateur doubles, shown with Guy Smith-Bingham and Tony Little, Headmaster.

FALKLAND PALACE

Built in 1539, this is the oldest existing Tennis court in the world, and also the only active open-air court. It is a Mecca for visiting players from all over the globe, who relish the opportunity to play on a court with no dedans, no tambour and no roof! For those who enjoy giraffe serves, the sky is the limit – literally.

King James V of Scotland built the court as a *jeu quarré*, as opposed to a court *à dedans*. Instead of a dedans it has four lunes (square openings) in the wall behind the server and an ais in the corner diagonally opposite the grille; all of these score winning points. There are no line galleries, entry to the court being by two doors on either side of the net at chase-the-door, and the penthouse roof has a pitch roughly 10 per cent steeper than usual.

The oldest existing and only active open-air Tennis court in the world, built in 1539.

The floor, consisting of thick paving slabs, has been re-laid twice, in 1628 and in the 1890s. There have been several restorations, the most important being that by the third Marquess of Bute near the end of the nineteenth century. By then the building had fallen into a sad state and needed excavation of the floor, a complete rebuild of the penthouses and total replastering of the walls.

It reopened with a match involving Sir Edward Grey, later to become foreign secretary. Since the Second World War, the National Trust for Scotland has maintained the palace, and it is thanks to them that the court continues to be playable. The Queen has visited the court twice, in 1958 (her first sight of Tennis) and in 1991.

In 1989, the 450th anniversary was celebrated by staging a tournament that brought together players from Australia, Belgium, France, Holland and the US, as well as several from English courts. The Earl of Wessex honoured the tournament with his presence, and played in a doubles match, partnered by Sally Jones. A temporary roof raised over the court guaranteed a week of brilliant sunshine which, coupled with the majestic surroundings, created a special and unforgettable atmosphere. The event was won, fittingly perhaps, by a team from the Falkland Palace Club, and the trophy is displayed in the exhibition room at the court. The year 2014 marked the 475th anniversary.

By the mid 2000s, two things adversely affected play at Falkland and caused the small number of local players to decrease even further. The first was a ban resulting from a wayward ball that cleared the wall and struck a visitor. Play was prohibited during opening hours. This ban lasted all of three years and coincided with the serious deterioration of the penthouse roof; closure of the club was contemplated. Meanwhile, an improvised rule called for a chase at whatever point the ball went through! The National Trust for Scotland once again played a helpful role in securing funding for a new penthouse roof, which will hopefully last longer than its predecessor. Due to its construction and materials which are designed to drain quickly and withstand rot, the penthouse roof has required an extra 50mm in height.

The club has discontinued its use of machine-manufactured balls, which in the past withstood wear from the coarse walls and had to be re-covered by the local cobbler, and has returned to the previous tradition of hand-sewn balls.

Play still takes place on a regular basis and the club sends a champion to the Chetwood Trophy each year. It warmly welcomes visitors from around the world.

LE JEU DE PAUME DE FONTAINEBLEAU

Reopened in 1990 after many lost years, the *jeu de paume* of the royal palace in Fontainebleau, built by King Henry IV of France in 1601, claims to be the world's oldest enclosed and complete Tennis court. With its outsized dimensions of 31.20m by 13.60m, it is also the largest, and its penthouse roofs are the highest and most steeply pitched.

It is a quirky, endearing, unheated, great old barn of a place, and until its renovation in 2000, its notoriously uneven floor of hard limestone blocks created a gloriously unpredictable bounce that brought many a modern professional to woe and gnashings of teeth. As if all that were not enough, it is a part of France's public domain, as open to tourists as are the museum, gardens and salons of the royal palace itself. As a result, gawping visitors commonly wander in and out of the galleries, chatting loudly, often snapping photos and invariably placing their innocent faces perilously close

The world's oldest enclosed and complete Tennis court, built in 1601.

During WW1 the court was painted white and turned into a physical therapy unit for the wounded.

to the netting. All in all, Fontainebleau is a special, even a unique court.

From 1601 until the French Revolution in 1789, the same family, the descendants of Nicolas Dupont de Compiègne (a companion in arms of Henry IV) occupied the concierge's lodgings near the court, drawing their revenues by renting rooms to players. Kings and future kings played there; as early as 1607, the personal physician of the future Louis XIII noted that the five-year-old Dauphin 'took volleys and played a good backhand'. Saint-Simon recorded that Louis XIV enjoyed strolling over to the court on rainy days to watch the best athletes play the game 'at which he had earlier excelled himself'. In August 1702, a terrible fire broke out in the nearby Pavillon des Armes, threatening the entire palace. To save the royal apartments and chapel, fire-fighters razed roofs to make fire-breaks, and directed the flames to the *jeu de paume* and the orangerie. This sacrifice was repaired thirty years later, when a new roof was installed and the present limestone floor laid. Although its physical aspect changed very little, the court was used only sporadically after the Revolution. The game was very much 'out' for the firebrands, just as many a noble head would be 'off' if caught playing, and it was 1812 before the court was repainted and put back into playing shape for the (very brief) imperial enjoyment of Napoleon I.

No Tennis event at Fontainebleau throughout the nineteenth century was more remarkable than the exploit of Edmond Barre, who walked from Paris (forty-three miles) in ten hours and immediately took on and beat his strongest challenger. The indefatigable Barre went undefeated for thirty-three years.

Use of the court was ceded to the club Le Sport de Fontainebleau in 1870, but there was less and less play there as the new rage, lawn tennis, grew in popularity. During the First World War it was painted white and turned into a physical therapy unit for wounded soldiers of the French Army, and after the war the American Art School took it over for the piano masterclasses of the composer and conductor Nadia Boulanger.

It was the mid-1980s before the building began the return to its true purpose, when a group of local enthusiasts formed the Cercle du Jeu de Paume de

The interior was restored and the court re-opened by The Earl of Wessex in 1990.

Rob Fahey signs an autograph at the 2005 world doubles.

Fontainebleau. They persuaded the city administration to join the Ministry of Culture and a few honorary founding members – notably Lord Aberdare and Richard Duvauchelle – in a vast project to restore the court to its original splendour.

In an official ceremony awash with champagne and graced by the presence of The Earl of Wessex, who whacked a few balls and pronounced himself satisfied, the court was reopened in the autumn of 1990. In 2001 a major exhibition was organised in the Musée du Château de Fontainebleau by Yves Carlier and Thierry Bernard Tambour about the history of tennis in France: *Jeu des rois, roi des jeux. Le jeu de paume en France*. For this occasion the court was massively restored to its last known historical condition in 1812 and to make it more suitable for play. The French royal coat of arms (from 1815) was also painted on the ceiling.

In September and October 2001, the court staged the Open national and the Ladies' and Men's French Open singles (won by Marc Seigneur, Charlotte Cornwallis and Rob Fahey respectively). Marc Seigneur served as the first pro for several years after the reopening. He was followed by various pros for brief spells including Mark Coghlan, Kees Ludekens and Jonathan Howell. In 1995 Ivan Ronaldson took up the post and was succeeded in 1998 by Anthony Scratchley. Angus Williams then joined him in 2005 and took over the helm the following year. Angus moved on to Paris in 2007 and was eventually succeeded by the current professional, Eric Delloye, in 2009.

In 2005 Fontainebleau hosted the world doubles championship, which was won by Rob Fahey and Steve Virgona. Three years later it was proud to host the world singles championship. This entailed a huge amount of organisation, with Bertrand Faure Beaulieu, assisted by Solange Sempere, acting as project manager and Guy Durand (then president of the club), assisted by Olivier Michel (leading Fontainebleau player), dealing with the palace and town authorities and court modifications. Many challenges had to be faced in the process, particularly increasing the seat capacity without breaching health and safety regulations. In the end it was a huge success and received massive media coverage, auguring well for the future.

Rob Fahey makes a giant leap towards winning the 2008 world championship.

GREENTREE

The Greentree Court, undoubtedly one of the finest in the world, was built by Payne Whitney in 1915 as part of a massive residential annexe to the family's private residence on the Greentree estate.

The annexe contains guest bedrooms, a library, an indoor pool and workout rooms. Payne Whitney died on court in 1927 and subsequently his son John Hay ('Jock') Whitney, a former US ambassador to London, continued to make it available to members. The court as well as the house, grounds and contents are now owned by the Greentree Foundation. Jock Whitney, who passed away in 1982, and his wife Betsey Cushing Whitney, who died in 1998, established the Greentree Foundation to host meetings and support non-profit programmes dedicated to peace, human rights and international cooperation. Shortly before she died, in 1996, Betsey had the foresight to do major renovations, such as restoring the roof and more than 350 glass ceiling panels and their steel encasements. Much of

The court was built by Joseph Bickley for Payne Whitney in 1915.

Betsey Whitney renovated the roof, the lighting structure and more than 350 glass ceiling panels in 1996.

the lighting structure was also replaced by specially moulded replicas.

For many years towards the end of the twentieth century, Clarence C. ('Clarry') Pell kept the court in use on behalf of the Whitney family with regular weekend play, along with the well-known Greentree weekend competition for the Payne Whitney Cup. During the weekend, the Whitneys would entertain players, wives and Tennis dignitaries from around the world, together with a great number of family relations. It was a huge loss to the Whitney family, the game of Court Tennis, and all of the Greentree players when Clarry Pell died in 1998.

Subsequently Peter di Bonaventura, a grandson of Betsey Whitney, then ably conducted the affairs of the Greentree Tennis court until the United States Court Tennis Preservation Foundation took over its operation in 1999 and continued the great traditions of the court. The members of the committee for Tennis at Greentree consisted of Peter di Bonaventura, Charles T. Johnstone, Peter Guernsey and William F. McLaughlin Jr, and they worked with the long-time professional, Jack Hickey, to foster steady and active play on the court, hold the annual Whitney Cup tournament and encourage the development of the game. Two important women's Tennis events were also held at Greentree in the 1999–2000 season: the Anne Boleyn and the US women's singles and doubles championships. Both were extraordinary successes for the women's game, and for Greentree as well. Notably, the 1999 Whitney Cup tournament was won for the first time in many years by the Greentree team. It was a hard-fought and much-appreciated victory for the home team.

The first professional at Greentree was Frank Forester, who was succeeded by William (Blondy) Standing in 1927. Eddie Stapleton succeeded him in 1958, followed by Pierre Etchebaster for a year in 1974. Jack Hickey took over from 1975 and continued until the court became inactive in 2001. The Whitney Cup competition was moved to the Racquet & Tennis Club in New York and has stayed there ever since.

HAILEYBURY

The 1970s were a golden era for Haileybury Rackets, with a succession of very talented players pressing for places in Haileybury teams. John Dawes, Robin Hollington, Robert Gradon, Peter Barber, Paul Hearn, Robert Wakely and William Hollington all won events at Queen's. Richard Ellis, son of Peter Ellis, had an outstanding record, with seven wins at Queen's – twice in Colts doubles (1974 with William Hollington and 1976 with Peter Wallis), Colts singles in 1975, Senior doubles with Wallis in 1978 and the Foster Cup three times in 1977, 1978 and 1979. Richard went on to represent Oxford at Rackets, Tennis and cricket and played for Middlesex in Mike Brearley's side.

In 1980, M.I. Tentori won the Level singles and in 1982 S.W.D. Heck and R.R.N. Bonallack won the Peter Gray Cup. The following year, T.R. Symonds and J.M. Dawes won the second-pairs event. In the 1990s, T.P. Faulkner won the Renny Cup in 1991 and a gifted left-hander, Rob Walker, reached the finals of the Jim Dear Cup in 1990, the Incledon-Webber Cup in 1991 and, with P.D. Stafford, the Peter Gray Cup in the same year. Walker's partnership with David Cruickshank made for a run of victories – securing the Colts doubles in 1992 and the Senior doubles in 1993, although they lost in the final the following year to Rugby. At Oxford, Walker set a record of five successive Varsity match doubles wins and was also a Tennis blue.

Duncan Stahl, son of the international squash player Chris Stahl, reached the finals of the Renny Cup in 1993 and the Foster Cup in 1994. All-rounder Richard Palmer reached the finals of the Jim Dear and Incledon-Webber cups in 1993 and 1994 respectively.

In 1996, Haileybury's idiosyncratic, droll and greatly admired professional, Peter Ellis, retired after thirty-three distinguished years as Rackets and cricket coach at the college. His famous one-liners enlivened many a Rackets gathering and caused several meetings of the Professional Rackets Association to come to a halt with laughter. He continued to mark many matches at Queen's after retirement. Peter Ellis was succeeded as professional at Haileybury by Howard Angus, the left-handed former world champion in both Real Tennis and Rackets. After five years as professional at the school, Howard went on to become head professional at Queen's Club.

Howard was in turn succeeded by Richard Ellis (son of Peter), the only player to have won Foster Cups three years in succession. Richard remained at Haileybury for two seasons, before his replacement by Old Cheltonian and ex-professional cricketer Mike Cawdron. In 2012 Haileybury boosted its professional team with the welcome addition of Andy Stout as trainee.

On-court success in recent years has centred around the Billings family. Tom Billings reached two Public Schools singles finals, along with Foster Cup and Public Schools semi-finals in two successive years. After leaving he won the US Amateur singles and was runner-up in the UK Amateur singles in 2014. In 2011, sister Jessica played in the final of the inaugural U16 Girls' trophy. Since the addition of the U16 and U18 Girls' championships at Queen's, popularity of the sport has grown amongst the girls at the school.

In 2011 Haileybury were fortunate enough to secure the teaching services of Will Hopton, in what turned out to be a vintage season for the young amateur. Will won a host of singles and doubles competitions, which meant that the trophy cabinet was full for the first time since R.G.P. Ellis graced the court.

In January 2012 a successful fundraising campaign to improve the condition of the court was completed. Repair work on the deteriorating front wall, suffering after periods of hard use, was carried out over the closed season.

As part of the 150th anniversary celebrations of the school, in early 2013 Haileybury hosted the Professional singles championship.

In recent years, Tom Billings has helped Haileybury score some notable victories. After leaving, he won the 2014 US Amateur singles.

HAMPTON COURT
THE ROYAL TENNIS COURT

No Tennis court in the world has a history as richly royal as this one, and it is more fully documented elsewhere in the book. Suffice it to say here that one English king built the court, another rebuilt it, three renovated it, one painted it white and turned it into a drawing room and Christopher Wren used it as a timber store – and all of that before 1720. In 1903, Edward VII consented to become its patron, as has every monarch since.

The first of its world championships was held in 1885, when Tom Pettitt took the title from George Lambert. By then the windows on both the west and east sides had been glazed, and soon afterwards the habit of darkening the floor with bullocks' blood was discontinued in favour of black paint.

By 1896, there was a cash crisis, and an annual subscription was introduced. Despite the club ceasing to function during the First World War, it flourished

One English king built the court, another re-built it and three renovated it – all before 1720.

Many alterations and restorations have occurred over the centuries but the service wall has been in constant use since 1529, or even earlier.

well enough subsequently for heating and lighting to be installed before the next war, during which the court suffered major bomb damage.

P.A. (Tony) Negretti ran the club almost singlehandedly after the war, filling the posts of honorary secretary and honorary treasurer from 1947 until 1973, when the club was reconstituted. He handed over to an active committee in what became known as the 'Palace Revolution', after which the lights were replaced, members redecorated the court and Negretti was elected president.

Howard Angus, who had taken the world championship from E.L. Scott in 1976, successfully defended it against him at Hampton Court in 1977. In 1979 Angus beat off the challenge from Chris Ronaldson, by 7–0, but went on to lose the world championship to the same opponent at Queen's Club in 1981 (Angus retired injured when behind 1–5). Ronaldson had by then become the Hampton Court professional.

Chris Ronaldson joined in 1979, after serving Oxford, Melbourne and the Sun Court at Troon, and soon had the court running at full capacity (operating some 5,000 court hours a year). New competitions were inaugurated (including the Seal Salver for those over fifty, where the handicap is on age only) and a club ladder was started. It was not long before the club was unable to cope with the flood of applications for membership, leading to the introduction of an entrance fee and a waiting list.

Only the eleventh head professional at the court since 1820, Ronaldson needed top-class practice to maintain his status as world champion. This led to first Wayne Davies and then Lachlan Deuchar working at the Royal Tennis Court – in the latter's case for six years, providing a feast of good tennis and coaching second to none. Ronaldson defended his world title at Hampton Court in 1983 against Wayne Davies, whom he again beat (at Queen's) in 1985 – the year, incidentally, in which the Hampton Court floor was painted red. In 2001, Chris Ronaldson was inducted into the International Court Tennis Hall of Fame in New York, becoming the nineteenth person so honoured.

The Keeper's house, built in 1636, extended in the mid-nineteenth-century and lost after the death in 1883 of the last Keeper, Major William Beresford, was recovered and refurbished in 1993. It provided clubrooms, a professionals' workshop, and an admirable flat for the head professional.

The club hosted the Amateur singles in 1982, 1983, 1984 and 1996. RTC also played host to the British Open in 1987, when Davies, having just taken the world title from Ronaldson, lost to Deuchar. In 1983 the inaugural Billy Ross Skinner Invitation mixed doubles was held on the court, and was played there for the next sixteen years.

From 1980, the club's Field Trophy team – infected with success and enthusiasm – were victorious for eleven of the next thirteen years, and again in 2004.

A new tournament was created in 1998, the Dresdner Kleinwort Benson Classic for the world's top eight professionals. It was won by Nick Wood, who had just left Hampton Court after ten years as assistant to take over at Holyport; for the following three years it was won by world champion Rob Fahey.

The world championship was again held at the club in 2002. An extraordinary last day saw Tim Chisholm recover from 2–6 down to 6 sets all, before succumbing to the reigning champion Rob Fahey 6–7. In terms of score, this was the closest anyone has come to defeating the champion.

Chris Ronaldson departed in 2008 to become the first professional at the new Tennis court at Radley School, after twenty-eight years of unparalleled service to the club and the game. Chris was succeeded by

Tim Chisholm takes Rob Fahey to the wire in the 2002 world championship.

Rob Fahey holds the 2002 world championship.

Head Pro Nick Wood with Peter Wright, winner of the Amateur doubles in 2009, 2010, 2011 and 2014.

a returning Nick Wood, who continues his mentor's traditions in his own inimitable way. Nick has the most elegant game – he defeated Rob Fahey in the 2002–03 Premier Division of the National League, en route to securing the title – and is an exceptional coach. In addition, he is chairman of the Real Tennis Professionals' Association (UK) and oversees the training and development of young professionals coming into the game.

The ladies' world championships were first held at the club in 1999, when the reigning champion, Penny Lumley, defeated RTC's Sue Haswell in the final in three close sets. The Ladies' Masters tournament was also played at the club in 1987, 1988 and 1991; the tournament's return in 2011 and 2012 was heralded by back-to-back victories for RTC's Sue Haswell.

Annual competitions within the club include the Barker-Camm Cup (formerly Camm Cup for the Level singles championship), the Harris-Watson Trophies (formerly Savage Trophies for Level doubles), the Lathom-Browne Cup (handicap singles), Wollaston Cup (Junior handicap singles) and the de Laszlo Bowl (doubles not crossing the centre line).

The tradition of Tennis courts being used as theatres was briefly revived at Hampton Court in 2003, for a single performance of Oliver Goldsmith's *She Stoops To Conquer*, which might possibly have staged its first ever performance in a Real Tennis court at Oxford.

The RTC has benefited from a succession of first-class assistants over the recent years. Prominent among these have been Ben Ronaldson, son of Chris; Camden Riviere, attached to the club for a single year in 2006, in which the two combined to win the Premier Division of the National League; Ben Matthews, who in 2012 participated in the eliminators for the world championship, and Chris Chapman, who has been in the world's top ten. Nick Wood's present team of assistants comprises Chris Chapman, Lesley Ronaldson and Josh Smith.

National League Premier Division champions in 2006, the equally hirsute Camden Riviere and Ben Ronaldson.

HARDWICK HOUSE

At the front of the Hardwick match book there is a lengthy cutting from *The Times* of 1896, reporting a new tennis court built by Mr Joseph Bickley for Mr C.D. Rose, 'a gentleman equally well known in yachting and racing circles':

Altogether the work seems to be nearly as perfect as human foresight and sagacity can make it and reflects the greatest credit on the builder. If we must find fault (and no criticism is good without a little spice of that kind) we should object to the extreme high finish of floor and walls, the object having been obviously to obtain an extremely quick surface. This no doubt has been secured – but is it an advantage?

The idea has probably come into the young Tennis world from that of Rackets, where quickness is the paramount point. It is not so in Tennis, which is sufficiently difficult with less rapid surfaces. But the difficulty used to be of another sort, involving more skill and less of the slap-bang, slash-and-smash style of the present day. It seems a pity to alter the game in that direction!

The first recorded match in the book was on 20 June 1896 between the Hon. Alfred Lyttleton, holder of the MCC Gold Racquet on numerous occasions, H.E. Crawley, twice Amateur champion in 1892 and 1894, E.F. Newton and Charles Rose, marked by the Prince's Club professional Edward Gray. Thus started

Sir Charles Rose built a second court in 1907 on his wife's vegetable garden, as he considered his first court too far from the house.

the golden period at Hardwick; there are many match entries and frequent singles between C.D. Rose and Gray, the latter having been installed as professional.

There was a memorable match in 1898 between world champion Peter Latham and Cecil 'Punch' Fairs, who between them held the world championship from 1895 to 1912. Such was Charles Rose's massive enthusiasm for the game that he commissioned Joseph Bickley to build another court at Suffolk House, his Newmarket home, to which Latham was duly lured away from Queen's.

Meanwhile, back at Hardwick, the splendid 1896 court was deemed just too far from the house, so for his greater convenience, Sir Charles Rose, as he now was, in 1907 invited a grateful Joseph Bickley to build another court beside the house, leaving the original to slowly fall into disrepair; now all that remains is the shell. It is notable that his guests not only had the opportunity to play Tennis; just off the stable yard there is an Eton fives court, and behind that the outline of a Rackets court is still just visible.

The new Hardwick court was now the centre of Sir Charles's attention, so when Edward Gray moved to Brighton, he brought Peter Latham to the new court. The noble proprietor and his star employee played the opening two-set match on 14 December 1907, with Latham so skilfully controlling play that Sir Charles (receive 30) won the second set 6–5. Thereafter they played several times a week for the next three or four years. From this high point in the court's history, sadly there would be no succession; at Mapledurham Church there is a window dedicated to his eldest sons, Charles and Bertram, who both died in South Africa during the Boer War, and also Adrian, killed in a road accident in 1908. This left the third son Frank, who was killed in Belgium in 1914.

It is not surprising that enthusiasm waned and entries in the match book after 1911 become very spasmodic; though some illustrious names appear in the late 1930s, including that of Latham in 1938, when he was seventy-five years old.

The court seemingly went to sleep, known to a few, and everything remained much as Sir Charles had left it when he died in 1913 – the lobby and spacious dedans hung with Tennis and racing prints; the marble fireplace; group lithographs, including one of Sir Charles chairing the Royal Automobile Club committee; the professional's quarters; the boiler room; racing scales. Soon ivy was growing through the windows.

It was not entirely forgotten, however, and there were occasional matches in the 1950s, including annual visits by a group of MCC members with Henry Johns, occasions that Lady Rose especially enjoyed. Then, in the 1980s, there was a resurgence of interest, and those fortunate to visit Hardwick were determined to see how they could help preserve a beautiful court, something that could only be done with the agreement of the Rose family. A 'committee of two', Adrian Snow and David Weston, held many meetings with Sir Julian and the Rose family estate with the objective of seeing whether a basis could be found for essential improvements, and how it all might be funded and managed.

This effort culminated in the Inaugural General Meeting of The Friends of Hardwick Tennis Court on Saturday 29 April 1989, during the annual handicap tournament. David was elected chairman and secretary, while Adrian became treasurer and clerk of works; they did explain that such an extraordinary amalgamation of titles was desirable in the early stages of the club's development – and so it was: the next item on the agenda was replacement of the roof.

In all of this, the support and encouragement of the club's president, Phoebe Lady Rose, was absolutely crucial. She had married the third baronet, Charles, son of Frank, and was very involved in the game. In the early days the ball basket was kept inside her front door and she was called to book the court, always twenty or more rings; then 'Hello' – a discussion on weather, the family, 'hold on while I look for the book'. She was always in the dedans with her dogs, barely ever missing a match or a committee meeting. It was a great loss when she died in 2003.

Over the years huge demands have been made on the clerk of the works – not just in terms of court maintenance, but also in continuous long-term development of all those other facilities. Sir Charles's guests could retire to the house and his plunge pool; others could not. There are now showers behind the grille penthouse. In the dedans there is a wood-burning stove, electric heating, a servery and french windows leading into the garden.

In June 2007, the centenary of the court was celebrated with a doubles tournament attracting players from other clubs and abroad. The finale of the occasion was a Grand Centenary Ball attended by The Earl and Countess of Wessex. It began with a champagne reception on court and then guests were persuaded to walk down to a marquee in the water meadow for an evening of dinner, speeches and dancing. Guest speakers, Sir Andrew Hamilton, chairman of the Tennis Committee of the T&RA, and Lord Coe, chairman of the London Organising Committee for the 2012 Olympic Games, reminded the guests that *jeu de paume* was contested at the 1908 Olympics. Vaughan Williams represented

A painting by the Hon. Neville Lytton, showing him at the hazard end and Charles Rose, grandson of the founder, at the service end.

Sir Julian Rose, while the captain, Gordon Robertson, and Adrian Snow spoke for the club.

Vaughan succeeded Adrian as chairman in 2009. His association with the court goes a long way back – the match book shows that his grandfather, Glynne Williams, had a lesson with Peter Latham on 18 September 1909. An important development during his tenure has been the construction of a car park below the court after fighting a personal battle with Japanese knotweed. The estate had long wanted to move the car park from the stable yard to its new location – not only does it provide an attractive new vista of the court, but as a consequence the club's licence has been extended to 2020.

In 2009, four Friends of Hardwick – Gordon Robertson and his sons Angus, Tom and Guy – played doubles for an hour at every club in Britain, starting at Falkland Palace and finishing at Hardwick. Transport was in one car with one of the four always driving. They completed the tour in five days six hours; £4,000 was raised for Multiple Sclerosis. To commemorate the event, the committee presented them with the Hardwick Round Britain Chase Salver, which has now become a challenge trophy for any group of four who can better that time. The salver has now passed to the Mjolnirs, a Queen's group of four who got round in three days thirteen hours.

Most recently, Angus Robertson has established The Haphazards, a club within a club at Hardwick that is attracting younger people to the game, and it continues to be the 'home' court for the Army. Also, the LRTA play many of their fixtures at Hardwick, and have presented the club with another match book, which will tell the story for years to come.

HARROW SCHOOL

Harrow's two Rackets courts were built exactly a century apart. The first opened in February 1865, at a cost of about £2,000; the second, the 'Crosby' court, in September 1965, after £33,455 had been spent. Not all of that sum was for the actual building work, though that did prove a problem. No courts had been built since Haileybury's in 1908, and the firm of Bickley, with its expertise in court construction, no longer existed.

Bickley's patent was discovered in the New York Public Library, and H.G. Harbour, one of the Bickley plasterers, provided some first-hand information, but there remained the difficulty of trying to suit modern materials to an old formula. Great credit is due to Charles Swallow, who stage-managed the project, to the architect Robert Bostock, and the builder, Donald Jones of T. Jones and Son, for accomplishing the task so successfully.

The original proposal and the offer of a most generous contribution towards the cost of a second Rackets court came from Old Harrovian Geoffrey Simmonds in 1963. More than 300 contributors followed his example.

The first professional, George Smale, coached the Harrow pair to win the Public Schools championship in 1871, and from then until 1888 Harrow dominated the championship, winning thirteen of their fifteen finals. Walter Gray, from the famous Cambridge cricket family, took over from Smales in 1872 (occasionally playing cricket for Middlesex at the same time), and when he left for Charterhouse in 1877, no resident professional was appointed until 'Judy' Stevens came from Prince's Club in 1885.

By this time the Crawley family had begun their march through Rackets history. First, three brothers played in winning pairs before the end of the nineteenth century – Ernest in 1883 (he later won the Amateur Tennis title three times), Eustace in 1885–86, and Stafford in 1895. He was the father of Cosmo, who played in the Harrow pair for three years with his cousin Leonard, and of Aidan, who was in the pair that reached the final in 1926.

Aidan's two sons both played for the school for two years, Andrew in 1964–65 and Randall in 1967 (when the pair lost 3–4 to the Eton pairing of Lord Wellesley and Mark Faber) and 1968. Randall Crawley subsequently formed an almost unbeatable partnership with Willie Boone (ex-Eton), dominating the British Open doubles through the 1980s. As celebrated a player as the Crawleys was Percy Ashworth who, after being in the winning Harrow pair of 1887, went on to win the Amateur singles in 1890 and the Amateur doubles seven times – four times with H.K. Foster and finally, in 1909, with Edgar Baerlein.

The school continued its triumphant progress to the end of the nineteenth century and beyond, winning six of eight finals between 1890 and 1903. It did not reach the championship final again until 1925, when it won, as it did in 1931 and 1932, on both occasions, with Roger Pulbrook in the pair (in 1933 he was still there, but lost to Rugby). No public school has won the championship more often than Harrow, and though its domination of the game had expired, Harrow continued to be successful after the war. Geoffrey Simmonds and Robin Treherne-Thomas won in 1947, Derek Taylor and Tom Pigott in 1948 and Christopher Strang and Roddy Bloomfield in 1954. Roddy Bloomfield also won the H.K. Foster Cup in 1954.

Success then became spasmodic, with a sixteen-year gap until Thatcher and Prenn won in 1971. It was another twelve years before David Dick and Steven Seagrave won in 1984 and fourteen before Tom Dunbar and Rupert Wilcox did it in 1999. John Prenn meanwhile had gone on to become one of the great players of the game, winning the Swallow Trophy (Under-24 singles) three times, the Amateur singles four times and the British Open a record six times (on each occasion beating Willie Boone in the final).

Though the doubles prize so often eluded the school, it hit another golden era for singles in the 1990s. Charles Danby won the Foster Cup in 1991, Harry Foster in 1992, Alex Titchener-Barrett in 1996 and 1997, and Tom Dunbar in 1999. Titchener-Barrett's record is remarkable: the only Harrovian to win the Foster Cup twice, he appeared in eight consecutive Queen's Club finals, including four wins.

Peter Warfield, a former England rugby international, was master-in-charge of Rackets from 1985 to 2013, and his enthusiasm has influenced the game greatly.

During his tenure Harrow won nine Foster Cups and six first-pairs doubles championships. But no name is more securely attached to Harrow's success than that of Crosby. Two of them, father and son, between them spent over eighty years there as Rackets professionals. Fred Crosby arrived in 1922 and Roger, at first his assistant, took over from him in 1962, retiring in 1996. Both were excellent motivators and great characters, exuding friendliness, and it is no wonder the new court was named after them. John Eaton is now the head professional. Roger's son Martin worked as assistant professional at Harrow from 1983 to 1988 before becoming the professional at Charterhouse.

Harrow's Thursday Rackets Club (which for two years ran on a Wednesday evening) has been notably successful, and was the forerunner of several similar clubs based at other schools. Most members are local people with a lawn tennis or squash background. The general standard has risen, and the spirit and level of enjoyment of the friendly matches between clubs is high. The Harrow Hammer has become a popular event each October, attracting entrants from all the other evening clubs.

Harrow enjoyed a successful period at Queen's in the Public Schools championships at the beginning of the twenty-first century. The Dunbar brothers were a key element in these successes. Both Tom and Peter had won the Colts singles in 1997 and 2000 respectively. Tom added the Foster Cup in 1999 and the Public Schools championship in 1999 (with Rupert Wilcox) and 2000 (with Oliver Craven), and Peter won the Public Schools championship in 2003 (with Joe Bone). Tom's four titles at Queen's drew him level with Harry Foster, who held the previous record in terms of winning titles at Queen's as a Harrow schoolboy. Tom proved himself to be a highly focused competitor with a strong temperament.

Joe Bone came to the fore when he won the Colts singles in 2002 and followed this with victories in the Foster Cup in 2004 and added a second win in the final of the Public Schools championship in 2005 (with Will Fortune). Joe emulated Tom Dunbar's achievement of winning the Foster Cup without dropping a game, tying Tom and Harry Foster's record of four titles at Queen's. He possessed excellent racquet skills and was a strong match player. Will Fortune achieved an unlikely and highly commendable double when he won the Foster Cup in 2005 and then the U18 National Real Tennis competition. In the final of the Foster Cup against James Rock (Cheltenham), with the help of unusual foul cut serves, he turned round a perilous position from 0–2 down, saving two match points in the third game and eventually winning 3–2. His ability to stay calm and think 'outside the box' was a defining factor in his success.

Sam Northeast burst on the scene by reaching the Junior Colts singles final in 2003 in his first term at

Joe Bone and Will Fortune win the Public Schools championship in 2005.

Sam Northeast and Glenn Querl win the 2007 Public Schools championship, after trailing 11–12 against Eton in the final game.

Harrow. In all he reached eight finals in nine appearances at Queen's, winning five titles in the process and setting a new Harrow record. Sam had a ferocious will to win and a lightning-fast eye. The highlights included a 3–2 win over Dan Shiner (Cheltenham) in the final of the Foster Cup in 2007. Sam overturned a 0–2 deficit by showing an unwillingness to accept defeat. In conjunction with Glenn Querl he won the 2007 Public Schools championship 4–3 against Eton. In a thrilling final game the Harrovians turned around an 11–12 deficit to win 15–12. The Etonian pair of Will Hopton and Chris Stefanowicz played a superb match, and the noisy and packed gallery made for a magnificent occasion. Both boys went to North America in 2006 with an inaugural Rackets touring party as Harrow School visited Chicago, Philadelphia and New York.

After a fantastic North American tour in Autumn 2012, Lalit Bose won the Foster Cup without dropping a game. He followed up by partnering Robbie White to a win in the Public Schools championship in 2013. Lalit has an icy cool temperament and is a devastating striker of the ball, especially on his backhand. Robbie White narrowly missed out in the Foster Cup final in 2013 in an intelligent, resourceful performance against Morales of Eton. In conjunction with Henry

Harry Foster won the Foster Cup in 1992 and went on to win the Open and Amateur singles many times, culminating in winning the world singles in 2005.

Goodfellow, he reached the final of the Public Schools championship in 2014. Robbie displayed tenacity and consistency in his displays at Queen's.

Harrow reached ten Foster Cup finals in the period from 1996 to 2014, winning seven of them. In the same period, Harrow reached eleven Public Schools championship finals, winning six in that period.

In the world of Old Harrovian Rackets, Harry Foster and Alex Titchener-Barrett were the dominant figures in the new century. Harry became world singles champion in 2005 by beating Guy Smith-Bingham in an eliminator and then Ali Robinson. He has a peerless temperament and an instinctive ability to find his best form at vital times. Harry added the world doubles crown with Mark Hue Williams in 2009 by defeating Neil Smith and Mark Hubbard.

Alex Titchener-Barrett became world doubles champion in 2011 with Tim Cockroft, having lost out to Jamie Stout in a world singles challenge in 2010. The Old Harrovians won the Noel-Bruce event for four consecutive years from 2006 to 2009, and again in 2012 and 2013. Charlie Danby played in all six events with Harry in 2006 and 2007 and with Alex in the other four years. Old Harrovian Real Tennis was spearheaded by John Prenn, who won the Bridgeman Cup (effectively the British Open for the Over-50s) in 2005, 2007, 2009 and 2013. In partnership with Charlie Danby, John also won the Henry Leaf Cup in 2011 for Harrow's first success since 1973.

Lalit Bose and Robbie White win the 2013 Public Schools championship against Cheltenham.

HATFIELD HOUSE

During the strong revival of Tennis in the Victorian era, it became fashionable for the aristocracy to add courts to their country houses. The court built at Hatfield House in 1842 by the second Marquess of Salisbury is a typical example, and the Cecil family used the Hertfordshire court exclusively for nearly a hundred years. It was inaugurated with a match between Lord Salisbury and the Rector of Hatfield, the Rev. F.G. Faithfull.

The fifth Marquess was probably the most accomplished player of the family, with a particularly fast overhead serve. He represented Oxford University (as Lord Cranborne) in 1914, and continued to play at Hatfield House until the closure of the court after the outbreak of war in 1939.

The court was used as a furniture store throughout the war and for several years afterwards, until in 1955 three local enthusiasts, Dick Granville, Francis Tufton and Norman Oliver, persuaded Lord Salisbury to let them form a club. They raised £600 for cleaning and refurbishing the court, and added electric light (fed by a coin meter).

No resident professional was appointed until Kevin King came in 1982, though an unbroken line of professionals had served Hatfield from its beginning until the Second World War. They included three of

The court was built by the second Marquess of Salisbury in 1842 and became a club in 1955.

the famous Lambert family. The founding father, Joseph (John) Lambert, was there from 1849 until his death in 1905 at the age of ninety-one.

He continued playing until well past eighty, and was first assisted and then succeeded by his youngest son, Charles. (Another of the brothers, George, was world champion from 1871 to 1885.) Jack Groom took over on Charles's death in 1915, to be followed – when he went to Lord's in 1924 – by one of Joseph Lambert's grandsons, Alfred.

A draft of an 1842 letter from the second Marquess throws fascinating light on the duties and rewards of the marker in those days. Lord Salisbury was writing to the father of Charles Phillips, the first professional at Hatfield:

I have been making some inquiry as to the payment of Tennis markers and from the best consideration I can give the subject I propose to give your son if it suits him 12s. a week and lodging and firing. That he should receive 3d. per set for marking and 6d. per set for playing with those gentlemen in the neighbourhood to whom I give permission to play in the court which I shall do by ticket (and to mark for the company in my house). I shall of course expect your son to repair the rackets and balls and to keep the court in good order. But there will still be a great deal of spare time upon his hands and I wish he had some employment which would lead to his advantage and keep him out of idleness. I would suggest to you for example, what I believe many markers are in the habit of doing, his learning to make Tennis shoes, which would probably be a source of considerable profit to him, or in short any other sedentary occupation which would not take him off the premises.

In 1987, the sixth Marquess generously granted the club security of tenure, enabling it to make substantial improvements to both the court and the off-court facilities. These developments benefited the membership greatly, and enabled the club to stage major tournaments, as well as to hold modest social functions. In 1994 major structural repairs were carried out by the estate; the following year the club formed itself into a limited company, which enabled it to enter into a formal lease with the owner. In 2006 roof replacements and renovations were carried out.

Among the most significant of professionals, after Kevin King, were Jiannis Hrysicos (from Ballarat), Matty Hayward (Hobart) and Mike Gooding (after six years in New York). The most successful player among them

Pros Will Burns and Jon Dawes.

was Mike Gooding who, during his time at Hatfield (1993–96), won the French Open, challenged for the world championship and, with Chris Bray, achieved the Open doubles Grand Slam – the French, British, American and Australian titles within a twelve-month period.

More recently Adam Phillips was professional for ten years until 2003, when he moved to Lord's to take over from David Cull. Jonathan Dawes moved up to become head professional at Hatfield, where he remains to this day. Jonathan was joined by Andrew Fowler from Melbourne, who stayed at Hatfield for 2½ years before he moved on to join Mike Gooding at The Racquet and Tennis Club, New York.

Will Burns then came to Hatfield from Middlesex University Real Tennis Club, where he had spent a one-year scholarship at the court while completing his Art degree at the university. Will remained at Hatfield for six years before returning to Middlesex at the start of 2012. Will was succeeded by Ben Matthews, who at the time of joining was ranked world No. 5 and is the first world-ranked player to join Hatfield since Mike

Pros Ben Matthews and Jon Dawes with club doubles champions Nick Lloyd and Simon Heck.

Gooding's departure in 1996. Ben had previously spent time at Hampton Court, Prested Hall and Bordeaux, having originally started at his local club of The Hyde in Dorset. In 2014 Ben was promoted to head pro at Leamington; James Law from Petworth replaced him.

Hatfield has a large active membership. As well as normal play between members, it holds a number of internal competitions, hosts three or four national tournaments each year, and competes in various national team events. During the last decade, Jonathan Dawes won Division 1 of the National League with both Andrew Fowler and Will Burns, and the club has also won Divisions 3, 5 and 6 during the last twelve years.

In 2012 Hatfield finally managed to win the Field Trophy under the dedicated captaincy of long-time club captain Nick Lloyd, beating Leamington in the final. The club also nurture their less advanced players, known as the Hatfield Angoras (a high class of rabbit), and for many years matches have been arranged for them too.

They are always centred around lunch, which may be quite lavish and is often very sociable. That tradition continues today, although these days the matches are likely to be mixed-ability and often mixed-sex.

The club hosted the event of the fiftieth anniversary of its formation in 2005 with a gala dinner in the Old Palace at Hatfield House, which was attended by the current Marquess and his wife, along with over 150 guests, including ex-professionals Jiannis Hrysicos, Matty Hayward, Kevin King and Adam Phillips. As a club it now has far greater ties with the Hatfield House estate, and it is part of the tour both for visitors and schools. It also takes part in corporate events held by the estate.

At Board level, in 2007 Colin Dean stepped down as chairman after many years of valuable service, initially as club captain and then as chairman. He has now taken up the role of vice president alongside another former club chairman, Basil Henson.

Hobart Tennis Club

Samuel Smith Travers, a London-based tea and coffee merchant, deserves credit for bringing the ancient game of tennis to Australia. He built his court in Davey Street, Hobart, in 1875, and at the same time published his acclaimed book *A Treatise on Tennis*. He enticed the experienced professional Thomas Stone from his billet at Oxford to teach a whole new generation of Tennis players down under.

By 1885 the club had produced a number of amateur players of very good standard. The Travers family retained a long association with the game and they, with the Butlers (direct descendants of Travers), were fine exponents of the game.

Following Thomas Stone's move to Melbourne in 1882, he was succeeded at Hobart by Bob Horne and then Percy Finch – the latter remaining the club's professional for more than sixty-five years.

The Champion Racquet was inaugurated in 1880 and the winner in 1882 was C.W. Butler, who went on to win it another eight times through to 1902. E. Maxwell then took the title sixteen times from 1903 to 1919, and C.T. Butler won it twelve times between 1911 and 1932. In the 1930s, C.C. Boag was dominant, winning eight times, and in the 1940s it was A.W. Knight, who won eleven times. The 1980s and 1990s were the era of Graeme Bradfield who has won an impressive thirteen times.

In 1967 an eighteen-year-old professional Barry Toates arrived from Cambridge, England, to take on the testing role of professional after years of relative inactivity at the club. Subsequently Toates moved to Boston, Newport and then to Melbourne, only to return to Hobart once again in 2007, where he remains as a well-respected doyen of Australian tennis.

Samuel Smith Travers, a London-based merchant, deserves credit for bringing Real Tennis to Australia, building the Hobart court in 1875.

Pro Barry Toates, well-respected doyen of Australian Tennis, with the Monk.

On the occasion of the club's centenary in 1975, Lord Aberdare unveiled the commemorative plaque, Pierre Etchebaster planted the grapevine that now cascades over the main entrance and the governor of Tasmania, Sir Stanley Burbury, presented the club with the Governor's Cup.

The club has produced a number of top players in recent times, including professionals Graham Hyland, Brad Dale and world champion Rob Fahey. In the amateur ranks, the club deserves credit for producing players of the calibre of Graeme Bradfield, Kieran Booth, Graeme Holloway and Pete Boyles. In the ladies' ranks, Judith Clarke became the first ladies' world champion and joined Barbara Baker, Karen Toates, Jane Hyland and Julianne Drewitt as Australian champions.

Like many historic buildings, the Hobart court and clubrooms need constant repairs and maintenance. In 1995 a complete replacement of the original flagstone and concrete floor of the Tennis court was undertaken. This was necessary to ensure that the 137-year-old club continues to be the venue for major Tennis events for which it has already proved successful. These include world title challenges, the Bathurst Cup, the ladies' world championship and the inter-club Percy Finch tournament versus the Royal Melbourne Tennis Club.

HOLYPORT REAL TENNIS CLUB

Now the home of the Royal County of Berkshire Real Tennis Club, the court at Holyport House was built for the owner, Sam Heilbut, in 1889. After initial trouble with the foundations, it proved to be one of the finest courts in the country, with spacious dedans and changing rooms and an adjoining swimming pool. Weekend parties were frequent until Mr Heilbut's death in 1913.

His successor, Major H.M. Martineau, continued to run the court, even though he was more interested in cricket. During the Second World War, troops were billeted in the house and played basketball in the court; it was also used for skating. In 1950, the Holyport Tennis Club was formed by Max Heilbut and Leslie Crispe. The support of Hubert Martineau and his daughter, Mrs Janne Cahill, and of more than fifty members enabled necessary repairs to be made and electric lighting to be installed.

The court reopened with a match between Alistair Martin, then the British and US Amateur champion, and his American compatriot Albert Johnson, a professional at Queen's Club. Later the legendary Pierre Etchebaster played exhibition matches there against Lord Aberdare, and it was at Holyport in 1954 that Jim Dear took his first step on the way to the world title by beating Henri St Germain of Bordeaux.

The court was built by Joseph Bickley for Sam Heilbut in 1889.

In 1985, Holyport House was sold and converted into a nursing home. The court was bought by a consortium consisting of Colin Lumley, Bryan Morrison, David Pearl and Chris Ronaldson. The roof was repaired, the changing rooms refurbished and the court brought up to championship standard, which entailed the building of a new side penthouse.

The new club opened for play in September 1986, with Kevin King as the enthusiastic professional and Lesley Ronaldson as manager. Holyport was transformed from a quiet Tennis backwater into a busy, modern facility, largely used by local residents who had previously known little of the game. Nick Wood, one of the world's leading players, became head professional in August 1998.

Nick Wood left in 2005 to go to Petworth. His departure was followed by a succession of professionals, none of whom stayed for more than a couple of years.

In due course the club was sold and passed through two subsequent owners. In 2012–13 the court came close to falling into the hands of a property developer, a fate from which it was saved by a determined effort by the T&RA in conjunction with Simon Talbot-Williams and the members. This alarming episode culminated in the purchase of the court by Holyport members and benefactors Colm O'Shea, Robert Peel, Simon Heywood and Christopher Figg. Under their enlightened and dynamic ownership, the club celebrated its quasquicentenary in 2014. The new management/professional team of John Evans and Claire Fahey will be at the forefront of the next chapter in Holyport's story.

The club continues to attract the world's top players and is the scene of a variety of major competitions, both amateur and professional. The British Open qualifiers, the Bathurst Cup and the LRTA International are three prominent events that the club has recently hosted.

The court came close to extinction in 2013 but is now under the new ownership of members and benefactors, Colm O'Shea, Robert Peel, Simon Heywood and Christopher Figg.

THE HYDE TENNIS CLUB

Restored and re-invigorated nearly seventy years after it was last used for Tennis, this old court came back to the game in 1998, the resident cows having been evicted and hay bales relocated. Joe Gundry, grandson of the man who had it built in 1883, gave the court and a parcel of land to the care of the Bridport and West Dorset Sports Trust; National Lottery and other generous funding arrived; the side and grille penthouses, demolished by the American Army, were rebuilt; and John Gundry, the great-grandson, took up the honorary secretaryship in time to welcome The Earl of Wessex to the reopening ceremony.

The pretty little village of Walditch, a mile or so outside Bridport, is the most improbable location for a Tennis club. The court stands next to the Victorian Gothic country home of its creator, Joseph Gundry, who played for Oxford in 1859 and whose racquet still hangs in the lobby. Mark Coghlan took on the challenge of running the club with only four known players, and soon attracted enough beginners to warrant a second

The court was built by Joseph Gundry in 1883 and restored for Tennis in 1998 after nearly 70 years of disuse, thanks to the extraordinary vision of Cleeves Palmer.

Interior of the court after massive restoration.

professional, Mark Hammersley. Between them they nurtured an atmosphere of enthusiasm and enjoyment that would be envied by many. By its third season, the club had some 175 members and a busy fixture list with twenty-five events, including the Brodie Cup final, which it has hosted since 1999.

There have been considerable changes at The Hyde since 2000. Cleeves Palmer, who had been instrumental in the success of the restoration project, stood down as chairman in 2000. If it had not been for Palmer's extraordinary vision in creating a plan that was to the satisfaction of the Gundry family and trustees, the court would very likely have ended up as a commercial building. In addition, Richard Salt, chairman of the Bridport and West Dorset Sports Trust, is to be commended for his bravery in selling the idea to his committee and taking on the ownership, despite a complete lack of Real Tennis knowledge.

Jamie Turner took the reins from Palmer, and almost immediately decided to install Derek FitzGerald as honorary secretary after John Gundry's retirement, as well as John Pearson as membership secretary and honorary treasurer. Turner stood down as chairman in 2009, and is now Director of Participation for the Tennis Committee at the Tennis & Rackets Association. He was replaced by his deputy, John Mackenzie.

In 2004 the main wall was rebuilt using thin concrete blocks, as for many years it had been suffering from damp. This solved the problem, and very little court space was lost. It was also an opportunity to square off the tambour, which had a rounded edge historically and was proving to be dangerous. In 2011 new LED lighting was installed, which has made a great cost saving.

Mark Coghlan, who had been head professional since the court reopened in 1998, was The Hyde's first professional since William Savage in the late nineteenth century. He was followed by Ben Ronaldson in 2008 and has been assisted by Neil Mackenzie, Adam Barratt and Jeremy Brodie. Ronaldson carried on the good work Coghlan had started, increasing court usage and the number of competitions, including Night Pennants and Auction doubles. During Coghlan's time, a young Ben Matthews applied for the post of assistant professional. Matthews has made his mark in international competitions and is currently in the top ten world rankings.

JESMOND DENE REAL TENNIS CLUB

Newcastle upon Tyne was one of the workshops of the world in the nineteenth century, so it is entirely fitting that the City's real tennis court was built by one of its leading industrialists. Sir Andrew Noble, inventor and businessman, was a Scotsman who moved to the northeast of England in the 1860s and was a close associate of the famous Lord Armstrong. He had the tennis court at Jesmond Dene built in 1894 as a private court for his family who lived at what is now Jesmond Dene House.

The court was described in *The Field* magazine as 'a beautiful court in every way'. The floors and wall are in the right relationship and the light is certainly good. Such praise is hardly surprising, as the court was built to the highest architectural standards by noted architect F.W. Rich and the floor was a Bickley floor.

The opening match on the court was played between professional Charles Saunders and the amateur Sir Edward Grey. At the time Sir Edward was parliamentary Undersecretary of State for Foreign Affairs. An exciting match took place as *The Field* reported. 'It is needless to say that Saunders was in good form, for that follows naturally from the facts, that he gave half 30 to his antagonist and came out of the contest victorious.'

Many other famous amateur players and professionals played at Jesmond before the First World War, as Sir Andrew and his family hosted house parties. Sir Andrew continued to use the court until he was over eighty years old, and the tradition continued through his four sons and three grandsons. Apart from the first few months of the court, Edgar Lambert was the professional there until 1928. He was succeeded by his

The court was designed by architect F. W. Rich and built by Joseph Bickley for Sir Andrew Noble in 1894.

In 1997, the court's use returned exclusively to Tennis and proper restoration took place.

son Charles, who was born in the professional's house adjoining the court and was of the fourth generation of that great line of Tennis professionals.

The fortunes of the court had been at a low ebb since the First World War, when it had been used for the making of airship gas bags and water ballast bags. In 1931 the Noble family sold the estate, which was taken over by Newcastle City Council. The court was adapted for use as two badminton courts, and the lease was held by the Northumberland Badminton Association, though very occasional Tennis play continued.

Lord Hothfield and Paul Butler were instrumental in founding the new Jesmond Dene Tennis Club in 1981. On a wonderful reopening day, the restored court was officially opened by Yseult Cochrane, the granddaughter of Sir Andrew Noble. The playing hours, however, were severely restricted, as many days and hours were devoted completely to badminton. There was no Tennis on the court after 7 p.m. on Mondays, Tuesdays and Fridays. Nevertheless, the club committee of Kiwi Craig, Ed Nicholl and Tim Bull held regular competitions, among them an Open amateur tournament for the Jesmond Dene Cup. Julian Snow was an early winner.

By the time the court's centenary dinner was held in October 1994, there was no professional and little money in the kitty, and no more than ten hours of tennis were being played in a week. A number of club stalwarts kept things going, including Freddie Such, John Duns, Alan Douglas, Richard Skinner and Richard MacAlister.

A breakthrough, however, came in 1997, when the club, with the help of keen member Mrs Annie Douglas, found alternative venues for the badminton players. When the court returned exclusively to the purpose for which it had been built, proper restoration could take place. Anthony Scratchley became the professional; he lovingly restored the floor with the help of the Craig family. When he left to take up a position in Bordeaux, Paul Hetherington managed the court in his spare time and enthusiasm rose again. Paul was succeeded by Peter Paterson from Cambridge, and he kept things moving until Peter Wiegand took over.

Peter, a French Canadian, assisted by Simon Harris, increased the court hours greatly to reach levels never seen before. In the early 2000s average court hours began to reach sixty hours per week. Peter left in 2008 to return to Canada and Paul Hetherington took over with Simon still in place. The successful development of the club has been pleasingly maintained and hours continue to average in the region of sixty.

Two notable features about the game at Jesmond Dene have developed over the last twenty-five years.

Jamie Douglas (thrice Amateur champion), Anthony Hothfield (Amateur champion 1964), Rob Fahey (world champion).

First, the club has managed to put on a very good and regular series of competitions, which have attracted players from around the country and further afield. The Invitation doubles in September continues to attract loyal support. The Jesmond Dene Cup has been won by champions such as Julian Snow, but more recently by Simon Shenkman, Simon Barker, Mark Seigneur and Duncan Hughes.

The club championship – during the 2000s in particular – has seen some successful young players win it and then move onto greater things, including Adam Dolman, the Newcastle University student, who eventually got down to below 10 handicap, and most significantly Jamie Douglas, who went on to become a British Amateur champion. From 1993 to 2005, the two names of Richard Skinner and Paul Hetherington dominate the honours board, although not always as winners! The club championship in most recent years has been won by students from Durham University: Charles-Antoyne Hurstel in 2012 and Charlie Harries-Jones in 2013.

The club's handicap tournaments have been most successful, and again the names of winners have been varied; however, it is notable that Jesmond Dene's husband-and-wife pairing of the Harrisons, Tony and Fiona, have won more than their fair share of competitions, as well as travelling far afield to spread the name of Jesmond Dene. Both Tony Harrison and Richard MacAlister have gone on to win the Chetwood Trophy.

Jesmond always make sure they enter both the Field Trophy and the Brodie Cup, even though success in the former has never been attainable. After a number of lean years in the Brodie Cup, Jesmond reached the final two years running, both times failing to clear the final hurdle. Perhaps they could blame it on jet lag from the journey to The Hyde!

Teams from the club have travelled extensively, and a number of members have now played all over the world, notably Alan Douglas, who has played on every court in the world except one.

Most recently there have been discussions with Newcastle City Council about the club's long-term future, the outcome of which is keenly awaited by all concerned.

Club stalwarts (left to right) *Simon Sanders, Fiona and Tony Harrison, Paul Raven.*

Lakewood
THE GEORGIAN COURT

Like a surprising number of clubs around the world, Lakewood is a quirky, unusual and enchanting place to play Real Tennis. The Tennis court is on the campus of Georgian Court University, a Catholic women's college, at the edge of a central New Jersey town dominated by a vibrant Orthodox Jewish community.

Of the eighteen proper Tennis courts built in the US, Lakewood is the only one at a private home that is still accessible and playable. It has a fascinating history.

In 1896 George Gould, the son of the infamous financier Jay Gould, purchased a plot of land in the weekend society colony of Lakewood, and with architect Bruce Price started to construct one of the Gilded

The court was designed by architect Bruce Price and built by Joseph Bickley for George Gould in 1896. It was massively restored in the new millennium and officially re-opened in 2009.

Age's most opulent estates. Price, who had built many of the buildings and homes at Tuxedo Park, including the still extant entrance gate lodge, designed Gould's mansion in a neo-Georgian style; it so dominated the estate that it was named Georgian Court.

After the mansion's completion in December 1898, the Goulds hosted a house party. It rained and rained. Gould, irritated that his guests had little to do, embarked on a fabulously quick project. In December 1899 he opened what was first called Bachelor's Court and later the Casino. For the cost of $250,000 (about $7 million today), Gould erected a masterpiece of athletic opportunity. The facility boasted a tanbark riding ring, the size of the old Madison Square Garden, where the Goulds could practise polo, show movies and put on chess matches using human actors as pieces. There was a steam room and swimming pool, three rosewood courts for the new American game of squash tennis (one for squash-tennis doubles), a Rackets court, a bowling alley and a billiards room. On the north side was a Real Tennis court.

In March 1900, Gould hired Frank Forester, a pro at Prince's in London, to coach his seven children in the Casino's racquet sports. One of the sons, Jay, proved to be particularly adept at tennis and went on to become one of the greatest amateur players in tennis history. At the age of eighteen, Jay Gould won the national Amateur title in 1906 and he didn't relinquish it until 1926. (Gould in fact only lost one singles match from 1907 until his retirement in 1926.) In London in 1908 he won a gold medal in the Olympic Games and, six years later, he captured the world championship in disputed fashion in Philadelphia, the first time the world championship had been held in America.

The Tennis court, home to such a celebrated player, sadly soon fell dormant. In May 1923, George Gould died on honeymoon with his second wife. He had become ill after visiting King Tutankhamun's newly discovered tomb in Egypt, an apparent victim of the so-called 'curse of the pharaohs'. Kingdon Gould, George's eldest son, soon disposed of Georgian Court. It had an asking price of $800,000, but Kingdon sold it for half that to the Sisters of Mercy. In 1908 the sisters had founded the College of Mount Saint Mary's, a small women's college in North Plainfield, New Jersey, and were looking for a larger campus. In the spring of 1924 the estate became the property of the Sisters of Mercy. They moved to Lakewood and named their school Georgian Court College (in 2004 it was renamed Georgian Court University).

'Silence Is Requested While the Ball Is in Play' reads the sign on the wall above the dedans, and for over half a century the court was silent. In 1982 Ed Hughes, later the president of the United States Court Tennis Association (USCTA), visited the Casino. The court was not in playable shape: the floor needed sanding, various wooden areas and wall markings needed paint, tape was needed for the chase line, the gallery netting was in tatters, the penthouses needed a wash and were a bit worn from water damage, especially in the corner where the service and grille penthouses met. The net was mouldering in the Rackets court. Hughes, along with Newport pro Barry Toates and his wife Karen, donated about $1,000 each to repair the court. In the autumn of 1982, they held a grand reopening. The ball trough had been filled in at some point after 1923 – evidence that the court was used for dances and other non-Tennis activities; the trough is still absent today, a memento of the fifty years during which the court was not in use.

Throughout the 1980s, play was sporadic at The Court, as the school is nicknamed. An annual singles tournament, the Jay Gould Cup, was started, and Lakewood was later the site for the Anne Boleyn tournament. But the court was still not in good shape – the roof was badly damaged – and Georgian Court didn't have the money or institutional willpower to restore it fully. In 1999 the US Court Tennis Preservation Foundation began to formally discuss renovations. Led by John McNamara and then Clarence McGowen, the initiative led to an innovative relationship between the foundation, the New Jersey Historic Trust and the college. In 2002 work began on restoring plaster and concrete, removing efflorescence and patching cracks. The ceiling was replaced, the floor refinished and remarked, netting replaced, windows recaulked and new seating installed.

In 2009 the court was officially back at The Court. The skylight is one of the most beautiful in the game (though it makes the service side a bit tricky on summer afternoons) and the court is in fine fettle. Under the careful guidance of Schuyler Wickes, with the help of Jim Zug, the court has again become alive with play. Some Tennis players with weekend homes nearby use it in the summer. The Jay Gould Cup, now a doubles event, returned to Lakewood and is an annual fixture.

The Lakewood Invitational, a season-opening event each September, is now a staple on the USCTA fixtures list, bringing players from Washington and Boston together at a halfway point along the Eastern Seaboard. Touring sides have returned – more than a dozen have come through in the past four years.

2011 Lakewood Invitational.

In the autumn of 2011, Neil Smith, the former Rackets world champion, began giving weekly Tennis clinics to the Georgian Court University (GCU) students. (Sadly for Smith, the Rackets court next door is now a student lounge; but the Casino is quite different today, with the Turkish bath now offices and the squash tennis courts now used as storage space; yet the bowling alley has also been restored.) These clinics, along with exhibitions and away matches at the Racquet Club of Philadelphia have begun to mobilise the school community. Tennis is now an official sport in GCU's intramural athletic programme and, with the school becoming co-educational in the autumn of 2013, great opportunities are now at hand at Lakewood.

Pro Neil Smith's first clinic, 2011.

GCU wins the 2012 Jock Whitney Intercollegiate Championship.

THE LEAMINGTON TENNIS COURT CLUB

One of the most important decisions made by the Leamington club in recent years was to admit lady members. The vote to do so went to those in favour by a comfortable margin. There were many in the Real Tennis world who did not understand the dilemma that faced members, but it should be remembered that Leamington was formed as a gentlemen's social club, with facilities for several games including Real Tennis, Rackets, billiards and cards, none of which were played by ladies at that time. In fact, it was unthinkable in the years in which the club was founded and built (1844 and 1846) that ladies should participate in sports and games. This did not change until towards the end of the nineteenth century, with the first Ladies' singles tournament at Wimbledon in 1884 being a landmark. It did not lead immediately to lawn tennis and golf clubs with large female memberships. The gentlemen's clubs of Pall Mall insulated themselves from these changes and Leamington, first and foremost a gentlemen's club, did the same. The possibility of admitting women – only raised on one or two occasions when the club's finances were in poor shape – was always summarily dismissed.

The gender question was raised at Leamington in 1921, and a sub-committee recommended the admission of ladies only to play squash rackets and bridge at certain times. The club's Rackets court had fallen into disuse by then, and had been converted into two courts for the new game of squash rackets. This concession did not amount to the creation of a special category of female membership, and some unsolicited suggestions from the ladies were not well received. As the club recovered from the deprivations of the 1914–18 war, any involvement of ladies melted away. The matter was raised again only fleetingly in the 1970s, and the decision to admit lady members was not finally made until 2008. A survey of the membership showed a high level of support and, with the committee of a like mind, there was little argument.

One of the benefits of the decision to admit lady members has been that the club has since hosted the ladies' national handicap doubles several times, and is now in line to host the ladies' world championship in 2015. There has not so far been an overwhelming rush of lady members joining the club, but such things tend to happen slowly in the early days of a major change, and numbers are increasing.

Leamington remains the oldest purpose-built Tennis club in the world still in existence. Those clubs that pre-date it, such as James Street (Haymarket), Prince's in London and Brighton have all disappeared. The Rackets court was never a success. It was an open court originally, integrated into the club premises at a time when the

The court was built in 1846 and is the oldest purpose-built Tennis club in the world still in existence.

rules of the game were not yet fully codified. A roof was added soon afterwards, but it was still little used. It is not known whether the conversion in 1921 into two squash courts led to anything approaching full usage, and the entire facility was sold to the printing business next door in 1939 for £800. By today's measure this is bound to look like a poor decision, which incidentally had nothing to do with the impending Second World War, and refurbishment would have required a similar amount (equivalent to more than one hundred annual subscriptions at that time).

The club retained its third squash court, which is still in use today, but the demise of Rackets there is a symptom of the difficulties that a Real Tennis club based in the provinces has in finding and developing talented racquet-game players. The club has a dominant champion in Tom Seymour Mead, and he has run up a sequence of championship wins that is likely to extend further in the years ahead. His few potential rivals find it difficult to balance the demands of their family, business and professional lives with the time commitment needed to improve their tennis.

The bulk of Leamington members very much enjoy weekend handicap tournaments, which keep winters warm. Open handicap tournaments for both singles and

Kevin Sheldon was Head Pro for nearly 50 years, before finally retiring in 2014.

doubles remain popular, even though rival events make it more difficult to attract the massive – and almost unmanageable – entries of the past. It was, of course, Leamington's Open singles tournament, which began in 1966, that led to the invention of the national and worldwide handicapping system.

Those who visit the Leamington club occasionally would detect few changes in the last fifty or sixty years. The main lounge and bar remain as they always have been, and dining at the club is always a special occasion. These facilities mean that the club can offer an exceptional venue for tournaments.

The popular Kevin Sheldon was head professional for approaching fifty years. He retired in September 2014 and was succeeded by Ben Matthews. The long-serving Chris Harrison retired as club manager in 2007.

Club stalwart Charles Wade invented the now internationally-accepted Tennis handicap system and also wrote the history of the club to mark its sesqui-centenary in 1996.

The club has a thriving golf society, which stages several tournaments during the season and books regular weekend tee times at The Warwickshire club. A younger generation of members is making its mark in the work of the Leamington committee and the organisation of many social events. Guy Stanton has become chairman, Ben Burbidge vice-chairman and Andy Dixon honorary secretary.

Lord's Marylebone Cricket Club

In 1898, sixty years after the first Tennis court was built at Lord's Cricket Ground, the court was demolished. W.G. Grace was still playing at the time and, two summers earlier, 30,000 spectators had somehow crammed into the ground to see the Australian Test. Something had to go. The Rackets court (built in 1844) went too, and the Mound Stand was erected. All was not lost, however. The freehold of an adjoining property in Grove End Road was purchased, providing space to replace both the Tennis and Rackets courts and also to build a squash court. The floor of the old Tennis court, which had been re-laid in 1866, was moved to the new site, the more worn flagstones being used near the net where the old chase lines may still be seen today. Owing to a legal dispute with a neighbour, it was not until 1 January 1900 that the new courts were opened. Sadly, there was little play on the Rackets court after the First World War and it fell into disuse. However, apparently in response to demand from members, the club added a second squash rackets court to an existing court constructed in 1898.

During the building hiatus, both Prince's Club and Hampton Court offered hospitality to MCC members, and the 1899 Gold and Silver Racquet prizes were played at Prince's. This competition is still one of the most prestigious amateur competitions in the game. Despite being open from 1870, in its first twenty-nine years it was only won by two players, J.M. Heathcote (seventeen times) and the Hon. Alfred Lyttelton (twelve), and only in its thirtieth year did Sir Edward Grey finally break their domination.

Two of the game's greatest and most memorable professionals, Jack Groom and Henry Johns, successively presided over the court for more than fifty years. Groom trained at Prince's and assisted at Hatfield House from 1907, returning there after 1918 before coming to head the team at Lord's in 1924. He was one of nature's gentlemen, whose Cockney good humour helped him mix on easy terms with everyone. During an Eton v. Harrow cricket match, a group of spectators wearing the traditional top hats customary in those days were watching Tennis from the upstairs gallery. One of the spectators leaned over a little too far and his hat fell onto the court. Spotting the falling object Groom, who was marking the match, instantly called it as chase two. He was also a fine player, running Edgar Baerlein close for the Open championship in 1931 and winning it the next year, and a wonderful coach, taking as great an interest in less able players as he did in the best.

During the Second World War, a bomb fell immediately behind the courts, destroying Groom's home and removing the roof of both courts. Groom installed his family in the professional's rooms between the two courts and he and the clerk of the works installed a corrugated roof to cover the Tennis court – a typically practical action that probably saved it from serious deterioration. The Rackets court, however, was beyond repair by the end of the war, and was converted into the Memorial Gallery (now the MCC Museum) in 1953.

Henry Johns took over in 1954 and remained in charge until 1975 (although he continued to work for the club part-time thereafter). He had first come to Lord's in 1936 after training at Prince's and spending two years with the Cazalets at Fairlawne. He was a masterly player on the Lord's court (champion of the world there, Jim Dear used to say), an excellent coach and a delightful personality. He trained many young professionals and was an outstanding marker, handling many of the most important matches of his time. Tennis also owes him a special debt of gratitude for making new balls after the war, which may have saved the game from a slow death.

Henry Johns was succeeded as head professional by David Cull, whom he had trained. David retired in 2002 and was succeeded by Adam Phillips, who had been the professional at Hatfield. Mark Ryan and Chris Swallow, who were trained by Johns and Cull and were the latter's assistants, are still the assistant professionals.

In 2008, Dave Woodman won the Gold Racquet and Spike Willcocks won the Silver Racquet.

Although MCC is primarily a cricket club, there are over two hundred Tennis-playing members and they keep the court and the club busy over eighty hours a week all through the year, both in the cricket season and out. Apart from its Gold and Silver Racquets and All-comers tournaments for the elite amateurs, the club holds a number of very popular tournaments in both doubles and singles in the R. Aird, Henry Johns, D.P. Henry and W.H. Ollis Cups. The annual Tennis Weekend, a creation of David Cull, is also much enjoyed, and its format of exclusively doubles matches played in twenty-five minutes is instrumental in bringing the members together in a competitive and social setting. In 2010, the D.W. Cull Trophy, a singles competition for its best amateurs, was created by the club in David's memory, following his death in 2009. New tournaments have been introduced in recent years and have proved a big attraction, including a series of Skills Nights and an annual Generations Cup, competed for by pairs comprising a parent and son or daughter.

MCC has always been keen to support the wider game. It has always entered teams in T&RA's sponsored competitions and in 2011 was the last winner of the Field Trophy in its previous format, and won the Pol Roger Cup in 2013. An MCC team has also won the Brodie Cup twice in the last seven years. A number of MCC members have served and continue to serve the sport at the highest level within the association. At the initiative of Adam Phillips, the club has also created an internship to encourage a young amateur player to improve his or her game and gain experience of the

In 2012, Jamie Douglas won the Gold Racquet and Conor Medlow won the Silver Racquet.

European Open Singles finalists 2013, Rob Fahey and Camden Riviere.

sport. Three interns have now held this position and one, Claire Vigrass, became ladies' world champion shortly after completing her term.

Lord's is frequently the setting for important events in the game. The annual Varsity Tennis match has been held at the club since 2000, when it returned to Lord's at the initiative of the then chairman, Brian Sharp. In 2008, the club hosted the dinner to celebrate the centenary of the Tennis & Rackets Association, which was attended by over 500 members. The MCC Locusts, captained by Roger Pilgrim, were the winners of the association's first Centenary Tournament. The professional game is not neglected: since 2005 the club has organised and hosted the European Open singles championship. After the first year, the club was fortunate to secure the support of Hiscox, thanks in major part to the then chairman, Andrew Beeson, and they continued as sponsor for four years. More recently, the competition has been privately sponsored, and held to support the Afghan Connection and Voices Foundation charities. The tournament attracts many of the world's best singles players and has been won by the world champion, Rob Fahey, five times and Camden Riviere, four times.

In 2011, with the support of the current chairman, Ronald Paterson, the club was able to secure the services of Fahey, now an honorary life member of the MCC, to play for it in the Premier Division of the National League, which it won for the first time.

Portrait of Rob Fahey, commissioned by the MCC and painted by Rupert Alexander in 2012.

MALVERN COLLEGE

OF ALL THE FAMILIES whose names appear on the Rackets roll of honour, none surely should be inscribed more firmly than that of Malvern's famous Fosters. The Rev. Henry Foster was the housemaster whose energy and enthusiasm led to the building of both the college's courts, next to his house, in 1881 and 1903. No doubt he also had some influence on the fact that his seven sons and four daughters all played the game.

In all but five of twenty-one years (from 1889 to 1909) there was a Foster, and sometimes two, in the Malvern pair for the Public Schools championship – and in one of those years Malvern did not enter. Three times in that period the college won the title – in 1892 with young Henry (always known as Harry) K. Foster and brother Wilfrid; in 1900 with Basil Foster and William Evans; in 1908 with another two Fosters, Maurice and Neville.

Harry was the outstanding player of the brood, and it is after him that the Public Schools singles championship trophy is named. He went on to reach the Amateur singles final the year after he left school, and then to win it for the seven years after that, twice demolishing in the final as fine a player as Eustace Miles by three sets to love, and once beating brother Wilfrid by the same margin.

In 1904, ten years after his first Amateur singles triumph, Harry reached the final again. He played the holder, the brilliant young Edgar Baerlein. Harry reckoned, knowing that he was not as fast as he had been, that he would have to hit Baerlein off the court in three sets if he were to win, and embarked on a flood of furious hitting. It worked.

The remarkable Harry (who also played cricket for Worcestershire) won the Amateur doubles eight times between 1894 and 1903 with a variety of partners including brothers Wilfrid and Basil. The latter was himself Amateur champion in 1912 and 1913, and won the doubles five times, once with Harry and once with Wilfrid. Some family!

Between the wars, Malvern won the championship three times: in 1920, 1936 and 1937. Desmond Manners recorded what might be a unique achievement – he played in the school pair for five successive years (1934–38) and reached the final in three of them, winning twice with Nigel Beeson. Manners also won Malvern's Prichard Racquet Trophy five times.

The courts were closed in 1940, suffered war damage, and were not reopened until 1954. It was twelve years before Malvern reached the final again, beating Radley for the title, but from 1973 to 1977 the school pair played in five consecutive finals. They won three of them – in 1974 with the Nicholls brothers, Mark and Paul; in 1975 with Paul Nicholls and Martin Tang; and in 1977 with Philip Rosser and Andrew McDonald.

Mark Nicholls also won the Foster Cup in 1973 and 1974 – a period of extraordinary success that was due, in large measure, to the outstanding coaching ability of Ronnie Hughes, the Malvern professional from 1956 to 1986. After Malvern, Mark Nicholls won the Army championship five times, and Paul took the Swallow Trophy (Under-24 Open singles) four times from 1979 to 1982.

Among many other Old Malvernians to prosper on the Rackets court, prime position is held by Mark Hubbard, who won the Swallow in 1997 and beat the world champion, Neil Smith, in the semi-final of the Professional singles championship in 1999. Hubbard was runner-up in the same competition again in 2000 and also competed in finals against James Male in 2001 and Harry Foster in 2002 and 2006 at the British Open singles, but lost on all three occasions. Hubbard

Mark Hubbard receives the 2011 Professional singles Cup from Richard Cooper.

(left to right) *Claire Vigrass, Alex Garside, Alex Kurkjian, Sally Jones at the Ladies Exhibition doubles to celebrate the re-opening of the Rackets courts in 2010.*

has since remained a consistent competitor in the past decade, reaching the finals of the Professional singles championship in 2003, 2004, 2005, 2009 and 2012, winning it in 2002, 2006–08 and 2010–11. Hubbard and Anthony Scammell won the Leonard Cup (Under-21 Open doubles) in 1994 and the Milne Hue Williams Cup (Public School Old Boys' Under-24 doubles) in 1997. Hubbard has been the Rackets professional at Radley since 1999.

Ron Hughes became professional at Malvern in 1956. His popularity and quality of teaching led to an increase in the participation of Rackets at the school, and roughly eighty boys of the student body participated regularly. Hughes emphasised the importance of gentlemanly behaviour on the court, as well as the enjoyment of the game and quality of footwork. He also instructed a huge number of students in the art of Rackets, including Tim Henman's brother, Mike. Hughes was able to demonstrate his skill at sixty-four years of age, when he was challenged by seventeen-year-old Mike Henman, and in turn beat him by 3 games to love after only twenty minutes. Hughes gave up in 1986 and was succeeded by old Malverian Roger Tolchard. Tim Roberts took over in 2006, passing on his position in 2011 to Noel Brett, who has been there since.

Of the masters-in-charge since the war, the most formidable name is that of Norman Rosser, who ran Rackets there from 1955 to 1983. He remained one of the national pillars of the game for many years after retiring. A recent master-in-charge who has played an essential part in the Rackets club at Malvern is Andy Murtagh, who retired in 2007 after being at the helm for ten years. Tom Newman then took up the role and has coordinated the club to the present day.

After the death of Ron Hughes in July 2008, his wife Vera decided to organise a very successful fundraising campaign in memory of the iconic man who was her husband. The revenue from the fundraiser and the generous addition from the OM Rackets Fraternity were dedicated to the complete refurbishment of the Ron Hughes Rackets courts, and they were opened in November 2010. Malvern organised a ladies' exhibition doubles match for the reopening ceremonies, which was the first ever official ladies' Rackets event. This was followed by hosting the inaugural Ladies' British Amateur doubles in 2013, and this is now a permanent fixture in their Rackets calendar.

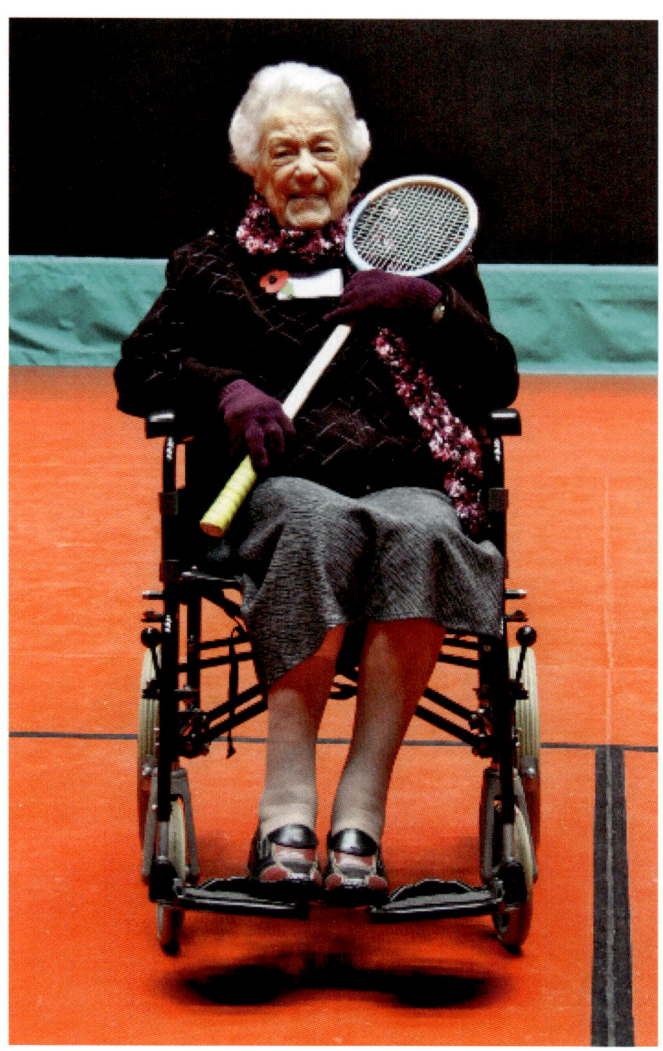

Vera Hughes, Ron's wife.

THE MANCHESTER TENNIS AND RACQUET CLUB

Few Rackets courts have had so short a life as the first pair built in Manchester. With funds raised after a public meeting in Manchester Town Hall, a site was bought in Miller Street, at the corner of Blackfriars Street and Chapel Street, Salford, where two courts were built. They opened in May 1876 with a match featuring three of the Gray professionals, Joseph (from Rugby), Walter (Charterhouse) and George (Haileybury), and Tom Attread of Prince's Club, London.

Little more than a year later, the club was gone, compulsorily acquired by the London and North-Western Railway Company. Another site was found, in Blackfriars Road, Salford, and one Rackets court, one Tennis court and a bowling alley were built. They changed the name of the club to include Tennis and opened in December 1880. The club premises stand on the same spot today, little changed but for the addition of a squash court, built in 1925.

Amateur championships were held at the club for Rackets (1878–82) and Tennis (1883–87), and a Professional Tennis championship from 1888 to 1894, won four times by Peter Latham. Latham had joined

The Tennis court was opened in 1880, having been built by Joseph Bickley.

the club as a boy in 1876, and won the first of his world championships in 1887, when he defeated Joseph Gray for the Rackets title on the Manchester Court, shortly before leaving to become head professional at the newly formed Queen's Club. Inter-club Rackets matches were also played, Manchester beating the Liverpool Racquet Club in every year but one from 1892 to 1911.

The Amateur Tennis singles championship for the Queen's Club Cup was first played at Manchester in 1922, after Queen's ceded its right to organise it, and has been played there several times since. The winner in 1922 was the greatest of all Manchester amateurs, Edgar Baerlein – one of the world's greatest players of both games. His record is so astounding that it merits careful reading.

Baerlein first won the national Rackets singles title in 1903, and twenty-eight years later, at the age of fifty, he beat Jack Groom for the first British Open Tennis championship. Within those twenty-nine years, Baerlein took the Amateur Tennis singles thirteen times and the Rackets singles nine times (despite the interference of the First World War). He also won the MCC Gold Racquet (for Tennis) ten times in eleven years, losing the 1930 final to Lord Aberdare, but reversing the result the following year. Eleven times he brought the Bailey Cup for inter-club Tennis doubles to Manchester, and six times he won the Amateur Rackets doubles.

Baerlein was not the first Manchester member to win the Amateur Rackets title. Percy Ashworth took it in 1890, and subsequently reached the final four times. He won the Amateur doubles seven times (four times with H.K. Foster, and once with Baerlein).

As Baerlein began (almost imperceptibly) to fade, Manchester's Lowther Lees bloomed. He won the Amateur Tennis singles eight times between 1928 and 1946 (with another World War removing six annual opportunities), and took the title from Baerlein in 1931. Quite astonishingly, there was not one Amateur Tennis singles final between 1912 and 1937 in which either Baerlein or Lees (or both) did not play. Lees's record of eleven Amateur Tennis doubles wins includes seven as Baerlein's partner; and on two other occasions he was partnered by one of the greatest sportsmen of his era, Max Woosnam, Wimbledon doubles champion, Olympic gold medallist and captain of Manchester City and England.

Lees lost the 1948 Tennis Amateur singles final to Peter Kershaw, the third of Manchester's outstanding players and another in Baerlein's mould, with equal facility for both games. His triumphs began at Rugby, where he won the 1934 Public Schools Rackets championship with Raymond Lumb. Kershaw played Tennis for Oxford against Cambridge for three years and Rackets for two years, in every match winning his singles and doubles. He won the Amateur Rackets singles in 1939 and the doubles three times with Geoffrey Atkins. He won the Amateur Tennis singles twice and the doubles seven times. With Robert Riseley as his partner, he never lost a doubles match.

Peter Kershaw was not content with his service on the court. He joined the club as an undergraduate in 1933, was honorary secretary from 1951 to 1978 (the position his father Harold held from 1909 to 1949), and then became president for three years. Incidentally, his uncle, G.G. Kershaw, won the Amateur Rackets doubles with Baerlein in 1914 and 1920.

Among the club's post-war professionals have been George Cooke (1949–1971), Graham Stephens, Derek Barrett and Frank Willis, an outstanding Tennis player who served the club from 1971 to 1977, and again from 1986 to 1999. Willis won the Field Trophy four times and was British Open champion from 1967 to 1970, when he was beaten by Howard Angus, as he was in the next three Open finals. Willis challenged G.H. ('Pete') Bostwick for the world title in 1969, losing by eight sets to eleven in New York and Manchester.

On Frank's retirement, Steve Brockenshaw joined as senior professional. Steve had been introduced to the game by Frank via the squash court, and joined as his assistant in 1985. He left to become senior professional at Moreton Morrell in November 1990 and his return was welcomed by all.

Frank's last assistant professional was Rod McNaughtan, who joined aged sixteen in 1996. Rod McNaughtan went on to Middlesex, and then to Paris, and was followed as assistant professional at the club by Craig Greenhalgh. The circle was then completed when Rod returned to the club as a senior professional in October 2012, after Craig's departure for Oxford.

Will Hopton joined the club as its senior Rackets professional in 2011, before leaving for Chicago in 2012. During his all-too-short a time at Manchester, he enjoyed a season of outstanding success – taking the Open singles and the Professional singles titles, as well as the Manchester Gold Racquet. Under the enthusiastic guidance of Will, the Rackets court saw a significant increase in usage. There has been some very high-quality play from the undergraduate members of the club and a good deal of enjoyment on the part of some of their elders, many of whom surprised both themselves, and their less adventurous brethren, by trying their hand at the game.

Club stalwarts (left to right) Head Pro Steve Brockenshaw, Brendan Hegarty, Tony Lawton, Senior Pro Rod McNaughtan and Stella Heap (Manager).

One of the major highlights of recent years was the choice of the club as the venue for the Bathurst Cup in 2004. After some much-needed refurbishment of the Tennis court in 2009, the club went on to host the International Real Tennis Professional singles in October of the same year – and in each of the following five years. Not to be outdone, the LRTA chose the Manchester court as the venue for the Ladies' singles and doubles world championships in 2007. The club has also provided the regular venue for the national Over-60s singles for the Kershaw Cup, which is usually held in conjunction with the Thomas Trophy, named after a much-esteemed former president of the club.

The Manchester Gold Racquet, instituted in 1966, had fallen into abeyance in 1999, but was revived as an Open Rackets tournament in 2006. In that year the club also celebrated its 130th anniversary. Over the years, most of the leading players of the day have competed in the tournament and enjoyed the hospitality of the club.

Also in 2006, most of the front wall of the Rackets court was replaced. The original finish had been repaired and patched over many years, but much of it remained intact and stubbornly resisted initial attempts to remove it, thus demonstrating the strength and durability of the original Bickley formula. Since then, the club has also hosted the Professional Rackets singles on two occasions and, perhaps most notably, in 2011, the Amateur Rackets singles.

Club Tennis also remains strong, with a regular Pennant team competition on Monday and Thursday evenings, as well as the annual handicap tournaments. Robin Barlow has particularly distinguished himself at senior level, winning the Kershaw Cup in 2006, and the World Masters Over-70s singles and doubles in 2012. He also gained representative honours for Great Britain in the Bostwick Trophy in 2006, 2008 and 2010 and captained the British Danby team in 2012. Jamie Bebb was another club member to be part of the Bostwick Team in both 2010 and 2012. In 2013, Mark Openshaw-Blower was selected to represent Great Britain in the Cockram Trophy, as was Jamie for the Bostwick and Robin for the Danby. In 2014, a team comprising Jamie Bebb, Simon Shenkman, Robert Shenkman, Mark Openshaw-Blower, Mark Seymour Mead, Adam Holloway and Richard Owen secured the Field Trophy for the club for the first time, defeating Holyport 3–2 in a close and exciting final at Moreton.

The social side of the club must not be overlooked, however. The dining room remains a second home for many members, where they can always be confident of enjoying good fellowship, good food and good wine. The club is particularly fortunate in its loyal and hard-working staff, under the firm but genial supervision of its manager, Stella Heap.

Celebrating the 130th Anniversary in 2006 (left to right) Derek Stevens, Jamie Bebb, Brendan Hegarty, Steve Brockenshaw.

MARLBOROUGH COLLEGE

More than sixty years after being converted into three squash courts, Marlborough's 1901 Jubilee Court was restored to Rackets in 1988, thanks to the generosity of the Ledger Hill Investment Company. The work was carried out in memory of an Old Marlburian, A.E.L. Hill (1901–86).

The college's first court, an open one, was built on the site of the present Memorial Library in 1860, but had to give way to new classrooms in 1899. Meanwhile, the first closed court was built in 1881, the gift of A.H. Beesly (first housemaster of Summerfield), to whom Marlborough Rackets owes a greater debt than to any other individual. Renovated in 1913, it proved to be one of the very best in the country.

The college's third court, the Jubilee, was the gift of Old Marlburians in 1901 and was built alongside the Beesly Court. Sadly, it was always too slow, and this was the court that turned to squash in 1925, and has now been restored.

Marlborough's first outstanding player was Eustace H. Miles. He never played Rackets for the school and concentrated on Tennis when he arrived at Cambridge. Nevertheless, he won the Amateur Rackets singles championship in 1902, and the doubles four times.

His Tennis record was extraordinarily good. He won the Amateur singles nine times between 1899 and 1910, losing twice in the final. He also won the MCC Gold Racquet fifteen times between 1897 and 1913, only once failing to reach the final. Among the great amateurs in Tennis, he indisputably succeeded J.M. Heathcote and Alfred Lyttelton as king of the game, preceding the legendary Edgar Baerlein.

Miles made a considerable contribution to the literature of both games, his best-known book being *Racquets, Tennis and Squash*, published in 1902. Aside from that, he was a vegetarian, a teetotaller and the purveyor of some rather eccentric theories about games.

In the early days, the school could not afford the services of a professional. It was not until 1895 that A.J. Crosby was appointed, and he served the school for twenty-seven years. To him goes the credit for the first two victories in the Public Schools championship, in 1901 and 1919. Crosby was a distinguished local citizen and was Mayor of Marlborough twice. Three of his four sons – Jim, Fred and Arthur – and one grandson (Roger, at Harrow), and one great-grandson, Martin, at Charterhouse, became Rackets professionals.

In 1928, one of the immortals of the game, D.S. Milford, arrived on the Marlborough staff and was immediately a tremendous asset to Rackets at the college. He first won the Amateur singles in 1930, took the title seven times before 1952, and held the Open championship from 1936 until it was revived after the war. During the same period, he held the world championship, beating Norbert Setzler 7–4 in 1937.

His doubles prowess was even more remarkable. After taking Marlborough twice to the Public Schools championship as master-in-charge, he first won the Amateur championship with P.M. Whitehouse in 1938. After the war, he began his remarkable, record-setting partnership with John Thompson, winning the Amateur doubles title ten times in twelve years.

A Tonbridge boy, Thompson joined the Marlborough staff in 1946 and guided the school's Rackets for several decades (as well as becoming British Open champion in 1959 and Amateur singles champion five times). Apart from that, Rackets owes him a considerable debt for his untiring efforts (in conjunction with Bill Gordon, the college professional from 1951) in developing a polythene-centred ball, without which Rackets might not have survived.

Gordon nursed three winning pairs to the Public Schools championship (two of them containing Mike Griffith, who won the Foster Cup in 1961 and later became the Sussex cricket captain). Gordon was succeeded in 1980 by Robert Wakely, whose success proved just as solid.

Two of his boys went on to be recognised among the best Rackets players in the history of the college. Alister Robinson and Guy Barker contested an all-Marlborough Foster Cup final in 1987 (Barker winning narrowly), after they had just lost the Public Schools doubles to Tonbridge (whom they beat 4–0 the next year).

From 1999 to 2005, Alister Robinson and Guy Barker enjoyed considerable success at the very pinnacle of the game. As a pair they won the Amateur doubles in 1999 (beating Willie Boone and Mark Hue Williams) and in the British Open doubles secured a hat-trick of victories in 2002, 2003 and 2004. That same year they retook the Amateur doubles, and again in 2010. The ultimate achievement was winning the world championship in 2005, defeating Guy Smith-Bingham and Tim Cockroft, after losing two years earlier to James Male and Mark Hue Williams.

When free from injury, Alister Robinson also enjoyed significant success in singles. Robinson appeared three times in the Amateur singles final, in 1999 as runner-up, but went on to become champion in 2001 and 2005. In 2004, he won the British Open, before narrowly losing to Harry Foster in the world singles championship in 2005. Guy Barker, meanwhile, was runner-up in the Amateur singles in 1997 and 2000.

In the Public Schools championships, Alex Brignall won the Foster Cup in 2003, the first time for Marlborough since 1987. Between 2008 and the present day, the school has been involved in many Colts singles and doubles finals. In 2014 Dom Coulson won the U15 singles for Marlborough. The game is flourishing, with a significant number of pupils playing at present.

Since 2008, Marlborough has hosted the qualifying tournament for the Invitation singles held at Queen's in November. Significant leading players have enjoyed a frenetic three days on the Marlborough Court, regarded as one of the finest in the world. In 2012, Marlborough proudly hosted the Amateur doubles while Queen's was undergoing major refurbishment. Alex Titchener-Barrett and Tim Cockroft defeated Harry Foster and Mark Hue Williams 3–2 in the final, which was a replay of the 2011 world championship.

Ali Robinson and Guy Barker win the world doubles championship in 2005, shown with Robert Wakely.

ROYAL MELBOURNE TENNIS CLUB

The Tennis court in Melbourne was located in Exhibition Street from the day it opened in 1882 as The Melbourne Tennis Club, until it was demolished in 1975. The court was opened by the governor of Victoria, the Marquess of Normanby, who was Queen Victoria's representative. Many of HRH's subsequent appointees became both patrons and players at the club. This was likely the reason that the game became known as 'Royal Tennis' within Victoria and Tasmania, a description that was enhanced by the granting of a royal warrant by Queen Victoria in 1897.

Thus, from this date, the club became known as The Royal Melbourne Tennis Club (RMTC).

Of all the governors of Victoria to make their mark at the club, Lord Stradbroke and Lord Somers stand out – the latter was a fine cricketer also who had captained Worcestershire, and both took considerable interest in the club facilities and its members. It was their influence that encouraged the committee to build one of the first squash courts in Victoria, in 1927.

As with many clubs around the world, the RMTC

The new premises, boasting two Real Tennis courts, were opened in 1975 by Lord Aberdare with Pierre Etchebaster in attendance.

has had its ups and downs, especially in the years that followed the two world wars.

The club was fortunate to have two loyal and long-serving professionals in Thomas Stone, who died in 1924, and his son Woolner, who died in 1964 whilst still in office.

The courageous decisions to move from the costly premises in Exhibition Street to new facilities in the suburb of Richmond in 1975, and to appoint a young and enthusiastic professional from England, Chris Ronaldson, probably saved the club from extinction. The new premises, boasting two Real Tennis courts, were opened by Lord Aberdare with Pierre Etchebaster in attendance.

Over the years, a number of world-class professionals have come through the ranks at RMTC, and include Colin Lumley, Lachie Deuchar, Wayne Davies, Chris Chapman, Paul Tabley, Kate Leeming and Frank Filippelli. In addition to the latter three, the current professionals include father and son Jonathan and Nick Howell.

The highest accolades for the amateur players are for the Gold Racket and Silver Racket, both inaugurated in 1882. In the early days, the names of J.B. Box, R. Cornish and C.H. Mollison are prominent, and in years prior to the move to Richmond, G.G. Hiller was the outstanding player. In recent times, Michael Happell, Ted Cockram, Chris Sievers, Mark Sayer, Bret Richardson, Rosie Snell and Amy Hayball have been dominant. The International Teams event, restricted to players over fifty, was first played at Leamington in 1996 and won by Britain. Now formally recognised as the Ted Cockram Trophy, it was played at Melbourne in early 1999 and won by Australia; however, Britain has been the successful team in recent years.

During its centenary celebration in 1982, the club hosted the Bathurst Cup, at which Australia won the

In 2014, Rob Fahey extended his record-breaking run to 12 consecutive world championship wins over an astonishing 21 years. Seen here with his fiancée Claire Vigrass.

event for the first time. Subsequently the club hosted the event in 2006, which saw Australia again successful against a powerful English team. In 2011 Australia defeated England in New York, and again in 2013 at Holyport. Kieran Booth, originally from Hobart and now resident in Melbourne, has been one of Australia's dominant amateur players for the Bathurst Cup and other international events.

The three most recent world champions, Chris Ronaldson, Wayne Davies and Robert Fahey, would probably credit the facilities at RMTC for much of their success on the international stage. In recent years the RMTC has hosted the world championship in 2010, and again in 2014, when Rob Fahey extended his record-breaking run to twelve consecutive wins over an astonishing twenty-one years.

For amateur players around the world, the club is renowned for the handicap doubles event, known as the Boomerang Cup and held every two years, at which RMTC is host to hundreds of international players for both Tennis and social events. Club facilities include an outdoor swimming pool, two Tennis courts, a squash court, library and dining areas.

Pros Kate Leeming, Frank Filippelli, Nick Howell.

MIDDLESEX UNIVERSITY REAL TENNIS CLUB

The creation of the court, including many state-of-the-art innovations, was masterminded and financed by Peter Luck-Hille in the late 1990s and opened by The Earl of Wessex on 16 January 2000. In the early years it was known as The Burroughs Club and managed by the university, with the professionals as university employees, but this proved less than satisfactory. In 2008 a new company, MURTC Ltd, was formed to run the club independently of the university. MURTC Ltd is now owned 50:50 by the university and members respectively.

Since then many big changes have taken place. In effect the club is now run by members for members. This fundamental change in approach has returned the club to financial solvency and greatly increased court usage. There has been a significant increase in university staff and student participation, in addition to the recruitment of more private members.

Paradoxically the relationship has much improved since the running of the club was separated from the university. In 2010, in the year it celebrated its tenth anniversary, the club and university signed an agreement for a further ten years' tenure, which gave the club a security that at one stage looked doubtful.

One example of the increasingly close and mutually beneficial relationship between the university and the club has been the installation of a seven-camera audio-visual recording system, jointly with the academic department of Sports Performance Analysis. Real Tennis has become a vehicle for academic study.

Over the years the club has seen many professionals passing through. The first was Frank Filippelli, followed by Steve Virgona and then Mike Gooding. Rod McNaughtan then followed, and while he was in post Rob Fahey was often to be seen on court. In 2009 Ged Eden was appointed head pro and when he left Matt Ronaldson took over with Will Burns as his deputy. Will is now the head pro.

The Luck-Hille foundation has also funded a scholarship or intern scheme for students at the university, to support those with potential talent to develop their Real Tennis skills and take their first steps towards becoming a pro. Several, including current head pro Will Burns, have gone on to successful Real Tennis professional careers.

Responding to the financial crisis of 2008, the university has had to restructure its facilities. In particular there has been real pressure on space as they have moved departments from two other campuses onto the Hendon site. Part of the negotiation regarding tenure involved the club contributing to a more efficient use of space. Thus, in an imaginative restructure, the professionals' area and hub of the club was moved to a new pro

Head Pro Will Burns in action.

The court was masterminded and financed by Peter Luck-Hille and opened by The Earl of Wessex in 2000. It has worn fantastically well thanks to the quality of the construction, including the now famous penthouse engineering.

a die. The court looks as good today as it did when it was built, with only slight wear to the floor in some areas. The court still plays better than ever and encourages good Tennis. If you cut the ball it comes down, if you don't it sits up, just as it should!

The club has become the home of the Henry Leaf and Cattermull trophies, the Under-21s and -24s tournaments, and 2013 saw the inaugural Middlesex University British Challenge, which is the only event in the calendar, save the world championship, to have a thirteen-set final. The plan is that this will be held every two years.

Briefly the court became a sound studio in 2012, as a setting for the recording of a radio play called *Singles and Doublets* by Martyn Wade. This is a comedy, which takes as its theme a Tennis match between two Elizabethan rivals, Philip Sidney and the Earl of Oxford. Queen Elizabeth I's response to a marriage proposal from the Duke of Anjou was to be decided by the result of the match. A witty play with some historical licence!

Peter Luck-Hille presents the trophy to Ricardo Smith at the inaugural British Challenge in 2013.

room in the gallery above the main wall. The club's main room behind the dedans is still there but with a better scale, and the club has access, by agreement, for major events, to the large studio space behind the club room which previously remained empty most of the time. In return for partially giving up some space, there are new and improved showers and changing facilities.

The court itself has worn fantastically well, testimony to the quality of the construction. The now famous 'penthouse engineering' has proved to set the standard for years to come and the bandeau is as straight as

THE MONTREAL RACKET CLUB

COURTS GALORE seem to have been built in various quarters of Montreal throughout the nineteenth century (including an open wooden one in 1836). The club was founded around 1800 but their first recorded professional marker, Johnny Mahon, was appointed as late as 1875. Albert Bridger from England served from 1881 to 1915, during which time the present court was built on Concord Street (1889). The original court was bigger than normal, and so was adjusted to regulation size in 1909.

Most remarkable of all their pros was Ken Chantler. His fifty years of service to the game was celebrated with a testimonial dinner on court in 1978. A superb Rackets player, Chantler won the Junior Professional

First leg of the 2011 world doubles championship (left to right) *Alex Titchener-Barrett, Tim Cockroft, Glenn Chamandy, Andrew Pepper, Mike McLernon, Mark Hue Williams, Harry Foster.*

championship at Queen's Club in 1928, came to Montreal in 1929, won the US Open in 1940, 1957 and 1960, and beat Bobby Grant III to win the North American Open in 1947. Jim Dear beat him 8–1 in the subsequent world title match.

Steve Tulley came from Charterhouse to take up the mantle in 1988, returning to England in 2000 to launch the Rackets programme at St Paul's School in London. He was succeeded by Derek Barrett. Ryan Tulley, son of Steve, had been a Fellow in Montreal and then succeeded Derek in 2006. After five years as the club professional, Ryan departed to take up the head professional post at Wellington. He was replaced in 2011 by James Rock, who had been a Fellow in Chicago. James's ability, energy and drive, coupled with experience on the Rackets circuit on either side of the Atlantic, has helped to take an active Rackets programme at Montreal to another level.

Among the club's outstanding amateurs, David McLernon's name is celebrated for his domination of the game in the late 1960s and throughout the 1970s (and he was still winning the club doubles in 1998 and 1999, with Karel Nemec). In the 1990s McLernon was supplanted by Bart Sambrook, more often than not the winner of both singles and doubles titles.

The Montreal Club has always been at the heart of Canadian Rackets, and the last weekend of January is

Mike McLernon, son of David and winner of the 2013 Canadian Amateur doubles (with Jonathan Larken).

reserved for the Canadian Amateur championships, which attract players from the US and the UK as well as from all over Canada. The weekend is the highlight of the year for the North American Racquets Association as well as for the club. In the new millennium, Jonathan Larken has dominated the singles, winning no less than six times.

The club has played host to a number of major Rackets matches in recent years, including the first leg of the 2005 world singles, in which Harry Foster (who would go on to become world champion in the second leg at Queen's) defeated his opponent Ali Robinson by four games to two.

In 2011 the club was again host of the first leg of a world championship – this time providing the venue for the world doubles. The first-leg match saw defending champions Harry Foster and his partner Mark Hue Williams go down by four games to three against Tim Cockroft and Alex Titchener-Barrett, who proceeded to win the world title in the second leg at Queen's.

Recently, the floor was redone, back wall replaced and a glass door added to the court. Further refurbishment of the club was made necessary after being damaged by construction next door. In 2014 the club celebrated the 125th anniversary of the building of the court.

Charles Hue Williams and Ron Kaulbach watch the 2011 world doubles.

Moreton Morrell Tennis Court Club

Few Tennis clubs, say the members here, can boast such a high percentage of handicappers below twenty, or such an imposing ambience in which to play. The court was built in 1905 by Charles Tuller Garland, an American citizen who later served with the British Army in the First World War and was the owner of Moreton Hall, the entrance gates of which face those of the court.

The Garlands trace their descent from the Garlands of Essex, whose coat of arms is displayed on the façade of the court building, while C.T. Garland's initials are incorporated in the mosaic floor within. Now part of Mid-Warwickshire College, a few miles south of Leamington, the hall (neo-William and Mary) and the estate were bought on Garland's death by Col. R.J.L. Ogilby, whose coat of arms is in the court itself.

The court was acquired by Major James Dance MP in 1949, and with the help of many supporters including Mr Garland's three daughters and Lord Willoughby de Broke, the Moreton Morrell Tennis Court Company was formed in 1963 to acquire the building and the surrounding grounds. In 1913 *The Field* described

The court was built by Joseph Bickley for Charles Tuller Garland in 1905 and became a club in 1963.

the court building as being ahead of any other in the country 'in luxury of appointment', and you can still see why. Over the moulded archway leading to the playing area is the bas-relief *Mercury and Pandora*, by the neo-classical sculptor John Flaxman RA, and elaborate cornices and pilasters decorate the dedans.

The first professional at Moreton Morrell was the legendary E.J. (Ted) Johnson, brought up by his father – for fifty years Lord Wimborne's professional at Canford – to do the job properly. Young Ted's first posts were at Prince's Club and Tuxedo Park, but when Charles Garland built this court, Ted came home, at the age of twenty-five, and stayed right there until he died in 1970, aged ninety-one.

The inaugural match was between Johnson and Peter Latham, five times world champion, and in 1908 Ted played 'Punch' Fairs for the world title at Brighton, losing 2–7. He later challenged Fred Covey for the championship. When the challenge was not taken up, Johnson was entitled to claim the title by default.

Major renovation had to be carried out in the 1990s.

Typically, he declined to accept an honour for which he had not fought.

By all accounts, he was the perfect professional – a player of exemplary style and strength, a man of charm and modesty, and a relentlessly efficient and devoted coach and marker. He spent more than seventy years in the game – and when he talked of having played before His Royal Highness, he was referring to the man who became King Edward VII.

Struggling to keep afloat during the difficult 1970s, the club was deeply indebted to the hard work of Sir Richard Hamilton, the honorary secretary at that time, whose translations of Albert De Luze's *La Magnifique Histoire du Jeu de Paume* and Pierre Barcellon's *Règles et Principes de Paume* are important additions to the game's rich literary history. Sir Richard, Roland Owen-George and Dr Anthony Hobson (well known for his portraits of Henry Johns and Howard Angus, and for *The Dinner Match*, which hangs in the bar at Leamington) organised two appeals for ongoing restoration work and were instrumental in the appointment of Jonathan Howell as full-time professional in 1978.

Despite his tender years, Howell (only the second professional at the court in seventy-three years) rejuvenated the club, encouraging new members and fostering improved playing standards. The world Invitation singles and doubles were held at the court in 1980, a tournament that culminated in the memorable final between Chris Ronaldson and Frank Willis. At 2 sets all and 5-all, Ronaldson saved match point by hurling himself to the floor to scoop a ball from the tambour. The match ended with Ronaldson beating a worse-than-a-yard chase laid by Willis.

By then on course to become one of the world's leading players, Howell moved on to Bordeaux in 1982. Among subsequent professionals were Andrew Davis, Steve Brockenshaw and the current head professional Tom Granville, who used to play at the club as an amateur.

In the early 1990s, the original Bickley floor and parts of the external structure began deteriorating at an alarming rate, and the club had to raise £100,000 for repairs. The fact that the work was completed and paid for by 1998 was a considerable achievement, and tribute not only to the energy of the members, but to the warmth with which the club is regarded by players across Britain.

In 2002 Lord Willoughby de Broke retired as chairman after twenty-nine years of service, since which time Sir Andrew Hamilton has taken over responsibility for stewardship of the court and club. His first major task was to coordinate undoubtedly the highlight of the club's recent history – the Centenary celebrations of 2005. The club hosted a world tournament, most generously sponsored by club member Jonny Cook, which attracted many of the leading players – the competition was needless to say won by the world champion, Rob Fahey, who beat Steve Virgona in the final.

A dinner was held at Moreton Hall, Charles Garland's mansion, built in 1909 (four years after the Tennis court!). At the time it was the largest Real Tennis dinner ever held, attracting over 400 guests, and attended by The Earl of Wessex. The committee was delighted to be joined by present and past world champions Rob Fahey, Howard Angus, Chris Ronaldson, Penny Lumley, Charlotte Cornwallis, Lesley Ronaldson, Moreton Morrell's Sally Jones, and her doubles partner Alex Garside. Also present were Tom Granville and the head professional's predecessors, Jonathan Howell, Andrew Davis and Steve Brockenshaw.

A singles tournament for members and visitors attracted forty-eight entrants and there were thirty-two pairs in the doubles competition. Financially, the fundraising element of the celebrations ensured stability for the long-term future of the club.

Other modifications have been made, including the renovation of the dining room, thanks to the generosity of Lady Hamilton in memory of her late husband Sir Richard. However, in 2007 the club was also severely hit when on a dark rainy evening, assistant professional Nick Jury suffered severe injuries when knocked off his bicycle by a car. With the support of the committee and members, he recovered well enough to continue in his job. In 2013 he announced his retirement from Tennis but still makes his superb trademark balls.

Junior Tennis provision has expanded in recent years, thanks to the professionals' input and the efforts of Tim Messer and Beverleigh Twohig-Howell. Warwick School and King's High School for Girls now receive coaching on Monday and Wednesday afternoons, and it has been encouraging that many of the pupils have continued to play in holiday time and in national competitions. The club is hoping to encourage another local school to involve their students in learning the game with help from The Dedanists' Foundation.

After major events like the centenary celebrations, there is always the danger of complacency, but thanks

(left to right) *David Bryant, Tom Granville, The Earl of Wessex, Sir Andrew Hamilton.*

to a T&RA-inspired initiative for management 'best practice', the committee surveyed the membership, as a result of which beneficial changes were introduced, not least the restoration of the American Squash Tennis Court and Gallery, which were reopened in 2012. Philip Shaw-Hamilton won the men's world tournament and Sally Jones the ladies' tournament. The game was in the past often incorrectly called Stické, but it has been established that it is American squash tennis, which was the precursor of modern Tennis.

In 2013, a group of club members led by Flo Holland transformed the bar area, with a judicious choice of colours and materials but in keeping with its Edwardian past.

After many years of service to the club, Jonny Cook and Richard Seymour Mead retired from the committee.

To celebrate fifty years of a club having been in existence, a celebratory weekend was held in June 2014 with a doubles tournament and a dinner. A grand total of £22,000 was raised, which will be a useful financial buffer in the likely event that the court's floor will need major renovation work.

Moreton Morrell remains a relaxed and welcoming club with a committee that continues to improve the playing and social experience for members and visitors.

NEWMARKET REAL TENNIS CLUB

Opened in 1901 and closed in 1923, this court remained out of Tennis use for seventy years. When the centenary of the inaugural match was held in June 2001, it had been in play for just twenty-five of its one hundred years. However, that was cause enough for celebration.

The court was built by Joseph Bickley for Sir Charles Rose at enormous cost – £6,000 compared with, for instance, the second court at Cambridge, built at around the same time for £2,000. It was the first to incorporate all the features of a modern court, and was the second of Sir Charles's three courts, the other two both being at Hardwick House (1896 and 1907). Its playing characteristics are often compared with those of the Bickley court at Moreton Morrell.

The first two professionals were the greatest players of their day, and both world champions: Peter Latham (1901) and Cecil 'Punch' Fairs (1908). On Sir Charles's death the court did not remain with the Rose family, and in 1923 it was converted into a garage workshop.

Its restoration, masterminded by John Shneerson, was completed in 1995, when it was opened as a privately owned club run for members. Kevin King and John Dawes were the professionals. They worked hard

The court was converted into a garage workshop in 1923.

When the centenary of the opening of the court was celebrated in 2001, it had been in play for just 25 out of its 100 years.

The court's restoration was completed in 1995. It was masterminded by John Shneerson, who also wrote about its history.

to achieve success, but running a new club in a small town was not easy, and financial problems caused the court to be put on the market again in 1998.

In 1999 the court was bought and then managed for the next eleven years by three local players, John Burnett, Chris Hollingsworth and Alex Riley, who formed a new club. Further improvements were made, including central heating, a small kitchen, better showers, an enclosed viewing area at the hazard end, and the first online booking and billing system to assist the members and professionals. John Shneerson, who has also written the book *Two Centuries of Real Tennis* about its history, was made honorary life member in recognition of his enormous contribution.

Andrew Knibbs, who had joined as professional just before the change of ownership, was joined by Mark Hobbs initially on a part-time basis, increasing to full time as the club's membership numbers and income increased. An enthusiastic membership entered teams into many of the handicap tournaments and leagues. In 2007 two Newmarket teams went to the Boomerang Cup in Melbourne and ended up as winners and semi-finalists (having had to play each other in the semis) out of an entry of thirty-seven international club teams.

In 2011 a scheme was implemented which made it possible for the membership to acquire the club with the help of Loan Notes subscribed for by 150 generous supporters from the Tennis community, repayable over a period of years by the playing members on a lottery basis. In March 2011, ownership was handed over to the new club committee.

One of the first major steps the new committee has taken is to replace the old sodium-based lighting system, which was effective but very costly to run, with a modern LED-based system which provides excellent light at a fraction of the running cost.

The New Club Committee comprising (left to right) *Alex Riley, Chris Hollingsworth, John Burnett, with Stuart Arrandale and Richard Dunn representing the New Members Club.*

Newport
The National Tennis Club

The National Tennis Club was formed in 1980 when the original court, destroyed by a series of fires in 1945 and 1946, was rebuilt, retaining the floor and some of the walls. The original court – designed by McKim, Mead and White, built by contractor David Perkins of Boston, and completed in 1880 – was situated alongside the lawn tennis courts of the Newport Casino Club, which was created by the publisher James Gordon Bennett as an alternative to the Newport Reading Room.

The first professional, Englishman Tom Pettitt, who had been the assistant in Boston, remained at Newport as head professional for forty-six years. While there he succeeded in becoming world champion in 1885 and retaining his title in 1890. He was succeeded by Dan Kenney, who presided until the 1945 fire. After that, the court lay in disrepair until 1979.

Then the reconstruction project commenced, due to the efforts of Clarry Pell Jr, Jack Slater, Sammy Van Alen and Allison Danzig. The first balls of the new era were struck by Clarry Pell, Philip Stockton, Alistair Martin and Lord Aberdare, and the official dedication of the court took place during the inaugural Tiffany Cup tournament in August 1980. This tournament, the longest running at the club, is now named the Pell Cup, after founder and former club president Clarry Pell.

In 1980, the court was re-built, having been destroyed by a series of fires. The original court had been part of the Casino Club for James Gordon Bennett in 1880, and designed by McKim, Mead and White.

The court with viewing galleries along the main wall and new windows above the grille penthouse.

The first professional at the reopened club was Barry Toates, who, like Tom Pettitt, is English and had come from Boston. Barry developed the initial core membership and schooled them in the proper form. He was succeeded as head professional in 1987 by George Wharton and, in turn, Josh Bainton and Richard Smith, who is the current head professional. The club has been fortunate to have had many qualified assistant professionals, including Jacques Faulise, Bryn Sayers, Tony Hollins, Richard (Ricardo) Hall-Smith, and many other visiting players who have served as summer assistants to the club.

The National Tennis Club has been considered the official court of the United States Court Tennis Association (USCTA) since its restoration in 1980. As the game has grown, new institutions have been formed, including the United States Court Tennis Preservation Foundation (USCTPF), to provide complementary organisation and funding for the public enjoyment of this unique game. As the National Tennis Club has matured, so have its congenial relationships with the International Tennis Hall of Fame (ITHOF), the owner of the court and beautifully manicured grounds; with the USCTA, the ruling body for the game in the United States; and with the USCTPF, with its important charitable and educational mission in support of the game.

The court was originally primarily a summer court, but as the membership has grown to more than one hundred, play is now year round. The club has hosted the Bathurst Cup, the Van Alen Challenge, the US national championships and many inter-club events.

In 2003, under Jay Schochet's leadership, the court underwent a major renovation whereby the club spaces were enlarged, and three enormous windows were cut into the back wall above the grille penthouse to allow for outstanding viewing. In 2004, the club hosted the

In 2004, the club hosted the world championship, where Rob Fahey was victorious over Tim Chisholm.

world championship, where Rob Fahey was victorious over Tim Chisholm in 7 sets to 1 in a bravura performance demonstrating his mastery of the game.

Creativity has been the hallmark of scheduling. There are active night leagues and extensive junior programmes. The club is one of the busiest in the United States, averaging eighty hours per week in bookings.

Since the club reopened, it has been ably led by Presidents Jonathan Isham, Barclay Douglas, Clarry Pell, James Wharton and Jonathan Pardee, Jane Lippincott, Joseph Tomaino, William Burgin, John Murphy, Ross Cann, Tom Rowe and Stephen De Voe, each of whom has seen the club through various stages of growth. Without their dedication, and that of the able Board of Governors, the National Tennis Club would not be the success it is today.

NEW YORK
THE RACQUET AND TENNIS CLUB

ONE OF THE LEADING CLUBS in the world, New York's Racquet and Tennis Club proudly occupies a full block on the west side of Park Avenue, a stark architectural contrast to the surrounding skyscrapers. Two fine Tennis courts and one Rackets court occupy most of the third (US fourth) floor, where the original second Rackets court has been converted into a doubles squash court.

The first indoor Rackets court in New York was in the Allen Street Club, 1800–50. The immediate ancestor of the present club was the Rackets Court Club, formed in 1875 when the city had been without a court since 1868. This club opened in 1876 at 55 West Twenty-Sixth Street, with two Rackets courts one above the other, each with two galleries. In 1890, the club moved to a new site at 27 West Forty-Third Street, changing its name to the Racquet and Tennis Club, since there was now one Rackets court and New York's first Tennis court. Second Rackets and Tennis courts were added in 1904. The club moved to its present site of 370 Park Avenue in 1918. The architects of this magnificent building were McKim, Meade and White, with the construction of the courts supervised by Bickley. In addition to its prestigious clubrooms and a great many other facilities, the second floor contains one of the finest libraries of sporting books in the world.

There is general consensus among the players and professionals that the club is enjoying a golden age of

Designed by McKim, Meade & White, the building was completed in 1918.

The victorious New York Whitney team in 2006 (left to right) *Lex Miron, Chris Arriz, Michael Flinn, Jim Ardrey, Nicolas Victoir, Howard McMorris, Alexis Hombrecher, Guy Devereux, Bruce Manson, Samuel Abernethy, Antony Smithie.*

sport in the early years of the twenty-first century. The number of players and hours of play in both Tennis and Rackets have increased substantially, with many more Tennis players also trying Rackets. The 2012–13 draws for the fourth class handicap in Tennis were 39 for singles and 18 for doubles, with over 250 members belonging to the United States Court Tennis Association.

The Tennis season starting in the autumn of 2001 was instrumental in establishing the schedule which has been continued in subsequent years. In addition to hosting a proportionate share of all regular USCTA tournaments, New York held the Silver Racquet in the second weekend in November, as is customary. This included the traditional Invitational Tennis singles draw of sixteen, in conjunction with the New York Open handicap singles, which routinely attracts sixty-four players. What made the 2001–02 season exceptional was the addition of two even larger events, the Whitney Cup, played for the first time at the Racquet and Tennis Club, 7–9 December 2001, and the World Overs, held the full week of 1–8 April 2002.

The Whitney Cup was started by Jock Whitney in 1930, and had been held almost continuously in early December at Greentree, the Whitney's family estate in Manhasset, Long Island. By tradition, the four teams of ten men each, playing as five doubles teams, were Greentree, New York, Philadelphia, and a combined team from Tuxedo, Newport, and Boston. Play started on Friday afternoon with only two matches of the Senior, Over-55, teams. The other eight matches were played all day Saturday, with the winning teams continuing on Sunday. With nearly all of the best forty players competing every year, and the Whitney family providing wonderful lunches for players, their wives/dates and Whitney friends, this was universally considered to be the major event of the amateur year.

With the passing of Betsey Whitney in 1998, the Greentree estate was redesignated as a United Nations meeting facility, with the result that the Whitney Cup had to move to New York, much to the initial regret of the family members and many of the players. And yet, this relocation resulted in changes – and perhaps even some improvements. With two courts available, the four teams could expand to six: Greentree (since combined with Aiken), New York, Philadelphia, Washington, Tuxedo (now joined with Chicago) and Newport/Boston (now reconstituted as New England). This required a new format, with two groups of three teams playing a full round-robin all day Friday/Saturday, thereby guaranteeing two matches for all players. The Racquet and Tennis Club is well equipped to provide a warm reception and luncheons for the players and their guests, and in subsequent years the annual USCTA dinner became a fixture on Friday night. A Captains' Committee was instituted, which has measurably improved the coordination behind the event. With the number of players now expanded to sixty, in addition to the USCTA dinner attended by over 100 supporters, the premier position of the Whitney weekend is stronger than ever. The New York Whitney team had disappointing results for the first several years, but emerged victorious in 2006 and 2007, to be repeated in 2011 and 2012.

This format of the Silver Racquet in early November, followed by the Whitney Cup in early December, has remained unchanged ever since. The Silver Racquet has continued to prosper; in 2009 draws of thirty in the Open A handicap, and forty-one in the Open B, necessitated the initiation of an Open C event in 2010. A positive development was the emergence of a new group of R&T players as winners, notably Lex Miron, Nicolas Victoir, Alexis Hombrecher, Addison West and Peter Pell.

The World Overs, started in Australia in 1985, was initially played in New York in 1989, although on a far smaller scale. The event in April of 2002 was an extravaganza, with fifty-two players from England, Australia and the US completing 110 matches in eight days. It started with the fourth playing of the Cockram team competition for seven players over 50, as well as the inauguration of the Pete Bostwick Cup, for five players over 50. Great Britain defeated the US in the Cockram finals 4–1, with the US reversing this in the Bostwick final by 3–0. This was followed by singles and doubles matches in the Over-40s, -50s, and -60s, with Howard Angus coming very close to winning both the singles and doubles in both the Over-40s and -50s. He nearly succeeded, losing only in the Over-50 doubles, quite an accomplishment at the age of fifty-eight.

Most of these senior players returned to New York once again, 2–13 April 2008, with additional evolutionary changes. Entries increased from fifty-two to sixty-seven, including twenty-nine from the US, twenty-three from the UK, and a stalwart group of fifteen from Australia. The name changed to World Masters, the age level of over 40 was dropped in favour of adding an over 70, and the number of individual tournaments increased from three to five, now over 50/55/60/65/70. The Bostwick Over-60 team event increased to three doubles teams and one singles match, and the amateur associations agreed to add the Danby Over-70 team competition, with three doubles teams per country.

The UK was simply too strong in the team competitions, defeating the US in all three finals, 4–1 in the Cockram and Bostwick, and 2–1 in the Danby, with the deciding match being a 4–6, 6–4, 6–5 win by Sam Leigh/Mick Dean over Pete Bostwick/John McLean at No. 1 doubles. The US had more success in the individual events, with Simon Aldrich/George Bell winning the 50s doubles, Philadelphians Dick Tanfield/Sam Howe the 65s doubles, McLean the 70s singles, and Bostwick/McLean the 70s doubles.

This all happened again in May of 2013, with the increasing scale of the event requiring that the team competitions be held during a first week, in Philadelphia for the Cockram, and Tuxedo Park for the Danby and Bostwick. The UK was again too strong, winning the Bostwick without losing a set, and beating Australia 4–1 and the US 5–0 in the Cockram. The only moment of drama was the deciding third match of the finals in the Danby, with the US and the UK tied 1–1. Ward/Wilks prevailed over McLean/Flinn, 6–4, 4–6, 6–1, making a clean sweep for England. For the individual tournaments in New York, John Prenn was dominant, winning four events, the 50/55 doubles and the 55/60 singles, thereby being the first competitor ever to win the maximum number of tournaments permitted.

The club championships in New York during these years witnessed the same evolution toward new and younger players as the Silver Racquet. For the first five years, Morris Clothier, Guy Devereux, Jonathan Larken and Simon Aldrich won nearly every tournament. The initial indications of change came in 2006, when Alexis Hombrecher, a new member recently arrived from London, combined with Peter Pell to win the club doubles. This continued in 2007, when Nicolas Victoir from France, also by way of London, won the singles, as well as the doubles with Lex Miron. Hombrecher, Pell, Victoir, Miron and Addison West would dominate these events through 2014. In the last two years, Spike Willcocks, yet another London transplant, teamed with Larken to win the doubles. Finally, a further indication of the depth of the programme is the very competitive first-class singles handicap, which has been won by ten different players during the last fourteen years.

These years also marked the end of Morris Clothier's long reign as the best Tennis player in New York. It is a fascinating bit of history that his record of winning twenty-three club championships, thirteen singles and ten doubles between 1988 and 2005 is a perfect match with the achievements of Alistair Martin, who captured three singles titles in 1939, 1949 and 1952, as well as twenty consecutive doubles events from 1949 to 1968.

Throughout the 1990s until 2003, the US Amateur singles and doubles were dominated by Nigel Pendrigh, Julian Snow and Ralph Howe. Once again, Clothier deserves mention as the winner of four singles, the last in 1991, and five doubles, the last with Simon Aldrich in 2005. In addition, in 2004 Chisholm and Clothier won the US Open, the first time an American amateur had won this event since 1989. Since 2004 the same group of emerging New York players as noted earlier has won these events eleven times. Older New York players continued to have success in multiple USCTA tournaments since 2001, notably Greg Van Schaack and Simon Aldrich in the Over-50/55/60s singles events, and Van Schaack, Aldrich, Chris Cline and Charles Johnston in the 50/60 doubles.

In 2003 the skylights were replaced in both Tennis courts, with technological improvements that made it possible to play during the day without lighting for much of the year. At the same time a new lighting system was installed, with both new technology and more lights in the corners. Finally, after prolonged debate, the pro shop converted to yellow Tennis balls.

In March 2011, New York hosted the Bathurst Cup. This team competition is played every two years, rotating among England, Australia, France and the United States. Originally scheduled for 2010, this event was postponed for a year due to the eruption of the Eyjafjallajökull volcano in Iceland. The US was represented by Addison West, Preston Quick, Alexis Hombrecher, Simon Aldrich and Lex Miron.

During these same years, Rackets has enjoyed a very similar trend, with the depth and quality of play showing definite improvement. There are now eighty-one players with established handicaps, with a weekly evening of continuous doubles for several hours with James Stout attracting new converts. The club singles and doubles championship for 2012–13 had draws of fourteen and eight, with first- and second-class handicap draws in singles each having eighteen entries. Without question, Jonathan Larken has dominated club singles play since 2001, winning every singles tournament except the three years he was in London, 2006–08. Even further, he has won the last six doubles events, five with Peter Pell, who is following in the footsteps of both his grandfather and great-grandfather. Fortunately, Guy Devereux and Clothier provided some variety to this routine by winning seven consecutive doubles titles between 1999 and 2005. The first-class handicap during these fourteen years was a more open affair, with Van Schaack, Hombrecher, and West winning once, and Pell four times.

Messrs. Larken and Devereux have also enjoyed success in the Rackets world beyond 370 Park Avenue. The two combined have won eight US Amateur doubles titles, thrice as partners; each has also won the US Open doubles. In 2001, Larken captured all

Jonathan Larken and Guy Devereux between them have won eight U.S. Amateur Rackets doubles, thrice as partners; each has also won the U.S. Open doubles.

major North American titles (the US and Canadian Amateurs, and the US and Western Opens), repeating in the US Amateur the following year. As a result, his challenge for a world championship was accepted by NARA, and he played James Male in 2003, winning the first match in Philadelphia 4–1, before losing the second leg at Queens 4–0. In addition, Larken has won six Canadian singles championships since 2001.

For the Silver Racquet weekend in 2012, New York hosted the US Open singles and doubles in Rackets, with a new format and philosophy which represented significant change. For the first time, there were qualifying tournaments in both singles and doubles, with matches played on a firm schedule. Total prize moneys for the pros was increased, with this event attracting six of the best seven players in the world.

New York professionals have played a central role in the Rackets world during these years. Neil Smith continued to be a force, taking the US Open three times and winning the world doubles in 2007, fifteen years after first winning that event in 1992. Smith had also won the world championship in 1999, before losing this to James Male in 2001. In addition, Neil has won the US Open doubles in four different decades, first in 1989 with Shannon Hazel, and last with Nick James in 2012. Despite these heroics, James Stout has clearly been the narrative of the last eight years.

Following several years as an international squash pro while based in Belgium, he joined the pro shop in 2006; only two years later James defeated Foster in the world Rackets championship in November 2008. In 2010, James successfully defended his title against Alex Titchener-Barrett; he has not been challenged since. In fact, Stout has lost only twice during these years, the US Open in 2009 and the British Open in 2010, each time to Titchener-Barrett. Finally, as an added attraction, James also defeated Tim Chisholm and Camden Riviere to win the US Open in Tennis in March 2010, only three years after starting to play that game; six days later he won the US Open in Rackets. The only players to have had similar success in these two sports in recent years are Howard Angus and James Male.

Tim Chisholm served as head Rackets and Tennis professional from 1999 until 2004 and was a major factor in Tennis, challenging Rob Fahey three times for the world championship (2002, 2004 and 2006). Mike Gooding succeeded Chisholm as head Rackets and Tennis professional, serving from 2004 to 2014 following a successful career in which he captured 17 major titles. Gooding had previously been in New York as an assistant to Wayne Davies from 1987 to 1993. In 2014, James Stout became head Rackets professional and Barney Tanfield became head Tennis professional. In addition to Stout and Tanfield, the highly capable Tennis and Rackets assistant professionals during this

In 2010 James Stout won the US Open Tennis singles and the US Open Rackets singles within 6 days of each other.

time included Josh Bainton, Ged Eden, Charlie Crossley, Andrew Fowler and Neil Smith. In recent years the Racquets, Tennis and Squash Committee, which oversees all games at the club, has been chaired by Samuel F. Abernethy (1996-2008), Morris W. Clothier (2008-2014), and Peter J. Pell, Jr. (from 2014).

Barney Tanfield, Mike Gooding, James Stout and Neil Smith with Morris Clothier, Chairman of Rackets, Tennis & Squash Committee.

THE ORATORY

The first Tennis court to be built in the UK for more than eighty years opened at The Oratory School, near Reading, in the final week of 1989. Since it was of modern construction, it was possible to introduce several novel features: the placing of glass panels above the court, thus increasing the number of potential spectators; the inlaying of court markings into the floor, thus saving time and money because the court does not have to close for re-marking lines; and the omission of natural light (and leaks) by the use of profile sheeting.

It was when The Oratory began playing cricket against Beaumont School at Lord's that they first became aware of Tennis, but it was not until David Weston became a school parent that the playing of Tennis there became a reality. Adrian Snow, the headmaster at the time, was persuaded to allow the boys to be introduced to the game and coached in it at Hardwick House, not far away at Pangbourne.

Mark Eadle, then the young assistant at Oxford University, gave his time freely to the boys, and it was not long before more wished to play than could be accommodated at Hardwick. With the help of Ron Womersley, an Oratory teacher, boys were also taken to the court at Oxford University.

The Oratory had moved during the war from its home at Caversham to Woodcote House, some eight miles north, a fine site with virtually no facilities. Considerable constructional development took place during the headmasterships of Father Adrian Morey (1952–67) and Adrian Snow (1972–88), one of the consequences of which was that the sporting facilities had become sufficiently attractive for people outside the school to want to use them.

It was clear to Adrian Snow that Tennis was a good game in itself, and one which could be played by pupils for almost the rest of their lives (unlike most other sports); and that it could also be a source of additional finance. The school's governing body accepted this line of argument and a Tennis court was included in the sports centre which was about to be constructed at Woodcote in 1988. Adrian Snow had been the contractor for many building projects at the school, and when he retired as headmaster he continued, as warden and managing director of Oratory Construction, to supervise all aspects of the creation of the Tennis court. The first game on the court was played, appropriately, between David Weston and Adrian Snow. The current headmaster, Clive Dytor (2000 to the present day), a keen supporter of Real Tennis, continues to encourage Oratorians to participate in the game.

As the popularity of the game and membership increased, the club designed and managed the conversion of an old storeroom behind the dedans and converted it into a member's clubroom, or Royal Dedans as it has became known. The room was opened in May 2004 by The Earl of Wessex, who became a regular player at The Oratory for a number of years.

More recently, The Oratory has been looking into improving the lighting of the court.

As its first professional, the school was lucky to recruit Jonathan Howell, at the time in his eighth year at Bordeaux. He was attracted not only by the prospect of participating in a new court, but also in returning to England to play cricket and coach the school XI. Against some expectations, the use of the court by outside personnel took off, and it was not long before Howell needed an assistant. Mark Eadle was available, and the partnership was an unqualified success. Throughout their time at Oratory, the fortunes of the club went from strength to strength, and Jonathan became a well-known figure on the touchlines, scouring the assembled groups of parents for likely and, in some cases, unlikely candidates for introductory Real Tennis sessions and subsequent membership, with great success. Not only did they establish a vibrant club with a large playing and social membership but they also oversaw the development of a number of talented junior Real Tennis players and established the National Schools Real Tennis tournament that continues to this day. In 2007 Jonathan decided that he could no longer postpone the longstanding commitment he had made to his wife, Julie, some ten years beforehand, to go back to her native Australia. In November 2007 a surprise farewell party was held, attended by over 250 people, including a host of fellow professionals, old friends from the Real Tennis and cricket worlds, members of the Royal Family and club members.

Full-width windows were fitted in the two rooms above the dedans so that viewing capacity could be increased to 240 for the 2006 world championship.

Amongst others, Chris Ronaldson gave tribute to his achievements at The Oratory and in the wider Real Tennis community.

The Oratory was lucky to have the help of Bryn Sayers and Ross Brown as assistant professionals at various times before and after Jonathan returned to Australia. In 2010 Mark departed from the club, signifying the end of an era spanning nearly two decades and the start of a new one. In April 2011, Andy Chinneck was appointed by the school as the Real Tennis head professional and his assistant Liam Taylor was appointed in the following August. Then, in 2014, Andy moved to Holyport. Meanwhile the tradition continues of nurturing junior talent from the school, as well as continuing to welcome old and new members as well as many visitors from around the world.

The club also hosted and sponsored the UK Professional singles tournament on four occasions, and it was the success of these tournaments that led to the club putting in a bid to host the 2006 world championship. The bid, driven by Mike Allaway, Mike Taylor, Jonathan and Mark was accepted. At that time the court had a spectator capacity of around 100, and it was decided that if full-width windows were fitted in the two rooms above the dedans then the viewing capacity could be increased to around 240. This was achieved, and the packed galleries witnessed Rob Fahey retain his title by beating Tim Chisholm 7–0.

Trophy presentation at the club singles championship in 2012, when Stuart Baxter beat Christian Whittaker.

The long list of club tournaments throughout the season continues. As well as the established singles and doubles competitions, such innovations as the Night Pennant, perpetually organised by Gerri Brooksbank and perpetually won by Pam Tomalin and her various teams, as well as the Over-100 doubles (combined age!) and the Village League tournaments have proved to be extremely popular. Additionally the annual Parents and Offspring tournament for the Gordon Bennett Trophy sees some of Jonathan's early recruits now playing with their offspring: Butlers, Allaways, Boughtons, Brownlees, Taylors, Gordons, Tomalins, Glynns, Nicksons, Macleans and Whittakers and others, all looking a lot happier for having discovered this wonderful game.

Oxford University

Although there were Tennis courts in Oxford in the fifteenth century, the first known Oxford University court was built by Christ Church around 1545. The present court at Merton Street was built about 1798. It was preceded, on the same Postmaster's Hall site, by one dating back to a lease of 1595.

The lease was held by the Wood family from 1608 to 1758, after which it was taken on by Edmund Tompkins of Waterperry, the first of a substantial family of Tennis players. In the time of Edmund Tompkins III, the court was rebuilt in its present form (except for the floor, which was not re-laid until shortly before the First World War). He left for Brighton in 1836, by which time the lease was held by Thomas Sabin.

The Tompkins link returned in 1866 in the form of Edmund Tompkins IV, who came to Oxford when London's James Street court closed. He brought with him that court's dedans benches, which remain at Oxford today, and in due course the lease passed on to his son-in-law, J.H. Dickinson, and then to his son, R.C.E. Dickinson.

After the Second World War, there was no resident professional at the university until Peter Ellis arrived from Queen's Club in 1961. The reign of Peter Dawes, who came from Lord's in 1965, was particularly successful, and his wife proved an expert re-coverer of Tennis balls. Chris Ronaldson, then a promising lawn tennis player, took over when Dawes left for Seacourt in 1972 and stayed for two years before going to the new court at Melbourne. He was followed at Oxford by Mick Dean, Mike Flanagan, Steve Ronaldson, Jerome Fletcher and Alan Oliver. A former Oxford United trainee professional footballer with no Tennis experience, Mark Eadle was taken on as assistant and took to the game so well that he moved on to Holyport.

Kees Ludekens, an enthusiastic young player at Ballarat, came to Oxford and stayed for five years, doing much to raise the profile of the Varsity match as well as starting the women's Varsity matches in 1992. He left for the Harbour Club in 1994, when Andrew Davis (from Leamington and Moreton Morrell) joined Alan Oliver as joint head professional.

The court at Merton Street was built about 1798.

Alan Oliver completed nearly three decades at the club when he retired in February 2011. Alan presided over this period with his own special blend of sardonic humour, distinctive organisational style and often frenetic sessions on court. He was succeeded as head professional by Andrew Davis and, shortly afterwards, Craig Greenhalgh joined the club from Manchester.

The university had a succession of strong sides in the 1990s, rarely being beaten by Cambridge. James 'Spike' Willcocks, the former Canford schoolboy, was the most prominent player – both as undergraduate and post-graduate – at that time. He worked on his game so successfully that he reached the highest standard ever achieved by a player still at university (handicap +2, and the second-ranked amateur in Britain).

Alan Oliver, seen here with Simon Stubbings, completed nearly three decades at the club when he retired in February 2011.

Professionals (left to right) Craig Geenhalgh and Andrew Davis.

Major improvements were made to the Club building in 1997.

Off the court, many have worked hard to maintain the game and its facilities over the years. In 1965, the Unicorn Club was founded to support the courts and it flourished under the guidance of Sir Peter Gretton, bursar of University College, and since 1978 under a succession of long-serving chairmen. In the early 1990s the Oxford University Tennis Foundation was formed to raise and manage funds for the benefit of the game, with John Cook, Martin Mercer and Lord Willoughby de Broke as trustees.

Accumulated funds from the Unicorn Club, augmented by an appeal led by Brigadier Hugh Browne, former bursar of Oriel College, led to major improvements to the club building. A new long lease was negotiated with Merton College, the landlord, and the new clubhouse was officially opened by Lord Aberdare in September 1997. The 400th anniversary of Tennis in Oxford was marked in 1995 by an international inter-club tournament, and a book, *Tennis and Oxford* by Jeremy Potter, was published at the same time, with all proceeds going to the appeal.

In 2007 the clubroom was completely refurbished and modernised, thanks to a generous donation from the Broadbent family. William and Camille Broadbent made the donation in honour of their children: Avery Broadbent, who played in the Ladies' Varsity match in 2005 and William Broadbent (junior) who played in the Varsity match in 2007.

In 2007 the club room was completely refurbished and modernised thanks to a generous donation from the Broadbent family, pictured here.

PARIS
SOCIÉTÉ SPORTIVE DU JEU DE PAUME ET DE RACQUETS

ONE TENNIS COURT remains in this city where once there were hundreds. Contemporary accounts at the end of the sixteenth century estimate the number wildly, three writers plumping variously for 250, 1,100 and 'more than 1,800'. Historians generally settle for the fact that there were at least 500, all of which have disappeared.

As late as 1907, the two courts at the Tuileries (built in 1862 and 1882) were converted into an art gallery. They were replaced the following year by two second-floor courts in rue Lauriston, thanks to investment support from a group of Real Tennis players.

In 1927, in light of the declining popularity of Real Tennis, the club converted one of the two Real Tennis courts into four squash courts. These were the first squash courts in France.

Charles Lesueur, formerly at the Tuileries, was the new courts' first *maître paumier* in 1908, succeeded on his death in 1916 by Ferdinand Garcin. His father, Séraphin, had been head professional at the Tuileries, and his great-uncle had managed the court at Fontainebleau. Young Garcin was a stylish player in the great French tradition, but not a strong man physically. Pierre Etchebaster took over from Garcin at Paris in 1925, and had become world champion by the time he went to New York in 1930.

Robert Desmet, who arrived at rue Lauriston in 1921, succeeded Etchebaster as *maître paumier*. When the Second World War broke out, Émile Planet replaced Desmet. He did everything in his power to prevent the closing of the Real Tennis club. His only resource then was to give lawn tennis lessons during the war years.

In 2009 Stefan Edberg visited the Club during a Senior ATP Event (left to right) *Matthieu Sarlangue, Stefan Edberg, Quint Mandil and professional Adrian Kemp.*

Sisters Claire and Sarah Vigrass in action at the 2011 Ladies French Open doubles.

Laredo Massip took over from Émile Planet in 1963. He remained at the Jeu de Paume de Paris until his retirement in 2005. He was followed by young *maîtres paumiers* of Anglo-Saxon origin: Gerard Eden, Matthew Ronaldson, Angus Williams, Rod McNaughtan and Adrian Kemp. They have brought up a new generation of French Real Tennis players.

On the rue Lauriston court, typically Parisian competitions are held, such as the Jacques Polton Cup or the BNP-Paribas Tournament with handicap, as well as national competitions like the Gold Racquet, the Silver Racquet (both inaugurated in 1899) or the French national Open. The Gould Eddy Cup, an international competition for doubles only created in 1922, is also held every year. The Jeu de Paume de Paris welcomed the Bathurst Cup in 1978, 1987, 2000 and 2008. The club has held ladies' international handicap tournaments since 1991.

In 2008, the Jeu de Paume de Paris celebrated its 100th Anniversary. On this occasion, a small book called *Histoire du Jeu de Paume de Paris 1908–2008*

The Vigrass sisters win the 2013 Ladies world doubles.

(History of the Jeu de Paume of Paris 1908–2008), written by Hubert Demory, was published; it is now a book of reference.

In 2011–12, the Tennis court, as well as the squash courts and the clubhouse space generally, were subject to a complete renovation: walls, galleries, floor and lighting.

In April 2013 the Jeu de Paume de Paris hosted the ladies' singles and doubles world championships, when Claire Vigrass retained her title against her sister Sarah, and then the two sisters retained their title in the doubles against Penny Lumley and her daughter Tara.

Then, in September 2013, the Jeu de Paume hosted the men's world championship doubles when Rob Fahey and Steve Virgona retained their title for the fifth time against Tim Chisholm and Camden Riviere in one of the best doubles matches ever.

The 320 members of the Jeu de Paume are proud of our historic club and look forward to continuing to build bridges with other clubs throughout the world.

Claire Vigrass wins the 2013 Ladies world singles, shown here with fiancé Rob Fahey.

Camden Riviere and Tim Chisholm win against Rob Fahey and Steve Virgona in the 2011 French Open doubles.

PETWORTH HOUSE

There have been as many as six Tennis courts at Petworth, the earliest dating from 1588. This record of more than 400 years as a site for Tennis is only exceeded at the royal palaces of Hampton Court and Falkland. Little is known about the first two courts. Records show that the third was built in the 'Cichen Yarde', and it was probably thatched. The dimensions of this court, as noted in *The Percies of Petworth 1574–1632*, are difficult to reconcile. The main wall was said to be 94ft long, the gallery wall 97ft, and the penthouse 101ft. A prominent contribution to Tennis history was provided by the owner of Petworth at that time, the ninth Earl of Northumberland, who in 1615 had drawn up a map giving the names and locations of fourteen courts in London showing the dimensions of each court, so that when he built his own court at Petworth it would compare well with others that existed.

This court was demolished in 1695 and a new court was built in 1700 by the then current owner, the sixth Duke of Somerset, who also rebuilt much of Petworth House. This court also occasionally served as the local courthouse. In 1797, it was torn down and moved stone by stone to a new position.

In the early part of the nineteenth century, there were several keen players in the town, led by the rector of Petworth, the Reverend Thomas Sockett. He recorded watching a match in London featuring the renowned Frenchman Barcellon. In 1822, the court was used as a dining room during the holding of a ball at the house, a function it was to fill again in 2010.

The current court was built in the mid-1870s. It was one of a number of such country house courts built at that time and it was very well rated by top players of the day, being faster than Lord Wimborne's Canford court and slower than Mr Garland's court at Moreton Morrell. In the early part of the twentieth century, the Petworth court suffered much from damp and condensation, which proved difficult to cure, a variety of solutions being proposed. The third Lord Leconfield was very keen on Tennis and enthusiastically welcomed users of his court, amongst whom were the Duke of Richmond and Gordon, who had his own court at Goodwood, and Mr J.F. Marshall, whose court was at Seacourt. Lord Leconfield also staged a number of top-class exhibition matches, featuring amongst others George Covey, who beat Peter Latham in 1910, and 'Punch' Fairs, who beat Edward Johnson in 1911.

During the First World War, the court was used to billet soldiers from the Rifle Brigade and the King's Royal Rifle Corps. From 1920 to 1928, Lord Leconfield continued to promote and host an annual exhibition match between top professionals.

Little is known about Tennis at Petworth after then, though the appointment of Frank Latham in 1938 suggests that there was still some interest. From 1941 to 1960, however, it is certain that no Tennis was played on the Petworth court.

The foundation of the club in 1960 was celebrated with a cocktail party on the court attended by over 100 people, whose signatures record their presence in the club album. An exhibition match was played featuring professionals David Cull (Lord's), Henry Johns (Queen's) and amateurs Lord Aberdare and Jimmy Whatman. Amongst those present were prominent Tennis players Dugald MacPherson, Edgar Baerlein, Max Heilbut and Frank Latham. A rump of players from the smaller court at Balcombe (The Penthouse Club) decamped to Petworth when the Balcombe court was closed, hence the derivation of Petworth's very popular Penthouse Cup.

Over the following years, many improvements were made to the court, including restoration of the dedans area, repainting of the floor (at least twice), and a complete rewiring of the entire building, with a new lighting system undertaken by the National Trust (the club's landlord) in 2012.

Petworth has been blessed with the services and enthusiasm of a number of leading professionals since the start of the twentieth century. The first recorded of these is Arthur 'Tennis' Smith, who was in post from 1902 to 1914. After training under Jimmie Fennell at Lord's, Smith featured in a number of high-profile challenge matches against Punch Fairs and Charles Williams, who went to the Chicago Racquet Club on the *Titanic*, and survived. Next came Harry Lambert;

Chris Bray and Alan Chalmers.

the Lambert family boasted ten professionals over many years. Harry became Petworth professional in 1918 and for the next few years the court was reasonably well used. Harry moved to Lord's in late 1927 and as far as can be told, there was no professional in post until Frank Latham, son of world champion Peter Latham, was appointed in 1938, so it looks as though the court was mostly unused between 1928 and 1938. Latham was also a product of Lord's and then went to the Paris court for a spell. As with Smith before him, his tenure as Petworth professional was terminated by the onset of a world war. Lord Leconfield served as President of the Tennis & Rackets Association from 1937 to 1949. Frank attended the reopening of the court in 1960, where he occasionally marked matches; he died in 1964.

Charles Osborne, latterly professional at Prince's Club in Brighton, also assisted the club in the 1960s by marking matches. In 1971, when George Cooke retired from Manchester, he moved to Petworth and offered his teaching services, but stayed firmly in the gallery or took a static position on the court. He died in 1978. In the 1980s, the membership of the club was fairly static and the court was not heavily used. Seacourt's Peter Dawes helped by making balls and marking matches, but there was no resident professional until Gerald Parsons moved from the Queen's Club and acted as part-time temporary replacement for a year. Seacourt's Rob Moyle took over in 1985 for three years.

A landmark year arrived in 1988 with the appointment of Chris Bray as full-time professional. Trained at Cambridge by Brian Church and at Seacourt by Peter Dawes, Chris rapidly established himself both as a dedicated coach and competition player. He set and maintained the highest standards of technique and etiquette amongst the members. Under Johnny Coote's chairmanship, the membership at Petworth increased quite rapidly and court usage moved commensurately. In the 1990s and the 2000s, Chris was active in international competition. His large range of top tournament wins includes being variously Open singles champion in Australia, France, the USA and Great Britain. He also accumulated fourteen Open doubles titles across the world. In the season 1997/1998, Chris won eight out of the top ten singles Tennis events, beating world champion Rob Fahey in three of them. Chris was officially world ranked No. 2 from 1996 to 2003. During this period, he took part in eliminator challenges for the world championship. In 2002, he played home and away against Mike Gooding from Burroughs, winning both ties but eventually losing in the last eliminator to Tim Chisholm (New York Racquet & Tennis Club). In February 2004, he again played home and away against Mike Gooding, winning both ties, but once again Chris lost both ties to Tim Chisholm, who was eventually defeated by Rob Fahey.

Chris left Petworth in 2005 to take a position in industry and his place was taken by Nick Wood, the professional at Holyport, to where he had moved after working as assistant professional at the Royal Tennis Court. In 2008, Nick was invited to return to the Royal Tennis Court as head professional. Chris Bray accepted the invitation to return to Petworth as head professional, where he remains today.

Under Chris's guidance, and ably assisted by senior professional Tom Durack and assistant professional Josh Dodgson, the club at Petworth made many advances, prominent amongst which is a thriving junior section. Boys and girls from four local preparatory schools regularly attend coaching sessions and several have joined the club along with their parents. Charlie Braham has already won the national Under-18 championship. In addition to his duties at Petworth, Chris – supported by Tom – has also been overseeing the development of the club at Holyport; since May 2011, they have divided their time between the two cubs. At the end of 2012, Josh Dodgson took up a new position at Tuxedo and was replaced by James Law. Then, from May 2014, with Holyport's future secured, Chris and Tom decided to devote their time wholly to Petworth and James Law moved to Hatfield.

PETWORTH HOUSE

The Founder Members taken at the Golden Jubilee Lunch in April 2010 (left to right) *John Miller, Simon Rees, David Godfray (Chairman), Tim Dawson, Cedric Gunnery, Paul Vine, Lady Egremont, Lord Egremont (President), John Page, Nick Dawson, Paul Danby, Chris Bray (Head Professional).*

The Petworth Board of Directors. Standing (left to right) *Chris Bray, Harvey Rawlings, Charles Fuente, Nigel Draffan.* Seated (left to right) *Carole Muir, Philip Robinson (Chairman), Robert Dolman (Vice-Chairman), Lucy Hutchinson (Membership Secretary), Julian Wilkinson (Treasurer), Carolyn Armstrong-Smith (Fixtures Secretary).*

In 2008 Petworth won the Field Trophy for the second consecutive year. The team comprised (left to right) Mark Drysdale, Charles Fuente, Will Bristowe, Harvey Rawlings, Andrew Page, Adam Dolman and Alastair MacKeown.

In 2009 Petworth staged an exhibition match in aid of SPARKS featuring Rob Fahey, organised by Gordon Woodman together with Oliver Harris and Stewart Newton. (left to right) Oliver Harris, Tom Durack (marker), Rob Fahey, Gordon Woodman, Stewart Newton.

The 6th Annual match between Petworth and the Old Carthusians to celebrate Bob Arrowsmith, the great Carthusian master and racquet sports enthusiast. (left to right) Josh Dodgson (marker), Mike Steward, Oliver Harris, Gordon Woodman, Robert Dolman, David Godfray, Robert Muir and David Fortune.

April 2010 saw the fiftieth anniversary of the re-establishment of Tennis on the Petworth court, and so a series of Golden Jubilee functions was planned for the summer. The highlight of these was a lunch held on the court and attended by 130 specially invited guests, including guests of honour Lord and Lady Egremont. As with the reopening in 1960, a signature book was provided, together with a comprehensive photo album, and these remain within the club archives. The main speaker was Andrew Page (HM Ambassador to Slovenia); other speakers were David Godfray, Lord Egremont, Tim Dawson and Chris Bray. In June the club held a summer reception attended by 120 members and, in September, an international field of club players took part in an Invitation doubles tournament. A golfing foursomes was hosted by David Godfray, and the festivities were concluded with a reception and dinner.

Tennis is played at Petworth by courtesy of the National Trust and of Lord Egremont. The club is controlled by a Board of Directors including a nominee from the National Trust and Lord Egremont, who is also the club's president. Several members who have given distinguished service to the club have been appointed as vice presidents. Since its formation in 1960, the club has had six chairmen. Andy Dawson was the prime mover in the formation of the club in 1960 and from 1962 he was the first chairman. He was succeeded in 1974 by Eddie Harrison, then came Captain Johnny Coote from 1987 to 1993, followed by Jack Phelps to 1994. David Godfray then took over and served with distinction until 2010 when Philip Robinson took up the reins of power.

Tennis thrives at Petworth, with more than 400 members and where court usage often reaches 95 per cent; the club is justifiably proud of its achievements and its international reputation as a club which warmly welcomes visitors.

THE RACQUET CLUB OF PHILADELPHIA

The Racquet Club of Philadelphia is considered the birthplace of US winter racquet sports. Squash came to the US in 1884 when St Paul's School, a boarding school in New Hampshire, put up four open-air squash courts, but the game took hold only because of the RCOP. In December 1900 the club, then on Walnut Street, erected the first squash court in the country besides St Paul's. It held tournaments, built three more courts, persuaded other clubs in Philadelphia to build courts, and in 1903 launched the Philadelphia Squash League, the world's oldest, continuously run inter-club league, still going strong today. A year later, the club hosted a meeting in which US Squash, the national governing body, was created. In 1907, the club invented the game of squash doubles when it built the world's first court at its present clubhouse on South Sixteenth Street. Today RCOP is still a leader in that vibrant sport, annually hosting a pro tournament (The Tompkins) and the national intercollegiate championships, and fielding winning teams in the Philadelphia district doubles league.

The present clubhouse was built in 1907.

The Tennis court is located on the fourth floor.

Rackets has always been a core sport at RCOP. The club put in two Rackets courts on Walnut Street in 1890; nine years later it inaugurated the US Amateur doubles championship. In 1907, when the club moved around the corner to its present location, it again put in two Rackets courts side by side (the eastern court was eventually converted into squash singles and then a squash doubles court, but its original door remains). Rackets was popular, especially after January 1900 when Peter Latham, the world champion, came for a doubles exhibition. In 1907 Jock Soutar arrived as the Rackets pro; Soutar was the world champion from 1913 to 1929. Since the 1980s the Jock Soutar Rackets tournaments, held each November at the RCOP, are a highlight of the winter Rackets schedule.

Some of the top US amateurs over the nearly century and a quarter of play have been at RCOP: Hugh and Edgar Scott (the former won the national Amateur doubles six times, the latter was known for his volley dropshot and underhand twist serve); George Brooke, a famous American football player and coach (he led Penn to two national titles), won the national Amateur singles and doubles. Joseph Wear who won the national Amateur doubles three times. The Pearson clan, Stan Sr, Stan Jr and Babe, all won national titles in Rackets and the first two also did so in squash.

Tennis, arriving with the new clubhouse in 1907, eventually became perhaps the dominant sport on the fourth floor. Fred Tompkins, of the famous English Tennis family, was hired in 1904 and played an instrumental role in creating and developing Tennis in Philadelphia. He launched the national Amateur doubles in 1909, hosted the 1914 world championship, mentored Jay Gould and welcomed Pierre Etchebaster for his first match on American soil, an eliminator against Jock Soutar.

Jimmy Dunn was the colossus of mid-century Philadelphia. A red-headed Irish-American from the East Falls neighbourhood of Philadelphia, Dunn came to the club as a young apprentice under Fred Tompkins in 1928. Tompkins retired in 1936 and his successor Jock Soutar stepped down in 1949, giving Dunn the

spot. He didn't relinquish it until 1985. Dunn was an irascible, feisty pro, tough on his assistants and his members (often a member's racquet would get oddly warped if he bought it at another pro shop), but beloved for his aphorisms, his stories and his ability to teach the games. More than thirty-five young men from East Falls apprenticed under Dunn. Four today still manage Tennis courts in America: Tommy Greevy at Tuxedo, Jimmy Burke in Boston, John Cashman in Chicago and Rob Whitehouse in Philadelphia. A fifth, Ed Noll, the head RCOP pro after Dunn, was the general manager at the club from 1998 to 2013. Ed's son Mike also became a professional for twelve years, both in Philadelphia and New York. Two others, Gabe Kinzler and Barney Tanfield, are the sons of RCOP members who have gone on to become professionals after training under Whitehouse.

Left: John Lumley, son of Penny and Colin, is assistant professional to Rob Whitehouse.

Below: In 2005 the club hosted the fiftieth anniversary golden jubilee of the founding of the USCTA.

Dunn taught Tennis to three generations of nationally renowned players, including the Van Alen clan (Sammy was the founder and first president of the USCTA), the Vogts (Peter is the present chairman of the Tennis Committee), the Bells, the Howes, the Clothiers and Bill Lingelbach. The club has won the Whitney Cup more than any other club, signifying its pre-eminence as a Tennis power. Dunn also founded the US Parent Child championship, in 1976, which has been won by Philadelphia families almost 90 per cent of the time.

Since Dunn's retirement, the game has experienced new growth. The club, under Andy Kinzler, launched the national Junior championships in 1992 and hosted it for the tournaments' first dozen years. In 2005 the club also hosted the fiftieth anniversary golden jubilee of the founding of the USCTA. A raft of new players has come to the fore, including Jon Crowell, who is presently the club champion in both Rackets and Tennis and chairman of the Rackets Committee.

Each year there are two big athletic weekends at the RCOP: the autumn Jimmy Dunn and Jock Soutar tournament (Tennis, squash and Rackets) and the spring Irish Invitational and Lord Percival Cup (squash and inter-club team Tennis). The club provides leadership in the USCTA and NARA, hosts many national championships, inter-club matches and international events and tours with aplomb, directs the Tennis at Lakewood and has an almost-full booking sheet each day.

Painting by Peter van Dyck in the Reading Room.

PRESTED HALL

Dreams do sometimes come true. Here, in rural Essex, the drive and passion of one man brought to life a dream that would not be out of place in a collection of fairy stories. In Feering, on a site previously earmarked for a golf course, an hour by train from the City of London, Mike Carter created the only pair of Tennis courts to be built in the northern hemisphere in the twentieth century, and the only privately funded courts in Britain since 1905.

Mike Carter had his first taste of Tennis as a Cambridge undergraduate in the 1960s. He was immediately addicted and determined to build a new court that would be accessible to a new generation of players, and one that would break the somewhat elitist image to which the scarcity of courts had inevitably led the game.

Frustrated by planning authorities when he tried to build a court near his home at Ipswich, Mike found Prested Hall, a sixteenth-century mansion halfway between Chelmsford and Colchester and close to the main A12 road. He converted the house to a hotel with eleven en-suite bedrooms and planning permission for a further forty, but was turned down for a National Lottery grant for the Tennis courts – the Sports Council felt that the game had recently had its fair share of funding, with the successful applications for a new court at Bristol and the restoration of an old one at Bridport.

In April 1998, the foundations were laid with Mike Carter as foreman of works, chief labourer and machine driver. By December, the first court was pretty much ready, and by the end of the year the former assistant professional at Melbourne, Adam Mickelburough, flew into Heathrow with his family, ready to coach new members. The second court (now the No. 1 court), with a glass grille wall, was finished in June 1999 and Prested was officially opened over the weekend of 26–27 June.

A clutch of champions from the Tennis and Rackets world were among those in attendance – Andrew Myrtle and Charles Swallow from the Tennis & Rackets Association, Howard Angus, Chris and Lesley Ronaldson, Penny Lumley, Sue Haswell and Ralph Howe. A Ton-up doubles tournament (won by Mike Carter and Chris Ronaldson) ran alongside handicap events.

As well as a large and comfortable clubroom, spacious changing rooms and the hotel facility alongside, Prested has some most unusual features – a large viewing area behind the glass grille wall, and no chase lines on the floor of the courts. These are replaced by half-yard stripes of alternating colours, so that most calls are 'worse than' something (if blue), or 'better than' something (if green). Only occasionally do exact yard or half-yard chases occur.

A high-tech gymnasium was opened in April 2000 and three new floodlit Astro lawn tennis courts in October 2000. A health and beauty treatment centre in November 2000, followed later by a 25-metre indoor swimming pool, completed the club's impressive leisure facilities.

By the end of only its second season, the club had over 100 members, mostly local and active, and many of whom had never played Tennis before. In 2001 the club sadly said goodbye to Adam Mickelburough as club professional on his return to Australia. He was succeeded in 2002 by Ivan Ronaldson, supplemented by Ricardo Smith the following year as assistant professional. After three years and taking the club to new heights, Ivan left for Washington in 2005 but, fortunately, was replaced by Matthew Ronaldson as senior professional. In 2007 Matthew moved on to Paris and Ricardo was promoted to senior professional. After a stint of over ten years, Ricardo left for Newport in January 2014 and was succeeded by Claire Vigrass for a few months. During his time at Prested, Ricardo moved up the world rankings and with partner Bryn Sayers was runner-up in the world championship doubles in 2009.

In 2004, Prested was proud to host the European singles for the first time, with Rob Fahey defeating Chris Bray to win the title.

The year 2009 heralded the tenth anniversary of the founding of the club, over the May Bank Holiday weekend. Anniversary celebrations included a champagne reception and dinner, an exhibition match between the top four professional players, a Pro-Am handicap doubles and an Amateur doubles.

In 2012 Prested was honoured to host the first leg of the world championship eliminator and witnessed an extraordinary match between Ben Matthews and Bryn

Prested has some most unusual features – a large viewing area behind the glass grille wall, and no chase lines on the floor of the courts. These are replaced by half-yard stripes of alternating colours, so that most calls are 'worse than something' (if blue), or 'better than something' (if green).

Sayers. Ben won the first leg but was defeated by Bryn in the final leg at Queen's.

Mention must also be made of the extraordinary achievements of club members Claire Vigrass and her sister Sarah. In 2002, Claire won the Girls U12 tournament at Queen's, a sure sign of great things to come. Two years later she repeated the feat in the U14. In 2008 she became the youngest ever winner of the US Ladies' Open at Aiken. By 2010 she had become the dominant force in the ladies' game and had taken it to a new level. In 2011 she became the youngest ever ladies' world champion at the age of nineteen, winning the singles and also the doubles with Sarah, who was singles runner-up. Claire has been the Ladies' British Open singles champion since 2010 (Sarah was runner-up in 2013 and 2014) and doubles champion with Sarah since 2012. Claire's best handicap to date is an amazing 4 and she has the ability and determination to improve on that.

THE QUEEN'S CLUB

London's heart of Rackets and Tennis for more than a century, the Queen's Club (known universally as Queen's) was founded in 1886 under the patronage of Queen Victoria, built on market garden land in West Kensington and opened in 1887. The amateur championships of both games were created there, and since 1888 nearly all the major national Rackets championships (including those of the Public Schools, from which most of Britain's great players have risen) have been played at Queen's.

In Victorian times there was a vast choice of sports for members. There were Eton fives courts, a running track, and pitches on which cricket, rugby, soccer, hockey and lacrosse were played. Croquet and billiards were available, of course, as well as lawn tennis, roller skating and (briefly) ice skating; and for a while, with difficulty, even golf.

Two squash courts were added in 1904, two more in 1924, and in 1926 one of the original two Rackets courts was converted into two more squash courts.

Among the great professionals who have served Queen's are several world champions: Charles Saunders (Tennis) and Charles Williams (Rackets), and three men who won the world titles of both, the phenomenal Peter Latham, Jim Dear and Howard Angus.

Norwood Cripps, an outstanding Tennis player, served as senior professional from 1962 until he went to Eton in 1979. He was succeeded by David Johnson. Among David's talented assistants were Neil Smith (who left in 1990 and later became world Rackets champion), Peter Brake and Andrew Lyons.

Between 1980 and 2000, a major development and building programme was carried out. This included the restoration of the second Rackets court to its proper purpose (since named the Bridgeman Court), the refurbishment of both Tennis courts and the dedans areas, the creation of a Tennis and Rackets museum and the rebuilding of the Rackets gallery, damaged by fire in 1979. Funding for all this work (more than £300,000) was raised by the Tennis & Rackets Association under the dynamic leadership of the then chairman, David Norman.

In the club's centenary year of 1986, in 2000 as part of the millennium celebrations, and again in 2012 to coincide with the London Olympics, Queen's hosted a quintathlon in which many North American players took part. The first one – the first ever held in this country – was organised by Garth Milne, the second by John Prenn and the third by Mark Agate, who has done so much to invigorate and spread interest in Rackets over the past decade. All three comprised a demanding schedule of social activities as well as competition in Rackets, Tennis, lawn tennis, squash and golf, and were memorably successful. The latest one attracted seventy-six participants, of whom half came from Australia, Canada and the United States.

The new millennium ushered in a period of considerable change at the club. In 1999, the chairman of the Board of Directors, Geoff Brown, who had held the post for nineteen years, was succeeded by Stuart Smith, who was to play a crucial role regarding the future of the club – these were LTA appointments as, since 1953, the LTA had owned Queen's. The first intimation that change was in the air came when, in the same year, the LTA announced that they were seeking an alternative site for a purpose-built national training centre and administrative headquarters. Both of these had been located at Queen's.

At the club AGM in 2001, the LTA announced that they intended to sell the club on the open market. However, due to the prolonged negotiations with the Bank of England, the owners of the preferred site in Roehampton, this did not take place until 2005. It was then officially announced that the club was for sale on a 120-year lease and called for bids.

It was at this stage that the LTA was reminded by David Norman of a facility agreement that he had negotiated with them in 1987, when he was chairman of the T&RA, whereby the members of the Queen's Club would be provided with a minimum of two Rackets courts and two Real Tennis courts for their use for a period of fifty years from that date. The LTA agreed to include this in their sales data.

The members gave overwhelming support to the club chairman, Alexander Anton, to submit a bid on their behalf. This amounted to £45 million and, despite the fact that this was below that of other bidders, one of which was rumoured to have offered in excess of £50 million, the LTA accepted the club's bid.

In the meantime, there was an increasing view among the members that the LTA had no right to offer the club on the open market, maintaining that they had bought it in 1953 in trust for the members.

The lack of clear documentation led to both parties agreeing to approach the High Court for a judgement on the legal position. Subsequently, the scope of the litigation was extended to cover the transfer to the LTA in 2004–05 of the right to hold the men's lawn tennis championships and a claim by former shareholders of Queen's Club Ltd.

In a situation of some drama, when the case came up for hearing in December 2006, the two parties were still in negotiations. The judge agreed to a limited postponement, during which a settlement was agreed and then approved by the court. The LTA offered to reduce the price to £35 million. A further £4 million of cash was to be made available to the club, provided that it was spent over the next three years for the benefit of the sports, playing and other facilities available at the club – this was subsequently to benefit the Rackets and Real Tennis facilities.

The LTA were by now in the process of moving to Roehampton and placed a five-month deadline for completion – May 2007.

Alexander Anton embarked upon a demanding timetable, inviting members to subscribe for one redeemable share in a new company, Queen's Club Holdings Ltd, at £8,000 each. Over 70 per cent of the membership subscribed.

On 22 May 2007, for the first time in its history, the club was owned by a majority of the playing members. Trustees were appointed, as was a Board of Directors, under the chairmanship of Lord Marshall of Knightsbridge. Within a year, the Board was wholly elected by the members by postal vote.

In all the changes, the system of committees – particularly in relation to the sports – was retained, and the loyalty, both of the members and the staff, ensured that the club's normal activities continued before and during the transition.

Now, the new-found enthusiasm and availability

Both of the Real Tennis courts were refurbished – with new roofs and improved lighting – very soon after the Members acquired the club in 2007.

of finance very soon allowed both of the Real Tennis courts to be refurbished – with new roofs and improved lighting. The viewing capacity of the Upper Gallery of the East Court was doubled, whilst the professionals' room was also expanded.

In the Rackets court area, the viewing gallery of both courts was massively upgraded in 2012. The brainchild of Sir Mervyn Dunnington-Jefferson more than a decade earlier, the galleries have greatly improved sight-lines and access as well as the potential for increased numbers of spectators for major matches. The courts themselves were also fitted with new lighting, and the walls continue to be looked after by Alan Neal, despite having retired as maintenance manager. This project also included the creation of a very pleasing terrace room behind the galleries, as well as a room linking the Rackets area to the clubhouse, both giving the opportunity to display a growing collection of artefacts nearly all relating to Rackets.

Interest in Rackets and Real Tennis memorabilia has increased steadily in recent years, to the extent that a dedicated exhibition was held at the club in 2004. The extensive range of paintings, prints, racquets, balls and ephemera were mostly loaned by private collectors and created considerable interest. The display of virtually all the trophies, competed for annually in both the sports was very eye-catching. The museum, behind the dedans of the west Real Tennis court, now includes a bookcase, primarily to build on E.B. Noel's collection of Real Tennis and Rackets books. It was only recently that David Best, while researching for his book, *The Official Story of the Tennis and Rackets Association*, published in 2008, established beyond doubt that the books had been bequeathed by his widow to the T&RA and that they should be kept at Queen's so long as the major Rackets and Real Tennis continued to be played there.

One effect of the renovation works was the relocation of some of the Rackets competitions to other courts during the 2011–12 season. The British Amateur singles was played at Manchester and the doubles at Marlborough, whilst the British Open went to Eton,

In 2013 Bryn Sayers and Tim Chisholm wrested victory in the British Open doubles from Rob Fahey and Steve Virgona, who had won it in the three previous years. Seen here with Robin Geffen, CEO of sponsor Neptune Investment Management.

as did the early rounds of the Public Schools singles events.

With all the works completed, the club can look forward to enjoying the facilities with great confidence. Its obligations, on both national and international levels, require the club to play host to an extraordinary number of regular tournaments. For Real Tennis, this includes the British Open singles and doubles and the Amateur singles and doubles. In 2012 Queen's hosted the world championship, which saw Rob Fahey successfully defend his title for the tenth time. Among the most recent highlights was club professional Bryn Sayers breaking Fahey's run of nine consecutive British Open championships in 2012. In the following year, Sayers again defeated Fahey, but this time in the semi-finals where he staged a Houdini-like recovery from two sets and 5–0 down in the third set, saving a handful of match points in the process. However, Steve Virgona was too great a challenge for him in the final.

For Rackets, the events played at the club include the world championships singles and doubles, the British Open singles and doubles and the Amateur singles and doubles. James Male retired in 2003 whilst still the holder of the world singles title, since when the title has been held by Harry Foster, followed by Jamie Stout, who is the current holder. The most recent highlight was Will Hopton clawing his way back from virtual defeat at 3 games down and defeating Alex Titchener-Barrett in the 2014 British Open.

Lead sponsorship has been generously provided in the past by Lacoste under John Prenn for Rackets and British Land under Sir John Ritblat for Real Tennis. In 2008 Neptune Investment Management (under the leadership of Robin Geffen, a club member) became lead sponsor for Real Tennis and, in 2010, for Rackets as well.

At club level, yet more events and competitions have been devised for members at all levels of ability, thanks to the now well-established handicap systems for both games.

All these events – in Real Tennis alone there are over fifty tournaments and matches annually – together with the ongoing requirements of the club members, place a huge demand on the club professionals and here, too, there have been many changes in the team over the past decade. In 2002, the well-established team of David Johnson, Peter Brake and Andrew Lyons was ended when Peter, who had been a talented and popular head Rackets professional since 1989, moved to Eton to run the Rackets there. In his place the club was very fortunate to employ Howard Angus, former

In 2013 Steve Virgona gained his first-ever British Open victory.

world champion of both Rackets and Real Tennis, whose experience and knowledge of all the different aspects of the game have been invaluable.

And then, in 2011, after thirty-two years of outstanding service, David Johnson hung up his racquet. He was a top-ranked Real Tennis player who reached No. 4 in the world and played the game with grace and style. Unfailingly courteous, he became a master of the 'client game', leaving his pupils that much more knowledgeable and that much better and happier.

A new team has taken over. Andrew Lyons, already with twelve years' service at the club, has taken over as head Real Tennis professional and Rackets manager. Bryn Sayers arrived at the club in 2010, having worked at Seacourt, Newport Rhode Island and The Oratory. Now the senior Real Tennis professional, he is ranked No. 4 in the world. In 2010, he reached the finals in the US Open singles and in 2012 the final eliminator for the world championships. Also in 2012 he won the US Open and defeated Rob Fahey to become British Open singles champion.

Ben Snell has taken over from Howard Angus, who retired in July 2012 having been a professional for more than ten years. Howard's contribution to Real Tennis and Rackets is legendary. He was a brilliant match-player, utterly overwhelming to his opponents, who came up against not only a wonderfully gifted left-hander with the finest serve, but also a winning temperament and exceptional fitness. He has devoted his life to both games, not just as a champion and a professional but also in improving the quality of the courts, racquets and balls and earning himself an MBE for services to Tennis. He continues to be the finest ambassador for both our games. Ben is an Old Cheltonian, who attended the University of Gloucestershire, where he gained a Sports Degree. A two-year stint at Rugby School teaching PE was followed by one year where he trained as a Rackets professional under Peter Brake. In 2013 he and Nick James won the British Open Rackets doubles championship. The team of professionals is completed by Andrew Fowler, who arrived in 2012.

Change amongst the staff was not confined there. In 2003, Jonathan Edwardes left after twenty-three years as club secretary. The current incumbent as chief executive is Major General Andrew Stewart, who was an accomplished cricketer and hockey player, representing the Combined Services in both sports. In 2008, he joined a club that went through a transition from single institutional ownership to having some 2,800 shareholders, 4,000 members and a new Board.

Any overview of the club should make mention of lawn tennis and squash, both of which have the same mix of international, national and members' activity. The opportunity for members to watch the four sports at the highest level at their club must be unique.

The club has much to celebrate. And so they did! On 8 July 2011, 750 members and their guests attended the club's 125th Anniversary Ball and celebrated in style. Four indoor courts were transformed into a brilliant venue for dinner, dancing and entertainment. To quote the then chairman of the Board of Directors, David Norman, who himself has done so much for Rackets and Real Tennis at Queen's: 'No Rackets sports club in the world has a history of such astonishing diversity, facilities, world champions, sporting achievements, opportunities and associated pleasures generated over the past 125 years, as our Queen's Club.'

The current team of professionals (left to right) *Ben Snell, Andrew Lyons, Bryn Sayers, Andrew Fowler.*

RADLEY COLLEGE

Real Tennis

Real Tennis began in the 1970s at Radley, when professional David Goldsmith would take boys to play at Oxford every week. Interest in tennis increased in 1978 when Mick Dean, an ex-Oxford professional and winner of the British Open and Amateur doubles titles, was recruited to teach geography and run Rackets at the school. Occasional matches started in 1979 with, arguably, the first ever inter-school fixture against Canford. This match coincided with the arrival of James Male and Julian Snow, both of whom won the Foster Cup for Rackets, and together the Public Schools doubles title. At Tennis, both went on to win the British Open and Amateur singles and doubles and earned challenges for the world Tennis title; Julian narrowly fell 4–7 to Rob Fahey in 1998, but won the world doubles with Tim Chisholm in 2001.

In 1987 Snow beat Howard Angus in the Amateur singles final. He won that title for an astonishing eighteen out of the next nineteen years, losing only in 1990 when Male beat him in the final. In 1996 and 1997, he won the US Open singles and doubles (with Male in 1997) and in 1998 the British Open.

Other notable Radleian Tennis players include Mark Drysdale, the 2012 world Over-50s singles finalist, Luke Danby, the 2006 Amateur doubles champion, Edmund Popplewell, the first ever national Under-18 champion in 1982, James McEwen, the Under-18 finalist in 2002, and Ben Boddington, Under-18 doubles winner in 2012. Many Oxbridge Blues, such as Jonathan Jee, Richard Taylor, Thane Warburg, Patrick Woods-Ballard, Henry Birts, Ben Dean, Tom Dance, Jamie Stallibrass and Alistair Mitchell-Innes also got their start at Radley.

Matches were, and still are, played against Magdalen College School, Stowe, Hampton, Haileybury and Oxford University (their best team famously beaten by Male and Snow in 1981). Radley dominated the Old Boys' (Henry Leaf) Cup from 1985 to 1994, with Male, Snow, Drysdale and Warburg winning the title nine times.

When The Oratory opened in 1990, more school matches became possible, and an embryonic National Schools doubles competition started, initially with The Oratory, Canford and Radley, but occasionally also including, Eton, Rugby, Kingston and Warwick. Clifton followed in 1997 with the new Bristol and Bath court. Initially played on handicap, this grew more competitive until played level in 1998, with Radley winning the title for the first time in 2000.

As fixtures increased, with moral support from Wardens (Headmasters) Dennis Silk (up to 1991), Richard Morgan (1991–2000) and Angus McPhail (2000–), all good players themselves, Mick Dean's campaign for a Radley court began to gain momentum. The support of College Governors Ian Balding, Christopher Clarke and Richard Morris-Adams also furthered the cause and, together, Balding and Dean became the fund-raising team for the Radley court.

Adrian Snow, the ex-headmaster of The Oratory and the overseer of the building of The Oratory court, provided invaluable advice to Bursar Richard Beauchamp and confirmed the benefit of an outside club to the college. When the college council finally gave permission for fundraising to start, it was Beauchamp, though not a player, who adopted the plan with great enthusiasm. By the end of 2006, the capital cost had been raised with donations and loans from the T&RA, RTC, MCC and Oxford, as well as with financial contributions from an eclectic assortment of Old Radleians, parents and Tennis players in general, many with no particular Radley connection.

Influential Old Radleians Michael Wigley and Mark Rushton were especially important in the final decision in late 2006 to commence building in October 2007. The builders were Beards of Oxford and Swindon, run by Real Tennis enthusiast Mark Beard.

In retrospect, the timing was very happy as, within a year, the credit crunch had struck, but as the promised funds had already been delivered, the project was safe and the building of the court imminent.

Although the first ball was struck on 10 June 2008, the court was officially opened in October 2008 by Prince Edward and celebrated with an exhibition between world champion, Rob Fahey, and Camden Riviere, as

The first ball was struck on 10 June 2008 (left to right) Mick Dean, Richard Beauchamp, Ian Balding, Chris Ronaldson.

The official opening in October 2008 was celebrated with an exhibition between Rob Fahey and Camden Riviere, as well as a doubles match with James Male and Spike Willcocks. Soon afterwards, Rob Fahey (so impressed had he been with Male) chose James as partner in the British Open and won.

A recent school team pictured with Chris Ronaldson and Mick Dean.

well as a doubles match with James Male and Spike Willcocks. Soon afterwards, Rob Fahey (so impressed had he been with Male) chose James when his British Open partner withdrew, and they won the title.

The new court has aquamarine walls, giving the court a uniquely modern feel. The floor has inlaid lines with a colour contrast behind the stroke line. The lighting, important for an enclosed court, is superb, while an upper viewing gallery provides more space for spectators and other club functions.

Chris Ronaldson, world champion 1981–87 and doyen of Tennis club developers (having masterminded the resurgence of clubs in Oxford, Melbourne, Troon, Bordeaux and Hampton Court) became the first head professional, assisted by Paul Knox. In 2010, Paul was succeeded by John Lumley, who has an extraordinary Tennis pedigree: his father Colin reached the world top five, while his mother Penny had been ladies' world champion. John then left for Philadelphia in 2013 and was succeeded by Mark Eadle.

Play on the new court was greatly encouraged by Chris Ronaldson. Ronaldson's extraordinary work ethic has been fundamental in making the club amongst the busiest in the world, with often over 100 hours' play per week, a membership of about 150 and a full fixture list, captained by Paul Kettle.

The club has a strong fixture list and also hosts the British Open qualifiers, the Over-60s doubles, and the Dutch and Irish championships. One tradition now firmly established is the Boxing Day Hangover doubles, with different odd rules each year (e.g. playing alternate shots or serving from the hazard end).

Real Tennis is lucky to have the court and programme at Radley as it will continue to encourage and support Tennis players for generations to come.

Rackets

Rackets at Radley made little impression on the outside world until after the First World War, but in the past four decades the phenomenal achievements of two Old Radleians, James Male and Julian Snow, have more than made up for the school's rather slow start. Though there had been a court at Radley since 1885, it was 1922 before a pair reached the Public Schools final and 1930 before the prize was won.

A taste for the game was established when in 1855 the warden had wing-buttresses built onto the clock tower, forming four courts in which the game of bat-fives became popular. In 1864, an acrostic appeared in the school magazine, appealing for funds for a Rackets court:

R   *Radleians old to us be kind*
A   *And money for our racquets find,*
D   *Do all of you some gold disburse*
L   *Long hidden in your private purse.*
E   *Each one may well some trifle spare*
I   *In slight remembrance of the care*
A   *And pains, which you all met with here,*
N   *Nor think your money ill-bestowed*
S   *Since it's a debt you long have owed.*

Eventually sufficient money was raised (£964) for a court, and a pair entered the championship in 1887. Real progress was made when Bertram 'Brahms' Abraham, from Prince's Club, became the professional in 1911, devoting his services to Radleian Rackets until 1948. He drew his richest reward when P.I. Van der Gucht and W.H. Vestey beat the Eton pair 4–1 in the 1930 final – the only Radley success until Male and Snow won the championship without conceding a game in 1982.

Ronnie Lay had joined Abraham as his assistant in 1925, later marrying his daughter, and in 1948 he succeeded his father-in-law. Before retiring in 1971 he had coached two pairs to the Public Schools final – Dexter and Dipple in 1953 and Rogers and Osborne in 1966.

Mick Dean, who reached his peak as an outstanding Tennis player in the 1980s, joined the teaching staff in 1978 and took charge of Rackets until December 1998.

It was in Mick Dean's time that Male and Snow came to the fore. Male, the elder of the two, took the first glittering steps by winning the Public Schools Under-16 prize (the Incledon-Webber Cup) in 1979. In 1980 and 1981 he won the H.K. Foster Cup, losing only one game throughout the two years' matches; in 1982 he and Snow brought the Public Schools doubles trophy back to Radley (not one game lost), and at the end of that year Snow won the Foster Cup.

There was little doubt that the pair of them, individually or in harness, were going to make a tremendous impact wherever they used their talents. Male, the more forceful and relentlessly determined player, immediately stormed the Rackets world. He won the Swallow Cup (Under-24 singles) in 1984, 1985 and 1987 (he did not enter in 1986); he won the British Amateur singles in 1985, 1986, 1988, 1990, 1992 and then a colossal seven times consecutively between 1994 and 2000, against Willie Boone on all occasions except three. He won the British Open singles in 1987–89, 1991, 1996 all against Neil Smith, then again in 2000–01. Finally, in 1988, at the age of twenty-three, he beat Willie Boone for the world championship by 6 games to 1, the youngest player to do so since Peter Latham in 1887, and remained world champion till beaten by Harry Foster in 2005 (with the exception of 1999 when he had to forfeit against Neil Smith through injury).

It was not surprising that Snow, the young master of court craft, turned early to Tennis. From 1987 to 2005 he dominated the amateur Tennis scene.

Since January 1999, Mark Hubbard, winner of the Professional singles six years between 2002 and 2011 and the world championship doubles in 2007, has been the Rackets professional at Radley.

In the 1999–2000 season Fred Bellhouse made his mark by reaching the final of the U15 singles and then winning the U15 doubles with Charlie Monbiot. The following year Monbiot attained the final of the U16 singles and doubles, again with Bellhouse. Then in the 2001–02 season, Alex Hackett burst on the scene, winning the U15 singles against Joe Bone from Harrow and the doubles with James Jeans. In the following season Hackett and Jeans made the finals of the U16 doubles, but lost to Wellington. That year Hackett was also finalist in the U16 singles but lost to Joe Bone, who had become his main rival. These two again crossed swords in the final of the Foster Cup in the 2004–05 season with Bone taking the crown. In the 2011–12 season George Buckley and Rupert Boddington reached the final of the U16 doubles but were beaten by Harrow.

Under the guidance of Mark Hubbard, and with a substantial history, Rackets at Radley is sure to continue to flourish.

ROMSEY

Newest of Australia's four Tennis clubs, this innovative building in the State of Victoria was the dream of vigneron and architect Gordon Cope-Williams. Opened in 1999, it is very impressive, with a complete glass grille wall, and is built in the style of an aisled barn, which gives the court, its central feature, an air of lightness and space. The court is six feet longer than others and the tambour made of slightly twisted timber.

Surrounding the court, but under the same roof, are the subsidiary and fascinating features of the complex. To the north is the 'cellar door' wine sales, overlooking the vineyard (mostly Chardonnay and Pinot); and there is a lounge room from which spectators may look through the glass wall. Upstairs, there is more viewing to be had through the glass above the grille penthouse. To the south are the members' rooms, including bar, billiard room and mezzanine area with glass wall for viewing. To the east, behind the main wall, are the changing rooms, gymnasium and administration offices (with more viewing above). To the west are the banqueting hall, restaurant and kitchens. The main walls of the court are a light battleship grey, and in keeping with Australian tradition the grille has a caricature – not of a monk this time, but a somewhat provocative portrait of a fifteenth-century lady tennis player, Margot of Hainault.

Robert Bartlett was engaged as professional and, thanks to his easy manner and maturity, soon attracted 150 members. The inaugural Romsey Open was staged in 2000 and restricted to the world's top eight players. In the final, Robert Fahey won a high-class match with England's Chris Bray. To support the increasing membership at Romsey, the club took on an assistant professional, Jacob Potts, in late 2000. Due to various reasons, membership sadly started to decline in 2002, as a result of which there has been no pro there since that time. The court is still available for hire but play is infrequent.

Opened in 1999, the court has a complete glass grille wall, and is built in the style of an aisled barn. The tambour is made of slightly twisted timber.

RUGBY SCHOOL

Here is a Rackets record that will take some beating – Rugby produced three players who between them held the world championship for thirty-four out of forty-four years. Rugby's great men were David Milford (1937 to 1947, without a challenge); Geoffrey Atkins (1954 to 1972, unbeaten through five challenges); and Willie Surtees, who took the title in 1972, lost it to Howard Angus in 1973, won it back in 1975 and held it comfortably until John Prenn beat him in 1981. Surprisingly, of the three, only Surtees won the Foster Cup, though Milford was twice in pairs that won the Public Schools championship.

Rugby played in four of the first eleven championship finals, winning in 1870 despite the handicap of the school court (built in 1864) being considerably above standard size. A second court was added in 1883.

For more than 100 years there was a Gray in charge of Rackets at Rugby. Joseph Gray, who held the world championship for ten years, served from 1868 to 1894. He was succeeded by his son Harry (1894 to 1937), during whose time Rugby won the championship six times and played in eleven finals.

Among his pupils (who included Milford and Atkins) were the remarkable Simpson brothers. The older of them, C.F.B. Simpson, who was killed in the First World War, held the extraordinary record of playing first string for Rugby for five years (1907–11). He reached the Public Schools final in 1908 and won it in 1911 with W.H. Clarke. It was at Oxford that his brother J.C.F. (later Sir Cyril) hit the heights, winning the University singles three years running (1920–22) and the doubles twice. He went on to become Amateur singles champion (1926–28) and Open champion (1929–32), as well as six times Amateur doubles champion.

Harry Gray sent both his sons, Peter and Ronald, to Rugby. Peter was captain of Rackets in 1930 and Ronald in 1932–33, reaching the schools final with Raymond Lumb the first year and winning it with him the second. Lumb was joined by Peter Kershaw in 1934 and won again. Kershaw, a fine player at both games, was a member of the winning pair of Old Rugbeians in the Noel-Bruce Cup twelve times (three with Lumb, eight with Milford and once with Atkins), and was in the winning trio in the Henry Leaf Cup

Old Rugbeian Guy Devereux has won the US Open Rackets doubles four times.

– the Tennis competition for Old Boys – an amazing fourteen times.

Of all Rugbeians, Geoffrey Atkins took all-round ability to the greatest heights. As well as his run as world Rackets champion, Open champion and Amateur champion, Atkins was also Amateur Tennis champion in 1960, 1962 and 1963.

Harry Gray, who trained him at Rackets, first retired in 1937 and was succeeded by his son Peter; however, Harry returned in 1939 for seven years, covering the war period. Peter Gray saw seven pairs through to the Public Schools championship final, winning in 1938, 1939, 1952 and 1965 (with Willie Surtees as first string). Surtees also took the Foster Cup the following year, as had two earlier pupils of Peter Gray, J.M.G. Tildesley (1955) and J.L. Cuthbertson (1959). Gray's own son Nigel played for the school in 1962–63.

Philip Rosser has been the Rugby professional since 1982. During his tenure, Richard Montgomerie won the Foster Cup in 1988. Also, the school reached the Public Schools championship final for three consecutive years in the 1990s. Richard Carter played in all three with different partners, winning in 1994 with Charlie Robards and in 1995 with Robin Hicks. This last pair did not lose a game until meeting Eton in the final, whom they beat 4–2. Carter also won the Foster Cup twice and is still one of only five players to have won both the singles and doubles twice. The annual tournament at Queen's Club is still the highlight of the year for Rugby's Rackets players.

The school has annual Rackets and Tennis trips to Seacourt and Manchester and Tennis trips to Moreton Morrell. All these trips have encouraged boys to understand the idea of playing Rackets for fun as well as competitively. They have also helped to introduce the boys to Real Tennis, a game that many will now wish to continue with after they have left school.

The school has also been on three successful tours to North America. During the latest tour in 2013 it was marvellously entertained in Chicago, Philadelphia, New York and Tuxedo – the latter being courtesy of old Rugbeian Guy Devereux, who has won the US Open doubles four times. Recently a number of leavers have also gained from the experience of working for several months in North American clubs and have arrived back much stronger players.

The year 2014 marked the 150th anniversary of the building of the Old Court, and 2019 is the 150th anniversary of the first Rugby School entry into the Public Schools Rackets championship.

ST PAUL'S SCHOOL

St Paul's School, founded in 1509 by Dean Colet in the shadow of the medieval cathedral, moved to West Kensington in 1884, and from there in 1968 to a 42-acre riverside site in Barnes, where there are now 790 pupils in addition to 440 at the preparatory school, Colet Court. An anonymous benefactor marked the new millennium by providing funds for the building of a Rackets court and for the employment of a professional. Steve Tulley arrived from Montreal to launch the sport at the school, and St Paul's thus became the first school whose pupils are predominantly day boys to make Rackets available. The St Paul's court was based on the No. 1 court at the Queen's Club. The architects, Barnsley, Hewett and Mallinson, combined the elements of a traditionally constructed court from a hundred years ago with up-to-date technology. The court walls, for example, are one-and-a-half bricks thick with a soft mortar, but the internal finish is modern.

On 20 January 2001, the court was officially opened when the school hosted the second leg of the world singles Rackets championship. It took James Male just two games to regain his title from the defending champion Neil Smith. To the delight of over 70 spectators the two players agreed to play a further two games for a crate of champagne.

Instead of the 40mm thick traditional Bickley formula, a 20mm thick render was used. The exact composition of the original is lost and would not in any case have complied with current health and safety legislation. The render used was more environmentally friendly and can withstand great force.

The position of the court and the link to the sports hall and five galleries were designed to encourage interest in the game. At first-floor level is a stand for up to seventy spectators. At ground level, the door to the court is glass to aid teaching and allow a view into the court for the resident professional, whose room faces it. The building was positioned so that mature trees were retained. At low level, polished blocks were used, and at high level western red cedar boarding was chosen, as it blended with the landscaping and provided texture, colour variation over time and low maintenance cost.

On 20 January 2001, the court was officially opened, when the school hosted the second leg of the world singles Rackets championship. The very high quality of the court was immediately apparent. It took the match contender, James Male, just two games to regain his title from the defending champion Neil Smith, but the games were keenly fought and included many long rallies. To the delight of over seventy spectators, the two players agreed to play a further two games for a crate of champagne, which James Male also won.

Within the school, Rackets had attracted so many pupils that Steve Tulley, the professional, hardly had enough hours in the day. At that time, St Paul's aimed to compete at the very top levels, and the high master was determined to support the sport so that all pupils who wished to play might do so. After the match, Lord Aberdare unveiled a plaque dedicating the court to the memory of E.P.C. 'Pat' Cotter, classicist, bridge writer and sportsman, who taught at St Paul's from 1928 to 1965. The day ended in magnificent style with a celebration dinner at the Queen's Club, sponsored, as had been the match, by the generous benefactor.

Just two months after the official opening and the second leg of the world singles championship match, St Paul's also hosted the second leg of the world doubles, between defending champions Neil Smith and Shannon Hazell, and challengers James Male and Mark Hue Williams. Leading 4–0 after the first leg in Philadelphia, the challengers needed only to win the first game to secure the title, and that they did 17–14 after facing a game point at 12–14.

The popularity of Rackets at St Paul's consequently resulted in its first big success within a remarkably short space of time. After just two years on the circuit, Tom Alway won the Jim Dear Cup for U15s in the 2002

Steve Tulley has been the professional ever since the court was opened.

Public Schools singles at Queen's Club, then repeated his triumph the following year, winning the Incledon-Webber Cup for U16 singles. In Easter 2004, Tom Alway and his partner, Mark Gibbor, won the Eric Angus Cup for U16 doubles. The following season St Paul's captured both Junior singles events, Dan Tristao won the U16 singles and Jamie Gibbor, the brother of Mark, won the U15 singles. This outstanding feat would make a total of five trophies won in two years of play, not to mention the two doubles finals that were narrowly lost in the 'set' of the final games of both the U16 and U15 at Easter 2005, nor to mention that St Paul's held the top seed positions in three of the four doubles events in 2006 and had four boys represent the school in the Foster Cup that same year

Tom Alway won the Jim Dear cup for U15s in the 2002 Public Schools singles, then repeated his triumph the following year winning the Incledon-Webber cup for U16 singles.

– an impressive start for the new boys on the block.

Since then things have settled down to a more realistic level, though St Paul's are consistently being represented in the Foster Cup and picking up high seeded positions in the Public Schools tournaments each year.

The speed of success in the junior ranks of Public Schools Rackets was undoubtedly astonishing for St Paul's, and in turn a brilliant platform on which to build a solid framework. It is now hoped that those successes can be transferred on to the senior end, with particular sights on the Foster Cup and the first-pair doubles.

The increase in popularity of Rackets at St Paul's in 2002 was linked to the foundation of two internal singles competitions – the Senior and Junior 'David Tate Cup', kindly given by former governor Mr David Tate to encourage healthy play and good competition within school. Tom Alway once again figures strongly on the honours boards, having won three Junior (U16) titles and two Senior titles, the three Junior titles he won are unlikely to be equalled due to him winning the first when only U14. In 2007 an U14 event was also introduced, which again promotes good competition for all new boys.

In 2002 an adult evening club was also formed after an evening's showcase to local people. This became a twice-weekly affair for many years, though more recently play has been reduced to once a week. The membership consists mainly of Old Boys from schools around the country rather than the local community, although it is hoped that eventually Old Paulines will become more involved here, as is the case with their involvement in Old Boy events such as the U21 and U24 singles, the Milne/Hue Williams and the Noel-Bruce doubles.

Another high-class event that was staged at St Paul's was in January 2004, when the British Professional singles championship was kindly hosted by the school, and generously sponsored by the benefactor. New York professional Neil Smith won the event when he defeated the Radley professional Mark Hubbard 3–2 in the final. The court was also used in conjunction with Queen's Club during the 2008 centenary, when many overseas players came to celebrate the week-long festivities.

In 2009 St Paul's celebrated its 500th anniversary. Many outstanding events were on show. At the Rackets court the history of the sport was displayed for the countless guests passing through during an action-packed day, but the highlight on the court was a world-class doubles match that included Will Hopton, Richard Spender, Ben Bomford and Joe Bone. This fabulous match kept the awe-inspired gallery riveted to their seats for ninety minutes during a five-game epic.

In January 2004 the British Professional singles championship was hosted by the school. New York Professional Neil Smith won the event when he defeated Radley Professional Mark Hubbard.

RMA SANDHURST

Up to the mid-1990s, Rackets flourished in the Army, where the game had been encouraged from its early formative years. By 1911, there were courts at all the main depots, including Aldershot, Chatham, Colchester, Portsmouth, Shorncliffe and the Curragh (Co. Kildare). The Army introduced the game to Canada and to India, where in 1930 there were some seventy courts.

The Royal Military Academy is credited with the first building of a closed court – by 1806 there were two courts at Woolwich, one covered and one open, at either end of the main block. The whole block was demolished in 1859 and two new courts built. At about the same time, the fives court at the Royal Military College, Sandhurst, was converted into a Rackets court.

The present Sandhurst courts were built about 1877, and two years later the first RMA v. RMC match was played – an annual encounter (except for war years) until about 1926. By 1940, the courts were being used for military purposes. One was restored in 1948 (by which time the two colleges were amalgamated into the RMA Sandhurst) but the other is now used as a state-of-the-art gym.

New strip lights were installed in 1978 and an Invitation doubles competition for the Sandhurst Cup was inaugurated, which proved very popular. It still survives as an annual event over a spring weekend, when Wellington College allow the Army the use of their court and thirty to forty military and civilian players take part. However, the ever-reducing number of Sandhurst cadets who played Rackets or Real Tennis at school, and the huge pressure of operational deployments, have proved challenging.

One noticeable effect of these two influences is that the Rackets element of the annual championships played at Queen's in February has reduced markedly. In an effort to stem this decline, the participation of Royal Navy, Royal Air Force and Reserves personnel in the singles and doubles competitions has been introduced, the effect of which has been very beneficial, and the Army championships have now been renamed as the Combined Services championships.

The Sandhurst Rackets court is in good order and being used quite regularly; a series of fixtures against other clubs continues to be played.

Paul Tennant serving in the Sandhurst Cup.

Real Tennis continues to flourish amongst personnel both present and past and Hardwick House continues to be the Army's 'Home' court. The dozen or so fixtures are well supported and the championships continue to have full entries. An increasingly popular fixture is the annual match between the MCC and a Combined Services Team, coinciding with the Inter Services Twenty20 cricket tournament at Lord's, and all the other fixtures against clubs throughout the UK continue to be keenly contested and enjoyed.

Another promising development has been a Services Tennis and Rackets tour to the United States in 2011. The tour party comprised players from all three services, most of whom had seen service in Afghanistan in recent months. The tour was successful in that they were victorious in all of their matches, playing in New York, Newport, Boston, Tuxedo Park, Philadelphia and Washington.

Players from the three services enjoy a practice session at the Newport court during their 2011 tour of the USA.

Pivotal to the sustainability and success of any organisation is its leadership and management. Brigadier James Illingworth, Colonel Paul Tennant, Lieutenant Colonel Andrew James, Majors Nigel Tench and Tom Mallinson have been on the ATRA scene holding key committee positions for twenty years or more, and have been key players as well as organisers.

The introduction of RN and RAF personnel has seen the dwindling band of Army players enhanced by light blue and dark blue players, and these have proved their worth, particularly for Real Tennis. Now there are worthy champions such as Lt Oliver Craven RN on the Rackets and Real Tennis silverware. The other benefit of this widening community is the involvement of RN and RAF personnel as organisers and match managers for what is effectively a Combined Services Tennis & Rackets Association. Commodore Philip Thicknesse RN and Captain Mark Garratt RN, and Air Vice-Marshal Aroop Mozumder RAF have all been key figures in promoting the games in their respective service. Young men and women from all three services are encouraged to continue to participate in these two great games and the future of the club remains positive. Real Tennis continues to flourish amongst personnel both present and past. The dozen or so fixtures are well supported and the championships continue to have full entries.

James Ilingworth defeats Haven Pell at the Washington court.

SEACOURT TENNIS CLUB, HAYLING ISLAND

THERE CAN HARDLY BE a more unusual and unexpected sports complex than this. The Tennis court in this south coast oasis was built in 1911 by J.F. Marshall, a talented player, at a cost of £10,000. The club was formed in the spring of 1966 with no more than twenty Tennis and badminton enthusiasts. By the end of that year there were seventy-eight members and today there are more than 800. The club boasts, in addition to the original court, a Rackets court built in 1980 with a glass door, four squash courts, two badminton courts, two floodlit hard lawn tennis courts, a fitness gym, a sports hall that is also used as a fencing salle and a pétanque area, as well as recently refurbished bar, restaurant and changing areas.

Marshall, who won the MCC Gold Prize in 1914, sunk the court three feet into the ground to avoid too obtrusive a building. It opened in June 1911 with a match between the former world champion Peter Latham and the man who had taken the title from him, Cecil 'Punch' Fairs. The surprising factor of that opening day was that the match that followed was a mixed doubles – a very mixed doubles, involving the two finest amateur players of the day, Eustace Miles and the Hon. Neville Lytton, partnering G.H.K. Bone and Mrs Lytton (later Baroness Wentworth). The lady was said to be a formidable opponent who practised with her own professional. He happened to be Fred Covey, at the time the best Tennis player in the world after Latham and Fairs. This unusual promotion of a female Tennis player set a standard that Seacourt has never lost.

In 1913 the club launched a handicap competition for ladies, and in 1978 the first Ladies' Open was staged there and has often been played there since. One of the leading female players in the world, Alex Garside, is a Seacourt member, competes in the club's annual Silver Racket competition and has represented Seacourt in the Field Trophy team. With Sally Jones, Alex Garside won the world doubles in 1989 and 1991, and in 1994 won the British Open and French Open singles titles. Her many doubles titles include the British Open (nine times), the French Open and the Australian, US, French and Scottish championships.

When the original Seacourt owner died after the Second World War, the property was bought by Charles Sylvester, who repaired the court after war damage and started a social club. Demolition threatened in the early 1960s, but in February 1966 Ned Danby, Francis Snell and John Parker formed the Seacourt Tennis Club Ltd, along with Paul and Nicky Danby. In 1998, Paul and Nicky Danby and John Parker stood down as directors of the company. Mrs Jenny Paterson was elected chairman, the first time that position had been held by anyone other than a member of the Danby family.

Derek Barrett served as professional from 1969 to 1970, when Peter Dawes took over. Peter made a significant contribution to the club's success and taught many assistants who are now club professionals – including Danny Jones, who joined him at Seacourt in 1991. Peter Dawes finally hung up his racquets in June 2003, after thirty years as the Seacourt head professional. The legacy he left was quite simple: give the young players room to develop and as much encouragement as possible, and the results will speak for themselves. He was succeeded by assistant Danny Jones, who has upheld Peter's philosophy.

About a quarter of Real Tennis professionals currently in the game started their Tennis or had their first job at Seacourt. Also, during the new millennium, over half of the national U12, U14, U16 and U18 singles titles have been won by Seacourt juniors. The numbers in these events are growing year on year and the trophies are being won by many different clubs now – the Dawes legacy is contagious! Those same juniors have also helped the club win the Brodie Cup in 2001 and 2013 and, as they grew, three Field Trophies (2003, 2006 and 2010) led by Paul Weaver, who also was Director of Junior Tennis for the T&RA through most of this period.

There have been four standout players at the club in recent times – though there have also been great wins from many others. Luke Danby has won the

In 2009 at Seacourt Bryn Sayers and Ricardo Smith reached the final of the world doubles against Rob Fahey and Steve Virgona.

Seacourt Silver Racquet twice, as well as the Amateur doubles with his cousin Charlie. Josh Dodgson and Conor Medlow have jousted on a number of occasions. Between them, they won every age group tournament in the last decade and usually ended up playing each other in the finals. Josh, who went on to be a pro at Petworth and then Tuxedo, has won the Under-24 doubles twice (with Tom Weaver, also from Seacourt), as well as the Seacourt Silver Racquet, the Taylor Cup and the IRTPA Satellite. Conor won the Seacourt Silver Racquet (twice) and, in 2011, the UK Amateur singles (the youngest ever winner); in the same season he got to the final of the British Open doubles with Tim Chisholm and represented the UK in the Bathurst Cup in New York. He has also won the Under-21 and Under-24 singles and, in both 2012 and 2013, won the UK Amateur doubles (with Julian Snow). In 2014 he won the MCC Gold and Silver Racquets.

The most successful player from Seacourt, however, has been Bryn Sayers. Since 2003 he has won the Under-21 and Under-24 singles titles multiple times, along with a record five Under-24 doubles titles (four with Ricardo Smith and one with Camden Riviere). In 2009, again with Ricardo Smith, he reached the final of the world doubles, having won an amazing semi-final in five sets against Nick Wood and Camden Riviere at Seacourt. In 2011, he achieved a world ranking of 3 and, after losing to Rob Fahey in a classic five-set match in the British Open final, he went on to win the 2012 US Open title in New York against Steve Virgona. This was followed by the final eliminator for the world championship, again against Steve Virgona, at Seacourt in March 2012. Bryn's outstanding career achievement has undoubtedly been his four-set triumph over world champion Fahey in the 2012 British Open – the first win by a British player in the tournament this century. Further, Bryn and Tim Chisholm won the British Open doubles in 2013.

Off the court, Seacourt was under new management from July 2005, with Paul Weaver taking the chairman's seat and Nick Jones becoming managing director. Since then, the club has strengthened financially and investment has been made in the facilities and buildings. This team, along with a mainly new board, have been responsible for bringing many events to the club (including the world doubles and final eliminator mentioned above) as well as many events in 2011 to celebrate the centenary of the Tennis court, which first opened on 27 June

Bryn Sayers's outstanding career achievement has undoubtedly been his four-set triumph over world champion Fahey in the 2012 British Open. Seen here with Robin Geffen, CEO of Neptune Investment Management.

In 2011 the club celebrated the Centenary of the Tennis court.

1911. In this period Paul won numerous singles and doubles Masters titles.

In 2003, Nick Danby was informed that there was a trophy up for auction in Bath which mentioned Seacourt. Upon doing some research, he found that it was an elegant solid silver trophy which was played for annually in the 1910s and 1920s, with engraving showing the victors' names and detailing their handicap. Nicky acquired the trophy and very kindly donated it to the club. Since then, it has periodically been presented to individuals who have made a sizable contribution to the club. Recipients to date are: Nick Jones, Nicky

Nick Danby found and donated to the club an elegant silver trophy which was played for annually at Seacourt in the 1910s and 1920s. Since then, it has periodically been presented to individuals who have made a sizable contribution to the club. Recipients to date are (left to right) Nick Jones, Nick Danby, Alf Fleming, Peter Dawes, Paul Weaver and Dougie Sharp.

In October 2011, new LED lights were installed giving crisp white light and saving over half of the electricity and maintenance costs traditionally associated with Tennis courts.

Danby, Alf Fleming, Peter Dawes, Paul Weaver and Dougie Sharp.

In October 2011, new lights were installed on the Real Tennis court. After much research, LED lights were fitted, giving crisp white light and saving over half of the electricity and maintenance costs traditionally associated with Tennis courts. Seacourt was the first club to take the plunge into this new technology and, following this initiative, several other UK courts have followed suit along with a couple overseas.

SOUTHWEST OF FRANCE

THE FOUR COURTS that make up the presence of Real Tennis in the southwest of France are the Beaumont in Pau, Hapette in La Bastide-Clairence, Saint-André in Bayonne and Urrugne. However, many other modern trinquet courts are used occasionally for Tennis.

The city of Pau was created at the foothill of the Pyrenees at the turn of the tenth century and remained a thriving but small city. On the site of Pau there was originally a hunting lodge for the viscounts of Béarn, who enjoyed its location due to the plateau overlooking the river from 40m above. The mountain stream that ran near the lodge was also convenient, in that it became wider near the walls of Pau and therefore acted as a moat. The hunting lodge's strategic position meant it was later converted into a barracks. In the early fourteenth century the viscount who ruled the Bearnese people defied the French King and created an independent state, named the principality of Béarn; they were adept at using their independence to mint money. Béarn coins were called *Vaquettes du Béarn* and were trusted all over Europe. Having allied themselves with the King of England and various Spanish kings, while also having blood ties to the King of France, these viscounts were granted power and soon became kings of Navarre, expanding the land of Béarn down to Pamplona.

In 1510 France and Castile, a region of Spain, were at war with each other. At the time Navarre, a kingdom independent of France and Spain, remained dislocated and detached from the conflict. However the Spanish King of Castile, Ferdinand II of Aragon, asked Jean d'Albret, King of Navarre, for permission to cross his territory in order to occupy a few strategic locations. Jean d'Albret refused. Within days and without a single battle, he had lost Pamplona – the capital of Navarre and the Spanish side of his kingdom (Navarre lay on both sides of the Pyrenees) – to Ferdinand's armies. The court moved to Pau, which became the new capital in 1512. The old military castle was beautifully transformed and the gardens soon became a European curiosity.

Pau was still the capital of Navarre when Henri IV was born in 1553; his grandfather, Henri d'Albret, better known as Henri II of Navarre, liked to call his tiny kingdom 'a louse between two monkeys'.

The current curators of the Château de Versailles, Yves Carlier, and of Musée National du Château de Pau, Paul Mironneau, have had access to numerous factual resources about the history of Real Tennis – in Pau in particular – and have found that at that time there were a selection of different courts and variations of the game being enjoyed in the luxurious gardens, created by Marguerite and Henri II, in and around Pau's castle. Over the years, these courts had also been used as acting and living space for theatre companies and comedians, though Tennis was still played on the court. In 1552, Henri II decided to restore one of these courts, which had originally been built around 1490 next to the castle. Several years later, after Henri IV became King of France, he followed his grandfather's lead and started sending funds to renovate the court before his arrival in Pau.

Soon after the departure of the Navarre court from Pamplona to Pau, the tennis court at La Bastide-Clairence was created by Salvador de Berrio, butler to the kings of Navarre in Pamplona. The poor lad lost his job when the kings of Navarre lost the southern part of their kingdom, after which he returned to La Bastide, his native village, and built the court.

The court at Pau was used for Tennis without interruption until 1840, when it was demolished to allow the extension and restoration of a section of the castle.

The Beaumont Real Tennis court was built in 1887 to satisfy the demands of a large colony of English who enjoyed spending long winters near the Pyrenees. This colony was initially created after Wellington's Spanish campaigns in 1814. At that time Wellington had expelled the Napoleonic armies from Spain and was pursuing them through the south of France, culminating in the battle of Orthez. After arriving at Pau, Wellington and his Army were amazed by the welcome they received from the local population, who decorated the streets with huge triumphal arches made of branches and flowers and huge banners saying, 'Welcome to our Liberator'. Pau being the birthplace of Henri IV, founder of the Bourbon dynasty, the people of Pau saw Wellington as the man who could restore the Bourbons to the throne of France – and above all help them get rid of Napoleon. As a result of the warm welcome, the British Army stayed in Pau and enjoyed the area for several months before leaving in July 1814. Wellington, like most Irishmen, was a fox-hunting fanatic; during his stay in Pau he discovered an ideal hunting ground and a large population of foxes. Some of Wellington's officers retired there, and were the first British to settle there as early as 1816.

Two other important visitors made Pau famous. The first was Lord Selkirk, who arrived in Pau on 19 September 1819. He was the founder of Winnipeg, as well as the Viceroy of Canada, but unfortunately had tuberculosis. After his doctor in London suggested he should settle in southern Spain to live the rest of his life out peacefully, Selkirk took the advice. Seven carriages soon left London. One contained Selkirk's family, the others contained his servants, the furniture and a young doctor named George Lefebvre who also suffered from tuberculosis. The morning after his arrival, Selkirk and Lefebvre went for a ride around Pau and soon found the city to be a superb place – in particular they loved the view of the mountains and consequently decided to stay there. The mild winter helped Lefebvre to fully recover, but Selkirk unfortunately died in June 1820. After his unexpected recovery, Lefebvre wrote an article to the medical journal *The Lancet*, stating how Pau's weather had been good for him and for his prestigious patient. The publicity surrounding the article was so huge that many people, including shopkeepers, chemists and grocers, left England and settled in Pau. Some of them proceeded to open businesses importing tea, Stilton and port.

Pau also owes its reputation to another man, Alexander Taylor, a doctor who fought during the Carlist wars and caught typhus in Saragossa. As a result he was sent to Bayonne, and during that time he decided to visit Pau to see the Bourbon château. He

The Beaumont court in Pau was built in 1887 as an exact copy of the Tuileries Court in Paris to satisfy the demands of a large colony of English who enjoyed spending long winters near the Pyrenees.

grew very attached to the city and its English colony. Taylor decided to live there, and started passing the time conducting studies of the weather. In 1842, he published a book called *Virtues of the Climate of Pau*. The book attracted a large number of wealthy British families, aristocrats and businesses to the Pyrenees. The increase in popularity of the city led to the creation of a fox-hunting gathering, the Pau Hunt, in 1843, and a racecourse, L'Hippodrome du Pont-Long, which is the equivalent of Cheltenham – the Pau and Cheltenham racecourses are very similar in appearance. A golf club was also founded by three members of St Andrews in 1856 – the first one in continental Europe – and ballooning also became an extremely exciting attraction. By the 1860s, Pau was the place to be seen.

In 1870, a young American tycoon James Gordon-Bennett, who was the founder of the *International Herald Tribune*, discovered Pau and quickly became Master of the Pau Hunt after saving it from bankruptcy. He also organised regular ballooning competitions and created the Automobile Club Basco Béarnais, the oldest club of its type in France. The result of his influence was a plethora of newspaper reports in the *International Herald Tribune* about the receptions and sporting events being held in Pau, and the activities of the Pau Hunt. At this time this newspaper was the only continental newspaper to be linked with the US by a sub-oceanic telegraph cable. The publicity, orchestrated by Gordon-Bennett, soon attracted a large numbers of Americans to Pau as well.

In 1886, in order to keep up its reputation of being the hub of the sporting world, and after the increase in popularity of Real Tennis in the Navarre kingdom, the city of Pau decided to build a new Real Tennis court using internationally agreed dimensions and proportions. An architect named Virant, who had previously built the Tuileries Court in Paris, was appointed for the job. He didn't waste time, quite simply reproducing an exact copy of the Tuileries Court on the edge of the ten-acre park of the newly acquired Villa Beaumont.

The increase in Pau's sporting popularity continued to attract many people, including Frederick Prince, a shrewd American businessman who was a central figure in Pau's social life for half a century, due to his position as Master of the Pau Hunt from 1910 till 1940. His secretary, a young French aristocrat named Henri de Vaufreland, wrote his own personal memoirs titled *60 Années de Sport*, in six volumes, some of which were written during the Second World War when he lived alone in his attic while his house in Central France was occupied by German officers. In 1994, Henri de Vaufreland's daughter, Madame B. Karsten, contacted the current head of the *Covedi* newspaper, Paul Mirat, to show him her father's manuscripts. Two years later, a collection of his writings titled *Carnets de la vie mondaine des Basses-Pyrénées* were published.

In August 1995, Paul Mirat was contacted by Frederick Prince, the great-grandson of the famous Master of the Pau Hunt, who wanted to order a couple of copies of *Carnets de la vie mondaine des Basses-Pyrénées*. While packing the books, Mirat added some information about Pau, as well as an invitation to a 'pilgrimage' retracing his ancestor's steps. Prince came to Pau in early February 1996. Mirat organised a fantastic week, with dinners, hunts and visits to stimulate Prince's passion for history. The Real Tennis court in Washington had just been built thanks to the generous support of Prince. After stepping into the Villa Beaumont Real Tennis court Prince said: 'This is a magnificent court. Paul, if you revive the game, I'll send you my team!'

While in Pau, Prince met up several times with Mr André Labarrère, mayor of Pau from 1971 till 2006, as well as a senator and MP of the Aquitaine region and minister in François Mitterrand's government from 1981 to 1986. Prince informed him about a possible restoration of the Beaumont court. However, it transpired that different plans were afoot. In 2000, bulldozers arrived and the five-star Hotel Beaumont emerged. Three years later, Labarrère and the renowned architect Zaha Hadid announced plans to build a multimedia library. Despite numerous discussions with the mayor and his deputies about preserving the old Real Tennis court, it was decided that it would be pulled down and relocated to give way to a parking facility. The court was temporarily closed. Meanwhile, Mirat had been asked to write the text for a small book illustrated with 140 old postcards showing photographs of Pau. He used one 1902 postcard, with a beautiful view of the Beaumont Tennis court, as a demonstration of his pledge to reintroduce Real Tennis in Pau.

In the winter of 2003, Julian Butcher, a member of the Petworth House Real Tennis club, whose wife Benedicte originates from Pau, discovered this small book and decided to meet with Mirat. In October 2004, Julian returned to Pau with Chris Bray and Simon Berry, armed with balls and racquets. Philippe Bordenave, an old schoolfriend of Benedicte's and a regular player of *pelota* at Beaumont, invited them to join him on court for the first Tennis ball to be struck there since the outbreak of the Second World War! In September 2005, with the mayor's approval and the support of the Comité Français, an event was held over the weekend of the Journées du Patrimoine. One hundred players from England and France were lured by the prospect of having a 'hit' on this sleeping court and helping with a possible restoration campaign. Much support was received from the Parc Beaumont Hotel, which had only recently been opened; they hosted a lecture on the history of Tennis in Pau by Yves Carlier and a gala dinner. A team of professionals, together with Olivier Michel (president of the Comité Français), gave demonstrations to a great number of Palois who had come to rediscover the court.

Some days later, Alexandre Boy started playing Real Tennis on the new court. He had previously been a Basque *pelota* champion. Having watched a few demonstrations, silently hypnotised by the display, he had been invited on court and had hardly left it during the whole day. After a year of training, he ranked in the top twenty French Real Tennis players and, along with a couple of his personal friends, created the Jeu de Paume de Navarre. In 2006, Zaha Hadid's project was cancelled due to lack of a suitable backer and the court in Pau was saved. Simon Berry and Paul Mirat have since enjoyed exploring nearby regions on quests to discover other old courts.

Having started by visiting the courts recommended by Albert de Luze, they soon realised that most of them had already disappeared. However, they were fortunate enough to find one still in existence when,

The wood for the pillars and beams at the court at La Bastide Clairence was cut down from a nearby forest in 1510 and assembled in 1512

Simon Berry and Paul Mirat enjoy exploring nearby regions to discover old courts.

in 2010, Berry visited La Bastide-Clairence, a small, once fortified village, created in 1312. During his visit, he found a trinquet – a court used by the locals to play Real Tennis for over four centuries and later converted to Basque *pelota*. A few days later, Mirat visited the ruined trinquet and noticed the magnificent carpentry, despite the court's poor condition after years of neglect and ruin. He went to the town hall to talk to the mayor, Leopold Darritchon. After hearing Mirat's pleas to renovate the court in a way that would enable Real Tennis to be played, the mayor described his restoration plans, revealing that he had no intention of aiding the sport. However, a few weeks later, Mirat was invited by Darritchon to a meeting at La Bastide-Clairence to argue his case for preserving and renovating the court to host Real Tennis. The modifications he suggested made quite an impact and were soon approved by the town hall. Within a few months, the mayor had funded wood-dating analyses on the quality and age of the existing pillars and beams, and hired a large quantity of workers to start building additions and renovating. From the analyses it was revealed that the wood for the pillars and beams had been cut down in a nearby forest in 1510 and assembled in 1512. Since its renovation, the Hapette court has attracted many keen players.

The Saint-André court in Bayonne can be traced back as far as 1610. Unlike the Beaumont and Hapette Real Tennis courts, not much is known about the origins of the one in Bayonne. It is known that Real Tennis was played regularly here until the mid-nineteenth century, when the court was converted into a Basque *pelota* court. Around that time rubber was invented, which gave birth to so many new ball games, including *pelota* and of course lawn tennis. To create a *pelota* court, the net and grille gallery were taken out and side-by-side play was introduced, using the grille wall as a main wall.

The Saint-André court was dedicated to Basque *pelota* until 28 September 1928, when Pierre Etchebaster, a former Basque *pelota* champion and by then a Real Tennis professional in Paris, gave a Tennis demonstration. Over eighty years later, Paul Mirat

In 2011 a week of tournaments was staged on the three courts in Pau, La Bastide and Bayonne. It was named Le Tournoi des trois Tripots. *On 28 September Rob Fahey and Claire Vigrass played a match in Bayonne celebrating Pierre Etchebaster's victory there over Edgar Baerlein on the same day in 1928. Here they are with Matthieu and Pierre Sarlangue.*

The Saint-André court in Bayonne can be traced back as far as 1610.

Since the spark of Freddy Prince's visit to Pau in 1996, the stubborn leaders of Jeu de Paume de Navarre (Simon Berry, Michel d'Arcangues, Paul Mirat and Alex Boy – all shown here except Simon) have been fighting hard for the development of the sport.

and Simon Berry had the idea of reintroducing Real Tennis to the club and convinced the club authorities to do so. Both men have since helped the club with its running and generated the idea of sending Real Tennis invitations to players around the world. This has stimulated popularity for the game in Bayonne.

In 2011 the club decided to host a unique tournament that would be played for a week on the three local courts in Pau, La Bastide and Bayonne. It was named *Le Tournoi des trois Tripots*, and was initiated and coordinated by Simon Berry and Paul Mirat. On 28 September, during the tournament, Rob Fahey and Claire Vigrass kindly agreed to play a match celebrating the anniversary of Pierre Etchebaster's victory over Edgar Baerlein, a match that had been played in Bayonne on 28 September 1928. This demonstration attracted a large number of people who were privileged to witness a skilful and exciting match.

The recent progress of Real Tennis in the south of France has been remarkable. Since 2005 Pau has held an international tournament each year, as well as various inter-club competitions, which include the likes of Bordeaux and Fontainebleau.

Since the spark of Freddy Prince's visit to Pau in 1996, the stubborn leaders of Jeu de Paume de Navarre (Berry, Boy, Arcangues and Mirat) have been fighting hard for the development of the sport and are always delighted to welcome visitors to Pau, Bayonne and La Bastide. Visiting players, mainly from Australia, the USA and England, are the best ambassadors for this area of France, as they have encouraged many more people to come.

TONBRIDGE SCHOOL

Until 2012 Tonbridge only had one Rackets court, the Dale Memorial Court, which had been built in 1897. Being located in the heart of the school, this court enabled boys of all ages to snatch occasional moments on the court at all times of the day, and over the years this proved an enormous advantage: much had been achieved by David Makey, the current Rackets professional, with just a single court. However, over the previous twenty-three years Rackets had become an increasingly popular sport in the school, so much so that too many boys found that they could seldom get on the court when they had the time to do so.

David Makey takes a novel but successful approach to the fund-raising process.

In 2006, when the new Tonbridge School Sports Centre was opened, the old school gymnasium, which adjoined the Rackets court, became vacant. It became apparent as the months passed that David Makey's dream of a new and much-needed second Rackets court was more than just a possibility. For some months discussions took place over whether the gym could be simply converted into a practice court for younger boys, at a relatively low cost, or into a Rackets court of the highest quality, which would be used for matches. The latter alternative was duly agreed upon, and the plans for a new court to be built within the old gym walls were drawn up and approved.

However, the finance necessary for the dream to become a reality still had to be raised. A committee was formed under the chairmanship of Tom Shields, an Old Tonbridgian parent and a great Rackets enthusiast, who was to become the driving force behind the venture. In February 2011 it was agreed that the target sum of £500,000 would be raised by the end of the summer term.

The generosity of Old Tonbridgians, parents, both past and present, and supporters of the game of Rackets, both in the UK and beyond, enabled the financial target to be achieved and, with additional finance from the school, the construction of the new court began in the first week of July 2011. The Appeal Court, as it has been named, only the fourth to be built in England since 1900, was officially opened on 19 March 2012 by Jonathan Cohen QC, the chairman of the Tonbridge School governors. This proved to be a very special occasion, with over 200 donors present for a champagne reception. It was also marked by an exhibition match between the school first pair, Jonny Maltz and George Moynihan, and John Prenn and Will Hopton. The court, with its beautiful roof and cherry-red floor, is a truly magnificent-looking building, and there was much to celebrate.

Since David Makey took over as professional in 1983, Tonbridge has won a total of forty-one Public Schools titles. Three different pairs won the doubles championship in three consecutive years, from 1985 to 1987, and in 1987 all four Tonbridge pairs reached the finals of their various age groups, winning three of them.

Some outstandingly talented boys have enriched the teams over the past twenty years. Adrian Spurling, beaten by Julian Snow in the Foster Cup final of 1982, won it in 1983 and, partnered by Rupert Owen-Browne, brought the doubles championship back to Tonbridge. Owen-Browne reached five Public Schools finals and won four of them, including the Foster Cup in 1984 and the doubles championship in 1985, partnered by Simon Davies.

Jonathan Longley, between 1984 and 1987, was the first – and remains the only – boy to win the main six Public Schools tournaments – the Under-15 and Under-16 singles and doubles, the Foster Cup (1985 and 1986), and the doubles championship (1986 and 1987) – eight titles and never a defeat at Queen's.

During the 1990s, Dan Cherry reached five national finals and won three of them, including the Public Schools doubles with Jamie Parker, who reached the second-pair final in his first year, having played Rackets for only two terms. Jamie Parker played in a further six national finals in his school career, winning five of the six majors, being unable to compete in the sixth because of a school cricket tour.

In 2009 and 2010 Jonathan Maltz reached all four Public Schools Junior finals, winning three of them. Also in this period, Tonbridge was once again represented in a Queen's final by a player with the name of Cowdrey. This was Fabian, following his father Chris and grandfather Colin. Partnered by Nick Spurling, he reached the final of the Under-16 doubles in 2009. This contributed, in the same season, towards Tonbridge winning the Mark Faber Cup for the third time; the cup was originally presented by the Faber family in memory of Mark Faber in 1993.

David Makey, a newcomer to Rackets in 1980, initially spent two years at Malvern learning from Ron Hughes – a master teacher with a master pupil. Rackets at Tonbridge pre-Makey had been in the hands of the Hull family since before the First World War, by extraordinary chance. James Hull was a friend of Walter Hawes of Wellington College, who introduced

The Appeal Court, only the fourth to be built in England since 1900, was officially opened on 19 March 2012.

Hull's elder son, Charles, to the game and then took him on as his assistant.

After three years Charles Hull moved to Prince's Club, and in 1913 he accepted a post as squash professional on the *Titanic*. Hawes persuaded him not to go, and in May 1914 he was appointed professional at Tonbridge. A year later he joined the Army, and by then he had bullied his younger brother, Arthur, into assisting him. Charles lost a leg in the war, and Arthur took over as senior professional in 1920. He remained there for the next forty-eight years, until his son Christopher took over from him in 1968. Then, fifteen years later, in 1983, David Makey took over.

Tonbridge first entered a pair for the Public Schools championship in 1878, but failed to reach the final until John Thompson and Peter Pettman took them there in 1937, followed by Colin Cowdrey and John Campbell in 1951. The first Tonbridge victory, however, came in 1957 from Miles Connell and Peter Rylands (who had won the Foster Cup in 1956).

Cowdrey had a distinguished, albeit brief, career in Rackets before cricket claimed him completely. He played first string for Oxford in 1952, 1953 and 1954, winning all his matches against Cambridge, and in 1952 – only one year after school – faced Geoffrey Atkins in the Amateur singles final. He three times helped Tonbridge win the Noel-Bruce Cup (1953, 1955 and 1957) in partnership with John Thompson, a player of exceptional skill.

Five times Amateur and once Open champion in the 1950s, Thompson was held in even greater awe for his performances on the doubles court. Playing with David Milford, he took the Amateur doubles ten times between 1948 and 1959, and then again with Tom Pugh in 1966. As well as his Noel-Bruce victories with Cowdrey, Thompson won it four times

The court, with its beautiful roof and cherry-red floor, is a truly magnificent looking building.

with Richard Gracey, thus getting the Tonbridge name engraved on the trophy seven times in nine years. Gracey then formed a stunning partnership with Martin Smith (another Amateur singles champion), winning the Old Boys' Cup every year from 1969 to 1974.

THE TUXEDO CLUB

THE TUXEDO CLUB was founded by Pierre Lorillard IV, together with others including Cecil Baring, third Lord Revelstoke, and his business partner Thomas Suffern Tailer. Tailer and Baring found the necessary subscriptions from fellow enthusiasts and employed the rising firm of Warren & Wetmore – future architects of Grand Central Station – to build the magnificent Tennis court, Rackets court and clubhouse on the site near Lake Tuxedo, north of New York. These were completed in 1899. That the commission went to Warren and Wetmore – who had been in practice only since 1896 – might have been because Whitney Warren had a family connection with one of the subscribers, William Kissam Vanderbilt, or perhaps because they had early caught the eye of J.P. Morgan, who gave Warren & Wetmore the commission for the New York Yacht Club at much the same time. Morgan was an old ally of Cecil Baring's. He had been one of the subscribers who had helped the Bank of England guarantee the firm during the Barings Crash in 1890, and Morgan and Barings had remained close trading allies ever since.

Warren & Wetmore – future architects of Grand Central Station – built the magnificent Tennis court, Rackets court and clubhouse, which were completed in 1899.

Tuxedo is the oldest American court still in continuous use.

The first game on the court at Tuxedo was played between Cecil Baring and Tommy Tailer on 31 December 1899. This match acquired an added symbolism when Tailer's wife, Maude Lorillard (daughter of Pierre Lorillard IV), divorced Tailer in 1902, and later in the same year was married to Baring in London.

The Tuxedo Club today is stronger in terms of its membership and facilities than ever before. The golf course, boathouse, swimming pool, recently renovated main clubhouse, golf house, and Tennis house, and courts for lawn tennis, Rackets, Court Tennis, squash, and platform tennis add up to one of the finest club facilities in the world. No other place offers as many sports in such a beautiful setting.

In 2011 a series of events were held to commemorate the club's 125th anniversary, including an international gala to celebrate the club's role in the creation of the tuxedo jacket, brought over from London's Henry Poole tailors in 1886. The Prince of Wales (later Edward VII) pioneered the wearing of what's now known as a dinner jacket or tuxedo when he ordered the first one in 1865 from Henry Poole & Co, bespoke tailors, who still operate from Savile Row. He wanted to wear something more informal in the evening than the customary white tie and tails. A few years later, in 1886, James Brown Potter, an original member of the Tuxedo Club, was invited to stay with the Prince of Wales at Sandringham. So as to respect the sartorial elegance of his host, he ordered a dinner jacket from the same tailors. On his return to the USA, he clearly reported to his fellow members at the club that this attire was now de rigueur in England, which resulted in many other members ordering the same from Henry Poole. So the dinner jacket became fashionable evening wear at the club, and diners beyond its walls saw and noted that this was what was worn at the Tuxedo. Exactly when the jacket itself started to be called *a tuxedo* in the USA remains a mystery, but the name gradually spread overseas and today is synonymous with the dinner jacket all over the globe.

Dan Laukitis and Ryan Carey at the club's 125th anniversary in 2011. A series of commemorative events were held, including an international gala to celebrate the club's role in the creation of the tuxedo jacket, brought over from London's Henry Poole tailors in 1886.

The historic tennis house was renovated for the 2002 Centennial Gold Rackets, with greatly improved locker rooms, air conditioning for the pro shop and dedans and a new heating system for the Rackets court.

The club recently commissioned a historian to begin to archive its vast collection of historic artefacts and related news articles. The hope is to have an in-house and digital library for future generations to enjoy.

A new golf house, the club's fourth in 112 years, was constructed in 1998. Designed by R.L. Hart, it includes luxurious changing rooms, a large bar, dining areas and covered porches. A master plan has been commissioned for significant renovations to the course and practice facilities; elements of the plan are already under way.

Two platform tennis courts were constructed near the new golf house in 1999, replacing original courts which had been located east of the main clubhouse and had been demolished in the 1970s. Two additional platform tennis courts were added in 2006, followed by a 'warming hut' in 2008.

The historic 1899 Warren and Wetmore tennis house was renovated for the 2002 Centennial Gold Rackets, with greatly improved locker rooms, air conditioning for the pro shop and dedans and a new heating system for the Rackets court. The club has commenced construction of two singles squash courts as well as a greatly expanded fitness area.

The boathouse has been replaced in its entirety, providing state-of-the-art facilities for boating, crew and sailing membership.

Tommy Greevy was Head Tennis professional at Tuxedo from 1968 to 2010, when he became professional emeritus. His Tennis career commenced as an apprentice to Jimmy Dunn at the Racquet Club of

Tommy Greevy was Head Tennis professional at Tuxedo from 1968 to 2010, when he became Professional Emeritus. His extraordinary dedication earned him the title of the world's longest serving Tennis pro.

Jonathan Larken achieved concurrent Tennis and Racket Gold championship wins in 2011, having previously won the Rackets Gold Championship in 2009 and 2010, and again in 2012 and 2013.

Philadelphia in 1956, when he was only fourteen. In 1968 he moved to Tuxedo, where his extraordinary dedication earned him the title of the world's longest serving Tennis pro.

When Greevy started at Tuxedo, there was so little to do in the winter that he would commute to New York and assisted Pierre Etchebaster. However, over time, he massively improved court use and introduced ladies and juniors to the game. His junior clinics became known as 'M&Ms' due to his reputation for munificence. He also had an extraordinary ability to tailor his adult lessons to the needs of the recipient in a flexible and enjoyable manner. He was an outstanding player, winning many championships, including the inaugural US Professional singles in 1973, and possessed a great sense of humour. For years, the name of 'Rains' appeared on Tuxedo tournament draws. A mysterious player without a home club or a handicap, Rains always seemed to lose in the first round. Only recently did Greevy reveal the truth, that Rains was just a filler name when someone dropped out of a draw mid-tournament, and Greevy had to shuffle players around. Rains was the lead in the 1933 classic *The Invisible Man*.

Tim Chisholm became Rackets Director in 2010. A consummate professional and uniquely talented in all racquet sports (former Real Tennis doubles world champion), Tim has done a phenomenal job in building up each of Tuxedo's five racquet sports – Real Tennis, Rackets, squash, lawn tennis and platform tennis – all of which are enjoying rapid growth in participation. Tim regularly attracts high-level assistants who come to train in Tuxedo's unique environment.

The Gold Racquet Real Tennis singles title remains a premier event, drawing players from all over the world. Guy Devereux won the Gold Racquet for Rackets every year between 1998 and 2008 except 2006, and in 2007 became the first person in the history of the club to win both Tennis and Rackets Gold championships concurrently. Jonathan Larken also achieved concurrent Tennis and Racket Gold championship wins in 2011, having previously won the Rackets Gold championship in 2009 and 2010, and again in 2012 and 2013. Spike Willcocks won the Tennis Gold championship every year between 2000 and 2008, except 2001, 2005 and 2007. In recent years there has also been an explosion of popularity of the Cuspidor and Spittoon doubles events.

Since 2004 the Hadden Tomes Invitational, held annually in October and notorious for its outlandish theme parties, has become a very popular event and marks the start of the national Real Tennis season.

In addition to a wide variety of club tournaments, Tuxedo continues to host many of the premier national Amateur and Professional events on a rotating basis.

Left: *Lisa Laukitis and Sara Devereux at the 2011 Hadden Tomes party, notorious for its outlandish themes, which has become a very popular event and marks the start of the national Real Tennis season.*

INTERNATIONAL TENNIS CLUB OF WASHINGTON

The International Tennis Club of Washington, known generally as Prince's Court, is located at the Regency Sport & Health Club in McLean, Virginia, six miles from Washington, DC. The club opened on 11 October 1997, and was the first new Tennis court built in the United States since the court at the Racquet Club of Chicago opened in 1924. Prince's Court started with fifteen members, and within ten years had grown into one of the busiest American clubs, boasting the most recorded matches per month in the United States in the Real Tennis online database. The court was created and built under the leadership of the United States Court Tennis Preservation Foundation, an organisation dedicated to bringing the sport to a wider public, and a small group of founding members, including Frederick H. Prince IV, whose generous support brought the project to fruition. The name Prince's Court is also in recognition of the several Prince's clubs built in London in the nineteenth century.

Numerous players who have been introduced to Tennis at Prince's Court have gone on to notable results in tournaments in the United States and abroad. The club routinely has several members in the list of the top twenty-five US amateurs. The club has twice come within two points of winning the Whitney Cup, fielding teams made up substantially of players who learned the sport at Prince's Court. Prince's also has many active female players in both singles and doubles, and hosted the ladies' world championship in 2001.

The court is often described as the most comfortable place to watch tennis. The main wall is made of plate glass, allowing dozens of spectators an unrivalled view of important tournament and exhibition matches. Prince's Court has hosted the annual US National Open in recent years, as well as a number of other tournaments

The main wall is made of plate glass, allowing dozens of spectators an unrivalled view of important tournament and exhibition matches.

Head pro Ivan Ronaldson stands astride his handiwork – a shattered glass panel. The dramatic event was caused by a hard shot hitting a metal ring attached to the net – the ring slammed against the glass, causing it to break. The design of the net's fixtures has since been modified.

and exhibition matches. Members and guests have seen spectacular rests from the world's top-ranked players, including Rob Fahey, Steve Virgona and Camden Riviere.

Prince's Court has had its own notable professional staff over the years, including current head pro Ivan Ronaldson, past head pro Will Simonds, and former assistant pro Phil Shannon. Both Will and Phil remain actively involved with the club. Ivan Ronaldson has been head professional at Prince's Court since June 2005. Originally from the UK, Ivan previously served as a professional at Holyport, Fontainebleau, the Royal Tennis Court, and Prested Hall. He is a two-time winner of the French national championship and is renowned as one of the fastest forces in the game. Neil McKenzie recently joined the club as assistant professional, succeeding Phil Shannon.

As a new model for how courts can be built and players developed, Prince's Court has encouraged innovation and creativity in its members. During the past few seasons, the club has pioneered the broadcasting of tournament and exhibition matches over the Internet, enabling small but global audiences to watch Real Tennis in real time. And two club members have won the George Plimpton Prize for literary and artistic achievement: James Zug in 2003 and Michael Do in 2007.

The club hosted a tenth anniversary dinner, held on the court itself, in September 2007, and in March 2011 the club threw a Tudor-themed dinner and costume party in honour of the court's twelve founding members. Eight founders attended the event: Temple Grassi, Charles T. Matheson, Haven N.B. Pell, Frederick H. Prince IV, Randall B. Roe, Robert Bland Smith, Stephen G. Smith and David Winstead, and a toast was raised in honour of the late Charles T. Cudlip; in addition, Robin B. Martin, Ian B.R. Fowler, and Francis de C. Hamilton sent along their best wishes for the continued success of the club.

Prince's Court has a diverse, active and highly social membership. It currently has nearly 100 resident members, a record for the club, including many representatives from around the world. Junior development is a priority at Prince's Court, which hosts some of the nation's best junior players. In 2013, club member Erik Barker (then 11 years old) won the US Under-12 singles and doubles, the US Under-15 singles and doubles, the US Under-18 singles and doubles, and the US Under-21 doubles.

The club's annual Cherry Blossom tournament, the brainchild of member Ryan Carey, is famous for its genial mad-hattery. It is named after a festival in Washington, DC that commemorates the gift of Japanese cherry trees by the Mayor of Tokyo to the city of Washington in 1912. Competitors from all the Tennis-playing nations have appeared in the tournament, and its ever-changing themes, including Easter-egg Tennis balls, a 3D webcast, viewable with special glasses, and Bingo, have proved to be very popular.

Camden Riviere playing in the club's annual Cherry Blossom tournament, the brainchild of Ryan Carey. It is famous for its genial mad-hattery and ever-changing themes, including Easter-egg Tennis balls, a 3-D webcast viewable with special glasses and Bingo, which have proved to be very popular.

WELLINGTON COLLEGE

Rackets at Wellington received an early boost when in 1867 Captain and Mrs Compton presented a challenge cup, to be contested annually. It was decided in 1870 that the winner of the cup should receive an additional prize of £2 – a rash decision that was swiftly rescinded, to be substituted by 'four dozen practising balls for the use of the two finalists before the Haileybury match'.

Wellington first competed in the Public Schools championship at Prince's Club in 1871, and first won the title in 1891. G.J. Mordaunt and R.H. Raphael, who had lost to Harrow the previous year, faced the redoubtable Foster brothers of Malvern in the final, H.K. and W.L., and beat them 4–2. George Smale was the school's professional at the end of the century ('One of the greatest teachers of play,' said Eustace Miles of Smales); he was succeeded in 1902 by the first of the great Hawes family, Walter. His extraordinary coaching ability led to championship wins in 1907 (again against Malvern, and another Foster brother), 1913, 1921 (with Lowther Lees in their pair, later to win the Amateur Tennis singles eight times) and 1926.

In 1933 a bath with a geyser was installed at the court, the Rackets Book recording that 'Visitors may now soak their tired limbs in a tiled bathroom concealed behind a rubber curtain.' Only boys in the VIII were allowed to use it, however, and they had to supply their own towels. Three years later, a new front wall was put in the court, the scaffolding standing in tubs filled with sand, and plasterers working continuously by

In 2011 the pair of Nick Hopcroft and Angus Boobyer won the Public Schools championship for Wellington for the first time since 1980.

the light of acetylene lamps. Walter Hawes, meanwhile, worked on re-surfacing the upper parts of the side walls.

The game continued to thrive during the war, and by 1944 there were fifty or sixty boys playing. Walter's son Ronnie returned from the war and took over from his father as Rackets professional, and immediately the school won the Public Schools doubles championship again, beating Harrow 4–1 in 1946. Ronnie's service to Wellington was as devoted and as skilled as his father's, and there was universal regret when he left for Eton in 1953, though not before he saw T.L. de Mesquita win the Foster Cup.

Peter Willey was the master-in-charge at the time, and reported the remark of a school governor – 'Glad to see you're taking over, Willey. Teach 'em how to stop hard balls – make 'em all the better at stopping hard bullets.'

In 1956, Wellington was fortunate to acquire the services of Jim Dear. The playing ability of this former world champion could not be doubted – and he held the British Professional championship from 1946 to 1974. He proved to be an admirable coach of teenagers, and did wonders in improving the standard of play at the school. G.B. Trentham won the Foster Cup in 1963, and C.N. Hurst-Brown in 1969.

Then Dear went to New York, and was followed at Wellington by Bob Mulliken from Dartmouth. He served Wellington splendidly, and was rewarded by the brothers Mallinson winning the Public Schools championship in 1980. The following year he had to retire through ill-health, and his place was taken by Shannon Hazell, who was trained at Clifton and won the Under-24 singles in 1983–84. Later he won the Professional singles and challenged James Male for the world title in 1991.

By then Hazell too had left for New York and was succeeded by Derek Barrett, then at Manchester. Chris Potter had two very successful and popular spells as master-in-charge, and the atmosphere he engendered has been maintained by his successor, Charles Oliphant-Callum. Barrett remained at Wellington until he moved to Montreal in 2001, having seen the college win four championships and appear in twelve other finals. After Walter Hawes, he had become Wellington's second longest-serving professional. Noel Brett arrived as Wellington's new professional, having just completed his training at Charterhouse.

The first decade of the twenty-first century proved one of the most successful in the history of Wellington Rackets. Over the next ten years, Wellington won ten trophies in the singles and doubles championships at Queen's Club, as a series of talented players came through the school. Nick Hopcroft dominated for five years, reaching three Foster Cup finals, winning twice.

In 2011 the pair of Hopcroft and Angus Boobyer won the Public Schools championship for Wellington for the first time since 1980. In the same year Old Wellingtonian Tim Cockroft, in partnership with Alex Titchener-Barrett, took the world doubles title, having together won the British Open doubles in the two previous years.

After presiding over one of the most successful decades in the history of Wellington Rackets, Brett moved on to Malvern in 2011. Brett was succeeded by Ryan Tulley, joining Wellington from Montreal.

In 2006 major refurbishment of the court took place and the gallery was restored to its original dimensions, accommodating the original honours boards, a library of racquet sport books donated by Sir David Scholey, and other memorabilia.

In recent years, Rackets has experienced greater popularity amongst girls at Wellington. Increasing female participation and interest in the game resulted in the inaugural U16 Ladies singles being won by Millie Pughe in 2011. India Cockroft – continuing a Rackets family legacy – succeeded Pughe as U16 champion in 2012. Pughe, meanwhile, claimed the Ladies' U18 singles in 2013.

In the 2012/13 season Chris Membrey, Millie Pughe, and Tom Membrey won the Jim Dear Cup, U18 Girls' singles and Renny Cup, respectively.

WINCHESTER COLLEGE

THE MOST STARTLING ACHIEVEMENT in Winchester's 144-year Rackets history was to win the Public Schools doubles three years running twice in nine years. The first hat-trick (1943–45) inspired an Old Wykehamist, K.O. Hunter, to pay for lighting to be installed in the old court; the second (1949–51) set what was then a unique record, with Mike Coulman playing in all three triumphant pairs. A rare family double was pulled off too, with Giles Myrtle in the 1944 and 1945 pairs, and his brother Andrew playing in 1950 and in 1951, in which year they also beat Oxford and Cambridge in the same week.

Only Eton and Harrow have a better record in the game than Winchester, who reached the championship finals in 1874 and 1875 and first won it in 1889 and again in 1904, with Clarence Bruce (later Lord Aberdare) as first string. The first court at the school had been built in 1871 at the expense of the headmaster, the Rev. George Ridding. A second court was added in 1910, with both courts built under Joseph Bickley's supervision. The new one had to be re-surfaced in 1929, but this lasted for the next 139 years. Lighting was installed in 1934.

The school was criticised in 1875, despite its successes, for being the only Rackets-playing school that did not employ a professional. They sent for Frederick Andre, an odd character intriguingly described by A.N. Palmer in his *Winchester 1900–1905*:

Always on the move, always with a grievance, always combining gloom and humour, and given to muttering devastating asides concerning even the most distinguished of our visitors, Andre was a typical Cockney. He was short and spare of figure; his face, with its scrubby dark moustache, expressed absolutely nothing but disillusionment and a determination not to be optimistic. His progress was a perpetual jog-trot. Even in the street he trotted, in the court he kept up a continuous shuttle, but always in the right direction, so that he rarely had to hurry, while as for running – I don't suppose he stretched his legs once a fortnight. If your ears were sharp enough to catch, if you had the key to his rapid, unending Cockney mumblings, he was an admirable teacher. But better still than his precept was his practice. He was a beautiful player with a model style, free and compact, graceful and devoid of flourish.

Longest serving of all the Winchester professionals was Guy Padwick, who was Jim Crosby's assistant from 1925 to 1939, and thereafter senior professional until 1975. He coached nine winning pairs during his fifty years, including all the hat-trick victors, three winners of the Public Schools singles in five post-war years, and the triumphant championship outsiders of 1953. That was when the unseeded partnership of Richard Whatmore and David Lowe beat the holders, Rugby, in the first round and Radley, with Dexter and Dipple, in the final.

The Nawab of Pataudi played in the finals of 1958, losing to the powerful Etonian pair of James Leonard and David Norman, and in 1959, when he and Christopher Snell beat Eton 4–3. And then, still in Padwick's time, along came Howard Angus. Though he won the Foster Cup in 1962, Angus was never in a championship-winning pair at Winchester, and indeed never dominated the world of Rackets as he did, for so many years, the world of Tennis. Angus won the Amateur Tennis singles in 1966, the year he left Cambridge, and won it for another fourteen consecutive years. In those fifteen finals, he conceded only six sets.

Alan Lovell took the title from him in 1981, but Angus regained it – for the last time – in 1982. Accompanied by Lovell and, for eight years, by Peter Seabrook, Angus led the Old Wykehamists to eleven successive Henry Leaf Cups from 1974. He had already had a major hand in four other Leaf wins while Lovell was still at school. Lovell and Seabrook, incidentally, won the Public Schools Rackets championship for Winchester in 1972, without conceding a single game. Meanwhile, at an even higher level of play, Angus held the British Open Tennis singles from 1970 to 1979, and was the world champion from 1976 until Chris Ronaldson beat him in 1981.

Various fates conspired to frustrate Angus in his attempt to emulate Peter Latham and become only

In 2005 Mike Bailey and Archie Fellowes reached the final of the Public Schools doubles.

the second player to hold the world championships of Rackets and Tennis at the same time. He was the Amateur singles champion of Rackets from 1972 to 1975, and won the British Open six times between 1971 and 1978. But though he played in four world championship finals against Willie Surtees, his only win was in 1973, before he held the Tennis title.

Peter Ashford succeeded Padwick in the role of head professional at the college in 1975. Ashford nursed the rise of an exceptional pair of players in Nick Hall and Matthew Segal, who won the Public Schools doubles in 1992, the Colts doubles in 1990, and the Junior Colts doubles in 1988. Hall beat Segal both for the Colts and Junior Colts singles titles. Between 1990 and 1999, Winchester reached the semi-finals of the doubles championship five times, a notable achievement. As well as Ashford's achievement with the boys, he also worked tirelessly in many ways behind the scenes, including administering the Public Schools championships and also by making most of the balls used within the game. Ashford held the position until 2002, when Tim Cawston took over after a former career in the BBC as a film editor.

The next highlight for Winchester Rackets took place in 2005 when the Prince's pair of Mike Bailey and Archie Fellowes reached the final of the Public Schools doubles. A truly golden period for Winchester was about to begin. In the 2005–06 season a powerful, fully engaged Christian Portz won the Under-15 singles and -15 doubles trophies being partnered by Ben Stevens. The following season Portz effortlessly added the Under-16 singles title. However, it was the following Easter of 2008 that history was made. Cawston took the brave decision of side-stepping an almost certain Colts doubles trophy by promoting Christian Portz to partner the older Sean Knight in the second-pair tournament. There they forged ahead and also managed to qualify for entry into the first-pair competition, where almost straight away they took out the number 3 seeds, Cheltenham. This put them up against Winchester's Prince's pair in the semi-final. This was a protracted affair with the two Portz brothers competing intensely against one another, with Tom Stevens being the strongest on court. Eventually, to the shock and surprise of the audience, the second pair won, the consequence of which was the challenge of having to tackle two finals the following morning.

The day started with disappointment, however, with Winchester's colts narrowly losing their final having had match points. Soon after came the second-pair final. Knight and Portz, perhaps tired from their recent ordeals, swiftly succumbed in the first two games. However, Knight recovered the situation with a string of untakeable serves, and ultimately the pair levelled and then won the title. Shortly afterwards they appeared on court once more and went head to head against a distinguished Harrow pair in the first-pair final. Still only in his third year at school, Portz seemed to have come of age and seemed fearless before the distinguished opposition. Knight, playing on the left, cleverly returned in a way to give an unusual amount of awkward exposure to the Harrow second string. The match swung back and forth between the two pairs. Eventually, before a packed, transfixed gallery, Knight and Portz managed to close the match out. They had become the first and only second pair to win the Public Schools doubles championship.

The following season also proved highly successful for Winchester, with Sean Knight managing to reach the final of the Foster Cup, having sustained a nasty facial injury in the semi-final which led to him needing several stitches to his nose. The match had to be suspended and was continued next day before the finals. Despite being one game down in the continuation of the semi-final match, Knight recovered to win, displaying considerable grit. The final took place a few hours later with Knight losing to Nick Hopcroft from Wellington. At Easter in the doubles competition, Christian Portz and Sean Knight successfully defended their first-pair title, with Winchester also winning the second-pair trophy.

In the following 2009–10 season, Winchester won the Under-15 singles with Henry Duxfield. Portz reached the final of the Foster Cup, coming up against defending champion Hopcroft. The two had experienced a close encounter the year before in the semi-final. This time Portz went on the attack from the start, serving with aggression and accuracy, ensuring he was never taken out for long. This approach bagged him the first two games in impressive manner, but Hopcroft began to fight back, winning game three. Portz stayed calm, however, repeating his initial strategy; this paid dividends in his closing out game four and the title. This was the first occasion in living memory that a competitor had beaten the holder of the Foster Cup. In the doubles, with the departure of Sean Knight from Winchester, Ben Stevens joined Portz, and they managed to defend the first-pair title for a third year running by winning a thrilling seven-game match, with Stevens serving out the concluding game. Winchester has now become the only school to have won the Public Schools doubles three times in a row, three times since the creation of the event in 1868.

Under the tutelage of Tim Cawston, Christian Portz's exceptional Rackets career at Winchester reads as follows. He won eight trophies: the Jim Dear Cup (Under-15 singles); the Peter Gray Cup (Under-15 doubles); the Incledon Webber Cup (Under-16 singles); the Foster Cup; The Palmer-Tomkinson Cup (second pairs) and the Public Schools doubles three times. Since leaving he has partnered Alex Titchener-Barrett to win the British Open doubles in 2014. Together they have won a world doubles title challenge to be played in spring 2015.

In recent years there has been some trophy success at Winchester, with Henry Duxfield capturing the Under-16 singles title. A large body of boys play the

In 2008 history was made when Christian Portz and Sean Knight became the first and only second pair to win the Public Schools doubles championship.

In 2012 Henry Duxfield captured the U16 Public Schools singles title.

In 2013 B.Cawston (right) *won the U15 championship for Westgate School near Winchester against A.Engstrom* (left) *from St Paul's.*

game, with the keenest managing to come to the courts most days.

In 2013 Cawston's son Ben succeeded in winning the Under-15 singles trophy for Westgate School, located in Winchester, and hopes to compete in future school doubles events.

There are two out-of-school evening clubs at Winchester, which have been operating with considerable success for over forty years. The Wykeham Rackets Club was formed in 1971 to encourage Old Wykehamists and others in the locality to play the game. They met on a Wednesday; in 1974 the Monday Club grew from them, the first real town – rather than Old Boys' – club to be so formed. Numbers are buoyant and the regular membership has been consistent and long-lasting.

Part IV

Further Information

BUCKHURST PARK (Above left) *Built in 1857, it is one of very few mid 19th century courts to have survived and is one of the earliest enclosed courts in existence. It is also the last remaining privately owned Rackets court in England.* (Above right) *The last time that the court was played on was in the 1960s when Clarence Clarry Pell played against Cosmo Crawley. The inside walls and floor, rather remarkably, remain in a very playable state. The family are currently exploring ways of raising sufficient funds to restore the Court to its former glory in the hope that Rackets can once again be played at Buckhurst.*

DARTMOUTH, BRITANNIA ROYAL NAVAL COLLEGE (Left) The player who asked for a let at match point, *commissioned by Richard Greenwood and painted by H. M. Bateman after a visit to Dartmouth in 1964.* (Above) *The courts were built about 1880 but fell into disuse after 1969. James Ford & Luke Danby are keen to promote Dartmouth Rackets. The building is structurally in good shape but in need of some repair work.*

COURTS BEING CREATED OR REVIVED

BUCKHURST PARK

The Rackets court at Buckhurst Park, with its richly coloured red floor, enjoys the distinction of being the last remaining privately owned Rackets court in England. It is one of very few mid-nineteenth century courts to have survived and is one of the earliest enclosed courts in existence. Built in 1857 by doting parents to commemorate the safe return of their eldest surviving son from the Crimean War's Siege of Sevastopol (1854–55), it reveals a fascinating history and insight into the Sackville family and the nineteenth-century game of Rackets.

The court was built for Major-General Charles Richard Sackville-West, who was later to become the sixth Earl De La Warr. Charles had been educated at Harrow School in the 1820s, where he had presumably developed a passion for the sport, as this was the time when Harrow became the first public school to take up the game of Rackets. Up until Charles's arrival at Harrow, there had been no particular tradition of racquet sports in the Sackville family. Indeed, if they can claim a contribution to the ranks of British sporting history, then it is through Charles's forebears, the second and third Dukes of Dorset, who were notable for their patronage of early English cricket: Charles Sackville, second Duke of Dorset, and his younger brother, Lord John Sackville, were at the first cricket match played at the famous Vine Cricket Ground in Sevenoaks, where for the first time cricket was played with three stumps rather than two. John Frederick Sackville, third Duke of Dorset, was a founder member of the Marylebone Cricket Club (MCC) and when, during his ambassadorship in France, he invited a team of English cricketers to lead a tour in 1789, they were met at Dover by the duke himself coming the other way – he was fleeing for his life from the French Revolution. So the intended first-ever overseas cricket tour became instead the first tour to be cancelled for political reasons!

The fourth Duke died aged twenty-one in a hunting accident in Ireland in 1815. The dukedom passed briefly to a distant cousin and subsequently died out, so that the extensive Sackville lands and estates passed to the fourth Duke's sister, Lady Elizabeth Sackville. Lady Elizabeth, the great Sackville heiress, had married the fifth Earl De La Warr, whose ancestor had given his name to the US State of Delaware. The run of bad luck followed in the family as Lord and Lady De La Warr's eldest son, George John Frederick, Viscount Cantelupe, died unmarried aged thirty-six in 1850. When, therefore, their second son and new heir, Charles, left to fight in the Crimea, the relief that his parents felt at his safe return resulted in the commission of an impressive new Rackets court in a perfect location, metres from the main house and the formal gardens. A brass plate in the gallery commemorates the return from Sevastopol of Colonel Lord West (interestingly, Charles did not take his late brother's title of Viscount Cantelupe – presumably thinking it to be unlucky – but instead styled himself as Lord West, referring back to an ancient De La Warr barony which has since ceased to exist). Luck was not to follow him, however, as the Rackets player, Charles, who never married, ended up drowning himself in the River Cam in 1863.

Unusually then, it was Lord and Lady De La Warr's third son, Reginald, who succeeded as seventh Earl in 1863. There is little record of Reginald – who until his succession to the earldom had been a vicar – ever having played Rackets in the Buckhurst court. There are, however, well-preserved records of the court being put to other uses. First in December 1863, when the new seventh Earl and his Countess arrived at Buckhurst, the *Tunbridge Wells Courier* describes lavish celebrations held in the court with '300 sat down to a bountiful repast of roast beef and plum pudding' and, a few days later, 'a Christmas Tree, lit up and of gigantic proportions with 577 children of estate staff and tenants filing past'. Later, in 1889, at the coming-of-age party of Lord and Lady De La Warr's eldest son, Lionel Charles Cranfield, who this time did style himself Viscount Cantelupe, a week of celebrations was held at Buckhurst with the Rackets court used again to stage a presentation ceremony from the estate tenants to Lord Cantelupe, and then, later in the week, for all the birthday presents to be laid out on tables for visitors to file past and view.

With a young family living at Buckhurst once again, it is likely that the court was played on frequently; it is unfortunate that, although there is still a copy of the visitors' book in the court, players stopped entering their names in the 1870s. We do know, however, that at around the turn of the century, Joseph Bickley re-faced the walls, and they remain in good condition today.

The run of bad luck continued in the family. Only a few months after his coming-of-age celebrations and subsequent marriage, the young Viscount Cantelupe drowned in his yacht during a storm off the coast of Belfast. So it was his younger brother, Gilbert, who eventually became the eighth Earl, but he too died at sea, in 1915, on his way back from fighting at Gallipoli. The Cantelupe title has not been used by an eldest son since, with three of the last four holders of the title having died on water.

Following the untimely death of the eighth Earl, Buckhurst was leased to a rich banking family called the Bensons (the family bank later became Kleinwort Benson). Although they made considerable improvements to the main house and gardens, there is little record of what happened to the Rackets court during their tenure in the first half of the twentieth century. We do know that during the Second World War, Buckhurst was requisitioned by the Canadian Army, who used the court to store tanks; in order to get them in and out they carved a large hole in one of the side walls, which was subsequently repaired. The last time that the court was played on was in the 1960s, when Clarence 'Clarry' Pell played against Cosmo Crawley. More recently, William Buckhurst used it when a boy to play games of indoor 'stump' with his younger brother!

Since then, the court has fallen into a state of disuse, with much of the original wooden staircase and viewing gallery rotted and no glass left in the roof. The court lights are no longer in place. However, the exterior walls are still in very good condition and the inside walls and floor, rather remarkably, remain in a very playable state. The family are currently exploring ways of raising sufficient funds to restore the court to its former glory in the hope that Rackets can once again be played at Buckhurst.

Charleston, South Carolina

The first traditional Real Tennis court to be built in the USA for almost 100 years will be created in South Carolina, after Court Tennis Charleston, chaired by Greg Van Schaack, secured an agreement with the Daniel Island Club.

The Daniel Island Club will donate the land required to build the court, as well as manage the court's running and meet its costs. The total costs of the construction have been estimated at $2.3 million and the court has been designed by leading local architect Eddie Fava.

Most importantly, a 99-year deed restriction has been agreed upon, which ensures its continued usage for only Real Tennis in the foreseeable future.

The new court is expected to function as a sister club to Aiken, which is two hours to the west by car, and would become only the second court south of the Mason-Dixon Line. It will attempt to further spread the popularity of the sport in the area by funnelling members across from Charleston's thriving squash club, whilst recruiting new players from the College of Charleston and The Citadel. Ben Cook, one of the Club's lawn tennis pros, is also a 12 handicap Real Tennis player at Aiken Tennis Club.

The Daniel Island Club currently has fifteen lawn tennis courts, two golf courses and many other facilities, only 12–15 minutes from downtown Charleston. A special membership will be available for Real Tennis only at a reasonable price. The island itself is a beautiful twenty-year-old gated community, having previously been a plantation belonging to the Guggenheim family.

Dartmouth, Britannia Royal Naval College

The two Rackets courts at Dartmouth are believed to have been built about 1880 to serve the training ship *Britannia* before the college was built. During the Second World War, one of the courts was converted for use by the Admiralty Interview Board and Rackets declined. Rackets was revived in the mid-1950s, and Bob Mulliken was appointed professional in 1957. After Bob left for Wellington in 1969, interest waned, and the courts fell into disuse. However, James Ford is keen to promote Rackets at Dartmouth, particularly with juniors. Luke Danby (son of Nick and nephew of Paul), lives a couple of miles away and is also enthusiastic. James, Howard Angus and Walter Thorpe inspected the courts in January 2012 and, bearing in mind that the building has been disused for so long, found that it is structurally in good shape but in need of some repair work.

Dublin, St Stephen's Green

Design and construction
In 1884/5, Sir Edward Cecil Guinness (later first Baron and Earl of Iveagh) of the famous brewing dynasty constructed a court at his St Stephen's Green city residence to designs supplied by Lord Wimborne of his court at Canford, Dorset. The two courts bear a remarkable internal resemblance, except that the Dublin court has a somewhat lower rafter height. However, Sir Edward chose to panel the entire court interior in black limestone sourced from Co. Galway in the west of Ireland, which was polished to a gloss marble finish by builders Sibthorpes under the supervision of brewery architect William Wilson. This finish was an Achilles heel in the design and was soon afterwards sanded back to a natural matt surface for more predictable ball behaviour! The hazard wall of the court, externally finished in bright orange brickwork, backs onto the pavement at Earlsfort Terrace. The court floor is three feet below pavement level. Recent research appears to confirm that a timber-panelled room at the service end was created as a billiard room, a further complement to the impressive range of sports facilities in the gardens adjoining the house, which included sunken Archery Grounds that could be flooded in winter to form an ice rink. The whole complex was overlooked by a folly lighthouse and Grecian statuary, all of which still survive as the publicly accessible Iveagh Gardens.

World championship, 1890
The court was chosen as a neutral venue for the match between Pettitt and Saunders held in the last week of May 1890. Pettit won by 7 sets to 5, thus retaining his title. Professional Frank Jewell, formerly of Prince's, London, served as Lord Iveagh's professional.

Bequest

The second Earl of Iveagh, Rupert Cecil Guinness, chairman of the brewery, decided to bequeath the house, gardens and Tennis court at St Stephen's Green to the Irish state in 1939, with the immortal words: 'I am of course loath to think of the tennis court being destroyed as I think it is unique in its way and might be appreciated by players in Dublin.' He must have had some foreboding following much procrastination as to the use of the site to expand the adjacent University College Dublin (UCD), but did not make continued use a binding part of the transfer. Three players at the court – Robert McNeile (brewery manager), Raymond Egan (Davis Cup player) and Sir Basil Goulding (industrialist) – formed the Irish Tennis Club and offered to keep up the court for play, inviting the Irish Prime Minister to see a promotional match at the court. The invitation was not taken up and the court's fate was sealed. The penthouses and limestone walls were demolished.

The court was initially pressed into use as wartime storage for important government printing/stamping equipment, after which it functioned until 1970 as a gymnasium for adjacent UCD. Gross interventions were made at this time, involving the creation of offices on two levels at the hazard end; greater damage was prevented by the advice of private consulting engineer Ian Roberts, which protected the limestone floor.

1998: The concert hall cometh/planning battles

In the late 1980s, following a nocturnal visit to the court, Ted Neville and Mike Bolton joined forces to lobby government for reinstatement of the court. There was little reception for this suggestion, until one day in March 1998 a notice appeared on the gable wall announcing plans to construct a music recital hall in the court. The necessary planning process involved would mean that the Real Tennis community now *had* to be heard – and was. Supportive submissions were received from all the national governing bodies around the world, that from the Comité Français being particularly noted by the media, who now gave regular coverage to the cause. This planning application was the catalyst for the formation of The Irish Real Tennis Association (IRTA) in October 1998, and since then its chief activity has been the pursuit of the return of the court to its original use.

In 1999 quite a stir was created when The Earl of Wessex asked permission to see the court on a planned visit to Dublin – alas the court visit wasn't approved. The first Tennis ball struck in the court since 1939 was played against the tambour during a filming by the Irish-language national TV station in 1999, which was shown in a half-hour special with interviews, supplemented with footage provided by Argent Films. The increased media interest led to the court receiving 'protected building' status for the first time as a Real Tennis court, a designation always denied it by government planners. The IRTA lost the local Dublin planning appeal, but pressed on and received a rarely awarded oral hearing at the highest planning appeal stage in spring 1999. This was also lost, the inspector's hands tied by the IRTA's 'non-status' in the face of government ownership.

Now facing rapidly dwindling time, the IRTA made an appeal to the Irish High Court with the great commitment of a leading conservation barrister (now a High Court judge). Two parliamentarians of the highest calibre lent their invaluable support and, following the intervention of the hitherto little-known Commissioners for Bequests in defence of the terms of the bequest, one of the IRTA's parliamentary friends, who had just assumed a key government role, was in a position to tell the Office of Public Works (OPW) to desist from any further works in pursuance of their planning permission until the matter had been resolved. The court was saved!

DUBLIN, St STEPHEN'S GREEN (Left) *At the Guinness (Iveagh) Court, Earlsfort Terrace (St Stephen's Green) Dublin, in the last week of May 1890, Pettitt (Boston) retains his title against Saunders (London). Sir Edward Guiness congratulates the winner. Among his personal guests is Lord Wimborne of Dorset on whose court the Dublin court is modelled. (sourced by Mr Brian Rich from 'The Graphic' magazine)* (Above) *The Guinness family built the court in 1884/85 based on the design of Canford. The IRTA has succeeded in saving it and has made proposals to restore the court at its own expense.*

Since then UCD has completely vacated the court, which has been gutted, apart from the office area. The open floor space has recently been used as a temporary display area for an Arts Exhibition.

A previous developer-driven plan to restore the court, which would be glass-cased in an enormous multi-storey office development, failed in 2009. This would have obliterated the distinctive annexe area of the court and involved greatly curtailed playing access and conditions. The Irish property crash was a blessing!

Most recently, the IRTA has made proposals to the OPW to restore the court at its own expense in return for a lifetime gratis lease.

HOLLAND

The Huis ter Kleef *kaatsbaan* (Dutch for Real Tennis court) in the city of Haarlem is, among covered courts, one of the oldest in the world, but to this day it has been used by the city primarily as a canteen. The club is centrally located and within easy reach of Haarlem's railway station as well as the major motorways and Schiphol Airport.

The court, complete with a proud little tower, was built around 1560 by Hendrik van Brederode next to his castle, and play regularly took place there in the first seventy years or so of its creation. At that time Hendrik was a close friend and ally of William of Orange and consequently took part in the rebellion against the Spanish in the turbulent year 1566. After Don Federico's siege of Haarlem in 1573, the castle was largely destroyed, but Hendrik's *kaatsbaan* was fortunately spared, not as a result of Federico's love of the game, but for the purpose of being used as a prison. Indeed, stories of the deaths of many prisoners on the actual Tennis court have been passed down through many generations. According to historical sources, Federico promised to spare the prisoners' lives but not their food. The last games on the Huis ter Kleef Tennis court took place around 1630, and then interest in playing there withered away and the space was gradually used more and more for public services.

In the late twentieth century, a collection of individuals, including the current Huis ter Kleef president Patrick Reuser, expressed desire to stimulate Real Tennis play in Holland once again. In December 2005 the mayor and aldermen of Haarlem approved the proposal to restore the decayed court. In autumn 2010 negotiations finally started and prices were discussed. The club is currently coordinated by Reuser, Niek Van Wijk, Arnoud Bernelot Moens, Toon Schipper, Frank van der Weijden and Steven Chapman, and although they originally hoped to pay just €1 for the monument, dire need of money caused the city to demand approximately €250,000. The club generously agreed. Just before the end of 2011, an agreement giving the club the right to acquire ownership of the court was made on the condition that the club organised and secured finance for the court's restoration by March 2013. The club has already established a tax-exempt charitable foundation, Stichting Huis ter Kleef,

HOLLAND *Built around 1560, it is one of the oldest covered courts in the world. The city of Haarlem is willing to sell it conditional on securing finance for restoration.*

which will own the court, and is currently pursuing various fundraising schemes and submitting financing requests to both public and private institutional funds that focus on restoring historic buildings.

After fundraising efforts across the Real Tennis world, around seventy-five members of the Dutch Real Tennis Association made membership deposits and donations for the restoration of the court. Their support has been a driving force behind the idea and the wealthy areas of Haarlem and Amsterdam offer further potential for recruiting new members. The aim is to generate a total of €1,450,000. For two years the Stichting has also been working in partnership with Stadsherstel Amsterdam, a National Trust-type organisation which is very interested in this unique project. The restoration of this registered national monument will be a major project, owing to the fact that the work needs to be done with a great degree of authenticity, following mid-sixteenth-century architectural practice. The original walls of the *kaatsbaan* still exist, but the interior structure requires substantial architectural changes. Such changes aim to ameliorate the dilapidated state of the roof and install upper windows as well as the various features of a Real Tennis court, including a flagstone floor and lighting. Plans include creating a bar/lounge, meeting room, changing facilities and a Real Tennis museum. The exhibits will guide the visitor through 500 years of Tennis history, starting with a game on the *kaatsbaan*, of which Holland had at least 150 in the seventeenth and eighteenth centuries.

JERSEY

The Association Jersiaise de Jeu du Court Paume et Rackets (Jersey Real Tennis and Rackets Association) hopes to build two Real Tennis courts, as well as one Rackets court, as part of a programme of development at the University of Jersey, which opened in 2014 initially as the Jersey International Centre of Advanced Studies.

The project was initiated and is led by John Lawton and Sir Nigel Broomfield, who are supported by a lively and committed working party, including most of the very successful Jersey Island cricket team.

Before commencing fundraising, the association first needs to finalise a location and obtain any necessary government consents. Jersey's Minister for Economic Development has already given the project his enthusiastic support.

Lambay

The Tennis court at Lambay, Co. Dublin, was built in 1921–22 for the Hon. Cecil Baring and his wife Maude Lorillard to designs by Sir Edwin Lutyens, who had previously remodelled and enlarged the island's sixteenth-century castle for the same clients.

The Lambay court, one of only two open-air courts in the world, sits above the west-facing beach adjacent to the island's harbour. During winter storms the sea breaks against and through the edifice. After seventy-five such winters, the court was declared unfit for use as the reinforced concrete and cement uprights and penthouses were cracked, crumbling and in danger of collapse. In 2005 the Barings' granddaughter Margaret Kelly and her husband, Patrick Kelly, had the edifice stabilised and repaired, in such a fashion that the penthouses and galleries could be reinstated in future. In 2012, members of the fourth generation of the family took over care of the island and began looking at plans to carry out a full restoration of the court, building new penthouses and laying a floor, with a view to making the court available to members of the Irish Real Tennis Association and clubs and players from all over the world.

Cecil Baring (later the third Lord Revelstoke), owner of Lambay from 1904 until his death in 1934, was one of the leading amateur Tennis players of his day. He was educated at Eton College and Oxford University and seems to have taken up the game in early adolescence. His father, Edward Baring, first Lord Revelstoke, built a Stické court in the early 1880s, when Cecil was sixteen or seventeen, on the family's Devonshire estate at Membland, near Plymouth.

For the rest of his life, Cecil Baring kept up his Tennis, either in London, where he had a court at Lord's every Saturday towards the end of his life and was president of Hampton Court, or in New York where he worked for the family bank, Baring Brothers, from the late 1880s until 1902. In August of that year, the *New York Times* described him as 'a prominent member of the Racquet Club' and 'a very good tennis player who excels in all outdoor sports'.

In 1899, with his business partner, Thomas Suffern Tailer, Baring was one of the main founders of a new Tennis club at Tuxedo Park, near New York City. The first game on the court at Tuxedo was played between Cecil Baring and Tommy Tailer on 31 December 1899. This match acquired an added symbolism when Tailer's wife, Maude Lorillard (daughter of the owner and founder of Tuxedo Park, Pierre Lorillard IV), divorced Tailer in 1902, and later in the same year was married to Baring in London.

In November 1903, Cecil and Maude Baring saw an advertisement in *The Field* magazine for the sale of Lambay, a small island north of Dublin, and completed the purchase the following April. The first phase of Lutyens's work at

LAMBAY (Above left) *Cecil Baring (later third Lord Revelstoke), who acquired Lambay in 1904, was one of the leading amateur Tennis players of his day.* (Above right) *Designed by Lutyens and built in 1921/22 for the Baring family, it is one of only two open air courts in the world. Members of the fourth generation of the family are looking at plans to restore the court.*

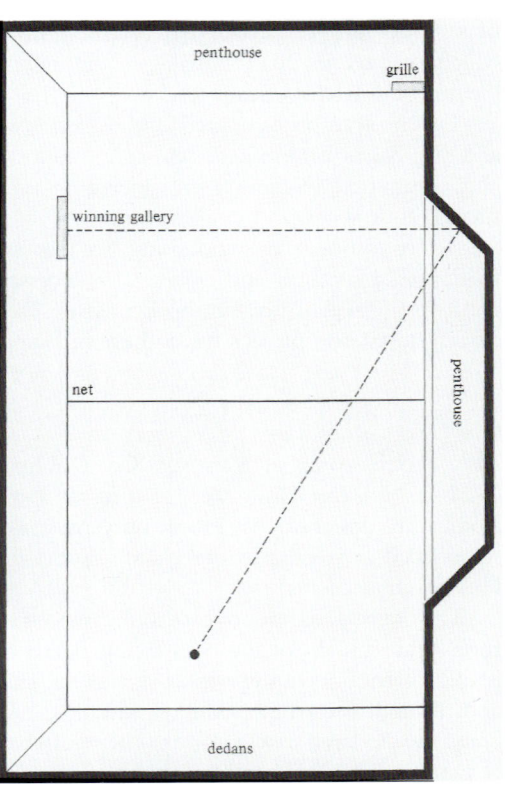

LAMBAY (Above) *The main wall has a penthouse running two thirds of the centre of its length, with angled walls at either end of the penthouse, providing, as it were,* super tambours. *The tambour itself is vestigial, rising no higher than the base of the grille, with an angled top along which one can run the ball up to it.* (Right) *One particularly interesting shot, from about Chase 3 in the middle of the court, strikes the main wall above the penthouse (on the super tambour at the hazard end) and enters the winning gallery.*

Lambay was the remodelling and enlarging of the castle between 1908 and 1910, a scheme which many scholars consider to be Lutyens's masterpiece in romantic domestic architecture. The Tennis court forms part of Lutyens's final phase of work at Lambay, the creation of a carefully articulated sea front.

From the start, the Lambay court was unusual. It was open air. It had no conventional main wall, but a wall – part masonry, part mesh – held in tension and a part gallery (matching the openings in the service wall opposite). The tambour was always vestigial, rising no higher than the base of the grille, with an angled top along which one can run the ball up to it. The walls as first built were no more than 15 feet tall, topped with an extra yard of mesh on the dedans service and hazard ends to stop the balls running out of court. The mesh main wall was presumably conceived to allow the prevailing wind to blow through the court. Plainly this low-profile arrangement proved unsatisfactory and, by 1926, when *Country Life* photographed Lambay for a second time, the main wall had been replaced with the striking angled, galleried main wall that we see today, with a penthouse running two thirds of the centre of its length, with angled walls at either end of the penthouse, providing, as it were, 'super tambours'. At the same time the walls were raised by three feet and iron uprights added on top to carry a further yard of netting to keep errant balls from escaping onto the beach and into the sea.

The final version of the main façade holds a fascinating quasi-modernist place in Lutyens's oeuvre. The court sits proud on a rubble bastion with massive angled surfaces. The angles of the main wall gallery recall the fortress severity of Lutyens's towering, chamfered windows at Castle Drogo, Devon (1910–30), while the overall design – whitewashed walls with quasi-military slit-openings onto the seafront – link it to the tenets of the international style (whiteness, less-is-more simplicity of detail), which were encoded by Mies van der Rohe and his cohorts at the Deutscher Werkbund estate built at Stuttgart in 1927. And there is no denying that form follows function at Lambay, as the angled walls serve to dissipate sideways the force of the storms that break against the façade in winter.

The want of a traditional main wall at Lambay means that the floor game is at a premium. (This chimed with Cecil Baring's own taste as a player: he honoured the floor game rather than the power game.) Forcing off the main wall into the dedans is far harder to do than on a conventional court, and possible only from roughly hazard the second gallery. One particularly interesting shot, from about Chase 3 in the middle of the court, strikes the main wall above the penthouse (on the 'super tambour' at the hazard end) and enters the winning gallery.

In the 1920s and 1930s, Lambay was host to most of the leading British pros of the day. They included Jack Groom, Arthur Twinn, Bill Cass and Henry Johns. Johns remembered in the 1990s that he often went to Lambay for a summer holiday, when still fifteen or sixteen, in order to give Cecil Baring his daily game. When he and his friend and contemporary Rupert Baring went swimming on the beach below the court, Rupert's sisters were not above hiding their clothes so that Rupert and Henry had to run naked up to the castle. In the 1990s, Johns taught Cecil Baring's great-grandson Louis Jebb to play the game, at Queen's Club.

Cecil Baring succeeded his brother John as third Lord Revelstoke in 1929 and died in January 1934. His son Rupert, and Rupert's wife, Flora Fermor-Hesketh (whose father, the first Lord Hesketh, had a Stické court at Easton Neston), took over care of the island, dividing their time between Lambay and London. Rupert succeeded his father as president of Hampton Court, and played regularly at Prince's Club up to and including the Second World War.

In 1992–94, Louis Jebb returned the court to use. This revival culminated in 1994 with a weekend visit from three Queen's Club pros – David Johnson, Peter Brake and Hugh Latham. The pros were fascinated by the special qualities of the court: the bite of the ball on the coarse cement floor and penthouses; the premium on the floor game; the high-lob service return to the dedans (a defensive shot made possible by the absence of a roof); and the new range of shots encouraged by the main wall penthouse and the vestigial tambour (which allows the ball to be rifled along the top of the waist-high tambour, past the receiving pair and on to the grille).

Rupert Revelstoke watched the pros in action in 1994 and recalled the legendary Peter Latham's advice: 'Never slice but, with lowering shoulder and bended knees, stroke the ball with power as if you were paring the peel off an orange.'

Sydney

The earliest record of Real Tennis courts in Sydney dates back to the 1820s, during the early days of European settlement. In 1836 a publican and Tennis player, Laurence Delaney, appeared in court to answer charges of 'placing the lives of the public in jeopardy' after a 30-foot-tall section of the wall of the Tennis court at the rear of his pub fell into Clarence Street, killing a passer-by and severely injuring two or three others.

More recently a court was built at Macquarie University in October 1997.

The financial involvement of former world champion Wayne Davies and his family was a catalyst in finding the necessary funds – more was needed after the opening when it was found necessary to rebuild both the floor and the main wall.

As part of the opening celebrations, Australia challenged Britain to compete for the Vice-Chancellor's Trophy. There was a narrow win for the home side (Robert Fahey, Frank Filippelli, Graham Hyland and Wayne Davies) against Julian Snow, James Male, Mike Gooding and Nick Wood. The following year the club hosted the Australian Open singles, in which Fahey beat Filippelli in the final.

Credit for motivating and nurturing the plans to build this court went to Robert Lawton, the executive officer at the university. With no experience of the game, he was inspired by what he saw at Melbourne and Hobart, and worked hard to obtain university approval for the complex.

In 2005 the Macquarie University Sports Association decided to use the premises for other sporting amenities. It did offer to provide the Tennis-playing community with their own piece of land within the grounds for a new court to be built. However, this offer was allowed to lapse when the membership decided to go after an alternative location at White City which turned out to be illusory.

Since then, a new club was incorporated in April 2011, and members of the committee have embarked on an extensive search for an ideal location for a replacement court. Many different sites have been identified and approached, and at the time of writing this book, there are a number of excellent prospects being pursued. In the meantime, the Sydney Real Tennis Club remains a club with no court and its annual programme of inter-club matches (against Melbourne, Hobart, Ballarat and the Melbourne Cricket Club) are all played away from home.

Wellington

Wellington College's landmark project to build what will be the second Real Tennis court constructed in the twenty-first century is being supported by influential players, both past and present, and chaired by James Mallinson. The reigning Real Tennis world champions, Rob Fahey and Claire Vigrass, are honorary ambassadors of the project alongside Chris Ronaldson, world champion 1981–87. Nick Jones and Peter Luck-Hille are providing their knowledge and experience of building courts to ensure that all the latest wisdom in court construction is being used.

HRH The Earl of Wessex is president of the fundraising appeal, dedicated to generating the estimated £1.1 million overall project costs required.

The new court will be situated adjacent to the existing squash and Rackets court complex and be part of the sports club, which currently has some 800 members playing squash, Rackets, lawn tennis, badminton and participating in other fitness activities. With the addition of Real Tennis, the club will be one of only two in the country able to offer all five racquet sports.

In particular, the hope is to encourage a base of schoolboy and -girl players from the college and neighbouring schools, as part of a wider aim to bring new generations to the sport. Wellington follows in the footsteps of Canford, The Oratory and, most recently, Radley, in becoming the fourth UK school to offer a Real Tennis facility.

The project is moving forward positively, expecting to break ground either in late 2014 or early 2015. The intention is for the grand opening to occur and play to commence before the end of 2015, the 200th anniversary of the Battle of Waterloo.

DISUSED COURTS

This list of disused courts is intended to be comprehensive for courts outside Continental Europe and the Indian subcontinent. Courts are only included where four walls are still intact or there is some chance of conversion. Versailles and Cawnpore have been added for interest purposes.

BALDERSBY PARK, THIRSK

Baldersby Park is now the home of Queen Mary's School. The Rackets court is used as a gym and also for lawn tennis, ballet, fencing and other sports.

BATH, MORFORD STREET

In 1777 Richard Scrace built the Real Tennis court at Morford Street with the active support of the Earl of Pembroke. It was a battle to keep the court financially viable, but it did remain active for about thirty-six years, going through various owners and a series of professionals, including Monsieur Hulet, Eleazer Hathway and John Maddick. The building is made of Bath stone and the original flagged floor survives to this day. It is now an industrial museum, with the tambour and the markings of three chases still visible. In 1972 Bill Stephens overheard Paul Danby saying to Howard Angus in the bar at Queen's, 'What a pity it is that the Bath Court

BALDERSBY PARK, THIRSK

MORFORD STREET, BATH (Above and right) *The tambour is still visible.*

is going to be demolished next week.' Bill, who was heavily involved with politics at the time, was briefed by Howard and managed to raise the matter the following evening with Geoffrey Rippon, the Environment Minister, who promised to list the building first thing in the morning, which he duly did. Because the listing was of the lowest grade, preventing demolition, Bath Council were able to seek other uses for the building. At Bill's behest Morys Aberdare then requested Geoffrey Rippon to raise the listing to a higher level, so that it could only be used for its original purpose. Before he got round to taking the decision, he lost his job as a result of the 1974 election.

Belmont House

In the late nineteenth century Antony Gibbs, grandfather of Lord Wraxall and a keen Rackets player while at Exeter College Oxford, gutted the centre block at Belmont House (near Bristol) to provide a Rackets court. Also the library was converted to a boiler house and changing rooms. A complete glass roof was built over the court to give maximum light. In 1920 a squash court was built across the middle of the Rackets court, rooms were rebuilt on the ground and first floors and a garage was constructed. The 1920 alterations have since been largely removed. The house is now owned by Mr and Mrs Bill Rossiter.

Brougham Hall

In 1852 W. Brougham (the future second Lord Brougham) built a Tennis court, thought to be modelled on the Paris court of Passage Sandrie, at Eamont Bridge near Penrith, Cumbria. It was located behind The Crown Hotel, which the Broughams owned along with much of the village of Eamont Bridge. Records show that the Prince of Wales paid a number of visits to Brougham from 1857 to 1905, and it is likely that he or his companions played Tennis there. Membership contained a fair share of those connected with the church and the military, such as the Earl of Lonsdale, the Lord Bishop of Carlisle, and many of the elite of Penrith and nearby villages. The club was very private, and all those desirous of joining the exclusive group had to be vetted personally by W. Brougham. In the 1930s the Brougham estates went bankrupt due to the profligacy of the fourth Lord Brougham. In 1985 Christopher Terry began a remarkable restoration project at Brougham Hall. The Tennis court space is currently occupied partly by housing, partly by a children's play area.

BROUGHAM HALL

BELMONT HOUSE (Above and right) *A complete glass roof was built over the court to give maximum light.*

BUENOS AIRES

BUENOS AIRES

BUENOS AIRES

The Rackets court is still standing at the Hurlingham Club. It was built by polo players and in use until about 1930.

CARDIFF RACQUET AND FIVES COURT COMPANY

The Rackets court was built in Westgate Street, adjoining Cardiff Arms Park, for £2,300 in 1878. The premises, known as Jackson's Hall, were later used as offices.

CHICAGO ATHLETIC ASSOCIATION

The Chicago Athletic Association, founded in 1890, erected an eleven-storey clubhouse on South Michigan Avenue in September 1893, in time for the 1893 World's Fair. Henry Ives Cobb designed the building with bowling alleys, swimming

CARDIFF RACQUET AND FIVES COURT COMPANY

CHICAGO ATHLETIC ASSOCIATION

pools, billiards rooms and, on the ninth floor, reached by an elevator, two fives courts, two Rackets courts and, in the rear of the building, a Real Tennis court. Under the skylights on the ninth floor of a city building without air conditioning or electric fans, it grew hot on summer days; at the same time play was often impossible during winter, with very little light making its way to the court. In 1901, eight years after its opening, the Chicago Athletic Association closed its Real Tennis court. The floor became bowling alleys and, eventually, the Real Tennis space became squash courts. One of the Rackets courts became a squash doubles court. The second Rackets court survived until 1931, when it and the squash doubles court were converted into three squash courts and one handball court. In 2010 the building, having been used as a hotel and health club, officially closed. It now sits empty. There are currently plans to convert it into a luxury hotel.

University Club of Chicago

When the club moved in 1909 to its current location at East Monroe Street, it was to a building that contained two Rackets courts. Professionals were engaged throughout the club's history, but in 1984 a fitness centre was created and in 1994 four squash courts were built. So both Rackets courts have ceased to exist, although the outlines of one can still be seen in the fitness centre.

In 1909 Harold F. McCormick, a member of the club, won the US Amateur singles, and in 1913 donated a court under the football stands to the university. It was used by scientists in the Second World War to house an atomic reactor and, incorrectly, came to be known as the 'Atomic Squash Court; on 2 December 1942 the first self-sustaining nuclear reaction occurred there. It was demolished in the 1950s.

CLEVELAND TAVERN CLUB

Cleveland Tavern Club

The club was founded in 1892. The current clubhouse was designed by the architect J. Milton Dyer in 1905. The former Rackets court has been converted to a doubles squash court.

Coombe Abbey

In 1817 the Earl of Craven built a Real Tennis court at Coombe Abbey, a magnificent building whose origins trace back to a twelfth-century Cistercian Abbey. Although the abbey has been converted into a hotel and conference centre, the exterior of the court, known as The Courthouse, remains unchanged. The interior has been converted to complement the other facilities on the property and serves as a reception centre for weddings and other events. Early prints of Tennis

UNIVERSITY CLUB OF CHICAGO

COOMBE ABBEY

375

COOMBE ABBEY

the edge of Epping Forest around 1920 so it was quite likely that he used the 'cherry-bob' at Copped Hall. There was at that time a game called Bat fives, which was played at many schools using a solid wooden bat and a small Rackets ball. So it may be that the 'cherry-bob' was actually a Bat fives ball and used at Copped Hall in view of its smaller dimensions.

The property was bought by the Copped Hall Trust in 1995, which saved it from the clutches of developers and is restoring it for educational and community benefit. The Rackets court is currently a tea room, but the Trust might consider using it for its original purpose if there was enough interest.

Crabbet Park

The Real Tennis court at Crabbet Park was built by Joseph Bickley in 1907, on property belonging to the Blunt and

scenes hang on the walls within The Courthouse to remind visitors of the building's original use.

Copped Hall, Epping

Copped Hall has the only known Miniature Rackets court in existence, measuring about 40ft by 23ft. It was built in 1905 by Ernest Wythes and continued to be played in until some time between the two world wars. The walls are almost identical to the Seacourt walls so suggest more Bickley magic.

Fortuitously, when the T&RA learnt about this court in 1984, it was also given a half-size Rackets ball. This was half the weight of the then standard leather-bound ball, but was seemingly identical in construction. The ball emanated from H.W. Leatham, twice Amateur champion and six times Amateur doubles champion, who called it a 'cherry-bob'. According to Aubrey Leatham, H.W.'s son, he was living on

CRABBET PARK

COPPED HALL, EPPING

COPPED HALL, EPPING

Disused Courts

CURRAGH ARMY CAMP, COUNTY KILDARE

Curragh Army Camp, County Kildare

A Rackets court was built at Curragh Army Camp in 1855–56 when it was a British Army base. Rackets continued there until 1933. Some time later it was converted into three squash courts. It is one of the earliest enclosed courts in existence.

Eastbourne Rackets

In 1870 a Rackets court was built as part of the recreational area known as Devonshire Park. The area also comprised two swimming pools, one for men and one for women, lawn tennis courts, Turkish baths, athletic facilities and, later, squash courts. Although no longer in use, the Rackets court still stands in Eastbourne at the Winter Gardens. Its walls are intact, but the glass roof has been partly replaced with corrugated iron. Partly walled in, the former court is currently used for storage by Eastbourne Theatres. Its past is easily remembered, though, as the words 'Racquet Court' are inscribed above the entrance.

Lytton family, located near Crawley in Sussex. The court, the exterior of which is roughly unchanged since 1907, can be seen on a hill beyond the Gatwick Worth Hotel. A short distance away is the old Crabbet Park country house, where amateur champion Neville Lytton lived with his wife Lady Wentworth, the best female Tennis player in the world in her time. In its short tenure during the first half of the twentieth century, Crabbet Park produced an English amateur champion (Neville Lytton) and a men's world champion (Fred Covey, the only professional at Crabbet).

When the playing days of these champions ended, so too did use of the court. It has since been converted to office space for a software company.

EASTBOURNE RACKETS

EASTBOURNE RACKETS

EASTON NESTON

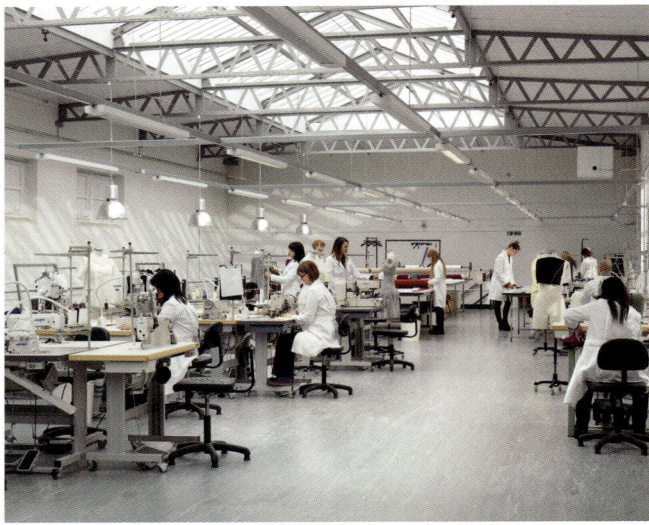
EASTON NESTON

Easton Neston

The longest Real Tennis court in England was built on Sir Thomas Fermor-Hesketh's estate in Northamptonshire in 1887, on the foundations of one dating back to the early seventeenth century. At Easton Neston, the game could be watched from the comfort of the adjoining smoking room, and the penthouse gallery, well furnished with armchairs and bookcases, acted as a comfortable forum for relaxation and conversation. When the court fell into disuse in the early 1900s, Sir Thomas's son, the first Baron Hesketh, converted it so that it could be used for Stické. Hesketh removed the penthouses and the tambour, and the court was later used for badminton. Since then it has been used as a library, furniture store, Formula One display room and workshop. More recently it has become a superbly restored building that can be converted to its original use at any time but for now is serving as an atelier for fashion designer Leon Max, the new owner of Easton Neston.

Eglinton

The thirteenth Earl of Eglinton built the very first covered Rackets court at his estate around 1839, which makes it the oldest surviving covered court in the world. Built before the standardisation of court size, the Eglinton Rackets court hosted its first match in 1846. The court floor was made of large granite slabs but is now hidden by a wooden floor. In 1860 the earl employed Rackets professional, John Mitchell, the owner of a pub and Rackets court in Bristol that became the Eglinton Arms. During the Second World War, the hall was used to store lorry batteries and, after the war, the shell of the court remained and was used for storage until the Irvine Development Corporation restored it as a centre for exhibitions and meetings. Today it serves as a centre for art shows, parties, meetings and small conferences and there is an archive in the upstairs viewers' gallery.

EGLINTON

EGLINTON

Disused Courts

EGLINTON

ESHER PLACE, SURREY

Esher Place, Surrey

The Tennis court at Esher Place in Surrey was built by Edgar Vincent Viscount d'Abernon in 1897. In 1930 he gave the house to the Ragged School Union, later the Shaftesbury Society. The house became the Shaftesbury Home for young children from 1930 until 1952, when it was sold to the Electrical Trade Union, now merged into Unite the Union, which currently uses it as its flagship training and conference centre. The former Tennis court was converted to two squash courts in the 1960s, but is now used for bedrooms and conference facilities and known as 'The Gallery'.

Fairlawne

Constructed by Edward Cazalet in 1879, this court remained in the family until the estate was sold in 1976. It is now owned by Saudi Prince Khalid Abdullah. The court is well maintained, but access is restricted for privacy and consequently

FAIRLAWNE

FAIRLAWNE

Tennis and Rackets

FAIRLAWNE

FULWOOD BARRACKS, PRESTON

Tennis isn't frequently played. However Chris Ronaldson, who was asked to help with the restoration in 1983, is usually granted permission to take a small group to play on the court once a year. While there, he usually gives advice on ongoing maintenance.

Fulwood Barracks, Preston

The Rackets court is one of the earliest covered courts, having been built around 1842–48. The barracks were built in response to anxiety over Chartist agitation. It is currently used for storage.

FYVIE CASTLE, SCOTLAND

FYVIE CASTLE, SCOTLAND

Disused Courts

FYVIE CASTLE, SCOTLAND

Fyvie Castle, Scotland

Alexander Forbes-Leith (later Lord Leith of Fyvie) bought Fyvie Castle in 1889 and built the Rackets court in 1903. Fyvie Castle was sold to the National Trust for Scotland in 1984 but is still occupied by the family (currently Sir George Forbes-Leith) The Rackets court currently houses a squash court and is also used for other sports and entertaining.

Gibraltar

The Rackets court on the Rock was built in 1871 and was used by members of the garrison. Between the wars, the Royal Navy used it for an annual match between the Mediterranean and the Atlantic Fleets. W.H. Hoare was the professional there for more than forty years, but interest fell away after the Second World War. The court was restored later and staged European Open championships in 1978 and 1979, won by Willie Boone the first year and John Prenn the next. The court has now been converted to squash, with a weights gym in the gallery, and called the Gibraltar Squash Association.

Greenwich Old Royal Naval College

The fabulous Pepys Building was built in 1874 to house two Rackets courts for use by naval officers. In 1905 it was converted to become the main mechanical engineering laboratory of the Royal Naval College. In 2010 a major

GIBRALTAR

refurbishment was carried out by Southstudio to transform the space into the Discover Greenwich Visitor Centre. The galleries in both courts were retained and one now serves as storage/staff changing for the restaurant/café, while the other has been converted into an office/storage space.

GREENWICH OLD ROYAL NAVAL COLLEGE

GREENWICH OLD ROYAL NAVAL COLLEGE

GREENWICH OLD ROYAL NAVAL COLLEGE

Disused Courts

HARBOUR CLUB

HARDWICK HOUSE – SECOND COURT

Harbour Club

At the time the Harbour Club was originally planned, the appointed contractor happened to be a Real Tennis aficionado. When he saw that a car park was planned in the basement he threw up his hands in horror and suggested that the space would instead be perfect for a Real Tennis court!

Located in 'the Dungeon' of the Harbour Club, the court was known fondly as the bane of every club visitor from elsewhere while being loved wholeheartedly by its members. With no natural light and a relatively low ceiling, the court was infamous amongst Real Tennis players. Despite its enclosed feeling, the court played very true, took cut well off the back wall, and the composition of the walls really suited the hard hitters. Daily usage on the court was high from seven in the morning onwards, and there were always club competitions going on at all levels. The first presentation of the Brodie Cup went to the Harbour Club in 1999 and over 250 members have enjoyed the game at the club. The Real Tennis court at the Harbour Club is now closed due to financial imperatives, a loss of Tennis players and a lack of support from non-playing members of the club.

Hardwick House – Second Court

Sir Charles Rose made his name in the Tennis world by building two courts at his home: Hardwick House in Berkshire. He considered that his first court, built in 1897, was too far from his house, and so he built another on his wife's vegetable garden ten years later. Both courts still stand, but the former is severely run down whilst the latter operates as a private club to this day. The second court is unlikely to be restored because it is situated on private property still owned by the Rose family, and the small membership has sufficient court hours at the other court on the property for all their playing requirements. Also on this property are the remnants of Sir Charles's Rackets court.

Hewell Grange

In 1820 a Tennis court was built at Hewell Grange, the home of the Windsor and earls of Plymouth families. Located just beyond the sunken French gardens, the court was upgraded in 1891, at which time the roof was raised to incorporate an arched glass top. The house and property now serve as a

HEWELL GRANGE

HEWELL GRANGE *The tambour is still visible.*

HEYTHORP PARK, CHIPPING NORTON

HEYTHORP PARK, CHIPPING NORTON

prison (certainly in the running for the most beautiful prison in the world) and the Tennis court acts as a training venue and gymnasium for the prisoners serving custodial sentences.

Heythrop Park, Chipping Norton

Originally owned by Charles Talbot, Earl of Shrewsbury, the house was gutted by fire in 1831. Wealthy industrialist Thomas Brassey purchased the remains of the estate at Heythrop Park for his son Colonel Albert Brassey in 1870. Brassey then had the mansion rebuilt using the original 1705 façade, and also constructed a Tennis court in one wing of the house. The court might not have had an active life, and it is doubtful that it was used at all after the Brassey family sold the estate in 1920. Heythrop Park has been tastefully restored to its former glory and has been converted into a hotel, golf and country club. The Tennis court is now the Enstone Suite.

Cawnpore, India

In 1991 Michael Garnett took a photo of the former Rackets court close to the Cawnpore Club. During the 1857 mutiny, the gallery was used by the Nunhey Nawab as his headquarters. The author has been unable to confirm whether it is still standing. There are likely to be many other Rackets courts still standing in India, in view of the great number built for the British Army.

CAWNPORE, INDIA

NEWCASTLE, JAMAICA

LEENAN FORT, COUNTY DONEGAL

NEWCASTLE, JAMAICA

A Rackets court was built in the former British Army Barracks in Newcastle, in the hills above Kingston, Jamaica. It is now owned by the Jamaica Defence Force.

LAKEWOOD RACKETS COURT

Although the Tennis court at Georgian Court University is now restored and in use, the Rackets court has been less fortunate and now serves as a lounge for the students.

LEENAN FORT, COUNTY DONEGAL

A Rackets court was built at Leenan Fort while it was a British Army base. The Fort is now derelict.

MELBOURNE RACKETS COURT

After a special general meeting in 1868, the Committee of Management agreed unanimously that a Rackets court should be built on the Little Collins Street frontage. However, it was not until G.T.W Freeman was commissioned to

LAKEWOOD RACKETS COURT

LAKEWOOD RACKETS COURT

MELBOURNE RACKETS COURT

MELBOURNE RACKETS COURT

build the court in 1876 that a court was finally built and opened at the Melbourne Club. In 1891 the Rackets court was restored and reopened to members after having been converted into a servants' dormitory for a period of time. In 1913 the Rackets court was again converted, this time into two squash courts. However, those courts were demolished in 1939 because of their infrequent use and their unofficial measurements. The building is on the register of historic buildings and was recently completely refurbished for use as an art gallery.

Milland Place, Liphook

This magnificent Rackets court was built in 1896 by a diamond merchant, Mr Seyches-Quinton. Play probably ceased after 1936 when the owner, Lady Massereene and Ferrard, died. A London ballet school used it during the Second World War, then some time later it became home for 8,000 broilers. In 1957 the estate was converted to a hotel. However, it ceased operating about twenty years ago and was passed to the current Indian owner.

MILLAND PLACE, LIPHOOK

Myopia Hunt Club

At the turn of the century, Hugh Whitney gathered a group of thirty Myopia friends and persuaded each to donate $1,000 to build a Real Tennis court. Constructed in 1902 and opened in 1903, the court is part of a country club that boasts lawn tennis, squash, golf and polo. Joshua Crane often played there at weekends and Quincy Shaw and George Fearing were also subscribers and regular users of the new court. Myopia's most famous player was Eleo Sears, the first American woman to ever play Real Tennis regularly. The court was mothballed during the First World War. In the early 1930s, the club converted the building into a stable, and in the 1950s the club pulled down the penthouse and galleries, tore out the dressing room, pro shop and squash tennis court and turned it into a maintenance shed for the golf course grounds crew. There are ball marks on some walls, the tambour still juts out from the north wall and one can see evidence of a grille, now bricked-in, but the sole purpose of the old court now is to house lawn mowers, water hoses and golf carts.

MYOPIA HUNT CLUB

MYOPIA HUNT CLUB *The tambour is still visible.*

MYOPIA HUNT CLUB

Tennis and Rackets

NORTH STREET EAST, NEWCASTLE

NORTH STREET EAST, NEWCASTLE

North Street East, Newcastle

The Rackets court was designed by Hubert Laws and opened in 1888. Play continued until 2001 when it became financially unsustainable. More recently the court has been used for badminton, judo and as a crèche.

Park Place, Remenham, Berkshire

The Rackets court was built by the Noble family around 1900. The family occupied Park Place until 1947 when it became a boarding school. The school converted the Rackets court into a swimming pool. The property was recently completely refurbished by Spink Property, which sold it in 2011.

PARK PLACE, REMENHAM, BERKSHIRE

PITTSBURGH ATHLETIC ASSOCIATION

PITTSBURGH ATHLETIC ASSOCIATION

The club was founded in 1908 by Frank Nicola. The building was designed for the association by the architect Benno Janssen and completed in 1911, including a Rackets court. In the early 1920s the Rackets court was converted to three squash courts. The gallery is still present and the Bickley walls still in good shape.

RANDOLPH HALL AT HARVARD UNIVERSITY

Archibald Cary Coolidge, a young Harvard graduate and assistant professor in the Department of History and Roman Law, proposed building a complex modelled upon Oxbridge, and in 1898 opened Randolph Hall, a luxury housing development for Harvard University students. A decade later Randolph drew closer to the Oxbridge model, when Coolidge built a large athletic building on the other side of the quad with a Real Tennis court, the only one to be built at an American university, a swimming pool, a Rackets court and two squash courts. Coolidge opened the Tennis court,

RANDOLPH HALL AT HARVARD UNIVERSITY

RANGOON, BURMA

ROSSALL SCHOOL

finished with Bickley cement and a first-class electric lighting system, with an exhibition between the world champion, Peter Latham, and the soon-to-be world champion, Jay Gould. In March 1909 Jay Gould and Joshua Crane faced off against Tom Pettitt and Alfred White in a doubles match which the professionals won 6–2, 1–6, 9–7, 9–7.

During the First World War the building was used as a gymnasium, and in 1919 Real Tennis and Rackets officially ended their brief collegiate encounter when Harvard tore down the Tennis and Rackets courts and built seventeen squash courts in their place. However, the exterior of the Real Tennis court can still be seen and is typical of an early twentieth-century court. In the mid-1990s the university gave the University Squash Courts to its Department of Visual and Environmental Studies, and in 1998, at a cost of $1.6 million, seventeen of the courts were turned into art studios. In some you can still see evidence of the old squash courts, but nothing remains inside from the era of Real Tennis. Today Randolph Hall is used by undergraduate art majors.

Rangoon, Burma

Two Rackets courts were built for the British Army at The Pegu Club. It was built in the 1880s to serve British Army officers and civilian administrators after the annexation of Upper Burma in 1885. It was one of the most famous gentlemen's clubs in Southeast Asia and the Pegu Club cocktail remains very popular around the world. Rudyard Kipling lunched and listened to soldiers' stories there, which were the inspiration for his poem *The Road to Mandalay*. The club is subject to a conservation order but in terrible shape.

Rossall School

Two Rackets courts were built here as part of a sports complex opened in 1883 during the headmastership of the Rev. H.A. James, who had come from Marlborough in 1875. In 1904, for the first and last time, a pair represented the school at Queen's Club. The courts deteriorated under the weather, maintenance costs were too high, and the game faded out in 1923. Squash courts now occupy the space.

St Louis Racquet Club

Designed by the architect Edward Gordon Garden in 1906. The former Rackets court was converted to a doubles squash court in 1926.

ST LOUIS RACQUET CLUB

ST LUCIA, WEST INDIES

SHORNCLIFFE

St Lucia, West Indies

The court was built by the War Office around 1890 and was played in until the late 1940s. After Sir John Stowe, administrator of St Lucia in 1947, left, it was converted into a squash court, then a radio broadcasting studio.

Sansome Walk, Worcester

Lamb's warehouse in Sansome Walk is a former hop warehouse from the late nineteenth century, more recently used for furniture storage and now converted into flats. It only became clear when a detailed record was made of the buildings that half of the warehouse was rather older, and in fact preserves the complete shell, including roof, of a mid-nineteenth century Rackets court. This in its turn incorporates the walls of an earlier open-air court. The inserted nine floors for the hop warehouse are carried on Hardy and Padmore cast-iron columns. The Worcester court is one of the oldest in existence.

Shorncliffe

A Rackets court was built at Burgoyne Barracks in Shorncliffe, Kent around 1867–73. The court appears to have replaced a three-sided structure, possibly an earlier court, shown on the 1867 site plan. It was still in use in 1914 and the building still stands today, but a squash court has been inserted. In 2013 the building was listed Grade II.

Stonehouse Royal Marine Barracks, Durnford Street, Plymouth

The Rackets court was built in 1788. In 1831 it was permanently converted into the Globe theatre and then enlarged in 1887.

SANSOME WALK, WORCESTER

STONEHOUSE ROYAL MARINE BARRACKS, DURNFORD STREET, PLYMOUTH

SUN COURT, TROON

VERSAILLES

Sun Court, Troon

In 1905 the Sun Court was built by Joseph Bickley for J.O.M. Clark, a thread manufacturer from Paisley. It fell into disrepair in the 1930s and formed part of a naval gunnery school during the war. Restoration on a historic scale took place after Alistair and Jill Breckenridge bought the house, which by then had been converted into a hotel. The court was reopened for Real Tennis in 1969. Chris Ronaldson arrived from Melbourne as the professional (succeeded by Walter Gregg and then Mike Gooding), and there was a solid fixture list. The first Scottish Open was held there in 1980, and again in 1981, 1984 and 1988.

However, the hotel was sold for conversion to a nursing home and, despite a specific clause in the missives of sale stating that Tennis was to continue, this sadly didn't happen and play ceased in early 1991. Fortunately a small group of players managed to have the court listed, which has at least saved it from demolition.

A demolition application was made in 2002, partly to make way for an extension to the nursing home, but various objections were lodged. The court is now listed as a 'Building at Risk' by the Royal Commission on the Ancient and Historical Monuments of Scotland (Historic Scotland).

Versailles

The original court at the royal palace of Versailles was demolished during the reign of Louis XIV and never replaced. Jean Bazin, *maître paumier du roi*, his son François and son-in-law Nicholas Crette, another Tennis professional, decided to remedy the omission and build a court in the town of Versailles. It was completed in 1686. More importantly, this was the scene of the famous *Serment du jeu de paume* on 20 June 1789 which marked the start of the French Revolution. For some time afterwards it fell into disuse and wasn't reopened as a court until 1855. Then, in 1883, it was inaugurated as a museum commemorating the Revolution. (*Author's note: the magnificence of the court, with tambour, galleries and other features still intact, persuaded me to include it in the list, even though it is in Continental Europe.*)

Westward Ho!

A Rackets court was built in Westwood Ho! for the Imperial Service College in 1901. ISC moved to Windsor in 1936 and then in 1942 it merged with Haileybury. The Westward Ho! court ceased to be played on in 1927 and has been altered for use as living accommodation.

WESTWARD HO!

WESTWARD HO!

STICKÉ

In the last quarter of the nineteenth century, a curious hybrid game developed called Stické – an abbreviation of sphairistike, the name given by Major Wingfield to his game of lawn tennis. It was a form of lawn tennis, played in a type of Tennis court, using lawn tennis racquets and a lawn tennis net.

The court was somewhat smaller than a normal Tennis court and constructed entirely of wood. Within the court there was no standard layout: some had a penthouse, some not; some had a grille, some a dedans, some a tambour; but none had chases. Rallies tended to go on for a long time, unless a player trained at Real Tennis knew how to cut the ball and bring it down sharply off the back wall. General Sir Desmond O'Callaghan is generally regarded as the man who invented the game.

The Royal Artillery built the first two courts at Shoeburyness in 1874 as a low-cost substitute for Rackets. The officers there and RE officers at Chatham (where another court was built) drew up a code of rules for the game. Other military courts were built at Gosport, Lydd, Dover, Spike Island in Cork Harbour, Freshwater, Bermuda, Darjeeling, Dalhousie (India), Jubbulpore, Rawalpindi, Halifax (Nova Scotia), Pretoria and Malta. Clearly, soldiers had carried the game overseas with them. None of these military courts exists any more. In its early days, Stické was played with a soft, uncovered India-rubber ball, 2¼–2½ inches in diameter and weighing 1¼–1½ ounces, supplied by L.H. Ayres.

There was at one time a court at Buckingham Palace, later converted into a swimming pool. Other courts existed at Easton Neston (the Tennis court converted), Membland Hall in Newton Ferrers, Cilymaenllwyd in Llanelli, Taplow Court, Kirtlington House, Greenlands, Clandeboye, Mongewell Park, Longford Castle in Wiltshire, Westbury Manor near

Cilmaenllwyd.

Membland Hall.

Taplow Court became known as the Desborough Patent Court.

Kirtlington House.

Buckingham (the last three destroyed by fire), Avon Tyrrell, Esher Place, Cliveden, Wildcroft Manor in Putney Heath, Ryston Hall, Digswell House in Welwyn and Queen's Club (the last seven all demolished).

The court at Membland Hall in Devon was built by the first Lord Revelstoke in 1880. The building still exists and has been converted into flats.

In Wales, Sir Stafford Howard built a court at his house Cilymaenllwyd in Llanelli, which he bought in 1910 from the Rees family. The game was played with lawn tennis balls coloured red. Play continued until the 1930s. The building still exists but is now used to store agricultural equipment.

Taplow Court was built in 1893 by Lord Desborough, who was an accomplished sportsman and president of Queen's. The design was founded on Lord Dufferin's court at Rideau Hall but he gathered the plans of all existing courts, collected improvement suggestions and then produced his own design, which became known as the Desborough Patent Court. This only had a side penthouse and became the model for twenty further courts across the south of England. Play continued until 1939. The building still exists and is now used as a staff restaurant by SGI, a Buddhist movement.

The court at Kirtlington House was built by the Earl of Leven and Melville in 1907. It is now owned by Christopher Buxton. The building still exists and is used for staff, storage and artists' studios.

The court at Greenlands was built by Viscount Hambledon and play continued till 1939. The building still exists and is now used by Henley Management College for badminton and squash.

The court at Mongewell Park near Wallingford was built by Howard Gould, son of George Jay Gould who built the Real Tennis court at Lakewood. It was destroyed by fire in the 1960s.

Greenlands.

Vice Regal Residence at Simla.

(Above left and right) Clandeboye. As well as Clandeboye, the first Marquess of Dufferin and Ava built courts at Rideau Hall in Ottawa, the Vice Regal Residence at Simla and Cooch Behar. He must have been extremely keen on Stické!

Overseas there were courts in Ottawa, Cooch Behar and at Vice-Regal Lodge, Simla (still playable and currently used for badminton), all built by the first Marquess of Dufferin and Ava. He built a court at his official residence at Rideau Hall in Ottawa in 1876, while he was Governor General of Canada, then while Viceroy of India built courts at the Vice Regal Residence at Simla in 1885 and Cooch Behar, then built one at Clandeboye in 1897 on his return home. He must have been extremely keen on Stické! The building at Clandeboye still exists and is now the James Frazer Room, which is used for banqueting and other functions.

At Rideau Hall the court was used for Stické during the day and for social events in the evening. A tent was

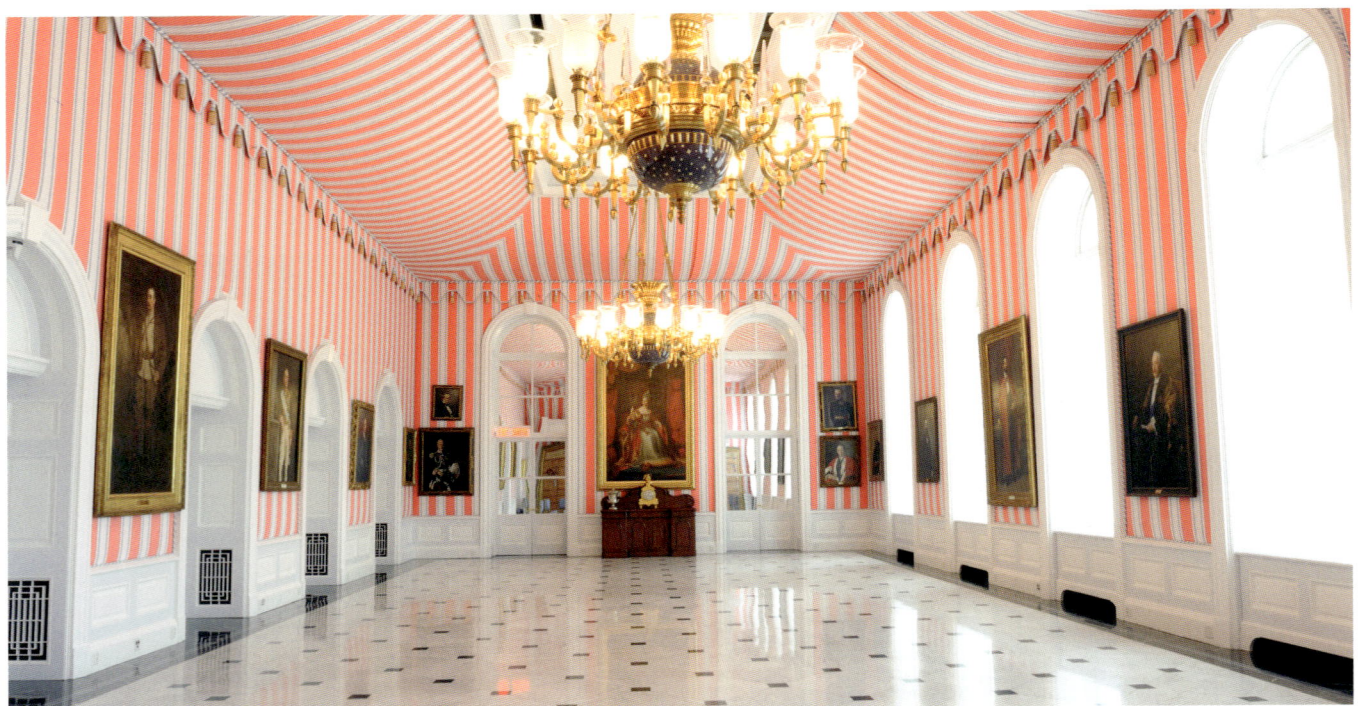

Rideau Hall in Ottawa.

Knighthayes is still working.

raised inside the room to transform it into a grand reception room for more formal events. Play continued at Rideau Hall until 1967. A major renovation was carried out in 1987. The decoration still respects the historic 'tent' character of the room.

The Heathcote-Amory family own an excellent court at Knightshayes, near Tiverton in Devon, built in 1907 and still actively used. It has a penthouse round three walls, and the game is played with lawn tennis balls dyed bright red.

The second Stické court still actively used is at Hartham Park, Corsham, in Wiltshire. It is built entirely of wood with a penthouse along one side only and is equipped with a changing room and upper gallery. It was built in 1904 by Sir John Dickson-Poynder, MP for Chippenham from 1892 until 1910 when, as Lord Islington, he was appointed governor of New Zealand. It is the only working example of a Desborough Patent Court remaining. It was bought by Jeffrey Thomas in 1997.

Hartham Park is the only working example of a Desborough Patent Court.

Hartham Park.

Building and Restoring Rackets and Real Tennis Courts

THE KEY TO BUILDING SUCCESSFUL Rackets and Real Tennis courts has always been the surface of the floor and, in particular, the walls. Anyone who has been unfortunate enough to have been hit by a fast-moving Rackets ball has a first-hand appreciation of the punishment that the walls of a Rackets court have to take on a daily basis. The floor must offer a consistent and desirable speed and bounce from the ball and the walls need to be as smooth and planar as possible, yet also durable. It is absolutely critical that the surface is polished and compacted to a very even and consistent surface, allowing the ball to skid off the surface in just the right way. Too little grip and the ball skids too much. Alternatively, excessive grip from the wall makes it a nightmare to anticipate the path of the ball. Worse still is a surface that is rough in places and smooth in others, leaving the player with little idea of where the ball might end up.

The front wall is usually finished with a matt paint, which is also conducive to achieving the desired grip, particularly from a cut ball.

The side walls of a Rackets court total almost 200 square metres in area, which is about the same area as a singles lawn tennis court or the wall area of two entire squash courts. To create a perfectly flat and consistently smooth polished surface to an area this size without any joins is no mean feat.

One of the earliest accounts of Tennis court surfacing can be found in *The Art of the Tennis-Racket-Maker* (1767) written by French zoologist, botanist and painter, François Alexandre Pierre de Garsault. He describes the perfect materials for blackening a court as a mixture of 'half a hogshead of ox blood, fourteen bushels of lamp-black, the gall of ten oxen to dissolve the lamp-black, and a bucket of urine to give sheen to the composition'.

Over a century later, an account of the composition of the Rackets court is found in J.R. Atkins's work, *The Book of Racquets* (1872). Atkins describes the Rackets wall as 'built for the most part of ordinary brickwork faced with Roman or Portland cement which is finally coated over with a kind of coarse black paint'. He also notes that 'the wall is sometimes lined wholly or in part with dark-coloured flagstones or with large slabs of slate riveted on to the brickwork at the back'. Other accounts of Rackets courts from around the world can be found in books which trace the histories of Rackets courts as told by Army officers who were stationed abroad. Whilst in England during the 1860s, Samuel Smith Travers recorded in his 'occasional book' an account of Lt. Col. Arthur Fisher on his experience with the building of a Rackets court near where he was stationed in Canton, China. His account of the Rackets court follows:

The great difficulty in a racquet-court is its expense, and the great expense consists in getting a sufficiently smooth hard surface for the end wall. It is usually constructed for this purpose of stone, or plaster made of the very best cement, which is, of course, expensive. Brick is neither hard nor smooth enough. After some trials we made ours as follows:– The whole of the walls were of brick and the floor of large square tiles, above an inch thick, laid on sand. As we were unable to get good plaster, the end wall was built with a number of wood bricks let in to receive nails; tiles were then prepared, having small furrows about three-quarters of an inch long and a quarter of an inch deep, cut in what would be the upper and lower edges of the tile, were it set up on edge; one at a short distance from either corner. Every tile was thus indented. The mode of fixing them was to set a course of the tiles, drive nails, with large flat square heads, into the wood bricks immediately above the top of the tiles placed on edge, slightly tap down the nail, until half the head was hidden in the groove cut in the tile; then another row of tiles was set in; the under grooves receiving the upper half of the nail's head; and thus the facing of the end wall was carried up perfectly fair, and with close joints.

The next thing was to colour it, for of course the red tiles did not allow of the players getting a fair sight of the ball.

We had an admirable mixture of this: lampblack boiled with rice, and a proportion of spirit added, and applied quite hot. It dried up immediately, was hand-rubbed as soon as dry, and after that never cracked, nor came off on the ball, and was never sticky, as paint might be.

It was really a most satisfactory affair altogether; and the plan is well worthy of a good trial, when a more perfect court cannot be obtained. Of course, the surface of a tile being only about fifteen inches square, you do not get so true a face, as with large stones, or plaster, but it really answered very well, and we used to have capital games.

In addition to his record of Lt. Col. Arthur Fisher's experience with a Rackets court, Travers, in his book *A Treatise on Tennis* (1875), includes a handwritten recipe for blackening the walls and floor of a Rackets court.

6lbs Lamp Black
1½ Ground Rice
2 oz Meth Spirits
Boil the Rice ¼ hr in two Galls Water – Stir the black in when cold & mix in the spirits

Although these formulae for cement and paint were sufficient for the time, they were not without flaws. Many courts flaked or chipped and frequently suffered from condensation on the walls. It was not until the introduction of Joseph Bickley and his technique for Tennis and Rackets court building that the games could be played in truly uncompromised conditions.

In the latter half of the nineteenth century, before the expertise of Bickley, flagstones were normally used for building the floors of Real Tennis courts. For Rackets courts, Atkins describes 'the best method for constructing the floor' as 'undoubtedly asphalte'. If not asphalt, due to the expense, 'stone pavement could be used'. Atkins, however, labels asphalt as 'more elastic to the foot of the player, and therefore less fatiguing'. The cheaper, less durable option of Portland cement could also be 'laid upon a bed of concrete', although it was likely to 'crack up' after some use. Finally, Atkins suggests that 'the cheapest and certainly the oldest kind of floor was a material composed of clay, lime, cinder-siftings and fine road-drift all mixed together like mortar.' However, 'this kind of floor [is] greatly inferior to asphalte for elasticity and durability.'

Born in England in 1835, Joseph Bickley (1835–1923) was a master plasterer who transformed the quality of Real Tennis and Rackets courts and, during his time, dominated their building. In the early days of Rackets court construction, Bickley was responsible for inventing a method of court building which could stand the test of time. He built up and ran a construction and plastering firm, and in 1888 his two courts at Queen's Club were opened and shortly followed by his court at the Tuxedo Club in New York State in 1889.

In the same year of 1889 he registered a patent for his process of covering the walls and floors of Real Tennis and Rackets courts. Of the twenty-six still active Real Tennis courts in the UK, at least fifteen can be attributed to him: Canford, one at Cambridge, Hardwick House, Hampton Court, Holyport, Jesmond Dene, Leamington, Lord's, Moreton Morrell, Newmarket, Oxford, Petworth, Seacourt and two at Queen's Club. Furthermore, of the ten active Real Tennis courts in the USA, at least eight can be attributed to him: Aiken, Boston, Chicago, Greentree, Lakewood, two in New York, and Tuxedo. His superior building techniques were not limited to the building of Real Tennis courts. Bickley was also involved with the construction of at least eight of the still active Rackets courts in the UK: Haileybury, Wellington, two at Marlborough, Queen's Club and Winchester, as well as virtually all of the still active courts in North America: Detroit, Montreal, New York, Tuxedo and two in Chicago.

In Eustace Miles's *Racquets, Tennis and Squash* (1902), Bickley's cement was acknowledged as 'being

Petworth c.1910 showing Joseph Bickley on the right. Arthur Tennis Smith, the first recorded professional there, is on the left.

by far the best'. Miles wrote: 'The Court is generally made of slabs of stone, or else of cement, Bickley's cement being by far the best. It may be mentioned that, when Bickley makes a Court, he guarantees that it shall be of the best kind. And eventually he always succeeds.'

In his book, *The Racquet Game* (1930), American sportswriter Allison Danzig wrote about Tennis and Rackets court construction pre- and post- Bickley.

Before Bickley went into the business, tennis and racquet courts were in the most instances poorly-lit, depressing looking structures whose walls were constantly sweating. His patented mineral black has almost entirely eliminated sweating of the floor and walls and has added to their durability. His composition floor, laid in six large slabs, gives a much livelier and truer bounce to the ball and also adds brightness to the court with its red color in place of black.

Danzig also detailed Bickley's technique:

The walls and floor are made of a concrete material that has a base of atlas cement mixed with sand that is screened through a sieve that has 2000 squares to the square inch. This base is soaked every twelve hours for a period of thirty days. When work is started on the finishing coat, which looks like lamp black, and whose composition remains a secret, it must be continued day and night to obtain the uniformly smooth, even surface. Both the material and the laborers are sent out by the company from London to America, France, Australia or wherever the court is to be built.

It appears to be a general consensus that, although the materials used by Bickley and his team were important to the successful construction of a court, it was Bickley's technique that resulted in the development of near perfect courts.

Alan Willingham writes: 'There is no great secret about this plaster, just Bickley's "atmospheric" patent which is non-specific regarding the type of cement he used. It was

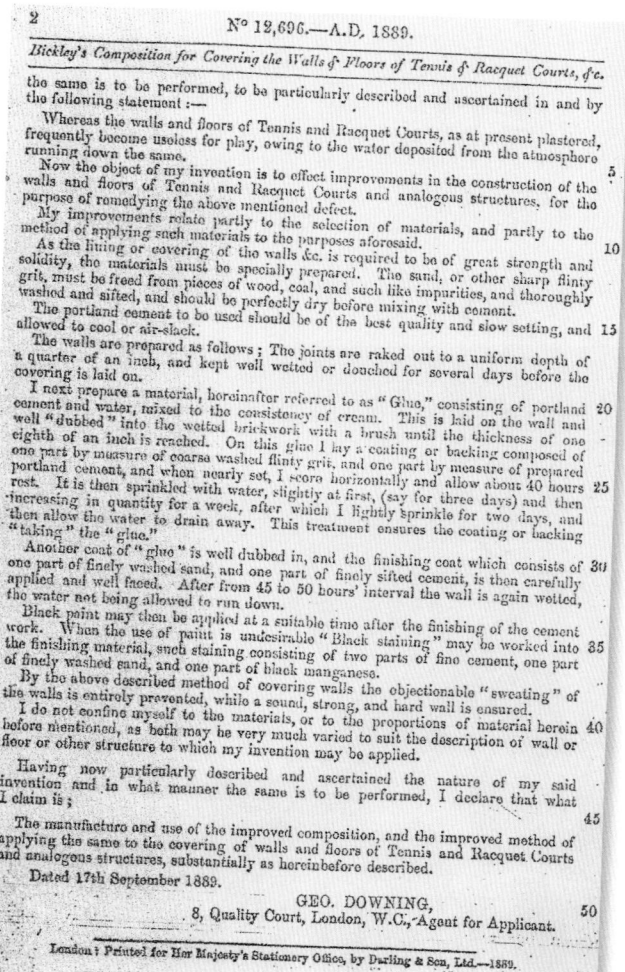

A copy of Bickley's patent was unearthed in the New York Public Library and forwarded to the builders of Harrow's second Rackets court.

the highly polished surface which reduced the likelihood of condensation of moisture on the walls in humid conditions.'

Condensation can occur if moist, warm air enters the court after a spell of very cold weather, so the moisture condenses and the court 'sweats'. Nowadays an easy solution to this is to heat the court.

Information on Bickley's work suggests that, once the rendering process had started, his men worked continuously day and night, plastering, rubbing and wetting and compacting the surface until the work was finished to Bickley's satisfaction. Bickley always controlled the mixing of the renders and topcoats himself. The patent application should have declared the complete process of Bickley's invention. However, it was thought by observers of his work that the process he used so successfully was not fully disclosed in his patent application and that, when Bickley died in 1923, he took the finer details of his 'invention' to the grave.

The courts in Bickley's time were built in 14- or 18-inch solid brickwork, in either English or Flemish bond, using a lime sand mortar. This traditional construction method helped to reduce the risk of cracking from settlement as the lime mortars were less hard and brittle and would allow minute movements between the individual bricks and thereby spread the movement across tens of thousands of hairline cracks around the bricks. Each crack was so imperceptible that substrate-induced cracking was rarely a problem.

Additional information on Bickley and his methods is found in notes made by the USCTA as a result of the renovation of the Greentree court. These notes provide further insight into the reasons for Bickley's success. They are as follows:

(i) His men always worked continuously day and night once they had started on the inside or on the floor of a tennis or racquet court.
(ii) The reliable witness of his work on a court built about 1905 says the men spent 24 hours at least on each square patch with continuous rubbing and application of water. It is said the object was to eliminate all air pockets and produce a very hard finish.
(iii) It is known he had at least one failure with a floor.
(iv) The mixing of the plaster was always done by Bickley himself. He used manganese dioxide as the blacking material, not vegetable dye. Samples of his plaster have been taken from several courts and tested. The tests do not show that the plaster had any special ingredients. Bickley's results appear to have been produced from workmanship.
(v) He appears to have worked only in the months when frost was unlikely.

Bickley's obituary, printed in *The Field* on 19 April 1923, reads:

It is hardly too much to say that Joseph Bickley, who has just died at the age of 88, indirectly had more influence on the games of tennis, rackets, and squash rackets than any other man in the last 50 years. Bickley was the great expert in the building and renovating of courts for these games, and the improvements he made were so far-reaching that they were in large measure responsible for the development and improvement of the games.

Clearly Tennis and Rackets owe much to Joseph Bickley and would not be the same sports they are today without his advancements.

There was no immediate replacement of Bickley and his method after his death. In fact, no Rackets courts were built in England from the First World War until Harrow began working on its second court in 1963. There are, however, some accounts of Rackets courts being built in other parts of the world during this time.

In his book, *Rackets in India* (1930), Colonel A.R. Winsloe wrote of the method the Army used to produce courts while stationed in various parts of India. Because the climate in India was certainly different from the climate back home, the builders had to use different techniques to ensure that the 'bricks on the inside of the face [were] really hard'. The courts in India also had to contend with 'the dust of the country', which required the walls to have a 'regular "spring cleaning"'.

Although they did not have to concern themselves with preparing their new court for dust storms, Harrow did face the challenge of having no clear record of Bickley's method of plastering. Bickley had died in 1923 and his stepson Mr Freeman had continued on with the business of building courts until the Second World War. However, when Harrow decided to build a second court in the 1960s, they had a difficult time locating any court-building wisdom left by Bickley.

Luckily, a copy of Bickley's patent was unearthed in the New York Public Library and forwarded to the builders at Harrow. Although they found that the patent provided some 'useful guidelines on timing and quantities', they also discovered that Bickley's formula was foreign 'to the ears of modern cement workers'.

The building of the Harrow court not only led to a rediscovery of Bickley's patent, but also put the Harrow cement workers in touch with Mr H.G. Harbour, the only living man who had actually worked as one of Bickley's plasterers. Mr Harbour explained that 'building a Rackets Court was not a job which could be hurried. The more time that was left for allowing not only the walls but also each of the three, successive coats of plaster to settle, the better.'

And thus, the second Harrow court was built with the combined efforts of modern cement workers, the long-lost Bickley patent and the advice of a former Bickley-employed plasterer.

In 1990, the Queen's Club realised the pressing need to re-surface the front and side walls of their championship court. There was a limited depth of knowledge available at the club at that time regarding who to approach for such a task, and the responsibility for the project passed to Sir Mervyn Dunnington-Jefferson, incoming chairman of the

Queen's Rackets Committee, which was known then, somewhat optimistically, as the Queen's Rackets Working Party.

Fortunately, Sir Mervyn had some commercial building experience and, through a firm of quantity surveyors he knew, an introduction was effected with Armourcoat Ltd, a company with an established record of polished plaster and high-performance surface finishes. Although Armourcoat had no specific product for producing the walls of a Rackets court, they did have experience of working successfully with squash court wall surfaces and, led by their managing director Jim MacKellar, they readily took on the challenge presented by the higher specification required for a surface that had to counter the violent impact of a Rackets ball.

Having first researched the Bickley Formula, and having understood the approach Joseph Bickley had taken, Armourcoat's research and development team set about creating a special high-strength black render for the Rackets courts. The material developed was a polymer modified render made from a mixture of crushed black granite, crushed black marble, washed and graded sands, cement and micro-silica. This formed the bulk of the render and was bonded onto the surface with a polymer cement slurry bonding coat. In order to create the final polished surface required for a Rackets court, Armourcoat developed a special topcoat mix that borrowed much from the polished plaster techniques that Armourcoat are so well known for.

The final topcoat is built up in four fine layers with each layer being less than 0.5mm thick. This final topcoat contained more than 50 per cent cement combined with fine black marble powder and black oxide pigments and is built up in progressively finer layers. The last layer is compacted and polished with stainless steel trowels to create a dense, hard polished surface. It is very skilled and labour-intensive work and to complete a side wall without any joints requires a team of sixteen craftsmen working together in an orchestrated way.

A small section of trial wall was built, which withstood the blows of a hammer delivered by ex-world champion John Prenn without indentation, and the new process, which was an entirely empirical solution, was duly declared fit for purpose and commissioned. It was an exciting time, as a planned finishing date could not be exceeded if Queen's was to host a forthcoming world singles challenge. The project was right on target and virtually finished when the floor protection was removed to reveal that a layer of dirt had penetrated right through to the floor itself. A light mechanical sanding was deemed to be the solution, but as well as removing the dirt, it also removed the top layer of the stone (or concrete) floor surface and rendered the court unplayable! Disaster loomed and Manchester was alerted as an alternative world championship venue.

However, the resourcefulness of Jim MacKellar had not been anticipated, and he arranged for a solvent-based acrylic spray to be brought to site and applied to the floor. Of course, with the floor not being entirely level, the spray 'pooled' in the lower areas and a huge quantity had to be applied to cover the entire surface. This powerful spray, applied in a confined indoor area, had the interesting potential to give off explosive fumes and was also very toxic. It would certainly be outlawed now by EU law, never mind by Health and Safety considerations. As luck would have it, though, Queen's Club did not blow up, and there were no reports of death by asphyxiation suffered by members with weak lungs. Moreover, the spray, when dry, entirely sealed the floor and restored the playing characteristics of the court in the nick of time. A good result. The new walls also played very favourably and the championship went ahead, but it had been a close-run affair.

Development and refinement of any product is usually evolutionary rather than revolutionary, and this has been very much the case with Rackets renders. From the first courts at the Queen's Club, much experience was gained, and the process has been continually refined and modified. Since then Armourcoat Ltd has gone on to surface the front wall of the Bridgeman Court at Queen's, and for years now has been firmly established in the field of court development, working on many Rackets projects, including courts at Manchester, New York, St Paul's School, and culminating in the new Rackets court at Tonbridge School with its beautiful black polished walls. Armourcoat's expertise also extends to Real Tennis courts – they did the walls for Burroughs and carried out repairs for Radley. We are fortunate that Jim's son Duncan (Armourcoat's technical director and himself a Rackets player) and his staff continue to be very approachable, bearing in mind that the firm's core business of polished plaster and other skills is truly worldwide.

No chapter on court development would be anything like complete, though, without highlighting the very valuable work done over many years by Arthur Cook and John Ford of A&J Services, who continue to specialise in Rackets court repairs and maintenance. They use a Belzona product which is, in effect, a resin-based chemical repair system. It is a difficult product to apply and requires the right mix for different environments, especially over large areas. It is, however, incredibly effective and strong. There is hardly a court in the country that has not used this material for either smaller repairs and/or whole walls and, amongst many others, Cheltenham, Haileybury, and most recently Malvern have benefited enormously from this expertise.

With both Armourcoat and A&J Services to call on for court construction and repair, Rackets and Real Tennis are now in a very strong position to maintain their facilities and to increase them wherever and whenever possible.

From the primitive techniques of mixing materials such as ox blood and urine to the present-day highly specific techniques of applying plaster and paint, it is clear that the production of a Real Tennis or Rackets court is no easy feat. However, when executed correctly, and generally with the help of guidelines left by Joseph Bickley, you are guaranteed a crack-free court that will entertain many years of competition, friendship and sport.

THE TENNIS & RACKETS ASSOCIATION

During the first few years of the twentieth century, the administration of Tennis and Rackets was shambolic, and it was becoming increasingly apparent that each game would benefit if a central authority could be established.

Tennis had been controlled for many years by a group of influential members of the James Street court in London's Haymarket, but in 1866 the court closed and responsibility for the game passed to the Marylebone Cricket Club at Lord's. Six years later the MCC drew up a new set of laws, but they were not universally accepted, and the resulting chaos led to the committees of the three London clubs with Tennis courts, Lord's, Prince's and Queen's, taking decisions independently.

Although the first club to have a Rackets court was the MCC, the old Prince's Club in Hans Place later built seven, and as a consequence had huge influence in the game. Because of its dominant position, Prince's handled virtually all matters pertaining to the game up until the club closed in 1886. However, before the members there could complete the construction of their new prestige club in Knightsbridge, the Queen's Club had opened and amongst its facilities were two Rackets courts. Needing a new home, the Public Schools Rackets championship, which had begun at Prince's in 1868, went first to Lord's and then a year later to Queen's. When the new Prince's Club opened, also with two Rackets courts, the championship stayed at Queen's.

It was Major Aston Cooper-Key who first suggested the idea of one central authority for the two games. Many people enjoyed playing both Tennis and Rackets and some clubs, including those in London, had courts catering for each game. Cooper-Key was a classic example: having represented Wellington in the school pair, he continued to play Rackets when he joined the Army, but in later life he migrated to Tennis.

Because of the rivalry between the London clubs, Cooper-Key had to tread carefully, but he came up with a clever scheme whereby each club in the capital would be represented by three nominees at meetings of the new association. The Manchester Tennis & Racquet Club was allowed two; other clubs were permitted one to represent them collectively, as were the public schools and the Army garrisons, but private owners could represent their own courts. His idea was welcomed by the London clubs as they would still be able to retain a great deal of influence. Buoyed up by the support he received, Cooper-Key drafted a letter which was sent on 1 October 1907 to all establishments with courts; it included the following paragraph:

The object of the Association will be in the first instance merely to act as an authority by which vexed questions of rules may be decided, representatives in international matches chosen, and regulations laid down to govern such matches; but it is hoped that steps may eventually be taken to put the professional championships of the two games on a more satisfactory footing than they are at present.

The response was encouraging. With the London clubs backing the scheme, Manchester agreed to support the new association, along with Hampton Court, Leamington, the Liverpool Racquet Club and Cambridge University. Of the public schools with Rackets courts, Charterhouse, Cheltenham, Eton, Haileybury, Harrow, Malvern, Marlborough, Wellington and Winchester all agreed to participate, as did the garrisons at Colchester, Chatham, Woolwich and the Royal Military College. Many of the owners of private Tennis courts also joined the new association: the Hon. Neville Lytton (Crabbet Park), Sir Charles Rose (Hardwick House and Newmarket), the Earl of Plymouth (Hewell Grange), Viscount Iveagh (Dublin), Lord Leconfield (Petworth House), Sir Andrew Noble (Jesmond Dene), W.M. Cazalet (Fairlawne) and J.O.M. Clark (Troon).

The first meeting of association was held at the Queen's Club on 18 December 1907. G.E.A. Ross, one of the Prince's Club nominees and the Tennis correspondent of *The Field*, was asked to chair the meeting. The Hon. Alfred Lyttelton was confirmed as the first president, Lord Alverstone and Sir Edward Grey as vice presidents, and the Queen's Club secretary, Edwin Biedermann, as the honorary secretary. It was agreed that each member would pay ten shillings a year. An executive committee was formed, which included Cooper-Key, and it was tasked with drafting a set of rules. These were approved at the second meeting on 5 February the following year, and at that meeting Sir William Hart Dyke agreed to become the third vice president.

The second meeting also agreed that the association should be known as the Tennis, Rackets and Fives Association and that the annual general meetings should be held on the first day of the Public Schools championships at Queen's. Squash rackets was to be included under Rackets, but why fives was included is a mystery, because no documentation survives. Also on the agenda at the second meeting was the subject of the Olympic Games, which were taking place the following year in London, with both Tennis and Rackets represented.

The spelling of Rackets caused a lot of confusion in the early years. Early on 'Racket' was sometimes used, as opposed to 'Rackets', and the first meeting of the association had used 'Racquets', which was occasionally found on official documents up until 1933. Lord Aberdare (the Hon. Clarence Bruce) then informed the association that 'Racquets' was incorrect and they should stop using it.

At the first AGM, held on 13 April 1908, it was agreed that sub-committees should be set up to draw up rules for squash and Rugby fives, and that a Professional Tennis championship should be established. The constant review of the laws of the games under its control is one of the present-day Tennis & Rackets Association's main functions. Another is to monitor the development of the equipment required for the games, and it was at this first AGM that problems with the production of Rackets balls were first raised. This was to turn out to be one of the biggest challenges for the association over the decades to come.

In 1910 it was agreed that any amateur prominent at Rackets or Tennis could become a member of the association, and the first Annual Report – a single sheet of foolscap – was produced that same year; subscriptions were also reviewed for the first time.

Establishments with Tennis, Rackets and squash courts had to pay £3, those catering for two games £2 and those with only one court £1. With these increases the association was able to record a surplus every year up until the First World War. The association also took over responsibility for Stické, which was extremely popular at this time, and new rules were drawn up for the hybrid game. These days the T&RA no longer has any responsibility for Stické.

The assumption by the association that it had the right to control the Tennis world championship led to the first of a number of disputes with the Lytton family. Neville Lytton and his wife Judith (Baroness Wentworth) were the owners of the Tennis court at Crabbet Park, where they employed the world champion Fred Covey. Briefly, for this incident was recorded earlier, Lytton did not agree with the association's insistence on controlling the 1913 championship challenge and the subsequent impasse led to his resignation. Later there were differences with Lady Wentworth over Covey's status as world champion following his defeat by Jay Gould in America just before the start of the First World War. The association recognised Gould as the champion when a second leg could not be arranged in Britain because of the conflict. And, having become the first lady member of the T&RA in 1923, by virtue of her sole ownership of Crabbet Park following her divorce from Lytton, she too resigned four years later over a difference in the way the prize money was to be apportioned for one of Covey's world championship defences.

The First World War was a disaster for the association. Many players were on active service and tragically some did not return, and the untimely death of its president just before the outset was another severe blow. Alfred Lyttelton had died following surgical complications after being hit in the abdomen by a cricket ball. During the conflict Edwin Biedermann wisely thought it sensible to cancel the Public Schools championships and not to convene any committee meetings: the association was effectively in hibernation.

Ten months after the cessation of hostilities Biedermann, having changed his name to Best because of the anti-German feeling in the country, decided to try and resurrect the association. He called a meeting which only four members of the old committee could attend. They decided to reconstitute the association along the lines that had been agreed just before the war. The London representation was reduced to two per club, Manchester one, one for Brighton and the private Tennis courts, one for the public schools, and one for the Royal Navy. The amateur champions of Tennis and Rackets, and the Army Rackets champion, were to be *ex-officio* members. However, six months later two representatives had been restored to Manchester, Hampton Court allowed one, Brighton's nominee was separated off from the private courts, and the public schools representation increased to two. Sir William Hart Dyke agreed to take on the role of president and Lord Grey to continue as a vice president. Lord Leconfield and G.E.A. Ross became vice presidents, filling the vacancies caused by Sir William's elevation and Lord Alverstone's death during the war years, and Henry Leaf became the honorary treasurer.

The first priority was to raise money. The association was virtually bankrupt, with only £5 in assets, but there were no liabilities because Biedermann had personally guaranteed them. He agreed to remain honorary secretary until the association could be reconstituted: he finally stood down in 1921, when Brigadier-General A.H.M. Taylor took over the role. When Biedermann resigned, the association suddenly needed a new address, because it had previously used his residence in Belgravia for all correspondence. No. 197 Knightsbridge, London SW7 was chosen, the home of the Prince's Club.

The reconstituted association was renamed the Tennis & Rackets Association, even though it still controlled fives and squash. But, with squash becoming increasingly popular, the administration of that game was taking up more and more of the committee's time; as a consequence at first one, and later two, representatives of the game joined the executive. In 1922 a squash rackets representative committee formed independently and immediately asked to be affiliated to the T&RA. Later this squash committee became the Squash Rackets Association, but after 1930 there is no mention of them again in the association's minutes. Similarly, because fives was not included in the reconstituted T&RA, the Fives Association was formed in 1923 and straight away asked for a formal link to be established. But by 1927 the Fives Association had started to fragment: firstly the Eton Fives Association was formed, followed soon after by the Rugby Fives Association. Thereafter fives is never recorded again in the minutes. However, fives and squash continued to have a representative on the association's executive committee until the Second World War. While those games were going their own separate ways, the Indian Rackets Association became officially affiliated to the T&RA in 1930 because of the popularity of Rackets there, and Colonel Winsloe was invited to join the committee in recognition of his work in promoting the game on the sub-continent.

Back in 1919 the pressing need for the reconstituted association was to raise about £200 a year to enable it to arrange tournaments for the professionals, as it was hoped this would attract new players and help to maintain standards. A membership drive was instituted, which involved approaching all of the pre-war members to ask for their support. The subscription of £1 for the individual member – which had been agreed just before the war – was reintroduced, but those who could afford it were encouraged to pay more. This initiative was successful and by the end of the first year income was approaching £300.

An agreement was reached with the Queen's Club that the T&RA would take control of both the Tennis and Rackets Amateur championships for three years, an arrangement that is now permanent. Other competitions were devised which enabled the association to announce that in addition to the Public Schools championships, there were to be five new Rackets and eight new Tennis tournaments in 1922.

Another welcome piece of news that year was the announcement that the Prince of Wales had agreed to become Patron of the Association. The Prince, like his father George V, was a member of the Prince's Club, and when the King died in 1936 he acceded to the throne as Edward VIII. When he abdicated a year later and his brother became George VI, the new King immediately agreed to continue the royal connection as patron. However, after he died in 1952, the T&RA had no patron until Prince Edward, The Earl of Wessex, agreed to honour the association by accepting the position in its centenary year.

The enthusiasm of the 1920s slowly started to evaporate as the next decade unfolded, not only because it was a period of severe economic difficulty in the country, but also because many of the men who had dedicated so much of their time to the association passed away. In 1930 the man who had been the driving force behind the establishment of the association, Major Aston Cooper-Key, died. The following year matters worsened when the president, Sir William Hart Dyke, died, along with the treasurer Henry Leaf and one of the influential founding members, G.E.A. Ross. What followed was extraordinary, because during the run-up to the Second World War, the association had no fewer than four different presidents and five honorary secretaries.

One of the vice presidents, Sir Edward Grey, by then Viscount Grey of Fallodon, stepped up to become president after the death of Sir William Hart Dyke, but he was to die two years later. The next president was Lord Revelstoke (the Hon. Cecil Baring), but within a year he had passed away, which resulted in an invitation to Percy Ashworth, president of the Manchester Tennis & Racquet Club, to take on the role. Three years later the committee was standing in silence in memory of its late president, which led to the fourth change in six years when Lord Leconfield became the association's sixth president.

The rapid changes of honorary secretary did not become a real problem until the second half of the decade. General Taylor had retired in 1930 because of ill health, but his successor Peter Kemp-Welch served for six years. After his resignation, Sir John Child took over, but business commitments forced him to give up after only two years. Vice Admiral G.N. Tomlin then assumed the role, but it may have been on a temporary basis because, eight months later, early in 1939, T.L. Lonsdale was appointed as the honorary secretary. But he too had to resign from the office when called upon to serve his country.

Before Percy Ashworth became president, committee meetings had always been chaired by the most senior member present; however, he was more of a hands-on individual, so he decided to act as chairman as well. When he died in 1937, the committee concluded that a permanent chairman was needed. They turned to Arthur Moon, a long-standing committee member and the association's honorary legal advisor; he accepted and therefore became the first T&RA chairman.

Two months after the outbreak of war, the committee met in Arthur Moon's chambers in London's Inner Temple. No. 4 Paper Buildings was to become the association's temporary address throughout the war years because the Prince's Club had closed six months earlier. At that meeting Edward Leaf, who had been the honorary treasurer since the death of his brother in 1931, agreed to combine the role with that of honorary secretary. It was resolved that they should continue to meet throughout the conflict, but that all competitions, except for the Public Schools Rackets championship, should be suspended. It was further agreed that members should continue to subscribe to the association, so funds would be in place to restart the games once the fighting stopped. Although it had been possible to arrange an AGM at Queen's in 1940, no others were held until 1946, but during that time members were kept informed of the association's activities through a folded single sheet of paper sent out annually. There was virtually no competitive play, but the committee felt that they should try and help with the war effort, and to that end a series of Rackets and Tennis matches was organised to raise funds for the Red Cross.

Having been largely responsible for the association's survival through the war years, Arthur Moon took the opportunity to step down after the cessation of hostilities. Although membership had dropped from its pre-war level of 247 to 161 by 1945, Edward Leaf's stewardship of the finances had resulted in a small surplus every year, so the reserves had grown from £2,684 to £4,372 during the period. This provided a firm foundation for restarting the games.

Rackets had survived the war in fairly good shape, but Tennis was in dire trouble. Only Lord's and Manchester had remained open throughout the war; several courts had been requisitioned and it would be years before many reopened;

some were lost forever, including the important Prince's Club. In the spring of 1947 Ronnie Aird, the MCC representative on the committee, produced a paper titled *The Future of the Game*. His principal concern was that, unless young Tennis professionals could be recruited, the game would cease to exist. He argued that the T&RA should decide what a fair wage was and encourage employers to guarantee their professionals matches with decent prize money. More also had to be done to persuade amateurs to take up the game and there needed to be a programme of matches instituted for all classes of player.

The association responded by allocating more money to Tennis than to Rackets for nine out of the following ten years. The university courts were considered to be the priority because they were the main source of new recruits. Oxford had reopened in 1946 and received immediate financial help, and when Cambridge restarted the following year they received the same amount, £200. Money was also allocated for repairing courts when help was needed to restore them to play, or to keep them functioning.

Kenneth Hunter succeeded Arthur Moon as chairman, and his immediate concern was that the committee was too cumbersome. He thought it should be reduced from a maximum of twenty-nine down to seven, but his colleagues decided this was too drastic and agreed a reduction of only five. Although these changes were approved, within five years the number had returned to twenty-nine.

The president, Lord Leconfield, was in poor health by 1949, and as a consequence resigned. They turned to the Marquess of Salisbury and he accepted an invitation to become the next president. Edward Leaf had stepped down as honorary secretary after the war, but remained the honorary treasurer until his death in 1956. Maurice Baring was the new honorary secretary, continuing until 1950 when Colonel Nigel Renny, later described as the 'heart and soul of the T&RA', took over. He was to serve in that office until he died in 1971; a few weeks before he was due to retire. As the years passed, the amount of work falling on Renny's shoulders slowly increased and this resulted in Richard Greenwood offering to share the workload as joint honorary secretary in 1964.

Although by 1950 membership had doubled since the end of the war, the association was eager to recruit more, looking upon the 300 members of the Royal Tennis Court at Hampton Court, and the 400 boys playing Rackets at the public schools, as potential new members. So, following another successful recruiting drive, membership doubled again to 625 by the end of the decade. However, while the membership level was regarded as healthy, the situation with the professionals at Queen's was not. The club was seen as essential for the survival of the games, but by 1958 there were no professionals employed there, and as a consequence there was very little play on the Tennis and Rackets courts. The T&RA was very concerned, so it designed a scheme to fund two professionals by asking its members interested in playing there to pre-pay for their courts. This proved so successful that four years later there were three professionals working at the club and the second Tennis court had been restored to play.

As the decade drew to a close, a secondary objective of the Queen's Club scheme, which was to entice youngsters into the games to train as professionals, led to the Young Professionals Fund (YPF) being set up. This was the brainchild of Dick Bridgeman and he organised a successful appeal that allowed two youngsters to be taken on. Ten years later, ten trainees had become professionals or assistant professionals and another three were in training.

As the 1950s drew to a close, Lord Aberdare (the Hon. Morys Bruce) was elected chairman after Kenneth Hunter had resigned due to ill health. One of his first actions was to draw up plans to reconstruct the association based on the principles of decentralisation and the delegation of responsibility. His idea was to create a General Council of no more than thirty members, each of whom would serve for three years, with ten being elected at each AGM. The council was to receive reports from a number of committees dealing with different aspects of the association's work. This restructuring was complex and took a long time to finalise. It eventually received approval at the 1966 AGM.

It was in 1964 that *The Field*, which had for more than a hundred years reported on Tennis and Rackets, donated the Field Trophy for a Tennis Invitation tournament. Although no prize money was forthcoming, it was the first time that a commercial organisation had contributed anything to either game. These days sponsorship is a very important source of revenue, with about £120,000 a year being donated, and T&RA members owe a debt of gratitude to the many that have helped in this respect. The list of sponsors over the years is too long to record fully here, but the major donors have been Daniel and John Prenn supporting Rackets, firstly through Celestion Loudspeakers and latterly Lacoste, David Norman through BNB Resources, while Tennis has benefited from the help received from the whisky company Cutty Sark, the dairy company Unigate, Sir Clifford Chetwood and Wimpey, Sir Derek Hornby and Rank Xerox, Sir John Ritblat and British Land, and the Prats family's Cos D'Estounel vineyard. The lead sponsor of both games today is Robin Geffen through his Neptune Investment Management, which has provided this key support since 2008 for Real Tennis and 2010 for Rackets. In addition, Pol Roger sponsor three inter-club team competitions and the Varsity matches.

The next decade was another that saw many changes in senior officers. In 1972 the Marquess of Salisbury died after twenty-two years as president; Lord Aberdare was immediately approached to take on the role, which he accepted. The resulting chairman's vacancy was filled by Peter Kershaw; he served in that capacity for seven years, but like so many before him his total contribution to the T&RA was immense, in his case fifty-one years. He was succeeded as chairman by Dick Bridgeman.

In 1971, Guy Bassett Smith had become joint honorary secretary when Nigel Renny died, sharing the responsibility with Richard Greenwood until the latter relinquished his secretarial duties two years later to concentrate on his other role, that of honorary treasurer. Bassett Smith was the last of the honorary secretaries, because Nigel Bruce, who was appointed secretary in 1975, received a small remuneration of £1,000 a year. The council had recognised that it had become unreasonable to expect anyone to fulfil the onerous role in an entirely voluntary capacity.

During the 1970s, membership rose from 800 to 900, despite a doubling of the subscription to two guineas a year. With ever more competitions to promote, the council, in 1971, took the decision to set up championship committees for each game. Two years later they were replaced by the Rackets sub-committee, under the chairmanship of Howard Angus, and the Tennis sub-committee, headed-up by David Warburg. The new sub-committees were later renamed the Rackets and the Tennis Committees. They had executive powers and operated with a number of sub-committees looking after various aspects of each game. A number of dedicated people have chaired these committees over the years. Garth Milne, Paul Nicholls, Charles Hue Williams, Sir Mervyn Dunnington-Jefferson, John Prenn and Guy Barker have been Rackets Committee chairmen, and currently Guy Smith-Bingham is serving in that capacity. Tennis chairmen have been: Alan Lovell, Colin Dean, Julian Snow, Sir Andrew Hamilton, and now, Roger Pilgrim.

Having assumed that the leadership of the T&RA was in good hands for years to come, it came as a terrible shock when Dick Bridgeman died unexpectedly in 1982 after only three years in office. But that was not the end of his contribution, for he left the association a large legacy. Some years earlier it had been recognised that his brilliant idea, the Young Professionals Fund, could not receive money from trust funds because of tax restrictions and charity legislation. As a consequence the T&RA Charitable Trust was established in 1965, and he was one of the original trustees, along with Lord Aberdare and Dugald Macpherson. As a result of his generosity and his involvement in establishing the endowment of the trust, it was renamed the Dick Bridgeman TRA Foundation (DBTRAF) after his death. Today the trust makes grants or loans to establishments with Tennis or Rackets courts that are registered charities, to help with training and court construction or repair. The current trustees are: James Bruce, Peter Mallinson, John Prenn and Giles Pemberton.

David Norman succeeded Dick Bridgeman, and over the sixteen years of his chairmanship a great deal was achieved. With the help of William (Bill) Stephens, who had succeeded Martin Scott as secretary – the latter having taken over from Nigel Bruce in 1981 – a new management committee was formed to facilitate administration. Changes to the constitution that had been proposed by Dick Bridgeman were approved at an EGM. These called for a council of between twenty-five and forty members, and the opportunity was taken to correct an anomaly when the Tennis professionals were allowed a representative, Rackets professionals having been permitted one since 1963.

Council members were busy. Charles Hue Williams was asked to review the laws of Rackets and to look into the question of the participation of ladies in competitions under the control of the T&RA, following the formation of the Ladies' Real Tennis Association. His sub-committee recommended that the LRTA should be permitted one representative on the council, but that the ladies should not play against men in the major competitions. Many new competitions were introduced in the 1980s, including a number of junior events for both games and a series of Tennis tournaments for various ages of senior player.

With the dynamism that characterised his period in office, David Norman produced a development plan for 1984 within a few months. Its aim was to increase membership by 200 during the year, improve the Annual Report and to negotiate with the Queen's Club so it could be recognised as the headquarters of the T&RA in return for injecting more money into the games. David Norman also contacted the sports editors of *The Times* and the *Daily Telegraph*, demanding to know why their coverage of the two games was so poor. His intervention had the desired effect.

The day-to-day implementation of the development plan fell on the shoulders of the hard-working secretary Bill Stephens. The Annual Report, which he edited, was transformed from a small 50-page booklet into an A4-size publication of some 100 pages, and the recruitment drive exceeded all expectations with membership nearly doubling to 1,500 in eighteen months. Another priority was to improve the value of membership, so handicap systems were developed for the two games, arrangements were put in place for members to play with proper introductions at most courts around the world, and privileged access to the Lansdowne Club in Mayfair was negotiated.

David Norman took personal charge of fundraising for the Queen's Club project. His ideas were far-reaching. Proposals were drawn up for the restoration of the second Rackets court, the complete refurbishment of the two Tennis courts, upgrading the two dedans and creating a museum in one, improving the professionals' workshop, and securing better office facilities for the association's secretariat. Added to the list was Queen's insistence on three new squash courts to replace the two that had been operating in the second Rackets court. Virtually single-handedly he raised more than £400,000 for the project, which was completed in 1988.

Two years earlier it had been agreed that a strategic review of the two games was necessary to ensure the T&RA was properly structured and financed over the coming decades. Charles Wade, the man primarily responsible for developing the Tennis handicap system, agreed to take on the task. A year and a half later he produced his report: *The Future of Real Tennis and Rackets*. The Wade Report, as it came to be known, contained some far-reaching recommendations which generated a great deal of heated debate. Most of the recommendations were eventually accepted, including a proposal that a chief executive should be appointed to focus on development, administration and fundraising. With Bill Stephens wishing to reduce his role, and Richard Greenwood wanting to retire after twenty-five years as honorary treasurer, this aspect of the report had become a priority, and as a result Brigadier Andrew Myrtle was appointed the T&RA's first chief executive at the beginning of 1989.

'The Brigadier', as he was affectionately known, set about implementing those aspects of the Wade Report that had been accepted. However, some proposals for restructuring the council ran into trouble at the 1990 AGM, when a number of members called them undemocratic. As a consequence the Brigadier was asked to carry out a comprehensive review of the rules. He recommended that in addition to the Wade proposals there should be four elected members on the council and each game's committee should have six elected members. With this change, the restructuring was approved at an EGM early the following year.

As the Brigadier had been tasked with broadening the association's base, one of the first things he did was to set about increasing the membership, and over the decade that followed numbers rose from 1,900 to 2,400. During his twelve years as chief executive, he drew up two four-year plans. The first, covering 1994 to 1998, was designed to try and gain a Sports Council grant by showing how the association could increase the number of Tennis courts, acquire new sponsors, improve standards of training and encourage Rackets players leaving school to continue playing the game. With the plan accepted, the association was able to employ, on a part-time basis, a Tennis court development officer and a training officer. By the end of the decade an astonishing nine new or restored Tennis courts had been brought into play, compared with the Wade Report's target of between three and five, plus two Rackets courts. Over the same period a basic certificate for young Tennis professionals was devised, and the foundations for advanced training put in place. Today the training of young Tennis professionals falls under the remit of the YPF, while a Club Professional Development programme, also funded by the T&RA, is designed to ensure the senior professionals have the skills necessary to run a club efficiently. The second four-year plan's objectives were similar to the first, but it additionally provided for the financing of a youth development officer.

The Brigadier had taken on the offices of secretary, treasurer and Director of the Young Professionals' Programme (DYPP), in addition to his duties as chief executive, but when he handed over to James Wyatt at the start of 2001, the council decided the extra responsibilities were too much for any one person. As a consequence Chris Cairns became the new honorary treasurer and Andrew Myrtle continued as DYPP, leaving James Wyatt to combine the role of CEO with that of secretary.

Having served fifteen years as chairman, David Norman stepped down in 1997. His successor was Charles Swallow, who pressed on with the policy of increasing the number of Tennis courts in play and encouraging more people to play Rackets. After five years he agreed to serve for another two, so long as a pre-existing business commitment did not take up too much of his time. Unfortunately for the T&RA, that did happen, which meant he had to retire slightly earlier than planned.

One of the last major problems that Charles Swallow had to deal with concerned the Tennis professionals. The association has always recognised the contribution made by the professionals and now ensures that they are represented at every level. Therefore there is a good working relationship, but friction can occasionally arise. Problems can revolve around the allocation of money raised through sponsorship, and in 2001 one such difficulty arose after the International Real Tennis Professionals' Association (IRTPA) announced it had secured contracts with all the leading players and a sponsor, and it was going to unilaterally take over the administration of the next world championship. Differences had arisen between the IRTPA and the National Associations of the Tennis-playing countries about the way the challenger was chosen and the venue determined. Alan Lovell, a former Tennis committee chairman, played a pivotal role in bringing all the parties together. It was agreed that the championship should remain a challenge and continue to be played as the best of thirteen sets, but the IRTPA proposals for determining the challenger and the venue were accepted. The IRTPA had already been given control of the upcoming 2002 challenge because it had everything in place; it was then appointed the executive to manage the next three challenges. With the new system working well, the agreement has since been extended.

The new chairman was Peter Mallinson; as a former investment banker he was immediately concerned about the association's long-term financial position. Although operating surpluses were being generated annually they were small, totalling just £12,000 over the previous five years. That was only one per cent of the association's turnover, and with government-sponsored grants coming to an end, new sources of income had to be found. One of the recommendations of the Wade Report sixteen years earlier had been that, as with many other sports, every active player should contribute to the governing body by way of a levy, but it had not been adopted because it was feared that it would be too difficult to introduce. In 2003 there were 2,400 members of the T&RA, but around 4,000 people were actually playing Tennis and Rackets in the country, and all were benefiting from the association's work. The new chief executive favoured a levy and, after some difficult discussions with the clubs, a few of which had special circumstances, an affiliation fee was agreed which would be collected by the clubs.

One of the major priorities for the T&RA is to encourage youngsters to play the games; during the first decade of the twenty-first century, huge strides were made in this respect. A new Rackets Development Squad was formed that combined coaching and fitness and was aimed at producing future champions. At Tennis, the employment of a youth development officer, now the Director of Junior Tennis, has led to a massive increase in the number of youngsters playing under the age of eighteen, with the very best now able to join a Junior Squad. The success with the youngsters is largely down to the efforts of Paul Weaver, the Director of Junior Tennis for the last thirteen years. On reaching the age of eighteen, those good enough are taken into the Tennis Development Squad, with the most promising able to progress to the British Real Tennis Academy, which is aimed at producing top-class players. The development squad and the academy were the idea of a group of Tennis enthusiasts calling themselves The Dedanists, who wanted to put something back into the game. They raise the funds that support these two programmes.

A major problem arose in 2004 when the Lawn Tennis Association (LTA) decided to sell the Queen's Club. Peter Mallinson immediately leapt into action and made sure he was at the centre of the tortuous negotiations that eventually led to the purchase of the club by its members, and in doing so managed to secure long-term legal protection for both games. This avoided what would have been a catastrophe for Tennis and Rackets had the courts there been lost; it also meant the association would not have to find a new home.

In January 2005 Lord Aberdare died. He had served the association for fifty-one years, initially on the old executive committee where he had looked after the interests of the private courts and small clubs. There followed twelve years as chairman and then thirty-two years as president: the longest anyone has served in the latter office. Lord Aberdare had resigned for health reasons a year earlier and had been succeeded by Richard Greenwood, who then held the office for the next seven years. After he stepped down, David Norman accepted an invitation to become the new president.

It was David Norman who orchestrated the successful centenary celebrations, which began at Lord's with a dinner in November 2007 when 550 members attended. The festivities climaxed in April the following year when huge doubles tournaments for both games were staged, necessitating the use of many different courts. The revelries concluded with a centenary ball at the Hurlingham Club. To coincide with the centenary, David Best wrote his much acclaimed *Official Story* and Roddy Bloomfield produced an enthralling DVD.

With the celebrations over, Peter Mallinson once again turned his attention to the future. Two important reviews were commissioned. The first, undertaken by Judge Brendon Hegarty, was charged with making recommendations on how to fund the T&RA's infrastructure and overheads. The second, a five-year strategic review, was carried out by Christopher Hopton. Both reports were adopted. The Hegarty Report proposed an enhanced club subscription – based on the number of active players at each club – to replace the affiliation fee. Since then great strides have been made towards universal membership, thanks to the current CEO's much improved relationships with the Tennis clubs. The Hopton Review found that the development of each game had stagnated, so it recommended targets. By 2015 there should be 1,000 new Tennis members, 50 per cent under 40 and 33 per cent women, and ten new Tennis courts built by 2020. The number of Rackets-playing members needed to rise from 900 to 1,400 by 2015, of which 80 per cent should be senior players, and one new Rackets court should be built in the period. Although some of these targets have been found to be too stretching, the Hopton Review has been the catalyst for significant progress in the overall health of both games.

Since the centenary there have been a number of changes of senior officers. James Wyatt had stepped down as chief executive just before the centenary celebrations concluded, having played a large part in their success. His seven years in office were characterised by his ability to forge stronger links with sponsors and the outside organisations. The honorary treasurer, James Walton, stepped in as acting CEO. During his time he oversaw the move into offices in Centenary House following the departure of the LTA, coped with the aftermath of a fire there that destroyed many of the association's files, and brought the T&RA into the IT era by introducing the online booking system and purchasing the Real Tennis Online database, a joint venture with the other national governing bodies. In June 2010 Chris Davies, a distinguished naval officer, was appointed the current CEO and secretary, and has already overseen a period of great change in the association. He is supported by Richard Dalzell, the present treasurer, who has transformed the finances since 2009.

After seven years as chairman, Peter Mallinson stepped down in 2010. William Maltby was approached and took up the chairmanship, and today, with the benefit of management skills honed in the banking industry, he continues to steer the association steadily forward. The new team has overseen improved financial integrity by streamlining many processes, introduced new media on the website, invested in life training for professionals and greatly enhanced the number of assistant Rackets professionals. In addition there has been a shift of emphasis towards encouraging juniors and schools, a direct consequence of the strategic review.

Another plan for attracting youngsters into Tennis was launched in 2011, when members of The Dedanists' Society, working in association with the T&RA, established The Dedanists' Foundation, a charity whose aim is to increase youth participation in Tennis, to complement and expand upon existing initiatives in youth Tennis. The foundation awards grants to clubs in order to help them to recruit young people into the game on an open-access basis and from all backgrounds.

A decision was taken in 2012 to incorporate the T&RA as a company limited by guarantee and this has necessitated a further restructuring. Apart from offering an opportunity to modernise the legal structure in line with current best practice, the new arrangement offers protection in this litigious age for the association's officers from legal action against them personally. The chief executive officer is now responsible directly to a Board of Directors, which has replaced the council. The Board consists of the chairman, treasurer, chairman of the trustees, the chairmen of the Rackets and Tennis committees, chairman of the LRTA, a representative of the vice presidents and four elected members. The president's role is mainly that of a figurehead, whose experience and wise advice is often invaluable. The vice presidents form a virtual privy council of external advisers, called upon as necessary. The current vice presidents are: Charles Hue Williams, Alan Lovell, Brigadier Andrew Myrtle, John Prenn, Sir John Ritblat and Charles Swallow. The CEO receives reports and advice from the Director of Junior Tennis and the child protection officer, who act as consultants.

Changes have also been made to the structures of the games' committees. The Tennis committee is now made up of the chairman, secretary, the DYPP, Director of Participation, chairman of the Real Tennis Professionals' Association, the LRTA chairman and the chairmen of two sub-committees – Tournaments & Fixtures, and Handicaps & Rankings. In addition, up to three elected club representatives and three elected members sit on this committee. The Rackets committee is made up of the chairman, secretary, the DYPP, Director of Tournaments, the chairman of the Rackets Professionals' Association, a further RPA representative, representatives of masters-in-charge of Rackets at public schools, each club with a Rackets court, Under-25s, old boys' associations and evening clubs, and not exceeding four elected members.

In April 2013 the T&RA introduced a new Benefactor Scheme so as to provide additional regular cash flow for the long-term benefit of both games. This received support from over fifty members and has already had a very beneficial impact on the financial support that can be provided, and been a key element in achieving the T&RA's goal of funding 10 per cent of a new court.

The T&RA lost two of its greatest servants in 2014. Over the course of fifty-two years, Richard Greenwood served the T&RA in a variety of roles, most notably as honorary secretary and then membership secretary from 1964 to 1989, and president from 2004 to 2011. Mervyn Dunnington-Jefferson served on the Rackets Committee for fifteen years, including five years as chairman. He also served many years on the Amateur Status Committee and the council. He had a deep understanding of the complexities of building and maintaining a Rackets court, and perhaps his most enduring legacy will be his enormous contribution towards the building of the new Rackets gallery complex at Queen's.

In spring 2014 the T&RA, in conjunction with NARA, appointed a committee chaired by Patrick Maxwell to review the existing World Championship Guidelines for Rackets. For a number of years, there had been an increasing mood that they needed revision, particularly concerning how challenges were determined. After months of intense debate, thorough analysis and wide consultation a new set of procedures was approved, the key components of which were that challenge matches would take place automatically every two years, singles challenges in each even year and doubles in each odd year and their identity would be determined by a new world championship Challenge Points System, based upon performance over the previous two seasons. The most significant change was that in future challenges would no longer be determined by a committee decision but by a points-based system similar to that adopted successfully by Real Tennis some fifteen years earlier.

As the Tennis & Rackets Association moves forward, the members are assured that their interests are being safeguarded, but it is easy to forget just how much is being done. Currently about £250,000 a year is spent on administering the games, but questions are regularly asked about how the money is spent. Recently the Tennis Committee chairman, Roger Pilgrim, broke the association's activities down into four sections: infrastructure, insurance, development and communication. Under infrastructure he included the maintenance of rules, standards and traditions, assessing the impact of new technology, safety issues, running the handicap and booking systems and managing a collective scheme for the purchase of ball cloth. Insurance activity includes a group scheme that clubs can join to protect themselves from claims, while another policy is in place to cover every member against public liability claims. In the development category there is help available for court restoration and repairs, advice and funding for new court projects, the organisation of tournaments, funding to get more people playing and train professionals, and importantly a great deal of time devoted to securing sponsors. The Annual Report is the traditional form of communication for members but, in this digital age, e-newsletters and email notification are of increasing importance, and up-to-date information is posted on the association's website. For the younger members, social media is a key means of communication.

In 2014 there were about fifty members voluntarily serving on the various committees, ensuring that all aspects of the association's work function properly. There is no doubt that the games would not be as enjoyable as they are today without the hard work done by the Tennis & Rackets Association and its army of volunteers.

Championship Records

Tennis

MEN'S WORLD SINGLES CHAMPIONSHIP

	Winner	Runner-up	Score	Venue
1740	Clergé			
1765	Raymond Masson			
1785	Joseph Barcellon			
1816	Marchisio	Philip Cox		James Street
1819	Philip Cox	Amédée Charrier		James Street
1829	Edmond Barre	Philip Cox		James Street
1862	Edmund Tompkins	Edmond Barre	6–4 (retired)	James Street
1871	Edmund Tompkins	resigned		
	George Lambert	claimed		
1885	Tom Pettitt	George Lambert	7–5	Hampton Court
1890	Tom Pettitt	Charles Saunders	7–5	St Stephen's Green, Dublin
1890	Charles Saunders	claimed		
1895	Peter Latham	Charles Saunders	7–2	Brighton
1898	Peter Latham	Tom Pettitt	7–0	Brighton
1904	Peter Latham	Cecil Fairs	7–5	Brighton
1905	Cecil Fairs	Peter Latham	5–1	Queen's & Prince's
1906	Cecil Fairs	Ferdinand Garcin	7–4	Brighton
1907	Peter Latham	Cecil Fairs	7–3	Brighton
1908	Peter Latham	resigned		
	Cecil Fairs	claimed		
	Cecil Fairs	Edward Johnson	7–2	Brighton
1910	Cecil Fairs	Fred Covey	7–6	Brighton
1912	Fred Covey	Cecil Fairs	7–3	Prince's
1914	Jay Gould	Fred Covey	7–1	Philadelphia
1916	Jay Gould	resigned		
	Fred Covey	claimed		
1922	Fred Covey	Walter Kinsella	7–3	Prince's
1923	Fred Covey	Walter Kinsella	7–3	Prince's
1927	Fred Covey	Pierre Etchebaster	7–4	Prince's
1928	Pierre Etchebaster	Fred Covey	7–3	Prince's
1930	Pierre Etchebaster	Walter Kinsella	7–1	Prince's
1937	Pierre Etchebaster	Ogden Phipps	3–1 (retired)	Tuxedo
1948	Pierre Etchebaster	Ogden Phipps	7–2	New York
1948	Pierre Etchebaster	J.P. Dear	7–4	New York
1949	Pierre Etchebaster	Ogden Phipps	7–1	New York
1950	Pierre Etchebaster	Alastair Martin	7–0	New York
1952	Pierre Etchebaster	Alastair Martin	7–2	New York
1955	Jim Dear	Jack Johnson	11–10	New York & Queen's
1957	Jack Johnson	Jim Dear	7–3	Queen's
1959	Northrup Knox	Jack Johnson	7–2	New York
1966	Northrup Knox	Ronald Hughes	7–0	New York
1968	Northrup Knox	Pete Bostwick	7–3	New York
1969	Northrup Knox resigned			
1969	Pete Bostwick	Frank Willis	11–8	New York & Manchester
1970	Pete Bostwick	Jimmy Bostwick	7–1	New York
1972	Jimmy Bostwick	Pete Bostwick	7–2	New York
1974	Jimmy Bostwick	Howard Angus	7–5	New York
1975	Jimmy Bostwick resigned			
1976	Howard Angus	Gene Scott	11–4	New York & Queen's
1977	Howard Angus	Gene Scott	7–2	Hampton Court
1979	Howard Angus	Chris Ronaldson	7–0	Hampton Court
1981	Chris Ronaldson	Howard Angus	6–1 (retired)	Queen's
1983	Chris Ronaldson	Wayne Davies	7–4	Hampton Court
1985	Chris Ronaldson	Wayne Davies	7–1	Queen's
1987	Wayne Davies	Chris Ronaldson	7–4	Queen's
1988	Wayne Davies	Lachlan Deuchar	7–1	New York
1991	Wayne Davies	Lachlan Deuchar	7–4	New York
1993	Wayne Davies	Lachlan Deuchar	7–6	New York
1994	Robert Fahey	Wayne Davies	9–5	Hobart & New York
1995	Robert Fahey	Wayne Davies	6–2 (retired)	Hobart
1996	Robert Fahey	Wayne Davies	7–1	Melbourne
1998	Robert Fahey	Julian Snow	7–4	Melbourne
2000	Robert Fahey	Wayne Davies	7–0	Hobart
2002	Robert Fahey	Tim Chisholm	7–6	Hampton Court
2004	Robert Fahey	Tim Chisholm	7–1	Newport, Rhode Island
2006	Robert Fahey	Tim Chisholm	7–0	Oratory
2008	Robert Fahey	Camden Riviere	7–5	Fontainebleau
2010	Robert Fahey	Steve Virgona	7–2	Melbourne
2012	Robert Fahey	Steve Virgona	7–3	Queen's
2014	Robert Fahey	Camden Riviere	7–3	Melbourne

MEN'S WORLD DOUBLES CHAMPIONSHIP

	Winners	Runners-up	Score	Venue
2001	Julian Snow and Tim Chisholm	Steve Virgona and Ruaraidh Gunn	5–1	The Burroughs
2003	Robert Fahey and Steve Virgona	Tim Chisholm and Josh Bainton	5–0	Hobart
2005	Robert Fahey and Steve Virgona	David Woodman and Neil Roxburgh	5–0	Fontainebleau
2007	Robert Fahey and Steve Virgona	Tim Chisholm and Camden Riviere	5–3	Boston
2009	Robert Fahey and Steve Virgona	Bryn Sayers and Ricardo Smith	5–0	Seacourt
2011	Robert Fahey and Steve Virgona	Ben Matthews and Julian Snow	5–0	Melbourne
2013	Robert Fahey and Steve Virgona	Tim Chisholm and Camden Riviere	5–4	Paris

LADIES' WORLD SINGLES CHAMPIONSHIP

	Winner	Runner-up	Score	Venue		Winner	Runner-up	Score	Venue
1985	Judy Clarke	Lesley Ronaldson	2-1	Melbourne	2001	Charlotte Cornwallis	Penny Lumley	2-0	Washington
1987	Judy Clarke	Katrina Allen	2-0	Seacourt	2003	Penny Lumley	Charlotte Cornwallis	2-0	Melbourne
1989	Penny Fellows	Sally Jones	2-1	Philadelphia	2005	Charlotte Cornwallis	Joe Iddles	2-1	Paris
1991	Penny Lumley (formerly Fellows)	Sally Jones	2-1	Hobart	2007	Charlotte Cornwallis	Penny Lumley	2-0	Manchester
1993	Sally Jones	Charlotte Cornwallis	2-1	Bordeaux	2009	Charlotte Cornwallis	Karen Hird	2-0	Newport
1995	Penny Lumley	Sue Haswell	2-1	Newport	2011	Claire Vigrass	Karen Hird	2-0	Melbourne
1997	Penny Lumley	Sue Haswell	2-0	Ballarat	2013	Claire Vigrass	Sarah Vigrass	2-0	Paris
1999	Penny Lumley	Sue Haswell	2-1	Hampton Court					

LADIES' WORLD DOUBLES CHAMPIONSHIP

	Winners	Runners-up	Score	Venue
1985	Judy Clarke and Ann Link	Lesley Ronaldson and Karen Toates	2-0	Melbourne
1987	Katrina Allen and Lesley Ronaldson	Judith Clarke and Jane Hyland	2-0	Seacourt
1989	Sally Jones and Alex Warren-Pipes	Katrina Allen and Penny Fellows	2-1	Philadelphia
1991	Alex Garside (née Warren-Piper) and Sally Jones	Penny Lumley and Helen Mursell	2-0	Hobart
1993	Charlotte Cornwallis and Penny Lumley	Alex Garside and Sally Jones	2-0	Bordeaux
1995	Sue Haswell and Penny Lumley	Sally Jones and Lesley Ronaldson	2-1	Newport
1997	Sue Haswell and Penny Lumley	Fiona Deuchar and Kate Leeming	2-0	Ballarat
1999	Sue Haswell and Penny Lumley	Alex Garside and Sally Jones	2-1	Hampton Court
2001	Jo Iddles and Penny Lumley	Charlotte Cornwallis and Alex Garside	2-1	Washington
2003	Penny Lumley and Jo Wood (née Iddles)	Charlotte Cornwallis and Kate Leeming	2-1	Melbourne
2005	Charlotte Cornwallis and Sue Haswell	Frederika Adam and Susan Castley	2-0	Paris
2007	Charlotte Cornwallis and Penny Lumley	Sue Haswell and Kate Leeming	2-0	Manchester
2009	Charlotte Cornwallis and Karen Hird	Amy Hayball and Juliette Lambert	2-0	Newport
2011	Claire Vigrass and Sarah Vigrass	Karen Hird and Rosie Snell	2-0	Melbourne
2013	Claire Vigrass and Sarah Vigrass	Penny Lumley and Tara Lumley	2-0	Paris

BATHURST CUP

International Competition

In Paris eight game sets were played up to 1927

	Winner	Runner-up	Score	Venue		Winner	Runner-up	Score	Venue		Winner	Runner-up	Score	Venue
1922	Great Britain	France	5-0	Queen's	1958	USA	Great Britain	3-0	Queen's		Great Britain	Australia	5-0	Queen's
1923	USA	France	3-0	Paris	1960	USA	Great Britain	3-2	Queen's	1991	Australia	France	3-2	Melbourne
	Great Britain	USA	3-2	Paris	1962	Great Britain	France	4-1	Paris		Great Britain	USA	5-0	Melbourne
1924	USA	Great Britain	3-1	Queen's	1966	USA	France	5-0	Paris		Great Britain	Australia	4-1	Melbourne
1925	Great Britain	France	5-0	Queen's	1969	Australia	Great Britain	4-0	Melbourne	1992	Australia	France	3-2	Bordeaux
1926	USA	France	3-0	Prince's		USA	Great Britain	3-2	Tuxedo and New York		Great Britain	Australia	5-0	Bordeaux
1927	USA	France	3-1	Paris						1994	USA	France	3-0	Newport
1928	USA	France	3-0	Queen's	1975	Great Britain	Australia	5-0	Melbourne		Great Britain	USA	3-2	Newport
	Great Britain	USA	3-0	Queen's		Great Britain	USA	5-0	Melbourne	1996	Australia	France	5-0	Leamington
1929	Great Britain	France	3-0	Paris	1978	Great Britain	France	4-1	Paris		Great Britain	USA	5-0	Leamington
1930	Great Britain	USA	5-0	Queen's		USA	Australia	5-0	Paris		Great Britain	Australia	5-0	Leamington
1931	USA	France	3-1	Paris		Great Britain	USA	3-2	Paris	1999	Australia	France	5-0	Hobart
	Great Britain	USA	3-1	Paris	1980	Great Britain	France	5-0	Lord's		Great Britain	USA	4-1	Hobart
1932	Great Britain	USA	3-0	Queen's	1982	Australia	USA	3-2	Melbourne		Great Britain	Australia	3-2	Hobart
1933	USA	France	3-2	Paris		Australia	GB	4-1	Melbourne	2000	Great Britain	France	4-1	Paris
	Great Britain	USA	3-0	Paris	1983	Great Britain	France	5-0	Bordeaux		Australia	USA	5-0	Paris
1934	France	USA	3-2	Queen's		Great Britain	Australia	4-1	Bordeaux		Great Britain	Australia	4-1	Paris
	Great Britain	France	3-0	Queen's	1984	Australia	USA	3-2	Newport Rhode Island	2002	Great Britain	USA	5-0	Aiken
1935	France	USA	3-1	Paris							France	Australia	4-1	Aiken
	Great Britain	France	3-0			Great Britain	Australia	4-1	Newport Rhode Island		Great Britain	France	5-0	Aiken
1937	Great Britain	France	4-0	Paris						2004	Great Britain	Australia	4-1	Manchester
1938	Great Britain	France	3-0	Queen's	1985	Australia	USA	3-0	Hobart Tasmania		USA	France	4-1	Manchester
1939	Great Britain	France	5-0	Paris		Great Britain	Australia	4-1	Hobart Tasmania		Great Britain	USA	5-0	Manchester
1947	Great Britain	France	3-2	Paris	1986	Great Britain	France	5-0	Queen's	2006	Australia	Great Britain	3-1	Melbourne
1948	USA	France	5-0	Queen's		USA	Australia	4-1	Queen's	2008	Great Britain	USA	5-0	Paris
1949	USA	France	3-2	Paris		Great Britain	USA	3-1	Queen's		Australia	France	4-1	Paris
	USA	Great Britain	3-2	Paris	1987	Australia	France	4-1	Paris		Great Britain	Australia	4-1	Paris
1950	Great Britain	France	5-0	Queen's		Great Britain	Australia	5-0	Paris	2011	Great Britain	France	4-1	New York
	Great Britain	USA	3-1	Queen's	1988	Australia	USA	5-0	Ballarat		Australia	USA	4-1	New York
1951	Great Britain	France	4-1			Great Britain	Australia	3-2	Ballarat		Australia	Great Britain	5-0	New York
1954	Great Britain	France	3-0	Bordeaux	1989	Great Britain	France	5-0	Philadelphia	2013	Australia	USA	5-0	Holyport
1955	Great Britain	USA	4-1	Queen's		USA	Australia	3-2	Philadelphia		Great Britain	France	5-0	Holyport
	Great Britain	Australia	3-0	Queen's		Great Britain	USA	3-2	Philadelphia		Australia	Great Britain	3-2	Holyport
1957	Great Britain	France	5-0	Paris	1990	Australia	France	3-2	Queen's					

CHAMPIONSHIP RECORDS

EUROPEAN OPEN SINGLES CHAMPIONSHIP
Invitation event until 2005 when it became open

	Winner	Runner-up	Score	Venue		Winner	Runner-up	Score	Venue
1995	Lachlan Deuchar	Mike Gooding		Bordeaux	2007	Rob Fahey	Ruaraidh Gunn	3–1	Lord's
1996	Mike Gooding	Chris Bray		Fontainebleau	2008	Camden Riviere	Rob Fahey	3–0	Lord's
1998	Nick Wood	Chris Bray		Paris	2009	Camden Riviere	Rob Fahey	1–2 *retired*	Lord's
2004	Rob Fahey	Chris Bray		Prested	2011	Rob Fahey	Bryn Sayers	3–1	Lord's
2005	Rob Fahey	Nick Wood	3–0	Lord's	2012	Camden Riviere	Bryn Sayers	3–0	Lord's
2006	Rob Fahey	Steve Virgona	3–0	Lord's	2013	Camden Riviere	Rob Fahey	3–2	Lord's

UNITED KINGDOM

MEN

THE PRINCE'S CLUB SHIELD
For the Open Championship (Challenge)

	Winner	Runner-up	Score		Winner	Runner-up	Score		Winner	Runner-up	Score
1931	E.M. Baerlein	W.A. Groom	3–2	1952	R. Hughes	H.D. Johns	5–3	1970	H.R. Angus	F. Willis	5–2
1931	E. Ratcliff	E.J.G. Johnson	3–1	1954	J.P. Dear	R. Hughes	5–2	1972	H.R. Angus	F. Willis	7–5
1932	W.A. Groom	E. Ratcliff	7–1	1962	J.P. Dear resigned			1975	H.R. Angus	F. Willis	7–6
1934	L. Lees	W.A. Groom	7–1	1962	R. Hughes	D.J. Warburg	5–1	1976	H.R. Angus	F. Willis	7–2
1935	L. Lees	W.A. Groom	7–2	1967	F. Willis	R. Hughes	4–3 (retd)	1979	H.R. Angus	C.J. Ronaldson	7–0*
1938	J.P. Dear	L. Lees	5–1	1968	F. Willis	H.R. Angus	5–2				

*H.R. Angus beat C.J. Ronaldson in a combined challenge for the British Open and World Championships. He relinquished the Open Championship so that it could become an annual event.

THE OPEN SINGLES CHAMPIONSHIP
(Annual)

	Winner	Runner-up	Score		Winner	Runner-up	Score		Winner	Runner-up	Score
1979	H.R. Angus	C.J. Ronaldson	3–0	1991	L. Deuchar	R.L. Fahey	3–2	2004	R.L. Fahey	R.G.A. Gunn	3–0
1980	C.J. Ronaldson	A.C. Lovell	3–0	1992	J.P. Snow	C.J. Bray	3–0	2005	R.L. Fahey	R.G.A. Gunn	3–0
1981	C.J. Ronaldson	W.F. Davies	3–2	1993	J.P. Snow	R.L. Fahey (retd)	0–1	2006	R.L. Fahey	S. Virgona	3–0
1982	C.J. Ronaldson	G.J. Hyland	3–2	1994	J.P. Snow	L. Deuchar	3–1	2007	R.L. Fahey	S. Virgona	3–1
1983	C.J. Ronaldson	L. Deuchar	3–0	1995	R.L. Fahey	L. Deuchar	3–0	2008	R.L. Fahey	C. Riviere	3–1
1984	C.J. Ronaldson	W.F. Davies	3–2	1997	C.J. Bray	R.L. Fahey	3–0	2009	R.L. Fahey	S. Virgona	3–1
1985	C.J. Ronaldson	W.F. Davies	3–2	1998	J.P. Snow	S. Virgona	3–2	2010	R.L. Fahey	S. Virgona	3–1
1986	L. Deuchar	C.J. Ronaldson	3–1	1999	J.S. Male	M.H.J. Gooding	3–1	2011	R.L. Fahey	B. Sayers	3–2
1987	L. Deuchar	W.F. Davies	3–2	2000	R.L. Fahey	C.J. Bray	3–0	2012	B. Sayers	R.L. Fahey	3–1
1988	L. Deuchar	C.J. Ronaldson	3–0	2001	R L Fahey	T. Chisholm	3–1	2013	S. Virgona	B. Sayers	3–2
1989	L. Deuchar	C.J. Ronaldson	3–2	2002	T Chisholm	R.L. Fahey	3–2	2014	C. Riviere	S. Virgona	3–2
1990	L. Deuchar	J.P. Snow	3–0	2003	R.L. Fahey	R.G.A. Gunn	3–0				

OPEN DOUBLES CHAMPIONSHIP

	Winners	Runners-up	Score		Winners	Runners-up	Score
1971	R. Hughes and N.A.R. Cripps	H.R. Angus and N.W. Smith	3–2	1984	L. Deuchar and W.F. Davies	C.J. Ronaldson and M.F. Dean	3–1
1972	F. Willis and C. Ennis	C.J. Swallow and N.A.R. Cripps	3–0	1985	L. Deuchar and W.F. Davies	C.J. Ronaldson and M.F. Dean	3–0
1973	C.J. Swallow and N.A.R. Cripps	F. Willis and C. Ennis	3–0	1986	W.F. Davies and L. Deuchar	C.J. Ronaldson and M.F. Dean	3–1
1974	C.J. Swallow and N.A.R. Cripps	F. Willis and C. Ennis	3–0	1987	W.F. Davies and L. Deuchar	N.A.R. Cripps and P.G. Tabley	3–1
1975	C.J. Swallow and N.A.R. Cripps	H.R. Angus and D.J. Warburg	3–2	1988	W.F. Davies and L. Deuchar	J.B.K. Howell and K. Sheldon	3–0
1976	F. Willis and D.W. Cull	C. Ennis and M.F. Dean	3–1	1989	W.F. Davies and L. Deuchar	J.B.K. Howell and K. Sheldon	3–0
1977 April	A.C. Lovell and N.A.R. Cripps	F. Willis and D.W. Cull	3–1	1990	W.F. Davies and L. Deuchar	R.L. Fahey and A.P. Meares	3–0
	A.C. Lovell and	F. Willis and		1991	C.J. Bray and M.H.J. Gooding	L. Deuchar and P.G. Tabley	3–2
Dec	N.A.R. Cripps	D.W. Cull	3–0	1992	L. Deuchar and W.F. Davies	F.J. Filippelli and J.S. Male	w/o
1978	A.C. Lovell and N.A.R. Cripps	C.J. Ronaldson and M.F. Dean	3–0	1993	C.J. Bray and M.H.J. Gooding	J.P. Snow and N. Wood	3–0
1979	A.C. Lovell and N.A.R. Cripps	C.J. Ronaldson and M.F. Dean	3–0	1994	C.J. Bray and M.H.J. Gooding	W.F. Davies and L. Deuchar	3–0
1980	A.C. Lovell and N.A.R. Cripps	B. Toates and F. Willis	3–0	1995	R.L. Fahey and F.J. Filippelli	C.J. Bray and M.H.J. Gooding	3–2
1981	C.J. Ronaldson and M.F. Dean	W.F. Davies and L. Deuchar	3–2	1996	C.J. Bray and M.J. Happell	L. Deuchar and M.H.J. Gooding	3–2
1982	A.C. Lovell and N.A.R. Cripps	C.J. Ronaldson and M.F. Dean	3–0	1997	J.S. Male and J.P. Snow	R.L. Fahey and M.H.J. Gooding	3–0
1983	C.J. Ronaldson and M.F. Dean	C.J. Lumley and L. Deuchar	3–1	1998	J.S. Male and J.P. Snow	R.G.A. Gunn and S. Virgona	3–0
				1999	R.G.A. Gunn and S. Virgona	J.P. Snow and J.S. Male	3–1

table continues

Tennis and Rackets

	Winners	Runners-up	Score		Winners	Runners-up	Score
2000	C.J. Bray and N. Wood	J.P. Snow and T. Chisholm	3-2	2008	R.L. Fahey and J.S. Male	N. Wood and C. Riviere	3-1
2001	R.L. Fahey and S. Virgona	C.J. Bray and J.P. Willcocks	3-0	2009	S. Virgona and N. Wood	R.L. Fahey and R.G.A. Gunn	3-0
2002	R.L. Fahey and S. Virgona	J.P. Snow and T. Chisholm	3-1	2010	R.L. Fahey and S. Virgona	T. Chisholm and C. Medlow	3-0
2003	R.L. Fahey and R.G.A. Gunn	J.P. Snow and A.J.M. Phillips	3-1	2011	R.L. Fahey and S. Virgona	B. Sayers and K. Booth	3-0
2004	M.H.J. Gooding and N. Wood	C.J. Bray and J.P. Willcocks	3-0	2012	R.L. Fahey and S. Virgona	B. Sayers and K. Booth	3-0
2005	R.L. Fahey and R.G.A. Gunn	S. Virgona and D. Woodman	3-0	2013	T. Chisholm and B. Sayers	R.L. Fahey and S. Virgona	3-2
2006	R.L. Fahey and R.G.A. Gunn	S. Virgona and J. Dawes	3-0	2014	T. Chisholm and C. Riviere	R.L. Fahey and B. Sayers	3-1
2007	R.L. Fahey and R.G.A. Gunn	S. Virgona and J.P. Willcocks	3-1				

OPEN INVITATION TOURNAMENT

	Winner	Runner-up	Score		Winner	Runner-up	Score		Winner	Runner-up	Score
1965	R. Hughes	J.P. Dear	3-0	1970 Jan	H.R. Angus	F. Willis	3-1	1974	H.R. Angus	N.A.R. Cripps	3-2
1966	F. Willis	N.A.R. Cripps	3-0	1970 Nov	F. Willis	D.W. Cull	3-1	1975	C. Ennis	N.A.R. Cripps	3-2
1967	F. Willis	G.W.T. Atkins	3-1	1971	N.A.R. Cripps	F. Willis	3-1	1976	H.R. Angus	N.A.R. Cripps	3-2
1968	H.R. Angus	F. Willis	3-2	1972	F. Willis	N.A.R. Cripps	3-0	1977	H.R. Angus	N.A.R. Cripps	3-0
1969	F. Willis	H.R. Angus	3-2	1973	N.A.R. Cripps	F. Willis	3-1	1978	C.J. Ronaldson	H.R. Angus	3-2

AMATEUR SINGLES CHAMPIONSHIP

Queen's Club Cup

Championship of Queen's Club 1888, Amateur championship since 1889
Played at Manchester 1922, 1926, 1931, 1947, 1951, 1964; Lord's 1946, 1958

	Winner	Runner-up	Score		Winner	Runner-up	Score		Winner	Runner-up	Score
1888	J.M. Heathcote	Sir E. Grey	3-1	1930	E.M. Baerlein	W.C. Wright (USA)	3-0	1976	H.R. Angus	J.D. Ward	3-0
1889	Sir E. Grey	E.B.C. Curtis	3-1	1931	L. Lees	E.M. Baerlein	3-0	1977	H.R. Angus	A.C. Lovell	3-2
1890	E.B.C. Curtis	Sir E. Grey	3-1	1932	Lord Aberdare	L. Lees	3-2	1978	H.R. Angus	J.D. Ward	3-0
1891	Sir E. Grey	Lord Windsor	scratched	1933	L. Lees	Lord Aberdare	3-1	1979	H.R. Angus	A.C. Lovell	3-0
1892	H.E. Crawley	Sir E. Grey	3-2	1934	L. Lees	Lord Aberdare	3-0	1980	H.R. Angus	A.C. Lovell	3-1
1893	H.E. Crawley	Sir E. Grey	3-2	1935	L. Lees	Lord Aberdare	3-0	1981	A.C. Lovell	H.R. Angus	3-0
1894	H.E. Crawley	Sir E. Grey	3-2	1936	L. Lees	C.M.N. Baker	3-0	1982	H.R. Angus	A.C. Lovell	3-0
1895	Sir E. Grey	H.E. Crawley	3-2	1937	L. Lees	R.H. Hill	3-0	1983	A.C. Lovell	H.R. Angus	3-0
1895	Sir E. Grey	H.E. Crawley	3-0	1938	Lord Aberdare	W.M. Ross-Skinner	3-0	1984	A.C. Lovell	M.F. Dean	3-0
1896	Sir E. Grey	H.E. Crawley	3-2	1939	W.D. Macpherson	L. Lees	3-1	1985	A.C. Lovell	H.R. Angus	3-2
1897	J.B. Gribble	H.E. Crawley	3-1	1946	L. Lees	W.D. Macpherson	3-1	1986	A.C. Lovell	J.P. Snow	3-2
1898	Sir E. Grey	H.E. Crawley	3-0	1947	Lord Cullen	P. Kershaw	3-0	1987	J.P. Snow	H.R. Angus	3-0
1899	E.H. Miles	J.B. Gribble	3-1	1948	P. Kershaw	L. Lees	3-0	1988	J.P. Snow	I.E.G. Snell	3-0
1900	E.H. Miles	J.B. Gribble	3-0	1949	O. Phipps (USA)	W.D. Macpherson	3-0	1989	J.P. Snow	M.J. Happell	3-1
1901	E.H. Miles	J.B. Gribble	3-0	1950	A.B. Martin (USA)	W.D. Macpherson	3-1	1990	J.S. Male	J.P. Snow	3-0
1902	E.H. Miles	J.B. Gribble	3-0	1951	P. Kershaw	D.J. Warburg	3-0	1991	J.P. Snow	A.J.W. Page	3-0
1903	E.H. Miles	V.H. Pennell (retd)	2-0	1952	Lord Cullen	R.C. Riseley	3-2	1992	J.P. Snow	A.J.W. Page	3-0
1904	V.H. Pennell	E.H. Miles	3-2	1953	Hon. M.G.L. Bruce	P. Kershaw	3-0	1993	J.P. Snow	N.J.J. Pendrigh	3-0
1905	E.H. Miles	V.H. Pennell	3-0	1954	Hon. M.G.L. Bruce	P. Kershaw	3-2	1994	J.P. Snow	N.J.J. Pendrigh	3-0
1906	E.H. Miles	Jay Gould (USA)	3-1	1955	R.C. Riseley	P. Kershaw	3-1	1995	J.P. Snow	N.J.J. Pendrigh	3-0
1907	J. Gould (USA)	V.H. Pennell	3-0	1956	Hon. M.G.L. Bruce	D.J. Warburg	3-0	1996	J.P. Snow	M.C. Howard	3-0
1908	J. Gould (USA)	E.H. Miles	3-1	1957	Hon. M.G.L. Bruce	D.J. Warburg	3-2	1997	J.P. Snow	N.J.J. Pendrigh	3-0
1909	E.H. Miles	Hon. N.S. Lytton	3-1	1958	N.R. Knox (USA)	Lord Aberdare	3-0	1998	J.P. Snow	N.J.J. Pendrigh	3-0
1910	E.H. Miles	Hon. N.S. Lytton	3-2	1959	D.J. Warburg	J.D. Whatman	3-2	1999	J.P. Snow	J.P. Willcocks	3-0
1911	Hon. N.S. Lytton	E.H. Miles	3-1	1960	G.W.T. Atkins	D.J. Warburg	3-1	2000	J.P. Snow	J.P. Willcocks	3-0
1912	E.M. Baerlein	Hon. N.S. Lytton	3-0	1961	D.J. Warburg	G.W.T. Atkins	3-0	2001	J.P. Snow	M.C. Howard	3-0
1913	Hon. N.S. Lytton	E.M. Baerlein	3-2	1962	G.W.T. Atkins	D.J. Warburg	3-0	2002	J.P. Snow	J.P. Willcocks	3-1
1914	E.M. Baerlein	J. Crane (USA)	3-0	1963	G.W.T. Atkins	D.J. Warburg	3-1	2003	J.P. Snow	J.P. Willcocks	3-0
1919	E.M. Baerlein	V.H. Pennell	3-2	1964	A.C.S. Tufton	D.J. Warburg	3-2	2004	J.P. Snow	I. Snell	3-0
1920	E.M. Baerlein	E.A.C. Druce	3-0	1965	D.J. Warburg	A.C.S. Tufton	3-2	2005	J.P. Snow	J.P. Willcocks	3-0
1921	E.M. Baerlein	C. Suydam Cutting (USA)	3-0	1966	H.R. Angus	D.J. Warburg	3-1	2006	D. Woodman	D.S. Harms	3-0
				1967	H.R. Angus	D.J. Warburg	3-1	2007	D.S. Harms	P. Wright	3-1
1922	E.M. Baerlein	W. Renshaw	3-1	1968	H.R. Angus	D.J. Warburg	3-0	2008	D. Woodman	R. Krznaric	3-1
1923	E.M. Baerlein	V.H. Pennell	3-2	1969	H.R. Angus	D.J. Warburg	3-1	2009	J. Douglas	P. Wright	3-1
1924	E.M. Baerlein	Hon. C.N. Bruce	3-1	1970	H.R. Angus	A.C.S. Tufton	3-0	2010	J. Douglas	P. Wright	3-0
1925	E.M. Baerlein	Hon. C.N. Bruce	3-0	1971	H.R. Angus	R.B. Bloomfield	3-0	2011	C. Medlow	J. Douglas	3-2
1926	E.M. Baerlein	Hon. C.N. Bruce	3-0	1972	H.R. Angus	R.B. Bloomfield	3-0	2012	J.P. Snow	M. Sarlangue (France)	3-2
1927	E.M. Baerlein	Hon. C.N. Bruce	3-1	1973	H.R. Angus	A.C.S. Tufton	3-0	2013	J. Douglas	J.P. Snow	3-1
1928	L. Lees	R.H. Hill	3-2	1974	H.R. Angus	A.C. Lovell	3-0	2014	M. Sarlangue (France)	J. Douglas	3-0
1929	E.M. Baerlein	L. Lees	3-1	1975	H.R. Angus	A.C. Lovell	3-0				

Championship Records

AMATEUR DOUBLES CHAMPIONSHIP
Inter-club doubles to 1953

Bailey Cup

Year	Winners	Year	Winners	Year	Winners
1920–22	E.M. Baerlein and W. Renshaw (Manchester)	1955–56	P. Kershaw and R.C. Riseley	1983–86	A.C. Lovell and M.F. Dean
1923	Hon. C.N. Bruce and R.H. Hill (Queen's)	1957	Hon. M.G.L. Bruce and Lord Cullen	1987	J.P. Snow and J.S. Male
1924	J. Gould and C. Suydam Cutting (Paris)	1958	A.B. Martin and N.R. Knox	1988	A.C. Lovell and M.F. Dean
1925	E.M. Baerlein and W. Renshaw (Manchester)	1959	Lord Aberdare and J.D. Whatman	1989–90	M.J. Happell and J.S. Male
1926	L. Lees and M. Woosnam (Manchester)	1960	N.R. Knox and W.E. Lingelbach Jr	1991–93	J.P. Snow and M.E. McMurrugh
1927	J. Gould and W.C. Wright (Philadelphia)	1961	Lord Aberdare and J.D. Whatman	1994	J.R. Acheson-Gray and N.J.J. Pendrigh
1928	L. Lees and M. Woosnam (Manchester)	1962–64	A.C.S. Tufton and J.W. Leonard	1995	J.P. Snow and M.E. McMurrugh
1929–31	E.M. Baerlein and L. Lees (Manchester)	1965	W.T. Vogt and E. Newbold Black IV	1996	J.P. Snow and S.P. Howe
1932–33	Lord Aberdare and W.D. Macpherson (Queen's)	1966	D.J. Warburg and R.L.O. Bridgeman	1997–2000	J.P. Snow and R. Acheson-Gray
1934–37	E.M. Baerlein and L. Lees (Manchester)	1967–70	D.J. Warburg and H.R. Angus	2001–3	J. Willcocks and A. Hombrecher
1938	Lord Aberdare and W.D. Macpherson (Queen's)	1971	*no competition*	2004	J. Willcocks and J. Acheson-Gray
1939	Lord Aberdare and R.C. Riseley (Queen's)	1972–74	D.J. Warburg and H.R. Angus	2005	J.P. Snow and J. Acheson-Gray
1946	L. Lees and P. Kershaw (Manchester)	1975	J.A.R. Clench and A.C. Lovell	2006	L. Danby and C. Danby
1947–49	W.D. Macpherson and Lord Cullen (Queen's)	1976	H.R. Angus and D.J. Warburg	2007	D. Woodman and N. Roxburgh
1950	R.C. Riseley and P. Kershaw (Oxford)	1977–79	A.C. Lovell and A.G. Windham	2008	D. Woodman and J. Douglas
1951	P. Kershaw and M.A. Pugh (Manchester)	1980	H.R. Angus and R.D.B. Cooper	2009–11	P. Wright and J. Douglas
1952–53	P. Kershaw and R.C. Riseley (Oxford)	1981	A.C. Lovell and M.F. Dean	2012–13	J.P. Snow and C. Medlow
1954	Lord Cullen and Hon. M.G.L. Bruce	1982	P.G. Seabrook and J.D. Ward	2014	P. Wright and J. Douglas

MCC PRIZES

Gold and Silver Racquet Cups
For members of MCC only 1867–96; J.B. Gribble Cup presented to winner of Gold Racquet from 1904

Year	Gold Racquet	Silver Racquet	Year	Gold Racquet	Silver Racquet	Year	Gold Racquet	Silver Racquet
1867	J.M. Heathcote	J. Marshall	1907	V.H. Pennell	E.H. Miles	1957	Hon. M.G.L. Bruce	D.J. Warburg
1868	J.M. Heathcote	G.B. Crawley	1908	E.H. Miles	E.B. Noel	1958	Lord Aberdare	D.J. Warburg
1869	J.M. Heathcote	Hon. C.G. Lyttelton	1909	E.H. Miles	W.M. Cazalet	1959	P. Kershaw	D.J. Warburg
1870	J.M. Heathcote	Hon. C.G. Lyttelton	1910	E.H. Miles	Capt. R.K. Price	1960	D.J. Warburg	P. Kershaw
1871	J.M. Heathcote	Hon. C.G. Lyttelton	1911	E.H. Miles	Maj. A. Cooper-Key	1961	D.J. Warburg	P. Kershaw
1872	J.M. Heathcote	Hon. C.G. Lyttelton	1912	E.H. Miles	Maj. A. Cooper-Key	1962	D.J. Warburg	Lord Aberdare
1873	J.M. Heathcote	Hon. C.G. Lyttelton	1913	E.H. Miles	Maj. A. Cooper-Key	1963	D.J. Warburg	P. Kershaw
1874	J.M. Heathcote	G.B. Crawley	1914	J.F. Marshall	Capt. R.K. Price	1964	D.J. Warburg	A.C.S. Tufton
1875	J.M. Heathcote	R.D. Walker	1919	E.A.C. Druce	Capt. R.K. Price	1965	D.J. Warburg	A.C.S. Tufton
1876	J.M. Heathcote	R.D. Walker	1920	Capt. R.K. Price	E.A.C. Druce	1966	H.R. Angus	D.J. Warburg
1877	J.M. Heathcote	R.D. Walker	1921	E.M. Baerlein	E.A.C. Druce	1967	H.R. Angus	D.J. Warburg
1878	J.M. Heathcote	C.E. Boyle	1922	E.M. Baerlein	Hon. C.N. Bruce	1968	H.R. Angus	D.J. Warburg
1879	J.M. Heathcote	C.E. Boyle	1923	E.M. Baerlein	Hon. C.N. Bruce	1969	H.R. Angus	A.C.S. Tufton
1880	J.M. Heathcote	Hon. A. Lyttelton	1924	E.M. Baerlein	E.A.C. Druce	1970	H.R. Angus	A.C.S. Tufton
1881	J.M. Heathcote	Hon. A. Lyttelton	1925	E.M. Baerlein	R.H. Hill	1971	H.R. Angus	A.C.S. Tufton
1882	Hon. A. Lyttelton	J.M. Heathcote	1926	E.M. Baerlein	Hon. C.N. Bruce	1972	H.R. Angus	A.C.S. Tufton
1883	J.M. Heathcote	Hon. A. Lyttelton	1927	E.M. Baerlein	Hon. C.N. Bruce	1973	H.R. Angus	A.C.S. Tufton
1884	Hon. A. Lyttelton	J.M. Heathcote	1928	E.M. Baerlein	Hon. C.N. Bruce	1974	H.R. Angus	R.D.B. Cooper
1885	Hon. A. Lyttelton	J.M. Heathcote	1929	E.M. Baerlein	Hon. C.N. Bruce	1975	H.R. Angus	A.C. Lovell
1886	J.M. Heathcote	B.N. Akroyd	1930	Lord Aberdare	E.M. Baerlein	1976	H.R. Angus	A.C. Lovell
1887	Hon. A. Lyttelton	J.M. Heathcote	1931	E.M. Baerlein	Lord Aberdare	1977	H.R. Angus	A.C. Lovell
1888	Hon. A. Lyttelton	A.J. Webbe	1932	Lord Aberdare	W.D. Macpherson	1978	H.R. Angus	A.C. Lovell
1889	Hon. A. Lyttelton	Sir E. Grey	1933	Lord Aberdare	R. Aird	1979	H.R. Angus	A.C. Lovell
1890	Hon. A. Lyttelton	Sir E. Grey	1934	Lord Aberdare	R. Aird	1980	H.R. Angus	A.C. Lovell
1891	Hon. A. Lyttelton	Sir E. Grey	1935	L. Lees	Lord Aberdare	1981	A.C. Lovell	H.R. Angus
1892	Hon. A. Lyttelton	H.E. Crawley	1936	L. Lees	Lord Aberdare	1982	H.R. Angus	A.C. Lovell
1893	Hon. A. Lyttelton	Sir E. Grey	1937	Lord Aberdare	W.D. Macpherson	1983	A.C. Lovell	H.R. Angus
1894	Hon. A. Lyttelton	Sir E. Grey	1938	R.H. Hill	W.D. Macpherson	1984	A.C. Lovell	J.D. Ward
1895	Hon. A. Lyttelton	Sir E. Grey	1939	W.D. Macpherson	R. Aird	1985	A.C. Lovell	H.R. Angus
1896	Sir E. Grey	Hon. A. Lyttelton	1946	W.M. Ross-Skinner	W.D. Macpherson	1986	A.C. Lovell	J.D. Ward
1897	E.H. Miles	Sir E. Grey	1947	W.D. Macpherson	R. Aird	1987	A.C. Lovell	J.D. Ward
1898	E.H. Miles	H.E. Crawley	1948	W.D. Macpherson	R. Aird	1988	A.C. Lovell	J.D. Ward
1899	E.H. Miles	Sir E. Grey	1949	W.D. Macpherson	R. Aird	1989	A.C. Lovell	J.D. Ward
1900	J.B. Gribble	Sir E. Grey	1950	R.C. Riseley	W.D. Macpherson	1990	M.J. Happell	J.D. Ward
1901	E.H. Miles	Sir E. Grey	1951	W.D. Macpherson	R.C. Riseley	1991	N.J.J. Pendrigh	A.J.W. Page
1902	E.H. Miles	Sir E. Grey	1952	W.D. Macpherson	Hon. M.G.L. Bruce	1992	A.J.W. Page	N.J.J. Pendrigh
1903	E.H. Miles	Sir E. Grey	1953	D.J. Warburg	Hon. M.G.L. Bruce	1993	N.J.J. Pendrigh	M.C. Howard
1904	E.H. Miles	Sir E. Grey	1954	Hon. M.G.L. Bruce	D.J. Warburg	1994	N.J.J. Pendrigh	M.C. Howard
1905	E.H. Miles	H.E. Crawley	1955	Hon. M.G.L. Bruce	P. Kershaw	1995	N.J.J. Pendrigh	H.R.P. Jarvis
1906	E.H. Miles	Maj. A. Cooper-Key	1956	Hon. M.G.L. Bruce	D.J. Warburg			*table continues*

415

Tennis and Rackets

	Gold Racquet	Silver Racquet		Gold Racquet	Silver Racquet		Gold Racquet	Silver Racquet
1996	N.J.J. Pendrigh	M.C. Howard	2000–05	J.P. Snow	J.P. Willcocks	2009–11	J. Douglas	J.P. Willcocks
1997	J.P. Snow	M.C. Howard	2006	J.P. Willcocks	D. Woodman	2012–13	J. Douglas	C. Medlow
1998	J.P. Snow	N.J.J. Pendrigh	2007	J.P. Willcocks	M.C. Howard	2014	C. Medlow	C. Medlow
1999	J.P. Snow	J.R. Acheson-Gray	2008	D. Woodman	J.P. Willcocks			

PROFESSIONAL SINGLES CHAMPIONSHIP

Lees-Scott-Chad Cup

1937	J.P. Dear (Prince's Club)	1987	C.J. Ronaldson (Hampton Court)	2001	R.L. Fahey (Melbourne)
1952	R. Hughes (Manchester)	1988	W.F. Davies (New York)	2002	R.L. Fahey (Melbourne)
1954	J.P. Dear (Queen's)	1989	C.J. Ronaldson (Hampton Court)	2003	R.L. Fahey (Melbourne)
1962	R. Hughes (Malvern)	1990	L. Deuchar (unattached)	2004	R.L. Fahey (Melbourne)
1966	F. Willis (Manchester)	1991	L. Deuchar (unattached)	2005	S. Virgona (Philadelphia)
1976	F. Willis (Manchester)	1992	C.J. Ronaldson (Hampton Court)	2006	R.L. Fahey (unattached)
1979	F. Willis (Unattached)	1993	L. Deuchar (Harbour Club)	2007	R.L. Fahey (unattached)
1980	C.J. Ronaldson (Hampton Court)	1994	L. Deuchar (Harbour Club)	2009	R.L. Fahey (unattached)
1981	C.J. Ronaldson (Hampton Court)	1995	L. Deuchar (Harbour Club)	2010	R.L. Fahey (unattached)
1982	C.J. Ronaldson (Hampton Court)	1996	W.F. Davies (unattached)	2011	S. Virgona (Philadelphia)
1983	C.J. Ronaldson (Hampton Court)	1997	L. Deuchar (Harbour Club)	2012	C. Riviere (unattached)
1984	C.J. Ronaldson (Hampton Court)	1998	C.J. Bray (Petworth)	2013	C. Riviere (unattached)
1985	L. Deuchar (Hampton Court)	1999	S. Virgona (Holyport)	2014	C. Riviere (unattached)
1986	C.J. Ronaldson (Hampton Court)	2000	N. Wood (Holyport)		

PROFESSIONAL DOUBLES CHAMPIONSHIP

	Winners	Runners-up	Score		Winners	Runners-up	Score
1982	P.L. Dawes and K. Sheldon	C.J. and S.J. Ronaldson	2-1	1995	L. Deuchar and J.B.K. Howell	C.J. Bray and M.H.J. Gooding	3-2
1983	P.L. Dawes and K. Sheldon	L. Deuchar and J. Fletcher	2-1	1996	C.J. Bray and M.H.J. Gooding	N. Wood and A.J.M. Phillips	3-1
1984	C.J. and S.J. Ronaldson	L. Deuchar and J. Fletcher	2-0	1997	L. Deuchar and M.H.J. Gooding	N. Wood and A.J.M. Phillips	3-1
1985	C.J. and S.J. Ronaldson	C. Lumley and K. Sheldon	2-0	1998	C.J. Bray and M.H.J. Gooding	J.S. Male and R.G.A. Gunn	3-0
1986	L. Deuchar and J. Fletcher	C.J. and S.J. Ronaldson	2-0	1999	C.J. Bray and M.H.J. Gooding	R.G.A. Gunn and S. Virgona	3-1
1987	L. Deuchar and J. Fletcher	C.J. and S.J. Ronaldson	2-0	2000	F.J. Filippelli and J.S. Male	N. Wood and A.J.M. Phillips	3-0
1988	C.J. and S.J. Ronaldson	C.J. Lumley and M.H.J. Gooding	2-1	2001	C.J. Bray and N. Wood	F.J. Filippelli and M.H.J. Gooding	3-0
1989	L. Deuchar and J. Fletcher	C.J. and S.J. Ronaldson	2-1	2002	M.H.J. Gooding and N. Wood	S. Virgona and L. Deuchar	3-0
1990	P.A.B. Brake and C.J. Bray	N. Wood and A.P. Meares	2-0	2003	M.H.J. Gooding and N. Wood	R.G.A. Gunn and S. Virgona	3-2
1991	C.J. Bray and C.J. Lumley	A.J.M. Phillips and K.R. King	2-1	2004	M.H.J. Gooding and N. Wood	A.J.M. Phillips and D. Jones	3-0
1992	L. Deuchar and R.L. Fahey	C.J. Ronaldson and S.J. Ronaldson	2-0	2005	M.H.J. Gooding and N. Wood	R.L. Fahey and D. Jones	3-1
1993	M.J. Devine and K. Sheldon	C.J. Bray and J.B.K. Howell	2-1	2007	R.L. Fahey and R. McNaughtan	M.H.J. Gooding and N. Wood	3-0
1994	L. Deuchar and R.L. Fahey	C.J. Bray and M.H.J. Gooding	3-1				

UNDER 18 SINGLES CHAMPIONSHIP

1983	E Popplewell	1989	A Lyons	1997	C Crossley	2003–04	P Knox	2010	J Lumley
1984	R Elmitt	1990–91	A Scott	1998	B Tanfield	2005	W Fortune	2011	L Williams
1986	I Snell	1992	J Dawes	1999–2000	B Allen	2006	T Weaver	2012	L Gale
1987	J-G Pratt	1993–94	A Blosse	2001	B Sayers	2007–08	C Medlow	2013–14	C Braham
1988	N Wood	1995–96	S Tomalinson	2002	R Greenland	2009	M Sarlangue		

LADIES

THE OPEN SINGLES CHAMPIONSHIP

	Winner	Runner-up	Score		Winner	Runner-up	Score		Winner	Runner-up	Score
1978	Anna Moore	Vivian Dawes	2-1	1991	Penny Fellows	Alex Garside (née Warren-Piper)	2-0	2002	Penny Lumley	Charlotte Cornwallis	2-1
1979	Lesley Ronaldson	Anna Moore	2-0					2003	Charlotte Cornwallis	Alex Garside	2-0
1980	Lesley Ronaldson	Katrina Allen	2-0	1992	Charlotte Cornwallis	Magda Groszek	2-0	2004	Penny Lumley	Charlotte Cornwallis	2-0
1981	Lesley Ronaldson	Katrina Allen	2-0	1993	Penny Lumley (prev. Fellows)	Alex Garside	2-0	2005	Charlotte Cornwallis	Jo Iddles	2-0
1982	Judith Clarke	Lesley Ronaldson	2-0					2006	Charlotte Cornwallis	Frederika Adam	2-0
1983	Katrina Allen	Lesley Ronaldson	2-1	1994	Alex Garside	Sally Jones	2-0	2007	Charlotte Cornwallis	Alex Garside	2-0
1984	Katrina Allen	Lesley Ronaldson	2-1	1995	Penny Lumley	Sally Jones	2-0	2008	Charlotte Cornwallis	Claire Vigrass	2-0
1985	Katrina Allen	Lesley Ronaldson	2-0	1996	Penny Lumley	Alex Garside	2-0	2009	Charlotte Cornwallis	Karen Hird	2-0
1986	Katrina Allen	Lesley Ronaldson	2-0	1997	Penny Lumley	Sue Haswell	2-0	2010	Claire Vigrass	Karen Hird	2-0
1987	Lesley Ronaldson	Sally Jones	2-0	1998	Penny Lumley	Sue Haswell	2-0	2011	Claire Vigrass	Karen Hird	2-0
1988	Sally Jones	Alex Warren-Piper	2-1	1999	Penny Lumley	Kate Leeming	2-0	2012	Claire Vigrass	Karen Hird	2-0
1989	Penny Fellows	Sally Jones	2-1	2000	Penny Lumley	Charlotte Cornwallis	2-0	2013	Claire Vigrass	Sarah Vigrass	2-0
1990	Sally Jones	Alex Warren-Piper	2-0	2001	Penny Lumley	Sally Jones	2-0	2014	Claire Vigrass	Sarah Vigrass	2-0

OPEN DOUBLES CHAMPIONSHIP

	Winners	Runners-up	Score
1982	Jill Cottrell and Sheila Macintosh	Evelyn David and Lesley Ronaldson	2-1
1983	Lesley Ronaldson and Gill Dean	Jill Cottrell and Sheila Macintosh	2-0
1984	Lesley Ronaldson and Gill Dean	Katrina Allen and Sheila Macintosh	2-0
1985	Katrina Allen and Sheila Macintosh	Robbie Bannerman and Lesley Ronaldson	2-0
1986	Lesley Ronaldson and Gill Dean	Katrina Allen and Sheila Macintosh	2-1
1987	Alex Warren-Piper and Sally Jones	Lesley Ronaldson and Gill Dean	2-0
1988	Alex Warren-Piper and Sally Jones	Katrina Allen and Lesley Ronaldson	2-0
1989	Alex Warren-Piper and Sally Jones	Katrina Allen and Penny Fellows	2-0
1990	Alex Warren-Piper and Melissa Briggs	Magda Groszek and Joanna Page	2-0
1991	Penny Fellows and Alex Garside (née Warren-Piper)	Lesley Ronaldson and Gill Dean	2-0
1992	Alex Garside and Sally Jones	Penny Lumley (prev. Fellows) and Charlotte Cornwallis	2-1
1993	Alex Garside and Sally Jones	Penny Lumley and Charlotte Cornwallis	2-1
1994	Fiona Deuchar and Mandy Happell	Sally Jones and Alex Garside	w/o by default
1995	Sally Jones and Sue Haswell	Fiona Deuchar and Emma Wood	2-0
1996	Penny Lumley and Sue Haswell	Alex Garside and Sally Jones	2-1
1997	Penny Lumley and Sue Haswell	Alex Garside and Sally Jones	2-0
1998	Alex Garside and Sally Jones	Fiona Deuchar and Charlotte Cornwallis	2-1
1999	Alex Garside and Penny Lumley	Sally Jones and Kate Leeming	2-0
2000	Penny Lumley and Jo Iddles	Charlotte Cornwallis and Alex Garside	2-1
2001	Penny Lumley and Jo Iddles	Charlotte Cornwallis and Alex Garside	2-1
2002	Penny Lumley and Jo Wood (née Iddles)	Charlotte Cornwallis and Alex Garside	2-0
2003	Penny Lumley and Jo Iddles	Alex Garside and Sally Grant (nee Jones)	2-0
2005	Charlotte Cornwallis and Sue Haswell	Jo Iddles and Jill Newby	2-0
2006	Jo Iddles and Frederika Adam	Charlotte Cornwallis and Sue Haswell	2-0
2007	Charlotte Cornwallis and Penny Lumley	Sue Haswell and Kate Leeming	2-1
2008	Charlotte Cornwallis and Penny Lumley	Sally Grant and Jo Iddles	2-1
2009	Charlotte Cornwallis and Karen Hird	Claire Vigrass and Frederika Adam	2-1
2010	Claire Vigrass and Frederika Adam	Alex Garside and Aldona Greenwood	2-0
2011	Karen Hird and Frederika Adam	Claire Vigrass and Sarah Vigrass	2-1
2012	Claire Vigrass and Sarah Vigrass	Karen Hird and Frederika Adam	2-0
2013	Claire Vigrass and Sarah Vigrass	Penny Lumley and Tara Lumley	2-0
2014	Claire Vigrass and Sarah Vigrass	Sue Haswell and Frederika Adam	2-0

UNDER 18 SINGLES PLATE

2004	S Slack
2005	S Vigrass
2006	K Hird
2011-12	T Lumley
2014	G Willis

THE UNITED STATES

MEN

OPEN SINGLES CHAMPIONSHIP

1919	J. Gould	1966	G.H. Bostwick Jr	1979	B. Toates*	1988-90	W.F. Davies*	2003-04	T. Chisholm*
1921	J. Gould	1967	J.F.C. Bostwick	1980	C.J. Ronaldson*	1991-92	L. Deuchar*	2005-08	R.L. Fahey*
1951	A.B. Martin	1968	G.H. Bostwick Jr	1981	G.J. Hyland*	1993	R.L. Fahey*	2009	C. Riviere*
1956-59	A.B. Johnson*	1969-70	J.F.C. Bostwick	1982-83	W.F. Davies*	1994-95	W.F. Davies*	2010	J. Stout*
1960-62	J.F.C. Bostwick	1971	G.H. Bostwick Jr	1984	C.J. Ronaldson*	1996-97	J.P. Snow	2011	S. Virgona*
1963	A.B. Johnson*	1972	J.F.C. Bostwick	1985	W.F. Davies*	1998	C.J. Bray*	2012	B. Sayers*
1964	R. Hughes*	1973-77	E.L. Scott	1986	C.J. Ronaldson*	1999	W.F. Davies*	2013-14	C. Riviere*
1965	A.B. Johnson*	1978	J.J. Burke Jr*	1987	G.J. Hyland*	2000-02	R.L. Fahey*		

* Denotes Professional

OPEN DOUBLES CHAMPIONSHIP

1959	A.B. Martin and R. Grant III	1980-81	O.M. Phipps and G.J. Hyland*	1998	R.G.A. Gunn* and S. Virgona*
1960	J.P. Dunn* and W.I. Forbes Jr	1982	O.M. Phipps and W.F. Davies*	1999	J.P. Snow and J.S. Male*
1961	G.H. Bostwick Jr and J.F.C. Bostwick	1983	B. Toates* and F. Faulderbaum	2000	J.P. Snow and N. Wood*
1962	J.P. Dunn* and W.I. Forbes Jr	1984	L. Deuchar* and K. Sheldon*	2001	C.J. Bray* and N. Wood*
1963	N.R. Knox and A.B. Martin	1985	J.J. Burke* and P. Clement	2002-03	M.H.J. Gooding* and N. Wood*
1964-67	J.P. Dunn* and W.T. Vogt	1986	W.F. Davies* and P.E. de Svastich	2004	T. Chisholm* and M. Clothier
1968-70	G.H. Bostwick Jr and J.F.C. Bostwick	1987	G.J. Hyland* and D.J.S. Collins	2005	R.L. Fahey* and R.G.A. Gunn*
1971	A.B. Martin and E.L. Scott	1988	W.F. Davies* and P.E. de Svastich	2006	T. Chisholm* and C. Riviere*
1972	S.P. Howe III and E.M. Noll*	1989	L. Deuchar* and P.E. de Svastich	2007-08	R.L. Fahey* and S. Virgona*
1973	R.J.B. Bijur and L.C. Dominguez	1990	R.L. Fahey* and A.P. Meares*	2009	C. Riviere* and N. Wood*
1974	S.P. Howe III and E.L. Scott	1991	W.F. Davies* and L. Deuchar*	2010	S. Virgona* and B. Matthews*
1975-76	J.F. Sammis III and R.W. Tuckerman	1992-93	J.P. Snow and R.L. Fahey*	2012	S. Virgona* and T. Chisholm*
1977	N.A.R. Cripps* and C.J. Ronaldson*	1994-95	C.J. Bray* and M.H.J. Gooding*	2013-14	C. Riviere* and T. Chisholm*
1978	O.M. Phipps and E.L. Scott	1996	J.P. Snow and N. Wood*		
1979	E.L. Scott and B. Toates*	1997	J.P. Snow and J.S. Male*		

*Denotes Professional

Tennis and Rackets

AMATEUR SINGLES CHAMPIONSHIP

1892	R.D. Sears	1927	G.D. Huband	1948-49	O.M. Phipps	1979	R.E. Howe III	2004	N.J.J. Pendrigh
1893	F. Warren	1928-29	H. Morgan	1950-56	A.B. Martin	1980-84	E.L. Scott	2005	C. Riviere
1894-95	B.S. de Garmendia	1930	Lord Aberdare	1957-58	N.R. Knox	1985-86	K.B. McCollum	2006-07	N. Victoir
1896	L.M. Stockton	1931-32	W.C. Wright	1959	J.F.C. Bostwick	1987-88	M. Clothier	2008	M. Porter
1897	C.R. Fearing Jr	1933	J.H. Van Alen	1960-63	N.R. Knox	1989	M. Happell	2009-10	A. West
1898-99	L.M. Stockton	1934-37	O.M. Phipps	1964	J.F.C. Bostwick	1990-91	M. Clothier	2011	K. Booth
1900	E.H. Miles	1938	J.H. Van Alen	1965-69	G.H. Bostwick Jr	1992	J.P. Snow	2012-13	P. Winthrop
1901-04	J. Crane Jr	1939	O.M. Phipps	1970	J.F.C. Bostwick	1993	T. Chisholm	2014	M. Mathias
1905	C.E. Sands	1940	J.H. Van Alen	1971	G.H. Bostwick Jr	1994	N.J.J. Pendrigh		
1906-17	J. Gould	1941	A.B. Martin	1972	J.F.C. Bostwick	1995	T. Chisholm		
1920-25	J. Gould	1946	R. Grant III	1973	H.R. Angus	1996-99	N.J.J. Pendrigh		
1926	C. Suydam Cutting	1947	E.M. Beals	1974-78	E.L. Scott	2000-03	J.P. Snow		

AMATEUR DOUBLES CHAMPIONSHIP

1909	J. Gould and W.H.T. Huhn	1958-59	N.R. Knox and S.H. Knox III	1984-85	G. Bell Jr and P. Clement
1910	G.R. Fearing Jr and Joshua Crane	1960	A.B. Martin and Robert Grant III	1986-87	G.R. Jones and K.B. McCollum
1911-17	J. Gould and W.H.T. Huhn	1961	N.R. Knox and S.H. Knox III	1988	H. Bunis and P.E. DeSvastich
1920-24	J. Gould and J.W. Wear	1962	A.B. Martin and W.T. Vogt	1989-91	M. Clothier and G.R. Jones
1925	C. Suydam Cutting and F. Cutting	1963-65	N.R. Knox and O.M. Phipps	1992-94	R.E. Howe and J.P. Snow
1926	J. Gould and J.W. Wear	1966	A.B. Martin and S.T. Vehslage	1995	M. Clothier and T. Chisholm
1927-29	J. Gould and W.C. Wright	1967	J.L. Van Alen and W.L. Van Alen Jr	1996	N.J.J. Pendrigh and P. Clement
1930	F.P. Frazier and G.W. Wrightman	1968	N.R. Knox and W.F. Talbert	1997	J.P. Snow and R.E. Howe
1931-32	J. Gould and A.B. Martin	1969	J.F.C. Bostwick and G.H. Bostwick Jr	1998	S. Aldrigh and N.J.J. Pendrigh
1933	G.R. Fearing and W.C. Wright	1970-71	N.R. Knox and A.B. Martin	1999	R. Devens and J. Capello
1934-39	W. Rand and O.M. Phipps	1972	N.R. Knox and E.L. Scott	2000	R.E. Howe and J.P. Snow
1940	J.H. Van Alen and W.L. Van Alen	1973	G.H. Bostwick Jr. and J.F.C. Bostwick	2004	L. Miron and P. Pell
1941	O.M. Phipps and R. Grant III	1974	R.E. Howe III and S.P. Howe	2005	M. Clothier and S. Aldrich
1946-47	E.M. Edwards and W.E. Lingelbach Jr	1975	E.L. Scott and R.E. Howe III	2006-07	N. Victoir and A. Hombrecher
1948	O.M. Phipps and A.B. Martin	1976	P.W. Clement and W.M. Shettle	2008	M. Porter and J. Wintersteen
1949-50	A.B. Martin and R.L. Gerry Jr	1977	N.R. Knox and O.M. Phipps	2009	A. Hombrecher and L. Miron
1951	A.B. Martin and E.B. Martin	1978	R.E. Howe III and W.J.C. Surtees	2010	P. Pell and A. West
1952	F.X. Shields and O.M. Phipps	1979	R.E. Howe III and O.M. Phipps	2011	B. Cook and P. Winthrop
1953-54	F.X. Shields and A.B. Martin	1980	N.R. Knox and J.F.C. Bostwick	2012	A.B. Miron and P. Pell
1955	W.L. Van Alen and F.H. Griffin Jr	1981-82	O.M. Phipps and E.L. Scott	2013	W. Barker and N. Mackensie
1956-57	A.B. Martin and N.R. Knox	1983	G.H. Bostwick and R.E. Howe	2014	T. McGinnis and A.B. Miron

PROFESSIONAL SINGLES CHAMPIONSHIP

Schochet Cup

1973	T. Greevy	1979	J.J. Burke	1985	L. Deuchar	1997	J.S. Male	2003-09	R.L. Fahey
1974	E.M. Noll	1980	J.J. Burke	1986-87	C.J. Ronaldson	1998	C.J. Bray	2010-14	C. Riviere
1975	C.J. Ennis	1981	C.J. Ronaldson	1988-90	No tournament	1999	J.S. Male		
1976	B. Toates	1982	J.J. Burke	1991	C.J. Ronaldson	2000	N. Wood		
1977	J.J. Burke	1983	W.F. Davies	1992	L. Deuchar	2001	R.L. Fahey		
1978	C.J. Ronaldson	1984	C.J. Ronaldson	1993-96	W.F. Davies	2002	T. Chisholm		

LADIES

OPEN SINGLES CHAMPIONSHIP

	Winner	Runner-up		Winner	Runner-up		Winner	Runner-up
1984	Lesley Ronaldson	Katrina Allen	1995	Katrina Allen	Karen Toates	2006	Charlotte Cornwallis	Sue Haswell
1985	Elizabeth Woordthorpe	Eleanor Douglas	1996	Sue Haswell	Kate Leeming	2007	Charlotte Cornwallis	Karen Hird
1986	Sally Jones	Julieanne Drewitt	1997	Penny Lumley	Jane Lippincott	2008	Claire Vigrass	Sue Haswell
1987	Jane Hyland		1998	Penny Lumley	Fiona Deuchar	2009	Charlotte Cornwallis	Frederika Adam
1988	Jane Lippincott	Evelyn David	1999	Jane Lippincott	Brenda Sabbag	2010	Claire Vigrass	Frederika Adam
1989	Sally Jones		2000	Penny Lumley	Jo Iddles	2011	Claire Vigrass	Aldona Greenwood
1990	Alice Bartlett	Jane Lippincott	2001	Penny Lumley	Charlotte Cornwallis	2012	Claire Vigrass	Karen Hird
1991	Charlotte Cornwallis	Lissen Thompson	2002	Penny Lumley	Brenda Sabbag	2013	Tara Lumley	Karen Hird
1992	Lissen Tutrone	Jane Lippincott	2003	Penny Lumley	Rose Snell	2014	Claire Vigrass	Amanda Avedissian
1993	Helen Mursell	Lissen Tutrone	2004	Charlotte Cornwallis	Penny Lumley			
1994	Jane Lippincott	Sheila Reilly	2005	Charlotte Cornwallis	Frederika Adam			

OPEN DOUBLES CHAMPIONSHIP

	Winners	Runners-up		Winners	Runners-up
1984	Lesley Ronaldson and Maggie Wright	Sheila Macintosh and Katrina Allen	2000	Penny Lumley and Evelyn David	Karen Toates and Prue McCahey
1985	Julie Talbert and Elizabeth Woodthorpe	Chris Rohner and Francoise Newman	2001	Penny Lumley and Jo Iddles	Charlotte Cornwallis and Alex Garside
1986	Sally Jones and Helen Mursell	Julieanne Drewitt and Penny Bland	2002	Penny Lumley and Evelyn David	Sheila Reilly and Angie Bernier
1987	Jane Hyland and Helen Mursell		2003	Penny Lumley and Evelyn David	Sheila Reilly and Jane Lippincott
1988	Jane Lippincott and Katherine Wooley	Evelyn David and Julie Rinaldini	2004	Charlotte Cornwallis and Alex Garside	Penny Lumley and Evelyn David
1989	Sally Jones and Alexis Warren-Piper		2005	Charlotte Cornwallis and Melissa Grassi	Frederika Adam and Susan Castley
1990	Jane Lippincott and Sheila Reilly	Evelyn David and Alice Bartlett	2006	Charlotte Cornwallis and Sue Haswell	Jo Iddles and Frederika Adam
1991	Catherine Castle and Lissen Thompson	Charlotte Cornwallis and Evelyn David	2007	Charlotte Cornwallis and Karen Hird	Rose Snell and Jane Lippincott
1992	Sheila Reilly and Jane Lippincott	Evelyn David and Lissen Tutrone	2008	Sue Haswell and Virginia Goodyear	Claire Vigrass and Margie Goodyear
1993	Jane Lippincott and Helen Mursell	Catherine Castle and Lissen Thompson	2009	Charlotte Cornwallis and Karen Hird	Amy Hayball and Aldona Greenwood
1994	Sheila Reilly and Eleanor Douglas	Jane Lippincott and Brenda Sabbag	2010	Claire Vigrass and Frederika Adam	Jane Lippincott and Amanda Avedissian
1995	Katrina Allen and Karen Toates	Jane Lippincott and Brenda Sabbag	2011	Claire Vigrass and Aldona Greenwood	Melissa Purcell and Kathy Carson
1996	Sue Haswell and Sheila Reilly	Jane Lippincott and Brenda Sabbag	2012	Claire Vigrass and Amanda Avedissian	Karen Hird and Frederika Adam
1997	Penny Lumley and Evelyn David	Jane Lippincott and Brenda Sabbag	2013	Karen Hird and Frederika Adam	Anne Gwathmey and Tara Lumley
1998	Penny Lumley and Fiona Deuchar	Jane Lippincott and Brenda Sabbag	2014	Claire Vigrass and Amanda Avedissian	Melissa Purcell and Kathy Carson
1999	Jane Lippincott and Brenda Sabbag	Sheila Reilly and Emily Boenning			

FRANCE

MEN

FRENCH OPEN SINGLES

	Winner	Runner-up		Winner	Runner-up		Winner	Runner-up
1990	Lachlan Deuchar	Mike Happell	1997	Chris Bray	Frank Filippelli	2004	Rob Fahey	Chris Bray
1991	Lachlan Deuchar	Rob Fahey	1998	Rob Fahey	Wayne Davies	2005	Rob Fahey	Steve Virgona
1992	Julian Snow	Rob Fahey	1999	Rob Fahey	Chris Bray	2006	Rob Fahey	Ruaraidh Gunn
1993	Rob Fahey	Frank Filippelli	2000	Rob Fahey	Tim Chisholm	2007–9	Rob Fahey	Camden Riviere
1994	Chris Bray	Wayne Davies	2001	Rob Fahey	Mike Gooding	2010–11	Robert Fahey	Steve Virgona
1995	Mike Gooding	Rob Fahey	2002	No tournament held		2012	Camden Riviere	Tim Chisholm
1996	Mike Gooding	Wayne Davies	2003	Tim Chisholm	Ivan Snell	2013–14	Camden Riviere	Steve Virgona

FRENCH OPEN DOUBLES

	Winners	Runners-up		Winners	Runners-up
2006	R.L. Fahey and R. Gunn	B. Sayers and C. Riviere	2011	C. Riviere and T. Chisholm	R.L. Fahey and S. Virgona
2007–08	C. Riviere and N. Wood	R.L. Fahey and R. McNaughtan	2012	C. Riviere and T. Chisholm	S. Virgona and J. Lumley
2009	R.L. Fahey and S. Virgona	B. Sayers and R. Smith	2014	C. Riviere and T. Chisholm	S. Virgona and R. Smith
2010	R.L. Fahey and S. Virgona	C. Riviere and R. Smith			

COUPE DE PARIS

1910	C.E. Sands
1911–13	Hon. N.S. Lytton
1914–20	Capt. R.K. Price
1921–25	E.M. Baerlein
1926–27	Hon. C.N. Bruce
1928	W.C. Wright
1929	L. Lees
1930	Marquis R. du Vivier
1931	W.C. Wright
1932–35	Lord Aberdare
1936	Marquis R. du Vivier
1937	R.H. Hill
1938	Lord Aberdare
1947	Lord Cullen
1948	R. Aird
1950	F. Alvarez
1962	D.J. Warburg
1976	H.R. Angus

OPEN NATIONAL SINGLES

1989	J.B.K. Howell
1990	M.P. Seigneur
1991	M.P. Seigneur
1992	R. Fahey
1993	R.G.A. Gunn
1994	R. Nicholson
1995	M. Seigneur
1996	I.O. Ronaldson
1997	M. Seigneur
1998	I.O. Ronaldson
1999	D. Grozdanovitch
2000–03	M. Seigneur
2004	N. Victoire
2005–09	M. Seigneur
2010	J. Bey
2011	R. McNaughtan
2012–14	A. Kemp

OPEN NATIONAL DOUBLES

2006	O. Michel and J. Bey
2007	M.P. Seigneur and T. Batten
2008	M.P. Seigneur and J-G. Prats
2009–10	M.P. Seigneur and T. Batten
2011–13	A. Kemp and L. Baldwin
2014	M. Brunoro and G. Dortu

COUPE DE BORDEAUX

1909	B.H. Seward	1938	M. Dupont	1967	A.F. Goulty	1985	J.D. Ward
1910-11	W. Bazin	1947-50	F. Alvarez	1968	D.J. Sloan	1986	M.J. Happell
1912-13	P. Deves	1951-52	M.A. Pugh	1969	M. Peuvrel	1987-96	J.P. Snow
1914 & 1920	Capt. R.K. Price	1953	G. Blanchy	1970	H.R. Angus	1997	N.J.J. Pendrigh
1921	E.M. Baerlein	1954	D.J. Warburg	1971	R.J. Potter	1998	J.P. Willcocks
1922-23	R.K. Price	1955	M.H. Searby	1972	M. Peuvrel	1999	C. Blanchot
1924	P. Deves	1956	N.F. Robinson	1973	Y. Faugère	2000	I.E.G. Snell
1925-26	Comte R. du Vivier	1957	W.E. Rawson-Shaw	1974	A.C. Lovell	2001	A. Hombrecher
1927-28	F. Blanchy	1958	B.H.I.H. Stewart	1975-76	B. Sarlangue	2002	A. Page
1929	Comte R. du Vivier	1959	M. Faugère	1977	H.R. Angus	2003	D. Hughes
1930	F. Blanchy	1960	N.W. Smith	1979	H.R. Angus	2004	N. Pendrigh
1931	Marquis R. du Vivier	1961	Hon. A.C.S. Tufton	1980	B. Sarlangue	2005	P. Sarlangue
1932	Comte F. du Vivier	1962	J.W.T. Wilcox	1981	W. Hollington	2006-09	P. Wright
1933	Capt. G.N. Scott-Chad	1963	M.H.L. Bowler	1982	J.D. Ward	2012	J. Douglas
1934	Lord Aberdare	1964-65	H.R. Angus	1983	A.C. Lovell		
1935-37	Marquis R. du Vivier	1966	J.Q. Greenstock	1984	R.C. McKenzie		

RAQUETTE D'OR

1899-1900	C.E. Sands	1933	Marquis R. du Vivier	1963	M. Peuvrel	1992	C. Chueka
1901	W. Bazin	1934	A.J. Drexel Biddle Jr	1964	A.G. Lawrence	1993	D. Grozdanovitch
1902	A.F. de Luze	1935-37	Marquis R. du Vivier	1965	M. Peuvrel	1994-95	J.G. Prats
1903-04	W. Bazin	1938	L.J. Aslangul	1966	L.M. Ravet de Marbaix	1996	D. Grozdanovitch
1905	A.F. de Luze	1945-46	F. Alvarez	1967	M. Peuvrel	1997	G. Ruault
1906-07	W. Bazin	1947	H. Cruse	1968	J. Strauss	1998	J.G. Prats
1910-11	W. Bazin	1949-51	F. Alvarez	1969	H. Faugère	1999	G. Ruault
1912	P. Devès	1952-53	Ch. Blanchy	1970	J. Strauss	2000	O. Michel
1913-14	W. Bazin	1954	H.R. Barton	1971-72	M. Peuvrel	2001	A.J.W. Page
1920	P. Devès	1955	Ch. Blanchy	1973	C. Ricard	2002-03	O. Michel
1921-22	J. Worth	1956	L.M. Ravet de Marbaix	1974	R.D.B. Cooper	2004	J. Bey
1923	P. Devès	1958	F. Laws Johnson	1975-84	B. Sarlangue	2005-07	O. Michel
1924	D. Lawton	1959	M. Faugère	1985-88	D. Grozdanovitch	2008-09	J. Bey
1925-29	Comte R. du Vivier	1960	R. Diani	1989	C. Chueka	2010-14	M. Sarlangue
1930-32	F. Blanchy	1961-62	J. Strauss	1990-91	D. Grozdanovitch		

LADIES

OPEN SINGLES CHAMPIONSHIP

	Winner	Runner-up		Winner	Runner-up		Winner	Runner-up
1986	Katrina Allen	Lesley Ronaldson	1996	Penny Lumley	Katrina Allen	2008	Charlotte Cornwallis	Karen Hird
1987	Danielle Barrabe	Katrina Allen	1997	Sue Haswell	Penny Lumley	2009	Karen Hird	Claire Vigrass
1988	Penny Fellows	Katrina Allen	1998	Penny Lumley	Katrina Allen	2010	Claire Vigrass	Frederika Adam
1989-90	Penny Fellows	Sally Jones	1999-2000	Penny Lumley	Charlotte Cornwallis	2011	Claire Vigrass	Sarah Vigrass
1991	Magda Groszek	Alison Cockcroft	2001-02	Charlotte Cornwallis	Penny Lumley	2012	Claire Vigrass	Karen Hird
1992	Katrina Allen	Alison Cockcroft	2003	Penny Lumley	Jo Iddles	2013	Claire Vigrass	Penny Lumley
1994	Alex Garside	Katrina Allen	2004-06	Charlotte Cornwallis	Jo Iddles	2014	Claire Fahey	Tara Lumley
1995	Penny Lumley	Sally Jones	2007	Charlotte Cornwallis	Sarah Vigrass		(née Vigrass)	

OPEN DOUBLES CHAMPIONSHIP

	Winners	Runners-up		Winners	Runners-up
1988	Alex Warren-Piper and Sally Jones	Danielle Barrabe and Katrina Allen	2003	Penny Lumley and Jo Iddles	Christine Anies and Louise Tant
1990	Alex Warren-Piper and Sally Jones		2004	Charlotte Cornwallis and Eleanor Harris	Susan Castley and Frederika Adam
1991	Magda Groszek and Bernadette Bidouze		2005	Charlotte Cornwallis and Sue Haswell	Jo Iddles and Frederika Adam
1992	Katrina Allen and Bernadette Bidouze	Margaret Allen and Alison Cockcroft	2006	Charlotte Cornwallis and Penny Lumley	Jo Iddles and Frederika Adam
1995	Penny Lumley and Sue Haswell	Sally Jones and Alex Garside	2007	Charlotte Cornwallis and Penny Lumley	Sarah Vigrass and Claire Vigrass
1996	Penny Lumley and Alex Garside	Kate Leeming and Fiona Deuchar	2008	Charlotte Cornwallis and Karen Hird	Claire Vigrass and Aldona Greenwood
1997	Penny Lumley and Sue Haswell	Alex Garside and Fiona Deuchar	2009	Claire Vigrass and Frederika Adam	Karen Hird and Nicola Cavill
1998	Penny Lumley and Alex Garside	Charlotte Cornwallis and Fiona Deuchar	2010	Claire Vigrass and Frederika Adam	Karen Hird and Aldona Greenwood
1999	Penny Lumley and Alex Garside	Charlotte Cornwallis and Jane Lippincott	2011	Claire Vigrass and Sarah Vigrass	Frederika Adam and Karen Hird
2000	Penny Lumley and Jo Iddles	Charlotte Cornwallis and Alex Garside	2012	Claire Vigrass and Alex Kurkjian	Frederika Adam and Karen Hird
2001	Charlotte Cornwallis and Alex Garside	Penny Lumley and Jo Iddles	2013	Claire Vigrass and Alex Kurkjian	Penny Lumley and Tara Lumley
2002	Penny Lumley and Jo Iddles	Charlotte Cornwallis and Alex Garside	2014	Claire Fahey and Irina Dulbish	Penny Lumley and Tara Lumley

AUSTRALIA

MEN

OPEN SINGLES CHAMPIONSHIP

1875-82	T. Stone	1956-58	R.W. Baker	1989	G.J. Hyland	2005	S. Virgona
1882-1902	T. Horne	1959-67	*No known challenges*	1990	L. Deuchar	2006	R. Gunn
1903-09	*No known challenges*	1968-76	B. Toates	1991	W.F. Davies	2007	S. Virgona
1910-31	W.T. Stone	1977-78	C.J. Ronaldson	1992	J.P. Snow	2008-09	R.L. Fahey
1932-35	H.P. Finch	1979	B. Toates	1993-94	R.L. Fahey	2010	R. Gunn
1935-38	H.A. Finch	1980-81	C.J. Lumley	1995	F.J. Filippelli	2011	S. Virgona
1938-47	H.P. Finch	1982	C.J. Ronaldson	1996-98	R.L. Fahey	2012	R.L. Fahey
1948-49	A.W. Knight	1983	W.F. Davies	1999	C.J. Bray	2013	S. Virgona
1950-51	*No known challenges*	1984-85	C.J. Ronaldson	2000-2	R.L. Fahey	2014	R.L. Fahey
1952-54	R.W. Baker	1986	L. Deuchar	2003	T. Chisholm		
1955	J.S. Barnett	1987-88	W.F. Davies	2004	R.L. Fahey		

OPEN DOUBLES CHAMPIONSHIP

1976	G. Hyland and B. Toates	1985	E.W. Cockram and G.J. Hyland	1994	R.L. Fahey and A.P. Meares	2007	J.P. Snow and N. Wood
1977	L. Deuchar and C.J. Ronaldson	1986	E.W. Cockram and G.J. Hyland	1995	C.J. Bray and M. Gooding	2008	R.L. Fahey and R.G.A. Gunn
1978	C.J. Lumley and G.I. Simpson	1987	E.W. Cockram and G.J. Hyland	1996-97	R.L. Fahey and A.P. Meares	2010	R.L. Fahey and R.G.A. Gunn
1979	A.K. Heard and B. Toates	1988	P.J. Tabley and M.G. Hayward	1998	R. Gunn and S. Virgona	2011-12	R.L. Fahey and S. Virgona
1980	W. Davies and L. Deuchar	1989	C.J. Bray and J.B. Howell	1999	C.J. Bray and S. Virgona	2013	S. Virgona and K. Booth
1981	E.W. Cockram and L. Deuchar	1990	C.J. Bray and A.P. Meares	2000-02	R.L. Fahey and B. Dale	2014	B. Sayers and K. Booth
1982	O. Phipps and G. Hyland	1991	W.F. Davies and B. Toates	2003	R.L. Fahey and S. Virgona		
1983	G. Hyland and D.J. Collins	1992	J.P. Snow and R.L. Fahey	2004	R.L. Fahey and R.G.A. Gunn		
1984	E.W. Cockram and A.W. Cockram	1993	W.F. Davies and M. Clothier	2005-06	S. Virgona and K. Booth		

MELBOURNE: GOLD AND SILVER RACKET COMPETITION

	Gold Racket	*Silver Racket*		*Gold Racket*	*Silver Racket*		*Gold Racket*	*Silver Racket*
1882	J.B. Box	F.R. Murphy	1917	C.H. Mollison	T.A. Quirk	1975	G.G. Hiller	A.K. Heard
1883	J.B. Box	T.A. Quirk	1918	C.H. Mollison	H.R. Flack	1976	A.K. Heard	R.M. Cowper
1884	J.B. Box	R. Travers	1919	C.H. Mollison	H.R. Flack	1977	A.K. Heard	R.M. Cowper
1885	J.B. Box	J.N. Webster	1920	C.H. Mollison	H.R. Flack	1978	R.M. Cowper	G.E. Limb
1886	J.B. Box	C.W. Butler	1921	C.T. Butler	C.H. Mollison	1979	A.K. Heard	R.M. Cowper
1887	J.B. Box	R. Cornish	1922	C.T. Butler	A.O. Henty	1980	R.M. Cowper	E.W. Cockram
1888	J.B. Box	R. Cornish	1923	C.H. Mollison	D.C. George	1981	E.W. Cockram	R.M. Cowper
1889	J.B. Box	R. Cornish	1924	C.T. Butler	D.C. George	1982	E.W. Cockram	R.M. Cowper
1890	J.B. Box	C.C. Malleson	1925	C.T. Butler	A.O. Henty	1983	E.W. Cockram	R.M. Cowper
1891	J.B. Box	W.T. Coldham	1926	A.O. Henty	E.C. Dyason	1984	M.J. Happell	E.W. Cockram
1892	J.B. Box	W.T. Coldham	1927	K. Tolhurst	E.C. Dyason	1985	E.W. Cockram	M.J. Happell
1893	J.B. Box	J.F. Strachan	1928	J.L. Hudson	E.C. Dyason	1986	E.W. Cockram	M.J. Happell
1894	J.B. Box	W. Travers	1929	R.C. Todhunter	K. Tolhurst	1987	M.J. Happell	E.W. Cockram
1895	J.F. Strachan	J.B. Box	1930	R.C. Todhunter	K. Tolhurst	1988	M.J. Happell	E.W. Cockram
1896	W. Travers	H.J. Hill	1931	K. Tolhurst	H.S. Forrest	1989	E.W. Cockram	C.M. Sievers
1897	W. Travers	J.B. Box	1932	K. Tolhurst	F. Strachan	1990	C.M. Sievers	E.W. Cockram
1898	H.J. Hill	J.B. Box	1933	G.L. Patterson	R.C. Todhunter	1991	C.M. Sievers	V. Eke
1899	J.B. Box	F.G. Travers	1934	K. Tolhurst	G.L. Patterson	1992	M.J. Happell	C.M. Sievers
1900	H.J. Hill	R. Cornish	1935	G.L. Patterson	R.A. Henderson	1993	M.J. Happell	C.M. Sievers
1901	T.A. Quirk	J.F. Strachan	1936	G.L. Patterson	R.A. Henderson	1994	M.J. Happell	C.M. Sievers
1902	T.A. Quirk	C.H. Mollison	1937	K. Tolhurst	Julian Smith Jr	1995	M.J. Happell	R. Dery
1903	C.H. Mollison	T.A. Quirk	1938	W.H. Vestey	*unknown*	1996	M.J. Happell	C.M. Sievers
1904	C.H. Mollison	T.A. Quirk	1952	R.H. Searby	M.H. Searby	1997	M.J. Happell	C.M. Sievers
1905	H.J. Hill	C.H. Mollison	1956	Hon. M.G.L. Bruce	S.H. Barstow	1998	M.J. Happell	C.M. Sievers
1906	C.H. Mollison	T.A. Quirk	1964	M.H. Searby	S.H. Barstow	1999	M.J. Happell	C.M. Sievers
1907	T.A. Quirk	C.H. Mollison	1965	R.H. Searby	M.H. Searby	2000	M.J. Happell	C.M. Sievers
1908	C.H. Mollison	T.A. Quirk	1966	R.H. Searby	M.H. Searby	2001	M.J. Happell	C.M. Sievers
1909	C.H. Mollison	T.A. Quirk	1967	J.P. Drummond	R.H. Searby	2002-04	M.J. Happell	M.J. Sayer
1910	C.H. Mollison	E. Maxwell	1968	G.G. Hiller	R.S. Allen	2005	K. Booth	M.J. Happell
1911	C.H. Mollison	C.T. Butler	1969	G.G. Hiller	D.G.D. Yencken	2006-09	J.P. Snow	M.J. Happell
1912	W.D. Gibbs	Lord Denman	1970	G.G. Hiller	G.E. Limb	2010-11	K. Booth	M.J. Happell
1913	W.D. Gibbs	C.H. Mollison	1971	G.G. Hiller	G.E. Limb	2012-13	K. Booth	J.P. Snow
1914	C.H. Mollison	T.A. Quirk	1972	G.G. Hiller	R.H. Searby	2014	K. Booth	B. Richardson
1915	C.H. Mollison	W.R. Clarke	1973	G.G. Hiller	A.K. Heard			
1916	C.H. Mollison	T.A. Quirke	1974	A.K. Heard	G.E. Limb			

Tennis and Rackets

HOBART CHAMPION RACQUET COMPETITION

1880	W.L. Dobson	1899	F.A. Dodds	1931-32	C.T. Butler	1967	J.S. Rogers	1998-99	P.J. Boyles
1881	A.L. Travers	1900	H.J. Hill	1933-39	C.C. Boag	1968-69	D.J. Martin	2000	K. Booth
1882	C.W. Butler	1901	F.A. Dodds	1940-50	A.W. Knight	1970	D.A. Shepherd	2001	K. Booth
1883-84	L. Travers	1902	C.W. Butler	1951-53	R.W. Baker	1971-72	D.J. Martin	2002	P.J. Boyles
1886	J. Macfarlane	1903-10	E. Maxwell	1954-55	J.S. Barnett	1973	C.C.A. Butler	2003	K. Booth
1887-92	C.W. Butler	1911	C.T. Butler	1956-58	R.W. Baker	1974-76	D.J. Martin	2004-06	P.J. Boyles
1893	W. Travers	1912-19	E. Maxwell	1959	C.A.S. Page	1977-80	J.S. Wilkinson	2007	A. Ramsay
1895	K. Maxwell	1920-27	C.T. Butler	1960	A.W. Knight	1981-84	G.G. Bradfield	2008-09	P.J. Boyles
1896	H.J. Hill	1928	S.H. Bastow	1961-63	C.A.S. Page	1988	G.G. Bradfield	2010-14	H. Booth
1897	C.W. Butler	1929	C.T. Butler	1964	G.G. Hiller	1989	R.D. Edwards		
1898	H.J. Hill	1930	C.C. Boag	1965-66	R.W. Baker	1990-97	G.G. Bradfield		

BALLARAT SILVER RACKET

1985	C.J. Ronaldson	1989	J.P. Snow	1993	J.P. Snow	1997	C.J. Bray
1986	G.J. Hyland	1990	F.J. Filippelli	1994	B. McFarlane	1998	J.B.K. Howell
1987	C.J. Ronaldson	1991	C.J. Bray	1995	J.P. Snow	1999	C.J. Bray
1988	L. Deuchar	1992	J.P. Snow	1996	F.J. Filippelli		

From 2000 there was no competition until 2004 when it became a handicap event.

GOVERNOR'S CUP, HOBART

1975	F. Willis
1979	C.J. Ronaldson
1982	C.J. Ronaldson
1985	G.J. Hyland
1988	G.J. Hyland
1999	R.L. Fahey

VICTORIAN OPEN SINGLES

Woolner Stone Memorial

1975-76	B. Toates	1984	M.J. Happell	1991	M.J. Happell	1998	F.J. Filippelli	2011	R.L. Fahey
1977-78	C.J. Ronaldson	1985	G.J. Hyland	1992	G.J. Hyland	1999	S. Virgona	2012	K. Booth
1979	B. Toates	1986	L. Deuchar	1993	M.J. Happell	2000-01	R.L. Fahey	2013	C. Riviere
1980	C.J. Lumley	1987	P.G. Tabley	1994	F.J. Filippelli	2002	A.B. Fowler	2014	K. Booth
1981	L. Deuchar	1988	L. Deuchar	1995	R.L. Fahey	2003	R.L. Fahey		
1982	C.J. Lumley	1989	G.J. Hyland	1996	F.J. Filippelli	2004	Not played		
1983	E.W. Cockram	1990	F.J. Filippelli	1997	R.L. Fahey	2005-10	R.G.A. Gunn		

LADIES

OPEN SINGLES CHAMPIONSHIP

	Winner	Runner-up		Winner	Runner-up		Winner	Runner-up
1990	Helen Mursell	Karen Toates	1998	Barbara Baker	Karen Toates	2006	Charlotte Cornwallis	Kate Leeming
1991	Penny Lumley	Alex Garside	1999	Prue McCahey	Rose Snell	2007-08	Kate Leeming	Laura Fowler
1992-94	Helen Mursell	Barbara Baker	2000-02	Prue McCahey	Karen Toates	2009	Charlotte Cornwallis	Laura Fowler
1995	Helen Mursell	Jo Edwards	2003	Penny Lumley	Charlotte Cornwallis	2010-12	Claire Vigrass	Sarah Vigrass
1996	Kate Leeming	Jo Edwards	2004	Prue McCahey	Rose Snell	2013	Kate Leeming	Amy Hayball
1997	Penny Lumley	Sue Haswell	2005	Kate Leeming	Prue McCahey	2014	Claire Vigrass	Kate Leeming

OPEN DOUBLES CHAMPIONSHIP

	Winners	Runners-up		Winners	Runners-up
1996	Kate Leeming and Jo Edwards	Barbara Baker and Julianne Drewitt	2006	Charlotte Cornwallis and Kate Leeming	Frederika Adam and Jo Edwards
1997	Penny Lumley and Sue Haswell	Fiona Deuchar and Kate Leeming	2007	Kate Leeming and Annabel Elwood	Laura Fowler and Xanthe Ranger
1998	Barbara Baker and Julianne Drewitt		2008	Laura Fowler and Xanthe Ranger	Kate Leeming and Jo Edwards
1999	Prue McCahey and Karen Toates		2009	Charlotte Cornwallis and E. Varigos	Kate Leeming and Jo Edwards
2000	Prue McCahey and Karen Toates	Hattie Dean and Laura Fowler			
2001	Prue McCahey and Karen Toates	Kate Brown and Julianne Drewitt	2010	Claire Vigrass and Sarah Vigrass	Kate Brown and Susan Castley
2002	Prue McCahey and Karen Toates	Rosemary Snell and Amy Hayball	2011	Claire Vigrass and Sarah Vigrass	Karen Hird and Rose Snell
2003	Charlotte Cornwallis and Kate Leeming	Karen Toates and Prue McCahey	2012	Claire Vigrass and Sarah Vigrass	Kate Leeming and Amy Hayball
2004	Rose Snell and Prue McCahey	Laura Fowler and Xanthe Ranger	2013	Kate Leeming and Amy Hayball	Prue McCahey and Rose Snell
2005	Kate Leeming and Amy Hayball	Rose Snell and Prue McCahey	2014	Claire Vigrass and Alex Brodie	Kate Leeming and Sue Haswell

RACKETS

WORLD SINGLES CHAMPIONSHIP
Eleven point games played in 1838, enclosed court used for first time in 1860

	Winner	Runner-up	Aggregate score	Venues
1820	Robert Mackay	claimed		
1825	Thomas Pittman	claimed		
1834	Thomas Pittman	resigned		
1834	John Pittman	claimed		
1838	John Lamb	John Pittman	8–4	Belvedere Gardens
1840	John Lamb	died – title vacant		
1846	John Mitchell	J.C.M. Young	5–0	Birmingham and Bristol
1860	Francis Erwood	John Mitchell	8–1	Woolwich and Bristol
1862	W.H. Dyke	Francis Erwood	8–3	Woolwich and Prince's
1863	Sir William Hart-Dyke	resigned		
1863	Henry Gray	claimed		
1866	Henry Gray	resigned		
1866	William Gray	claimed		
1875	William Gray	died		
1876	H.B. Fairs	Joseph Gray	8–3	Prince's and Rugby
1878	H.B. Fairs	died		
1878	Joseph Gray	claimed		
1887	Peter Latham	Joseph Gray	7–4	Rugby and Manchester
1888	Peter Latham	Walter Gray	6–3	Queen's and Charterhouse
1891	Peter Latham	George Standing	5–0	Queen's and Prince's
1897	Peter Latham	George Standing	6–3	Queen's and New York
1902	Peter Latham	Gilbert Browne	5–0	Queen's and Prince's
1902	Peter Latham	resigned		
1903	J. Jamsetji	Gilbert Browne	6–2	Queen's and Prince's
1911	Charles Williams	J. Jamsetji	5–0	Queen's and Prince's
1913	Jock Soutar	Charles Williams	6–4	Queen's and Philadelphia
1922	Jock Soutar	Charles Williams	7–4	Philadelphia and New York
1927	Jock Soutar	William Standing	8–1	Philadelphia and New York
1929	Charles Williams	Jock Soutar	7–3	Philadelphia and Chicago
1935	Charles Williams	died		
1937	David Milford	Norbert Setzler	7–4	New York and Queen's
1946	David Milford	resigned		
1947	Jim Dear	Kenneth Chantler	8–1	Montreal and Queen's
1948	Jim Dear	John Pawle	8–4	Queen's
1951	Jim Dear	John Pawle	8–2	Queen's
1954	Geoffrey Atkins	Jim Dear	6–5	Queen's
1963	Geoffrey Atkins	James Leonard	6–1	Queen's
1964	Geoffrey Atkins	Charles Swallow	7–5	Queen's
1967	Geoffrey Atkins	James Leonard	7–2	Chicago and Queen's
1970	Geoffrey Atkins	Charles Swallow	6–3	Chicago and Queen's
1972	William Surtees	Howard Angus	5–4	Queen's and Chicago
1973	Howard Angus	William Surtees	5–1	Chicago and Queen's
1975	William Surtees	Howard Angus	5–1	Chicago and Queen's
1977	William Surtees	Howard Angus	5–0	Chicago and Queen's
1979	William Surtees	Willie Boone	5–0	New York and Queen's
1981	John Prenn	William Surtees	6–4	New York and Queen's
1984	Willie Boone	John Prenn	7–2	Montreal and Queen's
1986	John Prenn	Willie Boone	8–6	New York and Queen's
1988	James Male	Willie Boone	6–1	Chicago and Queen's
1991	James Male	Shannon Hazell	6–2	Chicago and Queen's
1993	James Male	Neil Smith	6–5	Philadelphia and Queen's
1995	James Male	Neil Smith	6–2	Chicago and Queen's
1999	Neil Smith	James Male	4–2	Chicago *(James Male forfeited second leg through injury)*
2001	James Male	Neil Smith	6–1	New York and St Paul's
2003	James Male	J Larken	5–4	Philadelphia and Queen's
2005	Harry Foster	Ali Robinson	7–5	Montreal and Queen's
2008	James Stout	Harry Foster	6–1	New York and Queen's
2010	James Stout	Alex Titchener-Barrett	5–1	New York and Queen's

WORLD DOUBLES CHAMPIONSHIP

	Winners	Runners-up	Aggregate score	Venues
1990	James Male and John Prenn	Shannon Hazell and Neil Smith	8–5	Manchester and Queen's
1992	Shannon Hazell and Neil Smith	Willie Boone and John Prenn	7–3	Clifton and Queen's
1993	Shannon Hazell and Neil Smith	James Male and John Prenn	7–7 166 to 160 pts	New York and Queen's
1996	Shannon Hazell and Neil Smith	James Male and John Prenn	5–0	New York and Philadelphia
1998	Shannon Hazell and Neil Smith	Willie Boone and Peter Brake	7–6	Clifton and New York
2001	James Male and Mark Hue Williams	Shannon Hazell and Neil Smith	5–0	Philadelphia and St Paul's
2003	James Male and Mark Hue Williams	Ali Robinson and Guy Barker	6–6 136 to 134 pts	New York and Queen's
2005	Guy Barker and Ali Robinson	Tim Cockroft and Guy Smith-Bingham	7–4	Chicago and Queen's
2007	Neil Smith and Mark Hubbard	Harry Foster and Mark Hue Williams	5–0	New York and Queen's
2009	Harry Foster and Mark Hue Williams	Mark Hubbard and Neil Smith	7–5	New York and Queen's
2011	Tim Cockroft and Alex Titchener-Barrett	Harry Foster and Mark Hue Williams	8–5	Montreal and Queen's
2013	James Coyne and Will Hopton	Tim Cockroft and Alex Titchener-Barrett	6–2	Chicago and Queen's

UNITED KINGDOM

MEN

The Sheppard Cup
OPEN SINGLES CHAMPIONSHIP (Challenge)

From 1929 to 1975 the competition, for the Sheppard Cup, was a challenge event. In 1971 an Open Invitation Tournament for the Louis Roederer Trophy was initiated as an annual open event, but it was not the British Open. In 1975 H.R. Angus agreed to relinquish the British Open challenge championship in order that the Open Invitation event could become the annual British Open championship, which it did from 1975 onwards.

	Winner	Runner-up	Score		Winner	Runner-up	Score		Winner	Runner-up	Score
1929	J.C.F. Simpson	C.R. Read	5–1	1946	J.P. Dear	P. Kershaw	8–1	1967	J.W. Leonard	C.J. Swallow	7–4
1930	J.C.F. Simpson	C.R. Read	5–0	1951	J.P. Dear	J.H. Pawle	8–2	1970	C.J. Swallow	J.W. Leonard	7–4
1932	Lord Aberdare	J.C.F. Simpson	8–2	1954	G.W.T. Atkins	J.P. Dear	6–4		*C.J. Swallow resigned title*		
1933	I. Akers-Douglas	Lord Aberdare	4–0 (retired)	1959	J.R. Thompson	R.M.K. Gracey	3–1	1970	M.G.M. Smith	C.T.M. Pugh	*walkover*
1934	A.G. Cooper	I. Akers-Douglas	7–4	1960	J.P. Dear	J.R. Thompson	7–4	1971	H.R. Angus	M.G.M. Smith	6–2
1936	D.S. Milford	A.G. Cooper	8–3	1961	G.W.T. Atkins	*claimed*		1975	*H.R. Angus relinquished challenge title*		

OPEN SINGLES CHAMPIONSHIP

	Winner	Runner-up	Score		Winner	Runner-up	Score		Winner	Runner-up	Score
1975	H.R. Angus	W.J.C. Surtees	4–1	1989	J.S. Male	N.P.A. Smith	4–2	2003	G.J. Smith-Bingham	H.St.J.R. Foster	4–0
1976	H.R. Angus	J.A.N. Prenn	4–1	1990	N.P.A. Smith	W.R. Boone	4–0	2004	A.J. Robinson	H.St.J.R. Foster	4–2
1977	J.A.N. Prenn	W.R. Boone	4–1	1991	J.S. Male	N.P.A. Smith	4–1	2005	G.J. Smith-Bingham	A. Titchener-Barrett	4–3
1978	H.R. Angus	W.R. Boone	4–1	1992	S.M. Hazell	W.R. Boone	4–2	2006	H.St.J.R. Foster	M. Hubbard	4–0
1979	W.R. Boone	J.A.N. Prenn	4–1	1993	N.P.A. Smith	S.M. Hazell	4–0	2007	H.St.J.R. Foster	G. Smith-Bingham	4–2
1980	J.A.N. Prenn	W.R. Boone	4–2	1994	N.P.A. Smith	R. Owen-Browne	4–3	2008	J. Stout	A. Titchener-Barrett	4–1
1981	J.A.N. Prenn	W.R. Boone	4–0	1995	W.R. Boone	N.P.A. Smith	4–0	2009	J. Stout	H.St.J.R. Foster	4–1
1982	J.A.N. Prenn	W.R. Boone	4–2	1996	J.S. Male	N.P.A. Smith	4–0	2010	A. Titchener-Barrett	J. Stout	4–3
1983	J.A.N. Prenn	W.R. Boone	4–1	1997	W.R. Boone	M.G.N. Windows	4–1	2011	A. Titchener-Barrett	W.E.L. Hopton	4–0
1984	W.R. Boone	R.S. Crawley	4–0	1998	W.R. Boone	T.N. Sawrey-Cookson	4–0	2012	W.E.L. Hopton	A. Titchener-Barrett	4–2
1985	J.A.N. Prenn	W.R. Boone	4–1	1999	N.P.A. Smith	W.R. Boone	4–3	2013	A. Titchener-Barrett	J.R. Coyne	4–1
1986	W.R. Boone	J.A.N. Prenn	4–2	2000	J.S. Male	P. Brake	4–2	2014	W.E.L. Hopton	A. Titchener-Barrett	4–3
1987	J.S. Male	N.P.A. Smith	4–1	2001	J.S. Male	M Hubbard	4–0				
1988	J.S. Male	N.P.A. Smith	4–0	2002	H.St.J.R Foster	M Hubbard	4–1				

OPEN INVITATION TOURNAMENT
Louis Roederer Trophy

	Winner	Runner-up	Score		Winner	Runner-up	Score
1971	H.R. Angus	R.M.K. Gracey	3–1	1973	H.R. Angus	M.G.M. Smith	3–2
1972	H.R. Angus	M.G.M. Smith	3–1	1974	W.J.C. Surtees	H.R. Angus	3–1

CHAMPIONSHIP RECORDS

KBC Peel Hunt Trophy

Year	Winner	Year	Winner	Year	Winner	Year	Winner	Year	Winner
1996	A.J. Robinson	2000	J.S. Small	2003	H.St.J.R. Foster	2008	A.T.R. Titchener-Barrett	2011	J. Stout
1997–98	N.P.A. Smith	2001	J.A.N. Prenn	2004	G.J. Smith-Bingham	2009	J. Stout	2012–13	W.E.L. Hopton
1999	P. Brake	2002	J.S. Male	2005–07	H.St.J.R. Foster	2010	W.E.L. Hopton	2014	J. Stout

OPEN DOUBLES CHAMPIONSHIP

Year	Winners	Runners-up	Score
1981	W.R. Boone and R.S. Crawley	C.J. Hue Williams and J.A.N. Prenn	4–0
1982	W.R. Boone and R.S. Crawley	C.J. Hue Williams and J.A.N. Prenn	4–0
1983	W.R. Boone and R.S. Crawley	M.W. Nicholls and P.C. Nicholls	4–1
1984	W.R. Boone and R.S. Crawley	J.A.N. Prenn and J.S. Male	4–0
1985	W.R. Boone and R.S. Crawley	J.A.N. Prenn and J.S. Male	4–3
1986	J.A.N. Prenn and J.S. Male	W.R. Boone and R.S. Crawley	4–1
1987	J.A.N. Prenn and J.S. Male	W.R. Boone and R.S. Crawley	4–3
1988	J.A.N. Prenn and J.S. Male	W.R. Boone and R.S. Crawley	4–2
1989	J.A.N. Prenn and J.S. Male	N.P.A. Smith and S.M. Hazell	4–2
1990	J.A.N. Prenn and J.S. Male	N.P.A. Smith and S.M. Hazell	4–1
1991	N.P.A. Smith and S.M. Hazell	J.A.N. Prenn and J.S. Male	4–3
1992	N.P.A. Smith and S.M. Hazell	J.A.N. Prenn and W.R. Boone	4–1
1993	J.A.N. Prenn and J.S. Male	W.R. Boone and N.P.A. Smith	4–0
1994	W.R. Boone and T.B. Cockroft	J.A.N. Prenn and R. Owen-Browne	4–1
1995	W.R. Boone and T.B. Cockroft	N.P.A. Smith and P. Brake	4–3
1996	W.R. Boone and T.B. Cockroft	J.S. Male and J.A.N. Prenn	walkover
1997	W.R. Boone and P. Brake	T.B. Cockroft and R. Owen-Browne	4–1
1998	J.S. Male and C.M. Hue Williams	N.P.A. Smith and S.M. Hazell	4–1
1999	J.S. Male and C.M. Hue Williams	J.J.S. Larken and T.N. Sawrey-Cookson	4–0
2000	J.S. Male and C.M. Hue Williams	G.W. Barker and A.J. Robinson	4–2
2001	J.S. Male and C.M. Hue Williams	A. and G. Smith-Bingham	4–2
2002	G.W. Barker and A.J. Robinson	A. and G. Smith-Bingham	4–1
2003	G.W. Barker and A.J. Robinson	A. and G. Smith-Bingham	4–0
2004	G.W. Barker and A.J. Robinson	J.S. Male and J.A.N. Prenn	4–1
2005	H.St.J.R. Foster and C.M. Hue Williams	T.B. Cockroft and G. Smith-Bingham	4–2
2006	N.P.A. Smith and M.V. Hubbard	T.B. Cockroft and G. Smith-Bingham	4–2
2007	H.St.J.R. Foster and C.M. Hue Williams	M. Hubbard and N.P.A. Smith	4–1
2008	H.St.J.R. Foster and C.M. Hue Williams	W. Hopton and A. Titchener-Barrett	4–0
2009	T.B. Cockroft and A.T.R. Titchener-Barrett	J.R. Coyne and W.E.L. Hopton	4–1
2010	T.B. Cockroft and A.T.R. Titchener-Barrett	J. Stout and M. Gooding	4–2
2011	J.R. Coyne and W.E.L. Hopton	G. Tysoe and M. Bailey	4–1
2012	J.R. Coyne and W.E.L. Hopton	N.P.A. Smith and N.C.W. James	4–1
2013	B. Snell and N.C.W. James	J. Stout and M. Gooding	3–3 (retired)
2014	A.T.R. Titchener-Barrett and C. Portz	J.R. Coyne and M. Bailey	4–1

AMATEUR SINGLES CHAMPIONSHIP

Year	Winner	Runner-up	Score
1888	C.D. Buxton	E.M. Hadow	3–0
1889	E.M. Butler	C.D. Buxton	3–2
1890	P. Ashworth	Capt. W. C. Hedley	3–0
1891	H. Philipson	P. Ashworth	3–2
1892	F. Dames-Longworth	H. Philipson	3–0
1893	F. Dames-Longworth	H.K. Foster	3–1
1894	H.K. Foster	F. Dames-Longworth	3–1
1895	H.K. Foster	G.F. Vernon	3–1
1896	H.K. Foster	E.H. Miles	3–0
1897	H.K. Foster	P. Ashworth	3–2
1898	H.K. Foster	W.L. Foster	3–0
1899	H.K. Foster	E.H. Miles	3–0
1900	H.K. Foster	P. Ashworth	3–0
1901	F. Dames-Longworth	J. Howard	3–1
1902	E.H. Miles	F. Dames-Longworth	3–1
1903	E.M. Baerlein	E.H. Miles	3–2
1904	H.K. Foster	E.M. Baerlein	3–0
1905	E.M. Baerlein	E.H. Miles	3–0
1906	Maj. S.H. Sheppard	P. Ashworth	3–1
1907	E.B. Noel	B.S. Foster	3–2
1908	E.M. Baerlein	E.B. Noel	3–1
1909	E.M. Baerlein	H. Brougham	3–1
1910	E M. Baerlein	P. Ashworth	3–0
1911	E.M. Baerlein	H.A. Denison	3–0
1912	B.S. Foster	G.G. Kershaw	3–1
1913	B.S. Foster	H.W. Leatham	3–0
1914	H.W. Leatham	E.M. Baerlein	3–2
1920	E.M. Baerlein	Hon. C.N. Bruce	3–1
1921	E.M. Baerlein	Hon. C. N. Bruce	3–0
1922	Hon. C.N. Bruce	E.M. Baerlein	3–0
1923	E.M. Baerlein	Hon. C.N. Bruce	3–1
1924	Dr H.W. Leatham	Capt. T.O. Jameson	3–2
1925	C.C. Pell (USA)	Dr H.W. Leatham	3–0
1926	J.C.F. Simpson	Dr H.W. Leatham	3–2
1927	J.C.F. Simpson	Hon. C.N. Bruce	3–2
1928	J.C.F. Simpson	Hon. C.N. Bruce	3–0
1929	C.S. Crawley	H.D. Hake	3–0
1930	D.S. Milford	I. Akers-Douglas	3–0
1931	Lord Aberdare	I. Akers-Douglas	3–0
1932	I. Akers-Douglas	J.C.F. Simpson	3–1
1933	I. Akers-Douglas	C.S. Crawley	3–1
1934	I. Akers-Douglas	A.M. Hedley	3–0
1935	D.S. Milford	I. Akers-Douglas	3–1
1936	D.S. Milford	J.H. Pawle	3–1
1937	D.S. Milford	R.C. Riseley	3–0
1938	D.S. Milford	I. Akers-Douglas	3–0
1939	P. Kershaw	R.A.A. Holt	3–0
1946	J.H. Pawle	I. Akers-Douglas	3–1
1947	J.H. Pawle	D.S. Milford	3–2
1948	J.H. Pawle	D.S. Milford	3–2
1949	J.H. Pawle	D.S. Milford	3–2
1950	D.S. Milford	G.H.G. Doggart	3–0
1951	D.S. Milford	G.W.T. Atkins	3–2
1952	G.W.T. Atkins	M.C. Cowdrey	3–0
1953	G.W.T. Atkins	D.S. Milford	3–2
1954	J.R. Thompson	D.S. Milford	3–1
1955	J.R. Thompson	D.S. Milford	3–2
1956	G.W.T. Atkins	J.R. Thompson	3–1
1957	J.R. Thompson	M.R. Coulman	3–2
1958	J.R. Thompson	R.M.K. Gracey	3–0
1959	J.R. Thompson	J.M.G. Tildesley	3–2
1960	G.W.T. Atkins	J.R. Thompson	3–0
1961	J.W. Leonard	R.M.K. Gracey	3–0
1962	J.W. Leonard	G.W.T. Atkins	3–2
1963	G.W.T. Atkins	J.W. Leonard	3–2
1964	C.J. Swallow	G.W.T. Atkins	3–2
1965	J.W. Leonard	M.S. Connell	3–1
1966	C.J. Swallow	J.W. Leonard	3–1
1967	J.W. Leonard	C.T. Pugh	3–2
1968	C.J. Swallow	R.M.K. Gracey	3–0
1969	C J. Swallow	J.W. Leonard	3–0
1970	M.G.M. Smith	C.T.M. Pugh	3–1
1971	M.G.M. Smith	H.R. Angus	3–2
1972	H.R.Angus	M.G.M. Smith	3–1
1973	H.R. Angus	M.G.M. Smith	3–1
1974	H.R. Angus	C.J. Hue Williams	3–1
1975	H.R. Angus	D.M. Norman	3–1
1976	W.R. Boone	J.A.N. Prenn	3–2
1977	C.J. Hue Williams	W.R. Boone	3–0
1978	W.R. Boone	J.A.N. Prenn	3–2
1979	J.A.N. Prenn	W.R. Boone	3–0
1980	J.A.N. Prenn	W.R. Boone	3–0
1981	W.R. Boone	J.A.N. Prenn	3–2
1982	J.A.N. Prenn	W.R. Boone	3–2
1983	J.A.N. Prenn	W.R. Boone	3–0
1984	W.R. Boone	M.W. Nicholls	3–0
1985 Jan	W.R. Boone	J.A.N. Prenn	3–2
1985 Dec	J.S. Male	W.R. Boone	3–0
1986	J.S. Male	W.R. Boone	3–0
1987	W.R. Boone	M.W. Nicholls	3–0
1988	W.R. Boone	J.A.N. Prenn	3–1
1988	J.S. Male	W.R. Boone	3–0
1989	W.R. Boone	J.A.N. Prenn	3–0
1990	J.S. Male	W.R. Boone	3–1
1991	J.A.N. Prenn	W.R. Boone	3–0
1992	J.S. Male	W.R. Boone	3–1
1993	W.R. Boone	J.A.N. Prenn	3–1
1994	J.S. Male	W.R. Boone	3–1
1995	J.S. Male	W.R. Boone	3–0
1996	J.S. Male	W.R. Boone	3–1
1997	J.S. Male	G.W. Barker	3–0
1998	J.S. Male	W.R. Boone	3–0
1999	J.S. Male	A.J. Robinson	3–1
2000	J.S. Male	G.W. Barker	3–0
2001	A.J. Robinson	J.A.N. Prenn	3–2

table continues

	Winner	Runner-up	Score		Winner	Runner-up	Score		Winner	Runner-up	Score
2002	G. Smith-Bingham	H. Foster	3-0	2007	H.St.J.R. Foster	J. Larken	3-1	2012	A.T.R. Titchener-Barrett	T. Billings	3-0
2003	G. Smith-Bingham	T. Cockroft	3-1	2008	A.T.R. Titchener-Barrett	M. Farmiloe	3-0	2013	A.T.R. Titchener-Barrett	J.R. Coyne	3-2
2004	G. Smith-Bingham	R. Owen-Browne	3-0	2009	A.T.R. Titchener-Barrett	J. Coyne	3-0	2014	A.T.R. Titchener-Barrett	T. Billings	3-1
2005	A.J. Robinson	C. Danby	3-0	2010	A.T.R. Titchener-Barrett	W. Hopton	3-0				
2006	H.St.J.R. Foster	G. Smith-Bingham	3-2	2011	A.T.R. Titchener-Barrett	N. James	3-0				

AMATEUR DOUBLES CHAMPIONSHIP

1890	P. Ashworth and Capt. W.C. Hedley
1891	P. Ashworth and E.L. Metcalfe
1892	E.M. Butler and M.C. Kemp
1893	F.H. Browning and H.K. Foster
1894	H.K. Foster and C.S.C.F. Ridgeway
1895	F. Dames-Longworth and F.H. Browning
1896-97	H.K. Foster and P. Ashworth
1898	H.K. Foster and W.L. Foster
1899-1900	H.K. Foster and P. Ashworth
1901	F. Dames-Longworth and V.H. Pennell
1902	E.M. Baerlein and E.H. Miles
1903	H.K. Foster and B.S. Foster
1904-05	E.M. Baerlein and E.H. Miles
1906	E.H. Miles and F. Dames-Longworth
1907	W.L. Foster and B.S. Foster
1908	F. Dames-Longworth and V.H. Pennell
1909	E.M. Baerlein and P. Ashworth
1910-11	B.S. Foster and Hon. C.N. Bruce
1912	H.W. Leatham and H.A. Denison
1913	B.S. Foster and H. Brougham
1914 & 1920	E.M. Baerlein and G.G. Kershaw
1921	Hon. C.N. Bruce and Dr H.W. Leatham
1922-23	J.C.F. Simpson and R.C.O. Williams
1924-27	Hon. C.N. Bruce and Dr H.W. Leatham
1928	Hon. C.N. Bruce and A.C. Raphael
1929	J.C.F. Simpson and R.C.O. Williams
1930	Lord Aberdare and Dr H.W. Leatham
1931	J.C.F. Simpson and C.S. Crawley
1932-33	K.A. Wagg and I. Akers-Douglas
1934	Lord Aberdare and P.W. Kemp-Welch
1935	K.A. Wagg and I. Akers-Douglas
1936-37	C.S. Crawley and J.C.F. Simpson
1938	D.S. Milford and P.M. Whitehouse
1939 & 1946	C.S. Crawley and J.H. Pawle
1947	R.A.A. Holt and Maj. A.R. Taylor
1948	D.S. Milford and J.R. Thompson
1949	R.A.A. Holt and Maj. A.R. Taylor
1950-52	D.S. Milford and J.R. Thompson
1953	P. Kershaw and G.W.T. Atkins
1954-59	D.S. Milford and J.R. Thompson
1960	C.J. Swallow and J.M.G. Tildesley
1961-62	G.W.T. Atkins and P. Kershaw
1963	J.W. Leonard and C.J. Swallow
1964-65	R.M.K. Gracey and M.G.M. Smith
1966	J.R. Thompson and C.T.M. Pugh
1967-68	J.W. Leonard and C.J. Hue Williams
1969-71	R.M.K. Gracey and M.G.M. Smith
1972-73	H.R. Angus and C.J. Hue Williams
1974	G.W.T. Atkins and C.J. Hue Williams
1975-77	W.R. Boone and C.T.M. Pugh
1978-79	H.R. Angus and A.G. Milne
1980-84	W.R. Boone and R.S. Crawley
1985	J.A.N. Prenn and C.J. Hue Williams
1986	W.R. Boone and R.S. Crawley
1987	J.S. Male and R. Owen-Browne
1988-91	J.A.N. Prenn and J.S. Male
1992	W.R. Boone and T.B. Cockroft
1993	J.A.N. Prenn and J.S. Male
1994	W.R. Boone and T.B. Cockroft
1995	J.A.N Prenn and J.S. Male
1996	W.R. Boone and T.B. Cockroft
1997	T.B. Cockroft and R. Owen-Browne
1998	W.R. Boone and J.S. Male
1999	G.W. Barker and A.J. Robinson
2000-02	J.S. Male and C.M. Hue Williams
2003	T. Cockroft and R. Owen-Browne
2004	G.W. Barker and A.J. Robinson
2005	T.B. Cockroft and G.J. Smith-Bingham
2006-07	H.St.J.R. Foster and C.M. Hue Williams
2008	C.B. Cockroft and A.T.R. Titchener-Barrett
2009	H.St.J.R. Foster and C.M. Hue Williams
2010	G.W. Barker and A.J. Robinson
2011	W.E.L. Hopton and J.R. Coyne
2012-13	T.B. Cockroft and A.T.R. Titchener-Barrett
2014	H.St.J.R. Foster and C.M. Hue Williams

PROFESSIONAL SINGLES CHAMPIONSHIP
Scott-Chad Cup

	Winner	Runner-up	Score		Winner	Runner-up	Score		Winner	Runner-up	Score
1931	C.R. Read			1988	N.P.A. Smith	S.M. Hazell	3-0	2002	M.V. Hubbard	N.P.A. Smith	3-0
1932	A.G. Cooper			1989	N.P.A. Smith	S.M. Hazell	3-2	2003	N.P.A. Smith	M.V. Hubbard	3-2
1946	J.P. Dear			1990	S.M. Hazell	N.P.A. Smith	3-2	2004	N.P.A. Smith	M.V. Hubbard	3-2
In 1979 it was played as a knock-out competition for the first time				1991	S.M. Hazell	N.P.A. Smith	3-0	2005	N.P.A. Smith	M.V. Hubbard	3-0
				1992	N.P.A. Smith	S.M. Hazell	3-0	2006	M.V. Hubbard	N.P.A. Smith	3-0
1979	N.A.R. Cripps	T.S. Whatley	3-0	1993	N.P.A. Smith	S.M. Hazell	3-0	2007	M.V. Hubbard	D.J. Makey	3-1
1980	T.S. Whatley	N.A.R. Cripps	3-1	1994	P. Brake	N.A.R. Cripps	3-0	2008	M.V. Hubbard	N.P.A. Smith	3-1
1981	N.A.R. Cripps	T.S. Whatley	3-1	1995	P. Brake	N.P.A. Smith	3-2	2009	N.P.A. Smith	M.V. Hubbard	3-2
1982	S.M. Hazell	N.A.R. Cripps	3-1	1996	N.P.A. Smith	D.J. Makey	3-0	2010	M.V. Hubbard	D.J. Makey	3-0
1983	N.A.R. Cripps	S.M. Hazell	3-2	1997	P. Brake	D.J. Makey	3-0	2011	M.V. Hubbard	N.P.A. Smith	3-1
1984	S.M. Hazell	N.A.R. Cripps	3-0	1998	N.P.A. Smith	P. Brake	3-1	2012	W.E.L. Hopton	M.V. Hubbard	3-0
1985	N.P.A. Smith	S. Tulley	3-2	1999	T.N. Sawrey-Cookson	M.V. Hubbard	3-0	2013	W.E.L. Hopton	B. Snell	3-0
1986	N.P.A. Smith	N.A.R. Cripps	3-0	2000	T.N. Sawrey-Cookson	M.V. Hubbard	3-0	2014	W.E.L. Hopton	M.V. Hubbard	3-0
1987	N.P.A. Smith	S.M. Hazell	3-0	2001	N.P.A. Smith	T.N. Sawrey-Cookson	3-1				

PUBLIC SCHOOLS CHAMPIONSHIP
Played at Prince's 1868–86, Lord's 1887 and Queen's since 1888 except in 1941, when the final was played at Wellington

	Winner	Runner-up	
1868	Eton (C.J. Ottaway and W.F. Tritton)	Cheltenham (J.J. Read and A.T. Myers)	4-3
1869	Eton (C.J. Ottaway and J.P. Rodger)	Rugby (S.K. Gwyer and H.W. Gardner)	4-0
1870	Rugby (H.W. Gardner and T.S. Pearson)	Eton (J.P. Rodger and F.C. Ricardo)	4-2
1871	Harrow (G.A. Webbe and A.A. Hadow)	Eton (F.C. Ricardo and A.W. Ridley)	4-3
1872	Harrow (G.A. Webbe and A.A. Hadow)	Eton (E.O. Wilkinson and W.W. Whitmore)	4-1
1873	Harrow (P.F. Hadow and F.D. Leyland)	Rugby (J.J. Barrow and J. Harding)	4-0
1874	Harrow (F.D. Leyland and C.W.M. Kemp)	Winchester (H.J.B. Hollings and H.R. Webbe)	4-0

table continues

Championship Records

	Winner	Runner-up	
1875	Eton (J. Oswald and D. Lane)	Winchester (H.R. Webbe and A.L. Ellis)	4-1
1876	Harrow (H.E. Meek and L.K. Jarvis)	Eton (Hon. I.F.W. Bligh and V.A. Butler)	4-1
1877	Eton (C.A.C. Ponsonby and Hon. I.F.W. Bligh)	Marlborough (G.M. Butterworth and F.M. Lucas)	4-1
1878	Eton (C.A.C. Ponsonby and J.D. Cobbold)	Harrow (H.F. de Paravicini and M.C. Kemp)	4-0
1879	Harrow (M.C. Kemp and Hon. F.R. de Moleyns)	Rugby (C.F.H. Leslie and W.G. Stutfield)	4-0
1880	Harrow (M.C. Kemp and E.M. Hadow)	Eton (P. St. L. Grenfell and J.C.B. Eastwood)	4-2
1881	Harrow (E.M. Hadow and A.F. Kemp)	Marlborough (A.W. Martyn and H.M. Leaf)	4-1
1882	Eton (R.H. Pemberton and A.C. Richards)	Harrow (H.E. Crawley and C.D. Buxton)	4-2
1883	Harrow (H.E. Crawley and C.D. Buxton)	Eton (R.H. Pemberton and H. Phillipson)	4-2
1884	Harrow (E.M. Butler and C.D. Buxton)	Eton (H. Philipson and J.H.B. Noble)	4-3
1885	Harrow (E.M. Butler and E. Crawley)	Eton (H. Philipson and H.W. Forster)	4-3
1886	Harrow (E. Crawley and N.T. Holmes)	Haileybury(J.D. Campbell and H.M. Walters)	4-2
1887	Harrow (P. Ashworth and R.D. Cheales)	Charterhouse (H.L. Meyer and R. Nicholson)	4-1
1888	Charterhouse (E.C. Streatfeild and W. Shelmerdine)	Harrow (R.D. Cheales and E.W.F. Castleman)	4-2
1889	Winchester (E.J. Neve and T.B. Case)	Charterhouse (W. Shelmerdine and F.S. Cokayne)	4-2
1890	Harrow (A.H.M. Butler and W.F.G. Wyndham)	Wellington (G.J. Mordaunt and R.H. Raphael)	4-3
1891	Wellington (G.J. Mordaunt and R.H. Raphael)	Malvern (H.K. Foster and W.L. Foster)	4-2
1892	Malvern (H.K. Foster and W.L. Foster)	Harrow (B.N. Bosworth-Smith and F.G.H. Clayton)	4-2
1893	Charterhouse (E. Garnett and V.H. Pennell)	Eton (P.W. Cobbold and H. Harben)	4-3
1894	Charterhouse (V.H. Pennell and E. Garnett)	Malvern (C.J. Burnup and H.H. Marriott)	4-2
1895	Harrow (J.H. Stogdon and A.S. Crawley)	Clifton (R.O. de Gex and A.H.C. Kearsey)	4-0
1896	Rugby (W.E. Wilson-Johnston and G.T. Hawes)	Eton (H.C.B. Underdown and E.A. Biedermann)	4-3
1897	Harrow (L.F. Andrewes and W.F.A. Rattigan)	Winchester (E.B. Noel and R.A. Williams)	4-3
1898	Harrow (W.F.A. Rattigan and L.F. Andrewes)	Eton (E.M. Baerlein and J.E. Tomkinson)	4-2
1899	Eton (S. MacNaghten and I.A. de la Rue)	Harrow (F.B. Wilson and S.J.G. Hoare)	4-1
1900	Malvern (B.S. Foster and W.H.B. Evans)	Rugby (S.C. Blackwood and O. Fleischmann)	4-0
1901	Marlborough (A.J. Graham and L.E. Gillett)	Haileybury (S.M. Toyne and P.F. Reid)	4-0
1902	Harrow (G.A. Phelips and C. Browning)	Rugby (K.M. Agnew and J.V. Nesbitt)	4-2
1903	Harrow (G.A. Phelips and L.M. MacLean)	Rugby (K.M. Agnew and K. Powell)	4-2
1904	Winchester (Hon. C.N. Bruce and E.L. Wright)	Malvern (G.N. Foster and A.P. Day)	4-0
1905	Eton (J.J. Astor and M.W. Bovill)	Wellington (H. Brougham and T. Hone)	4-1
1906	Charterhouse (C.V.L. Hooman and R.M. Garnett)	Wellington (H. Brougham and E.C. Harrison)	4-1
1907	Wellington (H. Brougham and E.C. Harrison)	Malvern (M.K. Foster and F.T. Mann)	4-1
1908	Malvern (M.K. Foster and N.J.A. Foster)	Rugby (C.F.B. Simpson and C.C. Watson)	4-1
1909	Charterhouse (H.A. Denison and H.W. Leatham)	Eton (V. Bulkeley-Johnson and J.E. Craigie)	4-1
1910	Charterhouse (H.W. Leatham and H.A. Denison)	Eton (E.L. Bury and Hon. J.N. Manners)	4-0
1911	Rugby (C.F.B. Simpson and W.H. Clarke)	Winchester (L. de O. Tollemache and D.F. McConnel)	4-3
1912	Charterhouse (G.A. Wright and C.B. Leatham)	Wellington (E.G. Bartlett and W.G. Grenville Grey)	4-0
1913	Wellington (E.G. Bartlett and F.A. Carnegy)	Haileybury (D.H. Hake and L.F. Marson)	4-0
1914	Charterhouse (L.D.B. Monier-Williams and J.H. Strachan)	Wellington(E.A. Simson and C.P. Hancock)	4-3
1919	Marlborough (G.S. Butler and G.W.F. Haslehust)	Malvern (C.G.W. Robson and N.E. Partridge)	4-1
1920	Malvern (C.G.W. Robson and J.A. Deed)	Eton (H.P. Guinness and R. Aird)	4-1
1921	Wellington (P.N. Durlacher and L. Lees)	Eton (R. Aird and H.D. Sheldon)	4-1
1922	Eton (G.S. Incledon-Webber and O.C. Smith-Bingham)	Radley (F.C. Dawnay and A.E. Blair)	4-2
1923	Rugby (D.S. Milford and G.M. Goodbody)	Radley (F.C. Dawnay and A.E. Blair)	4-2
1924	Rugby (D.S. Milford and E.F. Longrigg)	Eton (C.J. Child and T.A. Pilkington)	4-2
1925	Harrow (A.C.Raphael and N.M. Ford)	Eton (C.J. Child and T.A. Pilkington)	4-3
1926	Wellington (R.C. Dobson and J. Powell)	Harrow (N.M. Ford and A.M. Crawley)	4-3
1927	Eton (K.A. Wagg and I. Akers-Douglas)	Harrow (R.H. Anstruther-Gough-Calthorpe and G.L. Raphael)	4-0
1928	Eton (I. Akers-Douglas and I. A. de Lyle)	Winchester (P.J. Brett and W.D.D. Evans)	4-3
1929	Winchester (N. McCaskie and R.H. Priestley)	Haileybury (E.N. Evans and R.W. Bulmore)	4-0
1930	Radley (P.I. Van der Gucht and W.H. Vestey)	Eton (R. Grant and J. de P. Whitaker)	4-1
1931	Harrow (R. Pulbrook and J.M.F. Lightly)	Eton (A. M. Hedley and J.C. Atkinson-Clark)	4-2
1932	Harrow (R. Pulbrook and J.H. Pawle)	Rugby (R.A. Gray and R.F. Lumb)	4-2
1933	Rugby (R.A. Gray and R.F. Lumb)	Harrow (R. Pulbrook and J.H. Pawle)	4-2
1934	Rugby (R.F. Lumb and P. Kershaw)	Haileybury (W.M. Robertson and F.R.E. Malden)	4-2
1935	Winchester (J.T. Faber and A.B. Kingsley)	Marlborough (P.M. Whitehouse and J.D.L. Dickson)	4-2
1936	Malvern (P.D. Manners and N.W. Beeson)	Clifton (W.E. Brassington and S.G. Greenbury)	4-0
1937	Malvern (P.D. Manners and N.W. Beeson)	Tonbridge (J.R. Thompson and P. Pettman)	4-3
1938	Rugby (A. Kershaw and J.D.L. Repard)	Malvern (P.D. Manners and D. Chalk)	4-2
1939	Rugby (J.D.L. Repard and W.H.D. Dunnett)	Winchester (A.R. Taylor and H.E.W. Bowyer)	4-0
1940	Haileybury (J.K. Drinkall and A. Fairbairn)	Rugby (L.G.H. Hingley and P.M. Dagnall)	4-1
1941	Haileybury (J.K. Drinkall and A. Fairbairn)	Clifton (R.J. Potter and L.J. Waugh)	4-0
1942	no competition		
1943	Winchester (G.H.G. Doggart and J.B. Thursfield)	Harrow (I.N. Mitchell and J.G. Hogg)	4-2
1944	Winchester (H.E. Webb and G.H.J. Myrtle)	Eton (A.J.H. Ward and J.R. Greenwood)	4-2
1945	Winchester (H.E. Webb and G.H.J. Myrtle)	Eton (J.A.R. Clench and W.H.R. Brooks)	4-1
1946	Wellington (C.B. Haycraft and J.E.L. Ainslie)	Harrow (G.R. Simmonds and J.A. Glynne-Percy)	4-1
1947	Harrow (G.R. Simmonds and R.K.F.C. Treherne-Thomas)	Eton (R.F.H. Ward and W.J. Collins)	4-2

table continues

	Winner	Runner-up	
1948	Harrow (D.W. Taylor and T.A.M. Pigott)	Wellington (A.H. Swift and R.L. Lees)	4-3
1949	Winchester (P.M. Welsh and M.R. Coulman)	Eton (I.C. de Sales la Terriere and A.C.D. Ingleby-Mackenzie)	4-3
1950	Winchester (M.R. Coulman and A.D. Myrtle)	Harrow (R.L.O. Bridgeman and R.J. McAlpine)	4-2
1951	Winchester (M.R. Coulman and A.D. Myrtle)	Tonbridge (M.C. Cowdrey and J.F. Campbell)	4-2
1952	Rugby (D.R.W. Harrison and J.G.H. Hogben)	Wellington (P. de Mesquita and M.W. Bolton)	4-2
1953	Winchester (R.T.C. Whatmore and D.B.D. Lowe)	Radley (E.R. Dexter and I.A.K. Dipple)	4-3
1954	Harrow (C.A. Strang and R.B. Bloomfield)	Marlborough (N.R.C. Marr and P.H.R. Anderson)	4-2
1955	Eton (C.T.M. Pugh and Lord Chelsea)	Winchester (C.N. Copeman and Hon. M.M. Mitchell-Thompson)	4-1
1956	Charterhouse (C.J. Swallow and J.J. Carless)	Tonbridge (M.S. Connell and M.R.V. Clinch)	4-2
1957	Tonbridge (M.S. Connell and P.D. Rylands)	Marlborough (C.P. Pyemont and N.C. Harris)	4-1
1958	Eton (J.W. Leonard and D.M. Norman)	Winchester (P.J.L. Wright and Nawab of Pataudi)	4-1
1959	Winchester (Nawab of Pataudi and C.E.M. Snell)	Eton (D.M. Norman and R.M. Bailey)	4-3
1960	Marlborough (A.J. Price and M.G. Griffith)	Winchester (C.E.M. Snell and P.B. Hay)	4-2
1961	Eton (G.P.D. Milne and B.A. Fitzgerald)	Marlborough (M.G. Griffith and J. Hopper)	4-2
1962	Marlborough (M.G. Griffith and J. Hopper)	Winchester (H.R. Angus and C.J.H. Green)	4-3
1963	Eton (R.A. Pilkington and M.D.T. Faber)	Winchester (H.R. Angus and C.L. Sunter)	4-1
1964	Eton (M.D.T. Faber and G.W. Pilkington)	Tonbridge (T.F. Tyler and A.H.V. Monteuuis)	4-3
1965	Rugby (W.J.C. Surtees and A.M.A. Hankey)	Eton (G.W. Pilkington and A.R. Bonsor)	4-3
1966	Malvern (P.F.C. Begg and P. D'A. Mander)	Radley (J.K. Rogers and B.M. Osborne)	4-0
1967	Eton (Lord Richard Wellesley and M.J.J. Faber)	Harrow (R.N. Readman and R.S. Crawley)	4-3
1968	Eton (M.J.J. Faber and W.R. Boone)	Rugby (S.R. Miller and J.C.A. Leslie)	4-0
1969	Eton (M.J.J. Faber and A.G. Milne)	Harrow (C.H. Braithwaite and G.R.J. McDonald)	4-0
1970	Eton (R.W. Drysdale and N.H.P. Bacon)	Rugby (T.H. Weatherill and J.H.M. Griffiths)	4-0
1971	Harrow (M. Thatcher and J.A.N. Prenn)	Clifton (J.P. Willcocks and D.G. Parsons)	4-2
1972	Winchester (A.C. Lovell and P.G. Seabrook)	Haileybury (J.E. Dawes and R.F. Hollington)	4-0
1973	Tonbridge (N.B.S. Hawkins and C.S. Cowdrey)	Malvern (J.G. Hughes and M.W. Nicholls)	4-1
1974	Malvern (M.W. Nicholls and P.C. Nicholls)	Eton (T.M. Brudenell and D.M. Lindsay)	4-2
1975	Malvern (P.C. Nicholls and M.A. Tang)	Harrow (A.C.S. Piggott and P. Greig)	4-0
1976	Marlborough (D.K. Watson and M.N.P. Mockridge)	Malvern (P.C. Nicholls and M.A. Tang)	4-3
1977	Malvern (P.J. Rosser and A.J.B. McDonald)	Marlborough (D.K. Watson and C.F. Worlidge)	4-3
1978	Haileybury (R.G.P. Ellis and P. Wallis)	Harrow (D.J.G. Thomas and M.J.L. Paul)	4-1
1979	Harrow (D.J.G. Thomas and M.J.L. Paul)	Eton (D.J.C. Faber and A.D. Pease)	4-1
1980	Wellington (J.H.C. Mallinson and R.A.C. Mallinson)	Marlborough (A.J. Naylor and M.R.C. Swallow)	4-0
1981	Tonbridge (G.R. Cowdrey and P.H. Reiss)	Clifton (P.B. Morris and T.R.V. Robins)	4-2
1982	Radley (J.S. Male and J.P. Snow)	Tonbridge (G.R. Cowdrey and A.M. Spurling)	4-0
1983	Tonbridge (A.M. Spurling and R. Owen-Browne)	Eton (A.C.B. Giddins and M.H. Brooks)	4-1
1984	Harrow (D.G. Dick and S. O'N Segrave)	Wellington (D.S.C. Mallinson and A.H. Gordon)	4-1
1985	Tonbridge (R. Owen-Browne and S.M.S. Davies)	Eton (P. Baily and M.C. Small)	4-0
1986	Tonbridge (J.I. Longley and J.A.G. Waters)	Clifton (G.J. Palmer and D.B. White)	4-0
1987	Tonbridge (J.I. Longley and J.L. Nance)	Marlborough (A.J. Robinson and G.W. Barker)	4-2
1988	Marlborough (A.J. Robinson and G.W. Barker)	Tonbridge (R.D. Gill and D.R. Penfold)	4-0
1989	Marlborough (T.P.W. Barker and J.J. Hey)	Radley (L.E. Danby and M.J. Lowrey)	4-0
1990	Clifton (M.G.N. Windows and J.A. Crane)	Eton (A.J. Smith-Bingham and J.J.S. Larken)	4-2
1991	Clifton (M.G.N. Windows and J.A. Crane)	Eton (A.J. Smith-Bingham and J.J.S. Larken)	4-2
1992	Winchester (N.R. Hall and M. Segal)	Marlborough (S. Gidoomal and T.C. Stewart-Liberty)	4-3
1993	Haileybury (R.E. Walker and D.A. Cruickshank)	Rugby (R.D. Carter and H.L. Green)	4-3
1994	Rugby (R.D. Carter and C.J.C. Robards)	Haileybury (R.E. Walker and D.A. Cruickshank)	4-2
1995	Rugby (R.D. Carter and R.J.A. Hicks)	Eton (N.A. Bailey and J.P.C. Wigan)	4-2
1996	Eton (N.A. Bailey and J.P.C. Wigan)	Winchester (E.D.C. Craig and H. Lloyd Owen)	4-0
1997	Eton (G.J. Smith-Bingham and H.J.H. Loudon)	Harrow (A.T.R. Titchener-Barrett and C.J.R. Wilson)	4-1
1998	Tonbridge (D.D. Cherry and J.W.R. Parker)	Harrow (A.T.R Titchener-Barrett and C.J.R Wilson)	4-2
1999	Harrow (R.J. Wilcox and T.G. Dunbar)	Tonbridge (J.W.R. Parker and N.G.H. Hutton)	4-1
2000	Harrow (T.G. Dunbar and O. Craven)	Cheltenham (G. Tyndall and M. Stout)	4-0
2001	Cheltenham (M. Stout and J. Stout)	Harrow (K. Behal and J. Willis)	w/o
2002	Cheltenham (J. Stout and A. Coldicott)	Eton (T. McCall and E. Watson)	4-1
2003	Harrow (P. Dunbar and J. Bone)	Eton (A. Barker and H. Franks)	4-1
2004	Eton (H. Franks and M. Readman)	Cheltenham (D. Hall and N. Abendanon)	4-3
2005	Harrow (J. Bone and W. Fortune)	Winchester (M. Bailey and A. Fellowes)	4-1
2006	Cheltenham (N. James and J. Rock)	St Pauls (T. Alway and D. Tristao)	4-1
2007	Harrow (S. Northeast and G. Querl)	Eton (W. Hopton and S. Stefanowicz)	4-3
2008	Winchester (S. Knight and C. Portz)	Harrow (S. Northeast and W. Jones)	4-1
2009	Winchester (S. Knight and C. Portz)	Cheltenham (C. Wooton and B. Shiner)	4-1
2010	Winchester (B. Stevens and C. Portz)	Cheltenham (R. Owen and C. Stout)	4-3
2011	Wellington (N. Hopcroft and A. Boobyer)	Cheltenham (R. Owen and C. Stout)	4-3
2012	Cheltenham (C. Stout and A. Duncliffe-Vines)	Eton (J. Giddins and M. Seely)	4-2
2013	Harrow (L. Bose and R. White)	Cheltenham (A. Duncliffe-Vines and A. Montagu)	4-0
2014	Eton (T. Morales and C. Braham)	Harrow (R. White and H. Goodfellow)	4-1

CHAMPIONSHIP RECORDS

PUBLIC SCHOOLS SINGLES CHAMPIONSHIP
H.K. Foster Cup
1951–54 on handicap, 1955 open competition

Year	Winner	Runner-up		Year	Winner	Runner-up
1951	A.D. Myrtle (Winchester)	M.D. Scott (Winchester)		1983	A.M. Spurling (Tonbridge)	A.C.B. Giddins (Eton)
1952	M.D. Scott (Winchester)	R.H.B. Neame (Harrow)		1984	R. Owen-Browne (Tonbridge)	D.G. Dick (Harrow)
1953	T.L. Mesquita (Wellington)	N.R.C. Marr (Marlborough)		1985	J.I. Longley (Tonbridge)	R.C.H. Bruce (Wellington)
1954	R.B. Bloomfield (Harrow)	R.J.L. Sidley (Harrow)		1986	J.I. Longley (Tonbridge)	A.J. Robinson (Marlborough)
1955	J.G. Tildesley (Rugby)	R.M.K. Gracey (Tonbridge)		1987	G.W. Barker (Marlborough)	A.J. Robinson (Marlborough)
1956	C.J. Swallow (Charterhouse)	P.R. Chamberlain (Marlborough)		1988	R.R. Montgomerie (Rugby)	A.C. Hiscock (Malvern)
1957	P.D. Rylands (Tonbridge)	J.W. Leonard (Eton)		1989–90	M.G.N. Windows (Clifton)	A.J. Smith-Bingham (Eton)
1958	J.W. Leonard (Eton)	D.M. Norman (Eton)		1991	C.B.J. Danby (Harrow)	H.St.J. Foster (Harrow)
1959	J.L. Cutherbertson (Rugby)	J.W.T. Wilcox (Malvern)		1992	H.St.J. Foster (Harrow)	G. Rees (Clifton)
1960	G.P.D. Milne (Eton)	J.W.T. Wilcox (Malvern)		1993	R.D. Carter (Rugby)	E. Behn (Radley)
1961	G.P.D. Milne (Eton)	M.G. Griffith (Marlborough)		1994	R.D. Carter (Rugby)	D. Stahl (Haileybury)
1962	M.G. Griffith (Marlborough)	J. Hopper (Marlborough)		1995	N.A. Bailey (Eton)	G.J. Smith-Bingham (Eton)
1963	H.R. Angus (Winchester)	R.P. Walker (Malvern)		1996	A.T.R. Titchener-Barrett (Harrow)	G.J. Smith-Bingham (Eton)
1964	G.B. Trentham (Wellington)	A.H.V. Monteuuis (Tonbridge)		1997	A.T.R. Titchener-Barrett (Harrow)	D.D. Cherry (Tonbridge)
1965	A.H.V. Monteuuis (Tonbridge)	J.M.M. Hooper (Charterhouse)		1998	J.W.R. Parker (Tonbridge)	E.P. Cazalet (Eton)
1966	W.J.C. Surtees (Rugby)	J.K. Rogers (Radley)		1999	T.G. Dunbar (Harrow)	G. Tyndall (Cheltenham)
1967	R.S. Crawley (Harrow)	M.J.J. Faber (Eton)		2000	J. Stout (Cheltenham)	A. Coldicott (Cheltenham)
1968 Jan	M.J.J. Faber (Eton)	C.J.M. Symons (Clifton)		2001	J. Stout (Cheltenham)	A. Coldicott (Cheltenham)
1968 Dec	M.J.J. Faber (Eton)	C.H. Braithwaite (Harrow)		2002	G. Tysoe (Wellington)	C. Monbiot (Radley)
1969	C.N. Hurst-Brown (Wellington)	R.W. Drysdale (Eton)		2003	A. Brignall (Marlborough)	J. Bone (Harrow)
1970	R.W. Drysdale (Eton)	J.P. Willcocks (Clifton)		2004	J. Bone (Harrow)	A. Hackett (Radley)
1971	M. Thatcher (Harrow)	J.H.M. Griffiths (Rugby)		2005	W. Fortune (Harrow)	J. Rock (Cheltenham)
1972	D.G. Parsons (Clifton)	J.E. Dawes (Haileybury)		2006	W. Hopton (Eton)	S. Northeast (Harrow)
1973	M.W. Nicholls (Malvern)	R.F. Hollington (Haileybury)		2007	S. Northeast (Harrow)	B. Shiner (Cheltenham)
1974	M.W. Nicholls (Malvern)	M.A. Szarf (Harrow)		2008	N. Hopcroft (Wellington)	S. Knight (Winchester)
1975	A.C.S. Pigott (Harrow)	P.C. Nicholls (Malvern)		2009	C. Portz (Winchester)	N. Hopcroft (Wellington)
1976	M.N.P. Mockridge (Marlborough)	P.J. Rosser (Malvern)		2010	N. Hopcroft (Wellington)	R. Owen (Cheltenham)
1977	R.G.P. Ellis (Haileybury)	J.C. Spurling (Tonbridge)		2011	C. Stout (Cheltenham)	J. Giddins (Eton)
1978	R.G.P. Ellis (Haileybury)	D.J.G. Thomas (Harrow)		2012	L. Bose (Harrow)	A. Duncliffe-Vines (Cheltenham)
1979	R.G.P. Ellis (Haileybury)	T.R.V. Robins (Eton)		2013	T. Morales (Eton)	R. White (Harrow)
1980–81	J.S. Male (Radley)	P. Tichener (Malvern)		2014	C. Braham (Eton)	T. Morales (Eton)
1982	J.P. Snow (Radley)	A.M. Spurling (Tonbridge)				

LADIES

OPEN SINGLES CHAMPIONSHIP

	Winner	Runner-up	Score
2011	Claire Vigrass	Barbara Vintcent	3-0
2012	Claire Vigrass	Alex Kurkjian	3-0
2013	Claire Vigrass	Alex Kurkjian	3-0
2014	Claire Vigrass	Alex Brodie	3-0

AMATEUR DOUBLES CHAMPIONSHIP

	Winners	Runners-up	Score
2013	Alex Brodie and Karen Hird	Ella Gaskell and Ashley Lenihan	3-0
2014	Alex Brodie and Karen Hird	Shinan Zhang and Chey West	3-2

UNDER 18 SINGLES CHAMPIONSHIP

	Winners	Runners-up	Score
2011	Lucinda Pigott (Clifton)	Emma Powell (Clifton)	2-0
2012	Lily Owen (Cheltenham)	Millie Pughe (Wellington)	2-0
2013	Millie Pughe (Wellington)	Lily Owen (Cheltenham)	2-0
2014	Lea van der Zwalman (Clifton)	India Cockroft (Wellington)	2-1

THE UNITED STATES

OPEN SINGLES CHAMPIONSHIP
Clarence Pell Racquet Cup

Year	Winner	Year	Winner	Year	Winner	Year	Winner	Year	Winner
1938	R. Grant III	1959	A.B. Johnson	1969–70	G.H. Bostwick Jr	1988	W.R. Boone	2004	J.S. Male
1940	K. Chantler	1960	K. Chantler	1971–79	W.J.C. Surtees	1989–90	J.S. Male	2005–06	N.P.A. Smith
1941	R. Grant III	1961	D.M. Norman	1980	J.A.N. Prenn	1991–96	N.P.A. Smith	2007	H.St.J.R. Foster
1947	R.A.A. Holt	1962–63	J.P. Dear	1981	W.R. Boone	1997–98	R. Owen-Browne	2008	J. Stout
1948	R. Grant III	1964	A.B. Johnson	1982	J.A.N. Prenn	1999	N.P.A. Smith	2009	A. Titchener-Barrett
1950	R. Grant III	1965	S.S. Cox	1983	D.H. McLernon	2000	J.S. Male	2010	J. Stout
1957	K. Chantler	1966–67	C.T.M. Pugh	1984–86	W.R. Boone	2001–02	J.J.S. Larken	2011	W. Hopton
1958	G.W.T. Atkins	1968	G.W.T. Atkins	1987	S.M. Hazell	2003	N.P.A. Smith	2012–14	J. Stout

OPEN DOUBLES CHAMPIONSHIP
The Bertolotti Cup

1976	W.J.C. Surtees and E.F. Ulmann	1989	S.M. Hazell and N.P.A. Smith	2002	J.J.S. Larken and G. Devereux
1977	W.J.C. Surtees and P.M.L. Hannen	1990	S.M. Hazell and N.P.A. Smith	2003	N.P.A. Smith and T. Chisholm
1978	W.J.C. Surtees and G.P.D. Milne	1991	N.P.A. Smith and J. Cashman	2004	G. Smith-Bingham and T. Cockroft
1979	W.J.C. Surtees and E.F. Ulmann	1992	N.P.A. Smith and J. Burke	2005	N.P.A. Smith and D. Makey
1980	W.J.C. Surtees and J.A.N. Prenn	1993	N.P.A. Smith and D.G. Anderson	2006	N.P.A. Smith and G. Devereux
1981	G.P.D. Milne and C.J.H. Green	1994	N.P.A. Smith and W. Bristowe	2007	H.St.J.R. Foster and A. Orchard
1982	R.A. Crawley and A. Crawley	1995	R. Owen-Browne and S. Tulley	2008	N.P.A. Smith and J. Stout
1983	D.H. McLernon and M.R. McMaster	1996	J.A.N. Prenn and J.S. Male	2009–11	J. Coyne and W. Hopton
1984	D.M. Norman and W.R. Boone	1997	N.P.A. Smith and P. Brake	2012	N.P.A. Smith and N.C.W. James
1985	J.A.N. Prenn and J.S. Male	1998	C.M. Hue Williams and M.G.N. Windows	2013	J. Stout and M. Gooding
1986	C.J. Hue Williams and J.A.N. Prenn	1999	J. Beaumont and G. Devereux	2014	J. Coyne and W. Hopton
1987	S.M. Hazell and N.E.C. Barham	2000	J. Beaumont and G. Devereux		
1988	S.M. Hazell and C.M. Hue Williams	2001	J.J.S. Larken and T.N. Sawrey-Cookson		

WESTERN OPEN SINGLES CHAMPIONSHIP
Johnson Cup

1938	R. Grant III	1950	C.C. Pell Jr	1982	D. McLernon	2001	J.J.S. Larken
1924	R.A. Gardener	1951	R.A.A. Holt	1983	A.R. Bonsor	2002–03	N.P.A. Smith
1925	C.J. Coulter	1952	J. Rolland	1984	A. Prenn	2004	D. Odds
1926	H.L. Dixon	1953	R. Grant, III	1985	K.A. MacGuire	2005	N.P.A. Smith
1927	R.A. Gardener	1954–57	G.W.T. Atkins	1986–87	N. Barham	2006	B.J. Sambrook
1928	H. Linn	1958	C.A. Lynch	1988	W. Davies	2007	J. Stout
1929–30	L.F. Williams	1959	G.W.T. Atkins	1989	S. Hazell	2008–09	A. Titchener-Barrett
1931–33	W.B. McIlvaine Jr	1960	T. Pugh	1990	P.A. Brake	2010	J. Bone
1934–36	J.H. Douglas	1961	M. Bailey	1991–93	N.P.A. Smith	2011	J.J.S. Larken
1937	W.B. McIlvaine Jr	1962	J. Rolland	1994	P.A. Brake	2012	J. Stout
1938–40	J.H. Douglas	1963	T. Pugh	1995	R. Owen-Browne	2013	W. Hopton
1941	R.F. Carney	1964–67	S.S. Cox	1996–97	N.P.A. Smith	2014	J. Stout
1947	R.A.A. Holt	1968–70	G.W.T. Atkins	1998	J.S. Male		
1948	R.F. Carney	1980	D. McLennon	1999	J.A.N. Prenn		
1949	W.J. Croul	1981	K.A. MacGuire	2000	J. Beaumont		

WESTERN OPEN DOUBLES CHAMPIONSHIP

1924–29	H. Linn and R.A. Gardner	1960	T. Pugh and M. Bailey	1995	J.B. Cashman and N.P.A. Smith
1930	L.F. Williams and W.B. McIlvaine Jr	1961	M. Bailey and D. Norman	1996	E.F. Ulmann and N.P.A .Smith
1931–34	H. Linn and R.A. Gardner	1962	E. Ewald and R. Turner	1997	T. Sawrey-Cookson and J.S.S. Larken
1935	T. Gregory and D. Cummings	1963	T. Pugh and T. Pugh	1998	J.S. Male and K.J. de Koning
1936	R.A. Gardner and H. Linn	1964–65	S. Cox and J. Watlyn Lewis	1999	R. Owen-Browne and P.A. Brake
1937	B.H. Paddock and C.H. Symington	1966–67	S. Cox and W.D. McSweeney	2000	J. Beaumont and K.J. de Koning
1938	W.B. McIlvaine Jr and H. Linn	1968	G.W.T. Atkins and W.B. Cutler	2001	N.P.A. Smith and B.J. Sambrook
1939	J.H. Douglas and R.A. Gardner	1980	D. McLernon and M. McMaster	2002	N.P.A. Smith and T.P. Howe
1940	H. Linn and R.A. Gardner	1981	A.A.B. Johnson and M. McDonald	2003	A. Titchener-Barrett and J. Beaumont
1941	W.B. McIlvaine Jr and W.S. Bromwell	1982	D. McLernon and M. Huband	2004	B.J. Sambrook and T.B. Price
1947	J. Pawle and C. Crawley	1983	D. McLernon and C.H. Pickwoad	2005	J.A.N. Prenn and B.J. Sambrook
1948–49	R.F. Carney and W.B. McIlvaine Jr	1984	A. Prenn and R.L. Brickley Jr	2006	K.H. Addington III and B.J. Sambrook
1950	C.C. Pell Jr and K. Wagg	1985	M. Riley and D. Mead	2007	D .Makey and R. Owen-Browne
1951	K. Wagg and R.A.A. Holt	1986	M.P. McDonald and N. Barham	2008	A. Titchener-Barrett and J. Coyne
1952	K. Wagg and R.R. McLernon	1987	N. Barham and R.E. Wood II	2009	J. Coyne and J. Beaumont
1953	D.F. Davis Jr and R. Grant III	1988	W. Davies and N. Barham	2010	R. Tulley and J. Shields
1954	W. Wood Prince and G.W.T. Atkins	1989	R.E. Wood II and S. Hazell	2011	N.P.A. Smith and J.J.S. Larken
1955	G.W.T. Atkins and W.D. McSweeney	1990	P. Brake and C. Green	2012	J. Coyne and A. Coldicott
1956	G.W.T. Atkins and W. Wood Prince	1991	N.P.A. Smith and S. Tully	2013	W. Hopton and J. Cashman
1957	G.W.T. Atkins and C.L. Kenrick	1992	N.P.A. Smith and W.A. Hargrave	2014	W. Hopton and J. Leonard
1958	C.A. Lynch and H. Loud	1993	N.P.A. Smith and T.D. Tieken Jr		
1959	G.W.T. Atkins and S. Colhoun	1994	N.P.A. Smith and E. Inselbuch		

Championship Records

AMATEUR SINGLES CHAMPIONSHIP

1890–91	B.S. de Garmendia	1916	S.G. Mortimer	1958	C.C. Pell Jr	1991–95	W.R. Boone
1892	J.S. Tooker	1917–22	C.C. Pell	1959–60	G.W.T. Atkins	1996–97	R. Owen-Browne
1893–94	B.S. de Garmendia	1923	S.G. Mortimer	1961–63	D.M. Norman	1998	J.J.S. Larken
1895	J.S. Tooker	1924–25	C.C. Pell	1964	P.B. Read	1999	J.A.N. Prenn
1896–97	B.S. de Garmendia	1926	S.G. Mortimer	1965	S.S. Cox	2000	J.S. Male
1898	F.F. Rolland	1927–28	C.C. Pell	1966–67	D.M. Norman	2001–02	J.J.S. Larken
1899	Q.A. Shaw Jr	1929	H.D. Sheldon	1968	J.W. Leonard	2003	A. Coldicott
1900	E.H. Miles	1930	S.G. Mortimer	1969–70	G.W.T. Atkins	2004	G. Smith-Bingham
1901	Q.A. Shaw Jr	1931–33	C.C. Pell	1971–72	W.J.C. Surtees	2005	R. Owen-Browne
1902	C.H. Mackay	1934	E.M. Edwards	1973	H.R. Angus	2006	J.J.S. Larken
1903	P. Whitney	1935	H.D. Sheldon	1974–79	W.J.C. Surtees	2007	A. Coldicott
1904	G.H. Brooke	1936	E.M. Edwards	1980	W.R. Boone	2008	M. Farmiloe
1905	L. Waterbury	1937–39	R. Grant III	1981	D.H. McLernon	2009	J. Coyne
1906	P.D. Houghton	1940	W. Ingersoll	1982	W.J.C. Surtees	2010	T. Meringoff
1907	R. Fincke	1941–46	R. Grant III	1983	W.R. Boone	2011	N.C.W. James
1908	Q.A. Shaw	1947	J.R. Leonard	1984–85	D.H. McLernon	2012	T. Meringoff
1909	H.F. McCormick	1948–51	R. Grant III	1986	W.R. Boone	2013	J.J.S. Larken
1910	Q.A. Shaw	1952	S.W. Pearson	1987	N.E.C. Barham	2014	T. Billings
1911–12	R. Fincke	1953	R. Grant III	1988	D.H. McLernon		
1913–14	L. Waterbury	1954–56	G.W.T. Atkins	1989	W.R. Boone		
1915	C.C. Pell	1957	C.B. Pearson	1990	W. Maltby		

AMATEUR DOUBLES CHAMPIONSHIP

1899	Q.A. Shaw, Jr. and H.H. Hunnewell Jr	1937–39	Robert Grant III and C.C. Pell Jr	1980	W.R. Boone and R.A. Crawley
1900	L.M. Stockton and G.R. Fearing	1940	J.R. Leonard and M.C. Kirkbride	1981	D.H. McLernon and M. McMaster
1901	Payne Whitney and Q.A. Shaw Jr	1941	Robert Grant III and C.C. Pell Jr	1982	J.A.N. Prenn and C.T.M. Pugh
1902	H.D. Scott and G.H. Brooke	1946	Robert Grant III and C.C. Pell Jr	1983	W.R. Boone and C.T.M. Pugh
1903	H.D. Scott and R.K. Cassatt	1947	R.A.A. Holt and A.R. Taylor	1984	D.H. McLernon and M. McMaster
1904	Q.A. Shaw Jr and Matthew Bartlett	1948	J.R. Leonard and M.C. Kirkbride	1985	W.J.C. Surtees and E.F. Ulmann
1905–06	H.D. Scott and G.R. Fearing Jr	1949–50	Robert Grant, III and C.C. Pell Jr	1986	W.R. Boone and V. Cazalet
1907	Reginald Fincke and R.D. Wrenn	1951	R.A.A. Holt and K.A. Wagg	1987	N.E.C. Barham and R.E. Wood II
1908	H.D. Scott and G.R. Fearing Jr	1952	K.A. Wagg and J.A. Rolland	1988	D.H. McLernon and D.H. Hamlen
1909	Q.A. Shaw Jr and P.D. Haughtonx	1953	D.S. Milford and J.R. Thompson	1989	E.F. Ulmann and W.R. Boone
1910	Lawrence Waterbury and Reginald Fincke	1954–55	G.W.T. Atkins and W. Wood Prince	1990	W. Maltby and P.E. de Svastich
1911	H.D. Scott and G.R. Fearing Jr	1956–57	S.W. Pearson and C.B. Pearson	1991–94	E.F. Ulmann and W.R. Boone
1912	Q.A. Shaw and G.R. Fearing Jr	1958	G.W.T. Atkins and K.A. Wagg	1995–96	R. Owen-Browne and K. Nemec
1913	H.D. Scott and P.D. Haughton	1959	C.C. Pell Jr and C.B. Pearson	1997	R. Owen-Browne and S.M.S. Davies
1914	J.W. Wear and D.F. Davis	1960	C.T.M. Pugh and R.M. Bailey	1998–99	W. Bristowe and J.J.S. Larken
1915	C.C. Pell and S.G. Mortimer	1961	R.L.O. Bridgeman and J.A.R. Clench	2000	J.A.N. Prenn and J.S. Male
1916	Lawrence Waterbury and J.C. Waterbury	1962	D.M. Norman and R.M. Bailey	2001–02	J.J.S. Larken and J.A.N. Prenn
1917	George H. Brooke and J.W. Wear	1963	C.J. Swallow and M.R. Coulman	2003	A. Coldicott and G. Smith-Bingham
1920	Jay Gould and J.W. Wear	1964	S.S. Cox and W. Lewis	2004–05	J.J.S. Larken and G. Devereux
1921–25	C.C. Pell and S.G. Mortimer	1965	C.H. Pickwood and A.J. Coote	2006	W. Bristow and T. Barker
1926	R.A. Gardner and H.A. Linn	1966	M. Sales and R. Turner	2007	A. Coldicott and N. Taylor
1927	C.C. Pell and S.G. Mortimer	1967–69	G.W.T. Atkins and S.S. Cox	2008	G. Devereaux and T. Barker
1928	Hon. C.N. Bruce and J.C.F. Simpson	1970	D.H. McLernon and M. Sales	2009	J. Coyne and A. Gourlay
1929	C.C. Pell and S.G. Mortimer	1971	W.J.C. Surtees and C.J. Hue Williams	2010	T. Spurling and J. Shields
1930	Lord Aberdare and Dr H.W. Leatham	1972–73	W.J.C. Surtees and R. Lightfine	2011	A. Gourlay and J. Rock
1931	C.C. Pell and S.G. Mortimer	1974	D.H. McLernon and J.J. Wagg	2012	T. Meringoff and M. Breuer
1932	S.W. Pearson and W.C. Wright	1975	W.J.C. Surtees and R. Lightfine	2013	J. J. S. Larken and G. Devereux
1933	W. Palmer Dixon and H.N. Rawlins Jr	1976	D.H. McLernon and C.H. Pickwood	2014	A. Coldicott and W. Morse
1934	H.D. Sheldon and J.W. Brooks	1977	W.J.C. Surtees and G.P.D. Milne		
1935–36	J.R. Leonard and M.C. Kirkbride	1978–79	W.J.C. Surtees and E.F. Ulmann		

CANADA

AMATEUR SINGLES CHAMPIONSHIP

1896	F.F. Rolland	1924-27	C.C. Pell	1961	R.M. Bailey	1993	B.J. Sambrook
1897	B.S. de Garmendia	1928	Hon. C.N. Bruce	1962	D.M. Norman	1994	W.R. Boone
1898	Q.A. Shaw	1929	A.S. Cassils	1963	M.S. Connell	1995	R. Owen-Browne
1899	F.F. Rolland	1930	Lord Aberdare	1964	J.A. Rolland	1996	T.B. Cockroft
1900	E.H. Miles	1931	W. Palmer Dixon	1965	S.S. Cox	1997	R. Owen-Browne
1901-02	F.F. Rolland	1932-33	Sir John Child	1966	C.T.M. Pugh	1998-99	T.B. Cockroft
1903	W.R. Miller	1934	H.D. Sheldon	1967	D.M. Norman	2000	M.G.N. Windows
1904-05	F.F. Rolland	1935	C.C. Pell	1968	G.W.T. Atkins	2001-02	J.J.S. Larken
1906	E. Hewitt	1936	H.D. Sheldon	1969	D.M. Norman	2003	R. Owen-Browne
1907	R.E. MacDougall	1937-39	R. Grant III	1970-72	D.H. McLernon	2004-05	J.J.S. Larken
1908-09	F.F. Rolland	1946	J.R. Leonard	1973-75	W.J.C. Surtees	2006	B. Sambrook
1910-11	R.E. MacDougall	1947	R. Grant III	1976	D.H. McLernon	2007	A. Coldicott
1912	F.F. Rolland	1948-49	J.R. Leonard	1977	W.J.C. Surtees	2008	M. Farmiloe
1913	E. Greenshields	1950-53	R. Grant III	1978	W.R. Boone	2009	R. Owen-Browne
1914	C.C. Pell	1954-56	G.W.T. Atkins	1979	J.A.N. Prenn	2010	A. Titchener-Barrett
1915	H.M. Smith	1957	C.C. Pell Jr	1980	W.R. Boone	2011	J. Coyne
1920	A.S. Cassils	1958	G.W.T. Atkins	1981-86	J.A.N. Prenn	2012-13	J.J.S. Larken
1921-22	C.C. Pell	1959	C.B. Pearson	1987-91	J.S. Male	2014	J. Coyne
1923	J. Gould	1960	G.W.T. Atkins	1992	J.A.N. Prenn		

AMATEUR DOUBLES CHAMPIONSHIP

1920	A. Wilson and H.M. Smith	1954-55	G.W.T. Atkins and K.A. Wagg	1985	R.S. Crawley and A. Crawley
1921	S.G. Mortimer and F.T. Frelinghuysen	1956	C.C. Pell and F.F. de Rham	1986	J.A.N. Prenn and C.J. Hue Williams
1922	C.C. Pell and S.G. Mortimer	1957	J.C. Cushing and C.E. Pacaud	1987	C.H. Pickwood and D.H. McLernon
1923	Jay Gould and L. du P. Irving	1958	G.W.T. Atkins and J.E. Price	1988-91	J.S. Male and N.E.C. Barham
1924	C.C. Pell and S.G. Mortimer	1959	J.A. Rolland and J.J. Wagg	1992	T.B. Cockroft and S.M.S. Davis
1925	J.C.F. Simpson and R.C.O. Williams	1960	G.W.T. Atkins and K.A. Wagg	1993	D.H. McLernon and B.J. Sambrook
1926-27	C.C. Pell and A.L. Corey	1961-62	R.M. Bailey and D.M. Norman	1994-98	T.B. Cockroft and R. Owen-Browne
1928	C.C. Pell and S.G. Mortimer	1963	M.R. Coulman and C.J. Swallow	1999	C.H. Pickwood and J.A.N. Prenn
1929	F.C. Dobell and S.H. Dobell	1964	C.E. Pacaud and J.V. Kerrigan	2000	B.J. Sambrook and M.G.N. Windows
1930	Lord Aberdare and Dr H.W. Leatham	1965	C.H. Pickwood and A.J. Coote	2001	K. Nemec and G. Smith-Bingham
1931	G.D. Huband and A.S. Cassils	1966-67	T.E. Price and D.M. Norman	2002	G. Devereaux and E. Novis
1932	A.R. Chipman and S.H. Dobell	1968	G.W.T. Atkins and J.A. Rolland	2003	T.B. Cockroft and R. Owen-Browne
1933-34	G.D. Huband and Sir John Child	1969-70	D.H. McLernon and M. Sales	2004	R. Owen-Browne and A. MacEchern
1935	J.R. Leonard and M.C. Kirkbride	1971	W.J.C. Surtees and W. Finkenstaedt	2005	G. Barker and T. Barker
1936	G.D. Huband and Sir John Child	1972	D.H. McLernon and M. Sales	2006	T. Price and B.J. Sambrook
1937-39	Robert Grant III and C.C. Pell Jr	1973	C.H. Pickwood and J.W.S. Chapman	2007	B. Bomford and A. Gourlay
1946	S.H. Dobell and C.E. Pacaud	1974	W.J.C. Surtees and R. Lightfine	2008-09	R. Owen-Browne and K. Nemec
1947	J.H. Pawle and G.S. Crawley	1975-77	D.H. McLernon and C.H. Pickwood	2010	B. Bomford and A. Gourlay
1948	J.R. Leonard and F.F. de Rham	1978-79	W.R. Boone and C.T.M. Pugh	2011	J.S. Male and P. Maxwell
1949	J.R. Leonard and C.C. Pell Jr	1980	W.R. Boone and R.S. Crawley	2012	J. Coyne and P. Maxwell
1950	C.C. Pell Jr and K.A. Wagg	1981	J.A.N. Prenn and C.J.H. Green	2013	J.J.S. Larken and M. McLernon
1951	J.R. Leonard and F.F. de Rham	1982	J.A.N. Prenn and C.J. Hue Williams	2014	N.C.W. James and P. Maxwell
1952	Robert Grant III and J.A. Rolland	1983	W.R. Boone and R.S. Crawley		
1953	D.S. Milford and J.R. Thompson	1984	J.A.N. Prenn and A.N.W. Beeson		

Important Bibliography

Author	Title
Atkins, J. R.	*The Book of Racquets*, 1872
Bernoulli, Jacob	*Ars Conjectandi*, 1713
Best, David	*The Royal Tennis Court*, 2002 *The Official Story of the T&RA*, 2008 *Disturb'd with Chaces*, 2009
de Bondt, Cees	*Royal Tennis in Renaissance Italy*, 2006
Butler & Wordie	*The Royal Game*, 1989
Chapus, Eugene	*Le jeu de paume, son histoire et sa description* (also by M. E. Fournier), 1862
Danzig, Allison	*The Racquet Game*, 1930 *The Winning Gallery*, 1985
Garnett, Michael	*A Chase Down Under*, 1999 *A History of Royal Tennis in Australia*, 1983 *Tennis-Reflections in Time*, 2014 *Tennis Miscellany*, 2006 *Tennis Anecdotes and Sketches*, 2010
Gillmeister, Heiner	*Kulturgeschichte des Tennis*, 1990
Hiller, Geoffrey	*The Bandies of Fortune*, 2009
Inglis, Simon	*English Heritage Series – Played in Britain*
de Luze, Albert	*La Magnifique Histoire du Jeu de Paume*, 1933
de Manivieux, Louis-Claude Bruyset	*Traité sur la Connoissance du Royal Jeu de Paume*, 1783
Marshall, Julian	*The Annals of Tennis*, 1878
Miles, Eustace	*Racquets, Tennis & Squash*, 1902
Morgan, Roger	*Tennis: The Development of the European Ball Game*, 1995 *Tudor Tennis*, 2001
Noel & Clark	*A History of Tennis*, 1924
Scaino de Salo, Antonio	*Trattato del Giuocco della Palla*, 1555
Tomkinson, Graham	*Stické Tennis*, 2004
Travers, S. Smith	*A Treatise on Tennis*, 1875

CONTRIBUTORS

The author would like to thank the following for their respective contributions:

Club, court or subject	Name
Aiken	Dacre Stoker
Australia	Mike Garnett
Bath	Bill Stephens
Bickley research	Michael Garnett, English Heritage Series-Played in Britain
Bordeaux	Simon Marshall
Boston	Jeremy Wintersteen
Bristol	Julian Hemming
Buckhurst Park	Will Buckhurst
Building Courts	Charles Swallow, Duncan MacKellar, Jim MacKellar, Mervyn Dunnington-Jefferson (deceased), Howard Angus, Allan Willingham
Cambridge	George Pearson
Canford	Steve Ronaldson
Charleston	Greg van Shaack
Charterhouse	Martin Crosby
Cheltenham	Karl Cook
Chicago	Davis Anderson, Bill Bickford
Cleveland	Davis Anderson
Clifton	Reg Williams
Copped Hall	Alan Cox, Bill Stephens
Crabbet Park	Robert Bruce
Creative writing and editing	Augusta Bruce, Robert Bruce, Julia Huschke, Charlotte Mungavin
Dartmouth	James Ford
David & Bathsheba paintings	Cees de Bondt
Detroit	Norb Madison
Disused Rackets courts	Nick Harding
Dublin	Ted Neville, Ben & Bear North
Eton	Paul Gillum
Falkland Palace	Robert Hammond
Fontainebleau	Thierry Bernard-Tambour, Eric Delloye
Greentree	Peter di Bonaventura
Haileybury	Mike Cawdron
Hampton Court	Geoffrey Russell
Hardwick House	Michael Parsons
Harrow	John Eaton
Hatfield	Jon Dawes
Holland	Patrick Reuser
Holyport	John Evans
Hyde	Derek Fitzgerald, Jamie Turner
Italy	Cees de Bondt
Jersey	John Lawton
Jesmond Dene	John Duns, Paul Hetherington
Knott Stephens	Bill Stephens
Ladies Rackets	Alex Brodie (née Kurkjian)
Ladies Tennis	Lucy Hutchinson, Sheila Macintosh
Lakewood	James Zug
Lambay	Louis Jebb
Leamington	Charles Wade
Lord's, MCC	Brian Sharp, Roger Pilgrim, Colin Maynard
Malvern	Tom Newman
Manchester	Brendan Hegarty
Marlborough	Robert Wakely
Middlesex University	Peter Luck-Hille, David Sloan
Montreal	Mike McLernon
Moreton Morrell	Andrew Hamilton
New Media	Chris Davies & Frederika Adam
New York	Howard McMorris
Newcastle, Jamaica Rackets Court	Charles Hue-Williams
Newmarket	John Burnett
Newport	Ross Cann
North American Rackets	Davis Anderson
Oratory	Ian Whittaker
Oxford	Marion Windsor
Paris	Wesley Johnson, Gil Kressmann, Pierre Heitzmann
Petworth	Alan Chalmers
Philadelphia	James Zug
Pittsburgh	Davis Anderson
Prested	Chris Vigrass
Queen's	Jonathan Edwardes & Andrew Stewart
Rackets racquets and balls	Howard Angus
Radley	Mick Dean, Mark Hubbard
Rugby	Peter Dewey, Philip Rosser
Sandhurst	James Illingworth
Seacourt	Nick Jones
South-West France	Paul Mirat
St Louis	Davis Anderson
St Paul's	Steve Tulley
Stické	Graham Tomkinson
Sydney	Chris Cooper
Tennis and Rackets 2000–14 review	Howard Angus
Tennis & Rackets Association	David Best, William Maltby, Chris Davies
Tennis racquets and balls	Steve Ronaldson
Tonbridge	David Makey and John Gibbs
Toronto Rackets court	David Best
Tuxedo	Dan Laukitis
Washington	Chris Hughey, James Zug
Wellington Rackets	Charles Oliphant-Callum
Winchester	Tim Cawston
Wise counsel	Evelyn Clothier

PHOTOGRAPHIC ACKNOWLEDGEMENTS

The author would like to thank the following for use of their respective photographs:

Photographer	Subject
Frederika Adam	Ballarat interior
	Fontainebleau exterior
	Fontainebleau 2005 Rob Fahey signs autograph
	Lord's, MCC 2010 – Real Tennis Online test
	Manchester 2011 web-streaming
	Matthieu Sarlangue, Rob Fahey 2009
	Prested interior
	Randolph Hall
	Rob Fahey and Claire Vigrass
	South-West France:
	Bastide and Bayonne courts
	Bayonne 2011 exhibition match
	Tournoi des trois Tripots
Peter Brake	2003 Eton Centenary match
	2004 Public School doubles Rackets winners
	2014 Amateur doubles final Rackets
	2014 Public Schools doubles finals Rackets
Rosie Brown	Amateur Rackets singles final 2013
	Foster Cup final 2013
	Ladies Rackets Singles Open 2014
	Tennis Amateur Doubles Final 2014
Michael Do	Lakewood – interior
	New York – Larken & Devereux
	New York – Morris Clothier with pros
	New York – Whitney Team 2006
	New York – Stout wins both Opens 2010
	Philadelphia – interior and exterior
	Tuxedo – interior
	Washington –Camden Riviere/ Bingo
	Washington interior
Tim Edwards	2010 James Stout
	2013 British Open Singles and Doubles Tennis
	2013 World Rackets Doubles
	2014 British Open Rackets Singles and Doubles
Michael Garnett	Ballarat – 2012 McFarlane, Fahey, Vigrass
	Cawnpore, India
	Melbourne Rackets exterior
	Melbourne Tennis
	Romsey
Nick Harding	Various disused rackets courts including:
	Cleveland
	Curragh
	Leenan
	Pittsburgh
	Plymouth
	St Louis
	St Lucia
	Worcester
Gil Kressman and Patricia Gallagher	Paris:
	Court interior
	Ladies World Doubles and Singles 2013
	Longue Paume
	World Doubles 2013

Subject	Acknowledgement
Aiken	Dacre Stoker
Author	Algernon Bruce
Baldersby	Queen Mary's School
Pierre Barcellon	All England Lawn Tennis Club Museum
H.M.Bateman cartoons	Richard Greenwood (deceased)
Belmont	Mark Wright, Tamsin Rossiter
Bickley	Petworth
Book of Hours	Agence Photographique de la Reunion des Musées Nationaux
Bordeaux	Simon Marshall
Boston	Jeremy Wintersteen
Bristol	David Pearce
Bristol Brunel Cup	Nick Ponsford
Brougham Hall	Christopher Terry
Buckhurst Park	Buckhurst Park Office
Buenos Aires – Hurlingham Club	Ben Stevens
Cambridge	George Pearson
Canford	Steve Ronaldson
Cardiff	Marilyn Walker
Charrier	Christies Images Ltd 1996
Charterhouse	Martin Crosby
Cheltenham	Karl Cook
Chicago	Davis Anderson
University Club of Chicago exterior	University Club of Chicago
Clandeboye	Marchioness of Dufferin and Ava
Clifton	Tamsin Rossiter, Reg Williams
Coombe Abbey	Lisa Pearson
Copped Hall	Philip Lobban, Alan Cox
Crabbet Park	Tiffani Rees
Dartmouth	James Ford
Death of Hyacinth	Cherbourg – Art Museum, Thomas Henry

Subject	Acknowledgement	Subject	Acknowledgement
Detroit	Norb Madison	Membland Stické court	David James
Dublin	Sile Reilly	Middlesex University	William Gillingham-Sutton, David Sloan
Dublin – 1890 sketch	Brian Rich		
Eastbourne	Eastbourne Theatres	Milland Place	Charles Hue Williams in memory of Geoff Sweatman
Easton Neston	Leon Max		
Eglinton	Eglinton Country Park	Montreal	Mike McLernon
Esher Place	Unite the Union	Moreton Morrell	Andrew Hamilton
Eton – Peter Brake & Norwood Cripps	Cameron Rose	Myopia	Rob McLane
		Newcastle	© English Heritage
Fahey Vigrass wedding	Ben Lavenham	Newmarket	John Burnett
Fairlawne	Prince Khalid Abdullah, James Swartz	Newmarket interior	Logan Crawford
Falkland Palace	Robert Hammond	Newport	A4 Architecture, Ross Cann
Fontainebleau	Thierry Bernard-Tambour, Eric Delloye	Newport 2004 world championship	© 2004 John Corbett Photography
Fulwood Rackets	Lancashire Infantry Museum	New York exterior	Howard McMorris
Fyvie	National Trust of Scotland Photo Library	North American Rackets	Davis Anderson
		Oratory	Ian Whittaker
Gibraltar Rackets	Barry Brindle	Oxford	Marion Windsor
Greenlands	Henley Business School	Paris – Edberg	Danny Mandil
Greentree	Amy Papola	Park Place	Spink Property
Greenwich	Paul Riddle, architectural photographer on behalf of Southstudio Architects	Petworth	Michel Chevis
		Philadelphia – 50th anniversary	Tim Smith of PDQ Graphics
Haileybury	Mike Cawdron	Philadelphia – John Lumley	Evelyn Clothier
Hampton Court	Geoffrey Russell, Murray Glover		
Hardwick House	Michael Parsons, Tim Tomalin	Philadelphia – van Dyke	James Zug
Harrow	John Eaton	Photographic editing	Robert Bruce
Hatfield House	Jon Dawes	Putti playing Pallone	© Herve Lewandowski and Thierry Bernard-Tambour Collection
Hewell Grange	HMP Hewell		
Heythrop Park	Heythrop Park	Radley	Mick Dean
Hobart – Barry Toates	Barry Toates	Rangoon Rackets Court	John Holsapple
Hobart interior	Graeme Bradfield	Rideau Hall	Colonel Chris Weicker © Office of the Secretary to the Governor General (2012)
Holland	Patrick Reuser		
Holyport	Tom Durack		
Hyde	Derek Fitzgerald	Rossall	Sharon Potts
Jamaica Rackets court	John Bailey	St Paul's	Steve Tulley
Jesmond Dene	John Duns	Sandhurst	Nigel Tench
Kirtlington	James Nicholson	Seacourt	Nick Jones, Victoria Wall, Paul Weaver
Ladies' Amateur Rackets doubles 2014	Tom Newman	Shorncliffe	© English Heritage, photographer Wayne Cocroft
		Simla	Indian Institute of Advanced Studies
Ladies' Rackets	Alex Kurkjian, Tom Newman	Southwest France – Pau court, Simon Berry & Paul Mirat, leaders of Jeu de Paume de Navarre	Paul Mirat
Ladies' Tennis	Jeremy Gilmore		
Lakewood	Schuyler Wickes		
Lakewood Rackets court	James Zug		
Lambay	Louis Jebb, Jamie Turner, Roger Pilgrim		
Lambay aerial	Tim Barraclough	Stické courts (Hartham, Knighthayes, Taplow, Cilymaenllwyd)	Graham Tomkinson
Leamington	Ray Spence FRPS		
Lord's, MCC	Adam Chadwick, Adam Phillips, Clare Skinner		
		Tonbridge	John Gibbs, David Makey
Lord's, MCC – 2012 & 2013 European Open Finals	Matt Bright	Troon	© Historic Scotland
		Tuxedo	Dan Laukitis
		Versailles	Office de Tourisme Versailles
Malvern	Tom Newman	Washington – Ivan Ronaldson	Chris Hughey
Manchester	Brendan Hegarty		
Marlborough	Robert Wakely	Wellington	Charles Oliphant-Callum, Ryan Tulley
Melbourne Rackets court interior	Jo Daniell		
		Westward Ho!	Norwood Cripps
Melbourne world championships 2014	Doug Grant	Winchester	Tim Cawston, Peter Sollars
		Woking Palace	David Best

Index

Figures in *italics* indicate captions.

A&J Services 402
Abendanon, Nick 223
Aberdare, Lord, 3rd Baron 94, 106, *170*, 217, 232, 277, 359, 404
   Amateur doubles 219
   Coupe de Bordeaux 207
   First Steps to Rackets 95
   MCC Gold Racquet 104, 277
   Rackets 158
      Amateur doubles champion 170
      Amateur singles champion 158, 170
      Open champion 158, 170, 171
      Public Schools champion 170
      US doubles champion 170
Aberdare, Lord, 4th Baron 105, *109*, *111*, *167*, 170, 172, 258, 259, 292, 309, 333, 373, 406, 409
   Amateur Tennis championship 105
   Cercle du Jeu de Paume de Fontainebleau 240
   MCC Gold Racquet 105
   opens courts 176, *281*, 282, 305
Abernethy, Samuel F. *296*, 299
Abraham, Bertram 'Brahms' 328
Acheson-Gray, James 114
Adam, Frederika 115, 226
Addington, Keene 191, 226, 227
advantage (score) 21
Agate, James 170
Agate, Mark 192, *192*, 320
Aiken Tennis Club 87, 92, 201-3, *201*, 399
Aird, Ronny *97*, 169, 232
   The Future of the Game 406
   Ronny Aird Cup 272
Aislabie, Mr 73
Akers-Douglas, Ian 157, 159, 162, 170, 232
   Rackets, Amateur champion 158, 171
   US tour 159, *160*, 161
Albert, Prince Consort 71-2
Alcazar Palace court, Madrid 50
Aldershot Rackets court 154, 335
Aldrich, Simon 297, 298
Alexander, Rupert *273*
Alexander III, King of Scotland 32
Alexander of Tunis, Lord 160
Alfred, Prince 143
Allaway, Mike 301
Allen, Bradley 209
Allen, Katrina 120, 122
Allen, Richard 87
Allen, Robin 173
Allerman, Ted 85
Altham, Harry 196
Alverstone, Lord 403, 404
Alway, Tom 333, *334*, *334*
Amateur Rackets Fellowship 230
American champions 105-7
Amr Bey 96, 162
Anderson, Davis 190, 226
André, F. 29, 359
Angus, Howard *101*, 114, 171, *175*, 182, 207, 226, *235*, 288, 289, 297, 299, 318, 366, 407
   Amateur singles champion 101, 214, 360
   Amateur Tennis champion 101, 168, 359

British Open champion 101, 105, 277, 359, 360
   Cutty Sark championship 101
   and Ladies' Rackets 183, 184, *184*
   MCC Gold Racquet 101, 168
   Open Tennis champion 101, 105
   professional 323-4
   Rackets 101, 172, 174
      v. Surtees 101, 167-8, *168*
      world champion 101, 168, 190, 214, 226, 243, 330
      v. J. Bostwick 101-3
      v. Ronaldson 103-4, 105, 108, 118
      v. Scott 103, 169, 245
      v. Snow 325
      world champion *102*, 104, 106, 169, *175*, 214, 243, 323, 359
Angus Cup 333
Anies, Christine *120*
Anne Boleyn women's tennis event 2, 210, 242, 267
Ansley, Anthony 40
Anton, Alexander 320
Antonio, Gian 48
Apollinaris, Sidonius 15
Appeal Court, Tonbridge School 347, *348*, *349*
Arcangues, Michel d' 346, *346*
Ardrey, Jim *296*
Argentine, Rackets 15
Argyll, Duke of 70, 72
Armitage, John 95
Armitage, Rackets player 137
Armourcoat Ltd 402
Armstrong, Lord 263
Armstrong, Richard 151
Armstrong-Smith, Carolyn *120*, *311*
Army and Navy Rackets Championships 159
Army championships 335
Army Open Rackets (Victory) competition 159
Arrandale, Stuart *291*
Arriz, Chris *296*
Arrowsmith, Bob *313*
Ashford, Peter 198, 360
Ashworth, Percy *86*, 169, 251, 277, 405
Astor, J.J. 155
Astor of Hever, Lord 160
Atherton, Claude 171
Atkins, Geoffrey *163*, *175*, 219, 277, 349
   Rackets 99, 105, 159, 171, *171*, 172, 173, *173*, 190, 191, 230
      Amateur singles championship 105, 164, 187, 188, 331
      British Open champion 164, 166
      Canadian Amateur champion 164, 189
      US Amateur singles champion 164, 219
      world champion 162, 164, 166-7, *166*, 169, 226, 227, 330, 331
Atkins, J.R.: *The Book of Racquets* 139-41, *140*, *141*, 195, 398, 399
Attread, Tom 276
Australia Tennis courts 76, 77, 87-8, 108
Australian Open championship 109, 110
Australian Royal Tennis Association 108

Avon Tyrrell Sticke court 394
Ayres, F.H., racquet maker 141
Ayres, L.H. 394

Baerlein, Edgar 95, *104*, *169*, 207, 219, 251, 274, 279, 309, 346, *346*
   Bathurst Cup 92, 105
   British Open champion 94, 271, 277
   Eton 169
   match played on bicycles 76
   MCC Gold Prize 104
   Prince's Club Shield 104-5
   Rackets 104, 154, 155, 169
   sporting record 232, 277
   v. Gould 92, 105
   v. Latham 90
   v. Lytton 85, 104
Baerlein Cup 121, 123
Bailey, Edmund 149
Bailey, Edward J. 195
Bailey, Mac 173, 174, 232
Bailey, Mike *180*, 181, 360, *360*
Bailey, Neal 233, *234*
Bailey balls 195, *198*
Bailey Cup 105, 277
Baily's Magazine of Sports and Pastimes 141
Bainton, Josh 293, 299
Baird, Maj. E.W. *86*
Bajot: *Eloge de la Paume* 13
Baker, Barbara 258
Bakloh, India, Rackets court 194
Balcerkiewicz, Anne *120*
Balcombe court (The Penthouse Club) 85, 309
Baldersby Park, Thirsk 372, *372*
Balding, Ian 325, *326*
ball games, early *12*, 13-16
Ballarat 108, 204-5, *204*
Ballarat Silver Racket *204*, 205
balls 28-30
   Racket balls 194, 195-8
   Tennis balls press 29
Bancroft, racquet maker 27
Barber, Peter 243
Barcellon, Guillaume 26, 63, 78, *126*, 309
Barcellon, Jean-Pierre 63
Barcellon, Joseph 78
Barcellon, Pierre, *Règles et Principes de la Paume* 63, 288
Barford, John 211
Baring, Hon. Cecil, 2nd Lord Revelstoke 87, 93, 350, 351, *369*, *369*, 370, 371
Baring, Edward, 1st Lord Revelstoke 369
Baring, Maurice 174, 406
Baring, Rupert 370-71
Barker, Ainsley *234*
Barker, Eric 356
Barker, Guy 177, 179, 180, 181, 279-80, *280*, 407
Barker, Pat 102
Barker, Simon 265
Barker-Camm Cup 247
Barlow, Robin 278
Barnéon 63
Barnes, Bertie 228-9
Barnsley, Hewett and Mallinson 332
Barratt, Adam 262

Barre, J. Edmund 26, 71, 72, 79, *79*, 80, 239
Barrett, Derek 277, 286, 337, 358
Barry, Douglas 159
Bartlett, Robert 204, 217, 329
Basque glove 25
Bassett-Smith, Guy 30, 406-7
Bateman, H.M. *217*, *364*
Bath, Morford Street, Tennis court 66-7, 372-3, *372*
Bath Club Cup 162
Bath Street, Birmingham, Rackets court 148
Bathurst, Lilias, Countess 92
Bathurst Cup 88, 92, 105, 108, 114, 205, 258, 260, 278, 282, 293, 298, 307, 338
Baxter, Stuart *302*
Bazin, François 393
Bazin, Jean 64, 393
Bazin, W. 85
Beale, Elenor 229
Beale, John 229
Beale, Sam 229
Beard, Mark 325
Beards of Oxford and Swindon 325
Beauchamp, Richard 325, *326*
Beaulieu, Bertrand Faure 240
Beaumont, James 190
Beaumont Court, Pau 112, 341, *342*, 343-4, 345
Bebb, Jamie 278, *278*
Bedford, Duke of 67, 71
Bedingfield, Thomas 45
Beesly, A.H. 279
Beeson, Andrew 190, 273
Beeson, Nigel 274
Belcher, Jem 134
Bell, George 210, 297
Bellhouse, Fred 328
Bell's Life 79, 149
Belmont House Rackets court 145, 373, *373*
Belvedere Rackets court, Pentonville 133, 141, *142*, 146, 148
Bennett, James Gordon 76-7, 292, *292*
Bennett, racquet maker 27
Beresford, Richard 65
Beresford, Major William 65, 72, 246
Berger, Milton 156
Bergeron 63
Berlin, Tennis court 60
Bermuda, Sticke court 394
Bernoulli, Jakob 69
Berry, Simon 343, 344, *344*, 346, *346*
Bertolotti, Tony 227
Bertolotti Cup 230
Bery, Rob 45
Best, David, *The Official Story of the Tennis and Rackets Association* 322, 409
Beton, George, ball maker 29
betting 49, 60, *68*, 69, 72, *125*, 138
Bevan, Julian 174
Biboche 26, 71, 74, 79-80, *79*, 89
Bickford, Bill 225, *226*
Bickley, Joseph 85, 86, *86*, 87, 143, 251, 399-402, *399*
   Aiken Tennis Club *201*, 399
   Boston Tennis and Racquet Club *208*, 399
   Buckhurst Park 365
   Cambridge court 399

437

Canford 399
Chicago 399
Crabbet Park 376
Detroit court 186, 230, 399
Greentree *241*, 399
Haileybury 399
Hampton Court 399
Hardwick House 248, 399
Holyport *259*, 399
Jesmond Dene 263, *263*, 399
Lakewood *266*, 399
Leamington 399
Lord's court 399
Manchester *276*, 278
Marlborough 399
Montreal 399
Moreton Morrell *287*, 288, 399
New York 399
Newmarket & Suffolk 290, 399
Oxford court 399
Petworth 399
Queen's Club courts 86, 399
Racquet Club of Chicago 227
Seacourt court 85–6, 399
Suffolk House court 249
Sun Court, Troon 393
Tuxedo Club court 186, 399
Wellington 399
Winchester 359, 399
Bickley Formula 278, 333, 402
Biddle, A.E. 162
Biedermann, Edwin (later Best) 403, 404
Bigelow, John 209, *209*, 210
Biggs 73
Billings, Jessica 243
Billings, Tom 187, 243, *243*
Billy Ross-Skinner British Invitation mixed doubles tournament 118, 246
Birch, Thomas 53
Bird, Ralph 56
Birgbauer, Ronald 230
Birmingham, Rackets courts 145, 148, 149
Birt, W., racquet maker 27
Birts, Henry 325
Blaber, Scott 214, 215, *215*
Bloomfield, Roddy *97*, 174, 251, 409
Bluck, E., racquet maker 141
BNB Resources 406
BNP-Paribas Tournament 307
Boag, C.C. 257
Boakes, Harry 77, 151–2, *152*, 186, 188
Boakes, Harry, Jr. 186
Boddington, Ben 325
Boddington, Rupert 328
Boileau Arms Rackets court, Hammersmith 141, 146
Bolster, Paul 210
Bolton, Mike 367
Bombay, India, Rackets court 193, 194
Bomford, Ben *191*, 221, *221*, 334
Bonallack, R.R.N. 243
Bone, G.H.K. 337
Bone, Joe 229, 252, *252*, 328, 334
Bonsor, Richard 190
Boobyer, Angus *357*, 358
Book of Hours of the Duchess of Burgundy 128
Boomerang Cup 215, 282, 291
Boone, Willie 172, *175*, 176, 177, 188, 232, 233, 251, 279, 325, 381
   Canadian Amateur champion 189
   Rackets Open singles champion 172, 176, 187, 233
   Rackets world champion 175
Booth, Kieran 258, 282

Bordeaux Tennis court 71, 85, 88, 109, 112, 206–7, *206*
Bordenave, Philippe 343
Borrelly, racquet maker 26
Bose, Lalit 253, *253*
Bostock, Robert 251
Boston, Buckingham Street court 76, 77
Boston Athletic Association 186
Boston Tennis & Racquet Club 77, 87, 186, 189, 208–210, *208*, 399
Bostwick, G.H. (Pete) 100, 174, 188, 201, 226
   Amateur doubles champion 100
   Amateur singles 100
   American Open champion 100, 107
   v. J. Bostwick 100
   v. Knox 100
   v. Willis 277
   world championship 106
Bostwick, G.H., Jr. *107*
Bostwick, J.F.C. (Jimmy) 100, 101–2, *101*, *107*, 174, 201
   Amateur doubles 100
   Amateur singles 100, 106
   American Open championship 100, 107
   v. P. Bostwick 100
   world championship 103, 106
Bostwick brothers 107
Bostwick Trophy 278, 297
Bosworth-Smith, B.N. 145
Box, J.B. 282
Boy, Alexandre 343, 346, *346*
Boyles, Pete 258
Boys, John 217, 218
Bracher, John 76
Bradfield, Graeme 257, 258
Braham, Charlie 235, *235*, 310
Brake, Peter 176, 177, 182, 198, 233, *233*, 234, *235*, 320, 323, 324, 371
Brandenburg, Albert, Marquis of 41
Brassey, Albert 71, 384
Brassey, Thomas 384
Bray, Chris 110, 205, 214, 255, *310*, 313, 329, 343
   Petworth professional 110, 310, *311*
Brearley, Mike 243
Breckenridge, Alistair 393
Breckenridge, Jill 393
Brett, Noel 184, 275, 358
Bretten, John 211, 212
Breuer, Matt 210
Brickley, R. (Dick) 209, *209*, 210
Bridgeman, Dick 173, 174, *174*, 175, 406, 407
Bridgeman Cup 124, 253
Bridger, Albert 189, 285
Briers, Mark 222, *223*, 224
Brighton 269
   Middle Street Rackets court 81
   Prince's Club 73
   tennis courts 72–3, 75, 80, 83, 89, 90
Brignall, Alex 280
Bristol & Bath Club 108, 211
Bristol Real Tennis Club 211–12, *211*
Bristowe, Tom 208
Bristowe, Will 312
Bristowe, William 190
Britannia Royal Naval College, Dartmouth *364*, 366
British Amateur championship 72, 75, 92, 105
British Amateur Doubles championship 115
British Amateur singles championship 113–14, *114*
British Junior Open championship *114*
British Ladies' Open 118, 119–20

British Ladies' Open doubles championship 118
British Land 323, 406
British Open championship 94, 96, 98, 105, 109, 110, 111, 113, 114
British Open Ladies' Rackets 183
British Rackets Open championship 155, 157, 180, *180*
British Rackets Open Doubles 180, *180*
Broadbent, Avery 305
Broadbent, Camille 305
Broadbent, William 305
Broadbent, William, Jr 305
Broadbent family 305, *305*
Brockenshaw, Steve 277, *278*, 288, 289
Broderick, Kevin 190, 230
Brodie, Alex (née Kurkjian) 183, *183*, 184, *184*, 275
Brodie, Jeremy 262
Brodie Cup 114, 124, 262, 265, 272, 337, 383
Broers, Lord 214
Brooke, George 315
Brooke, George H., World Rackets championship *156*
Brooksbank, Gerri 302
Broomfield, Sir Nigel 369
Brouaye, racquet maker 26–7
Brougham, H. 170
Brougham and Vaux, Lord 71
Brougham Hall tennis court 71, 373, *373*
Brown, Geoff 320
Brown, Nigel 214
Brown, Paul 115
Brown, Rawdon: *Four Years at the Court of Henry VIII* 40
Brown, Ross 301
Browne, Gilbert 153, 194, 220
Browne, Brigadier Hugh 305
Browning Cup 122
Bruce, Hon. C.N. *see* Aberdare, Lord, 3rd Baron
Bruce, Hon. M.G.L. *see* Aberdare, Lord, 4th Baron
Bruce, James 407
Bruce, Nigel 407
Brunel Cup 212, *212*
Bryant, David *289*
Buchanan and Malings, racquet maker 141
Buckhurst Park Rackets court 143, 179, *364*, 365–6
Buckingham Palace, Stické court 394
Buckley, George 328
Buenos Aires, Hurlingham Club, Rackets court 154, 374, *374*
Bull, Tim 264
Bulley, Ally 225, *226*
Burbidge, Ben 270
Burbury, Sir Stanley 88, 258
Burgin, William 294
Burke, J.J., Jr (Jimmy) 103, 107, 190, 191, 209, *209*, 316
Burma, Rackets court 390, *390*
Burnett, John 291, *291*
Burnham, Thomas 55
Burns, Will 255, *255*, 256, 283, *283*
Burr, Malcolm 172, 174
Burrell, Sir Peter 70
The Burroughs Club 283, 402
Butcher, Benedicte 343
Butcher, Donald 162
Butcher, Julian 343
Bute, 3rd Marquess of 237
Butler, C.T. 257
Butler, C.W. 257
Butler, Paul 264
Butler, Thomas 146

Buxton, Christopher 395
Byron-Evans, Sam 229

Cabart, racquet maker 27
Cahill, Janne 259
Cairns, Chris 408
Calcutta, India, Rackets court 193
Calhoun Witham doubles tournament 202, 210
Callot, Jacques 51
Cambridge, L.D. 158
Cambridge University 145, 213–15, *213*, 403
   Christ's College 47–8
   Clare and Trinity court 76, 213
   Corpus Christi College 47–8
   East Road tennis court 74, 76, 81, 144, 213
   Emmanuel College 47–8
   Jesus College 47
   King's College 47
   Pembroke College 47
   Pembroke College court 47–8, 76, 213
   Peterhouse College 47–8
   Queen's College 47
   Rackets courts 76, 143, 144, 154
   St John's College 47
   Rackets courts 144, 150, 175
   St John's College court 47
   tennis courts 46, 72, 213–14, *213*, 399
   Trinity College 47
   v. Oxford University 213
Cambridge University Press 215
Camm Cup 247
Campbell, John 349
Campbell, Major, Rackets player 135
Canada
   Rackets 188–9, 286
   tours to 174
Canadian Amateur championships 160, 189, 286
Candy, Captain 76
Canford School 204, 216–18, *216*
Canford tennis court 71, 87, 309, 399
Cann, Ross 294
Cannes tennis court 71
Caravaggio 49
Caravaggist painter: *The Death of Hyacinth* 127
Cardiff
   Jackson's Hall 154
   Racquet and Fives Court Company 154, *154*, 374, *374*
   tennis court 67
Carey, Ryan 115, *352*, 356, *356*
Carlier, Yves 341, 344
Carman, Richard T. 185
Carney, Rackets player 135–6
Carr, Jimmy 214
Carroll, Rowan 226
Carter, Mike 108, 318
Carter, Richard 178, 331
Case, Henry, racquet maker 27
Case, John, racquet maker 27
Case, Oliver 174
Cashman, John 190, 191, 225, 227, *227*, 316
Casino Club, Newport 76–7
Cass, Bill 370
Cassils, Angus 189
Castley, Susan 124
Catherine de Medicis 35, 37, 39
Cattermull Trophy 284
Caulfield, Lucy 207, *207*
Caulkins, Chuck 230
Cavanagh, John, obituary 133, 136–7
Cawdron, Mike 224, 243
Cawnpore, India Rackets court 384, *384*

Index

Cawston, Ben 362, *362*
Cawston, Tim 182, 360, 361, 362
Caxton, William 32
Cazalet, Edward 71, 379
Cazalet, Peter 159
Cazalet, Victor 190
Cazalet, W.M. 403
Cazalet family 271
Celestion Loudspeakers 174, 406
Cellini, Benvenuto 35
Cercle du Jeu de Paume de Fontainebleau 239–40
Chaban-Delmas, M. 88–9
Chalmers, Alan *310*
Chamandy, Glenn 191, *285*
Champion Racquet 257
champions
   19th-century Rackets 146–53
   20th century 89–94
   20th-century Rackets 154–8
   American 105–7
   post-war 95–105
   prominent players 104–115
Chantilly tennis court 61
Chantler, Kenneth 161, 162, 188, 190, 285–6
Chaplin, Thomas 65
Chapman, Chris 247, 282
Chapman, George, *An Humourous Day's Mirth* 45–6
Chapman, Steven 368
Chapus, Eugène: *Le Jeu de Paume – son Histoire et sa Déscription* 80
Charles I 53, 54, 55–6, 58
Charles II 40, 56–7, 58
Charles V 31, 33, 35, 41, 44, 50
Charles VI 32
Charles VII 32, 206
Charles VIII 32
Charles IX 35, 36, 37, *37*, 39
Charles d'Orléans 20
Charleston, South Carolina, court 366
Charleston Tennis Club 112
Charrier, Amédée 63, 64, 78, 79, *126*
Charrier, Janvier-Jacques *126*
Charterhouse Monks Rackets Club 220, 221
Charterhouse School 54, 196, 219–21, *221*, 403
Château d'Amboise 32, *33*
Château de Saint-Germain, tennis courts 35, 64
Château de Suze-la-Rousse 39
Chatham 403
   Rackets court 335
   Stické courts 394
Chaucer, Geoffrey: *Troilus and Criseyde* 25
Chawner, Mr 76
Cheltenham College 145, 175, 178, 179, 181, 182, 222–4, 402, 403
Cheltenham Gold Racquet 223, *224*
Cheltenham Masters Rackets Club *224*
Chepstow tennis court 67
Cherry, Dan 348
Cherry Blossom tournament 356, *356*
Chetwood, Sir Clifford *109*, 406
Chetwood Trophy 237
Chetwynd, William 65
Chicago
   Athletic Association 77, 186, 374–5, *374*
   Racquet Club 87, 156, 166, 168, 186, 191, 220, 225–7
   tennis courts 77, 87, 112, 116, 225, *225*, *226*, 227, 399
   University Club of Chicago 186, *375*, 375
Chignall, Major 221
Child, Sir John 162, 405
Chinneck, Andy 301
Chisholm, Tim 113, 207, 209, 210, 246, *246*, 284, *294*, 298, 299, 301, 308, *308*, 310, *322*, 325, 338, 353
Christ Church tennis court, Oxford 46
Christ's College, Cambridge 46, 47–8
Church, Brian 214, 310
Church, Rackets player 137
Cilymaenllwyd Stické court 394, *394*, 395
Clancy, Kevin 210
Clandeboye Stické court 394, 395, 396, *396*
Clarence Pell Cup 188
Clark, J.O.M. 85, 94, 393, 403
Clarke, Christopher 325
Clarke, Judith 120, 258
Clarke, Julia 215
Clarke, W.H. 330
Clergé 52, 63, 64
Clerici, Gianni: *500 Anni di Tennis* 15
Cleveland Tavern Club 375, *375*
Clifton and Bath court 325
Clifton Boasters 229
Clifton College 108, 145, 177, 178, 211, *211*, 212, 228–9, *228*
Cline, Chris 298
Cliveden Stické court 394
Clothier, Morris W. 297–8, 299, *299*
clothing 49, 52, 55, 61–2, 63, *63*, 139–40, *140*
Club Professional Development programme 408
Cobb, Henry Ives 374
Cochrane, Yseult 264
Cockcroft, India 358
Cockram, Ted 204, 282
   Ted Cockram Trophy 278, 297
Cockram Trophy 278, 297
Cockroft, Tim 177, 179, 180, *180*, 181, 189, 190, 227, 253, 280, *285*, 286, 358
Coe, Lord 249
Coghlan, Mark 240, 261, 262
Cohen, Jonathan 347
Cohen, W.H. 86
Colchester 403
   Rackets court 154, 335
Coldicott, Alex 222, 223
Coles, Anthony 108
Colhoun, Stephen 173, *173*, 174
Coligny, Admiral 36–7
Collin, Edmond, *Petit Manuel de la Longue Paume* 19
Collins, S.A.M. 97
Colman, O.J. 97
Cologne, tennis courts 60
Colquhoun, Duncan 215
Colvin, Dr Howard 41
Combined Services competitions 159
Compiégne tennis court 61, 64, 71
Compton, Captain and Mrs 357
Condé, Prince de 61
Connell, Mike 349
Connell, Miles 174
Cooch Behar Stické court 396, *396*
Cook, Arthur 402
Cook, Ben *203*, 366
Cook, John 305
Cook, Johnny 289
Cook, Karl 178, 222, 224
Cooke, George 29
Cooke, George, Manchester professional 277, 310
Cooke, Thomas 57, 58–9
Coolidge, Archibald Cary 389
Coolidge, H.J. 87
Coombe Abbey tennis court 71, 375–6, *375*, *376*
Cooper, Albert 157
   British Open champion 158, 171
   Professional champion 158, 161, 171
Cooper, Richard *274*

Cooper-Key, Major Aston 403, 404, 405
Coote, Captain Johnny 310, 313
Cope-Williams, Gordon 108, 329
Copped Hall, Epping 376, *376*
Cordier, Maturin, *Commentarius Puerorum* 19, 20
Corinthian Cup 214
Cornish, R. 282
Cornwallis, Charles 58
Cornwallis, Charlotte *120*, 121–4, *121*, *122*, *124*, 212, 240, 289
Corpus Christi College, Cambridge 22, 46, 47–8
Corsham, Wiltshire, Stické court 397
Cos D'Estounel vineyard 406
Cott, Georges 85
Cotter, E.P.C. 'Pat' 333
Cotterell, Clement 54
Cottrell, Jill 118
Coulman, Mike 97, 171, 173, *173*, 174, 359
Coulson, Dom 280
Coulter, Charles J. 158
'coup d'Orléans' 61
Coupe de Bordeaux 207
Coupe de Noel 207
Coupe de Paris 85
Coupe Duroy de Suduiraut 207
Coupe Gould Eddy 307
Court Tennis Charleston 366
courte paume 22, 31, 48
courts
   16th century 35–50
   17th century 51–60
   18th century 61–70
   19th century 71–84
   20th century 85–9, 108–111
   21st century 112–13
   building/restoring 87, 194, 365–71, 398–402
   disused 372–93
   plan 23
Covey, Fred *86*, 90, 91, 288, 337, 404
   v. Etchebaster 93–4
   v. Jay Gould 92, 93
Covey, George 309
Covey, G.F. 85
Cowbridge tennis court 67
Cowdrey, Chris 348
Cowdrey, Colin 348, 349
Cowdrey, Fabian 348
Cowdrey, Lord 196
Cox, Philip, racquet maker 27, 78, 79
Cox, W.J. 72, 79
Coyne, James 179, *179*, 180–81, *180*, 181, 183, *191*, 192, *192*, 223, 224, 227, *227*
Crabb-Robinson, Henry 145
Crabbet Park tennis court 85, 90, 376–7, *376*, 403, 404
Craig, Kiwi 264
Crane, J., Jr. 105
Crane, Joshua 387, 390
Crane, Justin 228
Craven, Earl of 71, 375
Craven, Oliver 252
Craven, Lt Oliver 336
Crawley, A.E. 21
Crawley, Aidan 251
Crawley, Andrew 230, 251
Crawley, Cosmo 157, 159, 160, *160*, 161, 170, 171, 251, *364*, 366
Crawley, E. 86
Crawley, Ernest 251
Crawley, Eustace 251
Crawley, H.E. 248
Crawley, Leonard 251
Crawley, Randall 176, 177, 230, 251
Crawley, Stafford 251
Crawley brothers 190

Craxford Mouldings Limited 196
Crette, Nicholas 64, 393
Cripps, Norwood 102, 103, 105, 107, 178, 229, *233*
   Eton professional 105, 192, *192*, 233, 320
Crispe, Leslie 259
Cromwell, Oliver 43, 44, 55, 56
Crosby, A.J. 279
Crosby, Arthur 279
Crosby, Fred J. 182, 220, 252, 279
Crosby, Jim 182, 279, 359
Crosby, Jim, Jr 182
Crosby, Martin 182, 198, 220, *220*, 221, 252
Crosby, R.J. 220
Crosby, Roger 178, 182, 252, 279
Cross, Greg 191
Crossley, Charles 299
Crowell, Jon 190, 192, 317
Cruickshank, David 243
Cudlip, Charles T. 356
Cull, David 255, 271, 272, 309
   D.W. Cull Trophy 272
Cullen, Charles 172
Cullen, Lord 105
Curragh Army Camp Rackets court, Co. Kildare 335, 377, *377*
Curren, Kip 210
Cuspidor Cup 354
Cuthbertson, J.L. 331
Cutting, C. Suydam 106
Cutting brothers 107
Cutty Sark 406
   championship 101, 104

d'Abernon, Viscount 379
Dale, Brad 212, 258
Dalhousie, India, Stické court 394
Dallington, Sir Robert 17, 29
Dalton, Mr 150
Dalzell, Richard 409
Dambach, George 230
Dames Longworth, F. 219
Danby, Charles 114, 181, 221, *221*, 251, 253, 338
Danby, Luke 114, 325, 337–8, *364*, 366
Danby, Ned 337
Danby, Nicky 337, 339–40, *339*, 366
Danby, Paul 120, *311*, 337, 366, 372–3
Danby Over-70 competition 278, 297
Dance, Major James 287
Dance, Tom 325
Daniel Island Club 366
Danzig, Allison 86, 98, 292
   The Racquet Game 95, 400
Darjeeling India, Stické court 394
Dark, J.H. 73
Darritchon, Leopold 344
Dartmouth, Britannia Royal Naval College *364*, 366
David, Evelyn 118, *120*
David, F.M. 189
David, Jacques-Louis 65
David Tate Cup 334
Davies, Chris 409
Davies, John 137, 146
Davies, Lucy 118, 119
Davies, Simon 190, 348
Davies, Wayne 108, 109, *109*, 110–111, *110*, 245–6, 282, 299, 371
   racket 27
   Tennis world champion 109
   US Open Tennis champion 110
Davis, Andrew 288, 289, 303, *304*
Davis, Dwight 186
Dawes, J.M. 243, 290–91
Dawes, John 243
Dawes, Jonathan 255, *255*, 256, *256*

439

Dawes, Peter 108, 120, 303, 310, 337, *339*, 340
Dawes, Vivian 118, 120, *120*
Dawson, Andy 313
Dawson, Geoffrey 159
Dawson, Nick *311*
Dawson, Tim *311*, 313
Day, Henry 143, 145
de Berrio, Salvador 341
de Bondt, Cees 17, 50
de Forrest, Elias 185
de Garmendia, B.S. 83, 186, *187*, 189
de Garsault, François Alexandre Pierre de 29
  The Art of the Tennis-Racket-Marker 26, *26*, 61, 62, *62*, 398
de Guevara, Antonio 50
de Koning, Kendrick 190
de la Baume Suze, Count François 39
de la Warr, Earl 143, 365
De Laszlo Bowl 247
de Luze, Albert 89, 344
  La Magnifique Histoire du Jeu de Paume 95, 288
de Manevieux 61, 62–3, 64
de Reignac, Comte 79
de Rham, F.F. 160, 161, 173
de Suduiraut, Duroy 89, 206
de Svastich, Peter 190
de Vaufreland, Henri
  60 Années de Sport 343
  Carnets de la vie mondaine des Basses-Pyrénées 343
De Voe, Billey 185
De Voe, Stephen 294
Dealtry, E. *86*
Dean, Ben 325
Dean, Colin 256, 407
Dean, Mick 178, 297, 303, 325, *326*, *327*, 328
Dear, Jim 88, 95–6, *98*, 160, *162*, *170*, 171, 188, 190, 196, 259, 271, 286
  British Open Squash champion 95–6
  British Open Tennis champion 96, 98, 105
  Eton professional 233
  Professional Squash champion 162
  Queen's professional 159
  Rackets
    British Open champion 96, 164
    world champion 96, 99, 103, 161–2
  v. Etchebaster 96
  v. Johnson 96, 99
  v. Pawle 161, 162
  Wellington professional 99, 358
  world champion 99, 103, 232, 233, 320
Dear, William 162
deaths and tennis 31–2
Deauville tennis court 71
The Dedanists 215, 409
The Dedanists' Foundation 289, 409
The Dedanists' Society 409
Delahaye, Charles *see* Biboche
Delahaye, Henri 80
Delaney, Laurence 371
Delloye, Eric 240
Demory, Hubert, *Histoire du Jeu de Paume de Paris 1908-2008* 307–8
Denison, H.A. 219
d'Erlanger, Baron *86*
Deruchie, Chris 192
Desborough, Lord 396
Desborough Patent Court 396, 397
Desmet, Robert 306
Detroit Racquet Club 186, 191, 230–31, *231*, 399
deuce, origin of the word 21
Deuchar, Fiona *120*

Deucher, Lachlan 109, 110, 205, 245–6, 282
Deutscher Werkbund 370
Devereux, Guy 190, *296*, 297, 298, *298*, *330*, 331, 354
Devereux, Sara *354*
Devine, Mark 201, *202*
Devitt, Patrick 149
Devoe, Billy 150
Devonshire, Earl of 41
Dexter 328, 359
di Bartolomeo, Dan 210
di Bonaventura, Peter 242
Dick, David 251
Dick Bridgeman TRA Foundation 407
Dickens, Charles 137
Dickinson, J.H. 76, 81, 303
Dickinson, R.C.E. 81, 159, 303
Dickson-Poynder, Sir John 397
d'Ierni, Francesco Gregory 17
Digswell House, Welwyn Stické court 394
Dijon, Salamander tennis court 52
Dipple 328, 359
Disraeli, Benjamin 141, 150
Ditton Place, Balcombe tennis court 85, 309
Dixon, Andy 270
Do, Michael 356
Dobbins, Tom 210
Dodgson, Josh 310, 313, 338
Dolman, Adam 265, *312*
Dolman, Robert *311*, 313
Dooley, Alfred *86*, 159, 162
Dorset, Dukes of 365
Douglas, Alan 264, 265
Douglas, Annie 264
Douglas, Barclay 294
Douglas, Jamie 114, *115*, 215, 265, *265*, 272
Dover, Stické court 394
D.P. Henry Cup 272
Draffan, Nigel *311*
Drane, Arthur 209, *209*
Dresdner Kleinwort Benson Classic 246
dress *see* clothing
Drewitt, Julianne 258
Dron, James 212
Drysdale, Mark *312*, 325
Drysdale, Robin 233
du Cerceau, Androuet 17
Dublin
  Kildare Rackets court 149
  St Stephen's Green 71, 82, 112, 366–8, *367*
  St Thomas' Street tennis court 54
  University Club Rackets court 150
  Vice-Regal Lodge Rackets court 150
Dufferin and Ava, Marquess of 396, *396*
Duffy, Patrick 230
Duleepsinhji, K.S. 222
Dumas, Alexandre, *The Three Musketeers* 51
Dunbar, Peter 252
Dunbar, Tom 251, 252
Duncliffe-Vines, Alex 223, *223*
Dunkley, Gitte *120*
Dunlop balls 30
Dunn, Jimmy 29–30, 87, 107, 190, 315–16, 317, 352
  Jimmy Dunn and Jock Soutar tournament 317
  tournament 210
Dunn, Richard *291*
Dunne, Peter 226
Dunnington-Jefferson, Sir Mervyn 401–2, 407, 410
Duns, John 264
Dunstan, Professor G.R. 34

Dupont de Compiegne, Nicolas 239
Durack, Tom 310, *312*
Durand, Guy 240
Durkes, Jeff 191
Durkes, Rick 190, 226
Dutch Real Tennis Association 368
Duvauchelle, Richard 240
Duvivier, Peres 206
Duxfield, Henry 361, *361*
D.W. Cull Trophy 272
Dyer, J. Milton 375
Dynan, John (father and son) 26, 58
Dytor, Clive 300

Eadle, Mark 212, 300, 303, 327
Eagle Tavern Rackets court, City Road 133, 141
Earle, J. 46
East Sheen tennis court 71
Eastbourne Rackets court 144, 154, 377, *377*
Easton Neston, Stické court 394; tennis court 71, 378, *378*
Eaton, John 252
Eckersley, Peter 172
Eckersley, Roger 172, 174
Edberg, Stefan *306*
Ede, Mr 149
Eden, Ged 283, 299
Eden, Gerard 207, 307
Edgar, Robert 185
Edinburgh, Duke of *167*
Edouard Kressmann Trophy 207
Edward, Prince 325
Edward III 33, 40
Edward IV 28
Edward VII 72, 75, 76, 158–9, 189, 244, 288, 351
Edwardes, Jonathan 324
Edwards, E.M. 158
Edwards, Richard 55
Egan, Pierce 146
  Book of Sports 133–7
  Finish to Life in London 132–3
Egan, Raymond 367
Eglinton, Lord 141, 148, 149
Eglinton Arms, Bristol, Rackets court 141, 148, 149, 378
Eglinton Castle, Rackets court 141, *148*, 149, 378, *378*
Egremont, Lady *311*, 313
Egremont, Lord *311*, 313
Egyptian ball games, ancient *12*, 13
Eliot, John, *The Parlement of Prattlers* 45
Elizabeth I 40, 44–5
Elizabeth II 237
Elliott, Tom 190
Ellis, Peter 178, 243, 303
Ellis, Richard 243
Elvaston Castle, Rackets court 145
Emmanuel College, Cambridge 46–8
Emmet, Robert 185
Emmet, William J. 185
Enfield, Edward 145
Engstrom, A. *362*
Ennis, Chris 105
Epping, Copped Hall 376, *376*
Erasmus, *Colloquies* 19, 20, 21, 26
Eric Angus Cup 333
Erle, General 188
Erwood, Francis 149, 150
Erwood, George 144, 147, 148, 149
Esher Place, Surrey 379, *379*
  Stické court 394
Essex, Earl 53
Etchebaster, Pierre 87, 88–9, 93, *94*, 96, 97–8, 107, 155, 201, 242, 258, 259, *281*, 282, 306, 315, 345, *345*, 346
  v. Covey 93–4
  v. Dear 96

v. Martin 96–7, 106
v. Phipps 94, 95, 96
Etchebaster tournament 210
Eton College 145, 151, 171, 172, 177–8, 182, 232–5, 403
Eton fives court 144, 320
Eton Tour 192, *192*
Eton Fives Association 404
European Open championship 113, *113*, 116
Evans, John 260
Evans, Philip 67
Evans, Robert, Jr 230
Evans, William 274
Evelyn, John 56

Faber, David 233
Faber, Julian 233
Faber, Mark 166, 172, 182, 233, 251, 348
Faber, Michael 233
Faber, Robert 109
  British Open, Tennis 111
  Tennis world champion 109–111
Faber Cup, Mark 233, 234, 348
Fahey, Claire *see* Vigrass, Claire
Fahey, Rob, v. Chisholm 294, *294*
Fahey, Robert 110, 112–13, *114*, 115, *116*, *117*, 205, *205*, 207, 212, 215, 225–6, 240, *240*, 246, *246*, 247, 258, *265*, 273, *273*, 283, 289, 299, 301, 308, *308*, 310, *312*, 318, *322*, 323, *325*, *326*, 327, 329, *338*, *345*, 356, 371
  British Open, Tennis 111, 323, 338
  Tennis world champion 110, *110*, 113, 246, *246*, 265, 282, *282*, 323
Fahey, Rob, v. Chisholm 294, *294*
  world doubles champion *114*
Fairbrother, Jeremy 214
Fairlawne tennis court 71, 87, 109, 379–80, *379*, *380*, 403
Fairs, Cecil 'Punch' *86*, 87, 89, *89*, 92, 233, 290, 337
  v. Johnson 90, 91, 288, 309
  v. Latham 85, 89–90, 249
Fairs, H.B. 'Punch' 151
Falkland Palace 46, 48, 85, 236–7, *236*, 250, 309
Falkner, Susie *120*
Faroe Islands, ball game 19
Farolais 63
Faulise, Jacques 209, 293
Faulkner, T.P. 243
Faull, John 205
Fava, Eddie 366
Fearing, George 387
Feldon, Charles 29
Fellman, Jim 77
Fellowes, Archie *360*
Fenn, Joseph 69
Fennell, J. *86*
Fennell, James 74
Fennell, Jimmie 309
Fennell, John 74
Ferdinand I 50
Ferdinand II 341
Ferguson, George, ball-maker 29, 229
Fermor-Hesketh, Sir Thomas 71, 378
Fern, George 230
Fernando, Gian 48
Ferro de' Rotai, Giovanni: *Teatro d'imprese* 125
Field, Horace 145
field tennis 69–70
Field Trophy 105, 114, 124, 215, 246, 256, 265, 272, 278, *312*, 337
Fife, Duke of 71
Figg, Christopher 260

Index

Filippelli, Frank 110, 205, 282, *282*, 283, 371
Finch, Percy 257
   Percy Finch Inter-club Trophy 258
Fincke, Reginald 187
Fink, Alexander 185
Fisher, Lt. Col. Arthur 398–9
Fisher, Dan 233
Fisher, John *43*, 57
Fitz-Roy, Charles 65
FitzGerald, Brian 233, 262
Fitzsimons, Will 226
fives 132, 136–7, 403–4
Fives Association 404
Flanagan, Mike 303
Flaxman, John 288
Fleet Prison Rackets court 131–2, *132*, 133, 134, 137, 138, 146, 147, 148
Fleming, Alf *339*, 340
Fletcher, Jerome 303
Flinn, Michael *296*, 297
Florin, F.P., *Grosser Herren Stands und Adelichen Haus-Vatters* 22
Florio, John 26
follis 14, *14*
Fontainebleau 10
   tennis courts *34*, 35, 39, 52, 61, 64, 79, 306
   see also Le Jeu de Paume de Fontainebleau
Forbes, W.I., Jr 107
Forbes-Leith, Alexander (later Lord Leith of Fyvie) 381
Forbes-Leith, Sir George 381
Forbet, book of rules 51
Ford, James *364*, 366
Ford, John 402
Forester, Arthur 87
Forester, Frank 87, 91, *91*, 186, 242, 267
Forton, Ken 209, 210
Fortune, David *313*
Fortune, Will 252–3, *252*
Foster, Basil 274
Foster, Harry K. 169, 179, 180, 181, 226, *227*, 235, *235*, 251, 252, 253, *253*, 274, 277, 280, *285*, 286, 299, 323, 328, 357
   see also Foster Cup
Foster, Reverend Henry 274
Foster, Maurice 274
Foster, Neville 274
Foster, Wilfrid 274
Foster, W.L. 357
Foster Cup 178
   Charterhouse 219
   Cheltenham 178, 179, 182, 222, 223
   Clifton College 178, 228, 229
   Eton College 178, 182, 232–3, 234, 235, *235*
   Haileybury 243
   Harrow 178, 182, 251, 252, 253
   Malvern College 274
   Marlborough College 279, 280
   Radley College 178, 325, 328
   Rugby School 178, 182, 330, 331
   St Paul's School 333–4
   Tonbridge School 178, 182, 348
   Wellington 182, 358
   Winchester 182, 359, 361
Foulkes, Fred 186
   v. Gray 150–51, 186
Fowler, Andrew 205, 212, *212*, 215, 255, 256, 299, 324, *324*
Fowler, Ian B.R. 356
Fowler, Laura 205
Fox, Julian 207
Foy, Joseph 150
France
   16th century 35–9, 48

17th century 52–3
18th century 61–5
19th century 71
20th century 85, 88–9
ball makers 28, 29
leading players 63–4, 77–8
longue paume 21, 31, *31*
Medieval game 31–3
southwest of France 341–6, *342*, *344*, *345*
Tennis Court oath 65
François, Dauphin 36
François I 28, 35, 36, 37
François II 36
Franks, Harry 234, *234*
Frederick, Prince of Wales 65
Freeman, G.W.T. 145, 385–6
French Open championship 109, 112, 207, *207*
French Revolution: Tennis Court oath 65
Freshwater: Stické court 394
Frissart, R., *Carmen de Ludo Pilae Reticulo* 19, 51
Fuente, Charles *311*, *312*
Fulwood Barracks, Preston 380, *380*
Fuzzy TV 116
Fyvie Castle, Scotland 380, 381, *381*

Gaby, R. 74
Gaby, Richard 74
Galen 15
Garcin, Ferdinand 85, 89, 93, 306
Garcin, Séraphin 306
Garden, Edward Gordon 390
Gardiner, Dave 186
Gardiner, Nick 190
Garland, Charles Tuller 85, 287, 288, 309
Garnet, Edward 219
Garnett, Michael 384
Garrard, John 60
Garrard, Samuel 60
Garratt, Captain Mark 336
Garsault, François de 29
The Art of the Tennis-Racket-Marker and of Tennis 26, *26*, 61, 62, *62*
Garside, Alex (née Warren-Piper) 118, 119, *119*, 120, *120*, 122, *124*, 183, *183*, 275, 289, 337
Gaskell, Ella 184
Gates, Garrett 210
Geddes, Jim 201
Geddes, Sir Reay 30
Geffen, Robin *322*, 323, 406
Gell, racquet maker 27
Gem, T.J. 148
Gentil, Pierre 51
George I 41, *42*, 65
George IV 72
George V 75, 159, 405
George VI 75, 159, 405
George Plimpton Prize 356
Georgian Court, Lakewood 87, 91, 108, 112, 186
Georgian Court University 266, 267, 268, *268*
Georgian Court College 267
Germany, tennis courts 60
Gerry, Robert L. 161
Gibbons, Charles 54, 56
Gibbons' Tennis Court 54
Gibbor, Jamie 333
Gibbs, Antony 145, 373
Gibbs, John 178
Gibraltar court 381, *381*
Gibraltar Rackets court 154
Giddins, Jamie 182
Gilbert, John 108, 204, *204*
Giles, Jack 220
Gillmeister, Dr Heiner 17, 19, 26
Tennis 16

Gilmore, Caroline and Jeremy 118
Giustiniani, Sebastian 40
Godfray, David *311*, 313, *313*
Gold, Rick 210
Gold Racket (RMTC) 282
Gold Racquet (France) 307
Gold Racquet (MCC) 73, 271, 272, *272*
Gold Racquet (US) 87
Goldie, Alex 229, *229*
Goldsmith, David 325
Goldsmith, William 230
Goodell, Mike 230
Goodfellow, Henry 253
Gooding, Mike 181, 218, 255–6, 283, 299, *299*, 310, 371, 393
Goodwood tennis court 67, 71, 309
Goodyear, Bobby 200, 201
Goodyear, Ginny *202*
Gopal, Harsha 210
Gordon, Bill 196, 197, *197*, 279
Gordon, D.R. 229
Gordon, Nigel 197–8
Gordon-Bennett, James 343
Gordon Bennett Trophy 302
Gosport, Stické court 394
Gosselin, Jean: *Déclaration de Deux Doubtes qui se trouvent en comptant dans le Jeu de Paume* 20–21
Gould, George 87, 186, 266, *266*, 267, 395
Gould, Howard 395
Gould, Jay 87, *91*, *106*, *156*, 158, 266, 315, 390, 404
   Bathurst Cup 92
   British Amateur Tennis singles 92
   US Amateur doubles 106
   US Amateur singles 105, 267
   US Open 92–3, 107
   v. Baerlein 92, 105
   v. Covey 92
   v. Kinsella 92
   v. Latham 91
   v. Miles 92
   v. Sands 91
   world championship 267
Gould, Kingdon 91, 186, 267
Gould Eddy Cup 307
Goulding, Sir Basil 367
Gourlay, Alistair 208
Governor's Cup 88, 258
Gracey, Richard 167, 171, 172, 174, 349
Gradige, ball maker 29, 152
Gradon, Robert 243
Graetzer, Kurt 190
Graham, Ian 178
La Grande Françoise, tennis court 35–6
Grant, Bobby, III 157, 160, *160*, 161, 162, 173, 187, 188, *188*, 189, 190, 192, 230, 232, 286
Grant, Joan: *Time Out of Mind* 85–7
Grant, Marsali 215
Granville, Dick 254
Granville, Tom 288, 289, *289*
Grassi, Helen 210
Grassi, Temple 356
Gray, Edward *86*, 248, 249
Gray, George 152, 219, 222, 276
Gray, H.J., & Son 27, 145
Gray, Henry John (Harry), racquet maker 27, 144, 145, 150, 182, *198*, 219, 330, 331
Gray, Joseph 150, *152*, 276, 330
   v. Boakes 151–2, 188
   v. H.B. Fairs 151
   v. Latham 277
   world champion 151, 182, 186, 219
Gray, Nigel 331
Gray, Peter 161, 330, 331

Peter Gray Cup 243, 361
Gray, Richard 182
Gray, Ronald 330
Gray, Walter 151, 152, 153, 219, 220, 251, 276
Gray, William 144, 219, 233
   Rackets champion of Ireland 150
   Rackets world champion 182
Grays of Cambridge, racquet maker 27, 141–2, 150
Great Britain v. United States 158
Greek ball games 13–14
Greene, Christopher 190
Greene, Molesworth 145
Greenhalgh, Craig 277, 303, *304*
Greenlands, Stické court 394, *395*
Greenstock, Mark 178
Greentree 87, 94, 106, 112, 241–2, *241*, *242*, 296, 399, 401
Greenwich Old Royal Naval College 381–2, *382*
Greenwich Palace tennis court 40
Greenwood, Richard *161*, *217*, 232, *364*, 406–8, 409, 410
Greenwood Trophy 121, 122
Greevy, Tom 87, 190, 191, 316, 352–3, *353*
Gregg, Walter 393
Greig, Col. J.G. 194
Gretton, Sir Peter 305
Grey, Sir Edward 237, 263, 271, 403, 404, 405
Griffin and Porter Butt, Bath 141, 148
Griffith, Mike 279
Griffiths, William 44
Groom, W.A. (Jack) 94, 105, 255, 271, 277, 370
Guernsey, Peter 242
Guest, Sir Ivor Bertie 71, 216
Guest, Sir John Josiah 216
Guild of Rackets- and Brush-Makers 37, *38*
Guinness, Sir Edward 71, 82, 366, *367*
Guinness, Sir Rupert Cecil 367
Gundry, Joe 71
Gundry, John 261, 262
Gundry, Joseph 261, *261*
Gundry, J.P.F. 150
Gunn, Ruarlaidh 113
Gunnery, Cedric *311*
Gustavus Adolphus II 60
Gymnasium Club, New York 150, 186

Haarlem, Holland: Huis ter Kleef tennis court 112, 368, *368*
Habina, Louis 190
Hackett, Alex 328
Hackett, R. *97*
Hadden Tomes Invitational 354, *354*
Hadid, Zaha 343, 344
Haileybury 145, 152, 175, 177, 243, 251, 393, 399, 402, 403
Halford, T.P. 174
Halifax, Nova Scotia, Stické court 394
Hall: *Chronicle* 32
Hall, Dan 222, 223
Hall, Nick 360
Hambledon, Viscount 395
Hamilton, Sir Andrew 249, 288–9, *289*, 407
Hamilton, Francis de C. 356
Hamilton, Lady 289
Hamilton, Ontario, Rackets court 189
Hamilton, Sir Richard 95, 288, 289
   and Anthony Hobson, *How to Make the Real Tennis Ball* 29
Hamlen, Devens 190, 208, *209*, 210
Hammersley, Mark 262

441

Hampton Court
  balls re-covered 29
  The Royal Tennis Court 41–2, *42*, 54, *55*, 56–9, 65, 71–2, 73, 77, 80, 81, 82, *101*, 103, 108, 109, *109*, 110, 244–7, *244*, *245*, 271, 309, 369, 371, 399, 403
handicap system 270, *270*
Hankinson, J.T. 217
Hapette Court, La Bastide-Clairence 112, 341, 344–5, *344*, 345
The Haphazards 250
Happell, Michael 282
Harbour, H.G. 251, 401
Harbour Club 108, 112, 383, *383*
Harding, Caroline *120*
Harding, E. *97*
Harding, Jem 137
Hardwick House tennis courts 71, 85, 89, 120, 211, 248–50, *248*, *250*, 290, 300, 335, 383, *383*, 399, 403
Harms, Dave 218
Harper, Tatham 215
Harradine, Henry 76
Harradine, James 84, *86*, 214
Harries-Jones, Charlie 265
Harrington, Earls of 145
Harris, Oliver *312*, *313*
Harris, Simon 264
Harris-Watson Trophies 247
Harrison, Chris 270
Harrison, Eddie 313
Harrison, Fiona 265, *265*
Harrison, Tony 265, *265*
Harrow School 15, 143, 145, 171, 172, 177, 178, 181, 182, 251–3, 403
  Harrow Hammer 252
  Rackets courts 143, 193, 251
  Thursday Rackets Club 252
Harrow Sports 27, 142
Hart, Rick 190
Hart, R.L. 352
Hart-Dyke, Sir William 144, *149*, 150, 157, 403, 404, 405
Harte, John 202
Hartgell, John 45
Hartham Park, Stické court 397, *397*
Harvard University
  Randolph Club 186
  Randolph Hall 389–90, *389*
  Randolph Tennis and Racquet Courts 87
Haswell, Sue *120*, *121*, 122, 247, 318
Hatfield Angoras 256
Hatfield House 71, 81, 82, 87, 214, 254–6, *254*
Hathrill, Archie 144
Hathway, Eleazer 372
Hatton, Charles 55
Hawes, Bill 196, 219–20
Hawes, Ronnie 232, 233, 358
Hawes, Walter 155, 157, 171, 219, 348–9, 357, 358
Hawthorne, Henry 45
Hayball, Amy 282
Hayden, Mark 142
Hayes, Ryan 210
Hayward, Matty 255, 256
Hazell, Shannon 176, 177, 190, 222, 230, 298, 333, 358
Hazlitt, William 146; 'The Indian Jugglers' 133
Head, Sir Edmund 188
Healey, George 186
Heap, Stella 278, *278*
Hearn, Paul 243
Heathcote, J.M. 73, *74*, 76, 83, 84, 271, 279
Heathcote-Amory family 397
Heck, Simon 256

Heck, S.W.D. 243
Hegarty, Brendan *278*, 409
Hegarty Report 409
Heilbut, Max 159, 309
Heilbut, Samuel 71, *86*, 259
Hemming, Julian 212, *212*
Henderson, Robert W. 92
  Ball, Bat and Bishop 13, 25, 95
Henderson Private Investors 174
Henman, Mike 275
Henman, Tim 275
Henri II 35, 36, 39, 48, 341
Henri III 17, 38
Henri of Navarre (later Henri IV of France) 28, 35, 37, 38–9, 238, 341
Henry, D.P.: D.P. Henry Cup 272
Henry, Prince of Wales 18, 43, 52, 53
Henry I of Spain 49–50
Henry II 16
Henry IV 33
Henry V 19, 20, 32, 40, 86–7
Henry VII 25, 40, *125*
Henry VIII 21, 22, 35, 40–41, *42*, *42*, 43, *43*, 44, 54, 56
Henry Johns Cup 124, 272
Henry Leaf Cup 105, 124, 218, 253, 284, 325, 330–31, 359
Henry Poole & Co 351, *352*
Henson, Basil 256
Hepworth, Bill 108
Herlihy, Shawn 209
Hertford College, Oxford 46
Hesketh, 1st Baron 378
Hetherington, Paul 264, 265
Hewell Grange tennis court 71, 76, 82, 87, 383–4, *383*, 403
Heythrop House, Chipping Norton tennis court 71, *384*, 384
Heywood, Simon 260
Hickey, Jack 242
Hickey, William 69
Hicks, Robin 331
Higgins, Eugene 186
Higginson, Thomas 66
Hill, A.E.L. 279
Hill, Brian 209
Hiller, G.G. 282
Hird, Karen 123, *123*, 184, *184*, 215
Hiscox 273
H.J. Gray & Sons 27, 145
Hoare, Sam 143
Hoare, W.H. 381
Hobart Tennis Club 88, 115, 257–8, *257*
Hobbs, Mark 214, 291
Hobson, Dr Anthony 288
Hobson, Anthony and Richard Hamilton, *How to Make the Real Tennis Ball* 29
Hogben, Jeremy 174
Holborn tennis court 66
Holinshed 44
Holland, Haarlem tennis court 368, *368*
Holland, Flo 289
Holland, Henry 67
Hollingsworth, Chris 291, *291*
Hollington, Robin 243
Hollington, William 243
Hollins, Tony 210, 293
Holloway, Adam 278
Holloway, Graeme 258
Holman, G.H. 217
Holt, R.A.A. 'Bimby' 159, 160, *160*, 161, 171, 173, *173*
Holt, Richard (or Robert) 46
Holvick, Olaf, II 230
Holyport Grange tennis court 71, 88, 98, 108, 109, 399
Holyport Real Tennis Club 259–60, *259*, 260

Hombrecher, Alexis 114, 214, 215, *296*, 297, 298
Honeck, Hank 202
Honeck Bisque 202, *203*
Hong Kong Rackets court 154
Hooker, John 55–6, 58
Hooker, Thomas 54, 55–6
Hooper, J.J.M. 219
Hopcroft, Nick *357*, 358, 361
Hope, William 45
Hopton, Christopher 409
Hopton, Will 179, *179*, 180–81, *180*, 191, *191*, 221, 223, 224, 226, 227, *227*, 234, 235, 243, 253, 277, 323, 334, 347
Hopton Review 409
Horine, Jeff 210
Horizon 115
Hornblower, Breton 210
Hornby, Sir Derek 406
Horne, Alderson 85
Horne, Bob 257
Hoskins, Rackets player 134–5
Hothfield, Lord (Anthony Tufton) 105, 174, 264, 265
Houghton, Percy *156*
Howard, Lord Edmund 41
Howard, John, *The State of the Prisons in England and Wales* 131
Howard, Sir Stafford 395
Howe, Ralph 297, 318
Howe, R.E. 106
Howe, Sam 297
Howe, Thomas P. 190, 230
Howe brothers 107
Howell, Jonathan 205, 240, 282, 288, 289, 300–301, 302
Howell, Nick 282, *282*
Howick, Lord 76
Hrysicos, Jiannis 255, 256
Huband, George 106, 158
Huband, Michael 190
Hubbard, Mark 179, 181, 229, 253, 274–5, *274*, 275, 328, 334, *334*
Hue Williams, Charles 167, 171, 172, 174, 190, 232, *286*, 407, 410
Hue Williams, Mark 177, *177*, 179, 180, 181, 235, *235*, 253, 279, 280, *285*, 286, 333
Hue Williams, Milne Hue Williams Cup 275
Hughes, Duncan 265
Hughes, Ed 267
Hughes, Ronald 98, 105, 178, 274, 275, *275*, 348
  Open Tennis championship 100, 107
Hughes, Vera 275, *275*
Hugo, Victor 71
Huhn, W.H.T. *156*
Hulet, M. 372
Hull, Arthur 349
Hull, Charles 349
Hull, Christopher 349
Hull, James 348–9
Hulpeau, C., *Le Jeu Royal de la Paume* 51, *52*
Hume, E.B. 145
Hunnewell, Hollis 76
Hunt, E. (Ted) 75, 76
Hunter, Kenneth 406
Hunter, K.O. 359
Hurley, Bob 209
Hurlingham Club, Buenos Aires, Rackets court 154, 374, *374*
Hurn, Jim 197
Hurst-Brown, C.N. 358
Hurstel, Charles-Antoyne 265
Hutchinson, Lucy 311
Hyde, Sir Edward 56
Hyde Tennis Club 71, 108, 261–2, *261*, *262*
Hyderabad, India, Rackets court 194

Hyland, Graham 109, 205, 258, 371
Hyland, Jane 258

Illingworth, Major James 336, *336*
Illinois Athletic Association 186
Incledon-Webber Cup 228, 229, 243, 328, 333, *334*, 361
India, Rackets 193–4
Indian Rackets Association 405
International Rackets match 158
International Real Tennis Professionals' Association 408
International Tennis Club of Washington 355–6, *355*
International Tennis Hall of Fame 293
Inverdale, John 229
Ireland
  racket players 135
  tennis courts 54
Irish Real Tennis Association 112, 212, 367, *367*, 368, 369
Irish Tennis Club 367
Ironmongers' Company: ball maker 28
IRTPA Satellite 338
Irvine Development Corporation 378
Isham, Jonathan 294
Islington, near Pie Bridge, Birmingham: Rackets court 146
Italy
  balls made in 28
  tennis in 49, 69
Iveagh, Viscount 366, 367, 403

Jackson, Daryl 87
Jacques Polton Cup 307
jai-alai 21
James, Lt Col Andrew 336
James, Rev. H.A. 390
James, Nick 181, *191*, 223, 298, 324
James I of Scotland 32
James I (VI of Scotland) 18, 54
  Basilicon Doron 52–3
James II (VII of Scotland) 56, 58–9
James IV of Scotland 32
James V of Scotland 46, 236
James Street Silver Racquet 72, 73
James Street tennis court 54–5, 58, 64, 66, 70, 72, 73, *73*, 76, 77, 78, 79, 80, 81, 269, 403
Jameson, J. 85
Jamsetji, J. 154, 155, 194
Janssen, Benno 389
Jarvis, D. 229
Jasani, Rakesh *203*
Jay Gould Cup 267
Jean II, the Good 31
Jeans, James 328
Jebb, Louis 371
Jee, Jonathan 325
Jefferies and Malings 144–5
Jefferies of Woolwich, racquet maker 141
Jeffries, Christopher 230
Jennings, T. 155
Jersey courts 368–9
Jersey Real Tennis and Rackets Association 368–9
Jesmond Dene Cup 264, 265
Jesmond Dene tennis court 71, 82, 108, 263–5, *263*, *264*, 399, 403
Jesters Rackets 174
Jesus College, Cambridge 47
jeu à dedans 48, 61, 62–3, 131, 236
jeu de Paume 17, 18, 21, 25, 67
Le Jeu de Paume de Bordeaux 206–7
Le Jeu de Paume de Fontainebleau 238–40, *238*, *239*, *240*
Jeu de Paume de Navarre 344, 346, *346*
Jeu de Paume et de Racquets, Paris Société Sportive du 306–8, *307*

Index

jeu quarré 46, *47*, 48, 51, 61, 62, *62*, 63, 66, 67, 131, 236
Jewell, Frank 366
Jim Dear Cup 228, 243, 333, *334*, *358*, 361
Jimmy Dunn and Jock Soutar tournament 317
Jock Soutar Rackets tournaments 315
Jock Whitney Intercollegiate Championship *268*
Johns, Henry 29, 44, *97*, 105, 159, 162, 249, 271, 288, 309, 370–71
 Henry Johns Cup 124, 272
Johns, Thomas 44
Johnson, Albert 'Jack' 98, *98*, 107, *162*, 188, 190, 227, 259
 v. Dear 96, 99
 v. Knox 99–100, 106
Johnson, Andrew 221
Johnson, David 320, 323, 371
Johnson, Edward, Jr 217
Johnson, E.J.G. 105, 159, 162, 217
Johnson, Ted 90, 91, 94, 98, 105, 159, 288, 309
Johnston, Charles 298
Johnstone, Charles T. 242
Jones, Danny 337
Jones, Donald 251
Jones, Michael 211
Jones, Nick 338, 339, *339*, 371
Jones, Sally (later Grant) 120, *120*, 122, *124*, 183, 237, *275*, 289, 337
Jones, Will 181
Jourdains 52
Joyce, William 77
Jubbulpore, India
 Rackets court 193, 194
 Stické court 394
Junior Professional championship 285–6
junior tennis 289
Jury, Nick 289

Karsten, Madame B. 343
Kaulbach, Ron 190
Keene, Foxhall 156
Keigwin, R.P. 229
Keiser, Mike 192
Kelly, Margaret 369
Kelly, Oliver 44
Kelly, Patrick 369
Kemp, Adrian *306*, 307
Kemp, David 178
Kemp-Welch, Peter 156, 158, 405
Kendrick, Charles 230
Kendrick Cup 210, 230
Kenilworth Castle tennis court 40
Kenney, Dan 292
Kenney, David 87
Kershaw, G.G. 169, 277
Kershaw, Harold 277
Kershaw, Peter 105, 161, 171, *171*, 172, 228, 277, 330, 406
Kershaw Cup 278
Kettle, Paul 327
Khalid Abdullah, Prince 379
Khan, Hashim 194
King, Kevin 115, 212, *212*, 254, 255, 256, 260, 290–91
King's Bench Prison Rackets court *130*, 131, 133, 134, 135, 137, 138, 139, 146
King's College, Cambridge 47
King's High School for Girls 289
Kinsella, Marty 192, *220*, 226
Kinsella, Walter 92–3, 94, 106, 107
Kinzler, Andy 317
Kinzler, Gabe 201, *203*, 316
Kirkbride, Malcolm *160*, 161
Kirtlington House, Stické court 394, 395, *395*

Kirton, Alfred 87
Knevet, Sir Edmund 33, 44
Knibbs, Andrew 214, 291
Knight, A.W. 257
Knight, Sean 181, 360–61, *361*
Knightshayes, Stické court 397, *397*
Knott, James, Jr 182, 192
Knott-Stephens tour 182, 192, *192*, 223
Knox, James 185
Knox, Northrup 88, 89, *99*, *107*, 201
 US Amateur single Tennis championship 99, 100, 106
 v. J. Bostwick 106
 v. Johnson 99–100, 106
Knox, Paul 327
Knox, Robert 185
Knox, Seymour 89
Knox, S.H., III *107*
Knox brothers 107
Kohat rackets court, India *194*
Kohn, David 210
Kressmann, Edouard 207
Kressmann, Roland 207
Kyd, Richard, ball maker 28
Kynwolmershe, Richard 44

La Force, Marshal de 37
La Fosse 63
La Lande 51
La Montagne, Auguste 150
La Montagne, Edward 185–6, *185*, 188
La Rochelle tennis court 51
Labarrère, André 343
Labbé, Louis 79
Lacoste 323, 406
ladies' Rackets 183–4
Ladies' Real Tennis Association 118, 119, 120, 122–4, 407
ladies' tennis 118–24
Lafforgue, Frank 186
Lafontaine, Sir Hippolyte 188
Lake, Ros *120*
Lakewood, the Georgian Court 87, 91, *108*, 112, 186, 266–8, *266*, 317, 385, *385*, 395, 399
Lakewood Invitational 267, *268*
Lamb, John 146, 147, 148
Lambay court, Co. Dublin 369–71, *369*, *370*
Lambay Island 112; tennis court 87, 112
Lambert, Alfred 82, 255
Lambert, Charles 82, 255, 264
Lambert, Edgar 82, 263
Lambert, George 73, 74, 75, 76, 81, *81*, *86*
 v. Pettit 82, 103, 244
 world champion 84, 244, 255
Lambert, Harry 309–310
Lambert, Henry Charles 82
Lambert, Joseph (John) 81, 255
Lambert, Stanley 77, 82
Lambert, Thomas 75, 82
Lambert, William 73, 74, 82
Landreth, Colt 191
Lansdowne Club 407
Lante, John 46
Larken, Jonathan 18, 177, *177*, 187–190, *192*, 228, 286, *286*, 297, 298, *298*, 353, 354
Latell 65
Latham, Emil 'Frank' 309, 310
Latham, Hugh 371
Latham, Peter 76, 82–3, *83*, *86*, 91, 95, 101, *156*, 158, 169, 172, 250, 276–7, 309, 310, 315, 371, 390
 Rackets champion 83, 99, 154
 v. Baerlein 90
 v. Fairs 85, 89–90, 249

 v. Harry Gray *198*
 v. Joseph Gray 277
 v. Pettitt 83, 89
 v. Standing 152–3, *153*, 186
 v. Walter Gray 152
 world champion 83, 90, 99, 169, 176, 277, 288, 290, 320, 328, 359–60
Lathom-Browne Cup 247
Laukitis, Dan *352*
Laukitis, Lisa *354*
Lavergne, racquet maker 26
Law, James 256, 310
lawn tennis 23, 24, 28, 86
Lawn Tennis Association (LTA) 320, 321, 409
Laws, Hubert 38
Lawton, John 369
Lawton, Robert 108, 371
Lawton, Tony *278*
Lay, Ronnie 328
Le Pape 52
Leaf, Edward 405, 406
Leaf, H.M. 404, 405
 Rackets 155
Leamington Rackets/tennis courts 154, 399
Leamington Tennis Court Club 72, 269–70, *269*, *270*, 403
Leatham, Aubrey 376
Leatham, Dr H.W. 158, 170, *170*, 187, 219, 376
Leclercq, racquet maker 26
Leconfield, Lord 71, 309, 310, 403–6
Ledger Hill Investment Company 279
Leeming, Kate *120*, *121*, 122, 214, *282*, 282
Leenan Fort, Co. Donegal 385, *385*
Lees, Lowther 105, 277, 357
Lefebvre, George 342
Leffingwell, Chris 192
Leicester, Earl 45
Leigh, Sam 297
Leipzig: tennis court 60
Leith of Fyvie, Lord 381
Lenihan, Ashley 184
Leonard, Dick 160–61, 173
Leonard, James *165*, 166, *166*, 167, 171, 172, 174, 359
 British Open Rackets champion 166, 219, 232
 Rackets Amateur champion 164, 232
Leonard Cup 275
Lesueur, Charles 85, 306
Leven and Melville, Earl of 395
Leveson-Gower, H.D.G. 145
Lewis, James 146
licences for tennis courts 45, 54, 60
Lingelbach, Bill 317
Lippincott, Jane *120*, 294
Lippomano, Jerome 17
Lisle's tennis court 54
literature between the wars 94–5
Little, Tony 235
Liverpool Racquet Club 144, 277, 403
 Rackets courts 144, 154
Liverpool tennis court 67
Llantrisant tennis courts 67
Lloyd, Martyn 221
Lloyd, Nick 256, *256*
Lockhart, David 191, 230
Lockhart, Grant 191, 230
London, tennis courts 41–4
Long, Darren ('Daz') 218, *218*
Long, Robert 57, 58, 59–60
Long, Robert, the younger 59–60
Longford Castle, Wiltshire, Stické court 394
Longley, Jonathan 178, 348
longue paume 21, 31, *31*, 48, 49, 64, 80, *128*, 131

Lonquet-Higgins, H.H. 228
Lonsdale, T.L. 405
Lord's Marylebone Cricket Club 271–3, 403
 media events 115–16
 Rackets court 73, 143, 154, 271
 Tennis court 43, 73, 81, 82, 85, 105, 271, 399
Lorillard, Maude 351, 369
Lorillard, Pierre, IV 350, 351, 369
Loudon, Hugo 233
Louis of France, Grand Dauphin 64
Louis I 69
Louis X, the Quarrelsome 31, 36, 49
Louis XI 28, 32
Louis XII 32
Louis XIII 19, 38, 51, 52, 64, 239
Louis XIV 52, 64–5, 69, 239, 393
Louis XV 61, 64, 65
Louis XVI 65, *208*
Louis of France, Grand Dauphin 64
Louis Roederer Open 172
Louvre tennis courts 16, 17, 31, 35, 36, 37, 39, 43, *47*, 48, 52, 64
Love, M.R.M. *97*
love (score) 21
Lovell, Alan 88, *102*, 105, 118, 359, 408, 410
Lowe, David 359
Loys, Etienne, *Guillaume Barcellon* 63, *126*
Lozier, Gideon 53
Luck-Hille, Peter 108, 225, 283, *284*, 371
Luck-Hille foundation 283
Ludekens, Kees 115, 214, *214*, 215, 240, 303
Ludington, N. *97*
Ludlow Castle, tennis court 45, 48
Lukin, Robert, *Treatise on Tennis* 72
Lumb, Raymond 277, 330
Lumley, Colin 109, 225, 260, 282, *316*, 327
Lumley, John 212, *316*, 327
Lumley, Penny 120–22, *121*, 124, *124*, 205, 247, 289, 308, *316*, 318, 327
Lumley, Tara 122, 123, 308
Lumsden, A. 115
Lutyens, Sir Edwin 369–70, *369*
Lydd, Stické court 394
Lyons, tennis courts 64
Lyons, Andrew 320, 323, *324*
Lyttelton, Hon. Alfred 73, 75, 84, 150, 158–9, 248, 271, 279, 403
Lytton, Hon. Neville 82, 85, 91, 104, *250*, 337, 377, 403, 404
Lytton, Judith (Lady Wentworth) 85, 90, 337, 404

MacAlister, Richard 264, 265
McClean, W.N. 87
McCormick, Harold F. 186, 375
McCray, Larry 210
McDonald, Andrew 274
MacDonald, Mark 190
McEwen, James 325
McFarlane, Brett 205, *205*
MacFarlane, Bruce 230
McGeoch, Ben 229, *229*
McGivern, Sarah 118–19, *119*, *120*
McGowen, Clarence 267
MacGuire, Kevin 190
Macintosh, Sheila 118, 119, *119*, 120, *120*
Mackay, Clarence 87, 187
Mackay (or Mackey), Robert 146
MacKellar, Duncan 402
MacKellar, Jim 402
Mackenzie, John 262
Mackenzie, Neil 262, 356

443

MacKeown, Alastair 312
McKim, Mead and White 77, 292, *292*
McLane, Rob 208, 209
McLaughlin, William F., Jr 242
McLean, John 297
McLernon, David 187, 189, *189*, 190, 192, 230, 286
McLernon, Michael 191, 208, *209*, *285*, 286
McMaster, Michael 190
McMorris, Howard *296*
McNamara, John 267
McNaughtan, Rod 212, 215, 277, *278*, 283, 307
McNeile, Robert 367
McPhail, Angus 325
Macpherson, Dugald 29, 105, 309
Macquarie University 108, 112, 371
Maddick, John *372*
Madison, Norb 191
Madras, India: Rackets court 193
Madrid, Alcazar palace: tennis court 50
Magrath, Billy 149
Mahon, Johnny 188, 189, 285
Makey, David 178, *179*, 182, 347, *347*, 348, 349
Male, James 110, 113, 175, *175*, 178, 188, 230, 274, 280, 298, 299, 323, 325, *326*, 327, 358, 371
 Amateur doubles Rackets champion 176–7, *177*
 Amateur singles champion 176
 Canadian Amateur champion 189
 Open singles champion 180
 Public Schools wins 325, 328
 world Rackets champion 176, 179, 181, 190, 191, 226, 229, *332*, 333
Maling, Jeffrey 195
Malings, Henry 145
Mallinson, Andrew 358
Mallinson, James 358, 371
Mallinson, Peter *234*, 408, 409
Mallinson, Major Tom 336
Malta
 Rackets court 81, 154
 Stické court 394
Maltby, William *181*, 190, 226, *229*, 409
Maltz, Jonny 347, 348
Malvern College 183, 274–5, 402, 403
Manchester
 balls re-covered 29
 tennis courts 116, *116*, *276*, 402
Manchester Gold Racquet 277, 278
Manchester Rackets courts 144, 154, 183, 276
Manchester Racquet Club 75, 152
Manchester Tennis and Racquets Club 75, 276–8, *276*, 403
Mandil, Quint *306*
Mann, Sir Horace 70
Manners, Desmond 274
Manown, Christopher 230
Manson, Bruce *296*
Mantua: tennis court 49
Marchisio 69, 78, 79
Margot of Hainault 25, 32, 88, 329
Mark Faber Cup 233, *234*, 348
markers 38, 48, 50, 51, 139, 145, 151, 255
Marlborough College 145, 157, 175, 177, 182, 196, 197, 279–80, 399, 403
Marriott, C.E. 145
Marriott, M.M. 217
Marshall, J.F. 85, *86*, 309, 337
Marshall, Julian *83*, 94, 95
The Annals of Tennis 83
Marshall, Simon 207, *207*

Marshall, William C. 213
Marshall of Knightsbridge, Lord 321
Martin, Alistair 95, 96–7, 98, *99*, *102*, 187, 292, 297
 British Amateur Tennis champion 96, 259
 US Amateur champion 96, 259
Martin, Robin B. 356
Martin twins 107
Martineau, Major Hubert M. 259
Mary II 59
Massereene and Ferrard, Lady 386
Massip, Laredo 307
Masson, Pierrette 63–4
Masson, Raymond 26, 63–4, *64*, 80
Master of the King's Tennis Plays 44
Master of the Queen's Tennis Plays 45
match of three 72
match player on bicycles 76
Matheson, Charles T. 356
Matthews, Ben 212, 247, 255–6, *256*, 262, 270, 318–19
Matthews, 'Fast Eddie' 182, 190
Max, Leon 378
Maxwell, E. 257
Maxwell, Patrick 410
MCC: *Rules of Tennis* 74
MCC Gold Prize 104, 105, 168
MCC Gold Racquet 228, 248, 277, 279
MCC Locusts 273
Mead, Mark Seymour 278
Mead, Richard Seymour 289
Mead, Tom Seymour 270
Mears, John *209*, 210
media coverage 114–16
Medlow, Conor 114, 212, *272*, 338
Melbourne Club *see* Royal Melbourne Tennis Club
Melbourne Rackets courts 204, 385–6, *386*
Melbourne tennis courts 77, 108, 109, 110, 116, *281*
Melvin, Bryan 230
Membland Hall, Newton Ferrers 394, *394*, 395
Membrey, Chris *358*
Membrey, Tom *358*
Mercer, Martin 305
Mercurialis, Hieronymus, *De Arte Gymnastica* 13–14, *14*
Meredith (fives player) 136
Meringoff, Todd 188, 190, *191*, 209, *209*, 210
Merrill, Tim 191
Merton College tennis court 46, 55
Mesquita, T.L. de 358
Messer, Tim 289
Meyer, R.J.O. 194
Meynell, Charles 65
Michel, Olivier 240, 343
Mickelburough, Adam 318
Middlesex University British Challenge 284, *284*
Middlesex University court 108
Middlesex University Real Tennis Club 283–4, *284*
Mies van der Rohe, Ludwig 370
Milan tennis courts 49
Miles, Eustace H. 82, 92, 169, 219, 274, 279, 337, 357
 Amateur Rackets singles champion 104, 279
 Canadian Amateur champion 189
 MCC Gold Racquet 104, 279
 Racquets, Tennis and Squash 92, 279, 399–400
 US Tennis singles champion 83
Milford, David 156, 158, 161, 162, 171, *171*, 173, *173*, 187, 230, 349

Amateur Rackets singles champion 156–7, 279
 Open singles champion 171, 279
 Rackets world champion 157, 161, 228, 279, 330
Milland Place, Liphook 385, *386*
Millen, Woody *202*
Miller, John *311*
Miller, Nick 210
Milne, Andrew 233
Milne, Garth 190, 232–3, 320, 407
Milne Hue Williams Cup 275, 334
Milton, Nicholas 215
Minshew, John, *Guide into Tongues* 18, 19
Mirat, Paul 343, 344, *344*, 345–6, *346*
Miron, Lex *296*, 297, 298
Mironneau, Paul 341
Mitchell, John Charles 141, *147*, 148, 149, 378
Mitchell-Innes, Alistair 325
Mjolnirs 192, 229, 250
Moens, Arnoud Bernelot 368
Mollison, C.H. 282
Monbiot, Charlie 328
Monday Club 362
Mongerson, Tyler 226
Mongewell Park Stické court 394, 395
Montaigne, *Essays* 39
Montgomerie, Richard 331
Montreal Racket Club 188, 189, 230, 285–6, *285*
 centenary 174
Montreal Rackets courts 188, 189, 399
Moon, Arthur 405, 406
Moore, Anna 124
Moore, Horatio 58, 59, 65
Moore, Robert 77, 87, 151, 186
Moore, Robert, Jr 87
Moore tennis court, Rickmansworth 40
Morales, Toni 235, *235*, 253
Mordaunt, G.J. 357
Moreton Morrell Tennis Club 85, 90, 98, 118, 277, 287–9, *287*, *288*, 290, 309, 399
Morey, Father Adrian 300
Morgan, Hewitt 106
Morgan Rackets 158
Morgan, J.P. 350
Morgan, Richard 222, 223, 325
Morgan, Roger 17
 Tennis 16
 Tudor Tennis 21
Morris, Rackets player 134
Morris-Adams, Richard 325
Morrison, Bryan 260
Morristown, New Jersey Rackets court 186
Mortimer, Stanley G. 157, 158, 187, *187*
Mosneron, M. 80
Moyle, Rob 310
Moynihan, George 347
Mozumder, Air Vice-Marshal Aroop 336
Mucklow, John 64, 66, 78
Muer, Tom 230
Muir, Carole *311*
Muir, Robert *313*
Mullan, Denis 212
Mulliken, Bob 358, 366
Multer, Gary 210
Multer, Nancy 210
Muneer, Mr 194
Murphy, John 294
Murtagh, Andy 178, 275
MURTC Ltd 283
Myopia Hunt Club tennis court 87, *387*, 387

Myrtle, Brigadier Andrew *178*, 318, 359, 408, 410
Myrtle, Giles 359
Napoleon I 71, 239
Narne, Alex 53
National Association of the Tennis-playing countries 408
National League 114, 124, 210, 215, 247, *247*
National Schools Real Tennis tournament 300
National Tennis Club, Newport 108, 292–4
National Trust for Scotland 237
Naylor, N. 145
Naylor's Racquet Court Wall Black 152
Neal, Alan 322
Neale, Thomas 60
Neale, William 60
Negretti, Tony 245
Neild, James 131–2
Nelson tennis court 67
Nemec, Karel 190, 286
Neptune Investment Management 184, *322*, 323, 406
Neville, Ted 367
New Sporting Magazine 146–7
New York
 Allen Street Rackets Club 185, 295
 Broadway Racquet Club 185
 Butchers Club 185
 Forty-Third Street Club 186
 Gymnasium Club 150, 186
 Rackets Court Club 77, 98, 295
New York Racquet and Tennis Club 13, 87, 92, 109, 186, 295–9, *295*
New York Racquet Club 94, 100, 109, 151, 157, 161
New York tennis courts 86, 399, 402
Newbold, Edgar 185
Newby, Jill *120*
Newcastle
 North Street East 388, *388*
 Rackets court 154, 175
Newcastle, Jamaica 385, *385*
Newman, Tom 275
Newmarket & Suffolk Real Tennis Club 214, 290–91, *290*, *291*, 399
Newmarket tennis court 54, 58, 89, 108
Newport Casino Club 292, *292*
Newport Casino tennis court 76–7, 108
Newport handicap 210
Newport National Tennis Club 209, 210, 292–4, *292*, *293*
Newton, E.F. *86*, 248
Newton, Stewart 312
Nicholas, Sir Edward 56
Nicholl, Ed 264
Nicholls, Mark 274
Nicholls, Paul 274, 407
Nichols, Bruce 378
Nichols, John, *The Progresses of Queen Elizabeth* 44
Nichols brothers 190, 295
Nicola, Frank 389
Noble, Sir Andrew 71, 263, *263*, 264, 403
Noble, Bob 220
Noble family 388
Noel, E.B. 154, 155, 169, 322
Noel, E.B. and Bruce, C.N., *First Steps to Rackets* 95
Noel, E.B. and Clark, J.O.M., *A History of Tennis* 94–5
Noel-Bruce Cup 196, 219, 221, 253, 334, 349
Noll, Eddie 190, 316

444

Index

Noll, Mike 190, 316
Norden, John, *Description of the Honor of Windsor* 40, *41*, 54
Norfolk, Duke of 40, 45, 54
Norman, David 103, *109*, 173, 175, *175*, 187, 189, 190, 219, 232, 320, 324, 359, 406, 407, 408, 409
Normanby, Marquess of 281
North American Racquets Association (NARA) 167, 190, 191, 197, 223, 227, 230, 286, 317, 410
Northeast, Sam 181, 234, *252*
Northumberland, Earl of 309
Norty Knox doubles tournament 202, *203*, 210, 330
Nusser, E., racquet maker 27, *86*

O'Brien, Gene 230
O'Brien, John 230
O'Brien, Joseph 230
O'Callaghan, General Sir Desmond 394
Ogilby, Col. R.J.L. 287
Old Carthusians 219, 221, *313*
Old Etonian Rackets and Tennis Club 232
Oliphant-Callum, Charles M. 358
Oliver, Alan 303, *304*
Oliver, Norman 254
Ollis, W.H., W.H. Ollis Cup 272
Olympic Games 92, 154–5, 190, 192, 249, 267, 320, 404
OM Rackets Fraternity 275
Openshaw-Blower, Mark 278
The Oratory 108, 115, 300–302, *301, 302*, 325
Oriel College tennis court, Oxford 46, 55
Orléans, Duke of 32, 36
Orléans tennis courts 35, 36, 51, 61
Orme, Judy *212*
Orme, Professor Nicholas 17
Osborne 328
Osborne, Charles 310
O'Shea, Colm 260
Ottawa, Rideau Hall Stické court 396, *396*
Ottaway, C.J. 232
Otterbourne, Thomas 32
Owen, Lily 223
Owen, Richard 223, 278
Owen-Browne, Rupert 176, 177, 178, 181, 187, 188, 189, 190, 348
Owen-George, Roland 288
Owens, Sheilagh *120*
Oxford & Cambridge Rackets court, Chalk Farm Road 141
Oxford City: tennis prohibited 33
Oxford Prize Racquet 75
Oxford University 145, 303–5, *304*
 Blue Boar Lane court 55
 Merton Street court 46, 55, 75, 76, 80, 81, *303*
 Oriel Street court 46, 55, 76
 Rackets courts 143, 144, 154
 tennis courts 46–8, 55, 72, 399
 Unicorn Club 305
 v. Cambridge University 303
 Varsity Tennis 303, 305
Oxford University Tennis Foundation 305

Padwick, Guy 359, 360
Page, Andrew *312*, 313
Page, John *311*
Pakistan: Rackets 194
'Pallacorda' courts 17
pallone (game) 14, 21, 43, 48, *127*, 131
Palmer, A.N., *Winchester 1900-1905* 359

Palmer, Cleeves *261*, 262
Palmer, Richard 243
Palmer-Tomkinson, Dominic 233
Palmer-Tomkinson Cup 361
Papouchado, Lou 201
Pardee, Jonathan 294
Paris
 Jeu du Grand Braque Latin 43
 Luxembourg Gardens 31, 80, *128*
 Société Sportive du Jeu de Paume et de Racquets 306–8, *307*
Park, John *231*
Park Place, Remenham, Berkshire 388, *388*
Parker, David 205
Parker, J. Harleston *208*
Parker, Jamie 348
Parker, John 337
Parsons, D.G. 229
Parsons, Gerald 310
Pasquier, *Recherches sur la France* 25
Passerat, Jean 39
Pataudi, Nawab of 359
Paterson, Jenny 337
Paterson, Peter 214, *215*, 264
Paterson, Ronald 273
Patriot Cup 209
Pau tennis court 38–9, 71, 85, 112, 341
Pawle, J.H. 228
Pawle, John 157, 159–62, *160*, 170, 171
Payne, W. *86*
Payne Whitney Cup 210, 242, 296–7, *296*, 317, 355
Pearl, David 260
Pearson, Charles 'Babe' 173, *173*, 174, 315
Pearson, George 215
Pearson, Janice 210
Pearson, John 262
Pearson, Stan 173
Pearson, Stanley W., Jr 315
Pearson, Stanley W., Sr 315
Peck, Josh 210
Peel, Robert 260
Peel Hunt plc 174
Peggs, B. 74
Pell, Clarence C. 157, 159, *160*, 161, 173, 174, 187, *187*, 188, 189, 190, 192, 230, 242, 294, *364*, 366
Pell, Clarence C., Jr 187, 292
Pell, Haven N.B. *336*, 356
Pell, Peter 191, 297, 298
Pell, Peter, Jr. 299
Pell Cup 292
Pell Racquet Cup 161, 210, 230
pelota 21, 49, 93, 131, 343, 344, 345
Pemberton, Giles 407
Pembroke, Earl of 372
Pembroke College, Cambridge 47–8, 76
Pendrigh, Nigel 297
Pennell, Vane H. 92, 155, 219
Pepper, Andrew *285*
Pepys, Samuel 57
Percival, John 228
Percival, Lord, tournament 210
Percival Cup 317
Percy Finch Inter-cup Trophy 258
Perino del Vaga, follower of, *Putti playing Pallone 127*
Perkins, David 292
Perlin, Etienne 44
Permar, Phil *200*
Perrier, Francisque 88
Peru (fives player) 136
Peshawar, Pakistan: Rackets court 194
Pete Bostwick Cup 278, 297
Peter Gray Cup 243, 361
Peterhouse College, Cambridge 47–8

Pettitt, Tom 75, 76, 77, 81–2, *81*, 87, *156*, 186, 293, 366, *367*, 390
 v. Lambert 82, 103, 244
 v. Latham 83, 89
 world champion 84, 244, 292
Pettman, Peter 349
Petworth House tennis court 27, 56, 71, 82, 87, 89, 309–313, *399, 403*
Phelps, Jack 313
Philadelphia
 Racquet Club 87, 186, 220, 226–7, 314–17, *314, 315*
 Walnut Street Racquet Club 81
Philip, Archduke of Austria and King of Castile 25, 40
Philip I of Spain 49–50
Philip II of Spain 36
Philip III 50
Philip IV of Spain 19
Philip V of Spain 69
Philippe IV of France 31, 33
Philippe Egalité 61
Phillips, Adam 214, 218, 255, 256, 271, 272
Phillips, Charles 76, 255
Phillips, James 76
Phillips, John 214
Phipps, Ogden 95, 188
 v. Etchebaster 94, 95, 96
 v. Van Alen 94, 106
Pignon, Melvyn *120*
Pigott, David 212
Pigott, Lucy 229, *229*
Pigott, Tom 251
Pilet (or Pillet), racquet maker 26, 64
Pilgrim, Roger 273, 407, 410
Pittman, G.J.E. 145
Pittman, John 133, 134, 141, 146–8
Pittman, Matthew 134, 146
Pittman, Matthew, Jr. 146
Pittman, racquet maker 27, 141
Pittman, Thomas 133–4, 141, 146, 148
Pittsburgh Athletic Association 389, *389*
Planet, Émile 306, 307
Plater, Thomas, *Description of Paris* 17
Pleasaunt, Timothy 58
Pleydell-Bouverie, E.O. 151
Plymouth: Stonehouse Royal Marine Barracks, Durnford Street 391, *391*
Plymouth, Earl of 71, 403
Pol Roger 215, 406; Trophy 114, 124, 272
Ponsford, Nick *212*
Ponz, A. 229
Popplewell, Edmund 325
Porter, Matt 210
Portsmouth Rackets court 335
Portz, Christian *180*, 181, 182, *191*, 360, 361, *361*
Poskanzer, Steve 209
Post, John A. 185
Potter, Chris 178, 358
Potter, James *156*
Potter, James Brown 351
Potter, Jeremy 228
 Tennis and Oxford 228, 305
Potter, W. Wilson *156*
Potts, Jacob 329
Powell, Emma 229, *229*
Powell, Rackets player 146
Prague: tennis courts 50, 60
Prats family 406
Prenn, Daniel 406
Prenn, John 172, 176–7, *177*, 181, 188, 190, 192, 226, 229, 251, 253, 297, 320, 323, 347, 381, 402, 406, 407, 410

 Canadian Amateur champion 189
 Open singles Rackets champion 172, 176
 Swallow Trophy 172
 world champion 175, *175*, 226, 230, 330
Prescott, Sir George 71
Prested Hall 108, 116, 318–19, *319*
Preston, Rick 201, *202, 203*
Pretoria, Stické court 394
Price, Bruce 266–7, *266*
Price, Timothy 182, 190
Prichard Racquet Trophy 274
Prince, Freddie 226, *343*, *346*
Prince, Frederick 343
Prince, Frederick H., IV 355, 356
Prince, George 149
Prince's Club, Brighton 73
The Prince's Club, London 72–5, 81, 82, 87, 89–94, 145, 269, 271, 403, 404
 Rackets courts 74, *75*, 143, 144, 154, 158–9, 162
 re-covering of balls 29
Prince's Club, Washington 218
Prince's Club Shield 94, 104–5
Prince's Court, McLean, Virginia 108, 355–6
Probyn, Peter 212
Professional Rackets Association 243
Professional single championship 113, *274*
Prosser, T.H., racquet maker 27, 141, 145, 152
Public Schools championships 143–4, 167, 168, 170, 172, 177, 181–2, 196, 198, 219, 222, 403
 see also Foster Cup; Henry Leaf Cup
Pugh, Michael 105, 172
Pugh, Tim 159, 172, 174
Pugh, Tom 171, 172, 349
 model for statuette 172
 Rackets 159, 167, 168, 174, 188, 232
Pughe, Millie 358, *358*
Pugin, A.C. and Rowlandson, T.: *Microcosm of London* 131
Pulbrook, Roger 251
Punjab Squash Club, Lahore 194
Punpa 198

Quadrathlon 190
Quancard, Claude 88
Quebec: Rackets courts 188
Queen's Bench prison Rackets court 146, 148
Queen's Club 75, 82, 83, 86, 89, 90, 98, 99, 101, 105, 109, 111, 115, 118, 124, 320–24, *321*, 409
 British Amateur championship 75
 Public Schools Rackets championships 143–3
 Quintathlons 190
 Rackets courts 75, 116, 143, 144, 154, 175, 183, 213, 320, 322, 399, 401–2
 re-covering of balls 29
 Stické court 395
Queen's Club Cup 277
Queen's College, Cambridge 47
Queen's Quintathlon 190
Querl, Glenn *252*, 253
Quick, Preston 298
Quintathlon 190, 192

RA Woolwich Rackets court 154
Rabelais, François 36, 43, 50
Raby, Peter 215
Rackets (game)
 history 131–42
 19th-century 143–53
 20th-century 154–78

Rackets (game) *continued*
  21st-century 179–82
  courts 75, 143
  in India 193–4
  Ladies' Rackets 183–4
  Olympic Games 154
  post-war revival 159–69
  prominent players 169–72
  Rackets balls 194, 195–8
  tours 173–4, 182
  in USA and Canada 185–92
  world champions 116
Rackets Development Squad 408
Rackets Fellows programme 209, 227, 230
Rackets Professional singles championship 181
The Racquet Club of Philadelphia 268, 314–17
racquets
  development 25–7
  French 26
  tennis 26–7, *26*, *27*
Radley College 108, 112, 175, 177, 178, 325–8, *326*, *327*, 402
Rambridge, Andrew 178
Randolph Tennis and Racquet Courts 87
Randolphe, Thomas 45
Rangoon, Burma, rackets court 390, *390*
Rank Xerox 406
Raphael, R.H. 357
Raquette d'Argent 207
Raquette d'Or 85, 93, 207
Ratcliff, E. 29, 94
Ratcliff, Willy 105
Raumann, Rick 218
Raven, Paul *265*
Rawalpindi, Pakistan
  Rackets court 193, 194
  Stické court 394
Rawlings, Harvey *311*, *312*
RE Chatham Rackets court 154
Read, Charles 170–71, *170*
  lawn tennis, Professional champion 157, 171
  Rackets, Professional champion 157, 158, 171
  squash, Professional champion 171
Read, Peter 173, 174, 190
Readman, Matt 234, *234*
Real Tennis Online database 409
Real Tennis Professionals Association (RTPA) 114, 247
Realtennis tv 115–16
rebot 19, 21–2
Rees, Simon *311*
Regensburg: tennis court 60
Reignac, Comte de 79
Reindel, G. *97*
Remenham, Berkshire: Park Place 388, *388*
Renny, Colonel Nigel 406
Renny Cup 222, 229, *229*, 243, *358*
Reuser, Patrick 368
Revelstoke, 1st Lord (Edward Baring) 369, 395
Revelstoke, 2nd Lord (Hon. Cecil Baring) 87, 93, 350, 351, 369, *369*, 370, 371, 405
Rich, Brian *367*
Rich, F.W. 263, *263*
Richard II 33, 40
Richards, John, *The Cowbridge Story* 67
Richardson, Brett 282
Richmond, Duke of 67, 71, 135, 309
Richmond Palace tennis court 40
Ridding, Rev. George 359

Rideau Hall, Ottawa Stické court 395, 396–7, *396*
Riehl, Andreas, *The story of David and Bathsheba* 125
Riley, Alex 291, *291*
Rippon, Geoffrey 373
Riseley, R.C. 228
Riseley, Robert 105, 157, 277
Ritblat, Sir John *111*, 323, 406, 410
Riviere, Camden 113, *113*, 115, 201, 202, *202*, 207, *207*, 209, 210, 247, *247*, 273, *273*, 299, 308, *308*, 325, *326*, 338, 356, *356*
Riviere, Tiger 115
Rivington, James 69
RMA Sandhurst 143, 335–6
RMA Woolwich Rackets court 154
RMC Sandhurst 403
  Rackets court 154
Robarts, Charlie 331
Roberts, Andy 210
Roberts, Tim 275
Robertson, Angus 250
Robertson, Gordon 250
Robertson, Guy 250
Robertson, Tom 250
Robinson, Alister 177, 179, 180, 181, 253, 279–80, *280*, 286
Robinson, Beverley 185
Robinson, N.F. *97*
Robinson, Philip *311*, 313
Rock, James 191, 223, 224, 252, 286
Rodgers, Eddie 77
Roe, Randall B. 356
Rogers 328
Rogers, Eddie *160*
Rogers, J.K. 174
Rolland, F.F. 186, 189
Rolland, J.A. 189
Roman ball games 14–15, *14*
Romsey 108, 112, 329, *329*
Ronaldson, Ben 247, *247*, 262
Ronaldson, B.J. 218
Ronaldson, Chris 88, 103–4, 105, 107, *108*, *109*, 111, 113, 115, 118, 217, 225, 226, 245–6, 247, 260, 282, 288, 289, 300, 303, 318, *326*, *327*, 359, 371, 380, 393
  Ballarat Silver Racket 205
  Hampton Court professional 245
  Melbourne professional 108
  Radley professional 327
  Tennis: A Cut above the Rest 108–9
  Tennis club developer 327
Ronaldson, Ivan 240, 318, 356, *356*
Ronaldson, Lesley 88, 115, 118, *119*, 120, *120*, 247, 260, 289, 318
Ronaldson, Matthew 283, 307, 318
Ronaldson, Steve 115, 217–18, *218*, 303
Ronan, J. 29
Ronnie Aird Cup 272
Rose, Alan 209
Rose, Sir Charles, 3rd Baronet 249, *250*
Rose, Sir Charles Day, 1st Baronet 71, 85, *86*, 89, 248, 249, 290, 383, 403
Rose, Sir Frank, 2nd Baronet 249
Rose, Sir Julian 249, 250
Rose, Lady, Phoebe 211, 249
Rose Street Rackets court, Edinburgh 143
Rosemary Branch Rackets court, Peckham 136, 141
Roslyn tennis court 87
Ross, G.E.A. *86*, 403, 404, 405
Ross-Collins, M.S. 174
Rossall School 390, *390*
Rosser, Norman 178, *178*, 275
Rosser, Philip 182, 274, 331

Rossiter, Mr and Mrs Bill 373
Rowe, Tom 294
Roxborough, Neil 114, 215
Royal Artillery Rackets court 144
Royal County of Berkshire Real Tennis Club 259
Royal Melbourne Tennis Club 87, 145–6, 205, 258, 281–2, *281*
Royal Military Academy *see* RMA Sandhurst
Rozier-Pamplin, Alex *227*
Rudolf II 50
Rugby Fives Association 404
Rugby fives court 144
Rugby School 145, 151, 177, 178, 182, 330–31
rules 16, 51, 72, 80
Rushmore, G.M. 185
Rushton, Mark 325
Russell, J.J. 76, *76*
Russell, Nelson 208
Rustall House tennis court 87
Ryan, Mark 271
Rylands, P.D. 174
Rylands, Peter 349
Ryston Hall Stické court 394

Sabbag, Brenda *120*
Sabin, Thomas 75, 81, 82
Sacks, Zach 192
St Germain, Henri 88, 98, 259
St James's Palace tennis court 44, 53, 54, 56, 58
St John's College, Cambridge 47, 48, 144, 175
St Louis Rackets court 186, 390, *390*
St Lucia, West India 391, *391*
St Martin's Street fives court 66, 136, 137
St Paul's School 175, 332–4, *332*
St Paul's School (New Hampshire) 314
St Petersburg tennis court 77, *78*
Saint-Simon 52, 239
Sainte-André court, Bayonne 112, 341, 345, *345*
Sales, Murray W. 190, 230
Salgin, Burak 215
Salisbury, Marquess of 71, 254, 255, 256, 406
Salt, Richard 262
Sambrook, Bart 189, 190, 286
Sanders, Simon *265*
Sandhurst Cup 335, *335*
Sands, Charles E. 91
Sangor, India, Rackets court 193
Sansome Wall, Worcester 391, *391*
Sarlangue, Matthieu 114, *114*, 115, *306*, 345
Sarlangue, Pierre 345
Satake, Eike 210
Sauerborn, Paul 201
Saunders, Charles 75, 76, 82, *82*, 83, 84, *86*, 159, 263, 320, 366, *367*
Savage, William 262
Savage Trophies 247
Sawrey-Cookson, Toby 177, *177*, 181, 229
Sayer, Mark 282
Sayers, Bryn 113, *113*, 293, 301, 318–19, *322*, 323, *324*, 338, *338*
Scaino da Salò, Antonio 131
  Trattato del Giuoco della Palla 16, 19, 20, 22, 43, *47*, 48–9
Scammell, Anthony 275
Schipper, Toon 368
Schochet, Jay 293
Scholarship Trust 212
Scholey, Sir David 174, 358
Schwartz, Suzy 210
scoring 20–22, *22*
Scotland: tennis 32, 46, 85

Scott, Christopher 191
Scott, Edgar *156*, 315
Scott, Eugene *102*, 103, 106, 107, 168
  v. Angus 103, 169, 245
Scott, Hugh 315
Scott, Martin 407
Scott-Chad Cup 171
Scrace, Richard 66, 372
Scratchley, Anthony 240, 264
Seabrook, Peter 359
Seacourt Silver Racquet 124
Seacourt Tennis Club, Hayling Island 85, 119–20, 124, 183, 309, 337–40, *340*, 399
Seacroft Silver Racket 337, 338
Seagrave, Steven 251
Seal Salver 245
Sealey, David 30
Searby, M.H. *97*
Sears, Eleo 387
Sears, R.D. 83
Segal, Matthew 360
Seigneur, Mark 240, 265
Selkirk, Lord 342
Sempere, Solange 240
Sercot 52
Setzler, Norbert 157, 279
Seyches-Quinton, Mr 386
Sforza, Galeazzo Maria 28, 49
Shabshelowitz, Eric 210
Shackleton, Derek 217
Shakespeare, William
  Henry V 32
  Much Ado about Nothing 29
Shannon, Phil 356
Sharp, Dougie *339*, 340
Shaw, Q.A. 189
Shaw, Quincy 387
Shaw-Hamilton, Philip 289
Sheen Palace tennis court 40
Sheldon, Kevin 115, 270, *270*
Shelton, Tom 147
Shenkman, Robert 278
Shenkman, Simon 265, 278
Sheppard, Major-General S.H. 193, 194
Sheppard, Robert 209
Sheppard Cup 170
Shields, Tom 347
Shiner, Dan 223, 253
Shneerson, John 108, 290, *291*
  Two Centuries of Real Tennis 291
Shoeburyness stické courts 394
Shorncliffe Rackets court 154, 335, 391, *391*
Shumaker, Thomas 230
Sidley, Sir Charles 55
Sidney, Sir Henry 48
Sievers, Chris 282
Silk, Dennis 325
Silver Racket (RMTC) 282
Silver Racquet (France) 307
Silver Racquet (James Street) 72, 73
Silver Racquet (MCC) 271, 272, *272*
Silver Racquet (New York) 296, 297, 298
Simla Vice Regal Residence, India, Stické court 395, 396, *396*
Simmonds, Geoffrey 251
Simonds, Will 356
Simpson, C.F.B. 330
Simpson, James 406
Simpson, J.C.F. (Sir Cyril) 155, 157–8, 170–71, 330
Sippel, George 60
Skelhorne, Ann *212*
Skinner, Richard 264, 265
Slater, Jack 292
Slater, Mark 209
Sloggett, Colonel A.J.H. 194
Smale, George *86*, 251, 357

INDEX

Smith, Arthur 'Tennis' 309, 310, *399*
Smith, Josh 247
Smith, Martin 167, 168, 171, 172, 174, 349
Smith, Neil 176, 177, 179, 181, 188, 190, 191, 229, 231, *231*, 253, *267*, 268, 274, 298, 299, *299*, 328, 334, *334*
   World Rackets champion 176, *176*, 298, *332*, 333
Smith, Rich 210
Smith, Richard 293
Smith, Richard (Ricardo) 284, 293, 318, 338, *338*
Smith, Robert Bland 356
Smith, Simon 58
Smith, Stephen G. 356
Smith, Stuart 320
Smith-Bingham, Alex 228, 233, *234*
Smith-Bingham, Guy 179, 180, 181, 198, 233, *235*, 253, 280, 407
Smith Travers, Samuel 77, 257, 398–9
   A Treatise on Tennis 257, 399
Smithie, Antony *296*
Snelgrove, Austin J. 218
Snell, Ben 181, 184, 198, 221, *221*, 223, 224, 233, 323, 324, *324*
Snell, Christopher 359
Snell, Francis 337
Snell, Rosie 282
Snow, Adrian 108, 249, 250, 300, 325
Snow, Julian 109, 110, *111*, 113–14, 205, 207, 264, 265, 297, 325, 328, 338, 348, 371, 407
Société Sportive du Jeu de Paume et de Racquets, Paris 306–8, *307*
Sockett, Reverend Thomas 309
Somers, Lord 281
Somerset, Duke of 309
Somerset, Earl of 53
Soutar, Jock 87, *89*, 93, 107, 155–6, *155*, *156*, 187, 315
Southwell, Clare *120*
Sowden, J., Rackets player 134, 146
Spain 29, 49–50
Spence, Alex 210
Spender, Richard 334
Sphairistike 13
Spike Island, Cork Harbour, Stické court 394
Spines, Jack 137
Spittoon Cup 354
Sports Council 318, 408
Spring, Wayne 205
Sprinz, Paul 230
Spurling, Adrian 348
Spurling, Nick 348
Squash Rackets Association 404
Stafford, P.D. 243
Stahl, Chris 243
Stahl, Duncan 243
Stair, Earl of 159
Stallibrass, Jamie 325
Standing, George 77, 87, *91*, 92, 152–3, *153*, 155, 156, *156*, 158, 186
Standing, William 'Blondy' 87, 156, 242
Standish, Captain 145
Stanton, Guy 270
Stapleton, Eddie 242
Steed, Darcy 217
Stefanowicz, Chris 253
Stephen, J.K., 'Parker's Piece' 83–4
Stephens, Graham 277
Stephens, William (Bill) 182, 192, *192*, 194, 372–3, 407
Stevens, Ben 181, 360, 361
Stevens, Derek *278*

Stevens, 'Judy' 151, 171, 251
Stevens, Sam 209
Stevens, Tom 360
Stevens, W. 86
Steward, Mike *313*
Stewart, Major General Andrew 324
Stewart, Sir Robert 32
Stichting Huis ter Kleef 368
Stické 369, 378, 394–7
Stockholm, tennis court 50, *59*, 60
Stockton, Phil 210, 292
Stoker, Dacre 201, *202*, *203*
Stokes, Simon 214
Stone, Edward 45
Stone, Thomas 77, 257, 282
Stone, Woolner 282
Stonehouse Royal Marine Barracks, Durnford Street, Plymouth 391, *391*
Stout, Andrew *222*, 224, 243
Stout, Chris 182, *222*, 223, *223*
Stout, Jamie 178, 179, 181, 182, *182*, 188, 190–91, *191*, 222, *222*, 223, *224*, 226, 231, *231*, 253, 298–9, *299*, 323
Stout, Michael 222, *222*, 223
Stout brothers 222–3
Stowe, Sir John 391
Stradbroke, Lord 281
Strain, W.S. 217
Strang, Christopher 251
Strasbourg, tennis court 60
Stratfield Saye, tennis court 71, 76, 77, 81, 214
Strutt, Joseph, *Sports and Pastimes of the People of England* 131
Stubbings, Simon *304*
Such, Freddie 264
Suffolk, Duke of 40, 44, 57
Suffolk House, tennis court 85, *86*, 249
Sullivan, Michael 201
Sun Court, Troon 245, *392*, 393
Surtees, Willie 101, 167, *168*, 171, *175*, 187, 189, 190, 192, 331
   Canadian Amateur champion 189
   world champion 168, *168*, 169, 175, 190, 226, 330, 360
Svabo, Jens Christian 19
Swallow, Charles 164, 166–7, 171, 174, 219, 232, 251, 318, 408, 410
   Amateur Singles Rackets champion 164, 166, 219
   British Open champion 166, 196, 219
   Foster Cup 219
Swallow, Chris 271
Swallow, Dr J.C. 196
Swallow Trophy 172, 251, 274, 328
Swantner, Gary 192
Sweden, tennis courts 60
Switzerland: tennis courts 60
Sydney: Macquarie University 371
Sydney Real Tennis Club 271
Sylvester, Charles 337
Symonds, T.R. 243

Tabley, Paul 282
Tailer, Thomas Suffern 350, 351, 369
Talbot, Charles, Earl of Shrewsbury 384
Talbot, John, Earl of Shrewsbury 89, 206
Talbot-Williams, Simon 260
Tancer, Manuel 191, 230
Tanfield, Barney 191, 299, *299*, 316
Tanfield, Dick 191, 297
Tang, Martin 274
Taplow Court, Stické court 394, 395, *395*

Tate, David, David Tate Cup 334
Taylor, Brigadier-General A.H.M. 404, 405
Taylor, Alexander 342–3
   Virtues of the Climate of Pau 343
Taylor, Derek 251
Taylor, John, *Journey through Wales* 67
Taylor, Liam 301
Taylor, Malcolm 217
Taylor, Mike 301
Taylor, Richard 325
Taylor, Ronnie 159, 160, *160*, 161, 171, 173, *173*
Taylor Cup 338
Ted Cockram Trophy 282
Tedeschi, Dave 210
Tench, Nigel 336
Tennant, Captain Paul *335*, 336
Tennis
   game
      chase 16, 21, 22, *22*, 23, 24
      principles of play 23–4
      scoring 20–22
      service 21, 23–4
   historic photographs 125–8
   history 31–117
      origins 13–19, *16*, *128*
      medieval period 31–4, *128*
      16th century 35–50, *125*, *127*
      17th century 51–60
      18th century 61–70, *126*
      19th century 71–84, *126*
      20th century 85–111
      21st century 112–17
Tennis & Rackets Association 89, 92, 103, 114, 167, *167*, 403–410
   Benefactor Scheme 410
   Board of Directors 409
   centenary 273, 409
   committees 410
   first meeting (18 December 1907) 403
   handicap system adopted 270
   membership 405–8
   new balls 196
   president's role 409
   Queen's 403, 405, 407, 409
   royal patronage 405
   vice presidents 409–410
Tennis and Rackets Charitable Trust 407
Tennis balls 28–31
Tennis courts *see* courts
Tennis Development Squad 409
Tennis, Racket and Fives Association (TRFA) 90–91
Tennis rackets 26–7, *26*, *27*
Tennis Singles Championship of America 83
Tentori, M.I. 243
Thatcher, Mark 172, 229, 251
Thatcher, Samuel 67
Thayer, Nathaniel 76
Theobald's Park tennis court 54, 71
Thibodeau, Robert, Jr. 190, 230
Thicknesse, Commodore Philip 336
Thomas, Jeffrey 397
Thomas Trophy 278
Thompson, Baker 192
Thompson, John 164, 171–2, *171*, 173, *173*, 178, 187, 195–6, 197, 230, 232, 279, 349
Thompson, Will 209
Thomson, E.A. 91
Thorpe, Walter 198, 366
Three Blackbirds, Bristol, Rackets court 141, 148
Throckmorton, Sir Nicholas 45
Tieken, Ted 190, 226, *226*
Tiffany Cup 292
Tildesley, J.M.G. 171, 331

Timbs, John, *Clubs and Club Life in London* 74
Tison, racquet maker 26
Titchener-Barrett, Alex 178, 179, 180, *180*, 181, *181*, 183, 190, *191*, *224*, 227, 251, 253, 280, *285*, 286, 299, 323, 358, 361
Toates, Barry 88, 108, 214, 257, *258*, 267, 293
   US Open Singles Tennis champion 107
Toates, Karen 258, 267
Todd, A. Thornton 188–9
Tolchard, Roger 275
Tomaino, Joseph 294
Tomkinson, Graham 198
Tomlin, Vice Admiral G.N. 405
Tompkins, Alfred 29, 74, 77, *77*, 80–81, 87
Tompkins, Edmund III 303
Tompkins, Edmund IV 72, 76, 80, *80*, 81, 87, 303
Tompkins, Frederick 77, 81, *86*, 87, 155, *156*, 187, 226, 315
Tompkins, J. Alfred 81
Tompkins, John 81
Tompkins, Peter 72, 75, 76, 79, 80
The Tompkins pro tournament 314
Tonbridge School 177–8, 179, 182, 347–9, *349*, 402
Tooker, J.S. 186
Toppin, C.G. 'Tim' 172
Toronto Club 188–9
Toronto Rackets courts 188–9
Torquay Rackets court 154
Toseland, Steve 191, 230, *231*
Le Tournoi des trois Tripots 345
Travis, J.N. 174
Treherne-Thomas, Robin 251
Trentham, G.B. 358
Trice, J.S.M. 217
Trinity College, Cambridge 47
Tristao, Dan 333
Troon tennis court 85, 108, *392*, 393, 403
Tübingen tennis court 22, *22*
Tufton, Anthony *see* Hothfield, Lord
Tufton, Francis 254
Tuileries tennis court 71, *72*, 80, 85, 213, 306, *342*, 343
Tulley, Ryan 191, 286, 358
Tulley, Steve 182, 190, 220, 286, *332*, 333
Turin tennis courts 49, 78
Turnbull, Henry 226
Turnbull, Robert 178
Turner, Edward 230
Turner, Jamie 262
Turner, Richard (Dick) 190, 230
Turner, William 145
Tutt, Bill 159, 162, 214
Tuxedo Club 86, 87, 100, 115, 186, 220–21, 350–54, *350*, *351*, *352*, 399
Tuxedo Gold Racquet 91, 106, 160, 173, 187, 232
Twinn, Arthur 27, 76, 214, 370
Twinn, Eric 214
Twohig-Howell, Beverleigh 289
Tyldesley, J.M.G. 219
Tyndall, Graeme 222, 223

UK Professional Singles 116, *116*
Ulmann, Edward F. 190, 192, 230
Ulster Club, Belfast 151
Unhoch, G. *97*
Unicorn Club 305
Unigate 406
United States
   ball making 29–30
   Rackets 139, 157–8, 173–4, 185–8
   Tennis courts 76

447

United States *continued*
 Tennis Singles championship 83–4
 v. Great Britain 158
United States Court Tennis Association 102, 103, 106, 107, 121, 210, 296
United States Court Tennis Preservation Foundation 210, 242
University Arms, Cambridge Rackets court 144, 150
University Club of Chicago 186, 375, *375*
University Club of Detroit 186
University College London Racquet Club 145, 154
University Hall, London 146
University of Jersey 112
Urrugne court 341
US Amateur doubles championship 107, 173, 230
US Amateur singles championship 83, 91, 94, 95, 96, 99, 100, 105–6, 230
US Court Tennis Association (USCTA) 102, 103, 106, 107, 121, 210, 267, 293, *316*, 317, 401
US Court Tennis Preservation Foundation 210, 242, 293, 355
US national doubles championships 87
US Open championship 92–3, 94, 98, 106, 107, 109, 110, 227, *227*, 230
US Parent Child championship 317
US professional championship 92, 98, 113
US Rackets doubles championship 161, 174
US Rackets singles championship 160–61
US tours 173–4, 182, 331

Van Alen, J., II 0*97*
Van Alen, James *97*
Van Alen, J.H. *107*
Van Alen, Jimmy 94, *102*, 106
Van Alen, J.L. 106
Van Alen, Sammy 29, 106, 292, 317
Van Alen, William L., Jr. *97*, 106, *107*
Van Alen Challenge 293
Van Alen tour 182
Van Alen Trophy *97*, 106
Van Brederode, Hendrik 368
Van der Berghe, Jan 20
Van der Gucht, P.I. 328
Van der Weijden, Frank 368
Van der Zwalman, Lea 229
Van Dyck, Peter *317*
Van Nice, Peter *226*
Van Schaack, Greg 190, 226, 298, 366
Van Wijk, Niek 368
Vanderbilt, William Kissam 250
Varsity matches 116, 273
Vatel, M. Charles 64, 65
Vaughan, Jane *120*
Velluti, Donato: *Cronica di Firenze* 18
Venice tennis courts 49
Vennat, Charles 192
Vennat, Fred 192
Verglas, François 201
Versailles tennis court 64–5, 71, 80, *392*, 393
Vestey, W.H. 328
Vice-Chancellor's Trophy 371
Victoir, Nicolas *296*, 297
Victoria, Queen 71, 143, 189, 281, 320
Victoria Club, Torquay, Rackets court 143

Vienna tennis courts 60, 77
Vigrass, Claire (later Fahey) 113, 115, *116*, *117*, 123, *123*, 124, 183, 184, *184*, 205, *205*, 212, 226, 260, 273, 275, *307*, 308, *308*, 318, 319, *345*, 371
Vigrass, Sarah 123–4, *123*, 215, *307*, 308, 319
Villiers, Henry 59
Villiers-Cotteret tennis court 61
Vincennes tennis court 31, 64
Vincent, Barbara 184
Vine, Paul *311*
Vines, Charlie 197
Virant (architect) 343
Virgona, Steve 110, 113, *114*, 226, 227, *227*, 240, 283, 289, 308, *308*, *322*, 323, *323*, 338, *338*, 356
Vivès, Juan Luis 50, 61
 Dialogues 26, 29, 43, 205
 Leges Ludi 22
Vogt, Peter 317
Vogt, W.T. 107

Wade, Charles *270*
 The Future of Real Tennis and Rackets (Wade Report) 407–8
Wade, Martyn: *Singles and Doublets* 284
Wadsworth, Ed 210
wages for professionals 74
Wagg, Kenneth 159, 161, 171, 173, *173*, 174, 232
Wakely, Robert 182, 243, 279, *280*
Wales tennis court 67
Walker, Catherine 120
Walker, Donald, *Games and Sports* 139
Walker, Rob 243
Wallis, Peter E.R. 243
Walpole, Horace 65
Walsh, Denis 182, 190, 192, 208, 209, *209*, 226
Walsh, J.G.M. 174
Walsh, Lucas 192, 209, *209*, 210
Walton, James 198, 409
Warburg, David *102*, 105, 407
Warburg, Thane 325
Warburg Salver 122
Ward, Anthony *161*, 232
Ward, John 207
Ward, Stephen 99
Warfield, Peter 178, 251–2
Warren, Whitney 350
Warren and Wetmore 350, *350*, 352
Warren-Piper, Alex *see* Garside, Alex
Warwick School 289
Washington court *336*, 343
Waterbury, Clarence 187
Watkins, racquet maker 27
Watson, Claire 215
Watson, James 215
Watters, T. 145
Wear, Joseph 186, 315
Weaver, Paul 337, 338–9, *339*, 340, 408–9
Weaver, Tom 338
Webb, John 53, 56, 58
Webb, William *86*, 159, 162
Wellesley, Lord Richard 233, 251
Wellington, Duke of 71, 76, 77, 214, 341, 342
Wellington College 99, 112–13, 144, 177, 182, 335, 357–8, 371, 399, 403
Wentworth, Lady (Judith Lytton) 85, 90, 337, 377, 404
Wesley, John 54
Wessex, Earl of 108, 112, *211*, 212, 237, 240, *240*, 249, 261, 283,

284, 289, *289*, 300, 367, 371, 405
West, Addison 191, 297, 298
West, Chey 184
West, Colonel Lord 143, 365
Westbury Manor Stické court 394
Western Amateur championships 160, 174
Western Open 190, 230
Westgate School 362, *362*
Westminster School 175
Weston, David 249, 300
Westward Ho! 393, *393*
W.H. Ollis Cup 272
Wharton, George 293
Wharton, James 294
Whatley, Terence 229
Whatman, Jimmy 309
Whatmore, Richard 359
Whetton, Arthur 171
Whiston, W.D. 217
White, Alfred 29, *86*, 87, 390
 racquet maker 27
White, Jack 87, 92
White, Robbie *235*, 253, *253*
White, T. *86*
White Bear Rackets court 141, *142*
White Conduit House Rackets court 133, 141
Whitehall Palace
 Brake Court 43, 44, 53, 54, 56, 57, 58
 tennis courts 41, 42–4, *43*, 53, 54, 57, 58, 59, 66
Whitehouse, P.M. 157, 279
Whitehouse, Rob 190, 316, *316*
Whitman, Malcolm D. 21
 Tennis Origins and Mysteries 95
Whitney, Betsey Cushing 241, 242, *242*, 296
Whitney, Hugh 387
Whitney, John Hay ('Jock') 241, 296
Whitney, Payne 87, *88*, 241, *241*
 Payne Whitney Cup 210, 242, 296–7, *296*, 317, 355
Whitney, William C. 87, 92, 201, *201*
Whittaker, Christian 302
Wickes, Schuyler 267
Wiegand, Peter 264
Wigan, Patrick 233
Wigley, Michael 325
Wilcox, Rupert 252
Wildcroft Manor, Putney Heath Stické court 394
Wildenstein, Graf von 69
Wilkinson, Julian *311*
Willcocks, James 'Spike' *114*, 218, *272*, 303, 322, 327, 354
Willcocks, J.P. 229
Willey, Peter 358
William III 59, 65, 368
Williams, Angus 240, 307
Williams, Charles 87, 155–6, *155*, *156*, 186, 187, 194, 227, 309, 320
 World Rackets champion 155, 169, 171, 226
Williams, Daniel 205
Williams, Glynne 250
Williams, Hugh, ball maker 28
Williams, Michael 205
Williams, R.C.O. (Roddy) 155, 157
Williams, Reggie 229, *229*
Williams, Vaughan 249–50
Willis, Frank 88, 100, 101, 105, 108, 277, 288
Willoughby de Broke, Lord 287, 288, 305
Wilson, Duncan Duncan 86, 87
Wilson, F.B. 169
Wilson, G., racquet maker 27

Wilson, J., ball and racquet maker 195
Wilson, P., racquet maker 141
Wilson, William 366
Wilson-Johnston, Col. W.E. 194
Wilson balls 195
Wimborne, Lord 216, *216*, 288, 309, 366, *367*
Wimpey 406
Winchester College 145, 170, 177, 181, 182, 359–62, 399, 403
Windham, Andrew 88
Windmill Street tennis court 66, 80
Windows, Matthew 178, 228, 229
Windsor, Duke of 75, 159, 404
Windsor Castle: tennis courts 40, *41*, 45, 58
Wingfield, Major Walter 13, 394
Winsloe, Col. A.R. 405
 Rackets in India 193, *193*, 194, 401
Winstead, David 356
Winter Gardens, Eastbourne: Rackets court 144
Wintersteen, Jeremy 209, 210
Woburn Abbey tennis court 67, 71
Woking Palace 125
Wollaston Cup 247
Womersley, Ron 300
Wood, Nick 212, 246–7, 247, *247*, 260, 310, 338, 371
Wood, Rob 190, *226*
Wood Prince, W. 173, 226
Woodcock, Roy 221
Woodman, David 114, 215, *272*
Woodman, Gordon *312*, *313*
Woods-Ballard, Patrick 325
Woodstock, tennis court 40
Woodward (fives player) 136
Woolwich 154, 403
Woosnam, Max 277
Wootton, Charlie 223
Worcester, Sansome Wall 391, *391*
world champions 78–83, 84, 89–107
world championship Challenge Points System 410
World Championship Guidelines for Rackets 410
world doubles championships 113, 280, *280*, *285*, *286*
World Masters 297
World Overs 210, 296, 297
World Rackets championship 83, 176
World Rackets Doubles 179, *179*
World Tennis championship 78, 79, 82, 83, 92, 98, 99–100, 110, 113, 114, 115, 116
 trophy 103
Worth, Jacques 93
Wraxall, Lord 145, 373
Wren, Sir Christopher 65, 244
Wright, Albert 222
Wright, Dom 192
Wright, Maggie *120*
Wright, P. *115*
Wright, Peter *247*
Wright, William C. 106
Wyatt, James 408, 409
Wykeham Rackets Club 362
Wynne, David: statuette *172*, 172
Wythes, Ernest 376

Yager, Jeff 191, 208
Yeatman, P.J. 209
Yorkshire Stingo Rackets court, Marylebone Road 141
Young, Samuel 148, 149
Young Professionals Fund 406, 408

Zhang, Shinan 184
Zug, Jim 267, 356